The Cambridge Companion to Irish Poets offers a fascinating introduction to Irish poetry from the seventeenth century to the present. Aimed primarily at lovers of poetry, it examines a wide range of poets, including household names, such as Jonathan Swift, Thomas Moore, W. B. Yeats, Samuel Beckett, Seamus Heaney, Patrick Kavanagh, Eavan Boland, and Paul Muldoon. The book is comprised of thirty chapters written by critics, leading scholars and poets, who bring an authoritative and accessible understanding to their subjects. Each chapter gives an overview of a poet's work and guides the general reader through the wider cultural, historical and comparative contexts. Exploring the dual traditions of English and Irish-speaking poets, this Companion represents the very best of Irish poetry for a general audience and highlights understanding that reveals, in clear and accessible prose, the achievement of Irish poetry in a global context. It is a book that will help and guide general readers through the many achievements of Irish poets.

GERALD DAWE is Professor of English and Fellow of Trinity College Dublin. A distinguished poet, he has published eight collections of poetry with The Gallery Press, including, most recently, *Selected Poems* (2012) and *Mickey Finn's Air* (2014). He has also published several volumes of literary essays, and has edited various anthologies, including *Earth Voices Whispering: Irish War poetry, 1914–1945* (2008).

A complete list of books in the series is at the back of this book.

THE CAMBRIDGE
COMPANION TO
IRISH POETS

EDITED BY
GERALD DAWE
Trinity College, Dublin

CAMBRIDGE
UNIVERSITY PRESS

CAMBRIDGE
UNIVERSITY PRESS

University Printing House, Cambridge CB2 8BS, United Kingdom

One Liberty Plaza, 20th Floor, New York, NY 10006, USA

477 Williamstown Road, Port Melbourne, VIC 3207, Australia

314–321, 3rd Floor, Plot 3, Splendor Forum, Jasola District Centre,
New Delhi – 110025, India

79 Anson Road, #06-04/06, Singapore 079906

Cambridge University Press is part of the University of Cambridge.

It furthers the University's mission by disseminating knowledge in the pursuit of
education, learning, and research at the highest international levels of excellence.

www.cambridge.org
Information on this title: www.cambridge.org/9781108420358
DOI: 10.1017/9781108333313

© Cambridge University Press 2018

First published 2018
Reprinted 2019

Printed and bound in the United Kingdom by Clays Ltd, Elcograf S.p.A.

A catalogue record for this publication is available from the British Library.

Library of Congress Cataloging-in-Publication Data
NAMES: Dawe, Gerald, 1952– editor.
TITLE: The Cambridge companion to Irish poets / edited by Gerald Dawe,
Trinity College, Dublin.
DESCRIPTION: Cambridge ; New York, NY : Cambridge University Press, 2017. |
Includes bibliographical references and index.
IDENTIFIERS: LCCN 2017030493 | ISBN 9781108420358 (alk. paper)
SUBJECTS: LCSH: English poetry – Irish authors – History and criticism. |
Irish poetry – History and criticism.
CLASSIFICATION: LCC PR8761 .C36 2017 | DDC 821.009/9415–dc23
LC record available at https://lccn.loc.gov/2017030493

ISBN 978-1-108-42035-8 Hardback
ISBN 978-1-108-41419-7 Paperback

CONTENTS

CONTENTS

NOTES ON CONTRIBUTORS

Nicholas Allen is director of the Wilson Center for Humanities and Arts and Franklin Professor of English at the University of Georgia. His books include *Modernism, Ireland and Civil War* (2009), *George Russell and the New Ireland* (2003), *The Cities of Belfast* (2003) with Aaron Kelly and *Coastal Works: Cultures of the Atlantic Edge* (2015), edited with Nick Groom and Jos Smith.

Fran Brearton is Professor of Modern Poetry at Queen's University Belfast and assistant director of the Seamus Heaney Centre for Poetry. She is author of *The Great War in Irish Poetry* (2000) and *Reading Michael Longley* (2006), and co-editor of *Incorrigibly Plural: Louis MacNeice and His Legacy* (2012), *Modern Irish and Scottish Poetry* (2011) and *The Oxford Handbook of Modern Irish Poetry* (2012). She edited the 1929 original edition of Robert Graves's *Good-bye to All That* for Penguin Classics (2014).

Terence Brown is Fellow Emeritus at Trinity College Dublin. He has published numerous volumes of literary and social criticism, including *Louis MacNeice: Sceptical Vision* (1975), *Northern Voices: Poets from Ulster* (1975), *Ireland: A Social and Cultural History* (1981, 2004), *Ireland's Literature: Selected Essays* (1988), *The Life of W. B. Yeats: A Critical Biography* (1999, 2001), *The Literature of Ireland: Culture and Criticism* (2010) and *The Irish Times: 150 Years of Influence* (2015). A member of the Royal Irish Academy and of Academia Europaea, he was made CMG for services to British–Irish relations in 2002.

Matthew Campbell is Professor of Modern Literature at University of York. His publications include *Irish Poetry under the Union, 1801–1924* (2013), and he is editor of the *Cambridge Companion to Contemporary Irish Poetry* (2003).

Lucy Collins is Lecturer in English Literature at University College Dublin, Ireland. She was educated at Trinity College Dublin and at Harvard University, where she spent a year as a Fulbright Scholar. She edited a special issue of the *Irish University Review* in 2012 on Irish poetry 1930–1970. Other recent publications include *Poetry by Women in Ireland: A Critical Anthology 1870–1970* (2012), *Contemporary Irish Women Poets: Memory and Estrangement* (2015) and a co-edited volume, *The Irish Poet and the Natural World: An Anthology of Verse in English from the Tudors to the Romantics* (2014).

Gerald Dawe is Professor of English and Fellow of Trinity College Dublin. He has published eight poetry collections, including *Selected Poems* (2012) and *Mickey Finn's Air* (2014). A volume of collected essays, *The Proper Word: Ireland, Poetry, Politics*, edited with an introduction by Nicholas Allen, appeared in 2007. He edited the anthology *Earth Voices Whispering: Irish Poetry of War 1914–1945* (2008). *Of War and War's Alarms: Reflections on Modern Irish Writing* was published in 2015.

John Dillon is a Notebaert Graduate Fellow in the English Department at the University of Notre Dame. His research and teaching interests include European Modernisms, Irish Studies and the Digital Humanities. Recently, he has published a translation of Seán Ó Ríordáin's aesthetic essay, 'What Is Poetry?' in *Selected Poems* (2014), and 'Mary Battle and W. B. Yeats – from Folklore to Gesamtlebenswerk' (*Folklore & Modern Irish Writing*, 2014). He is the co-founder and director of *Breac: A Digital Journal of Irish Studies* (http://breac.nd.edu).

Andrew Fitzsimons is a professor in the Department of English Language and Cultures at Gakushuin University, Tokyo. His publications include *The Sea of Disappointment: Thomas Kinsella's Pursuit of the Real* (2008) and *Thomas Kinsella: Prose Occasions 1951–2006* (ed., 2009). His poetry has appeared in Ireland, Italy, Britain, Japan and the United States, and he is the author of two collections: *What the Sky Arranges* (2013) and *A Fire in the Head* (2014).

Alan Gillis teaches at The University of Edinburgh and is editor of *Edinburgh Review*. He recently published his fourth book of poems, *Scapegoat* (2014), and was chosen as one of the Poetry Book Society's Next Generation Poets 2014. As a critic, he has written *Irish Poetry of the 1930s* (2005), and recently co-edited *The Edinburgh Introduction to Studying English Literature* (2014) and *The Oxford Handbook of Modern Irish Poetry* (2013).

Nicholas Grene is Professor of English Literature at Trinity College Dublin, a Senior Fellow of the College and a Member of the Royal Irish Academy. He has published widely on Shakespeare and on Irish literature. His most recent publications include *Yeats's Poetic Codes* (2008), the New Mermaids edition of *Major Barbara* (2008) and *Synge and Edwardian Ireland* (2011), co-edited with Brian Cliff. His book *Home on the Stage: Domestic Spaces in Modern Drama* was published in 2014.

Michael Griffin is a lecturer in eighteenth-century and Irish studies at the University of Limerick. He is the author of *Enlightenment in Ruins: The Geographies of Oliver Goldsmith* (2013). His is editor of *The Selected Writings of Thomas Dermody* (2012) and *The Collected Poems of Laurence Whyte* (2015). He is also co-editor with David O'Shaughnessy of the new *Cambridge Edition of the Collected Letters of Oliver Goldsmith* (2017).

Hugh Haughton is a professor in the Department of English and Related Literature, University of York. He is the author of *The Poetry of Derek Mahon* (2007) and numerous essays on modern and contemporary poetry. He is the editor of *Second World War Poems* (2004), Sigmund Freud, *The Uncanny* (2003) and, with Valerie Eliot, *The Letters of T. S. Eliot vols 1 and 2* (2009).

Florence Impens is a Leverhulme Early Career Fellow at the John Rylands Research Institute, University of Manchester. She has essays forthcoming in *After Ireland: Essays on Contemporary Irish Poetry* (2017), *The Oxford History of Classical Reception in English Literature* (2017), *Seamus Heaney in Context* (2018) and *Irish University Review*. She is currently working on a project on poetry in translation in the United Kingdom and Ireland after 1962.

Maria Johnston received her Doctorate in English Literature in 2007 and has since worked as a lecturer at Trinity College Dublin, the Mater Dei Institute (DCU) and Oxford University. Her reviews and essays have appeared in a range of publications, including *The Guardian, Poetry Ireland Review, Edinburgh Review, Poetry Review* and *Oxford Tower Poetry Matters*, and she has contributed essays to *The Oxford Handbook of Modern Irish Poetry* and *The Oxford Handbook of Contemporary British and Irish Poetry*. She is the co-editor of *Reading Pearse Hutchinson* (2011) and is currently working on a book on contemporary Irish poetry.

Benjamin Keatinge is Dean of the Faculty of Languages, Cultures and Communications and Head of English at the South East European University, Macedonia. He has published (as co-editor) *Other Edens: The Life and Work of Brian Coffey* (2010) and *France and Ireland in the Public Imagination* (2014), and is currently editing a collection of critical essays on Richard Murphy.

Seán Lysaght taught in the English Department at NUI Maynooth from 1990 to 1994, where he completed his PhD on the life and writings of the naturalist Robert Lloyd Praeger. He now lectures in Irish studies at the Galway-Mayo Institute of Technology, Castlebar. He has published seven collections of poems and translations, and a verse narrative of the life of Edmund Spenser. His *Selected Poems* was published in 2010.

Aodán Mac Póilin is the former Director of ULTACH Trust, and has published numerous articles on literature, cultural and linguistic politics, language planning and broadcasting, including 'The Irish Language in Belfast until 1900' and 'Irish Language Writing in Belfast after 1900', both in *The Cities of Belfast* (2003), 'The Universe of the Gaeltacht', in *Re-imagining Ireland* (2006), '"Something of a Cultural War"' in *Language Issues: Ireland, France, Spain* (2010) and 'Ghosts of Metrical Procedures: Translations from the Irish' in *The Oxford Handbook of Modern Irish Poetry* (2012).

John McAuliffe is Reader in Creative Writing and Modern Literature and director of the Centre for New Writing at the University of Manchester, and editor of the online journal *Manchester Review*. He has published three volumes of poetry – *A Better Life* (2002), which was shortlisted for a Forward prize, *Next Door* (2007) and *Of All Places* (2011), which was a Poetry Book Society Recommendation. He writes a monthly poetry column for the *Irish Times*, as well as contributing poems, reviews and essays to a wide range of other books and journals in Ireland, the United Kingdom and the United States.

Peter McDonald is Professor of British and Irish Poetry at the University of Oxford, and Christopher Tower Student and Tutor in Poetry in the English Language department at Christ Church, Oxford. He was born in Belfast. He has published several volumes of poetry, including *Collected Poems* (2012), and is the author of a number of critical books, including *Serious Poetry: Form and Authority from Yeats to Hill* (2002) and *Sound Intentions: The Workings of Rhyme in Nineteenth-Century Poetry* (2012). He has edited Louis MacNeice's *Collected Poems* (2007), and is currently editing a three-volume edition of *The Complete Poems of W. B. Yeats*.

Chris Morash is the Seamus Heaney Professor of Irish Writing at Trinity College, Dublin. He has published on a range of topics in the field of Irish writing, including Irish Famine literature (*Writing the Irish Famine*, ss1995), Irish theatre (his *History of the Irish Theatre* [2002] won the Theatre Book Prize) and the first comprehensive history of the Irish media, from the earliest printed word to the present (*A History of the Media in Ireland*, 2009). *Mapping Irish Theatre* (with Shaun Richards) was published in 2013, and he co-edited, with Nicholas Grene, the *Oxford Handbook of Modern Irish Theatre*. He is also currently writing a book on Yeats and theatre. He was elected to Membership of the Royal Irish Academy in 2007, and has chaired the Compliance Committee of the Broadcasting Authority of Ireland since 2009.

Louis de Paor is Director of the Centre for Irish Studies at the National University of Ireland, Galway, and author of numerous articles on modern and contemporary poetry and fiction in Irish. His most recent publications include a critical edition of the selected stories of Máirtín Ó Cadhain and an edited volume of essays on the poetry of Máire Mhac an tSaoi. He has also published a monograph on narrative technique in the short fiction of Máirtín Ó Cadhain and edited critical editions of the work of Liam S Gógan and Máire Mhac an tSaoi. He was a contributor to the *Cambridge History of Irish Literature* and the *Cambridge Companion to Irish Modernisms*. He is currently researching the diaries of Seán Ó Ríordáin and the Irish language element in the early work of Flann O'Brien.

Richard Pine worked in the Irish national broadcasting service for twenty-five years before taking early retirement, moving to Greece, and establishing the Durrell School of Corfu (2002–2014). He is now the Curator of the Durrell Library of Corfu, and an advisor to the British-Greek Research Centre of the Ionian University in Corfu. He is the author/editor of twenty books, including *The Diviner: The Art of Brian Friel* (2nd edn., 1999) and *Lawrence Durrell: The Mindscape* (1994), and editor of the essay collection *Dark Fathers into Light: Brendan Kennelly* (1997). He contributed 'Friel's Irish Russia' to the *Cambridge Companion to Brian Friel* (2006).

Justin Quinn is Associate Professor of American and English Literature, Charles University, Prague. His publications include *Gathered Beneath the Storm: Wallace Stevens, Nature and Community* (2002), *American Errancy: Empire, Sublimity and Modern Poetry* (2005), *Cambridge Introduction to Modern Irish Poetry, 1800–2000* (2008) and (as editor) *Irish Poetry After Feminism* (2008) and *Lectures on American Literature*, 3rd edn (2011). His translations of the Czech poet Petr Borkovec, *From the Interior*, appeared in 2008. He is currently writing a book on transnationalism and poetry during the Cold War, and translating the poetry of Bohuslav Reynek.

Maurice Riordan is Professor of Poetry at Sheffield Hallam University. He has taught at Imperial College and Goldsmiths College. He has published four collections of poems with Faber and Faber: *A Word from the Loki* (1995), a PBS Choice and shortlisted for the T. S. Eliot Prize; *Floods* (2000), shortlisted for the Whitbread Poetry Award; *The Holy Land* (2007), which received the Michael Hartnett Award; and *The Water Stealer* (2013), also shortlisted for the T. S. Eliot Prize. Among his other books are *The Finest Music: Early Irish Lyrics* (2014) and *A Quark for Mister Mark: 101 Poems about Science* (2000). He co-edited *Wild Reckoning* (2004), an anthology of ecological poems, with John Burnside, and *Dark Matter: Poems of Space* (2008), with astronomer Jocelyn Bell Burnell. *Confidential Reports*, his translations of Maltese poet Immanuel Mifsud, appeared in 2005. He has also published a collection for children, *The Moon Has Written You a Poem*, adapted from the Portuguese edition of José Letria. He was editor of *Poetry London* from 2005 to 2009, and became Editor of *The Poetry Review* in 2013.

Peter Sirr works as a freelance writer, teacher and translator. He teaches a seminar in literary translation in Trinity College, Dublin. He has published *Marginal Zones* (1984), *Talk, Talk* (1987), *Ways of Falling* (1991), *The Ledger of Fruitful Exchange* (1995), *Bring Everything* (2000), *Selected Poems* and *Nonetheless* (both 2004), *The Thing Is* (2009) and *The Rooms* (2014). A novel for children, *Black Wreath*, was published in 2014. He has written extensively on Irish and international poetry for leading Irish and European journals. He is a member of the Irish academy of artists, Aosdána.

Jeffery Vail is a senior lecturer of Humanities at the College of General Studies, Boston University. He has written widely on Romantic-era literature, especially that of Lord Byron and the Irish Romantic poet and songwriter Thomas Moore. He is the author of *The Literary Relationship of Lord Byron and Thomas Moore* (2001) and the editor of *The Unpublished Letters of Thomas Moore* (2013). He has lectured on British and Irish Romanticism in the United States and abroad, including Dublin, Galway, Belfast, Paris, Salzburg and the United Kingdom. He is currently preparing an edition of Moore's unpublished prose satire, *Sketches of Pious Women*.

Tom Walker is the Ussher Assistant Professor in Irish Writing at Trinity College Dublin. Born in Sydney and brought up in London, he completed his BA and DPhil at the University of Oxford, as well as an MPhil in Anglo-Irish Literature at Trinity College Dublin. He has published articles on several aspects of twentieth-century Irish literature, including the work of Louis MacNeice, Austin Clarke, Flann O'Brien, Denis Johnston, Derek Mahon, John McGahern and Patrick McCabe. His study on *Louis MacNeice and the Irish Poetry of His Time* was published in 2015. He is currently undertaking research into the relationship between the work of W. B. Yeats and the visual arts.

James Ward lectures in Eighteenth-Century Literature at the University of Ulster. He has published essays and articles on Swift and eighteenth-century literature, as well as on representations of the eighteenth century in modern film and fiction. He has written for the *London Review of Books* and the *Dublin Review of Books*, and served as academic director of the Trim Swift Festival.

David Wheatley is a senior lecturer at the University of Aberdeen. His *Contemporary British Poetry* was published in 2014. He has published four collections of poetry, and has edited the poetry of James Clarence Mangan (2003) and Samuel Beckett's *Selected Poems 1930–1989* (2009).

Guy Woodward was awarded a doctorate by Trinity College Dublin in 2012, and from 2012 to 2013 he held a Government of Ireland Postdoctoral Fellowship, awarded by the Irish Research Council. He has lectured at Trinity, the Institute of Public Administration, Dublin and at the Tecnológico de Monterrey, Mexico. He is the co-editor of the collection of essays *Irish Culture and Wartime Europe, 1938–48* (2015) and contributed the essay '"We Must Know More Than Ireland": John Hewitt and Eastern Europe' to *Ireland, West to East: Irish Literary and Cultural Connections with Central and Eastern Europe* (2014). His book *Culture, Northern Ireland, and the Second World War* was published in 2015.

CHRONOLOGY

Historical Events	Cultural/Literary Events
1537 Acts for the suppression of Irish monasteries	
1541 Henry VIII declared 'king of Ireland' by statute of Irish parliament	
1549 Order for use of English Book of Common Prayer in Ireland	
1550–7 Plantations in Laois (Leix) and Offaly (established respectively as Queen's County and King's County in **1556**)	**1550** The English Book of Common Prayer used in Ireland
1555 Papal Bull of Pope Paul IV declares Ireland a Kingdom	**1571** First printing in the Irish language, in Dublin
1561–7 Rebellion of Shane O'Neill; English campaigns led by Sussex and Sir Henry Sidney	**1577** The Great Comet recorded in Annals of the Four Masters
1588 Ships of Spanish Armada wrecked off Irish coast	**1580** Edmund Spenser in Ireland with Lord Leonard Grey, Lord Deputy of Ireland
1595–1603 Rebellion of Hugh O'Neill, earl of Tyrone	**1592** Charter incorporates Trinity College, Dublin
1601 Spanish army lands at Kinsale. Tyrone and 'Red Hugh' O'Donnell defeated at Kinsale; O'Donnell leaves Ireland for Spain	
1603 Surrender of Tyrone at Mellifont	

1607 Flight of the Earls (including Tyrone and Tyrconnell) from Lough Swilly

1608–10 Preparations for plantations in Ulster counties

1613 Opening of parliament in Dublin

1621 Patents granted for plantations in Leitrim, King's County (Offaly), Queen's County (Laois) and Westmeath

1641 Outbreak of rebellion in Ulster

1642–9 'Confederation of Kilkenny': government of Catholic Confederates

1649 Oliver Cromwell arrives in Dublin as civil and military governor of Ireland. Massacres at Drogheda and Wexford. Death of Eoghan Ruadh O'Neill (Owen Roe O'Neill)

1650 Cromwell returns to England

1652–3 Act for the settlement of Ireland; Cromwellian land confiscations

1663 First of series of acts restricting Irish trade and exports

1689 James II arrives in Ireland. Siege of Derry begins; ends in July

1690 Forces of James II defeated by those of William III at River Boyne

1691 Battle of Aughrim: Williamite victory. Treaty of Limerick, allowing evacuation of Irish army to France and promising toleration to Irish Catholics

1691–1703 Williamite land confiscations

1695 Beginning of 'Penal Laws': Acts restricting rights of Catholics to education,

1632 Compilation of the Annals of the Four Masters completed

1670 Possible birthdate of Aogán Ó'Raithille

1684 Foundation of Dublin Philosophical Society

1713 Jonathan Swift made Dean of St. Patrick's Cathedral, Dublin

to bear arms or to possess a horse worth
more than five pounds

1704 Further 'Penal Law' introduced,
including 'tests' on Catholics and Protestant
dissenters for holding of public office;
amended and strengthened August 1708

1718 Beginning of large-scale migration of
Ulster Scots to American colonies

1726 Jonathan Swift, *Gulliver's Travels*

1720 Declaratory Act defines right of English
parliament to legislate for Ireland

1731 Foundation of Dublin Society for
Improving Husbandry, Manufacturing, and
Other Useful Arts (from 1829, Royal
Dublin Society)

1740–41 'Bliadhain an Áir' ('The Year of the
Slaughter'): large-scale famine, with
mortality estimated at over 200,000 from
a population of approximately 2 million

1738 Death of Turlough O Carolan

1760 Catholic Committee established in
Dublin to advance Catholic interests

1763 Freeman's Journal (−1924)

1761 Beginning of Whiteboy movement in
Munster

1770 Oliver Goldsmith, *The Deserted Village*

1778 Beginning of Volunteer movement (local
independent military forces); first company
enrolled in Belfast. Catholic Relief Act
grants rights of leasing and inheritance

1771 Benjamin Franklin visits Ireland

1783 British Renunciation Act acknowledges
exclusive right of Irish parliament to
legislate for Ireland (inaugurates 'Grattan's
parliament', to 1800)

1791 Foundation of Society of United Irishmen
in Belfast

1785 First meeting of Irish Academy ('Royal
Irish' after January 1786)

1792–93 Catholic Relief Acts allow Catholics
to practise law and give parliamentary
franchise

1788 The Linenhall Library Belfast founded

1795 Foundation of Orange Order

1790 Edmund Burke, Reflections on the
French Revolution

1796 French fleet, with Wolfe Tone, at Bantry Bay

1798 United Irishmen rising: rebellion begins in Leinster (May); outbreaks in Ulster in June; French force lands in Killala (August); French force surrenders (September). Death of Wolfe Tone

1800 Act of Union dissolves Irish parliament and declares legislative union

1801 Act of Union takes effect

1803 Robert Emmet's rebellion in Dublin; Emmet executed in September

1816 Failure of potato crop leads to first major famine since 1742; widespread typhus epidemic continues until late 1819

1821 Failure of potato crop; fever follows in west of Ireland in summer 1822

1823 Foundation of Catholic Association by Daniel O'Connell

1828 Daniel O'Connell elected MP for Clare

1829 Catholic Emancipation Act enables Catholics to enter parliament and to hold civil and military offices

1837 Accession of Queen Victoria

1838 English system of Poor Law is extended to Ireland

1840 Repeal Association founded

1795 Act passed for establishment of Catholic Seminary at Maynooth

1796 Edward Bunting, Ancient Irish Music

1801 Copyright Act renders illegal the publication of pirate Irish editions of British publications

1808 Thomas Moore's *Irish Melodies* released in ten volumes (1834). George IV visited Ireland. Dún Laoghaire Harbour renamed Kingstown.

1825–41 Ordnance Survey of Ireland carried out

1831 State system of National Education introduced

1834 James Clarence Mangan contributes poetry to Dublin University Magazine

1838 Father Mathew founds Abstinence movement

1842 First number of The Nation

1841 Census of Ireland: population of island
8,175,124

1845 Arrival of potato blight in Ireland first
noted

1845–51 *An Gorta Mórr* ('The Great Irish
Famine'): mortality estimated at in excess of
1 million

1844 Queen's University founded, with
colleges in Belfast, Cork and Galway

1846 Repeal of the Corn Laws

1846 Recurrence of potato blight, leading to
large mortality in winter of 1846–7

1847 Death of Daniel O'Connell

1848 Abortive rising by William Smith O'Brien
at Ballingarry, Co. Tipperary: beginning of
short-lived Young Ireland Rebellion

1851 Census of Ireland: population of island
6,552,385

1848 John Mitchel establishes United Irishman
newspaper

1854 Catholic University of Ireland founded,
with John Henry Newman as rector

1856 Births of George Bernard Shaw and
Oscar Wilde

1858 James Stephens founds Irish Republican
Brotherhood (IRB) in Dublin

1859 *Irish Times* Newspaper founded

1859 Fenian Brotherhood established in the
United States

1861 Census of Ireland: population 5,798,967

1867 Fenian rebellion: disturbances in England
and Ireland in February; execution of
Fenian 'Manchester Martyrs' in November

1865 Birth of W. B. Yeats

1869 Irish Church Act disestablishes Church of
Ireland

1870 Isaac Butt founds Home Government
Association: beginning of Home Rule
movement. Gladstone's first Land Act

1876 Society for the Preservation of the Irish
Language Founded

1877 Charles Stewart Parnell elected president of Home Rule Confederation of Great Britain

1877 National Library of Ireland established

1879 Foundation of National Land League of Mayo by Michael Davitt

1880 Parnell elected chairman of Irish Parliamentary Party (IPP)

1880 'Boycotting' coined during the land war after Captain Boycott

1882 'Phoenix Park murders' of Lord Frederick Cavendish and Thomas Burke

1886 Gladstone's Home Rule Bill defeated

1884 Foundation of Gaelic Athletic Association (GAA) Announcement of 'Plan of Campaign' to withhold rents on certain estates

1890 Split in IPP, with majority opposing Parnell

1890 National Museum of Ireland opened

1891 Death of Parnell

1892 Labour Party established in Belfast

1892 National Literary Society established; Douglas Hyde's address, 'On the Necessity for De-Anglicising the Irish People'

1893 Second Home Rule Bill passed by House of Commons but defeated in House of Lords

1893 Foundation of Gaelic League (Conradh na Gaeilge) *Douglas Hyde, Love Songs of Connacht*

1898 Irish Local Government Act

1898 Queen Victoria visited Ireland

1900 Foundation of Cumann na nGaedheal led by Arthur Griffith

1899 First production by Irish Literary Theatre

1901 Census of Ireland: population 4,458,775

1902 W. B. Yeats's play *Cathleen Ni Houlihan* performed Cuala Press established (–1946)

1903 Wyndham Land Act

1907 Cumann na nGaedheal and Dungannon clubs become Sinn Féin League

1904 Opening of Abbey Theatre Ulster Literary Theatre founded

1908 Foundation of Irish Transport Workers' Union (later ITGWU)

1911 Census of Ireland: population 4,381,951

1907 J. M. Synge, *The Playboy of the Western World* performed at the Abbey Theatre. The Irish International Exhibition opened in Dublin. Marconi Trans-Atlantic Telegraphy starts between Clifden in County Galway and Cape Breton Canada

1908 Irish Women's Franchise League formed

1912 Third Home Rule Bill passed by House of Commons; twice defeated in House of Lords (January and July 1913) Solemn League and Covenant signed in Ulster

1912 The Titanic sinks on its maiden voyage

1913 Foundation of Ulster Volunteer Force Beginning of ITGWU strike in Dublin, becomes general lockout. Formation of Irish Citizen Army and Irish Volunteers

1914 James Joyce, *Dubliners* W. B. Yeats, *Responsibilities*

1914 'Curragh Mutiny': resignation by sixty cavalry officers in the British army at Kildare. Ulster Volunteer Force gun-running Foundation of Cumann na mBan (women's auxiliary league). Home Rule Bill passes again in Commons. Howth gun-running by Irish Volunteers. United Kingdom and Germany go to war. Home Rule Bill suspended; John Redmond calls on Irish Volunteers to support British war; movement splits into National (pro-Redmond) and Irish (anti-Redmond) Volunteers

1916 James Joyce, *A Portrait of an Artist as a Young Man*; Thomas Mac Donagh, *Literature in Ireland*

1915 Sinking of Lusitania

1916 Easter Rising (May) Execution of rebel leaders. Battle of the Somme (July)

1917 Death of Francis Ledwidge during third battle of Ypres, WWI (July)

1918 Sinn Fein victory in general election. Countess Markievicz elected to Westminster Parliament but refuses to take her seat

1919 Alcock and Brown completed first non-stop trans-Atlantic flight from Newfoundland to Clifden, Co, Galway

1919 First meeting of Dáil Eireann at Mansion House, with Eamon de Valera elected president. Irish Volunteer organisation increasingly known as Irish Republican Army

1919–21 Irish War of Independence/Anglo-Irish War (January) 1920. First recruits of British ex-soldiers and sailors ('Black and Tans') join Royal Irish Constabulary (December) 1920. Government of Ireland Act provides for creation of separate parliaments in Dublin and Belfast. George V opens Northern Irish Parliament. Truce between IRA and British Army, Anglo-Irish Treaty signed

1922 James Joyce, *Ulysses*

1922 Treaty approved by Dáil Eireann (sixty-four to fifty-seven): establishment of Irish Free State. Beginning of Irish Civil War between pro-Treaty (Free State) and anti-Treaty (Republican) forces

1923 Censorship of Films Act. W. B. Yeats is awarded the Nobel Prize for Literature

1923 Cumann na nGaedheal (political party) founded as first new post-independence party Suspension of Republican campaign. Irish Free State enters League of Nations

1924 BBC Northern Ireland first broadcast

1925 Findings of Boundary Commission leaked April 1926 Census of Ireland: population of Irish Free State 2,971,992; population of Northern Ireland 1,256,561

1925 George Bernard Shaw is awarded the Nobel Prize for Literature

1926 Foundation of Fianna Fail

1926 Radio Eifeann begin broadcasting

1927 Irish Free State Justice Minister, Kevin O'Higgins assassinated

1928 Irish Manuscripts Commission founded. Samuel Beckett moves to Paris. W. B. Yeats, *The Tower* Opening of The Gate Theatre First citizen of an independent Ireland Dr. Pat O'Callaghan wins a Gold Medal at the Olympic Games in Amsterdam

1930 Ireland elected to the Council of the League of Nations

1929 Censorship of Publications Act

1932 Fianna Fail wins general election. Thirty-First International Eucharistic Congress held in Dublin

1930 First Censorship Board appointed in Irish Free State

1933 Foundation of Fine Gael (replaces Cumann na nGaedheal)

1935 Samuel Beckett, *Echo's Bones and other Precipitates*

1936 IRA declared illegal

1936 W. B. Yeats Editor, *Oxford Book of Modern Verse 1892–1935*. Aer Lingus inaugural flight Dublin-Bristol (UK)

1937 De Valera's new constitution (Bunreacht na h Éireann) approved; Éire declared official name of state

1937 Charles Donnelly killed fighting with International Brigade during Spanish Civil War

1938 Douglas Hyde becomes first president of Ireland. Eamon de Valera elected president of the League of Nations

1938 Austin Clarke, *Night and Morning*

1939 Éire's policy of neutrality announced

1939 Death of W. B. Yeats in France. Louis MacNeice, *Autumn Journal*. Irish Red Cross Established Inaugural Trans-Atlantic Air Service to the United States

1939–45 'Emergency' years

1940 *The Bell* begins publication

1941 (April and May) Air-raids on Belfast. Approximately 700 people killed

1941 Samuel Beckett joins Paris-Based Resistance cell (Gloria SMH)

1942 Patrick Kavanagh, *The Great Hunger* Committee for the Encouragement of Music and the Arts (CEMA) founded in Belfast

1948 Fianna Fail loses overall majority; replaced by coalition government under John A. Costello. Republic of Ireland Act under which Éire becomes Republic of Ireland and leaves Commonwealth

1945 Samuel Beckett awarded the 'Croix de Coeur' and 'Medaille de la Resistance' by the French government

1948 Re-interment of W. B. Yeats in Drumcliffe, Co. Sligo

1951 Catholic hierarchy condemns 'Mother and Child' Scheme; resignation of Dr Noel Browne as Minister of Health

1949 *Envoy: A Review of Literature and Art* founded by John Ryan

1950 Thomas MacGreevy appointed director of National Gallery of Ireland (retires 1963)

1955 Republic of Ireland joins United Nations

1951 Arts Council of Ireland founded. Dolmen Press founded by Liam and Josephine Miller. Lyric Theatre founded by Mary and Pearse O'Malley

1956 IRA begins campaign on Northern border

1958 First Programme for Economic Expansion introduced, encouraging exports along with private and foreign investment in manufacturing

1959 De Valera elected president

1963 Terence O'Neill becomes prime minister of Northern Ireland Visit of John F. Kennedy Ian Paisley founds Democratic Unionist Party (DUP)

1966 Ulster Volunteer Force (UVF), loyalist paramilitary group (taking its name from the 1913 movement), founded January 1967 Foundation of Northern Ireland Civil Rights Association

1968 Civil rights marches in Northern Ireland; clashes between marchers and police in Derry mark beginning of 'the Troubles'

1970 IRA splits into Official IRA and Provisional IRA. Foundation of Social Democratic Labour Party (SDLP) in Northern Ireland

1971 Internment introduced in Northern Ireland

1972 Stormont parliament in Belfast suspended; direct rule from London introduced. 30 January 'Bloody Sunday': fourteen civilians killed and twelve wounded in Derry by British Army. 21 July 'Bloody Friday': twenty-two bombs set off in Belfast by IRA; nine people killed and some hundred and thirty wounded

1952 Séan Ó Ríordáin, *Eireaball Spideoige* [*A Robin's Tail*]

1953 BBC Northern Ireland TV broadcast Samuel Beckett *En attendant Godot*

1954 Richard Murphy settled in Cleggan, Co. Galway

1955 Austin Clarke, *Ancient Lights*

1957 John Hewitt appointed director of the Herbert Art Gallery and Museum, Coventry, England (retires 1972)

1960 Patrick Kavanagh, *Come Dance with Kitty Stobling*

1961 RTE (Radio Telefís Eireann) begins television service

1962 The Arts Council of Northern Ireland established

1963 Death of Louis MacNeice (55)

1963–73 Belfast 'Group' of poets meets at Queen's University

1967 Death of Patrick Kavanagh (63)

1968 Thomas Kinsella, *Nightwalker and other poems*. Honest Ulsterman, founded by James Simmons. (2003). Lyric New Theatre opens in Belfast

1973 Republic of Ireland joins European Economic Community (EEC)

1974 Ulster Workers' Council declares general Strike

1975 Suspension of internment without trial in Northern Ireland

1979 Pope John Paul II visits Ireland

1980 Hunger strikes in Maze and Armagh Prisons

1981 Ten IRA and Irish National Liberation Army (INLA) hunger-strikers die, including Bobby Sands (elected MP, April 1981)

1983 Amendment to constitution passed by referendum, seeking to prevent any possible legalisation of abortion

1984 Report of the New Ireland Forum is published

1985 Anglo-Irish Agreement signed by Garret FitzGerald and Margaret Thatcher

1986 Referendum upholds constitutional ban on Divorce

1987 Referendum approves Single European Act

1969 Samuel Beckett is awarded the Nobel Prize for Literature

1970 The Gallery Press founded by Peter Fallon.

1971 Seán Ó Riada dies

1973 Brendan Kennelly appointed first Professor of Modern Literature, Trinity College Dublin (retires 2005)

1974 Austin Clarke dies

1975 Eavan Boland, *The War Horse*. Paul Durcan, *O Westport in the Light of Asia Minor*. Seamus Heaney, *North* Michel Hartnett, *A Farewell to English*. Cyphers Magazine established. *Two Decades of Irish Writing: A Critical Survey* (ed. Douglas Dunn) published Arlen House, Ireland's first feminist press, founded by Catherine Rose

1977 *The Crane Bag* journal founded

1978 Poetry Ireland founded by John F. Deane who also founded Dedalus Press (1985)

1979 Medbh McGuckian wins the National Poetry Competition (UK)

1980 Field Day Theatre and Publishing Company established

1981 Nuala Ni Dhomhnaill, *An Dealg Droighin*. Salmon Poetry founded by Jessie Lendennie. Thomas Kinsella and Sean O'Tuama (eds), *An Dunaire' 1600–1900 Poems of the Dispossessed*. Aosdána, an

Irish association of artists established by the Arts Council

1982 Medbh McGuckian, *The Flower Master*

1983 John Hewitt made a Freeman of the City of Belfast

1986 Edna Longley, *Poetry in the Wars*

1987 Ciaran Carson, *The Irish for No*

1990 Mary Robinson elected president of Ireland, the first female president

1989 Samuel Beckett dies (83)

1992 Referendum held on three abortion-related issues: the right to travel and the right to information supported

1990 Paul Durcan, *Daddy, Daddy*

1993 Downing Street Declaration signed by Albert Reynolds and John Major

1991 Michael Longley, *Gorse Fires; Field Day Anthology of Irish Writing*

1994 IRA and Loyalist paramilitaries declare ceasefires (later suspended and restored)

1992 Derek Mahon, *The Yaddo Letter*

1995 Referendum allowing divorce is carried

1995 Seamus Heaney is awarded the Nobel Prize for Literature

1997 Mary McAleese elected president of Ireland

1996 Eavan Boland appointed Bella Mabury Knapp Professor in Humanities, Stanford University, USA. Ciaran Carson, *Last Night's Fun: About Time, Food and Music*

1998 Good Friday Agreement is negotiated and endorsed in referendums in Republic of Ireland and Northern Ireland (May)

1998 John Montague appointed inaugural Ireland; every three years a poet of honour and distinction is chosen to represent the Chair as Ireland's Professor of Poetry. Seamus Heaney, *Opened Ground: Poems 1966–1996*

1999 Northern Irish Assembly meets. Ireland adopts the euro

2001 Nuala Ni Dhomhnaill appointed first Irish Language Ireland Professor of Poetry

2002 Richard Murphy, *The Kick: A Life among Writers*

1997–2008 Economic boom years become known as 'Celtic Tiger'

2001 Amendment to Constitution provide universal ban on death penalty. Census of population of Northern Ireland: 1,685,267. Census of population of Republic of Ireland: 3,917,203

2008–11 Financial crisis leads to dissolution of 30th Dáil and election of coalition government to oversee programme of financial austerity and EU 'bail-out'. Election of Michael D. Higgins as thirteenth president of Ireland

2015 Referendum makes Ireland the first country to legalise same-sex marriage by popular vote: 62%–38%

2016 Centenary of the Easter Rising celebrated nationally and globally

2003 Paul Muldoon awarded Pulitzer Prize for *Moy Sand and Gravel*

2004 Seamus Heaney Centre for Poetry, Queen's University Belfast opened

2007 Thomas Kinsella received Freedom of the City of Dublin. Derek Mahon awarded David Cohen Prize for literature in recognition of an entire body of work written in English

2009 Derek Mahon awarded Griffin Poetry Prize for *Life on Earth*

2010 Michael Longley awarded Commander of the British Empire. John Montague made a Chevalier de la Légion d'honneur, France's highest civil award. Eilean Ni Chuilleanáin awarded Griffin Poetry Prize for *The Sun Fish*. *The Penguin Book of Irish Poetry* and *An Anthology of Modern Irish Poetry* (Harvard) published Harry Clifton appointed Ireland Professor of Poetry

2012 Death of Dennis O'Driscoll poet, critic and editor of *Stepping Stones: Interviews with Seamus Heaney* (2008)

2013 Death of Seamus Heaney (74). Paula Meehan appointed Ireland Professor of Poetry

'Historical Events' draws upon Margaret Kelleher and Philip O'Leary, eds. *The Cambridge History of Irish Literature* (Cambridge University Press, 2006)

2016 Deaths of John Montague (87) and Anthony Cronin (88). Opening of The Home Place, dedicated to Seamus Heaney in Bellaghy, Co. Derry. Eilean Ni Chuilleanáin appointed Ireland Professor of Poetry

PREFACE AND ACKNOWLEDGEMENTS

This volume aims to provide fresh and lucid accounts of twenty-nine Irish poets writing in English and Irish from the seventeenth century to the beginning of the twenty-first century. While the focus of the individual chapters varies from poet to poet, the intention of each contribution to this *Companion* is to give an overview of the poet's work and to guide the interested reader through the wider cultural, historical and comparative contexts, but without overloading or obscuring the primary concentration on the poet's work. Many of the contributors are poets themselves; others have written substantial monographs and studies of Irish poets other than those they have written about here. The critical and cultural exchange which takes place across the generations of Irish poetry and the resounding resonances and conversations between individual poets and their lives and times is a noteworthy though unintended feature of this volume.

As editor I would like to thank Ray Ryan of Cambridge University Press for his patience and support while the *Companion* gathered momentum, and Conor Linnie, a doctoral student with the School of English at Trinity College, who helped with the final formatting of the text and the 'Further Reading' section. Kyle Hughes, also a graduate student with the School of English, kindly stepped in at a critical moment when a technical issue confounded our best computer skills. I owe a debt of gratitude to Julitta Clancy for producing the Index, an epic poem all to itself. But my main debt of gratitude is to the contributors who responded to their tasks so enthusiastically despite carrying heavy workloads both within the academy and without. As the *Companion* was going into production we sadly lost one of our contributors, Aodán Mac Póilin, an inspirational presence whose love and knowledge of Irish poetry in both Irish and English was legendary. The book is testament to how we are all as readers still enthralled by what Seamus Heaney praised in his poem, 'Song' as 'the mud-flowers of dialect/And the immortelles of perfect pitch/ And that moment when the bird sings very close/To the music of what happens' (*Opened Ground: Poems 1966–1996*, 1998, p. 181).

Gerald Dawe

GERALD DAWE

Introduction

Never but imagined the blue in a wild imagining the blue celeste of poetry.

– Samuel Beckett[1]

This volume begins with a prolegomena – a critical or discursive introduction – not on an Irish poet but on Edmund Spenser. The reason is clear. The use of English in Ireland and how this colonisation came about, and what its effects were, carried throughout the following centuries to the present a lasting and unavoidable challenge, along with much else. It seemed appropriate, therefore, to raise the matter from the beginning of this *Companion to Irish Poets* since in one form or another this issue of language mattered so deeply to Irish poets from the earliest of times to the present, including *our* present in the twenty-first century. As will become obvious from reading the essays gathered here, how Irish-speaking Ireland was turned into a mostly English-speaking country by the turn of the nineteenth century and the role played in this radical political and cultural transformation by Irish poets – either as enraged chroniclers of the change, such as Aogán Ó'Raithille; or as reimagining the impact, such as W. B. Yeats; or recalling its bruising, brutal realities, such as John Montague and Thomas Kinsella – the language shift caused a deep and lasting wound which, perhaps only now, has been salved. Irish poetry has been part of that healing process.

It has also meant that Irish poets have since the time of Jonathan Swift been made conscious of the language they use in a manner and intensity that is reflected here in the work of such diverse literary talents as the London-based eighteenth-century playwright, novelist and journalist Oliver Goldsmith as much as in the haunted self-lacerating figure of the mid-nineteenth-century Dublin *poete maudit*, the short-lived James Clarence Mangan. While language in the hands of Mangan's contemporary, the superb lyricist Thomas Moore, became a bright and at times brittle medium to entertain, and yet, as Jeffrey Vail points out here, the shadows of history are never far below the surface.

It was W. B. Yeats, born in 1865, just a little over a decade after Moore's death, who transformed the fortunes of Irish poets and their standing in the world. Straddling the nineteenth-century traditions of both popular Irish and English literary culture, and publishing in both capitals of Dublin and London, Yeats produced an extraordinary volume of writing devoted to restoring the country's self-confidence, traumatised in the wake of failed political uprisings against British rule in Ireland in the eighteenth and nineteenth centuries but also, more importantly, shocked to the core by the devastating impact of the Great Irish Famine (1847).[2] The famine saw between 1 and 1.5 million dead of starvation and related disease and the emigration of approximately a further million people, leaving behind a hugely damaged society.

Yeats, along with other writers and artists, was the catalyst for a national movement of reconstruction, variously referred to as the Irish Literary Revival or the Celtic Revival. But behind the rhetoric and dedication of Yeats's indisputable nationalism there was an utterly committed writer, who, as Nicholas Grene amply demonstrates, was completely focussed on the making of poetry. Yeats' achievements, spanning the decades from the 1890s to his death in 1939, encapsulate one of the most intense moments of Irish history.

As the nationalist movement cohered increasingly around the agenda of political and cultural separatism from Britain, in the period leading into World War I (1914–18), other voices emerged such as Francis Ledwidge, a young 'peasant' poet who, like his somewhat younger contemporary, Thomas MacGreevy, would be exposed to the terrible brutalities of modern warfare in the trenches. MacGreevy survived his wounding at the Front to produce his own poetry of war, along with much else, and became a lasting friend and close confidant of Samuel Becket. Ledwidge, along with some 27,000 to 35,000 Irish soldiers, was tragically killed at the Front.[3]

In 1928 in Paris, MacGreevy introduced the young Beckett to James Joyce, author of the iconic novel of Irish self-analysis, *A Portrait of the Artist as a Young Man* (1916) in which the central character, Stephen Dedalus, famously responds to his fellow-student Davin's exuberant nationalism. 'When the soul of a man', Stephen 'vaguely' remarks, 'is born in this country there are nets flung at it to hold it back from flight. You talk to me of nationality, language, religion, I shall try to fly by those nets.'[4] The widespread catchment of these 'nets' would gather in the decades immediately after the Easter Rising of 1916 as a younger generation of poets, including Austin Clarke and Patrick Kavanagh, struggled, as both Lucy Collins and Tom Walker show here, to find a new *poetic* response to the society that was beginning to emerge by the time Ireland had won its independence in the mid-1920s. But for Yeats, the Rising and the loss of its leaders, many of whom were writers and poets personally known to him, had a profound impact upon his imagination; as he wrote in the wake of their executions in May 1916, in a letter to Lady Gregory, his patron and fellow dramatist: 'I had no idea that any public event could so deeply move me – and I am very despondent about the future. At the moment I feel all the work of years has been overturned, all the bringing together of classes, all the freeing of Irish literature and criticism from politics.'[5]

Not only was 'Ireland' by the late 1920s independent of Britain, it was also partitioned into two separate states – the Irish Free State and Northern Ireland. In the now-divided island, parallel lines of educational and cultural development started to take root, with poets born and bred in the North, such as Louis MacNeice and John Hewitt, placed in the incongruous (for the time) situation of being both Irish poets and citizens of Britain – a bifurcation that produced much tension in the years that followed. For by the late 1930s and early 1940s it was clear that the two parts of Ireland were beginning to go their separate ways. The Irish Free State, by the time of the declaration of World War II (1939–45), pursued a policy of neutrality, while the North would become an essential part of the Allied war effort. This critical division between the twin-states, notwithstanding the fact that many thousands of Irishmen and women from the south also enlisted, had produced, as Chris Morash explains, a deepening sense of difference, such as the ironic spleen of MacNeice's 'Autumn Journal' (1939) and the unapologetic rage of his stinging riposte, 'Neutrality' (1942):

> But then look eastward from your heart, there bulks
> A continent, close, dark, as archetypal sin,
> While to the west off your own shores the mackerel
> Are fat – on the flesh of your kin.[6]

By the time the Republic of Ireland was declared in 1948, it was one of John Hewitt's aesthetic and ethical priorities, as Guy Woodward charts, to try and recover some of the lost common ground in the Ireland of the 1950s and 1960s.

While maintaining his ongoing efforts in Belfast to promote a form of regional identity that drew upon the various strands of Northern Irish literary and cultural traditions from the Gaelic roots of the named landscape, the Scots vernacular of accent and ballad-making and the philosophical imperatives of Protestantism, Hewitt, along with John Montague, also attempted to challenge the unionist hegemony of the Northern Irish state. For Montague, as Maurice Riordain clearly demonstrates, the play of non-Irish influences has as much a role in shaping his poetry as the scars of local sectarian history, particularly for those of an Ulster catholic background.

One of the abiding features of the *Companion of Irish Poets* is the extent to which poets such as Montague, Richard Murphy and Thomas Kinsella are deeply conscious of a need to embrace literatures, languages and cultures other than Irish. This open-mindedness and cosmopolitan interest in poetry from very many different parts of Europe and beyond suggests how foolhardy it is to segregate Irish poets into neatly conforming boxes of 'traditional' and 'modernist'. For, as this *Companion* shows, more than anything else, Irish poets have been part of the global world while remaining keenly aware of the conflicts and developments of their individual presents and local and national cultural inheritances.

Michael Longley and Derek Mahon are perhaps two of the most notable figures in this regard, with their deeply felt engagement with, respectively, the Classics and the literature of France. Translation, therefore, can be seen as a key to the achievements of those poets born in and around the end of World War II and towards the second half of the twentieth century. One thinks here of the bilingual poet Michael Hartnett, alongside the multilingual Eiléan Ní Chuilleanáin as well as the prolific Ciaran Carson, whose versions of Dante, Baudelaire and Rimbaud are an integral part of his own very distinctive voice as much as his versions of Irish epics such as *The Táin* and Brian Merriman's *Cúirt an Mhéan Oiche/ The Midnight Court*.

The painful struggle of language-consciousness in Seán Ó Ríordáin, the production of a contemporary idiomatic Irish-language poetry so poignantly revealed by Louis de Paor's essay, should remind readers of the psychic and physical cost that remained such a telling part in the making of poetry solely *in Irish*, even as late as Ó Ríordáin's *Eireaball Spideoige* (1952) and *Brosna* (1964).

By the late sixties, the Northern 'Troubles' emerged as the over-arching narrative within which Irish poets, those based in Ireland and those living elsewhere, had to in one form or another contend. While Thomas Kinsella reacted against the notion of there being a 'Northern Poetry' separate and distinct from the rest of Irish poetry – he referred to the idea as 'journalistic'[7] – there was an abiding sense during the thirty years of the conflict in the North,[8] in which 3,600 people were killed and many thousands more injured from its beginnings in 1968 until it was effectively concluded with the Good Friday Agreement (1998), that poets from the province had caught the eye of the international literary world. In the figure of Seamus Heaney, his achievements as a poet, first and foremost, but also his negotiating with the contradictory tensions of historical conflict, proved captivating for both critical and popular audiences.

With the award of the Nobel Prize for Literature in 1995 Heaney's influence and significance was widely acknowledged and, as Terence Brown shows here, the moral felicity and formal control of his many volumes of poetry brought poetry itself to a global stage, such as it hadn't achieved since, one could say, the great age of Eliot or Auden. Heaney's influence is recorded too in the generation that followed his, in Medbh McGuckian, for instance, and Paul Muldoon – complicating figures made all the more excitingly accessible here in the essays of Maria Johnston and Peter McDonald.

Since his earliest successes of the 1960s until his untimely death in 2013, Seamus Heaney's legacy continues with the Seamus Heaney Centre for Poetry in Queen's University Belfast, the HomePlace library and community centre dedicated to his memory in Bellaghy, County Derry, and the Ireland Chair of Poetry which connects three universities in Belfast and Dublin with a mission of promoting the art of poetry. During this self-same half century, the social and political landscape of the Republic underwent substantial and, at times, deeply hurtful change, particularly in regard to the role and influence of the Catholic church but also the failings of government oversight of the economy which led to a major economic collapse in the mid-2000s.[9]

In his introduction to *The Penguin Book of Irish Poetry* (2012), Patrick Crotty identifies Brendan Kennelly, Eavan Boland and Paul Durcan with playing a major public role in 'the process of liberalization' in Ireland during the final decades of the twentieth and early part of the twenty-first centuries. It is a view Richard Pine, Justin Quinn and Alan Gillis fully corroborate in their respective essays here. In their contributions, for example, to the national broadcasting network, RTÉ, alongside very popular readings throughout the Republic, all three poets created a form of creative conversation about the state of the country and the unfolding issues of civic and social rights, particularly those involving women, the secularisation of a maturing democracy, the hypocrisies and mendacity afflicting the Catholic Church in Ireland as much as provocative revisions and satires of Irish history, including Kennelly's scurrilous re-reading, *Cromwell* (1983/87).

While taking a long backwards look at the various strands that make up Irish poetry from the 1210–1650 'bardic' period and its renaissance, where the present *Companion* begins, Crotty notes that 'it is hardly fanciful to say that there are vestiges' of an 'ancient primacy in the deference and public attention paid to poets and poetry in present-day Ireland'.[10]

Indeed, there is no better illustration of this view than in the achievement of Nuala Ni Dhomhnaill, who brings the *Companion* to its close – or maybe returns us to the beginning, as another way of putting it.

For there is no conclusion to be reached. In the post-Heaney world of Irish poets, slam/spoken voice festivals are currently hugely popular. The publication of *The Penguin Book of Irish Poetry* produced its own moment of 'public attention'[11] with heated responses to the editor's selection appearing in the leading Irish broadsheet newspaper, *The Irish Times*,[12] well-known for its ongoing publication of poems in its weekend edition.

Like most other parts of the literary world, the world of Irish poets has altered greatly, and with it the place and authority of the poet has had to adjust to these changes in the culture. The manifest challenges of popular entertainment and media expectations alongside the impact of global online publishing, the pull of marketing and the realities of the book-selling business are bound to affect the place of the poet in the twenty-first century in Ireland as much as anywhere else.

The Heaney generation that stretched from the final years of Patrick Kavanagh to the mature collections of John Hewitt, Thomas Kinsella, Richard Murphy and John Montague, and which embraced many of the poets with whom this *Companion* reaches into the twenty-first century, may be viewed as the last of their familial kind. For poets now born in the 1980s and '90s inhabit a very different map to the one this *Companion* attempts to outline. Responding to the much-changed and still-changing sense of mobility and place and of representations of self and gender, of global concerns and conditions substantially different from those which played out in 'the deeps of the minds'[13] of Patrick Kavanagh, say, or MacGreevy or Goldsmith or O'Raithille or O'Riordain, simply makes the tradition of Irish poetry all the more fascinating to think about.

However, as many of the poets included here – and the many more who are not, but could well have been, subjects of an essay – continue to produce work of the first order, one suspects that no matter what else happens, by way of the *poetic* legacy, if nothing else, 'Irish' will still have an unerring part to play in what Beckett's 'V' in *Footfalls* called 'it all'.[14]

NOTES

1. Samuel Beckett, 'Lessness', *The Complete Short Prose 1929–1989* (New York: Grove Press 1995), p. 199.
2. Alvin Jackson, *Ireland 1798–1998: Politics and War* (Chichester: Wiley-Blackwell, 2nd rev. edn. 2010) is a lucid, reliable and comprehensive study.
3. John Horne, 'Our War, Our History', *Ireland and the Great War: The Thomas Davis Lecture Series* (Dublin: Royal Irish Academy, 2008), p. 6.
4. James Joyce, *A Portrait of the Artist as a Young Man* ([1916] London: Penguin Books, 1992), p. 220.
5. W. B. Yeats, 'Letter to Lady Gregory, 11 May 1916', *Letters of W. B. Yeats*, ed. Allan Wade (London: R. Hart-Davis, 1954), p. 613.
6. Peter McDonald (ed.), *Collected Poems of Louis MacNeice* (London: Faber and Faber, 2007), p. 224.
7. Thomas Kinsella (ed.), *The New Oxford Book of Irish Verse* (Oxford: Oxford University Press 1989), p. xxx.
8. See David McKittrick, Seamus Kelter, Brian Freeney, Chris Thornton and David McVea, *Lost Lives: The Stories of the Men, Women and Children Who Died as a Result of the Northern Ireland Troubles* (Edinburgh: Mainstream Publishing, 2nd revised edn. 2004).

9. Diarmaid Ferriter, *The Transformation of Ireland* (New York: Overlook Press, 2005), explores aspects of these changing times in Irish society.

10. Patrick Crotty (ed.), *The Penguin Book of Irish Poetry*, with a preface by Seamus Heaney (London: Penguin Books, 2010), p. xlix.

11. There is a history to be written on the public spaces and 'roles' Irish poets have played in the modern past, such as (and at random) Yeats's controversial edition of the *Oxford Book of Modern Verse* (1936), the legal battles Patrick Kavanagh faced (and instigated) during the 1940s and 1950s, through to Thomas Kinsella's *Butcher's Dozen*, an excoriating response to the British government's Widgery Report on the 'Bloody Sunday' killings in Derry January 1972 and the poet's championing of Viking Dublin at Woodquay (1978), to Seamus Heaney's *Open Letter* (1983) on his inclusion in the *Penguin Book of Contemporary British Verse* (1982), to the controversies surrounding the publication of the *Field Day Anthology of Irish Writing* (1992) and which under-represented Irish women poets – poetry in Ireland has indeed been 'in the wars', to quote Edna Longley's collection of essays of the same name (*Poetry in the Wars* [Bloodaxe Books, 1986]), published in 1986 at the height of the arguments over poetry and politics in Ireland.

12. Patrick Crotty, 'The cut and thrust of Irish poetry', *The Irish Times*, 4 October 2010; Michael O'Loughlin, 'Missing: Have you seen these poets?' *The Irish Times* ('Culture', 26 October) and 'Exclusion and inclusion of Irish Poetry' ('Letters', 29 October 2010).

13. W. B. Yeats, 'Certain Noble Plays of Japan', *The Cutting of an Agate,* in *Essays and Introductions* (London: Macmillan Press 1961), p. 224.

14. Samuel Beckett, *Footfalls* (London: Faber and Faber, 1976), p.10.

I

SEÁN LYSAGHT

Prolegomena: 'Spenser's Island'

I declare this tower is my symbol; I declare
This winding, gyring, spiring treadmill of a stair is my ancestral stair;
That Goldsmith and the Dean, Berkeley and Burke have travelled there.[1]
W. B. Yeats 'Blood and the Moon'

When W. B. Yeats pronounced his definitive roll-call of Anglo-Irish tradition in 1927 he went back as far as Swift, but did not cast his net any farther than the Ascendancy society of the eighteenth century. And yet, if we review in our minds the late, historical poetry that Yeats wrote from his tower in south-east Galway, he was clearly haunted by an earlier figure, a tower-dweller like himself, who stands squarely within the Yeatsian formula of 'greatness' and 'violence', namely Edmund Spenser.

Spenser is the best-known Elizabethan careerist, but he was not the only courtier poet who had seen service in Ireland. During the late sixteenth century, several figures out of English literary history make lead or minor appearances on the stage of Irish conflict, such as Sir Philip Sidney, Sir Walter Raleigh and Sir John Harington.[2] Sidney's father, Sir Henry Sidney, had served on three separate occasions as Viceroy of Ireland, and young Philip had spent time in the west of Ireland during one typically inconclusive campaign chasing rebels. The Lord Deputyship may have been a thankless posting – Sir Henry would complain of being 'tired with toil of mind and body in that cursed country'[3] – but the title Pro-Rex of Ireland carried considerable prestige and was used prominently by Philip as a calling card on his diplomatic travels in Europe. By 1577, the poet of the *Arcadia* and of courtly love had come to a representative view of England's first colony: there should be no leniency in dealing with the Irish, who were 'that way as obstinate as any nation, with whom no other passion can prevail but fear'.[4] This sets the tone for colonial policy from that time onwards until at least the Cromwellian period. It was a harsh mood, shaped by religious prejudice and sectarian atrocities on both sides. Sir Henry once joked in a letter to Whitehall that he had lost count of the number of Irish 'varlets' he had killed.[5] Sir Philip was in Paris in 1572 during the St. Bartholomew's Day massacres of Huguenots, and was fortunate to have escaped.

Of all the Tudor courtiers and opportunists whose service to the queen brought them to the sister isle, it was Spenser who spent longest there, who wrote about Ireland with knowledge and whose imagination was, in several important respects, shaped by his Irish experience. While his friend Sidney had been his early source of first-hand accounts of Irish adventure, Spenser made that mission into an entire career. Part of this was shaped by necessity, because Spenser did not belong by birth to the noble families who brokered gifts and appointments in the 1570s, although he claimed kinship with the Spencers of Althorp in Northamptonshire. His family origins are obscure, but his father is thought to have been a 'free journeyman' involved in London's cloth trade.[6] It was through the support of scholarships that he was able to get an education at Richard Mulcaster's school in London and at Pembroke College, Cambridge. After graduation from Cambridge in 1576, and a spell in Kent working for the bishop of Rochester, we find him associated with Sidney and the Dudleys at Leicester House, and it was probably through this connection that he got his appointment as Secretary to Lord Grey de Wilton in 1580.

Spenser's Irish appointment was a considerable success in the social context of the time – 'an extremely good job', according to Andrew Hadfield.[7] He clearly had not wanted a church career, and university appointments were scarce; as Jean Brink puts it, 'competition for positions in government service was fierce, and those from privileged backgrounds who had travelled abroad had a definite edge'.[8]

Lord Grey's brief was to put down the Desmond Rebellion of 1579 and establish government in Munster, but before he moved south, he rashly engaged with the forces of Fiach McHugh O'Byrne in Wicklow and was roundly defeated. After this first lesson in warfare with Irish tories and woodkernes, Grey was in no mood for leniency more than two months later at Dún an Óir, on Smerwick Harbour in Kerry, where he presided over the notorious massacre of at least 600 Spanish and Italian mercenaries. Another figure with literary credentials, Sir Walter Raleigh, was among the commanders directing these operations.

With the St. Bartholomew's Day killings, the massacre at Smerwick was a landmark incident in the growing chronicle of violence through the late sixteenth century. Spenser was present at Smerwick, and was probably witness to the slaughter.[9] He returned to these events many years later, in *The Faerie Queene* and *A View of the Present State of Ireland*, to counter the opinion that Grey had acted too harshly. Spenser continued to defend Grey's actions and to argue that this draconian policy would have succeeded if it had been given a chance to operate. In the event, Grey was recalled after only two years.

In *The Faerie Queene*'s Book of Justice, Spenser's knight, Sir Artegall, frees Ireland/Irena from the tyranny of Grantorto and restores her to her kingdom. Artegall represents Lord Grey in the allegory, restoring order to Irena's realm:

> During which time, that he did there remaine,
> His studie was true Iustice how to deale,
> And day and night employ'd his busie paine
> How to reforme that ragged common-weale ...
> But ere he could reforme it thoroughly,
> He through occasion called was away,
> To Faerie Court, that of necessity
> His course of Iustice he was forst to stay   (V.xii.26–7)

It was on this first foray into Munster that Spenser witnessed the ravages of war on a once fertile landscape, an experience later recorded in the oft-quoted passage from *A View*:

> Out of every corner of the woods and glens they came creeping forth upon their hands for their legs could not bear them. They looked anatomies of death, they spake like ghosts crying out of their graves, they did eat of the dead carrions, happy were they could find them, yea and one another soon after.[10]

Among other effects, this passage was designed to show that the writer was under no illusions about the cost and conduct of colonial wars, unlike some of his genteel readers at court.[11]

Following the suppression of the Desmond Rebellion, and the recall of Lord Grey, Spenser stayed on in Ireland to exploit the rich pickings of confiscated lands on offer to the New English settlers. In the late 1580s he was involved in property transactions until the scheme for a Munster Plantation eventually brought him the seignory at Kilcolman in County Cork, an estate of 3,028 acres with a Norman tower house. Spenser thus became a landed country gentleman. Ireland had provided opportunities for enrichment that he could never have had in England, and the Plantation even gave him a community of New English like himself, including Raleigh, who snapped up an immense estate of 42,000 acres near Youghal. By 1591, Spenser clearly felt settled in Ireland, to the extent that his poem *Colin Clouts Come Home Againe* describes his pastoral surrogate returning home to Ireland after a visit to London.

Shortly after the grant of a life pension from the queen, 1591 also saw the publication of *Complaints*, a volume of miscellaneous poems including a satirical take on courtly life, *Mother Hubberds Tale*. This poem directed its attack against William Cecil, Lord Burghley's power at court, suggesting that

Burghley, as an opponent of Dudley, may have stood in Spenser's way for preferment back in England. *Mother Hubberds Tale* was Spenser's most daring intervention in the nervy relationship he always had with the court scene, and the breach which it caused with Elizabeth's most influential official meant that the door to promotion in London was now permanently closed.

After the heat of controversy generated by *Mother Hubberds Tale*, Spenser would seem to have lain low at his Irish estate and devoted himself mainly to writing the second part of *The Faerie Queene*, Books IV to VI. Whereas Raleigh had lost interest in his Irish lands, Spenser had many contacts within the settler community, including the family of Richard Boyle, first Earl of Cork. Boyle was the most successful of the colonists in securing titles to confiscated lands, and was on his way to becoming the largest landowner in the country. Following the death of Spenser's first wife Machabyas, about whom we know very little, Spenser met his second wife Elizabeth through his connections with the Boyles in the early 1590s, and they were married on 11 June 1594. By the end of that year, Spenser had completed *Amoretti*, a sequence of sonnets, and *Epithalamion*, a marriage hymn, both of them celebrating his relationship with Elizabeth. The year 1594 can be said to mark an apogee of security and personal happiness in Spenser's life, which would be overtaken by the outbreak of O'Neill's rebellion and the Nine Years' War.

Spenser made another visit to England in 1596–7, coinciding with the publication of the second edition of *The Faerie Queene* in six completed books. By this time, however, the situation in Ireland had deteriorated sharply, with Hugh O'Neill's rebellion threatening the position of the Munster settlers. These settlers 'lived as isolated farmers in an over-whelmingly hostile environment',[12] and many were deserting their hold-ings as danger loomed. Spenser's detailed analysis of policy in the troubled country, *A View of the Present State of Ireland*, dates from this time, with a series of prescriptions for the permanent subjection of Ireland. In fact, there was so much 'classified information' about the tactics and measures necessary to defeat the Irish clans, especially in the north, that the work was never published in the author's lifetime; instead, it circulated widely in manuscript form among influential peo-ple, to judge from the survival of about twenty copies, and, as Nicholas Canny has shown, it continued to be an influential reference point for Irish policy up to the Cromwellian period.[13]

As Tyrone's rebellion rumbled on during 1597, Spenser was back in Ireland, still involved in property deals, in a desperate gamble to secure a future for himself and his descendants. In that year, he bought a castle and almost 400 acres at Renny, about fifteen miles from Kilcolman, and a dis-established priory at Buttevant with a smaller plot of land. There are records of other properties, not all of which can be identified, which Spenser acquired in these years. He was doing on a smaller scale what his kinsman, Richard Boyle, had done with spectacular effectiveness in the late sixteenth and early seventeenth centuries, acquiring land at a time of confiscation and disturbance to secure a social position that would have been beyond reach in England.[14]

At this late stage of Spenser's life, there is little poetry in his output, unless we believe James Ware's claim that Spenser had finished *The Faerie Queene* after all, but that the extra sections (Books VII to XII) were lost in the confusion of those years.[15] There is just one surviving fragment from Book VII, 'Two Cantos of Mutabilitie', which shows Spenser's imagination to be focussed on Ireland as never before. In the first canto, Nature, Jove and Mutability sit atop Galtee Mountain debating the governing principle of the cosmos; the second canto relates a variation on the myth of Diana and Actaeon to explain the degraded condition of Ireland. Having been betrayed by one of her nymphs, who conspires with a faun to reveal the goddess bathing naked, Diana abandons Ireland, her former pleasure ground:

> parting from the place,
> There-on an heavy haplesse curse did lay,
> To weet, that Wolves, where she was wont to space,
> Should harbour'd be, and all those Woods deface,
> And Thieves should rob and spoile that Coast around.
> Since which, those Woods, and all that goodly Chase,
> Doth to this day with Wolves and Thieves abound:
> Which too-too true that lands in-dwellers since have found.

The closing lines are a bleak sketch of the exposed position of the settlers on the eve of disaster.

The Nine Years' War came to a head in August 1598, when Tyrone defeated the English forces at the Battle of the Yellow Ford; this left the field open for Irish rebels to overrun Munster, which they did through the month of October. Spenser's castle at Kilcolman was sacked and burned around 15 October; according to Ben Jonson's later account, 'the Irish, having robbed Spenser's goods and burnt his house and a little child new-born, he and his wife escaped'. Their young son Peregrine also survived the attack and went with his parents to Cork, to join other terrified settlers crowded into the town.

Our last evidence for Spenser's life is from the closing months of 1598, as he was entrusted with letters from Thomas Norris to the Privy Council. By the time he left Cork with his family on 9 December, English troops were pouring into southern ports in order to quell the rebellion. One of the documents in his possession, 'Certain pointes to be considered of in the recovering of the realme of Irelande', returns to the arguments of *A View*, and repeats the belief that only absolute devastation, including famine, will bring Ireland to its knees: 'Great force must be the instrument but famine must be the meane for till Ireland be famished it can not be subdued.'[16]

Spenser died at Westminster on 13 January 1599, hardly 'for lack of bread' as Jonson put it, but certainly bereft of the hopes of security he had invested in his Irish position. On the other hand, his reputation as 'our principall poet'[17] had been growing throughout the 1590s, and his funeral was a major occasion, bringing together both Elizabethan officialdom and the literary world. His burial in Westminster Abbey near to Chaucer confirmed his aspiration to inherit Chaucer's legacy and be recognised as the leading English poet of his age.

The story of Spenser's life, to the extent that we know it, is largely a construct of textual and historical scholarship, of inference and deduction. Recent scholarship has greatly increased our sense of Spenser as an official and businessman with many connections to the wider historical context. In the absence of intimate journals and letters, the raw materials of modern biography, Edmund Spenser is a dislocated, conjectural figure by comparison, whom we glimpse only fleetingly in the textual artefact. Much of that evidence, as we have seen, relates to an 'Age of Atrocity' in Ireland, where the Elizabethan state and its enemies played out a conflict of appalling cruelty, with militant Protestantism supplying a Biblical rationale for indiscriminate destruction.[18] With this narrative as the backdrop to the life of 'the new Poete', it becomes very difficult to comprehend in a single understanding both the careerist (Elizabeth's 'arse-kissing poet', in Karl Marx's phrase) and the Spenser celebrated by Coleridge as follows:

> As characteristic of Spenser, I would call your particular attention in the first place to the indescribable sweetness and fluent projection of his verse ... In Spenser, indeed, we trace a mind constitutionally tender, delicate, and, in comparison with his three great compeers [Chaucer, Shakespeare and Milton], I had almost said *effeminate*; and this additionally saddened by the unjust persecution of Burleigh, and the severe calamities, which overwhelmed his latter days.[19]

Whereas the modern genre of biography finds Spenser an intractable and elusive subject, he himself was committed to a form of self-reference that is very much of its time. His ambitious and programmatic early poem *The Shepheardes Calender* (1579) introduces the pastoral figure of Colin Clout in dialogue with other shepherds. The promotional introduction to the poem by the mysterious E. K. makes it clear that 'the Authour selfe is shadowed' under the figure of Colin.[20] The tone of the *Calender* is set by Colin, frustrated in his love for Rosalind, who has dropped him in favour of another shepherd. Colin's gloomy mood is in contrast to a lively earlier friendship he shared with Hobbinol, a pastoral vehicle for his college friend Gabriel Harvey. At this point the commentator E. K. intervenes to assure us that the relationship between Colin and Hobbinol was not homosexual, 'which the learned call paederastice'; E. K. disapproves of 'execrable and horrible sinnes of forbidden and unlawful fleshlinesse', while celebrating spiritual love between men. The curiosity of the modern biographer is led no further along the trail of Spenser's intimate relationship with Harvey, as public and private imperatives press on Spenser's career.

The year 1579 marked a watershed in Spenser's life with the publication of *The Shepheardes Calender* and marriage to his first wife, Machabyas. On the public front, 1579 saw an acute political crisis caused by the prospect of marriage between the queen and the French Catholic Duc d'Alençon. It was this threat to Protestant England that explains much of the sombre atmosphere of the *Calender*. Rosalind's disloyalty to Colin, representing the queen's favour to Alençon, is as much about wider politics as about personal affairs: in Spenser's own life, the friendship and collaboration with Harvey was about to be superseded by official duties as he was appointed secretary to Grey the following year.

It is typical of the conventions of the period that the most emotionally convincing section of the poem is the November elegy for Dido, the Carthaginian queen who is doomed by her failed courtship of the Trojan hero Aeneas in Virgil's epic:

> Up then *Melpomene* thou mournefulst Muse of nyne,
> Such cause of mourning never hadst afore:
> Up grieslie ghostes and up my rufull ryme,
> Matter of myrth now shalt thou have no more.
> For dead shee is, that myrth thee made of yore.
> *Dido* my deare alas is dead,
> Dead and lyeth wrapt in lead:
>   O heavie herse,
> Let streaming teares be poured out in store:
>   O carefull verse.
>
> Shepheards, that by your flocks on Kentish downes abyde,
> Waile ye this wofull waste of natures warke:
> Waile we the wight, whose presence was our pryde:

Waile we the wight, whose absence is our carke.
The sonne of all the world is dimme and darke:
The earth now lacks her wonted light,
And all we dwell in deadly night,
    O heavie herse.
Breake we our pypes, that shrild as lowde as Larke,
    O carefull verse.   (ll. 53–72)

Colin Clout appears again in *Colin Clouts Come Home Againe* (1595). This poem is one of Spenser's most cherished because of its peculiar transposition of the classical pastoral to an Irish setting. The meeting and musical contest between Colin and 'the shepheard of the Ocean' marks Spenser's acquaintance with Sir Walter Raleigh in Cork, where they were both estate owners.

One day (quoth he) I sat, (as was my trade)
Under the foote of *Mole* that mountaine hore,
Keeping my sheepe amongst the cooly shade,
Of the greene alders by the *Mullaes* shore:
There a straunge shepheard chaunst to find me out,
Whether allured with my pipes delight,
Whose pleasing sound yshrilled far about,
Or thither led by chaunce, I know not right:
Whom when I asked from what place he came,
And how he hight, himselfe he did ycleepe,
The shepheard of the Ocean by name,
And said he came far from the main-sea deepe.
He sitting me beside in that same shade,
Provoked me to plaie some pleasant fit,
And when he heard the musicke which I made,
He found himselfe full greatly pleasd at it:
Yet aemuling my pipe, he tooke in hond
My pipe before that aemuled of many,
And plaid theron; (for well that skill he cond)
Himselfe as skilfull in that art as any.
He pip'd, I sung; and when he sung, I piped,
By chaunge of turnes, each making other mery   (ll. 56–77)

There is a sense of liveliness and ease in the encounter that we do not always get in Spenser as his was habitually a scholarly and melancholic nature; the relationship with Raleigh seems to have brought back some of the energies of his earlier years with Harvey and shaken him out of a tendency to self pity. Elsewhere, he bewails his 'lucklesse lot:/That banisht had my selfe, like wight forlore,/Into that waste, where I was quite forgot' (ll. 181–3).

Colin Clouts Come Home Againe is also enlivened by a report of Colin's journey back to the court, where *The Faerie Queene* had been presented to queen Elizabeth. Colin has to explain what the sea and the sea-crossing are like to his land-bound listeners; the lines have a special facility and playfulness, and Spenser's language rises clear of the archaic usage that can inhibit the reader of the *Calender* or *The Faerie Queene*.

> So to the sea we came; the sea? that is
> A world of waters heaped up on hie,
> Rolling like mountaines in wide wildernesse,
> Horrible, hideous, roaring with hoarse crie.   (ll. 196–9)

The pastoral convention, which had been coloured by Kent and English country lore in *The Shepheardes Calender*, takes on an Irish complexion in *Colin Clout*; Spenser renames his local mountain range as Old Father Mole and recasts local rivers as nymphs from Ovid's *Metamorphoses*. Rather ominously, the allegorical wolves of the *Calender* are replaced by real Irish wolves threatening the flocks, and there are many insecurities in the new setting. Colin reports that England, now a foreign country, is very different from Ireland: 'No ravenous wolves the good mans hope destroy,/ Nor outlawes fell affray the forest raunger' (ll. 318–19).

From here it is a natural progression for Colin to describe, in humble swain's terms, the corruptions of the Elizabethan court. The rural shepherd has been bewildered by the showy decadence of courtly life and is relieved to return to 'single Truth and simple honestie' in the countryside, as was Sir Thomas Wyatt a generation earlier. At the same time, Colin repeats his devotion to the queen, whom he has idealised as Cynthia: this tension, between religious loyalty to the figure of the monarch and worldly criticism of those around her, is characteristic of Spenser.

Colin Clout makes a further appearance late in *The Faerie Queene*, in a key passage that dates from the early stages of the Nine Years' War (1593–1602). Book VI introduces Sir Calidore, the knight of Courtesy, in pursuit of 'the Blatant Beast', in territory apparently similar to the harsh dealings of Justice in Book V. But in the central section Calidore strays into a pastoral world, where he falls in love with the eponymous Pastorella; here he also witnesses Colin Clout playing music for the classical Graces, surrounded by 'An hundred naked maidens lilly white,/All raunged in a ring, and dauncing in delight' (VI, x, 11). At the heart of this major set piece is Colin's tribute to an early love, 'a countrey lasse', presumably Rosalind who had caused him such heartbreak in *The Shepheardes Calender*.[21]

At this late stage in his epic project, Spenser returns to the pastoral mode and to memories of early love. In a break with the Virgilian template, which took him from pastoral to epic poetry and allegory, he returns to a fruitful and harmonious world. However, Sir Calidore's arrival on the scene destroys the moment; the dancing nymphs and Graces vanish,

> All save the shepheard, who for fell despight
> Of the displeasure, broke his bag-pipe quight,
> And made great mone for that unhappy turne.   (VI, x, 18)

Nicholas Canny has argued with great insight that Spenser realised at this moment that poetry cannot operate in the disturbed context of his time and that, like Colin breaking his bagpipes, he is set to abandon *The Faerie Queene* after Book VI. By the time *The Faerie Queene* was published in its final six-book format, Spenser had switched to the business-like medium of prose to write his *View* in the summer of 1596.[22]

We meet Spenser as poet and citizen for the last time in *Prothalamion*, a pre-nuptial piece he wrote late in 1596 to celebrate the engagement of two daughters of the Earl of Worcester.[23] The poem has much of the customary ornateness we would expect: the daughters are depicted as swans in procession on the Thames, surrounded by nymphs throwing flowers, on their way to the house of the Earl of Essex. But there is an unusual intrusion as the poet drops his mask on this hot day:

> When I whom sullein care,
> Through discontent of my long fruitlesse stay
> In Princes Court, and expectation vayne
> Of idle hopes, which still doe fly away,
> Like empty shaddowes, did aflict my brayne,
> Walkt forth to ease my payne

The occasion must have been a poignant one, because Essex House used to be Leicester House, where Spenser and others had courted advancement in the 1570s:

> a stately place,
> Where oft I gayned giftes and goodly grace
> Of that great Lord [Dudley], which therein wont to dwell,
> Whose want too well, now feeles my freendles case   (ll. 137–40)

After all those years, Edmund Spenser still finds himself courting favours of noble patrons, still reminding people of his – tenuous – link to the Spencers of Althorp, 'an house of ancient fame'. Time has brought him back to 'mery London, my most kyndly Nurse', but his main stake is now in Ireland as the threats to the colony are growing. The refrain to *Prothalamion*, which T. S.

Eliot repackaged for the twentieth century, is shadowed by the poet's foreboding of the end of his literary career and impending disaster:

Sweete *Themmes* runne softly, till I end my Song.

The note of victimhood, of the isolated and indigent poet, is consistent with Coleridge's romantic view of Spenser, of a 'mind constitutionally tender and delicate.' This picture, like *Prothalamion* itself, conceals the official positions, fees and payments, the land deals and litigation that litter the biography of Edmund Spenser, gentleman. His interests in Ireland were such that his family returned there after his death to recover and manage their assets.[24] On the other hand, his literary reputation followed a completely different path for centuries, across English literary history, until modern scholarship in Britain and Ireland restored the connection between the poetry and the life.

During most of his active career, Spenser's imagination was framed by the disturbed country he lived in, and eventually both *The Faerie Queene* and its author succumbed to the Irish crisis. His involvement in violent times is something Spenser shares with Milton, and, like Milton, his legacy will continue to be politically charged. No-one with common sympathy can ever forget the draconian policy set out with elaborate care by the *View*, nor the extreme summary of that policy in 'Certaine pointes' (1598), nor the violence unleashed by Calidore in the name of Courtesy in *The Faerie Queene*, Book VI. At a time of utter desolation, Spenser's final notes chime with the private memorandum to 'Exterminate all the brutes!' added to Kurtz's report on 'the Suppression of Savage Customs' in Conrad's *Heart of Darkness*. These are despairing conclusions reached by a reforming and colonising mission at the end of its tether. We are unused to seeing poets compromised by such situations, either as persecutors or victims, but as we survey the tradition of Irish poetry in English, the figure of Spenser is one we can hardly avoid.

NOTES

1. W. B. Yeats 'Blood and Moon', *The Poems*, ed. Daniel Albright (London: J M Dent, 1990), p.287.
2. The entire context is reviewed by Andrew Carpenter in *Verse in English from Tudor and Stuart Ireland* (Cork: Cork University Press, 2003).
3. Alan Stewart, *Philip Sidney: A Double Life* (London: Chatto & Windus, 2000), p. 66.
4. Ibid., p. 160.
5. See David Edwards, 'The escalation of violence in sixteenth-century Ireland' in David Edwards, Pádraig Lenihan and Clodagh Tait (eds.), *Age of Atrocity: Violence and Political Conflict in Early Modern Ireland* (Dublin: Four Courts Press, 2007), pp. 34–78.

6. Andrew Hadfield, *Edmund Spenser: A Life* (Oxford: Oxford University Press, 2012), p. 22.
7. Ibid., p. 155.
8. Jean R. Brink, '"All his minde on honour fixed": The Preferment of Edmund Spenser' in Judith H. Anderson, Donald Cheney and David A. Richardson (eds.), *Spenser's Life and the Subject of Biography* (Amherst: University of Massachusetts Press, 1996), pp. 45–64 (p. 52).
9. Willy Maley, *A Spenser Chronology* (London: Macmillan, 1994), pp. 14–15.
10. Edmund Spenser, *A View of the Present State of Ireland*, ed. W. L. Renwick (Oxford: Oxford University Press, 1970), p. 104.
11. Hadfield, *Spenser*, pp. 171–2.
12. Ibid., p. 364.
13. Nicholas Canny, *Making Ireland British, 1580–1650* (Oxford: Oxford University Press, 2001), especially pp. 42–58.
14. Nicholas Canny, *The Upstart Earl: A Study of the Social and Mental World of Richard Boyle, First Earl of Cork, 1566–1643* (Cambridge: Cambridge University Press, 1982).
15. Hadfield, *Spenser*, p. 369.
16. Ibid., pp. 387–90.
17. Maley, *Chronology*, p. 80.
18. Brendan Bradshaw, 'Edmund Spenser on Justice and Mercy' in Tom Dunne (ed.), *The Writer as Witness* (Cork: Cork University Press, 1987), pp. 76–89.
19. Quoted in *The Spenser Encyclopaedia*, ed. A. C. Hamilton and others (Toronto: University of Toronto Press, 1990), p. 171.
20. Richard A. McCabe, *Edmund Spenser: The Shorter Poems* (Harmondsworth: Penguin, 1999), p. 28.
21. In the introduction to his selection of Spenser, W. B. Yeats praised 'that most beautiful passage ... which tells of Colin piping to the Graces', but astonishingly he did not include it in the book. See *Poems of Spenser*, selected with an introduction by W. B. Yeats (Edinburgh: T. C. and E. C. Jack, 1906), p. xx.
22. Canny, *Making Ireland British*, pp. 27–31 and 56.
23. McCabe, *Shorter Poems*, pp. 491–7 and notes.
24. Hadfield, *Spenser*, 'Appendix I: Spenser's Descendants', pp. 407–12.

SELECTED FURTHER READING

Canny, Nicholas, *Making Ireland British, 1580–1650* (Oxford: Oxford University Press, 2001).

Carpenter, Andrew (ed.), *Verse in English from Tudor and Stuart Ireland* (Cork: Cork University Press, 2003).

Edwards, David, Pádraig Lenihan and Clodagh Tait (eds.), *Age of Atrocity: Violence and Political Conflict in Early Modern Ireland* (Dublin: Four Courts Press, 2007).

Hadfield, Andrew, *Edmund Spenser: A Life* (Oxford: Oxford University Press, 2012).

McCabe, Richard A. (ed.), *Edmund Spenser: The Shorter Poems* (Harmondsworth: Penguin, 1999).

Maley, Willy, *A Spenser Chronology* (London: Macmillan, 1994).

Stewart, Alan, *Philip Sidney: A Double Life* (London: Chatto & Windus, 2000).

Tóibín, Colm, 'The dark sixteenth century', *The Dublin Review*, 43 (2011), 31–54.

2

JAMES WARD

Jonathan Swift

The Anti-poet

Every discussion of Swift the poet must contend with the long tradition that debars him from being one. In one of the earliest and most influential accounts of Swift's poetic career, Samuel Johnson concludes that there is 'not much' to say about the poems and popularises the apocryphal judgement of John Dryden that Swift would 'never be a poet'.[1] Dryden's prophecy has become a curse, its judgement neither fair nor accurate but always temptingly within reach. He may be the first Irish-born writer with a worldwide literary reputation and a substantial body of poetry in English, but Swift is usually set up in the Irish poetic tradition as a cautionary exemplar rather than a tutelary one. He comes down to us, Derek Mahon says, as 'a sort of anti-poet', nurturing what W. B. Yeats called 'bitter wisdom' in his imagination's 'dark grove'.[2] Both remarks are part of a manoeuvre which accords praise to Swift's work only after laboriously negotiating its accumulated criticisms, but each identifies a legitimate concern. Mahon attests how Swift's formidable of body of verse, which continues to grow as new attributions come to light, adopts measures and subjects that attract labels like 'sub-poetic' and 'close to doggerel'.[3] Yeats, by inverting a famous phrase of Swift's own coinage, suggests that anyone patient or perverse enough to press past such formal obstacles in search of philosophical content will be rewarded not with 'sweetness and light',[4] but something burdensome, bitter and dark. The suspicion endures that Swift's poetry, channelling nihilism and contempt through what looks to modern readers like 'light' verse, is by turns too serious and not serious enough. '[S]ome pieces are gross', to return to Samuel Johnson's judgement, 'and some are trifling', but a middle ground is lacking.[5] Whether apprehended as 'something fierce and repellent' or 'something joyous',[6] something in the poems repeatedly confronts and affronts cherished ideas of what poetry is for.

The Laureate of Rubbish

The following lines showcase both the exuberant virtuosity of Swift's poetry and its ability to provoke unease:

> An inundation, says the fable,
> O'erflowed a farmer's barn and stable;
> Whole ricks of hay and stacks of corn,
> Were down the sudden current borne;
> While things of heterogeneous kind,
> Together float with tide and wind;
> The generous wheat forgot its pride,
> And sailed with litter side by side;
> Uniting all, to show their amity,
> As in a general calamity.
> A ball of new-dropped horse's dung,
> Mingling with apples in the throng,
> Said to the pippin, plump, and prim,
> 'See, brother, how we apples swim.'[7]

They come from a poem called '*On the Words* – Brother Protestants, and Fellow Christians, *so familiarly used by the Advocates for the Repeal of the* Test Act *in* Ireland, 1733.' If nothing else, the title exhibits a healthy disrespect for the idea that poetry should aspire to transcendence or universal accessibility by encouraging multiple or subjective interpretations. Its precision conveys a distrust of specious universals which also animates the poem's political message. Political paranoia about Irish Presbyterians and their opposition to the temporal powers of the state church, shared by many of Swift's colleagues in the Anglican clergy, lends what Louis Landa, echoing Yeats's inversion, described as a 'dark and bitter tinge'[8] to his work.

This bitterness, along with the poem's exacting topicality and unwieldy title, may make it look atypical, but many features make it a representative and indeed classic example of Swift's poetry. It energetically combines two distinctive features – namely, an originality based on modification rather than novelty, and a surface jocularity layered over unpleasant depths. To bring Aesop's fable of the flooded barn to life, Swift's poem creates a tension between the water's sudden rush of energy and the meticulous detailing of the things which are 'borne' away on the flood. This participle, spelt without the 'e' in early editions,[9] along with 'dropped' and the noun 'litter', makes punning reference to birth as a figure for artistic fecundity and poetic originality. But birth is not the only means to life or motion: blasts of gas and torrents of liquid surge throughout Swift's work to animate inert or lifeless matter while the 'new dropped' dungball betrays a fascination with the motion of falling bodies shared with long-time adversary Isaac Newton. Gravity, in the sense of emotional weight, is in the details: Swift used the ambiguous term 'dropped' to mean both 'abandoned' and 'born' when discussing beggars and refugees, but he also applied it to himself.[10]

When the dungball speaks, inanimate matter comes to life within both the fiction of the poem and its organising rhetoric: it is a commonplace to say that political opponents are talking shit, but the poem invigorates the conceit by making the shit do the talking. The scatological dimension raises questions often discussed in idiopathic contexts of sexuality and gender, but the speaking object also dramatises questions of agency and subjectivity that received much wider attention in eighteenth-century literature and philosophy. Outside the poem's immediate sectarian context, then, it mounts larger protest against a modernity driven by the overlapping ontologies of empiricism, private property and novelistic fiction through which 'bodies and objects begin to acquire a private, individual nature'.[11]

In questioning the basis and extent of such individuation, readers' powers of discrimination must extend to the 'general calamity', which the poem presents not literally but as the tenor of a simile. The qualifying phrase 'as in' invokes not just role-playing theatrics, but also suggests that a specific crisis might underlie the generalised poetic fiction. Along with the dungball's misprision of superficial resemblance for sameness, it invites consideration of the nature and limits of analogy. The traditional derivation of 'calamity' from *calamus* (a stalk of wheat), and its association with crop failure, suggests one analogue – the wet summers, ruined harvests and outbreaks of famine of the years preceding the poem's composition. By so doing the poem implicates its opponents in subsistence crises as well as political ones, inflating the cost of their dissension until it threatens national survival. A moral fable that echoes the protagonist's experience at the hands of pirates in of *Gulliver's Travels*, the poem punishes presumption through a satiric fiction of scale and perspective. In both the poem and the prose fiction, assertions of identity that seem subjectively plausible are revealed as hapless platitudes, receding into silence as worthless detritus is flushed away.

The Debutant

'Brother Protestants' helped to cement Swift's status as popular figurehead when a target of its invective threatened Swift with violence and the poet's Dublin neighbours swore to defend his 'life and limbs'.[12] From a modern perspective, the poem, with its insistence on heterogeneity and its ability to animate lifeless matter, does many things that people like poems to do. This verve and variety are, however, subordinated to a programme of 'veto, voiding, ridding, cleansing, deletion' which, in Denis Donoghue's words, pretty much constitutes Swift's writerly mission.[13] At best this involves readers in a creative tension between an apparent celebration of copiousness and an underlying ethos which is in fact reductive and forbidding. Outside purely formal contexts, however, it is difficult to divorce this ethos from sectarian and even genocidal strains in Irish political history.[14] This aspect of the poem may represent an undercurrent of Swift's poetic imagination, but it has close links with the main stream, given that 'Brother Protestants' reworks the gesture with which Swift inaugurated his mature poetic style. Frequently anthologised, a favourite with critics and praised by its own author as 'the best thing I ever writ',[15] the climactic triplet of 'A Description of a City Shower' has achieved fame its own right:

> Sweepings from butchers' stalls, dung, guts, and blood,
> Drowned puppies, stinking sprats, all drenched in mud,
> Dead cats and turnip-tops come tumbling down the flood.
>
> (CP, 114)

While the momentum of these lines is irresistible, their tone is ambiguous. The speaker could come across as a sensual observer or an obsessive detailer, pursuing beyond reasonable limits the cultural imperative to itemise newly individuated objects. Tumbling bodies hang in the balance between pathos and disgust – an ambiguity that by the time of 'Brother Protestants' has arguably resolved into an antagonism, one which is also embodied in the division between narrator and protagonist in 'The Lady's Dressing Room'.

All three poems' interest in decaying materiality constitute Swift's literal rendering of a self-declared mission to expose in poetry 'the wrong Notion that *Matter* is exhausted' in a world that is 'wider to a Poet than to any other Man'.[16] This active affirmation of poetry as vocation and phenomenological quest is a pre-emptive riposte to judgements of posterity which cast Swift as 'simply ... not interested in "being a poet"'.[17] Swift styles his poetic self as a kind of virtuoso in that word's modern and historic senses: a technical adept and an enthusiastic collector. Poetic flair follows from an ability to seek out and treasure whatever is overlooked. This Addisonian pose of imaginative enthusiasm conceals the hard work that 'A Description of a City Shower' performs. It is a clearing of the decks, forcing through stylistic and generational shifts. Looking back on his own poem in 1735, Swift wrote that the closing triplet parodied 'a vicious way of rhyming wherewith Dryden abounded', chiefly because, he suggests, '[h]e was poor, and in great haste to finish his plays, because by them he chiefly supported his family'.[18] While no doubt heartfelt, this casting of Dryden as a hack inflating his word- and syllable-counts for extra pennies doesn't quite square with the ambition of the closing triplet. The poem, as distinct from Swift's later gloss on it, functions less as a personal attack than a form of poetic self-fashioning and self-presentation. With it Swift matches in poetry what other Irish-born contemporaries achieved in drama and prose. He was part of a generation of ambitious and copiously networked Irish writers in London that included Richard Steele (who collaborated with Swift on the poem's presentation in print) and George Farquhar, who were followed in time by Oliver Goldsmith and Richard Brinsley Sheridan.[19] Conscious of provincial and even foreign origins, they determined to outshine the competition by mixing radical, even outrageous, innovation with conspicuous displays of literary decorum and staged returns to generic origins. As well as helping to establish an enduring pattern for immigrant writers in London, Swift's poem, a city georgic paired with and preceded by the urban pastoral of its companion-poem 'A Description of the Morning', puts a personal spin on the *rota Virgilii* or wheel of Virgil, the traditional progress from bucolic to martial themes traced in imitation of the Roman poet's transition from eclogue to epic.[20] Like Alexander Pope, whose adherence to this model started out in more visible and conventional imitation, Swift's poetic career lacks an epic phase. Where it does surface in his work, the heroic mode emerges counter-intuitively not as climax but as juvenilia to be expunged. In this context, the 'Description' is a new start that expiates several false ones and propels a shy debutant onto the poetic stage at the age of forty-two.

Swift made an earlier and less successful effort at poetic self-invention and self-promotion with a series of Pindaric odes in the manner of Abraham Cowley. Counting W. B. Yeats among their few admirers, they are said to have occasioned Dryden's remark about never being a poet. Research on the incident suggests that the put-down may have been specifically directed at Swift's abilities to compose in this idiom.[21] This, along with the wider reception of the odes, provoked in Swift a reappraisal and rejection of what it meant to 'be a poet', which led ultimately to the pervasively ironic, 'anti-poetic' stance of his mature style.[22] Rather than a complete break, however, some of the poems suggest continuity with those of mid and late career. Swift's 'Ode to the King', addressed to William III in celebration of his victory over his son-in-law James II, shows how he expanded the Pindaric form to explore its 'satiric possibilities':[23]

How vainly (sir) did your fond enemy try
Upon a rubbish heap of broken laws
  To climb at victory
  Without the footing of a cause;
His laurel now must only be a cypress wreath,
 And his best victory a noble death;
His scrap of life is but a heap of miseries,
  The remnant of a falling snuff,
  Which hardly wants another puff,
 And needs must *stink* whene'er it dies (*CP*, 45–6)

 Despite their quite different subjects, this poem anticipates the others discussed so far in that all derive energetic charge from matter they hasten to discard, denigrate or disintegrate. Whereas 'A Description of a City Shower' itemises, memorialises and elevates forgotten products of daily life's routine violence, this poem contrives to grind an enemy into dust. In anticipation of similarly deconstructive efforts of late poems like 'A Beautiful Young Nymph Going to Bed', a body dissolves into a loose assemblage of materials. But although the aim of the Ode is to portray James II as lifeless and wasted, the apparently exhausted matter remains mobile and energetic, so that a scrap swells to a heap and shrinks back to a remnant. The specific image of the guttering candle is revisited in 'A Satirical Elegy on the Death of a Late Famous General', where the object of the satire is said to have 'burnt his candle to the snuff; / And that's the reason, some folks think, / He left behind *so great a stink*' (*CP*, 242). In both poems, Swift's own inversion of the 'sweetness and light' trope equates diminished or degraded masculinities with noisome darkness. Late poems like 'The Lady's Dressing Room' and 'A Beautiful Young Nymph Going to Bed', where Corinna is 'Surrounded with a hundred stinks' (*CP*, 454), famously politicise odour through representations of femininity that, as Tita Chico notes, 'have polarized critics for nearly three hundred years'[24] and which remain deeply contested. Gender in these poems is sometimes not quite as clear in its polarity as the critics have been in theirs. In images such as that of Strephon, who, 'if unsavoury odours fly, / *Conceives* a lady standing by' (*CP*, 451; emphasis added), there are punning references to conception, birth and even male pregnancy. In addition to gender, images of transgressive or equivocal generation also coalesce around the two other main preoccupations of Swift's poetic satire: bad poets and dissenting sects. In 'Brother Protestants', assumptions of Presbyterian kinship with Anglicans are dismissed as the claims of a parasite on a human host (Though born of filth and sweat, it / May well be said man did beget it' (*CP*, 538)). 'On Poetry: A Rhapsody' similarly fudges sexual and abiogenetic modes of production when the would-be poet is presented with 'The product of your toil and sweating; / A bastard of your own begetting' (525). These repeated images of ambiguous birth can be read in several ways. Often linked to English peers' adoption of increasingly scurrilous and misogynistic satiric modes, they also reflect on Swift's ambivalent embrace of his prominence and importance as an Irish poet. In this context they function partly as autobiographical projections of hybrid identity, and partly as representations of political crisis. Such imagery has wider currency in Anglo-Irish writing from this time, which, as Clíona Ó Gallchoir notes, abounds in images of a 'teeming and parasitic population, seemingly lacking legitimating fathers'.[25] Swift's late poetry combines this sense of social malaise with an impulse to appraise and evaluate a career reaching its final phase. With customary invocation of classically inflected models of poetry as public service, he had conceived his relocation to Ireland as a form of Horatian retirement from 'court and town' (CP, 170). At once self-ironising and self-aggrandising, the later poems complicate this sense of retreat with mixed postures of defeat and defiance.

The Tory Anarchist

Swift's poems often introduce dissident voices that undercut the traditional forms of authority on which they appear to rely. Famously discussed by George Orwell as a matter of temperament, this 'Tory anarchy' received a more nuanced interpretation from Edward Said. In the context of the late poems in particular, Said's interpretation of Swift as an essentially belated figure, 'haunted by the impermanence of events' and facing a political order in which he had 'no place except as outsider', is illuminating.[26] 'On Cutting Down the Old Thorn at Market Hill' exemplifies this ability to combine marginal and orthodox voices. The poem is traditionally grouped with others set around the estate of Sir Arthur and Lady Anne Acheson near Markethill, County Armagh, which comically foreground Swift's ability to test the limits of his hosts' hospitality. It uses folk beliefs about fairy thorns to stage a clash between the Anglican ruling class's proprietary ethic of agricultural 'improvement' and a competing sense that the lands it applied to remained hostile territory in a fragile grasp.

More often dramatised in the Markethill poems' comic exposition of Swift as an unruly and increasingly unwelcome guest, this conflict can also take on a mythic character. After a preamble describing Swift's determination to remove an ancient thorn from lands on the estate, the speaking voice is given over to the spirit of the tree. Female by convention, this nymph extends and complicates Swift's anti-pastoral aesthetic both by introducing vernacular folklore and by offering a vocal counterpart to the repressed female voices of 'The Lady's Dressing Room' and 'On a Beautiful Young Nymph Going to Bed'. She adopts an apocalyptic register to voice this vision of revenge:

'Pigs and fanatics, cows, and Teagues
Through all thy empire I foresee,
To tear thy hedges join in leagues,
Sworn to revenge my thorn and me.'   (*CP*, 355)

This prophecy of fallen empire takes in both Swift's personal celebrity status and the larger instabilities of his class. The hedges to be torn down appear elsewhere in his work as symbolic guarantors, Ian Higgins has shown, which lent biblical authority to the Anglican establishment in Ireland.[27] They enclose an embattled minority threatened economically by shifts from arable to pasture farming and politically by burgeoning numbers of dissenters and 'Teagues' (from the personal name Tadhg), a derogatory term for an Irish Catholic used freely in the poems, but which Swift had also applied ironically to himself. The lines also distantly echo a prophecy from near the end of Edmund Spenser's incomplete epic *The Faerie Queene*, where the goddess Diana departs Ireland in anger and determines that wolves and thieves will overrun the land.

Replaying Spenser's tragic alienation as slapstick, Swift the Tory anarchist surveys estrangement and devastation with a certain relish. Another Markethill poem finds him exhorting Acheson's tenants to 'cut his hedges down for fire' (*CP*, 430), while final reckonings, revolutionary upheavals, valedictions and maledictions are a much-visited theme. 'The Day of Judgement' offers a less localised version of impending chaos, while the 'Verses Occasioned by the Sudden drying up of St Patrick's Well' echoes the thorn poem in using a genius loci to voice what is effectively Swift's well-rehearsed resignation as patriot poet-in-chief. These poems' preoccupation with endings and exits is complemented by a tendency already discussed in earlier works to overlay topical or parodic content with a self-reflexive commentary on their own status as entrances, innovations and interventions. Swift's use of individual poems as staging posts suggests that being a poet, and in particular dramatising the process of announcing, acquiring or renouncing that status, was one of two central concerns in his career. The other – intervention in matters of controversy, habitually framed and focused on markers of identitarian difference – has ensured that the legacies left by his work have been political as much as they have been poetic.

The Legatees

Those modern Irish poets who have directly imitated Swift's voice have largely done so in contexts of frustration, violence or injustice. In 'The Holy Office', James Joyce borrowed the characteristic octosyllabics and excremental register to vent his frustration with censorship in the Ireland of the 1910s.[28] Later in the century, Thomas Kinsella's 'Butcher's Dozen' responded to the murder of unarmed civilians on Bloody Sunday 1972 and the subsequent judicial whitewash. Described as a 'deliberate poetic intervention in a particular political process',[29] the poem was self-published within three weeks of the Widgery tribunal's conclusion and distributed widely and cheaply. In its form as well as its manner of publication it recalls the urgent topicality of Swift's poems:

> Then from left and right they came,
> More mangled corpses, bleeding, lame,
> Holding their wounds. They chose their ground,
> Ghost by ghost, without a sound,
> And one stepped forward, soiled and white:
> 'A bomber I. I travelled light
> – Four pounds of nails and gelignite
> About my person, hid so well
> They seemed to vanish where I fell.'[30]

The protective ironies that cushion Swift's 'sub-poetic' style are here abandoned. Actual bodily violence supplants the merely verbal insults of Swift's mangled rhymes and comically distended syllables, which are almost but not completely absent. Although plain couplets predominate, 'soiled and white / travelled light / gelignite' offers a ghostly echo of Swift's use of multisyllabic terminal rhymes in triplet formations. The suggestion, perhaps, is of a literary heritage that adds to rather than relieves the weight carried by the poem's overburdened speakers. Kinsella's ability to recontextualise Swiftian topoi is also at work in a late poem which revisits the tableau of tumbling objects familiar from Swift's 'City Shower'. The speaker of 'Free Fall' (2011) describes 'falling helpless in a shower of waste'. At 'the last instant' before impact, the torrent slows and those caught up in it begin 'regarding one another in approval'.[31] The location of the authorial voice among rather than beyond the animate waste overcomes Swift's ironic distancing, perhaps reflecting a final dissipation of the tensions that informed 'Butcher's Dozen' as bitterly as they did Swift's own verse.

Something of Swift's fondness for pushing rhyme to its limits, along with a 'strong element of anti-pastoral',[32] is found in the poetry of Paul Muldoon. His own critical work on Swift imaginatively uncovers verbal and structural 'rhymes' between Swift's poetry and the Gaelic tradition.[33] Both can be found as separate but compatible presences in the work of Austin Clarke, who followed and considerably expanded on Swift's efforts in translating the Irish-language poetry of his day. Clarke's long narrative poem 'Mnemosyne lay in Dust' is one of two significant autobiographical works by twentieth-century poets set in St Patrick's University Hospital, the 'house for fools and mad' founded with a legacy from Swift and which is today Ireland's largest independent provider of mental health services. Along with Derek Mahon's 'Dawn at St Patrick's', it reflects the fact that Swift was an acute if not always compassionate observer of distressed states. By comparison with the traditional focus on Swift as a purveyor of satiric fictions and rhetorical flights of 'madness', these remain underexamined. In Clarke's poem Swift merges with and inhabits Dublin's Georgian architecture to impose an atmosphere of 'ribald gloom' that is a symptom of national as much as personal unease. Memory, signalled in Clarke's title and in the final emergence from hospital of his 'Rememorised' hero, is also a focus for Mahon.[34] Swift's marble bust, illuminated through 'Georgian windows shafting light and dust', becomes a focus of recovery in the sense of both personal healing and the wider cultural enterprise of unearthing and entering into a necessary reckoning with the past.[35] Set in Dublin's other Swiftian monument, St Patrick's Cathedral, Clarke's 'A Sermon on Swift' unfolds during the city's 1967 tercentenary celebrations, when Clarke delivered an oration from the Dean's own pulpit to a gathering of academics. Their preoccupations appear almost irreconcilably removed from the subversive, even countercultural frankness unearthed by Clarke in second-hand bookstalls: 'fables / And scatological poems, I pennied them on / The Quays'.[36] Baggage to be unpacked rather than discarded, Swift's poetry is made to carry a promise of release from repression and neurosis in both political and personal spheres.

Swift may appear at first blush an unlikely standard bearer for liberation in the summer of love. But Clarke's appropriation clearly builds on one of three personas central to his verse. These epitomise Swift the Irish poet. Firstly, there is the poet of sensory experience and description, enmeshed in material culture and bodily sensation. Secondly, and perhaps most famously, there is a public poet, articulating visions of nationhood and civic obligation in ways that were paradoxically personal and idiosyncratic. Finally, Swift is a poet of intimate correspondences, both literal and metaphorical. Readers derive mixed pleasure and discomfort from the sense that they are either intruding upon a private exchange or being presented with affinities and equivalences that have gone not merely unnoticed but unsought. In a broader cultural context, Swift's poetry is defined by its ability to bring together 'things of heterogeneous kind', as often to disconcert as to delight. His verse combines classical and vernacular forms and preserves aspects of Ireland's oral culture even while hastening the transition to print. It has also provided an opportunity to bridge the parallel poetic traditions in Irish and in English that were active and vibrant during Swift's lifetime. Above all, Swift's poetry is characterised by its currency and immediacy. His legacy endures in the insistence that Irish poetry aspire to be timely rather than timeless.

NOTES

1. Samuel Johnson, 'Swift', in John H. Middendorf (ed.), *The Lives of the Poets, The Yale Edition of the Works of Samuel Johnson*, 23 vols (New Haven: Yale University Press, 1955–), XXII, pp. 969–1023, p. 1022, p. 977.
2. Derek Mahon, 'Introduction', *Jonathan Swift: Poems Selected by Derek Mahon* (London: Faber, 2001), p. vii; W. B. Yeats 'Parnell's Funeral' (1935), in *W. B. Yeats: The Poems* (Dublin: Gill and Macmillan, 1983), p. 280.
3. Pat Rogers, 'Swift the Poet', in Christopher Fox (ed.), *The Cambridge Companion to Jonathan Swift* (Cambridge: Cambridge University Press, 2003), pp. 177–202, p. 181; Denis Donoghue, 'Swift as Poet', in Donoghue (ed.), *Swift Revisited* (Cork: Mercier Press, 1968), pp. 75–89, p. 79.
4. Jonathan Swift, *The Battle of the Books*, in *The Cambridge Edition of the Works of Jonathan Swift*, gen. eds. Claude Rawson et al., 18 vols (Cambridge: Cambridge University Press, 2007–), vol. I, *A Tale of a Tub and Other Works*, ed. Marcus Walsh, 2010, pp. 141–64, p. 152.
5. Johnson, 'Swift', p. 1022; on light verse, see Claude Rawson, 'Swift', in Rawson (ed.), *The Cambridge Companion to English Poets* (Cambridge: Cambridge University Press, 2011), pp. 213–34, p. 217.
6. Seamus Deane, 'Classic Swift', in Fox, *Cambridge Companion to Jonathan Swift*, p. 252.
7. Pat Rogers (ed.), *Jonathan Swift: The Complete Poems* (Harmondsworth: Penguin, 1989), pp. 537–8. Subsequent references given parenthetically in main text by the abbreviation *CP*.
8. Louis A. Landa, *Jonathan Swift and the Church of Ireland* (Oxford: Clarendon Press, 1954), 21. See also Christopher Fox, 'Swift and the Rabble Reformation: *A Tale of a Tub* and the State of the Church in the 1690s', in Todd C. Parker (ed.), *Jonathan Swift as Priest and Satirist* (Newark: University of Delaware Press, 2009).
9. *The Works of J. S., D. D.*, 4 vols (Dublin: George Faulkner, 1735), II, p. 355.
10. Swift wrote to the Earl of Oxford in 1737 that he had been 'dropped' in Ireland; *A Modest Proposal* refers to 'a Child, *just dropt from it's Dam*', while *The History of the Four Last Years of the Queen* (1714; first published 1758), discussing the 1711 Act for Naturalizing Foreign Protestants, describes German refugees as 'the same thing in great, as Infants dropped at the Doors'.
11. Mikhail Bakhtin, *Rabelais and His World*, trans. Hélène Iswolsky (Bloomington: Indiana University Press, 2008), p. 23.
12. Leo Damrosch, *Jonathan Swift: His Life and His World* (New Haven: Yale University Press, 2013), p. 457.
13. Denis Donoghue, *Jonathan Swift: A Critical Introduction* (Cambridge: Cambridge University Press, 1967), p. 33.
14. These are discussed in a wider European context in Claude Rawson, *God, Gulliver, and Genocide: Barbarism and the European Imagination, 1492–1945* (Oxford: Oxford University Press, 2001).
15. Abigail Williams (ed.), 'Journal to Stella', *The Cambridge Edition of the Works of Jonathan Swift*, IX (Cambridge: Cambridge University Press), p. 42.
16. Swift to John Gay, 20 November 1729, in Harold Williams (ed.), *The Correspondence of Jonathan Swift*, 5 vols (Oxford: Clarendon Press, 1963–5), vol. III, p. 360.

17. Oswald Johnson, 'Swift and the Common Reader', quoted in Louise K. Barnett, *Swift's Poetic Worlds* (Newark: University of Delaware Press, 1981), p. 16.

18. Swift to Thomas Beach, 12 April 1735, *Correspondence*, IV, p. 321.

19. David O'Shaughnessy, 'Tolerably Numerous: Recovering the London Irish of the Eighteenth Century', *Eighteenth-Century Life*, 39 (2015), pp. 1–13; Helen Burke, 'The Irish Joke, Migrant Networks, and the London Irish in the 1680s', *Eighteenth-Century Life* 39 (2015), pp. 41–65.

20. Ernst Robert Curtius, *European Literature and the Latin Middle Ages*, trans. Willard R. Trask (Princeton: Princeton University Press, 1990), p. 201n.35, p. 232.

21. Extant research on the anecdote is summarised and evaluated in Robert M. Philmus, 'Dryden's "Cousin Swift" Re-examined', *Swift Studies*, 18 (2003), pp. 99–103.

22. Anne Cline Kelly, *Jonathan Swift and Popular Culture: Myth, Media and the Man* (Basingstoke: Palgrave, 2002), pp. 13–20.

23. David Sheehan, 'Swift on High Pindaric Stilts', in John Irwin Fischer and Donald C. Mell (eds.), *Contemporary Studies of Swift' Poetry* (Newark: University of Delaware Press, 1981), pp. 25–35, p. 26.

24. Tita Chico, *Designing Women: The Dressing Room in Eighteenth-Century English Literature and Culture* (Lewisburg, PA: Bucknell University Press, 2005), p. 134.

25. Clíona Ó Gallchoir, '"Whole Swarms of Bastards": The Discourse of Economic Improvement and Protestant Masculinity in Ireland, 1720–1740', forthcoming in Rebecca Barr, Sean Brady and Jane McGaughey (eds.), *Ireland and Masculinities in History* (Basingstoke: Palgrave, 2017).

26. George Orwell, 'Politics vs Literature: An Examination of Gulliver's Travels', in Sonia Orwell and Ian Angus (eds.), *The Collected Essays Journalism and Letters of George Orwell*, 4 vols (Harmondsworth: Penguin, 1971), IV, pp. 205–23. Edward Said, 'Swift's Tory Anarchy', *Eighteenth-Century Studies*, 3 (1969), pp. 48–66, p. 51, p. 56.

27. Ian Higgins, 'A Preface to Swift's Test Act Tracts', in Kirsten Juhas, Hermann J. Real and Sandra Simon (eds.), *Reading Swift: Papers from the Sixth Münster Symposium on Jonathan Swift* (Munich: Wilhelm Fink, 1998), pp. 225–43.

28. James Joyce, 'The Holy Office', 'Gas from a Burner', in Richard Ellmann et al. (eds.), *Poems and Shorter Writings* (London: Faber, 1991) pp. 97–9, 103–5.

29. Derval Tubridy, *Thomas Kinsella: The Peppercanister Poems* (Dublin: University College Dublin Press, 2001), p. 23

30. Thomas Kinsella, *Collected Poems* (Manchester: Carcanet, 2001), p. 133.

31. Thomas Kinsella, *Late Poems* (Manchester: Carcanet, 2013), p. 75.

32. Jefferson Holdridge, *The Poetry of Paul Muldoon* (Dublin: Liffey Press, 2008), Kindle publication, ch 2, n.p.

33. Paul Muldoon, *To Ireland, I* (Oxford, Clarendon Press, 2000), pp. 115–18, 122–3.

34. Austin Clarke, *Collected Poems*, ed. R. Dardis Clarke (Manchester: Carcanet, 2008), p. 325, p. 348.

35. Derek Mahon, *New Collected Poems* (Loughcrew: Gallery, 1999), p. 150.

36. Clarke, *Collected Poems*, p. 457.

SELECTED FURTHER READING

Editions

Jonathan Swift: The Complete Poems, ed. Pat Rogers (Harmondsworth, Penguin, 1989).
The Essential Writings of Jonathan Swift, ed. Claude Rawson and Ian Higgins (New York: Norton, 2009).
Swift's Irish Writings: selected Prose and Poetry, ed. Carole Fabricant and Robert Mahony (Basingstoke: Palgrave, 2010).

Biography

Damrosch, Leo, *Jonathan Swift: His Life and His World* (New Haven: Yale University Press, 2013).
Ehrenpreis, Irvin, *Swift: The Man, His Works and the Age*, 3 vols (London: Methuen 1962–83).

Critical Studies

Barnett, Louise K., *Swift's Poetic Worlds* (Newark: University of Delaware Press, 1981).
Fabricant, Carole, *Swift's Landscape* (Baltimore: Johns Hopkins University Press, 1982).
Ferguson, Oliver W., *Jonathan Swift and Ireland* (Urbana: University of Illinois Press, 1962).
Karian, Stephen, *Jonathan Swift in Print and Manuscript* (Cambridge: Cambridge University Press, 2010).
Landa, Louis A., *Jonathan Swift and the Church of Ireland* (Oxford: Clarendon Press, 1954).
Mahon, Derek, 'Introduction', *Jonathan Swift: Poems Selected by Derek Mahon* (London: Faber 2001).
McMinn, Joseph, *Jonathan's Travels: Swift and Ireland* (Belfast: Appletree Press, 1994).
Rogers, Pat, 'Swift the Poet', in Christopher Fox (ed.), *The Cambridge Companion to Jonathan Swift* (Cambridge: Cambridge University Press, 2003), pp. 177–202.
Rawson, Claude, 'Swift', in Rawson (ed.), *The Cambridge Companion to English Poets* (Cambridge: Cambridge University Press, 2011), pp. 213–34.

3

AODÁN MAC PÓILIN

Aogán Ó Rathaille

Aogán Ó Rathaille (pronounced roughly Egan O'Rahilly) was the most significant Gaelic poet of the eighteenth century. His political sensibility was formed by what its English supporters called the Glorious Revolution – an enormously important step in the shift from absolutism to constitutional monarchy, but a disaster for Catholic and Gaelic Ireland. His cultural sensibility came from a belief that he belonged to a high culture and an aristocratic order that stretched back for millennia, and a recognition that both that high culture and the class which sustained it were being destroyed in his own lifetime. His poetic sensibility – or sensibilities – involved something rather more complex. Sometimes he was a traditional bard, offering praise-poems to patrons and composing formal elegies. Much of this stuff, often metrically intricate, highly musical, linguistically interesting, historically informative and with the occasional spark of vivid imagery, is dry enough for a modern reader. At other times, in poems that do come alive, he cursed some miscreant, and there are sparks of life in a couple of burlesque squibs in which he caricatured his own trade – among them a hundred-line praise-poem celebrating the gift of a pair of shoes. He was a passionate supporter of the deposed Stuarts, writing Jacobite poems on the politics of his day, the most potent of which are in the form of the *aisling*, or vision-poem. In these, a beautiful dream-woman, who represents the sovereignty of Ireland, promises a return of the Stuarts, but this message is undermined, and the poems themselves immeasurably enriched, by an underlying deep pessimism. For the modern reader, however, his most extraordinary achievement is in a handful of personal lyrics in which a cry of rage against the tragedy of his own life and the destruction of the Gaelic order melds with and becomes the best expression that we have of the tragedy of his country.

Or possibly not. One leading scholar, Breandán Ó Buachalla, has rejected any autobiographical reading of these works, blaming the first editor, Patrick Dinneen, for initiating a 'romantic impressionistic' and over-literal interpretation of his poetry which was then taken up and amplified by Daniel

Corkery and Seán Ó Tuama: 'Ó Rathaille's poetry', he writes, 'is not a realistic reflection of his life; but rather a textual delineation of the poetic world he created'.[1] He is particularly scathing about any autobiographical reading of the astonishing if problematic 'Cabhair ní ghairfead', assumed to be Ó Rathaille's last poem by Dineen, Corkery and Ó Tuama, and indeed by the scribes of the two earliest surviving manuscript versions of the poem, who identified it as 'The poet on his death-bed writing to his friend having from certain causes fallen into despondency'. Ó Buachalla asserts, correctly, that there is not an iota of proof that the poem was written at the end of Ó Rathaille's life, and argues that deathbed poems are a common trope in Gaelic poetry. However, it seems to this reader that 'Cabhair ní ghairfead' involves much more than the projection of a poetic persona. Nor does it follow the conventions of the deathbed poem by repenting past sins and crying to God for mercy. This poem spurns help from any quarter and mentions the Redeemer only for the purposes of historic comparison.

What follows are the first and last verses in the original with a reasonably literal translation:[2]

> Cabhair ní ghairfead go gcuirtear me i gcruinn-chomhrainn –
> dar an leabhar dá ngairinn níor ghaire-de an ní dhomh-sa;
> ár gcodhnach uile, glac-chumasach Shíl Eoghain,
> – is tollta a chuisle, 'gus d'imigh a bhrí ar feochadh. . . .

> Stadfadsa feasta – is gar dom éag gan mhoill
> ó treascradh dragain Leamhan, Léin is Laoi;
> rachad-sa 'na bhfasc le searc na laoch don chill,
> na flatha fá raibh mo shean roimh éag do Chríost.

I will not call for help until I'm put in a narrow coffin – / I swear if I called it would bring help no nearer; / our chieftain, the strong-handed descendent of Eoghan / – his pulse has been pierced, and his vigour withered. . . .   (ll. 1–4)

I will cease now, death approaches without delay / since the heroes of the Laune, the Laine and the Lee have been crushed; / with the beloved of champions I will join in death / the princes my ancestors served before the death of Christ.   (ll. 25–8)

Frank O'Connor's version is the best-known translation:[3]

> I shall not call for help until they coffin me –
>   What good for me to call when hope of help is gone?
> Princes of Munster who would have heard my cry
>   Will not rise from the dead because I am alone.

Mind shudders like a wave in this tempestuous mood,
   My bowels and my heart are pierced and filled with pain
To see our lands, our hills, our gentle neighborhood,
   A plot where any English upstart stakes his claim.

The Shannon and the Liffey and the tuneful Lee,
   The Boyne and the Blackwater a sad music sing,
The waters of the west run red into the sea –
   No matter what be trumps, their knave will beat our king.

And I can never cease weeping these useless tears;
   I am a man oppressed, afflicted and undone
Who where he wanders mourning no companion hears
   Only some waterfall that has no cause to mourn.

Now I shall cease, death comes, and I must not delay
   By Laune and Laine and Lee, diminished of their pride,
I shall go after the heroes, ay, into the clay –
   My fathers followed theirs before Christ was crucified.

This version captures much of the energy and key imagery of the poem, but, as with any translation, much is lost. There is of course no way to replicate the intricate Gaelic metrics, and O'Connor's vivid rendering into stately if vernacular English gives no idea of the almost baroque language of the original, with its compound words, allusive and occasionally arcane diction, and sometimes jagged syntax. Many cultural references that deepen its impact but would have little or no resonance for a modern anglophone audience have been elided. To take but one instance, where O'Connor has 'The waters of the west run red into the sea', the original cites Tonn Tóime – one of the mythical waves of Ireland that, among its other functions, roared when a rightful king died, an inference that would not have been lost on Ó Rathaille's contemporaries

Modern readers may also need to adjust some of their other aesthetic preconceptions. The wailing of nature in this poem is more than a pathetic fallacy; it is rooted in an ancient belief that the righteous and rightful lord brings social harmony, prosperity and fruitfulness to the land he rules. Conversely, the rule of the unrighteous brings chaos, injustice and oppression, and nature itself suffers. In this case unrighteous rule can be traced to William III, characterised here as a *cuireata* – the knave in a pack of cards – who fleeces James II, the (rightful) Stuart king, but could equally stand for George I vis-à-vis the Old Pretender, or any of the English landowners who have displaced the rightful lords of Munster. Here, as so often in Ó Rathaille, an archaic and seemingly obsolete tradition is brought to bear with considerable force on the contemporary situation.

In O'Connor's slightly shortened version, one admittedly problematic key theme has been flattened out into a generalised 'princes of Munster', a reference to the 'descendants' of Eoghan, a third-century king of Munster and founder of the important *Eoghanacht* line. Ó Rathaille here is referring to the McCarthys, his exemplars of Gaelic aristocracy, princes of south Munster between the twelfth and sixteenth centuries, former kings of the entire province, patrons of Ó Rathaille's Mac Aogáin ancestors and, in his poetry, symbols of the entire Gaelic order.

Genealogy, real or invented, was enormously important in the value-system of the Gaelic aristocracy. In a 272-line elegy on the death of the chief of the O'Callaghans in 1724, Ó Rathaille devotes a mind-numbing 100 lines to his subject's pedigree, including the tenth-century Donnchadh, common ancestor of the O'Callaghans and the McCarthys, through the possibly mythical Eoghan to the definitely mythical Goidel Glas, ancestor of the Gaels and a contemporary of Moses, and finishing with Japheth, Noah and Adam. Ó Rathaille himself could claim an impressive aristocratic lineage through his mother, a Mac Aogáin (Egan, Keegan), from a line of scholars and poets that for five centuries had been Ireland's most notable literary family. One genealogy runs through Aogán, the sept's tenth-century pro-genitor, to pre-Christian times. Another tradition traces the family to the *Soghain*, a prehistoric population group who were vassals to the *Eoghanacht*, the descendants of Eoghan. Or, to put it another way, this poem is even stranger than we knew. That resounding last line – borrowed by Yeats for 'The Curse of Cromwell'[4] ('And there is an old beggar wander-ing in his pride – / His fathers served their fathers before Christ was crucified') – was more than a rhetorical conceit. Ó Rathaille, in one mood anyway, meant it to be taken literally.

Aside from what has survived of his poetry, Ó Rathaille has left little trace, and it could be useful to compare his fate to that of another close contemporary. Both Jonathan Swift and Aogán Ó Rathaille were born in Ireland, both engaged with the condition of Ireland and 'savage indigna-tion' is as fitting a description of one as the other, but one belonged to the rising Protestant and anglophone middle class, the other to the doomed Catholic Gaelic aristocracy. The record reflects the difference in their status. We know to the day when Jonathan Swift was born and died (30 November 1667–19 October 1745), and where. Ó Rathaille may or may not have been born in 1670, and appears to have died some time between 1727 and 1729. The consensus that he was born in the Sliabh Luachra district of Kerry is based solely on the fact that all manuscript and oral sources are in agreement. Ó Rathaille was never in print until three poems were published in 1849, well over a century after his death, while Swift was extensively published in his own lifetime. There are several large collections of Swift's manuscripts, and even collections of the very books he owned. We have none of Ó Rathaille's poems in his own hand, and his only surviving manuscript is a copy made in 1722 of Keating's history of Ireland. A single contemporary reference to him has been found, a sad little note in the Kenmare Manuscripts: 'September 1727 paid Egan O Rahilly when his only cow was appraised last winter 1726 by James Curtaine for composing songs for Master Thomas Browne and the rest of his Lordship's children at John Rierddanes prayer and request: £1.10.0.' No songs celebrating the birth of Master Thomas Browne in 1726 or referring to any of his siblings have come down to us, and we have no idea what else may have been lost. Ó Rathaille's surviving work, about forty poems and a short prose satire, is found in manuscripts written by scribes of various levels of learning and reliability, many of them written well after his death. Another forty manuscript attributions to Ó Rathaille have been rejected by scholars, and there is a small number of non-attributed poems which experts in the field believe are likely to have been composed by him.

The brief entry in the Kenmare Manuscripts is nonetheless revealing. It supplements the evidence of the poetry itself to show that towards the end of his life Ó Rathaille was living in reduced circumstances and was continuing to attempt to function as a professional Gaelic poet, writing poems for patrons. In this case the patron was Valentine Browne, 3rd Viscount Kenmare (1695–1736). The payment for the poems was meagre enough, thirty shillings in old money, and, from the tone of the entry, was less a reward than an act of charity.

This wasn't the first time Ó Rathaille had sought the patronage of Valentine Browne. The Brownes had first settled in Ireland early in Elizabeth's reign and built up an enormous estate, initially through grants of confiscated land and ultimately through purchases from improvident Gaelic landowners. They were nevertheless Catholics who had intermarried extensively with Gaelic and Norman families – in an elegy on Valentine's uncle John, who died in 1709, Ó Rathaille notes that he was doubly related to all the Gaelic princes of Ireland (and was specially blessed in that his grandmother was a McCarthy). Valentine's father had been exiled for his Jacobite activities and his estates confiscated during his lifetime. When he died in 1720, Valentine inherited the family's vast, albeit debt-ridden estates, marrying Honora Butler of Kilcash the same year. Whatever expectations Ó Rathaille had of Browne's patronage – two surviving poems celebrate his engagement and marriage – they were clearly not fulfilled. He responded to his humiliation in an extraordinarily eloquent outburst of racial snobbery:

Do leathnaigh an chiach dhiachrach fám sheana-chroí dúr
ar thaisteal na ndiabhal iasachta i bhfearann Chuinn chughainn;
scamall ar ghrian iarthair dár cheartas ríocht Mhumhan
fá deara dhom triall riamh ort, A Bhailintín Brún.

Caiseal gan cliar, fiailteach ná marcraí ar dtúis
is beanna-bhruigh Bhriain ciar-thuilte 'mhadraibh úisc,
Ealla gan triair triaithe de mhacaibh rí Mhumhan
fá deara dhom triall riamh ort, A Bhailintín Brún.   (ll. 1–8)

A mist of despair spread over my old dour heart / since the alien devils have overrun our land, / there's a cloud on Munster's rightful lord, the western sun / or I never would have come near you, Valentine Browne.
    Cashel bereft of its poets, guest-house, horsemen, / Brian's turreted mansion black-flooded with greasy curs / Duhallow without the three royal chieftains of Munster / or I never would have come near you, Valentine Browne. . . .

Frank O'Connor has captured some of the ferocity of this poem in the three verses he translated:[5]

> That my old bitter heart was pierced in this black doom,
> That foreign devils have made our land a tomb,
> That the sun that was Munster's glory has gone down
> Has made me a beggar before you, Valentine Brown.
>
> That royal Cashel is bare of house and guest,
> That Brian's turreted home is the otter's nest,
> That the kings of the land have neither land nor crown
> Has made me a beggar before you, Valentine Brown.
>
> Garnish away in the west with its master banned,
> Hamburg the refuge of him who has lost his land,
> An old grey eye, weeping for lost renown,
> Have made me a beggar before you, Valentine Brown.

One of the challenges in reading Ó Rathaille today is that his frame of reference is often well outside the experience of his modern readers. Cashel formerly belonged to the McCarthy kings of Munster, and Garnish [*recte.* Dairinish – Valentia Island] is one of the territories confiscated from McCarthy Mór, titular chief of the sept. The Hamburg reference is to Donough McCarthy, the Oxford-educated Earl of Clancarty, in exile in Germany for Jacobite activities, and making a living stripping shipwrecks on the mudflats of the Wadden Sea.
    Valentine Browne in 1720 was an opera-loving, flute-playing, thoroughly anglicised 25-year-old who had been brought up in London and suffered badly from constipation. Unlike his father and grandfather, he seems to have

had no feel for Gaelic culture. He also carried an upstart English name that, compared to the kind of long-tailed genealogy revered by Ó Rathaille, had no cultural purchase. Contempt drips from repetition of the ineffably cissy forename Valentine and the Gaelic form Brún (pronounced, as in the Thompson comic-strip, *Broon*). One verse has fish fleeing the sunlit stream, and another deals with the effect of an unjust ruler on the land: 'The down of nimble bird-flocks floats on the breeze / like ashes discarded over a waste of heath / cattle refuse to give their milk to their calves / since Sir Val usurped the noble McCarthys' land.'

The epithelium had drawn on the same trope, but in reverse; fish leap in the streams, bees swarm and trees bloom in winter: Valentine Browne is called Lord Kenmare, the title given to his grandfather by James II; he is a *saorfhlaith*, a noble prince, and *Rí Chille hAirne*, the king of Killarney, while the final line wishes long life to him *ina réim chirt* – in his rightful patrimony.

There is nothing surprising in this swift turn from praise to satire. In the bardic ethic espoused by Ó Rathaille, probably the last poet to try to live by its principles, a patron was to be praised according to his generosity and dispraised according to his niggardliness. James Carney (using the term 'ollav' for the high-status poet) has traced this ethic from its pre-Christian religious roots through to the early modern period:

> A king married his territory: if he was effective and behaved as a king should, according to this ethical system, his land was fertile and bore fruit. If a king was bad, according to this ethical system, the land was barren. ... [the ollav] is the intermediary between the prince and the mysterious powers of nature. ... If an ollav satirises a prince he is in effect telling him that the forces of nature, with which he, the ollav, is in communion, are not satisfied ... when a poet praises a king he is assuring him that the powers of nature find him pleasing and that the marriage is going well.[6]

Such an important function could not come cheap, and the professional poets, described by Carney as the oldest trade union in Europe, should clearly be well rewarded for their labours. Self-interest, of course, played its part in these exchanges. However, the broader responsibilities of the nobility – any nobility – included protecting the environment and those in their care. Ó Rathaille's protests against the destruction of ancient woodlands, sold off at sixpence per tree, and his criticism of the new masters for failing to protect the poor and weak are informed by the poet's ancient function as a moral arbiter.

Ó Rathaille was temperamentally a conservative, responding to current realities by invoking ancient mores and principles that were now redundant, but his conservatism is not that of the defender of privilege. Like Yeats and

Eliot, he responded to the political and social upheavals of his time with poetry that was in many ways radical, while at the same time shoring an idealised set of traditional values against the ruins of the world he had known, and simultaneously providing a devastating critique of the deplorable present.

The bardic ethic allowed Ó Rathaille to countenance and adapt to the newer ruling class, provided they also subscribed to the principles of noblesse oblige. In one poem he praises the lavish hospitality of the recently installed Englishman who now owned Castle Tochar, former stronghold of a minor branch of the McCarthys, Mac Carthaigh na Féile (the Munificent McCarthys). Significantly, he praises the new owner in terms of how well he replicates the hospitality of his famously open-handed forerunners: '*Do mheasas im aigne is fós im chroí / an marbh ba mharbh gur beo do bhí*' – I thought in my mind, and also in my heart, that the dead who were dead were still alive. In another long elegy he commemorates John Blennerhasset, from a Protestant family which had been in Kerry for only a hundred years or so, but whose home, according to the poem, was open to scholars, poets, musicians, bishops, princes and viscounts. Valentine Browne's crime was less that he was an upstart Englishman than that he had neglected his social obligations, and, in particular, had neglected to honour the poet who had honoured him.

Free-market pragmatists and Marxist determinists would find Browne's neglect understandable enough. In the chaos of the post-Williamite settlement, penal laws, confiscations, banishments and bankruptcies, all members of the old order had to come to terms with the new realities. Under the Penal Laws Catholic property had to be divided among all sons, and many Catholic landowners converted to Protestantism to keep their estates intact, among them Randal McCarthy Mór, titular chief of the sept, although he subsequently managed to mortgage off and finally lose a large part of his holdings. The Brownes, who remained staunchly Catholic, avoided subdivision by being sparing with their male offspring, but under Valentine and his son they became pillars of the new order. Supporting a ferociously Jacobite poet was much lower on Valentine's priority list than clearing the debts on his inheritance. Some Gaelic aristocrats escaped to the Continent, or to England, where Catholics and Jacobites were safer than in their own country. Others again, including McCarthy Mór's son, joined the British army, while the irreconcilable enlisted in the armies of other European states. In the scramble for survival, loyalty to the Crown, rejection of the Jacobite cause and anglicisation were all part of the survival package of Catholic and Gaelic families (the Jacobite movement of the eighteenth century was led by Protestants from long-established colonial families, while, as the Governor of Kerry reported to Dublin Castle, the Gaelic families were notably quiescent). Opportunists thrived in this chaos, and Ó Rathaille directed some of his most savage invective against enterprising middlemen of Gaelic extraction, the Catholic Teigue Cronin (a turbulent, twisted, vile, fraudulent, foul-smelling satan-visaged churl) and the former Catholic Murty Griffin (mercenary thug, serpent who embezzles from the weak, upstart voluptuary, seducer of women).

In these turbulent times, the greatest losers were those who either would not or could not adapt, and while Ó Rathaille equivocated as best he could, he had neither the saleable skills nor the temperament to succeed in the new order. In everything except his poetry, he can be definitely counted among the losers.

That poetry reveals a man who was literate, knew English, was familiar with Greek and Roman mythology and history and had some, possibly indirect, acquaintance with more recent European literature (he cited Sancho Panza in a prose satire). His mastery of the Irish language was extraordinary, encompassing the complex and arcane poetic register of his bardic ancestors at one pole and an earthy demotic at the other. Judging from the range of his references, he had a profound knowledge of mythology, genealogy and the traditional version of Irish history.

Ó Rathaille was probably raised in relatively comfortable circumstances as an under-tenant of Valentine Browne's grandfather (another Valentine) in the Sliabh Luachra region, a rolling upland plateau interspersed with glens and occasional peaks on the Cork/Kerry/Limerick border, mostly poor land, but with fertile patches. It is possible that they lived there at a peppercorn rent; the Brownes rented an estate of 3,600 acres to a neighbour, Captain Eoghan McCarthy, for two shillings a year. Ó Rathaille may have received part of his education here. In a 250-line poem lamenting McCarthy's loss of his lands to 'sheepmongers' such as Murty Griffin, he celebrated McCarthy's former hospitality to poets, bards, learned men and aged authors, adding, with bardic ebullience, druids and seers to the list. He may also have attended classical schools in nearby Killarney, part of the 140,000 acre estate owned by Valentine's grandfather, and a centre of learning for aspiring priests. The area was also a centre of Gaelic learning; Ó Rathaille's Mac Aogáin relatives had land a few miles from Killarney, possibly as tenants of the McCarthy Mór (who had managed to hold on to 10,000 or so acres). The O'Donoghues of Glenflesk, described by Ó Rathaille as *tearmainn d'éigsibh* – refuge of bards – and themselves descendants of a notable poet, were also close at hand.

Wherever he gained his education, and however he learned his trade, Ó Rathaille was a master of the techniques of Gaelic accentual verse, which is based primarily on elaborate patterns of assonance (a fragment of a tract on prosody survives along with his copy of Keating). Through most of the Valentine Browne poem, lines follow the same vowel pattern (a-ia-ia-a-í-ú) over all six stressed syllables:

> scamall ar ghrian iarthair dár cheartas ríocht Mhumhan
> fá deara dhom triall riamh ort, a Bhailintín Brún.

Monotony is avoided through varying the rhythm by what would be called sprung rhythm in English, alternating occasionally with clusters of unstressed syllables, and an occasional lapse in the pattern.

His most admired technical achievement, and his most popular poem in the manuscript tradition, is *Gile na Gile*, one of the *aisling* poems (twice as many copies of this work survive than of any other). The poem has attracted modern translators such as Seamus Heaney, Thomas Kinsella, Frank O'Connor, Michael Hartnett and Brendan Kennelly, as well as James Clarence Mangan (1849) and George Sigerson (1897). O'Connor suppressed his version for more than thirty years, defeated by the intricacy of the original: 'In Irish the poem is pure music, each line beginning with assonantal rhymes on the short vowel "i" (like "mistress" and "bitter"), which gives it the secretive, whispering quality of dresses rustling or of light feed scurrying in the distance.'[7] It is indeed an extraordinary technical feat; the matching short stressed vowels at the beginning of lines (not always an 'i') combined with clusters of unstressed syllables do have the effect identified by O'Connor, while each line is slowed down by its ending: two long stressed syllables in 'í' and 'ua' followed by an unstressed neutral vowel. There are patterns of assonance between lines, much use of alliteration and compound words, and the doubling of words, used as an intensifier (roughly equivalent to the English bravest of the brave, time of times, day of days) is echoed by near-homonyms (*finne / fionnadh; glaine / gloine; tigim / tuigim; bruinneal [broinn-gheal] / broinnibh / broinnire / broinn-stuacach*) in an extraordinarily complex sound-scape.

> Gile na gile do chonnarc ar slí in uaigneas,
>   criostal an chriostail a goirm-roisc rinn-uaine,
>   binneas an bhinnis a friotal nár chríon-ghruama,
>   deirge is finne do fionnadh 'na gríos-ghruannaibh.
>
> Brightness of brightness I saw on a lonely path, / crystal of crystal in the lustrous blue-green of her eye, / sweetness of sweetness her speech not mournful with age, / redness with fairness seen in the glow of her cheeks.

In densely wrought Gaelic metres sense is sometimes sacrificed for sound, but while the reader (or listener) attuned to the genre can discount the words which have been inserted mainly for their aural effect, readers depending on a literal translation can be distracted not just by that which is untranslatable, but by much that is essentially meaningless (as are most of the adjectives in Ó Rathaille's O'Callaghan genealogy). One of the great achievements of *Gile na Gile* is that sound is very rarely sacrificed to sense.

Of the many versions in English, that by Kinsella generally wins on accuracy, while Hartnett made heroic attempts to be both literally faithful and to capture some measure of Gaelic assonantal rhyme. For its time, Mangan's nineteenth-century version, from a translator who knew no Irish, is worth noting:[8]

> The Brightest of the Bright met me on my path so lonely;
> The Crystal of all Crystals was her flashing dark-blue eye;
> Melodious more than music was her spoken language only;
> And glories were her cheeks, of a brilliant crimson dye. . . .   (ll. 1–4)

> o'er mountain, moor and marsh, by greenwood, lough and hollow,
> I tracked her distant footsteps with a throbbing heart;
> Through many an hour and day did I follow on and follow,
> Till I reached the magic palace reared of old by Druid art.   (ll. 17–20)

Heaney's *The Glamoured*,[9] in that it fails better than any of the others, is the version that best balances meaning and rhythm against an echo of the music of the original, and comes close to capturing the poet's almost physical disgust – that of the betrayed lover – at the state of Ireland:

> A gang of thick louts were shouting loud insults and jeering
> And a curly-haired coven in fits of sniggers and sneers:
> Next thing I was taken and cruelly shackled in fetters
> As the breasts of the maiden were groped by a thick-witted boor.

> I tried then as hard as I could to make her hear truth.
> How wrong she was to be linked to that lazarous swine
> When the pride of the pure Scottish stock,[10] a prince of her blood,
> Was ardent and eager to wed her and make her his bride.

The maiden, the sovereignty of Ireland, is here ravished – and allows herself to be ravished – by King George, thick-witted boor, hornmaster (he was commonly regarded as a cuckold), and in one untranslatable phrase, *slibire slím-bhuartha* – a gaunt, fretful string of slime, rendered here as 'lazarous swine'. Her rightful spouse, of course, was the Old Pretender, the son of James II.

Scholars have noted that none of the motifs in this or Ó Rathaille's other *aisling* poems is new. There were vision-poems in Irish long before his time,

Ireland's sovereignty has long been portrayed as a woman and Seán Ó Tuama, probably the best literary analyst of Ó Rathaille's work, has also traced debts to the Pastourelle and Reverdie tradition of troubadour poetry and to certain passages in Ronsard. However, Ó Rathaille's handling of inherited themes and motifs in this genre is indeed original, and was never surpassed. What most strikes today's reader about Ó Rathaille's oeuvre is the contrast between the pedestrian, if highly wrought, quality of his more conventional verse and the extraordinary power of those poems where, in his rage and sorrow, he transcends the conventions he inherited. Auden's phrase is possibly even more true of Ó Rathaille than of Yeats, mad Ireland hurt him into poetry.

NOTES

1. Ó Buachalla, New Introduction, in Patrick S. Dineen and Tadhg O'Donoghue (eds.), *Dánta Aodhagáin Uí Rathaille / The Poems of Egan O Rahilly*, London: ITS, 2004, p. 30.
2. *The Poems of Egan O'Rahilly*, pp.114–17
3. Frank O'Connor, *Kings, Lords and Commons*, London: MacMillan, 1961, p.107.
4. W. B. Yeats, *New Poems*, Dublin: Cuala Press, 1938.
5. 'A Grey Eye Weeping', *Kings, Lords, Commons*, p.102.
6. James Carney, *The Irish Bardic Poet*, Dublin: Dolmen, 1967, 11.
7. O'Connor, *Kings, Lords and Commons*, p. 104.
8. '[The Brightest of the Bright]', *The Collected Works of James Clarence Mangan: Poems, 1848–1912*, edited by Jacques Chuto [et al] (Dublin: Irish Academic Press, 1999), p. 143–4.
9. *Index on Censorship magazine*, September 1998, https://www.indexoncensorship.org/2013/08/seamus-heaney-1939–2013/
10. Heaney follows Kinsella's mistake in making James Stuart a *Scottish* rather than a *Scottic* prince. For Ó Rathaille and his contemporaries he was of Irish descent through Fergus mac Erc, mythical founder of the Scottish royal line, and ultimately from the Egyptian princess Scotia, supposed female ancestor of all the Gaels.

SELECTED FURTHER READING

Editions

Dineen, Patrick S. and Tadhg O'Donoghue (eds.), *Dánta Aodhagáin Uí Rathaille / The Poems of Egan O Rahilly*, London: Irish Texts Society, 1911, new edition, 2004 (which includes Breandán Ó Buachalla's *New Introduction*).

Ó Buachalla, Breandán (ed.,) *Aogán Ó Rathaille*, Dublin: Field Day Publications, 2007.

Secondary Works (Translations, Biographical and Critical Works)

Corkery, Daniel, *The Hidden Ireland*, Dublin: Gill, 1924.

Hartnett, Michael, *Ó Rathaille*, Loughcrew: Gallery Press, 1998.

Jordan, John, 'Aogán Ó Rathaille', in: Seán Mac Réamoinn (ed.), *The Pleasures of Gaelic Poetry*, London: Allen Lane, 1982.

Lillis, Michael, 'Riddled with Light', *Dublin Review of Books*, http://www.drb.ie/essays/riddled-with-light, 2012.

Ó Beoláin, Art, 'Aogán Ó Rathaille', *Merriman agus Fílí Eile*, Dublin: An Clóchomhar, 1985.

Ó Buachalla, Breandán, *Aisling Ghéar, Na Stiobhartaigh agus an tAos Léinn, 1603–1788*, Dublin: An Clóchomhar, 1996.

O'Connor, Frank, *Kings, Lords and Commons: An Anthology from the Irish*, London: Macmillan, 1961.

Ó Tuama, Seán, *Fílí Faoi Sceimhle*, Dublin: Oifig an tSoláthair, 1978.

'The World of Aogán Ó Rathaille' and 'Gaelic Culture in Crisis: The Literary Response', in *Repossessions: Selected Essays on the Irish Literary Heritage*, Cork: Cork University Press, 1995.

Ó Tuama, Seán and Thomas Kinsella, *An Duanaire, Poems of the Dispossessed, 1600–1900*, Dublin: Dolmen Press / Bord na Gaeilge, 1981.

4

MICHAEL GRIFFIN

Oliver Goldsmith

Raised in the Irish midlands, along and astride the borders of counties Longford, Roscommon and Westmeath, and educated at Trinity College Dublin, Goldsmith arrived in London in 1756 at the age of twenty-eight, and over the following eighteen years became one of the best-known poets, essayists, novelists, dramatists and popular historians of his age. In February of 1766 the 'Great Cham' Samuel Johnson, of whose famous literary club Goldsmith would become a core member, declared of Goldsmith's long philosophical poem *The Traveller; or, a Prospect of Society* (1764) that 'There has not been so fine a poem since [Alexander] Pope's time'.[1] With such praise, Johnson validated the appeal of Goldsmith's verse to his eighteenth-century English audience. With this English appeal in mind, it is worth asking at the outset: just how Irish a poet was Oliver Goldsmith?

To some readers, then and since, he was an Irish writer by birth only. To the younger William Butler Yeats, he was too English in his manners to be a considered a proper part of the national canon. For the older Yeats, however, he would become a beacon of Irish Anglican wisdom. In 'The Seven Sages' (1932) Goldsmith appears as one of those eighteenth-century Irish thinkers who, along with Edmund Burke, Jonathan Swift and George Berkeley, best embodied an anti-Whiggish, anti-mercantile mentality. It is *The Deserted Village* (1770) which informs Yeats' image of Goldsmith, and it is that poem, more so than *The Vicar of Wakefield* (1766) or the plays, into which his Irish origins are most amenably read; it is also the poem most readily associated with the Irish midlands which produced him. For the older Yeats, Goldsmith's Irishness was exemplary; his conservatism and poetic pastoralism consolidated an aristocratic paradigm, consisting of a responsible elite and a noble, sturdy peasantry:

> Oliver Goldsmith sang what he had seen,
> Roads full of beggars, cattle in the fields,
> But never saw the trefoil stained with blood,
> The avenging leaf those fields raised up against it.[2]

Yeats was increasingly dismayed at what he saw as a prehensile, urban (and Catholic) turn in post-revolutionary Ireland; by contrast, Goldsmith's world suggested an older decency, one not harried by any rebellious or revolutionary distemper. Averse to political abstraction, Goldsmith's pastoralism in the happier passages of *The Deserted Village* was understood to be rooted in, and defensive of, a pre-modern and ostensibly very Irish ideal of community.

In Yeats' adaptation, and the change of mind which made that adaptation possible, the difficulties which precede a consideration of Goldsmith as an Irish poet are evident; in order to present a singular image of a writer with as varied an *oeuvre*, there are inevitable issues of selectivity, emphasis and occlusion. In his 2010 essay on the Irishness, and even more specifically again, the Longfordness – if such a thing could be said to exist – of Goldsmith's best-loved and for Irish readers most resonant poem, W. J. McCormack challenges a romantic tendency of Irish scholars to attach poetry too readily to (Irish) place. For McCormack, there is a danger that the poem might be inappropriately Irishised or parochially co-opted; as such, he wishes to complicate too enthusiastic an association between the 'Auburn' of *The Deserted Village* and the Irish midlands: a 'cooler examination' is called for.[3] The proposition of an Irish Goldsmith, or of *The Deserted Village* as an Irish poem, however, need not be too heated with national ardour. In this chapter an Irish Goldsmith and his finest poem are situated in the contexts of emigration and adaptation to London, and London-Irish, literary and cultural life; his correspondence and his works – *The Citizen of the World* (1762), *The Traveller; or a Prospect of Society* (1764) and *Retaliation* (1774) – are touched upon briefly to preface a reading of *The Deserted Village* which will make the case for that poem's Irish qualities and origins, and for its continued appeal as such.

Goldsmith's self-description in his breakthrough poem *The Traveller; or a Prospect of Society* as 'half a patriot' is appropriate for critic Dustin Griffin primarily because of the poet's ambiguities of 'national identity and local attachment'.[4] He was not convinced by British or English patriotism in the midst of the Seven Years War (1756–63); and whatever Irish patriotism Goldsmith felt, whether influenced by the late or post-Swiftian milieu that surrounded him in 1740s Dublin while a student at Trinity College Dublin, or imbued by the Jacobite ambience of his rural upbringing along the Longford/Westmeath border, was equally halved by his quest for literary fame in London, and relatedly by his chagrin at aspects of his Irish background. He left Ireland for good in 1752, and his letters from that period onwards were often characterised by a strange mixture of dismissiveness about aspects of the culture that he had left behind and a concern regarding social upheaval in a country which he suspected he could no longer fully understand. Prior even to his becoming a man of considerable literary fame, he felt that the best of his memories of home were idealised, or connected with family and friends rather than the society at large. His conflicted attitudes towards Ireland may have influenced his choosing not to write about it as directly as Irish onlookers might have expected at the time, or since. But that should not necessarily mean that autobiographical and political Irish subtexts did not infuse his works.

By the time he arrived in London after his Scottish and European travels and studies, Goldsmith was already feeling distanced. In a letter of 27 December 1757, addressed from the Temple Exchange Coffee House in London to his brother-in-law Daniel Hodson in Lissoy, near Ballymahon, County Longford, Goldsmith fancies to himself 'strange revolutions at home', but finds that it is 'the rapidity of my own motion that gave an immaginary one to objects really at rest'.⁵ This sense of worry-in-displacement is reproduced in the words of Lien Chi Altangi, the Chinese traveller and philosopher through whom Goldsmith ventriloquises *Citizen of the World* (1762), his series of 123 satirical letters on the *moeurs* of contemporary London:

> In every letter I expect accounts of some new revolutions in China, some strange occurrence in the state, or disaster among my private acquaintance. I open every pacquet with tremulous expectation, and am agreeably disappointed when I find my friends and my country continuing in felicity. I wander, but they are at rest; they suffer few changes but what pass in my own restless imagination; it is only the rapidity of my own motion gives an imaginary swiftness to objects which are in some measure immovable.   (2:261)

The Citizen of the World has been, and could be considered further, to be the work that trades most tellingly in Goldsmith's experience as an Irishman in London; as such, it adds to our understanding of his two major poems. He writes in his third letter to Fum Hoam, his most cherished correspondent, that his travels have prompted an exilic melancholy. 'The ties that bind me to my native country', he writes, 'are still unbroken. By every remove, I only drag a greater length of chain' (2:21) – a sentiment which Goldsmith recycles in the opening lines of *The Traveller* when he exclaims that his 'heart untravell'd fondly turns' to his brother Henry in Ireland, while the distance between them 'drags a lengthening chain' (4:249, ll. 8, 10).

Bound to family, he nonetheless felt that his aspirations to sophistication were stymied by his origins, his missives mixing increasing literary self-regard and nostalgia, the latter a psychic ailment by which he professed himself baffled, given the social disabilities with which he felt his nationality had left him. In his 1757 letter to Hodson, he wrote despondently of the difficulties and confusions of settling in a city 'where my being born an Irishman was sufficient to keep me [unem]ploy'd. Manny [sic] in such circumstances would have had recou[rse to] the Friar's cord, or suicide's halter' (27).[6] Paradoxically, he is troubled by his residual affection for his country, his 'maladie du Pays'. It was '[u]naccountable', Goldsmith mused, that 'he should still have an affec[tion for] a place, who never received when in it above civil [contem]pt, who never brought out of it, except his brogue [an]d his blunders' (28). His nationality burdened him with a self-consciousness in London which many of his company would remark upon throughout his career, along with a tendency to try to shine in conversations on topics where he had no purchase – a misguided overcompensation, perhaps, for a more general social awkwardness. Though he never would, Goldsmith expressed a desire to return to Ireland, in spite of his native region's limitations (as he saw them) in conversation, culture and learning:

> Then perhaps ther's [sic] more wit and [lea]rning among the Irish? Oh Lord! No! there has been more [money] spent in the encouragement of the Podareen mare there [in on]e season, than given in rewards to learned men since [the ti] mes of Usher. All their productions in learning amount [mayb]e to, perhaps a translation, or a few tracts in labo[rious div]inity, and all their productions in wit, to just nothing at all. [Why the p]lague then so fond of Ireland! (29)

His fondness, he explains to himself, is largely due to a longing for the home comforts, the landscape and the companionship of friends and family in his native region. Though he felt that his home country, from which he felt increasingly removed and about which he felt increasingly ambivalent, was characterised by a low vulgarity, Goldsmith surrounded himself with Irishmen throughout his London career. He was ever available as a host to any compatriots who showed intellectual or social promise.

One fellow Irish expatriate in London was William 'Conversation' Cooke (1740–1824), who gathered a rich fund of anecdotes about Goldsmith's milieu, Irish and otherwise. Cooke had emigrated from Cork to London in 1766, with strong recommendations to the Duke of Richmond, and to Burke and Goldsmith. Like many of Goldsmith's Irish friends, he came to London to study law at the Inner Temple, and became something of an observer of Irish literary and social life in the city. Cooke gives us the most intimate insight into the geographies of *The Deserted Village* as they were conceived. In his account of the circumstances of the poem's conception, Cooke recalls Goldsmith's remark two days into composition: 'Some of my friends', he told Cooke, 'differ with me on this plan, and think the depopulation of villages does not exist – but I am myself satisfied of the fact. I remember it in my own country, and have seen it in this.'[7]

Cooke would claim to be a close friend of Goldsmith's, though his anecdotes and reminiscences, published in the *European Magazine*, played a role

in perpetuating the image of Goldsmith as peevish and foolishly self-regard-
ing. It was Cooke who reported Goldsmith's vain reaction to the fame and
acclaim afforded *The Traveller* upon its appearance late in 1764. Fellow
Irishman, playwright Hugh Kelly, invited Goldsmith to dinner, an invitation
to which, in Cooke's report, Goldsmith responded haughtily:

> to tell you the truth, my dear boy, my 'Traveller' has found me a *home* in so
> many places, that I am engaged, I believe, three days – let me see – today I dine
> with Edmund Burke, to-morrow with Dr Nugent, and the next day with
> Topham Beauclerc – but I'll tell you what *I'll do for you*, I'll dine with you
> on Saturday. (171)

Kelly accepted the supercilious offer, and the two men would remain friends
until the success of his 1768 play *False Delicacy* created a rift between them.
Nugent, of course, was Robert Nugent, later Lord Clare, an Irishman and a
poet of Goldsmith's native region – originally from Westmeath. Onlookers
felt that it was Nugent – 'a jovial and voluptuous Irishman, who had left
Popery for the Protestant religion, money, and widows' – who best understood Goldsmith.[8] Goldsmith would have had more in common with
Nugent, but it is possible also that Goldsmith saw him as less of a threat to
his literary status than higher-profile playwrights such as Kelly or Arthur
Murphy. Goldsmith's Irish milieu in the later 1760s was characterised by
equal measures of exilic companionability and competition.

Goldsmith's famous, posthumously published *Retaliation* (1774), composed in response to an epigrammatic slight on his rough brogue by the actor
David Garrick, featured a series of references to, and commentaries on, the
personalities of Irish figures which demonstrate that curiously friendly
friction.[9] The grouping about which Goldsmith wrote, which met at St
James's coffee house, was characterised by its emphasis on mildly insulting
epigrams. In Goldsmith's case, many of the insults levelled — and not just by
Garrick — were predicated on nationality. As an anonymous letter to George
Kearsly, the publisher of the poem's first edition, frames it: 'Dr Goldsmith
belonged to a club of *Beaux Esprits*, where wit sparkled sometimes at the
expence of Good-Nature. — It was proposed to write Epitaphs on the Doctor;
his Country, Dialect and Person, furnished Subjects of Witticism' (4:351).
His poetic response casts a fascinating light on Goldsmith's social interac-
tions with his fellow Irishmen, and on that milieu's political multivalence.
Among the Irish figures described and gently (or, in the case of Edmund
Burke, rather less gently) mocked or threatened with mockery were the three
Burkes (Edmund, William and Richard), Thomas Barnard, the Dean of
Derry, and Edmund Burke's legal advisors Joseph Hickey and John Ridge.
Barnard and Ridge had been Trinity College Dublin students in the same

period as both Burke and Goldsmith, and there is more than a suggestion of the collegially clubbable in the poem's good-natured needling of its Irish personalities. The poem is not merely the emanation of an émigré clique, however; *Retaliation* captures a sort of metropolitan sociability that could incorporate both Irish and English social networks. The most famous lines of *Retaliation* refer to Edmund Burke's narrowing his mind so that he could give up to party 'what was meant for mankind' (4:353). Goldsmith knew better than most the nature of that narrowing. While a contemporary at Trinity College Dublin in the later 1740s, he would have been very much aware of, if not influenced by, the political content, and in particular the anti-absentee stance, of Burke's student paper *The Reformer* (1748). His slight in *Retaliation* implied that the public spirit – and with it the desire to see an absentee tax – recommended in *The Reformer* had been compromised in later life by Burke's party affiliation, which would see him oppose a 1773 proposal for an Irish absentee tax in accordance with the will of the Marquess of Rockingham.[10] Goldsmith subtly reminds Burke that he has betrayed previously held convictions for political advancement in England.

Like Burke, Goldsmith knew that what was good for English political and economic interests was not necessarily good for the Irish poor. *The Deserted Village* baffled English readers and critics for that very reason. Goldsmith himself anticipated such a response in his dedication of the poem to Joshua Reynolds: 'I know you will object (and indeed several of our best and wisest friends concur in the opinion) that the depopulation it deplores is no where to be seen, and the disorders it laments are only to be found in the poet's imagination.' He claims nonetheless to have investigated fully, in his 'country excursions' over the previous four or five years, the realities of what he has described: 'all my views and enquiries have led me to believe those miseries real, which I here attempt to display' (4:285). Though certainty is claimed in these lines, there is overcompensation too for the dedication's subtle conces-sion to the poet's critics. The disorders, they have charged, may have been generated by his imagination.

The poem's imagery is compelling but unsettling to contemporary English critics, 'for we cannot believe, that this country is depopulating, or that commerce is destructive of the real strength and greatness of a nation'.[11] Another reviewer doubts 'whether he here shows himself as accurate a politician and philosopher, as he is a poet of a rich and elegant fancy' before claiming that 'England wears now a more smiling aspect than she ever did; and few ruined villages are to be met with except on poetical ground'.[12] It was controversial to English reviewers in its own time because they could not see the desertion of villages which Goldsmith described taking place in their own country; indeed, they could only see English villages flourishing. The poem did not speak to their national sense of self as part of an expanding empire of trade. No English villages, so far as they could tell, were sliding into ruin, their inhabitants America-bound. But, as Goldsmith understood, the discrepancy between the happy and the deserted village was a discrepancy between his English and Irish observations. Thomas Babington Macaulay proposed that the poem is English only in its arcadian dimensions. The English village is an idyll, but its ruination is an Irish phenomenon which, though it will strike the English reader as strange, expresses best Goldsmith's exilic sensibility and his anxiety about social changes happening at home.[13] Macaulay is suggesting, intriguingly, that the harsher actualities of the poem are being projected from Irish memory onto an English rural landscape which has yet to experience them.

Whatever the precise locations of Goldsmith's Auburn, the political world-view of his major verse was coloured with a peculiarly Irish dissidence. Goldsmith distrusted the contemporary British ideology of liberty, and his distrust, which in some ways echoed (albeit in a gentler register) Swift's perspective, is most evident in *The Traveller* and *The Deserted Village*. In these poems, Goldsmith uses prospect and pastoral genres to compare and contrast across time and space the progress of societies; his conclusions are dismayed. Indeed, Goldsmith's *oeuvre* as a whole constitutes a generically various critique of self-congratulatory discourses of liberty. Developing Macaulay's point, R. W. Seitz argued in the 1930s that *The Deserted Village* challenged Whiggery by describing an English idyll from an Irish perspective. Seitz framed his argument by making the perfectly valid point that Goldsmith took many of his key phrasings and ideas from his formative years in Ireland; those ideas and phrasings, 'if not already formed before he left Ireland, at least predetermined by the traits of character and mind that he developed there'.[14] With its contrast of faded utopias with unsettling realities, *The Deserted Village* performed the discrepancy between Goldsmith's adopted home and the one he had left behind.

Whereas *The Traveller* surveys and compares European nations and their landscape to a philosophical end, *The Deserted Village* creates the enlivened landscapes of an idealised past, reminiscent of Ireland, though ostensibly English, and contrasts this landscape with its withered present and a violent, dangerous American wilderness to which its inhabitants have emigrated due to the socially destructive negligence of a new landowning elite. The present tense in the poem is a vehicle for dismay; the past tense, for wistfulness. There is nothing in the poem's postlapserian state for the rural peasantry to do as the need for intensive rural labour has been overtaken by enclosure, by the displacement of tillage by grazing and by the new monied elite's demand for pleasure gardens. Such is the damage that erstwhile scenes of rural labour have been given back to nature.

Amidst thy bowers the tyrant's hand is seen,
And desolation saddens all thy green:
One only master grasps the whole domain,
And half a tillage stints thy smiling plain;
No more thy glassy brook reflects the day,
But choked with sedges, works its weedy way.

(4:288, ll. 37–42)

Rural productivity has been undone by the contiguous arrogance, pride and wealth of a nearby landowner, the despoiler from whose hand the surrounding population shrinks, leaving for the city and the emigrant ship. Thus, the 'bold peasantry, their country's pride', is disbanding, and 'When once destroyed, can never be supplied'. At this point in the poem, Goldsmith betrays an ostensibly English preoccupation, which disguises the poem's Irish concerns, for Goldsmith looks back to a time ''ere England's griefs began,/ When every rood of ground maintained its man', and when labour was reasonably apportioned and life was frugal, untouched by ambition. In his idealisation of what had gone before, Goldsmith is disingenuous. The image of 'light labour' (4:289, ll. 56–9) being enough, and of ambition never outreaching a measured frugality, is a wilful misremembering, or a false remembrance of something that never was. The management of the contrast and alternation between that utopia and a new and dismaying social order is the poem's crucial achievement: Goldsmith moves deftly back and forth between the idyllic past and the damaged present, the quality of the oscillation obscured only by the will of the reader – Irish or English – to luxuriate in its gorgeous backward look. In fact, the poem only rests in these idyllic passages; they are pleasant stations from which Goldsmith proceeds to make his more determined, energised sallies against the new oligarchy whose pride has corrupted landscape and memory alike; thus, remembrance 'turns the past to pain' (4:290, l. 82).

One of the more identifiably Irish parts of the poem is that part which participates in the trope of retirement, as Goldsmith expresses his desire to return to the home place 'from whence at first' he 'flew' (4:291, l. 94), his life's labours done. The retirement poem in the eighteenth century was a version of pastoral, treating the prospect and possibility of retirement as a pure good: a redress from the tribulations of working life and a celebration of rural virtue. As in other respects, Goldsmith involves himself in generic expectations only to move away from them. Here too he diverges from a version of pastoral by suggesting that return, retirement and their accompanying consolations might not, for him, come to pass; they will, rather, be denied to him by accelerating social change, as 'the sounds of population fail'. Only one figure in the remembered community to which he would have returned remains: a 'widowed solitary thing', a 'wretched matron' left, like the nation itself, without sons or rural subsistence, driven to the scant foods of Irish famine, the 'mantling cresses' (4:292, ll. 125–32) which constituted the desperate diet of the rural poor during the Irish famines of the early eighteenth century, and in particular the famine of 1740–1, the effects of which Goldsmith witnessed as a child.

Relieving the reader of this distressing image, two of the best-loved passages of the poem ensue. One portrays the village preacher, modelled on the poet's own father and brother, both of whom were Anglican vicars (it was the latter to whom Goldsmith was particularly devoted, and to whom he dedicated *The Traveller*). The other portrait is the village schoolmaster, based on a teacher named Thomas Byrne – a soldier returned from the war of the Spanish Succession who taught Goldsmith as a child. Such lines, particularly those describing the school master, have long been memorised in Irish schools, the better to insinuate the intellectual and moral authority of elders. The village teacher, or master, is memorably fixed in a pastoral ambience. His 'little school', the modest institution which prepares the village's future, is situated amidst useless and bucolic beauty, or 'blossomed furze unprofitably gay', and the master's methods, appropriately, are not designed to drive ambition, but to impart practical knowledge, the art of persuasion and learning for its own sake:

> The village all declared how much he knew;
> 'Twas certain he could write, and cipher too;
> Lands he could measure, terms and tides presage,
> And even the story ran that he could gauge.
> In arguing too, the parson owned his skill,
> For even tho' vanquished, he could argue still;
> While words of learned length and thundering sound
> Amazed the gazing rustics ranged around,
> And still they gazed, and still the wonder grew,
> That one small head could carry all he knew. (4:295, ll. 207–16)

If he is loved as an Irish poet, it is largely because of the evocative qualities of passages such as this, and it explains why *The Deserted Village* is so beloved, as John Montague has remarked, of Irish agriculture ministers.[15] Its pastoral idealisations can be found in Eamon De Valera's famous, or infamous, St Patrick's Day speech of 1943, in which the life of the rural community was celebrated against the corruptions of the commercial world. The essence of DeValera's speech was a celebration of social health; for all of its social archaisms, it was at its core an essay in pastoralism which drew upon the tradition to which Goldsmith's best-known poem was an essential contribution. The pastoralism of Goldsmith's portraits of the village preacher and master is almost cloying, but it prepares by contrast the sustained political complaint of the poem's remaining sections, in which the luxuries and splendours of the age are critically juxtaposed with the hardships and displacements which sustain them. There is a crucial difference, Goldsmith proposes, between 'a splendid and an happy land' (4:297, l. 268). Trade may boom, and *some* men may prosper, but society is in decline. The rural virtues of the many give way to the rural vistas of the few, creating a 'barren splendour' (4: 298, l. 286) in a landscape described through simile as akin to an ageing woman forced into gaudy dress by a prevailing and treacherous luxury. Gradually, the simile gives way to a stark image of the famine-stricken peasant forced out of the rural scene to an unforgiving city or an infernal American wilderness.

Towards its conclusion, the poem trades in the broadly philosophical, lamenting the effect which the decline of the rural virtues will have on poetry itself, and proposing, albeit in a tone which hovers between fatalism and defiance, frugal self-sufficiency as society's only remaining defence. By this point, the poem seems unmoored from any original location or landscape; nonetheless, it should not be seen simply as a generic exercise in self-reflexive pastoral: it is too unusual a mix of the idyllic and the politically disgruntled to be merely that. Goldsmith was, ultimately, coming from somewhere, geographically *and* politically, with *The Deserted Village*.

Similar scenarios were evoked in the poetry of fellow midlander Laurence Whyte (d.1753), whose *Poems on Various Subjects* (1740, expanded and republished in 1742) was widely read in Goldsmith's Trinity College milieu between 1745 and 1750. In (arguably) the collection's best poem, 'The Parting Cup, or, the Humours of Deoch an Doruis', Whyte laments the decline of rural society and hospitality in Westmeath from 1688 down to the present. In the fourth canto, he derides the absentee landlord class, whose negligence and insistence on new, less labour-intensive modes of farming, he claims, has had the result of 'Depopulating ev'ry *Village*'.[16] For Goldsmith biographer James Prior, Whyte's poem is an important antecedent to *The Deserted Village*, 'having been supposed to impress Goldsmith's mind at an early period with strong commiseration for the state of the peasantry, and to have suggested passages', in the later poem.[17] The fact of Whyte's influence may not help to provide an exact locale for the complaints of *The Deserted Village*, but it does provide enhanced evidence for reconsidering the extent to which the 'strange revolutions' which Goldsmith imagined at home infused a poem which was intended also to influence an English audience, and to warn of the dangers of rural denudation wrought by negligent landowning elites. Goldsmith claimed to have seen in his 'own country' the ills he had described, and he was surrounded with Irishmen when he wrote it. He coupled his Irish experience with the experience of displacement in order to comment on the tendency to social destruction wrought by the new economics taking hold in a more accelerated fashion in Ireland, plagued as it was by the additional burdens of famine and absenteeism in the decade before he left.

Though the poem describes historical and geographical displacements, the idyll of Auburn is, ultimately, nowhere, and in the most technical sense of that word a utopia: the good place which is no-place, or even more pointedly, no longer there. Nonetheless, it has, as a poetic locale, appealed to the Irish reader since the poem's publication. One of the best expressions of Auburn's Irish appeal in recent times is Vona Groarke's introduction to the 2002 Gallery Press edition. Groarke, a native of the very same townland (Lissoy) as Goldsmith, writes fondly of her awareness of the poem as she grew up: 'It was quoted in wedding speeches, homilies, at the hustings, and even when locals were giving directions to altogether bemused drivers. In this way, the poem was held in the close embrace of a folk affection that ensured that it stayed used and vital.' Such sentimental identifications with the poem, continues Groarke, may have obscured the poem's political charge – those 'qualities which made it so controversial on its publication'. Groarke proposes the continued political relevance of the poem in the present, as it is a poem which 'finds resonance in every debate about the degradation of the communal impulse in the face of greater opportunities for personal wealth in the last ten years'.[18]

Ultimately, it should not matter whether Goldsmith was thinking of Lissoy or Longford specifically when he wrote *The Deserted Village*. We do know, via Cooke, that he was thinking of Ireland; and the continuing relevance and resonance of the poem for Irish readers which Groarke describes, particularly in times of economic distress and emigration, is unworthy of condescension by literalist conclusions or denials about its particular geographical coordinates. It is possible to see in his writing more generally an expression not just of Irishness, but of *London*-Irishness – an expression, that is, of an exilic sensibility which sought also to communicate its political concerns to a metropolitan readership. Goldsmith's self-image in London was that of an Irishman among Englishmen *and* among expatriate Irishmen. That a dual perspective deriving from ambiguities of national affiliation should inform his major poetry is one of his abiding attractions.

NOTES

1. James Boswell, *Life of Johnson* (Oxford: Oxford University Press, 1791, 2008), 355.
2. W. B. Yeats, 'The Seven Sages', *The Poems*, ed. Daniel Albright (London: Everyman, 1990), 291.

3. W. J. McCormack, 'Oliver Goldsmith's Deserted Village (1770) and Retrospective Localism', in Martin Morris and Fergus O'Ferrall (ed.), *Longford: History and Society. Interdisciplinary Essays on the History of an Irish County* (Dublin: Geography Publications, 2010), 259–281.

4. Dustin Griffin, *Patriotism and Poetry in Eighteenth-Century Britain* (Cambridge: Cambridge University Press, 2002), 206. Goldsmith's 'half a patriot' is in 'The Traveller; Or, a Prospect of Society', *The Collected Works*, ed. Arthur Friedman, 5 vols (Oxford: The Clarendon Press, 1966), 4: 266. All subsequent references to the works are to this edition, and are given in parenthesis.

5. Goldsmith, 'To Daniel Hodson', *The Collected Letters*, ed. Katharine C. Balderston (Cambridge: Cambridge University Press, 1928), 30. All subsequent references to the letters are to this edition, and are given in parenthesis.

6. Public opinion in London in the 1750s was not without its anti-Irish dimensions. In 1754 an anonymous 24-page pamphlet titled *A Candid Enquiry why the Natives of Ireland, which are in London, are More addicted to Vice than the People of Any Other Nation; Even to the Dread and Terror of the Inhabitants of this Metropolis. With some Considerations how to remedy the like Evil for the future* was published in London, reflecting a generally held view that the Irish tended towards violent and debauched behaviour. The alarmist title of this piece is belied, however, by its improbably sociological analysis, which attributes Irish misbehaviour not to defective national character, but to the negligence and oppressiveness of Ireland's landowning class, which, it is argued, had systematically failed to encourage or reward tenant self-improvement.

7. William Cooke, 'Table Talk', *European Magazine*, 24 (1793): 171–2.

8. Richard Glover, *Memoirs of a Celebrated Literary and Political Character* (London: John Murray, 1813), 47.

9. See Roger Lonsdale's headnote, in *The Poems of Thomas Gray, William Collins, and Oliver Goldsmith*, ed. Roger Lonsdale (London: Longman, 1969), 741–745 n.

10. For an extended account of this episode, see Michael Griffin, *Enlightenment in Ruins: The Geographies of Oliver Goldsmith* (Lewisburg: Bucknell University Press, 2013), 113–51.

11. Anonymous review of 'The Deserted Village. A Poem. By Dr. Oliver Goldsmith', *The Town and Country Magazine; or, Universal Repository of Knowledge, Instruction, and Entertainment*, 2 (1770), 168.

12. Anonymous, review of 'The Deserted Village. A Poem. By Dr. Oliver Goldsmith', *The Critical Review*, 29 (1770), 436–42.

13. Thomas Babington Macaulay, 'Life of Goldsmith', in Walter Scott, Thomas Babington Macaulay, and William Makepeace Thackeray, *Essays on Goldsmith*, ed. G. E. Hadow and C. B. Wheeler (Oxford: The Clarendon Press, 1918), 30.

14. R. W. Seitz, 'The Irish Background of Goldsmith's Social and Political Thought', *PMLA*, 52.2 (June 1937), 408, 409.

15. Montague, 'The Sentimental Prophecy: A Study of *The Deserted Village*', in *The Art of Oliver Goldsmith*, ed. Andrew Swarbrick (London: Vision Press, 1984), 91.

16. Lawrence Whyte, *Poems on Various Subjects, Serious and Diverting* (Dublin: S. Powell, 1740), 92.
17. James Prior, *The Life of Oliver Goldsmith M. B.*, 2 vols (London: John Murray, 1837), 1:40
18. Vona Groarke, 'Introduction', in Oliver Goldsmith, *The Deserted Village* (Oldcastle: Gallery Books, 2002) [no page numbers].

SELECTED FURTHER READING

Editions

The Collected Letters of Oliver Goldsmith, ed. Katherine C. Balderston, Cambridge: Cambridge University Press, 1928
The Collected Works of Oliver Goldsmith, ed. Arthur Friedman, 5 vols, Oxford: The Clarendon Press, 1966
The Poems of Gray, Collins and Goldsmith, ed. Roger Lonsdale, London: Longman, 1969

Secondary Works

Biographical

Prior, James. *Life of Oliver Goldsmith, M. B.*, 2 vols, London: John Murray, 1837.
Ginger, John, *The Notable Man: The Life and Times of Oliver Goldsmith*, London: Hamilton, 1977.
Sells, A. Lytton, *Oliver Goldsmith: His Life and Works*, London: George Allen & Unwin, 1974.
Wardle, Ralph, *Oliver Goldsmith*, Lawrence: University of Kansas Press, 1957.

Critical

Bell Jr., Howard J., '*The Deserted Village* and Goldsmith's Social Doctrines', *Publications of the Modern Language Association of America* 59 (1944), 747–72.
Kiberd, Declan. 'Nostalgia as Protest: Goldsmith's *Deserted Village*', in *Irish Classics*, London: Granta, 2000.
Goldstein, Laurence. 'The Auburn Syndrome: Change and Loss in "The Deserted Village" and Wordsworth's Grasmere', *English Literary History* 40.3 (Autumn, 1973), 352–71.
Kazmin, Roman. 'Oliver Goldsmith's *The Traveller* and *The Deserted Village*: Moral economy of landscape representation', *English Studies* 87.6 (December, 2006), 653–68.
Lonsdale, Roger. 'A Garden and a Grave: The Poetry of Oliver Goldsmith', in *The Author in His Work: Essays on a Problem in Criticism*, ed. Louis

L. Martz and Aubrey Williams, 3–30, New Haven: Yale University Press, 1978.

Lutz, Alfred. 'The Politics of Reception: The Case of Goldsmith's *The Deserted Village*', *Studies in Philology* 95 (1998), 174–96.

McCormack, W. J., 'Goldsmith, Biography and the Phenomenology of Anglo–Irish Literature', in *The Art of Oliver Goldsmith*, ed. Andrew Swarbrick, London: Vision Press, 1984, 168–94

Swarbrick, Andrew, (ed.). *The Art of Oliver Goldsmith*, London: Vision Press, 1984.

5

JEFFERY VAIL

Thomas Moore

Thomas Moore was one of the most beloved and widely read poets of the nineteenth century, in Ireland, Great Britain, Europe, the United States and beyond. His *Irish Melodies*, which consist of Moore's original lyrics written for traditional Irish airs, appeared in ten 'numbers' between 1808 and 1834 and achieved worldwide popularity, establishing him by the middle of the 1810s as 'the National Poet of Ireland'. Ronan Kelly observes that Moore was more than a 'mere ambassador' of Ireland to the rest of the world: to many he actually *was* his country, 'the living, breathing incarnation' of his native land.[1] He was a lyric poet, a songwriter, a musician and a performer, but also a prolific political satirist in verse and prose, a historian, a biographer, a scholar of Church history and theology, a diarist and one of the most charming and charismatic men of his era. Across the Atlantic, Edgar Allan Poe testified to the global reach of Moore's works, calling him in 1840 'the most popular poet now living – if not the most popular that ever lived'.[2]

In the decades following his death in 1852, however, Moore's literary stock crashed with remarkable rapidity. By the twentieth century, changing aesthetic tastes and new political imperatives had led to a severe overcorrection: Moore's poetry was by then generally considered inauthentic, tawdry tinsel and his politics meek, servile and toothless. William Butler Yeats replaced Moore as Ireland's national poet. James Joyce's Stephen Dedalus passed Moore's statue in Dublin and contemptuously compared the poet to 'a firbolg in the borrowed cloak of a Milesian'.[3] Moore was 'an ineffectually Anglicised Irish bard, wailing tunefully and noncontroversially of his nation's injuries'.[4] Howard Mumford Jones's biography of Moore described the poet's desolate burial site in 1937: 'To the grave of the Catholic buried in a Protestant churchyard, of the Irishman at rest in Wiltshire, of the genius once thought to be immortal and now no longer read, almost no one comes'.[5] As Francesca Benatti and Justin Tonra have recently observed, 'for much of the twentieth century, Thomas Moore's name was anathema to literary scholarship . . . Moore was a ghostly figure from the past and the twentieth century dismissed his former popularity and prominence as a perplexing or embarrassing misjudgement on the part of its forebears.'[6] Fortunately, the twenty-first century has been much more equitable in its assessment of Moore. The new millennium has brought a reawakening of scholarly interest in his life and works, with books, articles, conferences and musical recordings now appearing at a steady clip. Moore is now widely seen as a 'significant influence on Irish Catholic cultural and nationalist political development',[7] a figure of great importance to Irish literature and British Romanticism and an often-brilliant artist.

Poe's review of *Alciphron* (1839), Moore's late, epistolary Egyptian-themed long poem, acclaimed the author as a poet of the highest rank. His enumeration of Moore's poetry's distinctive qualities reflected the broad critical consensus of the era.

> While Moore does not reach, except in rare snatches, the height of the loftiest qualities of some [poets] whom we have named, yet he has written finer poems than any, of equal length, by the greatest of his rivals. His radiance, not always as bright as some flashes from other pens, is yet a radiance of equable glow, whose total amount of light exceeds, by very much, we think, that total amount in the case of any cotemporary writer whatsoever. A vivid fancy; an epigrammatic spirit; a fine taste; vivacity, dexterity and a musical ear; have made him very easily what he is, the most popular poet now living – if not the most popular that ever lived – and, perhaps, a slight modification at birth of that which phrenologists have agreed to term temperament, might have made him the truest and noblest votary of the muse of any age or clime.[8]

By speaking of Moore's 'radiance of equable glow', Poe was employing a photic trope often used by critics to distinguish Moore's 'glowing', 'sparkling' style from the 'burning' or 'fiery' intensity of more determinedly 'sublime' or profound poets. To the *Edinburgh Review*, the poetry of Moore's intimate friend Lord Byron blazed like Vesuvius erupting, whereas Moore's shimmered like the aurora borealis, but 'the light that plays around Mr. Moore's verses, tender, glancing, and brilliant, is in no danger of being extinguished even in the sullen glare of Lord Byron's genius'.[9] In Moore's *Lalla Rookh, An Oriental Romance* (1817), the eponymous heroine observes,

> It is true ... few poets can imitate that sublime bird, which flies always in the air, and never touches the earth: – it is only once in many ages a Genius appears, whose words, like those on the Written Mountain, last for ever: but still there are some, as delightful, perhaps, though not so wonderful, who, if not stars over our head, are at least flowers along our path, and whose sweetness of the moment we ought gratefully to inhale, without calling upon them for a brightness and a durability beyond their nature.[10]

Moore is undoubtedly referring to himself here, as the earthbound 'delightful' poet who does not aim to soar always at 'sublime' heights. The 'Genius' he has in mind is most likely Byron, the poet with whom Moore would be more closely linked than any other. (The two poets were paired in the public mind for many reasons: their similar Whig politics; Byron's gushing dedication of *The Corsair* (1814) to Moore; Byron's lyric tribute to Moore beginning 'My Boat is on the Shore' (1817), which became a popular song, struck up by bands and orchestras for decades when Moore made an appearance; Moore's unwilling involvement in the destruction of Byron's *Memoirs* in 1824; Moore's monumental 1830 biography of his late friend, *Letters and Journals of Lord Byron, with Notices of his Life*; and the often-similar themes, styles and subject matter of their writings.) Moore's comparative modesty about his own works sometimes extended as far as self-satire, as in his *Tom Crib's Memorial to Congress* (1819), which features a comical imitation of Moore's poetry supposedly written by Bob Gregson, the famous boxer. The volume's fictional editor notes with approval that 'Gregson' in one place has 'contrived to collect the three chief ingredients of Moore's poetry, viz. dews, gems, and flowers, into the short compass of two lines'; in another, the editor observes that a 'Jail-bird' mentioned by 'Gregson' is 'the only bird in the whole range of Ornithology, which the author of Lalla Rookh has not pressed into his service'.[11]

Moore's self-effacing wit was one element of his near-legendary personal charm. The Catholic son of a Dublin grocer, Moore left Ireland for London in 1799, at the age of 19, intending to study law at the Middle Temple; by August 1800 he had published his first book of poems, *Odes of Anacreon*, been presented to the future King George IV and was welcomed into the most rarified circles of London high society. Despite his serious social disadvantages in this milieu – he was Irish, Catholic, a commoner, perpetually short of money and very short and slightly built (he was five feet tall or slightly smaller) – his ebullient gregariousness, inexhaustible fund of Irish stories and jokes and passionate performances of his own songs at parties and fêtes made him the perpetual dinner-guest of the London glitterati for decades. From the beginning of his career, the fictional personae of his poems bled into the public perception of the real man, so that Moore, the translator of Anacreon, became known for the rest of his life as 'Anacreon Moore': the living embodiment of convivial hedonism, the seductive amatory poet who celebrated wine, love, female beauty and all sublunary sensual delights.

When Moore left Ireland for England, he was escaping the grim aftermath of the 1798 Irish Rebellion, which killed tens of thousands of people and led to the incarceration, deaths and disappearances of family friends. Moore's best friend at Trinity College, Dublin, was Robert Emmett, the revolutionary who would be hanged and beheaded in 1803. While a college student, Moore secretly took the oath of the United Irishmen, the illegal revolutionary society, though belonging to that group was punishable by death. He published a long, anonymous 'Letter to the Students of Trinity College' in the United Irish newspaper *The Press*; it praised Napoleon, condemned the English and the Protestant Ascendancy and called for a violent uprising. Moore's actions and exact whereabouts during the 1798 Rebellion remain a mystery, but his subsequent disillusionment with violent radicalism along with his disgust at sectarian intolerance would thereafter manifest itself in many of his works. The spectre of 1798 would haunt Moore's entire literary career; it hovers over such works as the *Irish Melodies*, *Lalla Rookh*, his satires, *Memoirs of Captain Rock* (1824), *The Life and Death of Lord Edward Fitzgerald* (1831) and his autobiographical writings, such as the unfinished *Memoirs of Myself* (1833).

Moore's first book of poetry explicitly rejected martial themes in favour of drink, love, pleasure and convivial revelry. The odes of Anacreon that Moore 'translates' are in fact from a collection now known as the *Carmina Anacreontea*, and are ancient imitations of Anacreon's style written over a span of several centuries, rather than poems by Anacreon himself. (That the *Anacreontea* were not in fact written by Anacreon was not demonstrated conclusively until the mid-nineteenth century.) Nevertheless, Moore's preface, in which he dwells on the traditional depictions of the Teian poet as a life-embracing hedonist, is as much about establishing Moore's own poetic persona as it is about the ancient Greek. Moore deliberately presented himself in his early works and in his public appearances and interactions as the modern-day Anacreon, 'the smiling bard of pleasure', as the first line of Moore's 'Ode I' declares. Moore's first three volumes of poetry – the *Odes*, *The Poetical Works of the Late Thomas Little, Esq.* (1801) and *Epistles, Odes and Other Poems* (1806) – each used the vivid, amorous personality of the speaker of the poems as a unifying device.

In *Odes of Anacreon*, the horrors of 1798 and the war with Revolutionary France are firmly and intentionally put aside, as 'Ode II' proclaims:

> Give me the harp of epic song,
> Which Homer's finger thrill'd along;
> But tear away the sanguine string,
> For war is not the theme I sing.   (ll. 1–4)

In 'Ode XXIII' the poet expresses regret at his inability to celebrate heroic deeds and sublime subjects, before he renounces that guilt and commits himself to amatory themes:

I often wish this languid lyre,
This warbler of my soul's desire,
Could raise the breath of song sublime,
To men of fame, in former time.
But when the soaring theme I try,
Along the chords my numbers die,
And whisper, with dissolving tone,
'Our sighs are giv'n to love alone!'
Indignant at the feeble lay,
I tore the panting chords away,
Attun'd them to a nobler swell,
And struck again the breathing shell –
In all the glow of epic fire,
To Hercules I wake the lyre!
But still it's [sic] fainting sighs repeat;
'The tale alone of love is sweet!'
Then fare thee well, seductive dream,
That mad'st me follow Glory's theme;
For thou my lyre, and thou my heart,
Shall never more in spirit part;
And thou the flame shalt feel as well
As thou the flame shalt sweetly tell!   (ll. 1–22)

The Anacreontic poems allow Moore to employ the ancient poetic device of *recusatio*, or the banning of specific reference to certain topics: 'Anacreontic *recusatio*', writes Patricia A. Rosenmeyer, 'consistently rejects epic and tragic themes for sympotic and erotic pleasures'.[12] The image in both of these poems of strings being torn from a lyre recurs years later in 'The Minstrel Boy' (1813). The Irish Minstrel Boy, falling in battle, tears the chords of his harp asunder, declaring that its songs of 'the pure and free' 'shall never sound in slavery'. Though the poet of *Odes of Anacreon* seems determined to exchange the nightmare of history (or the 'seductive dream' of 'Glory') for 'pleasure's soft dream', works such as 'The Minstrel Boy' imply that the 'warrior-bard's' silence is ultimately forced upon him by the conditions of his 'enslavement'. In 'Oh! Blame not the Bard' (1813), Moore's arresting apologia for his career, the half-repressed guilt of the Anacreontic poet in 'Ode XXIII', bursts forth:

Oh! blame not the bard, if he fly to the bowers,
Where Pleasure lies, carelessly smiling at Fame;
He was born for much more, and in happier hours
His soul might have burned with a holier flame.
The string, that now languishes loose o'er the lyre,
Might have bent a proud bow to the warrior's dart;

And the lip, which now breathes but the song of desire,
Might have poured the full tide of a patriot's heart.

But alas for his country! – her pride is gone by,
And that spirit is broken, which never would bend;
O'er the ruin her children in secret must sigh,
For 'tis treason to love her, and death to defend.   (ll. 1–12)

Moore's anger at England's mistreatment of his country is often carefully concealed (or half-concealed) in his poetry and songs through imaginative acts of historical displacement, mask-wearing and strategic elision. In *The Fudge Family in Paris* (1818), his brilliant epistolary satire on post-Waterloo politics, the most dangerous of the angry denunciations of England and its allies by Phelim Connor, an Irish Catholic tutor, are obscured by masses of asterisks, allowing Moore to make visible the European monarchies' censorship of political dissent. Moore's fascination with veiled faces in his orientalist poems is concomitant with his employment of veiled political meanings in the *Irish Melodies*, such as in 'When First I Met Thee' (1815), a half-disguised but electrifying attack on the Moore's perennial target, the Prince Regent; 'The Irish Peasant to his Mistress' (1810), an allegory of the oppression of the Irish Catholic religion by the Protestant Ascendancy; and 'Oh Breathe not his Name' (1808), which refers to Lord Edward Fitzgerald, the Irish revolutionary killed in 1798. The glint of concealed blades quietly awaiting their historical moment is briefly visible in the third stanza of 'Oh! Blame not the Bard':

Then blame not the bard, if in pleasure's soft dream,
He should try to forget, what he never can heal:
Oh! give but a hope – let a vista but gleam
Thro' the gloom of his country, and mark how he'll feel!
That instant, his heart at her shrine would lay down
Every passion it nurst, every bliss it adored;
While the myrtle, now idly entwined with his crown,
Like the wreath of Harmodius, should cover his sword.   (ll. 17–24)

A startling suggestion, namely that under different circumstances the Anacreontic poet could have been (or still could be) a patriotic tyrannicide, like the ancient Greek Harmodius. As Ronan Kelly remarks of the broken harps and enforced silences in the *Melodies*, 'keeping silent, and keeping faith, may also imply keeping one's powder dry'.[13]

Moore was consciously fashioning a public image for himself when he described Anacreon as

the elegant voluptuary, diffusing the seductive charm of sentiment over passions and propensities at which rigid morality must frown. His heart, devoted to indolence, seems to think that there is wealth enough in happiness, but seldom happiness enough in wealth. ... the disposition of our poet was amiable; his morality was relaxed, but not abandoned; and virtue, with her zone loosened, may be an emblem of the character of Anacreon.[14]

Moore's second book, popularly known as *Little's Poems*, further tested the limits of 'relaxed morality' in poetry. The unnamed 'editor' of the work describes the deceased young poet, 'Thomas Little', as a cheerful philanderer bursting with natural joie de vivre. His poems depict him as merrily promiscuous, with scores of lovers. The book was both enormously successful and, in later years, a stain on Moore's reputation that he struggled to efface. Though mostly tame by modern standards, *Little's Poems* were furiously denounced by conservative reviewers and critics as borderline pornography.

In 1803 Moore's influential connections won him the post of Admiralty Registrar on the island of Bermuda, an office that he occupied for only a few months in 1804 before appointing a deputy to carry out his duties there. (This decision would come back to haunt him, when in 1818 it was revealed that Moore's deputy had criminally abused his position, leaving Moore with a debt of £6,000; Moore moved to Paris to escape arrest, only returning in 1822.) From Bermuda Moore travelled through the United States, visiting Washington, Baltimore, Philadelphia and other cities, and at one point being introduced to President Thomas Jefferson. Moore visited Niagara Falls and Canada before finally returning to England at the end of 1804. His travels resulted in *Epistles, Odes and Other Poems* (1806), which contained love poems addressed to various women, harsh satires in Popeian couplets on the hypocrisies and corruption of American democracy (including one explicitly referring to Jefferson's rumoured sexual relationship with his slave, Sally Hemings), descriptive pieces, natural reveries and the 'Odes to Nea', beloved by Percy Bysshe and Mary Shelley. This volume featured the lyrics 'Ballad Stanzas' (popularly known as 'The Woodpecker Tapping') and 'A Canadian Boat-Song', both of which became enormously and lastingly popular as songs, especially in Canada. However, by strongly implying that the (evidently) sexually promiscuous speaker of these latest poems was Moore himself *in propria persona*, and that the women the poet makes love to were actual women that he had romanced while on his travels, Moore took his hedonistic aesthetic a step too far. In July 1806, *Epistles* suffered a withering critical fulmination from the *Edinburgh Review*, courtesy of Francis Jeffrey, who accused Moore of deliberately trying to corrupt the morals of young readers. Moore's reaction was to challenge Jeffrey to a duel, but when the author and critic met to fight, the duel was interrupted by the police, who took Moore and Jeffrey into custody. Both men were humiliated by newspaper reports the following day that the duel was a sham and that neither gun was properly loaded. Moore strenuously denied the stories, but his reputation was becoming increasingly tarnished; instead of being known as the 'smiling bard of pleasure' he was becoming notorious as an 'indecent' and 'impious' poet, and was now branded a coward to boot. One of his attackers was Byron, who, despite his love of Moore's poetry, poked fun at Moore's and Jeffrey's duel in his satirical *English Bards and Scotch Reviewers* (1809). This attack provoked Moore to challenge Byron to a duel, but by then Byron had left England for his first Grand Tour. The dispute between the two poets would be settled over dinner with Samuel Rogers in 1811, after which Moore and Byron became close friends.

Byron loved Moore's songs, which Moore sang in person at innumerable social gatherings and dinners before the *bon ton* of London for decades, performing them as an unusual kind of recitative rather than singing in a conventional style. Here again, *Odes of Anacreon* had laid the groundwork for Moore's unique style of performance, which Mary Shelley called 'Something New & Strange & Beautiful'.[15] In the preface to that work, Moore claimed that

> In the age of Anacreon music and poetry were inseparable. These kindred talents were for a long time associated, and the poet always sung his own compositions to the lyre. It is probable that they were not set to any regular air, but rather a kind of musical recitation, which was varied according to the fancy and feelings of the moment.[16]

By all accounts, Moore's effect on his audiences was spellbinding, even though Moore was in the delicate position of singing to the English about their own country's unjust oppression of the Irish. Leaving London drawing rooms full of English listeners weeping at songs about Irish suffering and defeat, all the while insinuating into their minds an image of the Irish as 'heroic, dignified, even – amazingly – respectable',[17] was, in Moore's mind, one of his most important contributions to the Irish cause. Moore believed in a concept of gradual political progress through art that he would return to again and again: the notion of the captive melting the heart of his conqueror through the mournful power of his music. The preface to *Odes of Anacreon* claims that 'by the influence of [Anacreon's] amatory songs, he softened the mind of Polycrates into a spirit of benevolence toward his subjects'.[18] The final stanza of 'Oh Blame not the Bard' articulates the hope that the bard's songs can kindle compassion and sympathy in Ireland's English 'masters':

> But tho' glory be gone, and tho' hope fade away,
> Thy name, loved Erin, shall live in his songs;
> Not even in the hour, when his heart is most gay,
> Will he lose the remembrance of thee and thy wrongs.

> The stranger shall hear thy lament on his plains;
> The sigh of thy harp shall be sent o'er the deep,
> Till thy masters themselves, as they rivet thy chains,
> Shall pause at the song of their captive, and weep!   (ll. 25–32)

In an appendix on Irish music subjoined to his 1808 political satire *Corruption and Intolerance: Two Poems*, Moore drew a parallel between colonised Catholic Ireland and the fourth-century Antiochians under the harsh rule of the Christian Roman emperor Theodosius, who oppressed them because of their unorthodox modes of Christian worship:

> At length [writes Moore], Flavianus, their bishop, whom they had sent to intercede with Theodosius, finding all his entreaties coldly rejected, adopted the expedient of teaching [the] songs of sorrow which he had heard from the lips of his unfortunate countrymen to the minstrels who performed for the Emperor at table. The heart of Theodosius could not resist this appeal; tears fell fast into his cup while he listened, and the Antiochians were forgiven.

Though the *Melodies* were designed for both Irish and English audiences, it was Moore's hope that his songs and performances would gradually awaken the compassion of the English towards the Irish, one listener or reader at a time, while inculcating an idea of Irish culture as dignified, valorous and artistic. In 1952, the Irish prime minister Eamon de Valera paid tribute to this hearts and minds strategy, declaring that

> during the dark and almost despairing days of the nineteenth century, Thomas Moore's songs kept the love of country and the lamp of hope burning in millions of Irish hearts here in Ireland and in many lands beyond the seas ... [His works] made Ireland's cause known throughout the civilized world and won support for that cause from all who loved liberty and hated oppression.[19]

Moore struggled throughout his career to balance his two roles, as the anti-Tory, anticolonialist Irish Catholic patriot and the poet of smiles and wine par excellence. In 1818 John Murray's conservative *Quarterly Review* attacked the 'Epicurean system' of Moore, Byron, Leigh Hunt and other poets, which linked sensuousness of form and sensuality of subject matter to liberal politics. The Epicurean label was alternately embraced and resisted by Moore; in his narrative poem *The Loves of the Angels* (1822) and his novel *The Epicurean* (1824), Moore tried to graft Christian themes onto his customary plenitudes of sensual and erotic imagery. In the latter work, a pleasure-loving third-century Greek Epicurean named Alciphron eventually converts to Christianity; however, the proximate cause of his conversion, as one might expect from a work of Moore's, is his sexual desire for a beautiful young Christian girl. Conservative critics generally condemned what they saw in these works (as in *Sacred Songs*, Moore's two collections of Biblical-themed songs published in 1816 and 1824) as the eroticisation of religion. In *Lalla Rookh*, erotics, religion and politics intermingle in four long narrative orientalist poems linked by a prose framing narrative. The poems are 'sung' to Lalla Rookh, the princess of the seventeenth-century Mughal Emperor Aurangzeb, by the bard Feramorz, who is revealed at the end of the work to be Aliris, Prince of Bucharia, Lalla Rookh's intended husband. Feramorz (whose name contains 'Moore') is a liberal-minded, anticolonial bard like Moore himself, which lends added significance to the story of *The Fire-Worshippers*, the third of the four poetic tales, and Moore's greatest long poem. The story of a doomed, bloody rebellion of the Persian fire-worshippers against their Muslim oppressors, who have outlawed the Persians' ancient religion, is an allegory of the struggle of the Irish Catholics against the English, and as such achieves a tragic and moving intensity. *Lalla Rookh* as a whole is uneven, and exhaustingly overloaded with dazzling sensual imagery, but Jane Stabler is right to remark that in many parts of the work, Moore is 'a dream-weaver of sustained hypnotic power'.[20] Whereas *The Fire-Worshippers* depicts a morally justified armed struggle for national independence, *The Veiled Prophet of Khorassan* is a nightmarish Eastern allegory of the French Revolution. The hideously disfigured false prophet Mokanna hides his features behind a silver veil, while promising to emancipate the oppressed peoples of the earth. He is a bloodthirsty rapist and murderer masquerading as a holy deliverer, and as such can be seen as the furious violence of French Jacobinism personified. The ghost of the bloody 1790s lurks behind the scenes of the 'Oriental Romance', as it does in the case of so many of Moore's works.

'In my strong and inborn feeling for music,' Moore wrote, 'lies the source of whatever talent I may have shown for poetical composition; and . . . it was the effort to translate into language the emotions and passions which music appeared to me to express, that first led to my writing any poetry deserving of the name.'[21] Some of Moore's greatest songs have sometimes been unfairly and inaccurately evaluated in modern times, because they are read on the page, shorn of their music, in a way that they were never intended to be experienced. Moore insisted that the songs were 'intended rather to be sung than read';[22] they were 'compound creations, in which the music forms no less essential part than the verses . . . . [those] occasional breaches of the laws of rhythm, which the task of adapting words to airs demands of the poet, though very frequently one of the happiest results of his skill, become blemishes when the verse is separated from the melody'.[23] Moore greatly disliked seeing his songs printed without their music in editions of his collected works, and hoped that such an emasculation might 'exempt them from the rigors of literary criticism'.[24]

Moore's literary importance, cultural impact and poetic merit seem now to be receiving their due after a century of scholarly neglect. Though Jane Moore's edition of Moore's major satirical works appeared in 2003, and Emer Nolan's edition of *The Memoirs of Captain Rock* in 2008, we are badly in need of new, modern editions of the rest of Moore's vast literary corpus. Modern scholars still must rely for the most part on the 10-volume 1840–1 Longmans edition of Moore's works, which was edited by Moore himself; that edition leaves out a significant amount of the poetry as well as all of his prose works, including his three biographies, *Travels of an Irish Gentleman in Search of a Religion* (1833), *The Epicurean* and his four-volume *History of Ireland* (1835–46). I am currently at work on an edition of *Sketches of Pious Women*, an early satirical prose work which Moore suppressed and never published. There is an exhilarating amount of new ground to be ploughed in Thomas Moore studies, and the continuing rediscovery of his importance greatly enriches our overall understanding of nineteenth-century Irish poetry and its legacies.

NOTES

1. Ronan Kelly, *Bard of Erin: The Life of Thomas Moore* (Dublin: Penguin Ireland, 2008), p. 427.
2. Edgar Allen Poe, *Burton's Gentleman's Magazine*, January 1840, p. 56.
3. James Joyce, *A Portrait of the Artist as a Young Man*, ed. Seamus Deane (London: Harmondsworth, 1992), pp. 194–5.
4. Michael O'Neill, 'Mournful Ditties and Merry Measures: Feeling and Form in the Romantic Short Lyric and Song', in *A Companion to Romantic Poetry* (Oxford: Wiley-Blackwell, 2011), p. 12.
5. Howard Mumford Jones, *The Harp that Once – : A Chronicle of the Life of Thomas Moore* (New York: Henry Holt & Co., 1937), p. 325.
6. Francesca Benatti and Justin Tonra, 'Introduction', in *Thomas Moore: Texts, Contexts, Hypertext* (Bern: Peter Lang, 2013), p. 1.
7. Robert Portsmouth, 'Thomas Moore, Whig Propaganda and the Demise of Conciliatory Emancipation', in *Thomas Moore: Texts, Contexts, Hypertext*, p. 81.
8. Edgar Allen Poe, *Burton's Gentleman's Magazine*, January 1840, p. 56.
9. 'Review of *The Loves of the Angels* and *Heaven and Earth*', *Edinburgh Review*, February 1823, p. 27.
10. Thomas Moore, *Lalla Rookh, an Oriental Romance* (London: Longmans, 1817), p. 130.
11. Thomas Moore, *Tom Crib's Memorial to Congress* (London: Longmans, 1819), pp. 75, 77.
12. Patricia A. Rosenmeyer, *Anacreon and the Anacreontic Tradition* (Cambridge: Cambridge University Press, 1992), p. 99.
13. Kelly, *Bard of Erin*, p. 167.
14. Thomas Moore, *Odes of Anacreon* (London: John Stockdale, 1800), p. 11.

15. Mary Wollstonecraft Shelley, *Journals of Mary Shelley* (Baltimore: Johns Hopkins University Press, 1995), p. 502.
16. Moore, Odes of Anacreon, p. 15.
17. Kelly, *Bard of Erin*, p. 164.
18. Moore, Odes of Anacreon, p. 7.
19. Kelly, *Bard of Erin*, p. 523.
20. Jane Stabler, 'Second-generation Romantic Poetry I: Hunt, Byron, Moore', in *The Cambridge History of English Poetry* (Cambridge: Cambridge University Press, 2010), p. 497.
21. Thomas Moore, *The Poetical Works of Thomas Moore, Collected by Himself*, 10 vols. (London: Longmans, 1840–1), vol. 5, p. xv.
22. Ibid, vol. 4, p. 128.
23. Ibid, vol. 5, pp. xix–xx.
24. Ibid, vol. 4, p. 128.

SELECTED FURTHER READING

Editions

The Poetical Works of Thomas Moore, Collected by Himself, 10 vols, London: Longmans, 1840–1.

The Poetical Works of Thomas Moore, ed. A. D. Godley, Oxford: Oxford University Press, 1910.

The Letters of Thomas Moore, ed. Wilfred S. Dowden, 2 vols, Oxford: Oxford University Press, 1964.

The Journal of Thomas Moore, ed. Wilfred S. Dowden, 6 vols, Newark: University of Delaware Press, 1983–91.

British Satire 1785–1840, Volume 5: The Satires of Thomas Moore, ed. Jane Moore, London: Pickering and Chatto, 2003.

Memoirs of Captain Rock, ed. Emer Nolan, Dublin: Field Day, 2008.

The Unpublished Letters of Thomas Moore, ed. Jeffery W. Vail, 2 vols, London: Pickering and Chatto, 2013.

Secondary Works

Biographical

Jones, Howard Mumford. *The Harp that Once – : A Chronicle of the Life of Thomas Moore*. New York: Henry Holt & Co., 1937.

Jordan, Hoover H. *Bolt Upright: The Life of Thomas Moore*. 2 vols. Salzburg: Institut für Englische Sprache und Literatur, Universität Salzburg, 1975.

Kelly, Linda. *Ireland's Minstrel: A Life of Tom Moore, Poet, Patriot and Byron's Friend*. New York: I. B. Tauris, 2006.

Kelly, Ronan. *Bard of Erin: The Life of Thomas Moore*. Dublin: Penguin Ireland, 2008.

Critical

Benatti, Francesca, Sean Ryder and Justin Tonra, eds. *Thomas Moore: Texts, Contexts, Hypertext*. Bern: Peter Lang, 2013.

Davis, Leith. *Music, Postcolonialism and Gender*. Notre Dame: University of Notre Dame Press, 2006.

Leersen, Joep. *Remembrance and Imagination: Patterns in the Historical and Literary Representation of Ireland in the Nineteenth Century*. Cork: Cork University Press, 1996.

Moore, Jane. 'Thomas Moore, Anacreon, and the Romantic Tradition'. *Romantic Textualities* 21 (Winter 2013). www.romtext.org.uk/articles/rt21_no2/

Nolan, Emer. *Catholic Emancipations: Irish Fiction from Thomas Moore to James Joyce*. Syracuse: Syracuse University Press, 2007.

Vail, Jeffery W. *The Literary Relationship of Lord Byron and Thomas Moore*, Baltimore: Johns Hopkins UP, 2001.

'Thomas Moore in Ireland and America: The Growth of a Poet's Mind'. *Romanticism* 10.1 (2004), 41–62.

'The Standard of Revolt: Revolution and National Independence in Moore's *Lalla Rookh*'. *Romanticism on the Net* 40 (2005). www.erudit.org/en/journals/ron/2005-n40-ron1039/012459ar/

'Thomas Moore: After the Battle'. *The Blackwell Companion to Irish Literature*. Ed. Julia M. Wright. 2 vols. New York: Wiley-Blackwell, 2010; vol. 1, 310–25.

White, Harry. *Music and the Irish Literary Imagination*. Oxford: Oxford University Press, 2008.

6

JOHN MCAULIFFE

James Clarence Mangan

James 'Clarence' Mangan is as much a myth as a poet, especially as we read him now, at second or third-hand, in national anthologies, or in the biographical essays of contemporaries, including John Mitchel, or by later figures including James Joyce, or in poems by Thomas McDonagh, or Thomas Kinsella, or Susan Howe.[1] And, if we do get past the second-hand projections of successive generations of editors and writers, there are other complicating matters: Mangan himself used many pseudonyms and worked often at the edges of translation, translating from the Irish language via cribs, translating Turkish and Arabic via German translations of those languages, insinuating original poems among those translations, framing all of them with witty, occasionally piercingly intelligent prose commentaries. His extensive collected poetry and prose, in a notable new Irish Academic Press edition,[2] is just beginning to re-shape his critical reception and our ideas of him as an original and iconoclastic poet whose formal and rhythmic innovations – in his sociable anacreontics, his translations and his landscapes – should emphatically mark our understanding of Irish poetry.

The Mangan Inheritance

In the critical literature Mangan has instead become, for theorists, a figure whose work is amenable to the ideas of Walter Benjamin and Jacques Derrida; for literary historians there is a similarly prospective sense of his achievement. That is, he is named, chiefly, as a precursor, a writer whose experiments and potential were developed more fully by Joyce, by poets of the Irish mode, by the fantastical writing of James Stephens and Flann O'Brien. And most significantly, as is the case with so much Irish writing, he becomes a figure in the intellectual autobiography of William Butler Yeats, which has cost Mangan the kind of serious, independent analytical attention reserved for his successors.

'Davis, Mangan, Ferguson': thus, in 'To Ireland in the Coming Times', W. B. Yeats pins together a set of Irish poets which acts as an opening to his own futurological project. Yeats's poem knits together his national and unusual supernatural interests but insists that, despite them, he is a 'true brother of a company / that sang to sweeten Ireland's wrong'. This would not be the last poem marked by Yeats's knack for assembling a memorable national team but, as in the other instances, his tactical acumen is not matched by the fairness of his selection methods. A more scrupulous assessment of that trio of Ferguson, Davis and Mangan is evident in his introduction to *A Book of Irish Verse*:[3]

> [Mangan] is usually classed with the Young Ireland poets, because he contributed to their periodicals and shared their political views; but his style was formed before their movement began, and he found it the more easy for this reason perhaps to give sincere expression to the mood which he had chosen, the only sincerity literature knows of; and with happiness and cultivation might have displaced Moore. (xxii)

Yeats's careful wariness about his predecessors is a natural part of his ambition for his own work. Just as he was understandably keen to put off any possible identification between his work and Thomas Moore's, fearful of the diminishment of seeming merely musical, he liked to present the nineteenth century as a sort of prologue. On Mangan, his commentary is revealing about his anxieties concerning the earlier poet. He emphasises the national nature of Mangan's achievement and writes, controversially, 'He translated from the German, and imitated Oriental poetry, but little that he did on any but Irish subjects is permanently interesting' (xxii). As he puts it later, 'Except some few Catholic and mystical poets and Prof. Dowden in one or two poems, no Irishman living in Ireland has sung excellently of any but a theme from Irish experience, Irish history, or Irish tradition' (xxii).

In his groundbreaking work on Mangan, David Lloyd was one of the first to question Yeats's emphasis.[4] Lloyd carefully showed that the idea of Mangan as a Young Ireland or nationalist poet was a posthumous projection which did no justice to the Dublin poet's critical relation to his material and his contemporaries. Lloyd's argument was subsequently borne out by the scholarly editions of Mangan's work, itself one of the signal achievements of Irish Studies in recent decades, which laid out the extent and nature of Mangan's work, as well as its relation to British and Irish contemporaries and predecessors, necessitating yet another review of the limitation of considering Mangan primarily alongside David and Ferguson in Yeats's triumvirate.

And other, more recent and equally notable interventions into the Irish nineteenth century allow us to see clearly the way that later myths have obscured Mangan's work. In *Strange Country*, Seamus Deane reads Mangan as the writer – in his fragmentary *Autobiography* – of a type of nationalist and Catholic gothic, but also as the victim of biographers who use him as the antithesis to Thomas Moore's successful career.[5] Deane sees Mangan's fate as inevitable and pre-ordained, but later critics have sought ways of telling Mangan's story in a way that does more justice to the diversity of his writing career.

In *Words Alone: Yeats and His Inheritances*, Roy Foster is equally aware as Deane that Mangan has become part of other men's stories. He uses Mangan as part of an argument which reads Yeats less as a modernist innovator than as a creative reader of his peers and predecessors: reading Yeats's poetry and poetics back into the culture he grew out of, Foster finds similar tensions in the various nationalist publications to which Mangan sent work and also observes of Mangan: 'In the period of Yeats's apprenticeship, it was Mangan who meant most to him and whom he hailed as a "strange, exotic, different" (thus buying into Mangan's cult of himself, from which later critics have tried to disentangle him).'[6] Aside from noting that Yeats was much more indebted to Mangan than, say, Davis or Ferguson, Foster also suggests that Yeats learnt from Mangan the power of a poet who concocts a dramatic public image, as Mangan certainly did.

More recently, Matthew Campbell also uncouples Mangan from Yeats, the critic and literary historian of nineteenth-century Irish poetry. He separates Mangan out from the poet-contemporaries who Yeats identified with him, and he asks us, as Foster does, to see that Yeats learnt from these poets and then, to a certain extent, misdirected readers about their influence on him. Campbell points to Yeats's description of 'Davis, Mangan and Ferguson' as patriots rather than as artists: 'no one of them wrote out of mere vanity or mere ambition, but ever from a full heart,' Yeats wrote.[7] By moving his discussion of their work away from poetry, Yeats seems to re-imagine Mangan and others as naifs whose work forms a sort of raw material which he – the artist – will quarry and re-make. Campbell's book, however, even more than Foster's or Deane's or Lloyd's, allows us to see that Mangan's poetics and rhythmic innovations strongly influenced the later poet.

Campbell shows that Mangan's poems are fascinated by an apocalyptic sense of end-times, which he associates as much with European millenarianism as Mangan's experience of political nationalism and the famine. It is a theme or note or type of historical *moment* to which Yeats, of course, returned throughout his writing life. And, in one key argument about the mish-mash of translation and music which characterised the development of a distinct Irish mode, Campbell suggests a way of liberating Mangan from the national narratives which have limited the ways in which his poems are read. Campbell asks us to read Mangan's style both in relation to precursors he parodied, like Thomas Moore, and to those he emulated, for example Fr Prout, whose parodies were the creation of Cork-born, London-based journalist F. S. O'Mahony. O'Mahony's parody of Thomas Moore, 'The Shandon Bells', is – Campbell shows – itself based on Richard Milliken's 'The Groves of Blarney', which, circuitously, shares a tune with Moore's setting of 'The Last Rose of Summer.' O'Mahony/Prout's inventively free and plundering attitude to translation is not dissimilar to Mangan's, while the way that O'Mahony/Prout *sets* the poems in essays or as part of broader arguments also resembles Mangan's presentation of his work, and the line-by-line music and oddness of what Campbell calls the characteristic 'synthetic form' of nineteenth-century Irish poetry (and after), defines O'Mahony/Prout's aesthetic as much as Mangan's. Immersing Mangan's work in its contemporary influences allows us to reconsider the integrity and originality of his life's work.

Mangan's Profession

It is, somehow, unsurprising that O'Mahony/Prout's grave is located in St Anne's Church in Shandon, under the bells his parody extolled. More unsettlingly, visitors who climb the stairs to see the bells' mechanism will find that its makers' name, still clearly engraved, is 'James Mangan 1847'. The poet Mangan, of course, was born and grew up in Dublin, although his father hailed from Shanagolden in west Limerick. Biographer Ellen Shannon-Mangan writes that Mangan himself rarely left the city centre where he lived and worked almost all his life, apart from visits to his mother's family in Meath. The family's grocery business prospered initially, and Mangan's early schooling introduced him to Latin, French, Spanish and Italian, and he had begun to publish poems by the age of fourteen. However, at the time that Mangan's formal education ended, his father's property speculation went awry, which seems to have imposed tensions and pressures which Mangan found difficult to bear and which his autobiography and first biographers describe vividly, as they do his death by cholera in 1849. Mangan's unhappy youth and death might be said, though, to unduly darken the story of his success as a writer.

Apprenticed as a scrivener, and later working at a solicitor's office, Mangan spent his days copying out legal documents, but he also began to publish more and more in the increasingly lively magazine culture of the 1830s, in *The Comet*, the *Dublin Penny Journal* and the *Dublin University Magazine*, where his 'Anthologia Germanica' essays ran for twenty-two instalments, showcasing his mastery of another language but also allowing him to explore persona and parody as his distinctive style developed. By 1838, Mangan had left his copyist work. He began to work with the intellectuals and cultural entrepreneurs who were re-shaping ideas about Irish culture, often through the medium of the magazines to which Mangan was contributing. He worked on John O'Donovan's *Annals of the Four Masters* and under George Petrie in the Ordnance Survey project, before taking up employment at Trinity College Library, his last job before alcoholism reduced him to penury and reliance upon freelance payments, in a much more politically charged environment, for journal publications including the *Nation* and the *United Irishman*.

While the editors of the Irish Academic Press edition still find most notable the work of Mangan the 'poet-patriot',[8] a different emphasis – on Mangan's *style* – clarifies the distinctive originality of his poems, and their origin in the professional writing life of nineteenth-century Dublin. In his classic poem, 'Twenty Golden Years Ago', it was this style he saw as identifying him as the 'Tortured torturer of reluctant rhymes' (in Ryder, p. 93). His earliest publications were puzzle poems and riddles, written for almanacs and competitions: they treat stock subjects, but the stock rhymes are reached in a contorted, occasionally grotesque manner, hinting at the effects in which Mangan will later specialise:

> For long o'er his darksome and pillowless bed,
> Have the sorrowing winds of the evening been sighing;
> Full often alas! hath the passenger's tread
> Pressed on the sad spot where his remains are lying.
>
> ('Rebus, Emmet' in Ryder, p. 23)

A decade later, Mangan's professional writing life took a turn towards translation. James Hardiman and Samuel Ferguson had established a format for such work with their essays (and counter-essays) on Irish-language poetry, which also featured translations of the poems. Mangan presented his versions in a similar format, albeit his tone is less scholarly and closer to the tone of what readers today might see in fan fiction.

German poems, and then Turkish and Arabic poems, which Mangan seems to have read in German translation, proved to be the field where Mangan could develop an aesthetic which drew out his intense, rhyming, refrain-led style, often in relation to poems that celebrate social occasions, coffee-drinking, alcohol, snuff and tobacco, and great feasts. Mangan continues a type of Irish poem which Thomas Moore had popularised and which Jane Moore discusses as an Irish tradition of anacreontic poems. Jane Moore notes that Mangan's Oriental versions borrow from her poetic namesake's 'sensationally popular' *Lalla Rookh*,[9] but the range of Mangan's writing about food and drink, like so much else in his extensive oeuvre, remains critically underdescribed and barely analysed.

Mangan and the Society of the Poem

Mangan's anacreontic poems include comic extravaganzas like 'The Ruby Mug' and 'The Khalif's Song', but he wrote about this subject under the shadow of Fr Mathew's massively influential Temperance movement: 'Song for Coffee-Drinkers' is as wonkily strung along its lines and rhymes as anything Mangan wrote, and seems to adopt an Eastern accent when it has its speaker declare 'I, YAKINI, state too!':

> The man who, in his prime, and long
> Ere guzzling makes him sick, quits
> The Chian flask as overstrong
> Displays most poli-tic wits;
> But if he'd live *in* or *by* song,
> He must bow out *all* liquids
> Save coffee, ere he'll swell the throng
> Of geniuses and quick wits.   (Ryder, pp. 64–5)

If this seems a suspiciously effervescent espousal of temperance, another of his heteronyms, Drechsler, is altogether grimmer in 'Fragment of Another [Drinking Song] XI':

> Albeit we smile
> When we behold
> A beerless pot
> Or a punchless bowl,
> Yet that is bile;
> Such smile is cold;
> It brightens not
> The sunken soul.   (Ryder, p. 61)

A later heteronymic poem, written in the guise of Selber, is called 'The Coming Event', and begins: 'Curtain the lamp, and bury the bowl – / The ban is on drinking! / Reason shall reign the queen of the soul / When the spirits are sinking', and its picture of an alcohol-free world is stark: 'Nights shall descend, and no taverns ring / To the roar of our revel; / Mornings shall dawn, but none of them bring / White lips and blue devils' (Ryder, p. 139) And if 'Eighteen Hundred Fifty' is more resigned to the goods it consumes, its glimpses of plenty are tantalisingly set in the near future: 'For myself, if Eighteen Hundred Fifty / Still shall find me sighing o'er a lack / Of rixdollars, Rhenish, and taback' (Ryder, p. 168).

Wayward Echoes: Translating the Present

If Fr Mathew looks over the shoulder of these poems, the most obvious other context for their hyperbolic and guilty representations of feasting, drinking and smoking is the famine. Although 'Siberia' has recently been identified as a version of a poem by Ernst Ortlepp, David Wheatley's contention holds true that that, like many of his great poems of the 1840s, it is 'reflective of the onset of famine.'[10] Melissa Fegan goes farther: '"Siberia" is Famine Ireland, recognised by Mangan as what always waited for him in the future, a wasteland of dull death and pain.'[11] Fegan's point here is that Mangan's poems do not so much describe the famine as find tones and analogies for famine; his apocalyptic imagination, by a sort of historical accident, is charged and distorted by its immediate context. The opening stanza establishes a scene far from Mangan's Dublin workplaces:

> In Siberia's wastes
>   The ice-wind's breath
> Woundeth like the toothèd steel;
> Lost Siberia doth reveal
>   Only blight and death.

The 'breath/death' rhyme is, clearly, not unexpected, but Mangan's poems typically respond to such clichés by doubling down on their effect, and this happens here when the third line's 'Wound*eth*' and 'too*thèd*', and the fourth line's '*doth*', reflect and reverse that obvious rhyme, intensifying the way that *death* resounds through the scene it describes.

Succeeding stanzas are more cumbersomely rhymed, but the pained stretch of 'soft/aloft' draws greater attention to polarising images of greenness, softness and sands, while the slow triple stress or molossus of 'gaunt ice-blocks' is a characteristic Mangan effect:

> In Siberia's wastes
>   Are sands and rocks.
> Nothing blooms of green or soft,
> But the snow-peaks rise aloft
>   And the gaunt ice-blocks.
>
> And the exile there
>   Is one with those;
> They are part, and lie is part,
> For the sands are in his heart,
>   And the killing snows.   (Ryder, p. 213)

When the saw-like teeth of the opening stanza return in an explicit famine setting, Mangan withholds any elegiac or final accounting, drawing out the poem's pre-apocalyptic moment, a life which is 'scarce more than a corpse':

> And such doom each sees,
>   Till, hunger-gnawn,
> And cold-slain, he at length sinks there,
> Yet scarce more a corpse than ere
>   His last breath was drawn.   (Ryder, p. 213)

Writing about 'Siberia', 'Dark Rosaleen' and the 1844 poem 'Moreen: A Love Lament' which Mangan subsequently re-published as a famine poem newly titled 'The Groans of Despair' in 1849, Fegan describes Mangan's 'dualistic quality, referring simultaneously to the far past, and to present Famine Ireland'.[12] This is an astute reading of Mangan and the productive ambiguities of his poetry, although it may be over-optimistic in its hope that Mangan can be read seriously as a poet of the 'far past' of, say, the Ottoman empire or the Bardic period in Ireland: Mangan's versions of poems from those areas are, rightly, understood as being more engaged with his own immediate position as a poet at work in an empire's second city. The 'dualism' of Mangan's work, its mysterious ability to evade paraphrase and simplification, has less to do with its distant subjects than with Mangan's artful aesthetic. It is their *formal* quality which distinguishes his poems, their self-consciousness about the art of poetry and the existing tradition of rhyme- and image-making. And what is most uncanny about these powerfully *coincidental* poems is Mangan's artful and sometimes perplexing reflection on this process.

The back-story of his most famous poem, 'Dark Rosaleen', is a complex affair within Mangan's work. As part of his and John O'Daly's *Poets and Poetry of Munster* project, he also adapted two other Irish-language poems which draw on the same images, 'Black-haired Fair Rose' and 'Little Black-haired Rose', noting of the latter: 'The allegorical allusions to Ireland under the name Roisin have long been forgotten, and it is now sung by the peasantry merely as a love song' (Ryder, p. 343). Prefacing his 1846 version for the *Nation*, however, Mangan wrote, 'The true character and meaning of the figurative allusions with which it abounds ... the intelligent reader will of course find no difficulty in understanding' (Ryder, p. 222), a statement which picks up on a central controversy of the previous decade when Samuel Ferguson had critiqued James Hardiman's translation of this poem:

> This says Mr. Hardiman, is an allegorical political ballad – it seems to be the song of a priest in love, of a priest in love too who has broken his vow, of a priest in love who was expecting a dispensation for his paramour, of a priest in love who was willing to turn ploughman for his love's sake – nay, to practice the very calling of a priest to support her.[13]

Mangan used Hardiman and Thomas Furlong's translation as a crib, but as Sean Ryder states, with some restraint, Mangan 'makes free with the structure and sense of the poem' (p. 470). In fact, he turns Furlong's dozen lines into seven twelve-line stanzas. Mangan also carries across and preserves Ferguson's more erotic than allegorical reading in lines like 'Your holy delicate white hands / Shall girdle me with steel. / At home ... in your emerald bowers / From morning's dawn till e'en, / You'll pray for me, my flower of flowers' (Ryder, p. 224). But it is the intensity of the opening line and the refrain which have guaranteed the poem its central place in the history of Irish poetry. The first line begins and ends with long vowels Mangan engineers into his refrain as well, as 'O, my Dark Rosaleen' becomes 'My dark Rosaleen! / My own Rosaleen!'

The second stanza offers another example of Mangan's ability to drive a sound pattern through somewhat contorted and resistant phrasing. His strong and effective combination of alliteration and assonance carries across the rhymes so that 'sailed with sails' picks up on *hills* and *dales* and *all* and *sake* and *lake*, pitching the poem's emotional ardour high so that the reader may not initially notice the redundancy of the phrase 'sailed with sails' and the geographical oddity of placing the Erne (one of the few overlaps with Furlong and the original) among 'dales':

> Over hills and through dales
>   Have I roamed for your sake;
> All yesterday I sailed with sails
>   On river and on lake.
> The Erne, at its highest flood,
>   I dashed across unseen,
> For there was lightning in my blood,
>   My Dark Rosaleen!
>   My own Rosaleen!
> Oh! there was lightning in my blood,
> Red lightning lightened through my blood,
>   My Dark Rosaleen!   (Ryder, p. 223)

The red lightning calls to mind the apocalyptic scenery of other Mangan poems and the likewise typical sense of an imminent but unseen future which his poems so often project. It also draws the reader's attention to the unusually prominent use of colour in this poem, with its 'dark' addressee, her 'white hands', 'emerald bowers', 'golden throne' and its 'ocean green', although it is the 'red' of the rose which returns in the closing stanza:

> O! the Erne shall run red
>   With redundance of blood,
> The earth shall rock beneath our tread,

> And flames wrap hill and wood,
> And gun-peal, a slogan cry,
> Wake many a glen serene,
> Ere you shall fade, ere you shall die,
> My Dark Rosaleen!
> My own Rosaleen!
> The Judgement Hour must first be nigh,
> Ere you can fade, ere you can die,
> My Dark Rosaleen!   (Ryder, p. 224)

Again the sound of the 'red' is matched by the rhyming 'tread', but also by the alliterative variations of 'blood', 'wood', 'wrap' and 'rock', and the unusual pairing of 'Erne/earth', as well as the brilliantly unusual noun '*red*undance' (which also seems to mimic the poem's few other trisyllabic nouns: 'emerald', 'delicate' and, most notably, 'Rosaleen'). The 'gun-peal' and 'slogan cry' assert the bloodiness of the poem, its strong element of 'political allegory', what Fegan calls Mangan's 'dualism', but the poem's occasionally stray vocabulary (those 'dales' and that '*red*undance') and insistent sound patterns also dramatise its speaker's wildly passionate expressiveness. It is easy to read Mangan as iconic Young Irelander into this poem's speaker, but to do so asks readers to set aside Mangan's artifice, wit, learning and the range of his other writing.

As we have seen, in his essays and translations Mangan experimented with heteronyms of his own, passing off original poems as the work of invented figures, including Drechsler and Selber, and writing about those poets' imagined biographies and contemporaries in his prefatory remarks to the poems. Those remarks show a keen appreciation of the way in which a poem may be 'turned' to a particular occasion which may not have occurred to its maker (imagined, or otherwise). In the case of 'Siberia', a poem written by Ortlebb about Polish rebels sent to Siberia is turned dramatically to the subject of Irish famine, while Mangan's adaptation of 'Roisin Dubh' applies a frenzy of sound effects which distinguish it dramatically from the original *and* from competing translations by Furlong, Ferguson and Aubrey de Vere, as well as Mangan's own other responses to the figure of Ireland as Roisin Dubh.

While it is important to reckon with Mangan's death, whether it was by cholera or by starvation, alongside our knowledge of the tumultuous decade in which he published his best work, they should not be the only prisms through which his work is read. To do so is to the detriment of our understanding of him as a maker whose artfulness is, perhaps, more consistent and sustained and developed than even his best critics allow.[14]

In one short poem, an imagined Turkish poet, Lamii, voices an idea about the art of making poems, of the creative act, which speaks directly to Mangan's practice:

> I was parrot, mute and happy, till,
> Once on a time,
> The fowlers pierced my woods and caught me;
> Then blame me not; for I but echo still
> In wayward rhyme
> The melancholy wit they taught me.
> ('Lamii's Apology for his Nonsense', Ryder, p. 76)

Here, with the typically off-kilter rhythms he used to foreignise his speaker's idiom ('I was parrot'; 'Once on a time'), Mangan's self-conscious wit discovers a contrary and paradoxical image for itself: the parrot who is still the creature of his initial discovery.

Mangan's gift was to introduce this note to the stock scenes of post-Romantic, post-Moore poetry in Ireland. In the posthumously published 'The Nameless One', he asks the reader to remember one who 'fell far through that pit abysmal / The gulf and grave of Maginn and Burns':

> Tell thou the world, when my bones lie whitening
> Amid the last homes of youth and eld,
> That there was once one whose veins ran lightning
> No eye beheld.   (Ryder, p. 323)

The sombre sense of the lines co-exists with the awkward rhyme and the pun, suggested by the title, on 'eye' / I.

Mangan Country

That same, rapid and rapidly adjusting self-consciousness distinguishes another of Mangan's substantial areas of achievement, the poetry of landscape and the Irish landscape in particular, which in Mangan's poems is almost always set up as a lost land, to be viewed from elsewhere: in 'Duhallow', the speaker says, simply, 'Through sunshine and storm / Corrach's acres lie fallow; / Would Heaven I were warm / Once again in Duhallow!' (Ryder, p. 302); in the more complex litany of 'An Elegy on the Tironian and Tirconnellian Princes Buried at Rome', Mangan laments the impossibility of grieving the dead in their native country: 'Red would have been our warriors' eyes / Had Roderick found on Sligo's field / A gory grave' (Ryder, p. 109), while 'To the Ruins of Donegal Castle' encapsulates present loss: 'The clay-choked gateways none can trace, / Thou fortress of the once bright doors!' (Ryder, p. 197).

Another of his circuit of Ireland poems, 'Prince Aldfrid's Itinerary Through Ireland', again offers a counterpoint to its writer's famine context across its fifteen quatrains:

> I found in Connaught the just, redundance
> Of riches, milk in lavish abundance;
> Hospitality, vigour, fame,
> In Cruachan's land of heroic name. (Ryder, p. 195)

A similarly bereft scene is imagined, more extensively, in 'O'Hussey's Ode to the Maguire', whose landscape is an abandoned one: 'The lawns and pasture-grounds lie locked in icy bonds, / So that the cattle cannot feed. // The pale bright margins of the stream are seen by none' (Ryder, p. 203). Mangan's eye on his present moment is even more explicit in 'A Vision of Connaught in the Thirteenth Century': 'the sky / showed fleckt with blood, and an alien sun / Glared from the north, / And there stood on high, / Amid his shorn beams, A SKELETON!' (Ryder, p. 229).

These are still, recognisably, the landscapes of W. B. Yeats's haunted west, Kavanagh's satires, Thomas Kinsella's 'Ballydavid Pier', Michael Hartnett's 'A Visit to Castletown House', Muldoon's Brownlee, of Eavan Boland's and Peter Sirr's and many other twentieth-century poets' deserted pastorals. No one has yet, though, advanced into the temporal and geographical shifts of Mangan's astonishing 'Khidder', another of his very free translations whose 'ever young' protagonist tours through 'ancient town', 'fair city', 'dark rolling mere', 'pleasant shade', 'forest wide', each one displacing the other until the speaker arrives, in the welter of noises Mangan introduced to Irish poetry, at 'lo! A town –

> And spires and domes, and towers looked proudly down
> Upon a vast
> And sounding tide of life,
> That flowed through many a street, and surged
> In many a market-place, and urged
> Its way in many a wheeling current, hither
> And thither.
> How rose the strife
> Of sounds! the ceaseless beat
> Of feet!
> The noise of carts, of whips – the roll
> Of chariots, coaches, cabs, *gigs* – all
> Who keep the last-named vehicle we call
> *Respectable* – horse-trampings, and the toll
> Of bells; the whirl, the clash, the hubbub-mingling
> Of voices, deep and shrill; the clattering, jingling,
> The indescribable, indefinable roar; (Ryder, p. 189)

When Khidder asks, as is his wont, 'How long / The city whereabouts had stood, / And what was gone with pasture, lake and wood', he is met with no answer to his disappearing landscapes: 'some did laugh and shake / Their heads, me deeming mad.' Then one voice ungraciously tells him, 'As it is now, / So was it always here, and so will be for aye.' Khidder resolves to leave them to their immutable lives, but with the foreknowledge that he will certainly meet us again further along the way: 'Them, hurrying there, I left, and journeyed on – / / But when a thousand years are come and gone, / Again I'll pass that way' (Ryder, p. 191).

NOTES

1. Melissa Fegan expertly demolishes many of these myths and projections of poète maudit stereotypes onto Mangan in *Literature and the Irish Famine 1845–49* (Oxford: Oxford University Press, 2002), p. 168–75.
2. Augustine Martin, gen. ed., *The Works of James Clarence Mangan*, with a Biography and Bibliography (Dublin: Irish Academic Press, 1996–2004). See also Sean Ryder, ed., *James Clarence Mangan: Selected Writings* (Dublin: UCD Press 2004) (hereafter 'Ryder', citations in parentheses in text).
3. *A Book of Irish Verse* (London: Methuen, 1900).
4. *Nationalism and Minor Literature: James Clarence Mangan and the Emergence of Irish Cultural Nationalism* (Berkeley: University of California Press, 1987).
5. *Strange Country: Modernity and Nationhood in Irish Writing since 1790.* Oxford: Oxford University Press, 1997. 122–39.
6. R. F. Foster, *Words Alone: Yeats and His Inheritances* (Oxford: Oxford University Press, 2011, p. 147).
7. *Irish Poetry Under the Union, 1801–1924* (New York: Cambridge University Press, 2013), p. 3.
8. *The Collected Works of James Clarence Mangan: Poems 1845–47.* Jacques Chuto, Rudolf Patrick Holzappel, and Ellen Shannon-Mangan, eds. vol. 3 (Dublin: Irish Academic Press, 1997), p. xvi.
9. Jane Moore, 'Nineteenth-century Irish Anacreontics: The Literary Relationship of James Clarence Mangan and Thomas Moore', *Irish Studies Review*, vol. 21, Iss. 4, 2013, pp. 387–405, at 389.
10. *James Clarence Mangan: Poems*, David Wheatley, ed. (Loughcrew: Gallery, 2003), p. 13.
11. Melissa Fegan, *Literature and the Irish Famine 1845–49* (Oxford: Oxford University Press, 2002), p. 192.
12. Fegan, Literature and the Irish Famine, p. 194.
13. *Dublin University Magazine*, vol. 4, Aug. 1834, p. 158.
14. In Sinead Sturgeon's excellent recent essay collection, even David Lloyd writes, 'Despite my frequent misgivings about the achievement of the poetry I was reading, misgivings amplified by the widespread assumption that few of Mangan's poems were worth critical consideration any more, the work refused to let me go.' *The Man in the Cloak: Essays on James Clarence Mangan.* Basingstoke: Palgrave Macmillan, 2014. p. 14.

SELECTED FURTHER READING

Works Cited

Campbell, Matthew, *Irish Poetry Under the Union, 1801–1924* (New York: Cambridge University Press, 2013).

Chuto, Jacques, Rudolf Patrick Holzappel, and Ellen Shannon-Mangan, eds. *The Collected Works of James Clarence Mangan: Poems 1845–47.* (Dublin: Irish Academic Press, 1997).

Deane, Seamus, *Strange Country: Modernity and Nationhood in Irish Writing since 1790.* (Oxford: Oxford University Press, 1997).

Fegan, Melissa, *Literature and the Irish Famine 1845–49* (Oxford: Oxford University Press, 2002).

Foster, R. F., *Words Alone: Yeats and His Inheritances* (Oxford: Oxford University Press, 2011).

Lloyd, David, *Nationalism and Minor Literature: James Clarence Mangan and the Emergence of Irish Cultural Nationalism* (Berkeley: University of California Press, 1987).

Moore, Jane, 'Nineteenth-century Irish Anacreontics: The Literary Relationship of James Clarence Mangan and Thomas Moore', *Irish Studies Review*, vol. 21, Iss. 4, 2013, pp. 387–405.

Martin, Augustine, gen. ed., *The Works of James Clarence Mangan*, with a Biography and Bibliography (Dublin: Irish Academic Press, 1996–2004). 2003).

Ryder, Sean, ed., *James Clarence Mangan: Selected Writings* (Dublin: UCD Press 2004)

Shannon-Mangan, Ellen, *James Clarence Mangan: A Biography* (Dublin: Irish Academic Press, 1996).

Sturgeon, Sinead, ed. *The Man in the Cloak: Essays on James Clarence Mangan* (Basingstoke: Palgrave Macmillan, 2014).

Wheatley, David, ed. *James Clarence Mangan: Poems* (Loughcrew: Gallery, 2003).

7

NICHOLAS GRENE

W. B. Yeats

> The intellect of man is forced to choose
> Perfection of the life, or of the work[1]

In this late disconsolate lyric, 'The Choice', Yeats laments the lost possibilities of life, the meagre rewards and bitter regrets of his own commitment to perfection of the work. But the lines in fact construct a false binary. Yeats never did choose work over life, and perfection was never on offer in any case. The choices, both human and aesthetic, were always between different orders of being, different styles, with the chosen one imperfect by reason of the very existence of the alternatives. This was a poet for whom transcendental worlds of vision always held sovereignty over the mere actuality of the phenomenal. Yet in spite of his lifelong belief in the revealed truths of magic and the occult, his poetry never freed itself of the pull of bodily sensation and its stubborn manifestations. His theory of masks posited a psychological taxonomy of character in which the individual personality was always animated by the awareness of its opposing anti-mask.[2] So Yeats the poet, whose emblem was the solitary lonely tower, was simultaneously a gregarious gossip, a clubman, a literary controversialist, a writer of manifestos and leader of artistic movements. He was a notorious reviser of his own poems, and defended this practice against critics: 'when ever I remake a song', he declared, 'it is myself that I remake' (*Variorum*, 778). Again and again, throughout his career, he turned against his previous style, forging his new modes on the rebound from the old. The greatness of Yeats as a poet was based on his sustained capacity to reinvent himself and his work, always aware of the deficit between imagination and execution.

Awarded the Nobel Prize in 1923, Yeats still had some of his best work to come. Since his death in 1939 he has received ever growing critical attention.[3] His multiply active life is the subject of R. F. Foster's authoritative two-volume biography as well as many other biographical studies.[4] There have been specialist studies on his cultural nationalism, his controversial politics, his collaboration with his wife George in the automatic writing which generated *A Vision* and his formal skills and techniques.[5] As well as the scholarship published in the dedicated journal the *Yeats Annual*, there is an enormous body of archival material now available.[6] In 2015, the 150th anniversary of Yeats's birth was celebrated with many events across Ireland and around the world.[7] For the purposes of this brief overview, I have concentrated on a number of focus poems to illustrate key Yeatsian choices: choices between opposed visions of the world, and the stylistic choices that enabled the late Victorian poet to turn himself into one of the outstanding high modernist writers.

'When I first wrote I went here and there for my subjects as my reading led me, and preferred to all other countries Arcadia and the India of romance, but presently I convinced myself . . . that I should never go for the scenery of a poem to any country but my own' (*Variorum*, 843–4). In the section of early work which Yeats entitled *Crossways* in his *Collected Poems*, 'The Stolen Child' appears as one of the first fruits of that new conviction. Each stanza of the fairies' mesmeric call to the child to come away with them names specific places in the Sligo countryside that Yeats, staying with his mother's family, the Pollexfens, made his imaginative homeland: 'Where dips the rocky headland / Of Sleuth Wood in the lake . . . Far off by furthest Rosses / We foot it all the night . . . Where the wandering water gushes / From the hills above Glen-Car' (*Poems*, 44–5).[8] The magical moonlit beauty of this silvered landscape, conjured up through the first three stanzas, has its desired effect in the opening of the last one: 'Away with us he's going, / The solemn-eyed'. But at the moment when we first actually see the child, we are made aware of just what he is losing in forsaking a 'world more full of weeping than he can understand':

> He'll hear no more the lowing
> Of the calves on the warm hillside
> Or the kettle on the hob
> Sing peace into his breast,
> Or see the brown mice bob
> Round and round the oatmeal-chest.   (*Poems*, 45)

This is no pastoral idyll that the child is led to leave; who wants mice bobbing round their oatmeal-chest? But it summons up the medley of homely sights and sounds of an ordinary reality that renders the inhuman realm of the fairies sinister in retrospect. That antithesis of world and anti-world, with their competing values, reappears repeatedly in Yeats in very different forms.

Influenced by his mentor, the veteran Fenian John O'Leary, Yeats was converted to Irish cultural nationalism in the 1880s. But he remained equally committed to magical studies, as he passionately affirmed in a letter to the sceptical O'Leary. Magic, he said, 'next to my poetry [is] the most important pursuit of my life. . . . The mystical life is the centre of all that I do & all that I think & all that I write' (*CL*, I, 303). The trick was to reconcile the belief in magic and the belief in Ireland. This is the endeavour of 'To Ireland in the Coming Times', the concluding poem of *The Rose*, the second section of the *Collected Poems*. The varying significance of the rose, the central symbol of Rosicrucianism, Yeats's then preferred mystical doctrine, is worked through in lyrics such as 'To the Rose upon the Rood of Time' and 'The Rose of the World'. In 'To Ireland...' Yeats somewhat defensively claims:

> Nor may I less be counted one
> With Davis, Mangan, Ferguson,
> Because, to him who ponders well,
> My rhymes more than their rhyming tell
> Of things discovered in the deep,
> Where only body's laid asleep.   (*Poems*, 71)

The poet maintains that the deeper meanings of his poetry, which well up from the unconscious mind and are adumbrated in the mystical image of the rose, do not bar him from the nationalist pantheon of his nineteenth-century predecessor poets. However, in his later work it became increasingly difficult to align this underpinning vision with what he called '[t]he seeming needs of my fool-driven land' (*Poems*, 147), and the clash between the two energises many of his poems of the twentieth century.

The Wind among the Reeds, published in 1899, comes as the culmination of late Romantic Yeats, by turns wispily pre-Raphaelite, as in 'He wishes for the Cloths of Heaven', and apocalyptic, as in 'He mourns for the Change that has come upon him and his Beloved, and longs for the End of the World'. Yet the volume closes with what was to become one of his most popular lyrics, 'The Fiddler of Dooney':

> When I play on my fiddle in Dooney,
> Folk dance like a wave of the sea   (*Poems*, 91)

For all the arcane symbolism of so much of early Yeats, throughout this period he produced simple ballads, some of quite conventional Victorian sentimentality, such as 'The Ballad of the Foxhunter' or 'The Ballad of Father Gilligan'. His extraordinary technical skills are on display in what were to emerge as his cherished anthology pieces, 'The Song of Wandering Aengus' and 'The Lake Isle of Innisfree'. Though Aengus was the Celtic god of poetry, the 'Song' seems to stand free of any mythological setting, its intricately woven verbal texture making it a natural for vocal setting. Though the disproportionate fame of 'Innisfree' came to irritate Yeats, he did admit that it was 'my first lyric with anything in its rhythm of my own music'.[9] That music gives the escape poem its plangent appeal, though the poet, poised between the 'pavement grey' and the imagined lake isle, stands only at the point of resolution to depart: 'I *will* arise and go now' (*Poems*, 60, my italics). It is a threshold state, as in so many other Yeats poems down to 'Sailing to Byzantium'.

'Then in 1900, everybody got down off his stilts; henceforth nobody drank absinthe with his black coffee; nobody went mad; nobody committed suicide.'[10] So Yeats, in the Preface to his *Oxford Book of Modern Verse*, jauntily summed up the aesthetic effect of the end of the *fin de siècle*. Certainly, in the case of his own lyric poetry, the stilts were gone after 1900, as he moved to a new style closer to ordinary speech. In fact, for much of the first decade of the twentieth century, absorbed in his work with the Abbey Theatre, he wrote relative few poems, some of them, like 'The Fascination of What's Difficult' expressive of his frustration at having to devote so much of his time to the distracting grind of '[t]heatre business, management of men' (*Poems*, 143). The vicissitudes of his relationship with Maud Gonne at the time – the disaster of her marriage to John MacBride in 1903, his rapprochement with her after the break-up of the marriage in 1905 – inspired a whole series of poems, several of them as if deliberately misshapen sonnets: truncated to 12 lines in 'No Second Troy' and 'Reconciliation', lengthened to 15 in 'King and No King'.

Yet, in any plotted graph of poetic development for Yeats, there comes a poem out of its time, of an achievement beyond anything else of its period. Such is the great poem 'Adam's Curse' from 1902. Based on an actual conversation between himself, Gonne and Gonne's sister Kathleen Pilcher, it begins in apparently casual style:

> We sat together at one summer's end,
> That beautiful mild woman, your close friend,
> And you, and I, and talked of poetry. (*Poems*, 106)

The dialogue with its run-on syntax masks the rhyming of the couplets, as the 'friend' and the poet compare notes on the laboursome nature of poetry, of feminine beauty and of love. It is only as the talk dies into silence that the presence of the third unspeaking person becomes felt and the poem moves into another mode, with the image of the rising moon 'worn as if it had been a shell / Washed by time's waters as they rose and fell / About the stars and broke in days and years'. That is the cue for the poem's conclusion:

> I had a thought for no-one's but your ears:
> That you were beautiful, and that I strove
> To love you in the old high way of love;
> That it had all seemed happy, and yet we'd grown
> As weary-hearted as that hollow moon. (*Poems*, 107)

With an unprecedented directness and simplicity, the middle-aged poet enacts the farewell to a lost life, a past style of imagination.

Responsibilities (1914) is generally taken to be a watershed volume in Yeats's career, when disillusionment with Ireland brought a new acerbic energy to his work as a public poet. The immediate occasion was the 1913 controversy over the building of a municipal gallery to house Hugh Lane's collection of modern paintings and the decision by the Dublin Corporation not to approve it; but before that there had been the violent reaction against Synge's *The Playboy of the Western World* in 1907. Such Philistine rebuffs had opened up for Yeats the gap between '[w]hat I had hoped 'twould be / To write for my own race / And the reality' (*Poems*, 197), as he put it in the later poem 'The Fisherman'. A sequence of poems written in 1913 voiced his disenchanted mood with the vigour of satiric denunciation. 'To a Shade' is addressed to the ghost of Parnell, who is aligned with Lane as the elite leader betrayed by the Irish people. A powerfully controlled syntax organises the poem's 24 lines of apostrophe into just three sentences. In his topical reference to the recently erected Parnell monument – 'I wonder if the builder has been paid' – the poet glances at the hypocrisy of contemporary nationalism. William Martin Murphy, the newspaper owner who had led the opposition both to Parnell and to Lane's gallery, is dismissed as 'an old foul mouth'. The poem gathers force to its culminating peroration:

> Go unquiet wanderer,
> And gather the Glasnevin coverlet
> About your head till the dust stops your ear,
> The time for you to taste of that salt breath
> And listen at the corners has not come;
> You had enough of sorrow before death –
> Away, away! You are safer in the tomb   (*Poems*, 161–2)

There is daring in the image of Parnell's grave in the national cemetery of Glasnevin as a bed in which he should huddle beneath the blanket of earth. But there is a hint, also, of a time to come – though definitely not the present – at which he might return, as the lost leaders of so many countries are imagined returning to redeem their people.

The most famous of these 'poems written in discouragement', as Yeats entitled them when they were first collected, is of course 'September 1913', where it is Yeats's own friend John O'Leary who is the type of the heroic past contrasted with the grubbily materialist present: 'Romantic Ireland's dead and gone / It's with O'Leary in the grave' (*Poems*, 159). But as early as July 1916, Yeats was forced to admit that '"Romantic Ireland's dead and gone" sounds old-fashioned now. It seemed true in 1913, but I did not foresee 1916'

(*Variorum*, 820).[11] At that point he had begun to write his great poem 'Easter 1916', which is in some sort a retraction of 'September 1913'. Its refrain, 'All changed, changed utterly: / A terrible beauty is born' (*Poems*, 228), talks back to the refrain of the earlier poem. For political and strategic reasons, Yeats held back the publication of 'Easter 1916' and it was not collected until *Michael Robartes and the Dancer* (1921),[12] but it represented his troubled recognition of the significance of the event at the time. The opening stanza sketches in the 'casual comedy' of a social everyday in which the retrospectively 'vivid faces' of the revolutionaries had been slight acquaintances, subjects '[o]f a mocking tale or a gibe / To please a companion / Around the fire at the club' (*Poems*, 228). The second stanza gives brief life histories of some of these figures: Constance Markievicz, Padraic Pearse, Thomas McDonagh, even the hated John MacBride, previously thought of by Yeats as a 'drunken, vainglorious lout'. Yet even he 'has been changed in his turn / Transformed utterly: / A terrible beauty is born' (*Poems*, 229).

The poem recognises the transfiguration of the men and women of the Rising by the historical significance of the event that they created. But the poem's third stanza, formally unlike the others in the absence of the refrain, takes us somewhere quite unexpected.

> Hearts with one purpose alone
> Through summer and winter seem
> Enchanted to a stone
> To trouble the living stream.

What follows are lines of astonishing beauty that summon up that living stream of ever-moving phenomenal reality:

> The horse that comes from the road,
> The rider, the birds that range
> From cloud to tumbling cloud,
> Minute by minute they change   (*Poems*, 229)

It is this ever-changing actuality that is disturbed by the fixed resolution of the revolutionaries' purpose. There is a hint of the inhuman fanaticism of such fixity in the opening of the poem's final stanza: 'Too long a sacrifice / Can make a stone of the heart'. But the dubiety of weighing up the political issues – 'For England may keep faith' – and testing attitudes towards the deaths – 'What is it but nightfall?' (*Poems*, 230) – are overtaken by the clanging return of the refrain and its acknowledgement of the epochal historical change quite unlike the normal mere transience of things.[13] The poem's salute to the heroic frieze into which the leaders have been transmuted by revolution comes with a sense of the cost to their lives and to the free spontaneity of the living stream they have troubled.

The Wild Swans at Coole (1919) was one of Yeats's richest and most varied volumes, even though the Easter 1916 poems were excluded from it. The title poem finely evokes the mood of despondent middle age; 'Broken Dreams' is one of Yeats's most telling Maud Gonne poems. This was the period in which the poet proposed one last time to Gonne, widowed by the execution of MacBride for his part in the Rising, and subsequently to her daughter Iseult, addressed in 'To a Young Beauty' and 'To a Young Girl'. But in 1917 he married George Hyde-Lees and the change that brought in his life, with her automatic writing, inspired poems such as 'Under the Round Tower' and 'Solomon and Sheba'. The wartime death of Robert Gregory, only son of his closest friend, demanded an elegy, and Yeats in fact wrote three: 'An Irish Airman Foresees his Death', the pastoral 'Shepherd and Goatherd' and 'In Memory of Major Robert Gregory'. It is in this last that he developed the extended stanzaic meditation that Helen Vendler helpfully calls the 'spacious lyric'.[14]

The eight-line stanza form – first used by the seventeenth-century poet Abraham Cowley – gives the poet a capaciousness that allows his thoughts to move ruminatively in something like standard speech rhythms but controlled by the very precise formal shape, the variation in line length and rhyming pattern facilitating an intricate syntax. As in later examples of this type of poem – 'A Prayer for My Daughter', 'Among School Children' and 'The Municipal Gallery Re-visited' – an anchor location is used, in this case the housewarming of the tower at Ballylee into which he and George have just moved: 'Now that we're almost settled in our house'. The first six stanzas are designed to summon up the memory of the long dead 'friends that cannot sup with us' (*Poems*, 181). Each of those remembered – Lionel Johnson, Yeats's friend and fellow poet in the 1890s; J. M. Synge, his collaborator in the Abbey; and his uncle George Pollexfen – has a self-contained stanza devoted to him, a life summed up. It is only when we move into the second half of the poem, the elegy for Gregory which takes up another symmetrically balanced six stanzas, that the design of the whole is revealed. Johnson, Synge and Pollexfen all had some disparity between life and achievements, each related to one another and anticipating the eulogy of Gregory, 'Our Sidney and our perfect man' (*Poems*, 182). In the final stanza, the sense of the tragic deficit in each destiny, of the arbitrariness of mortality itself, which the poem's design has so artfully built up, is undone in the unspeakable blankness of grief:

I had thought, seeing how bitter is that wind
That shakes the shutter, to have brought to mind
All those that manhood tried, or childhood loved
Or boyish intellect approved,
With some appropriate commentary on each;
Until imagination brought
A fitter welcome, but a thought
Of that late death took all my heart for speech.   (*Poems*, 184)

At what point did Yeats become a modernist poet? There can be little doubt that by the time of 'The Second Coming' (1920) that is what he was. The poem is expressive of that mood of post-war cataclysm which is pervasive in so much modernist art. Though Yeats refused to write directly about World War I, and notoriously excluded the British war poets from his *Oxford Book of Modern Verse*, he was as deeply affected as Eliot or Pound by the sense of a world torn apart, all past certainties undone. 'The Second Coming' was most immediately inspired by the Russian revolution, but its lines seem to sum up prophetically the mood of the whole inter-war period: 'The best lack all conviction, while the worst / Are full of passionate intensity' (*Poems*, 235).[15] For Yeats, this marked the onset of a new era within a cyclical theory of history by which every two thousand years there was a fundamental shift in human culture. The birth of Christ had marked one such epoch; two millennia on, the second coming was no triumphant return bringing peace and the end of the world, but a terrible destructive time heralding a changed state of being. 'Leda and the Swan' (1924) imagines another such annunciation, the birth of Helen that ushered in the Trojan War: 'A shudder in the loins engenders there / The broken wall, the burning roof and tower / And Agamemnon dead' (*Poems*, 260). Both 'The Second Coming' and 'Leda and the Swan' assault the reader with dramatic scenes that come out of nowhere; the vatic tone and violently foreshortened images produce the effect of apocalypse now.

The Tower (1928), considered by many to be Yeats's greatest single volume of poetry, defies summary. This is partly because of the sheer depth, complexity and resonance of the form of poetic sequence Yeats here developed. After the accomplished finish of the opening lyric 'Sailing to Byzantium', the book continues with three multi-part poems, 'The Tower', 'Meditations in Time of Civil War' and 'Nineteen Hundred and Nineteen', each of them made up of a series of formally disparate poems that collectively create a collage. In 'The Tower', the poet moves from his personal situation in anguished awareness of his ageing body to the tower, not just as his personal habitation but as it stands for the history of the country. The three sequence poems spiral outward in a movement like that of 'The Second Coming': 'Turning and turning in the widening gyre'. 'Meditations in Time of Civil War', still situated within the tower, with lyrics entitled 'My House', 'My Table', 'My Descendants', places the bitter conflict that had broken out in 1922 between former comrades in the Republican movement within a broader context of civilisation and destruction. There is an acknowledgement of complicity in the most beautiful poem of the sequence, 'The Stare's Nest by my Window': '*We* had fed the heart on fantasies / The heart's grown brutal from the fare' (*Poems*, 251, my italics). In the deceptively misdated 'Nineteen Hundred and Nineteen' – it was written in 1921 – the scope is still wider again: its first title was 'Thoughts Upon the Present State of the World'.[16] The present experience of horror contrasted with past innocence – 'Now days are dragon-ridden, the nightmare / Rides upon sleep' – is universalised into the blankly general summation: 'Man is in love and loves what vanishes / What more is there to say?' (*Poems*, 253–4). But such a traditional statement of philosophical pessimism is not enough to contain the turbid anarchy of the sequence, which concludes with the terrifying section beginning 'Violence upon the roads, violence of horses' (*Poems*, 256). There can be no resolving chord for this imagination in which the violence on which the poet reflects draws him in to its vortex.

Yeats remained astonishingly productive for the last decade of his life. In *The Winding Stair* (1933), there were elegiac retrospectives such as 'Coole Park, 1929', and 'Coole and Ballylee, 1931', celebrating the achievements of his own generation and the gracious ideals the poet increasingly came to associate with the eighteenth-century country house. There were dramas of internal conflict in 'A Dialogue of Self and Soul', and in another outstanding multi-part poem, 'Vacillation'. Most strikingly, perhaps, there was a return of the repressed in metaphysical poems of the body in which Yeats went back to ballad form, using grotesque personae for his masks, most notably Crazy Jane. The poet channelled his own frustrations through the voice of Crazy Jane, but she was also made to speak for a changed attitude towards sexuality in the poet. In early Yeats, the love object was always a shadowing of the transcendental beauty of the eternal Rose. 'Pale brows, still hands and dim hair', are the nearest we get to seeing an actual woman in this period (*Poems*, 78). Crazy Jane, by contrast is bawdily unrepentant about her youthful affair with Jack the Journeyman, and argues fiercely against the Bishop's homiletic asceticism. The famous last stanza of 'Crazy Jane talks with the Bishop' is radically subversive:

> 'A woman can be proud and stiff
> When on love intent;
> But Love has pitched his mansion in
> The place of excrement;

> For nothing can be sole or whole
> That has not been rent.' (*Poems*, 310)

The anatomical explicitness of the language here and the deliberate inde-corum of its vocabulary –'mansion' juxtaposed with 'excrement' – are used to reinforce the challenge both to patriarchal ideology and to orthodox Christian belief.

Creative energies never died in Yeats; if anything, they became wilder and more multifarious in his final collections of verse, *Parnell's Funeral* (1935), *New Poems* (1938) and *Last Poems* (1939), yielding new personae like the hermit Ribh in the 'Supernatural Songs' series or 'The Wild Old Wicked Man', the remarkable modernist lyric 'Long-legged Fly', the despondent 'Man and the Echo' and the attitudinising legacy poem 'Under Ben Bulben'. In 'The Circus Animals' Desertion', he could turn a dejection ode at the loss of poetic capacity – 'I sought a theme and sought for it in vain' (*Poems*, 394) – into a denunciation of his past work, his circus animals of masks and symbols, and make of that a bitter renewal of inspiration:

> Now that my ladder's gone
> I must lie down where all the ladders start
> In the foul rag and bone shop of the heart. (*Poems*, 395).

Perhaps most startling of all is 'Cuchulain Comforted', the poem written within two weeks of his death. Cuchulain was the heroic figure of the medieval Irish sagas that had preoccupied Yeats throughout his career from the early narrative poem 'Cuchulain's Fight with the Sea' (1892) to *The Death of Cuchulain*, his last completed play written in 1938, to which 'Cuchulain Comforted' is a pendent. The poem, composed in Dantean *terza rima*, a form Yeats had never used before, begins abruptly and without explanation:

> A man that had six mortal wounds, a man
> Violent and famous, strode among the dead (*Poems*, 379)

Cuchulain, so terrifying in battle that no-one dared approach him until a bird lit on his shoulder, convincing his enemies he was dead, after death continues as in life:

> He leant upon a tree
> As though to meditate on wounds and blood.

Gradually, certain mysterious Shrouds, souls of the dead, approach him and persuade him to follow their lead: 'Obey our ancient rule and make a shroud'. Improbably, the dead hero picks up a needle and begins to sew. The Shrouds then confess to him who his new companions are, 'convicted cowards all'. This done,

They sang, but had nor human tunes nor words,
Though all was done in common as before,
They had changed their throats and had the throats of birds.

(Poems, 380)

This accords with Yeats's doctrine of the afterlife in which there is a purgatorial stage beyond death requiring 'that the dead person experience the opposite of the emotional and moral code he has adopted during his life on earth':[17] so here the warrior Cuchulain is assimilated into the ethos of the antitypical cowards. But it also represents one last palinode for Yeats, who throughout his career had been so drawn to the intensity of the heroic, to witness the dissolution of that extraordinary individuality into the common chorus of birdsong.

Yeats 'was one of those few [poets] whose history is the history of their own time, who are a part of the consciousness of an age which cannot be understood without them'.[18] This much-quoted tribute by T. S. Eliot is quite surprising in some ways. Yeats, with his Celtic Twilight associations with the Irish literary revival, and the obscure hermeticism of his occult theories, might not at first seem obviously engaged with the mainstream consciousness of his own time. However, Eliot's statement is governed by what he says just before this final conclusion. Yeats was exemplary in showing 'that an artist, by serving his art with entire integrity, is at the same time rendering the greatest service he can to his own nation and to the whole world'.[19] That extraordinary integrity in Yeats, the never-satisfied pursuit of formal excellence, made him capable of the creative self-renewal which is one major dimension of his greatness as a poet. At the same time, his recurrent dissatisfaction with his own past work, his need to revise it and to move on to other modes, was matched by his inability to rest secure in any one vision of himself, Ireland or the wider world beyond. 'We make out of the quarrel with others, rhetoric, but of the quarrel with ourselves, poetry'.[20] It is a false distinction, like that of the choice between perfection of the life and of the work: Yeats was capable of creating magnificent poetry out of the quarrel with others. But it was indeed the never-resolved tension between self and anti-self, the imagination of a transcendent Other counterpoised with sublunary reality, the need for engagement and the yearning for escape, that made Yeats the outstanding modern poet he was.

NOTES

1. W. B. Yeats, *The Poems*, ed. Daniel Albright. 2nd edition (London: J. M. Dent, 1994), p. 296. All quotations from Yeats's poetry are taken from this edition, cited parenthetically in the text as *Poems*. For variants in Yeats's often revised poems, see W. B. Yeats, *Variorum Edition of the Poems*, ed. Peter Allt and Russell K. Alspach (New York: Macmillan, 1957), cited herein as *Variorum*.

2. Yeats's theory of masks was conceived as early as 1909 but most fully developed in *A Vision*: see W. B. Yeats, *Memoirs*, ed. Denis Donoghue (London: Macmillan, 1972), p. 191, and W. B. Yeats, *A Vision*, 2nd edition (London: Macmillan, 1937), pp. 67–184.

3. For overviews of Yeats criticism, see Declan Kiberd, 'Yeats and Criticism', in Marjorie Howes and W. B. Yeats (eds.) *Cambridge Companion to W. B. Yeats* (Cambridge: Cambridge University Press, 2006), pp. 115–128, and Edna Longley, 'Critical Debate, 1939–1970', and Rob Doggett, 'Critical Debate, 1970–2006', in David Holdeman and Ben Levitas (eds.), *W. B. Yeats in Context* (Cambridge: Cambridge University Press, 2010), pp. 385–395, 396–405.

4. R. F. Foster, *W. B. Yeats: A Life*, 2 vols. (Oxford and New York: Oxford University Press, 1997–2003); see also Terence Brown, *The Life of W. B. Yeats: A Critical Biography* (Oxford: Blackwell, 1999).

5. For representative examples, see Marjorie Howes, *Yeats's Nations: Gender, Class and Irishness* (Cambridge: Cambridge University Press, 1996), Elizabeth Butler Cullingford, *Yeats, Ireland and Fascism* (Basingstoke: Macmillan, 1981), Margaret Mills Harper, *Wisdom of Two: The Spiritual and Literary Collaboration of George and W. B. Yeats* (Oxford: Oxford University Press, 2006), Helen Vendler, *Our Secret Discipline: Yeats and Lyric Form* (New York: Oxford University Press, 2007).

6. Four volumes of the *Collected Letters* have been published under the general editorship of John Kelly (Oxford: Oxford University Press, 1986–2005), cited here as *CL* I–IV, and the rest of the letters are available in the InteLex Electronic Edition. The Cornell Yeats has made available the manuscript materials for each volume of Yeats's poems: see www.cornellpress.cornell.edu/collections/?collection_id=143, accessed 22 December 2015, for complete listing.

7. See http://yeats2015.com/, accessed 22 December 2015

8. For a fuller analysis of the effects, see my *Yeats's Poetic Codes* (Oxford: Oxford University Press, 2008), pp. 81–2.

9. W. B. Yeats, *Autobiographies* (London: Macmillan, 1955), p. 153.

10. W. B. Yeats (ed.), *The Oxford Book of Modern Verse* (Oxford: Clarendon Press, 1936), ix.

11. The admission was made in a note on 'September 1913' in the expanded trade edition of *Responsibilities* (London: Macmillan, 1916).

12. The fullest account of the context for this deferral is given in Wayne K. Chapman, *Yeats's Poetry in the Making* (Basingstoke: Palgrave Macmillan, 2010), pp. 78–96.

13. For one of the finest analyses of this much interpreted poem, see Brown, *W. B. Yeats*, pp. 227–34.

14. See Vendler, *Our Secret Discipline*, 291–7 for her illuminating reading of the poem.

15. On the context for the poem's composition, see Brown, *W. B. Yeats*, pp. 270–1.

16. On 'Nineteen Hundred and Nineteen', see Michael Wood's superb book *Yeats and Violence* (Oxford: Oxford University Press, 2010).

17. Vendler, *Our Secret Discipline*, p. 371.

18. T. S. Eliot, *On Poetry and Poets* (London: Faber, 1957), p. 262.

19. Ibid.

20. W. B. Yeats, *Mythologies* (London: Macmillan, 1959), p. 331.

SELECTED FURTHER READING
Editions

Oxford Book of Modern Verse (Oxford: Clarendon Press, 1936).
A Vision, 2nd edition (London: Macmillan, 1937).
Autobiographies (London: Macmillan, 1955).
Variorum Edition of the Poems, ed. Peter Allt and Russell K. Alspach (New York: Macmillan, 1957).
Mythologies (London: Macmillan, 1959).
Memoirs, ed. Denis Donoghue (London: Macmillan, 1972).
Collected Letters, 4 vols., ed. John Kelly (Oxford: Oxford University Press, 1986–2005).
Poems, ed. Daniel Albright. 2nd edition (London: J. M. Dent, 1994).

Biographical

Brown, Terence, *The Life of W. B. Yeats: a Critical Biography* (Oxford: Blackwell, 1999).
Foster, R. F., *W. B. Yeats: a Life*, 2 vols. (Oxford and New York: Oxford University Press, 1997–2003).

Critical

Chapman, Wayne K., *Yeats's Poetry in the Making* (Basingstoke: Palgrave Macmillan, 2010).
Cullingford, Elizabeth Butler, *Yeats, Ireland and Fascism* (Basingstoke: Macmillan, 1981).
Eliot, T. S., *On Poetry and Poets* (London: Faber, 1957).
Grene, Nicholas, *Yeats's Poetic Codes* (Oxford: Oxford University Press, 2008).
Harper, Margaret Mills, *Wisdom of Two: The Spiritual and Literary Collaboration of George and W. B. Yeats* (Oxford: Oxford University Press, 2006).
Holdeman, David and Ben Levitas (eds.), *W. B. Yeats in Context* (Cambridge: Cambridge University Press, 2010).
Howes, Marjorie, *Yeats's Nations: Gender, Class and Irishness* (Cambridge: Cambridge University Press, 1996).
Vendler, Helen, *Our Secret Discipline: Yeats and Lyric Form* (New York: Oxford University Press, 2007).
Wood, Michael, *Yeats and Violence* (Oxford: Oxford University Press, 2010).

8

FRAN BREARTON

Francis Ledwidge

In his 1979 collection *Field Work*, Heaney includes a number of elegies for, variously, friends, relatives and fellow artists: his cousin, Colum McCartney ('The Strand at Lough Beg'), shot in the head by the UVF in August 1975; Sean Armstrong ('A Postcard from North Antrim'), a Belfast social worker killed in his south Belfast flat by what Heaney calls 'A pointblank teatime bullet' in June 1973; Louis O'Neill ('Casualty'), killed in an explosion in Stewartstown in February 1972; the musician and composer Sean O'Riada ('In Memoriam Sean O'Riada'), who died prematurely in 1971, shortly after his fortieth birthday; and Robert Lowell ('Elegy'), who died in 1977 and who steered, in Heaney's phrase, a 'course set wilfully across / the ungovernable and dangerous'.[1] In *Field Work*, these five elegies precede the 'Glanmore Sonnets' sequence at the centre – in more ways than one – of the collection. Not until the penultimate poem of the book do we find his sixth elegy, 'In Memoriam Francis Ledwidge'. That his elegy for Ledwidge sits at a remove from the elegiac impulse dominating the first half of *Field Work* is unsurprising: the first five elegies are for people Heaney knew, for his (Irish) contemporaries. The exception, Lowell, is still an acquaintance, and cast in an almost paternal role (Lowell, he tells us 'found the child in me' when he 'took farewells / under the full bay tree / by the gate in Glanmore').[2] Those deaths all occurred in the 1970s, and the elegies are ones through which Heaney reflects, implicitly and explicitly, on his own aesthetic in a 'troubled' period of history. They seek to 'answer' the times, even if that quest takes him only to the powerful 'Question me again' at the close of 'Casualty';[3] the 'idea of an answering poetry as a responsible poetry' in times of crisis has, Heaney writes later in *The Redress of Poetry*, 'been one of my constant themes'.[4]

Francis Ledwidge shares characteristics with some of the other subjects of elegy in *Field Work* – not least that he died a violent death, as a relatively young man, in complex political circumstances. And, in some respects, he might seem a likely subject for Heaney given Heaney's own rural background. Born in 1887 the son of a farm labourer in Slane, Co. Meath,

Ledwidge, leaving the national school at fourteen, worked on the farmlands and the roads of Meath; he also began, in the early years of the twentieth century, to write that landscape into poetry – indeed, as his biographer Alice Curtayne points out, to write poetry onto the landscape itself: 'Whenever a verse came into his head, he would stop in his tracks to scribble it down anywhere handy, perhaps on the pier of a gate, a fencing-post, or on a boulder in a field.'[5] A prolific publisher of poems in newspapers, and promoted by Lord Dunsany as a 'peasant poet', Ledwidge published his first volume of poems, the appropriately titled *Songs of the Fields*, in 1915, to 'laudatory reviews'. It comprises some 50 poems written up to 1914, dealing predominantly with rural life and love, and according to the *Bookman* made Ledwidge's name 'beloved in the hearts of all those to whom Nature is really and truly their mother'.[6] Thus far at least, Ledwidge could be a potential source of inspiration for Heaney – the 'field work' poet himself, in the manner of Patrick Kavanagh (advocate of 'important places'), or Hardy (about whose 'landscape' Heaney says he 'always felt something familiar'), or Frost.[7]

But the Ledwidge story that might have emerged here – of the rural Catholic 'peasant poet' who possessed the characteristics Daniel Corkery would later identify as the essential qualities of 'Irishness' (religion, nationalism, love of the land[8]); who seemingly epitomised the Revival desire to find in the peasant the voice of 'authenticity'; and who might, as with Kavanagh, in achieving poetic maturity have destabilised both Irish-Ireland and Revivalist perceptions of the peasant poet – was not to be. Ledwidge, for reasons much debated,[9] joined the Royal Inniskilling Fusiliers in October 1914, one of more than 140,000 Irish men – including those, like Ledwidge, who were passionately committed to Irish independence from Britain, and sympathetic to the Irish Volunteers who later engineered the Easter Rising – to enlist in the British Army during World War I. He is also one of the c.35,000 Irishmen who died in that war.[10] Following service in Gallipoli and Salonika in 1915–16, he was invalided back to Britain in April 1916, then in December 1916 sent to the Western Front. He was killed in the third battle of Ypres on 31 July 1917, 'blown to bits' just over a fortnight before his thirtieth birthday.[11] (As Dermot Bolger notes, in a 'cruel irony', he was 'working at the same job he had spent so much of his early manhood in Meath doing, building a road through mud near Ypres'.[12]) His *Songs of Peace* appeared posthumously in 1917, followed by *Last Songs* in 1918, both edited by his patron and literary adviser Lord Dunsany.

Prior to the outbreak of war, Ledwidge was a compulsive, rather conventional versifier who was growing in popularity; if his stature was not equal to that of some of the other Georgian poets with whom he shares the pages of the second of Edward Marsh's *Georgian Poetry* anthologies, his appeal may be understood in some of the same terms. In 'A Rainy Day in April', we find nature sprinkled with innocence, and served up in the late romantic style for which 'Georgianism', however unfairly, was later derided:

> When the clouds shake their hyssops, and the rain
> Like holy water falls upon the plain,
> 'Tis sweet to gaze upon the springing grain
> And see your harvest born.
>
> And sweet the little breeze of melody
> The blackbird puffs upon the budding tree,
> While the wild poppy lights upon the lea
> And blazes 'mid the corn.[13]

More justice is done to Ledwidge by the inclusion in the same anthology of 'The Wife of Llew', which for all its Yeatsian imitativeness, demonstrates, as Heaney has noted, 'a finer, more objective way with verse-craft':[14]

> And Gwydion said to Math, when it was Spring:
> 'Come now and let us make a wife for Llew.'
> And so they broke broad boughs yet moist with dew,
> And in a shadow made a magic ring

A poem moistened but not drenched with dew, there is a freshness and immediacy attributable not only to the 'in medias res' spontaneity of its opening, but also to its handling of monosyllable, alliteration and assonance, and to its balancing of rhyming couplets in the centre of the poem ('They built a mound of daisies on a wing, / And for her voice they made a linnet sing') with the ABBA pattern of its opening and closing lines. The momentum of the whole poem (as if it begins to have a life of its own) is heightened by its insistent 'And', 'And':

> And over all this they chanted twenty hours.
> And Llew came singing from the azure south
> And bore away his wife of birds and flowers.[15]

Nevertheless, in 'In Memoriam Francis Ledwidge', when Heaney describes the poet as 'Literary, sweet-talking, countrified', a figure who belongs 'among the dolorous / And lovely: the May altar of wild flowers, / Easter water sprinkled in outhouses', there is a delicacy, almost a prettiness to the lines that may be read as both tribute to Ledwidge and an implicit, even if unconscious, judgement by Heaney on some of the earlier poet's limitations.[16] Even Ledwidge's sorrow comes ('dolorous') in the language of romance for Heaney; and the colloquial 'sweet-talking' reflects too that 'sweeter strain', in Ledwidge's own phrase,[17] of some of the early verse in *Songs of the Fields*.

But it is not the 'sweetness' that prompts Heaney's imaginative engagement with Ledwidge in *Field Work* so much as the 'strain', a 'strain' Heaney
finds not in the work but in the life. As neither ally nor artistic influence,
Ledwidge thus sits slightly uneasily in the elegiac pantheon of *Field Work*;
and his life choices, despite his rural Catholic background, place him at odds
with Heaney's own sense of 'belonging'. World War I, for someone of
Heaney's generation, background and upbringing, was predominantly,
through to the 1980s and 1990s, associated in the North with the loyalist
community, for whom the unionist sacrifice in the Great War is part of the
founding myth of Northern Ireland. In Heaney's elegy for Ledwidge, the war
is associated with the 'loyal' (loyalist) names on the Portstewart war memorial ('this vigilant bronze'), and with the 'eternal vigilance' of a loyalism that
claimed – and still claims – the July 1916 Battle of the Somme as peculiarly its
own; in this context, Ledwidge is a misfit who 'belonged' in Slane, but whose
'haunted Catholic face' is, incongruously, found 'Ghosting the trenches with
a bloom of hawthorn'. That it all 'meant little to the worried pet / I was in
nineteen forty-six or seven' carries the broader implication that the Great
War 'meant little' to Heaney's community too – or, at least, was perceived to
do so. In 'Casualty', Heaney asks the politically fraught and emotive question
about Louis O'Neill 'How culpable was he ... when he broke / Our tribe's
complicity?'[18] In the early drafts of 'In Memoriam Francis Ledwidge', it is
evident that he is also, in a sense, asking Ledwidge to 'puzzle [him] / The right
answer'[19] in terms of how to read the war memorial: cancelled lines in the
poem read 'Come, Francis Ledwidge, dead at Ypres, say / How my bewildered [beleaguered] caste should read this sign, / The stiff, proud vigilance of
this effigy?'[20] That questioning is, for Heaney, about coming to terms with
the legacy of World War I in Ireland, and one senses some frustration with
the absence of any decodable 'sign' from his subject:

> In you, our dead enigma, all the strains
> Criss-cross in useless equilibrium
> And as the wind tunes through this vigilant bronze
> I hear again the sure confusing drum
>
> You followed from Boyne water to the Balkans
> But miss the twilit note your flute should sound.[21]

Ledwidge does not produce a powerful music that counters or complements
the loyalist 'drum'. Instead, he seems here almost the passive focal point for
conflicting strains of music, from which his own 'twilit note' is simply
missing. For Heaney to 'miss' that note works in two ways – it acknowledges
the loss that is Ledwidge's death, so that a note once heard has now gone; but
it is also to be unable to hear that note clearly amidst the other 'tunes' of the

poem: Ledwidge, we might infer, unlike Heaney, does not 'strike [his] note' clearly enough.[22]

Heaney's poem reverberates more broadly in the fraught issue of Irish nationalist involvement in World War I, appearing as it did at a time when the Irish contribution to the war effort was still subject to some collective historical amnesia. His elegy for Ledwidge has embedded within it much of the problematic response in Ireland to the Great War, and that Ledwidge is the exemplary case here – exemplifying, that is, the problem as well as the solution – is not without relevance in terms of the reception and profile of Ledwidge's own poetry. Unveiling a statue of the poet at Richmond Barracks in July 2016, Martin McGuinness noted that there had been a 'national amnesia about what happened during the First World War', and that remembering Ledwidge was part of 'get[ting] over that'. That a Sinn Fein deputy first minister unveiled a statue of 'an Irish man who served in the Royal Inniskilling Fusiliers' was itself seen to add another 'layer of complexity' to the story of Ledwidge.[23] Characteristic of these and other responses to the poet is the fact that the layers of complexity are attributed to Ledwidge's life, but not, generally speaking, to his work. A poet often and contradictorily labelled – 'peasant poet', 'minstrel boy', 'poet of the blackbird', 'soldier poet', 'war poet', 'Irish nationalist rebel' – Ledwidge, it seems, stands for, or at times stands in for, the multiple and contradictory threads in the tapestry of Irish history in the tumultuous decade 1912–22. Coming to terms with Ledwidge's life story has been a means for a society to rethink its own 'malaise', its own selective amnesia in relation to World War I. The attention to the layered complexity of his life – a story worth telling, worth remembering and understanding – has thus dominated the heightened profile he has acquired in the late twentieth and early twenty-first centuries.

Ledwidge was much celebrated as a popular poet in 1912–13 (and the interest in his life was then an interest in his 'peasant' background) – 'one of the company', Padraic Colum called him, 'of old Irish poets who sang of the deer on the hillside', who 'gets the atmosphere that is in the old Fenian poetry'. Yet the more cautious voices of the time also set the tone for reservations about his stature expressed later in the century – or if not explicitly voiced, then evident in the way in which Ledwidge's life experiences have warranted attention where his verse has not. 'I do not believe', James Stephens wrote, 'that he will ratify [his] promise. I don't believe that his thought will equal his faculty for utterance'.[24] In the introduction to Ledwidge's *Selected Poems*, Heaney is also critical of what he describes as 'something regressive in the way [Ledwidge] often seems to be holding on to the skirts of a maternal landscape', and of a 'melodiousness [that] can at times verge upon the infantile'. He argues too that Ledwidge's early influences – 'the Keatsian idiom he inherited and Dunsany's ambitions for him as a writer' – were at too great a remove from his working life 'as a road surfaceman ... in the coppermines ... his involvement with trade-union politics'.[25] His pre-1916 poems often read as (lesser) variations on a Keatsian (tempered by early Yeatsian) theme. Take the following from Keats's 'I stood tip-toe upon a little hill':

> The soul is lost in pleasant smotherings:
> Fair dewy roses brush against our faces,
> And flowering laurels spring from diamond vases;
> O'er head we see the jasmine and sweet briar,
> And bloomy grapes laughing from green attire;
> While at our feet, the voice of crystal bubbles
> Charms us at once away from all our troubles:
> So that we feel uplifted from the world,
>   . . .
> Poor nymph – poor Pan – how did he weep to find,
> Naught but a lovely sighing of the wind
> Along the reedy stream; a half-heard strain,
> Full of sweet desolation – balmy pain.[26]

From these lines we might recognise many of the more imitative characteristics of Ledwidge's earlier poems: the rhyming couplets; his echo of the insistently romantic adjectival impulse (lovely, reedy, sweet, balmy); the dim 'half-light' ('half-heard strain') of the Celtic Twilight; the sound (or 'sighing') of a Yeatsian 'wind among the reeds'; the habitual musical motifs – cleverly echoed and reinterpreted by Heaney – which are also manifest in the proliferation in Ledwidge's *oeuvre* of songs and ballads. Ledwidge's 'To a Linnet in a Cage' is one of many poems that evidence the Keatsian/Yeatsian debt,

> When Spring is in the fields that stained your wing,
> And the blue distance is alive with song,
> And finny quiets of the gabbling spring
> Rock lilies red and long,
> At dewy daybreak I will set you free
> In ferny turnings of the woodbine lane,
> Where faint-voiced echoes leave and cross in glee
> The hilly swollen plain.
>   . . .
>   . . . your song shall fall
> When morn is white upon the dewy pane,
> Across my eyelids, and my soul recall
> From worlds of sleeping pain.[27]

For all their spontaneity of utterance – the verse simply coming into his head – the idiom in such poems is rather more second-hand than 'intertextual'. Dermot Bolger, a life-long devotee of Ledwidge's work (Ledwidge is the subject of Bolger's poignant one-act play *Walking the Road* (2007)), who once consumed '[e]verything that Ledwidge had written … with the uncritical openness of youth', also acknowledges that '[m]uch of his work suffers from the flaws of its time'.[28] And as Liam O'Meara, editor of his *Complete Poems*, pragmatically observes:

> Ledwidge, anxious to have his work published, was writing for a particular market. The success rate of poems appearing in both newspapers [*The Drogheda Independent; The Irish Weekly Independent*] shows how well he knew his readership. The poems, in style, theme and language, were typical of the ones written by his contemporaries. The traditional flavour of these poems was exactly what the public demanded.[29]

Nevertheless, Bolger, rightly, also affirms 'the lyric grace and beauty of the best of Ledwidge's poetry'.[30] For Alice Curtayne, '[t]he best feature of his style is simplicity, not achieved without immense effort and for that reason deceptive to the uninitiated. … He preferred not only short words, but short lines, too, and short poems'. 'A Little Boy in the Morning', written on leave in 1916, is a lyric which she describes as 'near perfect':[31]

> He will not come, and still I wait.
> He whistles at another gate
> Where angels listen. Ah, I know
> He will not come, yet if I go
> How shall I know he did not pass
> Barefooted in the flowery grass?[32]

This is the art that conceals art, with its monosyllables, its transparent yet unanswerable question; its caesuras that hold the moment of indecision between staying and going, life and afterlife. In lyrics like these it is possible to see Ledwidge as the contemporary of a poet such as Robert Graves, who sought this kind of simplicity in some of his wartime and post-war lyrics, a simplicity which is also, in Graves's poem of that title, a way of 'Flying Crooked'.

Jim Haughey, noting the increased interest in Ledwidge's work which followed the 80th anniversary of his death (and which has been notable again on the 100th), argues that 'it appears that Ledwidge's poetry, especially his war poetry, has regained an audience chiefly due to its cultural and ideological significance' – which also appears to confirm Heaney's point that Ledwidge's is 'neither a very strong nor very original talent'.[33] In a recent study by Terry Phillips of Irish war literature, Ledwidge's poems are trawled for what they tell us of the soldier's 'range of experiences': the 'sense of camaraderie' is found in several poems; 'Jim West' is 'a poem which gives a sense of the battlefield itself'; 'In a Café' offers 'a valuable insight into life behind the lines'; many poems express a 'sentiment shared by almost all soldiers – homesickness'; the poems sometimes show him to be disillusioned with life; he developed 'a growing understanding of the suffering and loss which war involved'; nevertheless, a couple of poems 'express the pleasanter aspects of the soldier's experience', and so on.[34] Without disputing the validity of any of these observations, they do no more than find in Ledwidge sentiments typical of serving soldiers (British, Irish, French or German) – and could as well be taken from the letters home or diary entries of any thoughtful junior officer as from Ledwidge's poems. More tellingly, Haughey himself makes a case for the pastoral and more 'escapist' elements in Ledwidge as culturally revealing: he suggests that they are indicative of a 'concerted ... attempt to preserve his memory of a rural world untainted by the destruction of war', and the 'preoccupation with scenes of rural tranquillity indicates how desperate he was to locate oases of order and coherency amid the prevailing chaos and bloodshed of the front'.[35] He rightly notes too that some of Ledwidge's poems which directly address the war 'celebrate the type of chivalric piety we associate with cenotaph inscriptions', as well as with Rupert Brooke or Julian Grenfell.[36] So, for instance, in 'Soliloquy', a poem whose rhyming couplets give it a slightly jingling tone at odds with its title's more reflective ambitions, Ledwidge writes:

> Tomorrow will be loud with war,
> How will I be accounted for?
> . . .
> A keen-edged sword, a soldier's heart,
> Is greater than a poet's art,
> And greater than a poet's fame
> A little grave that has no name,
> Whence honour turns away in shame.[37]

In some respects, Ledwidge's poems are revealing in terms of what they don't say, as much as what they do. Given the extent to which Ireland was riven by political tensions during World War I, it may seem surprising to find little or no such tension evident in the work of Ledwidge, or others of Ireland's 'soldier poets'. That could be the fault of anachronistic expectations, so that while Heaney, from the vantage point of 1970s Northern Ireland, finds Ledwidge an 'enigma' in terms of the choices he made, there is nothing particularly enigmatic about the decision of an Irish nationalist to enlist: the 'strain' of doing so becomes evident in Ledwidge not in 1914–15, but after the Easter Rising changed the course of Irish history. He speaks of it directly in his letters, writing in June 1917:

I am sorry that party politics should ever divide our own tents but am not without hope that a new Ireland will arise from her ashes in the ruins of Dublin, like the Phoenix, with one purpose, one aim, and one ambition. I tell you this in order that you may know what it is to me to be called a British soldier while my own country has no place among the nations but the place of Cinderella.[38]

In 1913, as noted above, Stephens commented 'I don't believe that his thought will equal his faculty for utterance'. In 1916, and with the challenges to Ledwidge's 'thought' posed by the events of 1916, one might be tempted to reverse the critique, proposing instead that his 'faculty for utterance' in poetry is not, as Heaney implies, fully adequate to the complexities of his 'thought' as evidenced in his letters – particularly if we take 'thought' in its more Yeatsian sense, as holding contrarieties ('reality and justice') in balance.[39] Ledwidge's poems don't contain 'the quarrel with ourselves'[40] that might issue in a more discordant music than the 'twilit note', although that he *felt* such discordance ('to be called a British soldier', which Heaney turns into a self-contained lament in his own poem, is not the same as 'to be a British soldier') is not really in doubt.

That said, it is also possible to suggest that in 1916–17, and in the last 18 months of a short but prolific writing career, the beginnings of some new formal capabilities in Ledwidge are indeed evident. Haughey argues that in some of Ledwidge's wartime poetry, '[w]e see the strain of maintaining the standards of a prewar aesthetic ideal in his poetry which can no longer inoculate itself against the obscenity of the war'.[41] In the analysis of 'A Fear' which follows, he suggests that the allusion to Dante in the poem ('I roamed the woods today and seemed to hear, / As Dante heard, the voice of suffering trees') 'goes beyond the decorative to cross-connect pictures of suffering that communicate to us the subsequent violence, mass murder, and trauma of war'. If this perhaps overstates what the poem itself achieves, the broader point that more 'ominous images' begin to work their way into Ledwidge's poems is persuasive.[42] And beyond such 'strains' there are also developments in his verse-craft and idiom which enable the writing of a poem generally recognised as his most enduring lyric – the elegy for Thomas MacDonagh, who had been executed on 3 May 1916 for his part in the Easter Rising.

MacDonagh was one of Ledwidge's heroes, whom he had met in the pre-war years at Dunsany Castle, and whose work and ideas clearly influenced the younger, aspiring poet. In *Literature in Ireland*, published posthumously in 1916, MacDonagh advocates an 'Irish Mode' in poetry, objecting to what he describes as 'inversions' and 'artificialities' (traits found in Ledwidge's 'salon idiom'), and making a case for Irish writers as 'more direct, more modern, than such writers as Robert Bridges, Henry Newbolt and William Watson, on whom have fallen the mantles of older English writers'. He praises instead 'natural diction' and 'the wonderfully intricate thing, Gaelic versification', pointing towards its rhyming patterns and employment of monosyllabics.[43] Ledwidge's elegy, simply titled 'Thomas McDonagh', was written when he was invalided back to England from Serbia, shortly after MacDonagh's execution, and it is a poem which does justice to the ideas and literary ideals of its subject:

> He shall not hear the bittern cry
> In the wild sky, where he is lain,
> Nor voices of the sweeter birds
> Above the wailing of the rain.
>
> Nor shall he know when loud March blows
> Thro' slanting snows her fanfare shrill,
> Blowing to flame the golden cup
> Of many an upset daffodil.
>
> But when the Dark Cow leaves the moor,
> And pastures poor with greedy weeds,
> Perhaps he'll hear her low at morn
> Lifting her horn in pleasant meads.[44]

The 'bittern' is a reference to MacDonagh's translation of the Gaelic poem *The Yellow Bittern*.[45] As Curtayne notes, Ledwidge 'had begun to model his verse on Irish poetry, using the metre with the *aicill*-rhyme, from the end of one line to the middle of the next', as evident here. The craft, she writes, is 'perfected by suffering'.[46] The 'sweeter' sounds of this poem are drowned out by the 'wailing of the rain'; its monosyllabic simplicity – particularly telling in the opening line of each stanza – encompasses more by saying less; its internal and assonantal rhymes fall into place to complicate its surface: 'sweeter' finds an echo in 'greedy'; 'lain' and 'rain' shift us from the 'wild sky' to bodies trodden in the mud; the gentle winds of earlier poems are more forcefully 'Blowing to flame'. A poem of grace and musicality, it is also, on closer inspection, surprisingly noisy, the 'sweeter strain' taking on a new shrillness.

From his hospital bed in Manchester, Ledwidge wrote to friends both of 'hardships in Serbia', of 'the cold, the blizzards, the frost and the hunger' as almost beyond words; and of his grief that 'MacDonagh and Pearse … two of my best friends … are dead, shot by England'.[47] The poem, with all its indebtedness to the 'Irish mode', is one of the outstanding elegies for the dead of Easter 1916. Yet it contains within it, in its 'wailing of the rain', 'loud March blows', and 'fanfare shrill', a lament for the dead of the war too: this is the language of World War I, of spring offensives, of the call to arms, with the 'wailing' of shellfire creeping into the Irish tradition. It predates Owen's 'Anthem for Doomed Youth' (1917) with its 'Shrill, demented choirs of wailing shells',[48] but it begins to intimate what Owen brought to fruition, in terms of reworking the Keatsian idiom to powerful effect in the context of modern war. Where April is the month enshrined in the rhetoric of the Rising, with its sacrificial connotations, 'March' resonates more obviously in the context of war. It is a poem uncertain of any potential for pastoral healing ('Perhaps'); it offers none of the traditional consolations of God or country or duty; and it avoids the sacrificial rhetoric that was as characteristic of Padraic Pearse as it was of Rupert Brooke. These are telling absences that Yeats, in equally difficult but very different circumstances, elegising Major Robert Gregory, would more directly espouse, in a poem whose complexities are also embedded in its stark monosyllabic mode: 'Nor law, nor duty bade me fight ... In balance with this life, this death'.[49] In what 'Thomas McDonagh' leaves unsaid as well as in what it does say, it serves as a self-elegy too, anticipating Ledwidge's own death on the Western Front less than a year later and disallowing any too-easy assumptions about what 'bade [him] fight'.

'Thomas McDonagh' has stood the test of time because it is one of the few poems by Ledwidge that inscribes within its own language and form some of the 'layers' that render his biography so compelling within the context of Irish history; that draws together – without compromising its surface simplicity of utterance – his lived experiences with the tangled threads of English and Irish literary traditions. 'I mean to do something really great if I am spared', Ledwidge wrote in June 1917, a few weeks before his death.[50] He was not spared; but although his *oeuvre* is uneven and his full potential unrealised, this poem stands as a poignant reminder of what he might have accomplished in a more sustained fashion had circumstances permitted him to do so.

NOTES

1. Heaney, *Field Work* (London: Faber, 1979), pp. 19, 32.
2. Ibid., p. 32.
3. Ibid., p. 24.
4. Seamus Heaney, *The Redress of Poetry: Oxford Lectures* (London: Faber, 1995), p. 191.
5. Alice Curtayne, *Francis Ledwidge: A Life of the Poet* (London: Martin Brien & O'Keefe, 1972), p. 26.
6. See Curtayne, *Francis Ledwidge*, p. 136.
7. See 'Seamus Heaney, The Ministry of Fear', *North* (London: Faber, 1975), p. 63; Heaney quoted in Tara Christie Kinsey, 'Seamus Heaney's Hardy', *The Recorder*, 17:1 (Summer 2004), p. 119; for extensive discussion of the relation between Frost and Heaney, see Rachel Buxton, *Robert Frost and Northern Irish Poetry* (Oxford: Clarendon Press, 2004).
8. In the introduction to *Synge and Anglo-Irish Literature* (1931) Corkery writes that: 'The three great forces which, working for long in the Irish national being, have made it so different from the English national being, are: (1) The Religious Consciousness of the People; (2) Irish Nationalism; and (3) The Land.' See http://ricorso.net/rx/library/criticism/classic/Anglo_I/Corkery_D/Corkery_D.htm (accessed 26 September 2016).

9. At a meeting of Navan Rural Council on 19 October 1914, Ledwidge argued against the position taken by John Redmond in his Woodenbridge speech ('The interests . . . of the whole of Ireland, are at stake in this war') and in the split in the Volunteers that occurred following that speech, between the National Volunteers following Redmond, and the Irish Volunteers following Eoin MacNeill, he positioned himself with O'Neill. Yet only five days later he joined up himself. Whatever his motivations, it seems clear that he expected the war to be of short duration. Curtayne observes 'It is difficult to avoid the conclusion that the poet did not even read the daily papers'. Ledwidge later says of his enlistment that 'I joined the British Army because she stood between Ireland and an enemy common to our civilisation and I would not have her say that she defended us while we did nothing at home but pass resolutions'. See Curtayne, *Francis Ledwidge*, pp. 76–83, 111.

10. The figures are tentative. For more information, see Keith Jeffery, *Ireland and the Great War* (Cambridge: Cambridge University Press, 2000), pp. 6–7, 35. The enlistment figure does not include those Irishmen already serving in the army when war was declared.

11. Father Charles Devas, S. J., army chaplain, recorded in his diary on 31 July 1917: 'Ledwidge killed, blown to bits; at Confession yesterday and Mass and Holy Communion this morning. R.I.P.' Quoted in Curtayne, *Francis Ledwidge*, p. 188.

12. Dermot Bolger, 'Editor's Note' to Francis Ledwidge, *Selected Poems*, ed. Dermot Bolger (Dublin: New Island Books, 1992), p. 7

13. The other two poems included in *Georgian Poetry 1913–1915* (London: The Poetry Bookshops, 1915), pp. 161–3, also from *Songs of the Fields*, are 'The Wife of Llew' and 'The Lost Ones'. The version of 'A Rainy Day in April' in Francis Ledwidge, *The Complete Poems*), ed. Liam O'Meara (Newbridge, Ireland: Goldsmith Press, 1997), p. 46, has seven rather than four stanzas.

14. Heaney, 'Introduction' to Francis Ledwidge, *Selected Poems*, ed. Dermot Bolger, p. 16.

15. *Complete Poems*, ed. O'Meara, p. 76.

16. Heaney, 'In Memoriam: Francis Ledwidge', *Field Work*, p. 59.

17. Ledwidge, 'To Lizzie' ('Eilish of the Fair Hair'), *Complete Poems*, ed. O'Meara, p. 135.

18. Heaney, *Field Work*, p. 23.

19. Heaney, 'Casualty', *Field Work*, p. 23.

20. The framed manuscript of the poem is displayed on the wall of the Francis Ledwidge Museum in Slane. See www.francisledwidge.com/. The typed 'beleaguered' has been scored out and 'bewildered' handwritten over it; this, and a following stanza, do not appear in the final version of the poem.

21. Heaney, *Field Work*, p. 60.

22. '"Now strike your note"' is Heaney's self-exhortation (mediated through 'Joyce') in section XII of the Station Island sequence. *Station Island* (London: Faber, 1984), p. 93.

23. *Irish Times*, 27 July 2016; www.irishtimes.com/culture/heritage/statue-of-francis-ledwidge-unveiled-at-richmond-barracks-1.2736182 (accessed 26 September 2016).

24. Quoted in Curtayne, *Francis Ledwidge*, pp. 47–8.

25. Heaney, 'Introduction', Ledwidge, *Selected Poems*, pp. 13, 15.

26. John Keats, *The Complete Poems*, ed. John Barnard (2nd edn. London: Penguin, 1977), pp. 79–80.
27. *Complete Poems*, ed. O'Meara, p. 30.
28. Dermot Bolger, 'Editor's Note' to Ledwidge, *Selected Poems*, p. 8.
29. O'Meara, preface to Ledwidge, *Complete Poems*, n.p.
30. Bolger, 'Editor's Note', Ledwidge, *Selected Poems*, p. 8.
31. Curtayne, *Francis Ledwidge*, p. 193.
32. *Complete Poems*, ed. O'Meara, p. 128.
33. Jim Haughey, *The First World War in Irish Poetry* (Lewisburg: Bucknell University Press, 2002), p. 75.
34. Terry Phillips, *Irish Literature and the First World War* (Bern: Peter Lang, 2015), pp. 26, 28–33.
35. Haughey, *The First World War in Irish Poetry*, p. 77.
36. Ibid., p. 83.
37. *Complete Poems*, ed. O'Meara, p. 238.
38. Ledwidge, letter to Lewis Chase, 6 June 1917, quoted in Curtayne, *Francis Ledwidge*, p. 180.
39. See W. B. Yeats, 'Introduction' (1928), *A Vision* (London; Macmillan, 1962), p. 25.
40. See W. B. Yeats, 'Per Amica Silentia Lunae' (1917), *Mythologies* (London: Macmillan, 1952), p. 331.
41. Haughey, *The First World War in Irish Poetry*, p. 81.
42. Ibid., pp. 82, 79.
43. Thomas MacDonagh, *Literature in Ireland: Studies Irish and Anglo-Irish* (New York: Frederick A. Stokes, 1916) pp. 75, 78.
44. *Complete Poems*, ed. O'Meara, p. 175.
45. The intertextual dialogue opened up makes it tempting to read lines from MacDonagh's translation as an epitaph-in-advance for Ledwidge himself: 'It's not for the common birds that I'd mourn, / The black-bird, the corn-crake, or the crane, / But for the bittern that's shy and apart.' See *The Poetical Works of Thomas MacDonagh* (Dublin: Talbot Press, 1916).
46. Curtayne, *Francis Ledwidge*, p. 156
47. Ledwidge, letter to Bob Christie, 4 May 1916 quoted in Curtayne, *Francis Ledwidge*, p. 131.
48. Wilfred Owen, *The Poems of Wilfred Owen*, ed. Jon Stallworthy (London: Chatto & Windus, 1990), p. 76.
49. W. B. Yeats, 'An Irish Airman Foresees His Death', *Collected Poems* (London: Macmillan, 1950), p. 152.
50. Ledwidge, letter to Lewis Chase, 6 June 1917, quoted in Curtayne, *Francis Ledwidge*, p. 182.

SELECTED FURTHER READING

Brearton, Fran, *The Great War in Irish Poetry* (Oxford: Oxford University Press, 2000).
Curtayne, Alice, *Francis Ledwidge: A Life of the Poet* (London: Martin Brien & O'Keefe, 1972).

Dawe, Gerald, *Of War and War's Alarms: Reflections on Modern Irish writing* (Cork: Cork University Press, 2015).

Dunn, Hubert, *The Minstrel Boy: Francis Ledwidge and the Literature of his Time* (Ireland: Booklink, 2006).

Haughey, Jim, *The First World War in Irish Poetry* (Lewisburg: Bucknell University Press, 2002).

Ledwidge, Francis, *Complete Poems*, ed. Alice Curtayne(London: Martin Brian & O'Keefe, 1974).

Selected Poems, ed. Dermot Bolger (Dublin: New Island Books, 1992).

The Complete Poems, ed. Liam O'Meara (Newbridge, Ireland: Goldsmith Press, 1997).

O'Meara, Liam, *A Lantern on the Waves: Francis Ledwidge, Poet, Activist and Soldier* (Dublin: Riposte Books, 1999).

Phillips, Terry, *Irish Literature and the First World War* (Bern: Peter Lang, 2015).

9

DAVID WHEATLEY

Thomas MacGreevy

He is a quintessential minor writer: a World War I poet, but often over-looked by anthologists and critics of war poetry; a modernist, but eclipsed by his more famous friends – a Rosencrantz or Guildenstern to their Hamlet; a radical who found himself at odds with the politics of his times; the victim of a truncated career, leaving subsequent generations with a tantalising sense of what might have been; and a much-invoked name in debates over experimental poetry and its mainstream foes, with or without any reference to his actual work. He is T. E. Hulme, Thomas MacGreevy's senior by a decade. Both men served in the war: MacGreevy, who was wounded twice, at Ypres and the Somme, and Hulme in West Flanders, where he was killed by a shell in 1917. Hulme lingers in the background of the Anglo-American modernist family photograph, over-shadowed by the achievements of Eliot and Pound – achievements which would not have been possible without his innovating example. *Mutatis mutandis*, the same holds in Irish writing for the Tarbert-born MacGreevy (1893–1967), a writer who, unlike Hulme, cannot plead early death in extenuation of his neglect. A further commonality between Hulme and MacGreevy is their Francophilia. Though MacGreevy was thirteen years older than his friend Samuel Beckett, the pair overlapped as language assistants at the École Normale Supérieure in Paris, where MacGreevy introduced Beckett to James Joyce in 1928. MacGreevy's studies had been preceded by a spell in the civil service, before his enlisting with the Royal Field Artillery in 1917. His service in the British Army, despite strong nationalist sympathies, is one of many dissonant elements in MacGreevy's character and career. Writing of similar contradictions in another Irish World War I poet, Francis Ledwidge, Seamus Heaney proposes that 'all the strains' of the time, political and cultural, 'criss-cross in useless equilibrium' in his melancholy example.[1] MacGreevy's 'strains', I would like to suggest, are less melancholy than dynamic and transgressive, if not without an unhappy ending of their own.

By the time of his encounter with Beckett, MacGreevy had published his poetry in *The Criterion* and would shortly do so in other journals frequented by Beckett, including *The European Caravan, transition* and, on home ground, George Russell's *The Irish Statesman*. He had previously attracted the interest of Yeats, who called him 'the most promising of all our younger men'[2] and included two poems of his in the *Oxford Book of Modern Verse*. While in Paris he was recruited by Joyce to contribute to the festschrift *Our Exagmination Round His Factification for the Incamination of Work in Progress*; Joyce would later pay him the further compliment of rewriting some of 'Crón Tráth na nDéithe' in *Work in Progress*. Two short monographs by MacGreevy, on T. S. Eliot and Richard Aldington, were published by Chatto and Windus in their Dolphin Series in 1931, the same year as Beckett's study of Proust with the same publisher. *Poems*, MacGreevy's single collection of poetry, was published by Heinemann in 1934 and enthusiastically greeted by Beckett, who simultaneously (in 'Recent Irish Poetry') hailed him alongside Denis Devlin and Brian Coffey as part of 'without question the most interesting of the youngest generation of Irish writers'.[3] As Beckett assured the readers of the *Dublin Magazine*, MacGreevy was a poet of 'endopsychic clarity, uttering itself in the prayer that is a spasm of awareness' (*D* 69).

Beckett's name has now already occurred with some – perhaps excessive – frequency. It is courting heresy to suggest that MacGreevy has not entirely profited from his close connection to Beckett, but a quasi-serious argument can be mounted to this effect. MacGreevy kept all of Beckett's letters and Beckett kept none of his, and by the time Beckett has moved away from Dublin and MacGreevy is inclining homeward (he would re-settle permanently in Dublin in 1941), the temptation is strong to cast MacGreevy in the role of the modernist who refuses, the recidivist nationalist who swaps the excitements of 1920s Paris for the torpor of the Free State. This does less than complete justice to MacGreevy's case, but Beckett's letter of 31 January 1938 to his friend puts the charge succinctly, holding forth on his 'chronic inability [*viz.*, unlike MacGreevy] to understand as member of any proposition a phrase like "the Irish people", or to imagine that it ever gave a fart in its corduroys for any form of art whatsoever'.[4] With the banning of *More Pricks Than Kicks* fresh in Beckett's memory he was in unforgiving mood, but the idea of the irreconcilability of modernism and nationalism does not survive a comparison with the work of Máirtín Ó Cadhain in Ireland, Caradoc Evans in Wales, or Hugh MacDiarmid in Scotland. By the end of the '30s Beckett and MacGreevy found themselves on different trajectories, but luckily we are not required to generalise either choice into the one true path for Irish experimental writing.

MacGreevy the poet is, initially at least, MacGreevy the war poet. Irish criticism has grown accustomed to thinking of the modernist poem and the war poem as separate categories, not always with happy results. Praise for MacGreevy as a modernist has tended to be at the expense of attention to MacGreevy the war poet: 'Thomas MacGreevy fits into the 1930s Modernist tradition', as Fran Brearton notes in her *Irish Poetry and the Great War*.[5] An anthology of *Poems of Ireland Since 1916*, telling the national story from the Easter Rising to the present day, also finds no place for MacGreevy (or Beckett, poetic modernism remaining incompatible with received categories of the political poem).[6] In his study of Richard Aldington, MacGreevy stresses the solitude that is the soldier's lot, both in combat and its aftermath; soldiers and veterans are bound together by a 'solitude in companionship' that is 'part of the misfortune'.[7] One critic who has taken pains to relieve MacGreevy of his outsider status in the Irish canon, Gerald Dawe, stresses the painterly aspect of this detachment in 'De Civitate Hominum', one of two poems (along with 'Nocturne') awarded a section to themselves in *Poems* as products of the war. There is a distancing quality to MacGreevy's description of the sky above Belgium as 'a Matisse ensemble' but, as Dawe argues, there is a 'strange contradictory beauty' in the focus on the colour-palette of the skies, lakes and hills amid so much horror even without the reference to the Fauvist painter[8]. Shell-holes make 'Black spots in the whiteness', and 'whitened tree stumps / Are another white. // And there are white bones' (*CP* 2): the landscape already wears its resemblance to a charnel house as though a fact of nature. The aestheticisation of the battlefield is the response of a shell-shocked soldier, but also (on some level) a response to the taboo-ridden nature of a culture where Yeats can argue, notoriously, that 'we should not attribute a very high degree of reality to the Great War'.[9]

Soldiers in war graves are 'known unto God', but the God of 'De Civitate Hominum' is not much minded to share his thoughts with humanity. 'Holy God! / 'Tis a fearful death', a sergeant exclaims at the end of the poem, before the poet silently corrects him with 'Holy God makes no reply / Yet.'[10] Knowing and unknowing are conjoined, as memory and forgetting of the war would become, in Ireland. The heroes of Beckett's *Mercier and Camier* encounter a park-ranger described as a 'hero of the great war'[11] in the Irish National War Memorial Gardens in Islandbridge, adjoining the Liffey. Designed by Edward Lutyens, it was allowed to fall into disrepair by the Free State government, for whom Irish participation in the war had become a politically inconvenient memory. The Temple at its centre is inscribed with lines by Rupert Brooke – not an author calculated to reassure nationalists of the Irish dimension of a conflict in which up to fifty thousand Irishmen perished. 'De Civitate Hominum' might have made a more appropriate choice, but its politics are not more noticeably anti-imperial than anything by the jingo bard of 'The Soldier'. The speaker of Yeats's 'An Irish Airman Foresees His Death' disowns his cause ('Those that I fight I do not hate'), but MacGreevy the nationalist enters no such disclaimer. He speaks as a combatant in ways the civilian cannot hope to understand (the anacoluthon of these lines only adding to the difficulty):

> Those who live between wars may not know
> But we who die between peaces
> Whether we die or not. (CP 2)

Later British poets than Brooke have set the tone for public perceptions of World War I poetry, especially Wilfred Owen's declaration that 'the Poetry is in the pity'. There is much that is pitiful in MacGreevy's descriptions of war, but the rhetorical sequel in which the poet casts off artifice in favour of emotional appeals to the reader is not forthcoming; God's silence stands in for the poetry of direct (and powerful) appeal we find in Owen and Sassoon. 'Nocturne' places its soldier 'in a barren place, / Alone, self-conscious, frightened, blundering', but rather than offer his thoughts on the rights and wrongs of conflict the poem turns to the far-away stars and – with an impeccably punctilious inversion – 'About my feet, earth voices whispering' (CP 1). The contrast with British war poets should not be exaggerated (I have mentioned T. E. Hulme, after all, and David Jones too might be suggested as a kindred spirit), but whatever the voices of 'Nocturne' murmur to themselves, in protest or despair, it is not for us to know.

Among MacGreevy's highest achievements, and the closest Irish writing comes to a modernist long poem born of wars and peaces of the revolutionary period, is 'Crón Tráth na nDéithe'. The Irish-language title is best rendered as *Götterdämmerung*; the poem's affinities with Wagner extend to musical quotations from *Tannhäuser* and *Das Rheingold*. T. S. Eliot spoke of the 'mythical method' of Joyce's *Ulysses* as a way of accommodating the 'immense panorama of futility and anarchy which is contemporary history',[12] and MacGreevy assumes an Olympian perspective as he moves between the 'Wet lurching lamplight' of post-Civil War Dublin and the '*Seven hundred years*' ordeal since Ireland's '*last absolution*' (CP 15). The poem allows the reader to reconstruct an exact itinerary, from Mayo to Broadstone Station on Dublin's once grandiose north side, to Merrion Square, passing 'wrecks wetly mouldering under rain' on all sides (CP 15), or the 'squalid elements of Civil War' as Beckett called them (D 69). Circulating through Dublin and its imperial statuary brings MacGreevy out in a rash of Joycean onomatopoeia, with assistance from another laureate of the imperial city, Virgil: 'Ter-ot. Stumble. Clock-clock, clock-clock! / *Quadrupedante, etcetera*' (CP 14). Taken out of context,

MacGreevy's use of the '*seven hundred year*' shorthand for nationalist grievance would be a merely pugnacious gesture, but 'Crón Tráth na nDéithe' displays a sensitive intimacy with Ascendancy Dublin, and the Georgian grandeur of James Gandon's Customs House and Four Courts. MacGreevy's sympathies in the Civil War had been on the anti-Treaty side – a position he shared with Peadar O'Donnell, Sean O'Faolain and Francis Stuart, to name but three contemporaries. As the Free State embarked on the mundane business of statebuilding, MacGreevy embraces fragmentation as a truer reflection of the tragic dimension of the Irish present and past. The Civil War further inflects MacGreevy's Catholicism: the severity of the Free State crackdown on the Anti-Treaty side was matched by the Catholic Church, which refused the sacraments to the insurgents. MacGreevy's distress at this has led critics including David Lloyd and Nicholas Allen to read MacGreevy, in both faith and politics, as a rejectionist, keeping the faith with a purer vision of Republican values than embodied in the fledgling state.[13] Seeking a mythic framework for his alienation, MacGreevy again turns to Wagner. The similarity of MacGreevy's poem to the 'Sirens' chapter of *Ulysses* should encourage scepticism towards its use of music; in 'Sirens', Bloom resists the easy patriotism of a nationalist ballad. Wagner promises national renewal, though his visions of rebirth are tied up in darkly tribal myth. Wagner also features in *The Waste Land*, where the suppression of life has assumed the form of a curse, but one that is dramatically broken in the poem's final part. The fifth part of 'Crón Tráth na nDéithe' displays resistance, however, to moving from 'Blest, fabled unreality' into what Yeats might term the 'desolation of reality'. 'Oppression' (*CP* 22) is the continuing reality, unchecked by the ending of Civil War hostilities, while the possibility of release trickles away into incoherence ('How long? / How long? / How long since? / Long till? // Long // Trot // Tr . . . ', *CP* 24).

In Beckett's 'Recent Irish Poetry' it is axiomatic that recourse to Irish myth by the Revivalists signals a refusal to engage with the 'breakdown of the object' touted as a condition of the modernist artwork. His lauding of *The Waste Land* as an exemplary statement of modernity underlines that it is the Irish rather than the mythic aspect of this syndrome that most troubles Beckett. Yet if MacGreevy's poetry can be such a potent influence on Beckett's own ('Crón Tráth na nDéithe' has much in common with the cantankerous cityscapes of *Echo's Bones and Other Precipitates*), readers should feel licensed to take or leave its nationalist dimension as they see fit. Further, in rescuing MacGreevy from the limiting equation of Ireland with the smothering of his talent, it is worth noting how closely Ireland and Europe interact in his work, rather than standing lifelessly apart from each other. In 'Aodh Ruadh Ó Domhnaill' the exiled Red Hugh O'Donnell is woven into a vision of Golden Age Spain, while the grotesque visions of

'Homage to Hieronymous Bosch' form the medium for MacGreevy's protest against the execution of the young Republican Kevin Barry. Though subject to enfeeblement in the nineteenth century, the ballad tradition on which MacGreevy draws was heavily invested in support for the Irish cause arriving from France or Spain. In 'The Six Who Were Hanged', written on the eve of the execution of six Republic prisoners during the War of Independence, MacGreevy quotes James Clarence Mangan's 'Dark Rosaleen' (*'Tis you shall have the golden throne!*'), a writer whose patriotism had been praised by Yeats, if on the understanding that its fevered Young Ireland rhetoric was a thing of the past. Mangan's visions of aristocratic Catholic resistance to the English crown produced one of his most arresting poems in 'O'Hussey's Ode to the Maguire'; Aodh Mag Uidhir, otherwise known as Hugh Maguire, fell in battle in 1600, and his brother was a party to the Flight of the Earls to Genoa in 1607, as prefigured by Hugh O'Donnell's escape to Spain. Despite its melancholy subject, the combination of political disaffection, exile, and cultural encounter prove irresistible to the MacGreevy of 'Aodh Ruadh Ó Domhnaill'.

I have noted the importance of music in 'Crón Tráth na nDéithe', but painting is also central to MacGreevy's art, as befits a curator of the National Gallery in Dublin. When MacGreevy titles a short lyric 'Giorgionismo' or 'Giaconda', a knowledge of art history significantly enhances the reader's experience. In its seven short lines, 'Giorgionismo' resembles a caption to an absent canvas, and in the crepuscular, solitary state it explores the poem tallies all too well with the existential inwardness proposed by Beckett as MacGreevy's stock-in-trade. 'Giorgionismo' fails to exfoliate its vision sufficiently to admit of any illumination, nor does its darkness glow with sufficient memorability to compensate. 'Giaconda' is better developed, assembling a landscape before over-determining it into incompatibility with human concerns ('The sun did not rise or set / Not being interested in the activities of politicians', *CP* 50). The key word comes in the last line, where 'white manes' of water and 'bluish snakes' slide 'Into the dissolution of a smile'. 'Dissolution' places MacGreevy in accord with Beckett's letter to him of 8 September 1934 on Cézanne's anti-anthropomorphic or non-relational art. Paradoxically, its 'dissolution' is the first reference in the poem to the smile, connecting us at the death with the title 'Gioconda' and providing a human referent that has been missing up to this point.

My opening comparison of MacGreevy to Hulme extends to one further aspect not much remarked by his critics: gender. When Hulme's acolyte, Ezra Pound, defected from Imagism, he couched his disaffection in terms of a desire to return poetry to a state of manly vigour. Hulme before him had theorised his critique of Romanticism in strongly masculine terms, having grown suspicious of the vague and watery female lyric. MacGreevy's poems honour the imagist creed in the conscientious parsimony of their verbal economy, but engage generously and consistently with female presences. These are not limited to the nationalist gendering of Ireland as a woman, but capture the shadows of ideological phantoms such as Cathleen Ni Houlihan falling across real lives. In 'The Other Dublin' MacGreevy paints a *soirée* with an Anglo-Irishwoman unmoved by the national ferment. While his political poems are capable of unguarded anger (cf. 'Homage to Vercingetorix'), here MacGreevy needs only the 'delicious little coffee-cups of soup' (*CP* 27) to communicate the latent violence of Ascendancy values (a Crippenesque fellow guest 'made one think he murdered women in his dreams'). In 'The Six Who Were Hanged' the poet attends a protest outside Mountjoy Prison ahead of the titular execution, but notices 'There are very few men. / Why am I here?' (*CP* 8). MacGreevy disputes the identification of mourning with woman's work, and the cult of the lachrymose Madonna that would fire the anti-Free State satire of Louis MacNeice's 'Valediction'. In 'Homage to Hieronymus Bosch' it is a ghoulish male presence who preys on the living woman, inverting the familiar necrophilia of Mother Ireland goading her male servitors.

'Crón Tráth na nDéithe' describes the prostitution of Molly Malone to British soldiers, but in 'Homage to Jack Yeats' women too are allowed their (unflattering) part in the pageantry of war ('The brave stupidity of soldiers, / The proud stupidity of soldiers' wives', *CP* 28). 'Ten Thousand Leaping Swords' is a high-flown love-lyric, ending on a note of chaste non-consummation; 'Dechtire' fuses the Catholic and the Celtic in another Romantic agony of incompletion; and 'Arrangement in Gray and Black' delicately imagines a frustrated woman clinging to 'A hope / Of unfailing life / In unfailing love' (*CP* 53). 'Moments Musicaux', one of the late poems, repeats the phrase 'You thought she had left you alone', referencing the ebbing of inspiration MacGreevy had suffered in recent decades, but is suggestive of unfinished business in spiritual and temporal realms: MacGreevy ties 'her' departure to that of a god who has gone 'Through the flames that leaped and sang' – a possible allusion to Ernie O'Malley's memoir of his Civil War service, *The Singing Flame*. For Austin Clarke, living through the same repressive years of Archbishop McQuaid's Ireland, representations of the feminine are channelled largely through the disjunction between the Catholic Madonna–whore complex and the poet's struggling sexuality, but this is one arena of conflict we seek out in vain in MacGreevy (his sexuality remains a matter of conjecture). A MacGreevy satire on sexual politics and the role of the church in shaping government policy would be as engrossing to read as it is difficult to imagine. Poems such as Beckett's blasphemous

'Ooftish', with its denunciation of the sadist-creator and its dwelling on sins of the flesh, must have distressed him greatly. MacGreevy's working relationship with the church is also a factor here. Convention places Free State intellectuals in the anti-clerical camp, or at least in the pages of Sean O'Faolain's *The Bell*, but in 1943 MacGreevy joined the staff of the *Capuchin Annual*. His commitment to a Catholic intelligentsia places MacGreevy in the company of Fr Alfred O'Rahilly, brother of the revolutionary, and Monsignor Pádraig de Brún, poet and translator: overlooked but hardly negligible figures in Irish intellectual history. All special pleading aside, however, the *Capuchin Annual* falls short of Eliot's *Criterion* as a platform for Christian modernist debate; the chances of MacGreevy's launching himself as an Irish François Mauriac or Paul Claudel were sadly minimal.

Matters of postcolonial politics loom large in discussions of MacGreevy, but it is often the simplest things in his poems that evince his most enduring worth. Two of his finest poems – 'Gloria de Carlos V' and 'Nocturne of the Self-Evident Presence' – exemplify his skill with the shortest of lines, as though MacGreevy had discovered Projectivist poetry *avant la lettre*, and its creed of one perception leading directly to the next. 'Gloria de Carlos V' is a poem of return from the war and confrontation with the anti-climax of all that follows that cataclysm ('When we come back from first death / To our second life here', *CP* 36). Revisiting the nightmare ground of conflict, he registers a contamination of memory ('My rose of Tralee turned gray in its life, / A tombstone gray') but breaks free for a moment of 'equable radiance', as Beckett called it, praising this poem (*D* 68):

> But a moment now, I suppose,
> For a moment I may suppose,
> Gleaming blue,
> Silver blue,
> Gold,
> Rose,
> And the light of the world.   (*CP* 36)

The insistence on 'And' before the poem's last words locates the preceding illuminations on a higher than earthly plane. Though I began by hinting at some of the differences between Beckett and MacGreevy, smoothed over too often in the rush to bracket the pair as 1930s modernists, the otherworldly visions and daring enjambments of 'Gloria de Carlos V' could scarcely belong to another Irish poet of that decade, if not the author of *Echo's Bones*.

There remains the question of MacGreevy's creative silence. 'Oh well, I suppose it's not the place's fault', concedes the speaker of Philip Larkin's 'I Remember, I Remember', after cataloguing the shortcomings of his home, through which he is passing on a train.[14] For many readers of MacGreevy the temptation is to assume that it *was* the place's fault when his inspiration ran dry: modernist maverick poet into independent Ireland would not go. *Collected Poems* records only four poems after his 1934 volume, though three of them, 'Homage to Vercingetorix', 'Moments Musicaux' and 'Breton Oracles', are considerably developed (by MacGreevy's standards of brevity), and in the first two cases at least do not read as the poems of a writer struggling with a creative block. The state of ex-poet – as experienced by Rimbaud, John Crowe Ransom, Laura Riding and Kenneth Slessor, to name but four writers – is not so unusual that disappointed readers need rush to blame post-independence Ireland. A significant factor is his falling out of print, with all the consequences this entails for younger poets who might otherwise have responded sympathetically to his work. The 1950s are not among the most dynamic periods in Irish poetry, and when the '60s generation of Northern Irish poets achieved recognition, MacGreevy's was not a line to which they felt any allegiance. In interview with Dennis O'Driscoll, Seamus Heaney dismisses the 'fantasy of a "tradition" of Irish "modernist"', 'foisted on us' by Beckett's 'Recent Irish Poetry', writing off the work it produced as 'generally of period interest'.[15] Most receptive of the Ulster poets is Derek Mahon, who has praised MacGreevy generously, rating his and Denis Devlin's work 'higher than any "Movement" poet',[16] but in his own lyric practice Mahon is reluctant to exchange the rhyming, metrical lyric for the more free-form pleasures espoused by MacGreevy. The audacious short lines of 'Gloria de Carlos V' find their closest counterpart in the work of Maurice Scully and Trevor Joyce, Joyce having been an important agent in the revival of MacGreevy's fortunes through his work on the journal *Lace Curtain* (1969–78).

The collage effects and European allusions deployed throughout MacGreevy's work ensure a high degree of continuity between his poems and his translations, a side of the *oeuvre* that remains neglected. As with Beckett's translations of the 1930s, there are whole stanzas one can imagine having strayed onto the page from the author's own work; both men are in some sense writing towards, as well as out of, their foreign models, reworking their English as they did so. When Don Paterson translates Antonio Machado, the candour of the Spanish's poet vocabulary makes for a tonal contrast with streetwise contemporary poetic diction, but the moons, souls, shadows and heavens of MacGreevy's Spanish poets are reproduced without embarrassment or awkward regressions to a Celtic Twilight style. The ability to combine simplicity and sensuousness with a *superficies* of foreignness and other art forms was always among MacGreevy's principal strengths. A fine example of this, and among MacGreevy's best poems, is 'Homage to Marcel Proust'. On one level, the lyric presents an uncomplicated family memory, conjuring the poet's mother in a landscape where 'the sea gleamed deep blue in the sunlight' (*CP* 39). An allusion to Thomas Moore ('*Those endearing young charms*'), that laureate of the Irish Victorian drawing-room, adds a sepia tinge to proceedings, while recalling satirical jibes at the same writer in both Joyce and Beckett. A family walk leads to an 'island . . . dreaming in the sun across the bridge', and a Syngean vision of a young islander visiting the mainland ('tall / And slim / And curled, to the moustaches'). We are now recognisably in the territory of Yeats's 'The Fisherman', but resorting to a musical reference again MacGreevy chooses this moment to quote Byron's 'Maid of Athens, Ere We Part'. Byron's feat of swimming the Hellespont, commemorating Leander's watery visits to Hero, was an important part of his public myth. There is nothing in MacGreevy's narrative to suggest doom is in the air until the final five lines:

> The young sailor is dead now.
> Miss Holly also is dead.
> And Byron . . .
> Home they've gone and . . .
> And the waves still are singing. (*CP* 40)

In Ovid's myth Leander tragically drowns, and the currents of time have now borne away all MacGreevy's *dramatis personae*. The ideal republic has miscarried and the poet has turned to self-consoling elegy. J. C. C. Mays has argued that Beckett's stress on his friend's introspection 'led him to understand MacGreevy as a more self-absorbed writer than he is',[17] but if 'Homage to Marcel Proust' adumbrates defeat, it does not reflect any lessening of the poet's commitment to his lost vision or mere self-delusion in his revisiting of the past. Something else remains. In the closing section of another late poem, 'Breton Oracles', the poet acknowledges defeat and 'mournful solitude', before becoming aware of a second presence sharing his darkness and, as time passes, the daybreak too. Amid visionary flashes reminiscent of 'Gloria de Carlos V' ('The dark green, touched with gold', *CP* 70), this presence petrifies into a classical statue. MacGreevy's art becomes its own monument, the shrine to a lost classical order, unresigned to the filthy modern tide, stony and exemplary:

> And crouching at the foot of a renaissance wall
> A little cupid, in whitening stone,
> Weeping over a lost poetry.

NOTES

1. Seamus Heaney, 'In Memoriam Francis Ledwidge', in *Field Work* (London: Faber and Faber, 1979), p. 60.
2. Yeats to Harriet Monroe, 30 December 1928, quoted in Susan Schreibman (ed.), *Collected Poems of Thomas MacGreevy* (Dublin: Anna Livia Press, 1991), xxxiii; hereafter cited in-text as *CP*.
3. Samuel Beckett (as Andrew Belis), 'Recent Irish Poetry', *The Bookman* August 1934; reprinted in *Disjecta*, pp. 70–6 (76); hereafter cited in-text as *D*.
4. Samuel Beckett to MacGreevy, 31 January 1938, in Martha Dow Fehsenfeld and Lois More Overbeck (eds.), *The Letters of Samuel Beckett 1929–1940* (Cambridge: Cambridge University Press, 2009), p. 599.
5. Fran Brearton, *Irish Poetry and the Great War* (Oxford: Oxford University Press, 2000), p. 40.
6. Niall MacMonagle, *Windharp: Poems of Ireland Since 1916* (Dublin: Penguin Ireland).
7. Quoted in Gerald Dawe, *Of War and War's Alarms: Reflections on Modern Irish Writing* (Cork: Cork University Press, 2015), p. 27.
8. Dawe, *Of War and War's Alarms*, p. 30.
9. George Mills Harper and Margaret Mills Harper, assisted by Richard W. Stoops, Jr (eds.), *Yeats's Vision Papers IV* (Basingstoke: Palgrave, 2001), p. 18.
10. The poem prefigures the ending of Beckett's 'Dante and the Lobster', which also touches on the mysteries of sudden death. Nor is this the only textual anticipation of Beckett in MacGreevy's poems: 'Fragments', dating from January 1931, uses as its epigraph the punning line from Dante's *Inferno* XX ('*Qui vive la pietà quando è ben morta*') which causes Belacqua such amusement, also in 'Dante and the Lobster'. Adding to the tally, Gerald Dawe finds 'the slightest hint' of MacGreevy's 'Nocturne' in Beckett's 'Gnome' ('Nocturne: Thomas MacGreevy and World War One', in Susan Schreibman (ed.), *The Life and Work of Thomas MacGreevy: A Critical Reappraisal* (London: Bloomsbury, 2013), pp. 3–16 (15).
11. Samuel Beckett, *Mercier and Camier* (ed. Seán Kennedy, London: Faber and Faber, 2010), p. 10.
12. T. S. Eliot, '*Ulysses*, Order, and Myth', *The Dial* 75 (1923), p. 483.
13. Cf. David Lloyd, 'Republics of Difference: Yeats, MacGreevy, Beckett', *Field Day Review* (2005), pp. 42–66, and Nicholas Allen, *Modernism, Ireland and Civil War* (Cambridge: Cambridge University Press, 2009).
14. Philip Larkin, *The Complete Poems* (ed. Archie Burnett, London: Faber and Faber, 2012), p. 42.
15. Dennis O'Driscoll, *Stepping Stones: Interview with Seamus Heaney* (London: Faber and Faber, 2008), p. 239.
16. Derek Mahon, letter to *The Irish Times*, 10 July 1982.
17. J. C. C. Mays, 'How is MacGreevy a Modernist?', in Patricia Couglan and Alex Davis (eds.), *Modernism and Ireland: The Poetry of the 1930s* (Cork: Cork University Press, 1995), pp. 103–128 (p. 115).

SELECTED FURTHER READING

Edition

Collected Poems of Thomas MacGreevy, ed. Susan Schreibman (Dublin: Anna Livia Press, 1991).

Critical Work

Beckett, Samuel, *Disjecta: Miscellaneous Writings and a Dramatic Fragment*, ed. Ruby Cohn (London: John Calder, 1983).

Cronin, Anthony 'Modernism not Triumphant', in *Heritage Now Irish Literature in the English Language* (Dingle: Brandon: 1982), pp. 155–60.

Schreibman, Susan, *The Life and Work of Thomas MacGreevy: A Critical Reappraisal* (London: Bloomsbury, 2013).

Smith, Stan, 'From a Great Distance: Thomas MacGreevy's Frames of Reference', *The Lace Curtain* 6 (Autumn 1978), pp. 47–55.

10

LUCY COLLINS

Austin Clarke

One of the most important Irish poets since W. B. Yeats, Austin Clarke remains a critically neglected figure. He has often been characterised as an insular poet whose commitment to the re-working of Gaelic verse forms increased the obscurity of both his poetic style and his subject matter. Yet his originality can also be seen as productively challenging, both for readers of his own time and of ours. Clarke's career is exemplary of the tensions in modern Ireland between tradition and innovation, between community and individualism. From his work we can learn much about the conditions of writing and publishing poetry in modern Ireland and observe the aesthetic and political tensions that helped to shape the literature of the mid-century years.

Clarke's first book, *The Vengeance of Fionn*, was published in 1917 and this, like most of the work he would produce in the first half of his career, showed the influence of Revivalist aesthetics. A transition from mythic to historical material can be traced in his work from the later 1920s, indicating Clarke's preoccupation with Ireland's medieval past as a period that linked religious devotion with aesthetic achievement. Though at first Clarke's poetry drew praise from critics, he found it increasingly hard to place his work with publishers: Allen and Unwin brought out his *Collected Poems* in 1936, but two years later he published *Night and Morning* with a small Dublin publisher, Orwell Press. After this, Clarke published no more poems for seventeen years; yet the range of his literary output during this period remained considerable, as dramatist, as critic and as literary journalist in Dublin and London. The 1950s marked Clarke's return to poetry and his transformation into a potent satirist of modern Ireland, publishing work of great formal variety and moral force first under his own imprint, the Bridge Press, and later with Dolmen Press. Peter Denman sees the gap in Clarke's poetic history as a challenge to achieving a 'unified perception of . . . his place in Irish poetry',[1] but the aesthetic variety of his work suggests that it is Clarke's evolution as a writer that is most significant in any such assessment.

The difficulties attending his creative process are evident in his comment 'I load myself with chains and try to get out of them'.[2] In this respect Clarke is exemplary of a period of Irish literary history where poets were especially challenged by their social and economic conditions. The mid-century years were marked by depression and censorship; Ireland's cultural isolation meant that writers had to be especially resilient, even controversial, in order to produce work of lasting merit. Clarke's writing life must be understood in the context of these conditions. This essay will re-evaluate Clarke's achievement by exploring the thematic and formal risks that shaped his career and what these tell us about his significant position in modern Irish literary life.

Clarke's earliest poetry demonstrates the importance of national identity as a shaping force on twentieth-century Irish poetry. In keeping with Revivalist aesthetics, mythological and folk materials exerted a strong influence on the young poet. His early engagement with Irish language materials set him apart from many precursors, including W. B. Yeats, who could neither read nor speak the language. It also prompted Clarke to think about the implications of the dual language tradition for the style and technique of poetry in English, an issue that would shape his formal innovations in later years. Clarke acknowledged the significant role of the Revival in encouraging new writers, and was aware that the political and social energies of the time were an important stimulus for creative innovation.[3] As a young poet he worked hard to perfect his use of the epic, unearthing tensions and controversies in his chosen materials, juxtaposing long and short poetic forms and re-interpreting key mythological figures. Yet he adopted these Revivalist modes at the very moment when their power and popularity was beginning to wane. From the beginning, then, Clarke's career is untimely, his originality leaving him out of step with the latest artistic developments.

Clarke's first major publication came just a year after the execution of the poet and revolutionary, Thomas MacDonagh, who had taught the young poet at University College Dublin. The extent to which the events of Easter Week would herald a period of upheaval is acknowledged in Clarke's memoir, *A Penny in the Clouds*. Clarke's early epics, published between 1917 and 1925, also obliquely chart the personal and political struggles of the revolutionary period and suggest the fusion of private and public turmoil that affected Clarke's personal life at the time. Indeed, Clarke's prolonged engagement with Revivalist aesthetics may be due in part to his reluctance to engage with the realities of Ireland's difficult birth as a nation state, as well as with his own traumatic experiences. While his early work on epic facilitated his engagement with shorter forms by the mid-1920s, Clarke struggled to bring coherence to the long narrative. One early reviewer of *The*

Vengeance of Fionn noted the absence of 'firm lines of construction that mark a deep imaginative grasp', indicating the close links between intellectual engagement and aesthetic achievement.[4] Some of the formal shortcomings observed by critics were also related to the subject matter of the Irish epics: themes of prolonged enmity and of intergenerational violence reflect the intensity of this historical moment – its symbolic power as well as its real effects. It could be argued, too, that Clarke's breaching of formal expectations indicates his awareness of the tension between Revivalist aesthetics and the need to express the breakdown of political and social order.

During his first decade as a published poet, Clarke's aesthetic remained unsettled. His mastery of the contained simplicity of traditional forms in poems such as 'Praise' and 'If There Was Nothing Noble' is balanced by the restlessness of the itinerary poems. Alan Gillis has attributed the dissociated quality of 'The Itinerary of Ua Chleirigh' to Clarke's alienation after the foundation of the state – he supported the republican side during the civil war.[5] However, these poems reflect a more fundamental destabilisation of the relationship between thought and action, between the inner life and the physical, sensuous world. This psychic disturbance had its roots in the uncertainties in Clarke's creative and personal life. After a failed marriage to Lia Cummins, and the loss of his lecturing job at University College Dublin, Clarke left Ireland in 1921 to work in London as a reviewer. This decision offered him the opportunity to participate in an international literary culture, but the experience was isolating – he returned to Dublin often to visit family and friends, including F. R. Higgins and Seamus O'Sullivan, and to attend performances at the Abbey Theatre. Yet he remained an outsider in Ireland too. Hostile both to modernism and to literary realism, Clarke needed to create an alternative aesthetic for his own particular expressive needs, and this convoluted process would contribute significantly to his neglect by readers and critics, both during his lifetime and later.

Clarke's publication history gives some indication of the challenges he faced in finding a readership for his challenging and idiosyncratic work. His early work readily found a publisher; Maunsel Press, a Dublin-based firm, published many late Revivalist writers. When the press began to experience serious financial difficulties, Clarke sought publication in London and moved to Allen and Unwin for his third foray into Irish epic, *The Cattledrive in Connaught and Other Poems* (1925). Stanley Unwin published Clarke's prose and poetry until he returned to Dublin in 1937, though the readership – in both England and Ireland – remained small. The relationship between publisher and poet was at times fractious, but Unwin's support was essential to Clarke's continuing visibility as a writer, and to his capacity to attract readers internationally. The arrangement also reinforced his position as a writer between cultures – as an outsider to the Irish Free State, as well as to the competitive world of London literary journalism. Yet it was Clarke's detached position that would enable his relentless critique of Irish political and cultural life in the decades that followed.

For most of the 1920s Clarke continued to concentrate on mythological material; rhythm and rhyme became the chief focus of his innovation. His practice of rendering Irish sound patterns in the English language was unique, but it owed something to Thomas MacDonagh's concept of the 'Irish mode'. In MacDonagh's view, the musicality of language should not be bound by fixed rhythms, but used instead to facilitate the meaning of words. Clarke was attracted to the subtle sounds of Gaelic verse and relished the study of this tradition: 'It was pleasant,' he wrote, 'to escape from the mighty law and order of English poetry into that shadowy, irresponsible world of delicate rhythm and nuance.'[6] 'Secrecy', from *The Cattledrive in Connaught*, encapsulates the best of Clarke's intricate, even convoluted, approach to language at this time. It also signals his interest in the aesthetics of early Christian Ireland, which would be a key theme of the next phase of his poetic career. The concept of secrecy itself was a continuing preoccupation of Clarke's too, reflecting the lack of openness that would be the hallmark of the Free State, but also the poet's own particular difficulties in integrating private matter into the public narrative of art. This eight-line poem comprises one sentence only: its syntactical elaboration evidence of Clarke's attempts to forge unity in diversity.

> Had we been only lovers from a book
> That holy men who had a hand in heaven
> Illuminated: in a yellow wood,
> Where crimson beast and bird are clawed with gold
> And, wound in branches, hunt or hawk themselves,
> Sun-woman, I would hide you as the ring
> Of his own shining fetters that the snake,
> Who is the wood itself, can never find. (*Collected Poems* 113)

'Secrecy' explores the relationship between nature and artifice, demonstrating how art at once conceals and reveals aspects of the human condition. The first effect of the poem is to obscure the realities of human love, displacing the flesh-and-blood lovers into their fictional counterparts. The immediacy of sexual experience is thus overwritten by 'holy men', and concealed within an artwork that is both beautiful and allegorical. Yet in spite of the outward splendour of the representation, the beasts and birds are the agents of their own capture and destruction. Concealment within this text is both subversive and self-defeating, just as Clarke's own acts of creative rebellion are impediments to his reputation as a writer.

Clarke's concern with the relationship between religion and sexual free-dom would intensify in the years that followed. *Pilgrimage and Other Poems*, published in 1929, marked his growing interest in the artistic and intellectual legacies of the monastic movement in medieval Ireland, which, in his view, marked Ireland's highest aesthetic achievement within a European intellectual and religious culture. The title poem draws formally on the style of Clarke's shorter poems, such as 'The House in the West' or the beautifully modulated 'The Lost Heifer'. The devotional context of this new phase of Clarke's work is integrated closely with the Irish landscape:

> Grey holdings of rain
> Had grown less with the fields,
> As we came to that blessed place
> Where hail and honey meet.
> O Clonmacnoise was crossed
> With light: (*Collected Poems* 151)

This landscape is different to the mythic terrain of the early poems. Instead of panoramic views, crowded with detail, nature is rendered in simplified terms, showing the extent to which the human subjects and their environment are mutually involved. Two long poems, 'The Confessions of Queen Gormlai' and 'The Young Woman of Beare' examine the representation of women within the context of this dichotomy. These texts renew Clarke's interest in the long form but use the life of the individual woman as a way of focusing the tensions between freedom and containment, and between individual and community.

Night and Morning (1938) intensified Clarke's engagement with sexual guilt as a theme. Many of the poems in this collection were written at the time of his decision to return to Ireland and reflect the renewed imaginative significance of memory and return to the feelings of entrapment that were generated in the early years of the Free State. The title poem expresses the increasingly contorted nature of Clarke's religious doubt: 'Thought can but share / Belief – and the tormented soul, / Changing confession to despair, / Must wear a borrowed robe' (*Collected Poems* 181). It is significant that even after more than a decade in England, Clarke is still concerned with the scruples of Catholic observance, in particular with its long tradition of necessary atonement. The four lines of 'Penal Law' rehearse the subversive duality of language when faced with such restrictions:

> Burn Ovid with the rest. Lovers will find
> A hedge-school for themselves and learn by heart
> All that the clergy banish from the mind,
> When hands are joined and head bows in the dark.
>
>   (*Collected Poems* 189)

Here the brevity of the verse works in Clarke's favour, compelling him to a powerful economy of expression that characterises his best work. As Denis Donoghue has remarked, Clarke 'loves to find one sound releasing two words',[7] and the capacity for an apparently contained space to invoke a wider world of possibility is at the centre of Clarke's poetic achievement. In 'Penal Law' irony links the repressive character of Catholic doctrine with that of the British government during penal times. Ovid's banishment from Rome has a hinted counterpart in Clarke's exile in England and the censorship of his prose works from this period. Clerical attempts to restrict the mind prompt a physical outlet for expression in a new religion of intimacy and love, however. Here the very forms that repressive clergy use to maintain purity may be subverted by wayward lovers.

The striking containment of this poem foreshadows the important relationship between wit and formal simplicity in the later satires. In 'Penal Law' Clarke demonstrates the productive tension between regularity of form and subversive language. Similarly, 'The Straying Student' employs subtle variations of rhythm and rhyme to affirm the need to transmute temporary escapism into lasting freedom from oppression. The poem is a rewriting of the aisling form, in which a beautiful woman appears to the poet requesting his help in restoring Ireland to her rightful leaders. In 'The Straying Student' the woman's appearance seems to suggest a liberation that is at once sexual and intellectual – for Clarke freedoms of body and mind are closely linked:

> On a holy day when sails were blowing southward,
> A bishop sang the Mass in Inishmore,
> Men took one side, their wives were on the other
> But I heard the woman coming from the shore;
> And wild in despair my parents cried aloud
> For they saw the vision draw me to the doorway.
>
> (*Collected Poems* 188)

Here the binary opposites of land and sea, clergy and laity, are matched by a fundamental separation of male and female. The vision woman crosses these boundaries by drawing the student across the threshold, yet the form of the poem barely registers this momentous change. The six-line stanzas preserve full or half-rhymes, their broad vowels anchoring the poem and framing its sensuous crosscurrents of 's' and 'w' sounds. The woman's transgressive potential traverses space and time, offering an experiential understanding that far surpasses traditional forms of learning. In blessing 'the noonday rock that knew no tree' the student rejects the ideas of suffering and atonement that follow from the crucifixion, embracing instead the immediacy of the body; his failure in logic is further indication of his removal from a cerebral to a sensuous context.

The power of clerical restriction never leaves the student, however. He does, after all, only temporarily stray from the influence of the Church, and his fear of abandonment suggests the extent to which he has internalised fixed moral positions. Alan Gillis judges the poems of *Night and Morning* to be 'locked and bound' by the schism between reason and faith,[8] but this is a contest which must be undergone in order that Clarke may move on to the more distanced perspective of the later poems. The vision of containment in this collection is more powerfully articulated than the freedoms that precede it, and this becomes the hallmark of Clarke's interrogation of clerical power later in his career. At this stage, though, his investigation of guilt and anxiety remains displaced from present to past, through his use of memory and history as key nodes of moral investigation.

After *Night and Morning*, Clarke published no further poetry collections for seventeen years. This silence, coinciding as it did with Yeats's death, reinforced the impression of the 1940s as a barren decade for Irish poetry. Clarke was active in other ways, though. His return to Dublin was marked by an increasing interest in drama, and in 1944 he co-founded the Lyric Theatre Company with Robert Farren. He published seven plays between 1939 and 1953; all but one of these appeared in London with Williams and Norgate, and in Dublin under Clarke's own imprint, the Bridge Press. When he returned to poetry in 1955, he again used the Bridge Press as his means of publication, in the absence of another publisher. Clarke was critical at this time of what he perceived as a lack of commitment by British readers and publishers to Irish poetry, even as he promoted the notion of an Irish aesthetic.[9] He was disparaging too about the declining literary interest in Ireland, where he saw poetry as 'neglected and despised'.[10] *Ancient Lights: Poems and Satires* (1955) gives poetic form to his critique of contemporary Ireland. In these new poems Clarke uses formal containment to powerful effect, sublimating the confused and emotional language of some of his earliest work into a clearer and more concise form. The linguistic play of Clarke's middle period is still in evidence here, but a number of key elements of his satirical verse are established early, including the removal of definite and indefinite articles, and the coining of verbs from nouns. This syntactical risk-taking gave Clarke a new purpose and confidence as well as a productive channel for his feelings of repression. This work combines sharp social criticism with empathy for the victims, allowing the poet to obliquely link this material to his own experiences.

Clarke's anatomisation of the lives of the most vulnerable in Irish society is especially prominent at this stage in his career, and he is alert to the systemic failure of institutions to protect the marginalised. In *Ancient Lights* a particular concern for the fate of children can be traced. 'Three Poems about Children', a triptych on this theme, exposes the bitter consequences of theological rigidity. It starts by praising the practical faith of the penal era – which at least had the virtue of honesty – over the glib apportioning of eternal life with which modern religion is obsessed:

> Though offerings increase, increase,
> The ancient arms can bring no peace,
> When the first breath is unforgiven
> And charity, to find a home,
> Redeems the baby from the breast.
> O, then, at the very font of grace,
> Pity, pity – the dumb must cry.
> Their tiny tears are in the walls
> We build. (*Collected Poems* 196)

The separation of mother and child in the name of charity both removes the child from the love of the parent and consigns the mother to feelings of guilt and shame. Balanced repetition of the words 'increase' and 'pity' calls attention to the need to resist domination, demanding that the avarice of the Church be equalled by our compassion for its victims. The poem also sets the freedom of a 'roofless faith' against the containing walls of Church institutions that separate the vulnerable from love and support. Some of the impact of this revelation is lost in the obscure closing lines, but its anticlimactic nature is fitting – these ideals, like the incarcerated children, 'turn to dust so soon'. The speed with which these children die, and their memory is lost, is taken up in the second poem in the concept of limbo, which holds that unbaptised babies cannot go to heaven. The brevity of this text is deliberate: like the infants' death the text is 'too quick' to provide consolation or understanding.

These two poems are important precursors to the third, which takes as its subject matter a specific contemporary event – the destruction by fire of an orphanage in Co. Cavan, which resulted in the death of thirty-five children. The subsequent enquiry found that lack of leadership and inadequate rescue services were responsible for the loss of life, and did not attach any blame to the nuns who ran the orphanage. Clarke's satire is directed at the Bishop of Kilmore who, at the funeral of the children, suggested that death had preserved them from sin: 'Dear little angels, now before God in Heaven, they were taken away before the gold of their innocence had been tarnished by the soil of the world.'[11] The capacity of the bishop to turn a tragedy of negligence into a thing of advantage for the children outraged Clarke, not only in its complacency but also in its denial of life itself.

Has not a Bishop declared
That flame-wrapped babes are spared
Our life-time of temptation?
Leap, mind, in consolation
For heart can only lodge
Itself, plucked out by logic.
Those children, charred in Cavan,
Passed straight through Hell to Heaven.

(*Collected Poems* 197)

The Church's punitive attitude towards children born outside marriage is a particular target for Clarke in this collection, and political circumstances offered opportunities for him to address the collusion of Church and State in this matter. One of his most biting satires, 'Mother and Child', addressed the controversial failure of Dr Noel Browne's proposed Mother and Child Scheme. The scheme provoked the displeasure of the bishops on several grounds. They argued that it gave the State the right to interfere in the private morality of the people; in particular, they feared that the proposed 'gynae-cological care' would mean advice on birth control or abortion. They also objected to the fact that the bill failed to differentiate between legitimate and illegitimate children.

Clarke uses the commemoration of the Marian Year in 1954 to highlight the irony of this discrimination. This poem, of fifteen short lines, reveals the instability of the contested power relations of politicians and clergy, and dwells on its fundamental injustice. Half-rhymes show the slippage between intention and result – the prominent pairing of 'mended' and 'amended' suggesting the ease with which political ideals are diverted by the clerical agenda. The value of pity, which Clarke views as a necessary empathy, is first distorted by rhetoric, then directly negated by the votes of politicians. Language and action are shown to be interdependent, a circumstance that legitimises the satirical turn in Clarke's work and its indirect claims for a public poetry.

Clarke's *Later Poems*, published by Dolmen Press in 1961, played an important role in re-establishing the poet both in Ireland and abroad. The volume gathered work from 1929 onwards, thus bridging the long silence in Clarke's poetic career and highlighting his change in aesthetic direction.[12] It forms an interesting counterpart to the *Collected Poems* of 1936, which prematurely characterised Clarke as an inheritor of the Irish Revival, a poet of Celtic styles and subject matter. *Later Poems* consolidated Clarke's relationship with Dolmen Press and suggested his role as precursor to the new generation of poets emerging from Dolmen at this time.[13] It also attracted the attention of readers outside Ireland: English critic Charles

Tomlinson described its publication as 'the literary event of 1961'.[14] The poems of *Flight to Africa*, published two years later, represent a direct development of the satiric strand in Clarke's work, but one tempered by a new diversity. The collection followed a period of travel undertaken by Clarke, which released him from Ireland's political and moral confinement, and resulted in a broadening of vision and a resurgence of poetic energy. This is vividly expressed in 'Mount Parnassus', the volume's opening poem, which concludes: 'I stray from American, German, tourists, / Greek guide, feel in my two wrists / Answer for which I have come, / The Oracle, not yet dumb' (*Collected Poems* 251). Many of the poems in this volume were written in a ten week period in which Clarke reports experiencing 'a continual, voluptuous state of mind'.[15] His distrust of the ease with which the poems came reveals how accustomed he has become to the laborious process of crafting, which was only now beginning to recede.

In spite of these new freedoms, this volume is also in dialogue with Clarke's earlier work, indicating both the extent of his development as a poet and his willingness to engage once more with familiar themes and characters. 'Martha Blake at Fifty-One' is a counterpart to the earlier 'Martha Blake' from *Night and Morning*, revisiting the pious woman of the earlier poem to reveal the folly of the search for certainty in religion. Both poems draw attention to the role of the sacraments in defining Martha's relationship with belief, and, while the bond is a continuous one, the joy that Martha obtains is substantially diminished: 'To her pure thought, / Body was a distress / And soul, a sigh. Behind her denture, / Love lay, a helplessness' (*Collected Poems* 269). Her sublimation of pleasure mimics the sacrifice of a religious vocation but, since it is entirely private, it remains without meaning. Like the earlier poem, the perspective of this text remains close to that of Martha herself – in her engagement with the nuns who finally care for her shades of bitterness can be traced, a counterpart to the naivety of the earlier poem:

> Unpitied, wasted with diarrhea
> And the constant strain,
> Poor Child of Mary with one idea,
> She ruptured a small vein,
> Bled inwardly to jazz. No priest
> Came. She had been anointed
> Two days before, yet knew no peace:
> Her last breath, disappointed. (*Collected Poems* 274)

The bitter experience of religious institutions has kept containment and loss of control at the forefront of Clarke's writing. In spite of this, he resisted engaging directly with his own experience of institutionalisation when, aged 23, he spent almost a year in St Patrick's Hospital. What Beckett termed Clarke's 'flight from self-awareness' became more evident as international currents moved towards self-revelation from the 1950s onwards. In Clarke's case the decision to remain silent was a particularly strange one, since the moral issues raised by his work could be investigated powerfully through the medium of personal witness. *Mnemosyne Lay in Dust*, which appeared in 1966, was thus a landmark text for Clarke in its direct confrontation of early autobiographical experience.

Since this is a poem of incarceration and release, the representation of space is a key determinant in the treatment of subjectivity in the poem. The protagonist, Maurice Devane, enters a mental institution to receive treatment; he can only recover his full selfhood through separation from the world. The poem begins in darkness and ends in light, with a final homecoming involving Maurice Devane's emergence into the world, his acceptance of the past and return to the potentiality of language. The eerie street scenes with which the poem begins juxtapose St Patrick's Day celebrations with the shadowed streets and imposing institutions of Dublin's past, indicating the importance of the passage of time in the process of healing. This is a poem of disorientation and memory loss, yet the past is interwoven in Maurice's thoughts and observations, affirming its significance throughout Clarke's creative life. The experiences of the poem mirror Clarke's own; *Mnemosyne Lay in Dust* is an important part of his own acceptance of the past, which has not, until this point, been fully acknowledged.

In the absence of regenerative language, the overwhelming emphasis of the poem is on sensory experience, so the violence that is meted out to Maurice as he enters the hospital is especially traumatic:

> Straight-jacketing sprang to every lock
> And bolt, shadowy figures shocked,
> Wall, ceiling; hat, coat, trousers flung
> From him, vest, woollens, Maurice was plunged
> Into a steaming bath; half-suffocated,
> He sank, his assailants gesticulating,
> A Keystone reel gone crazier;
> The terror-peeling celluloid,
> Whirling the figures into vapour,
>   Dissolved them. All was void. (*Collected Poems* 326)

Real events take on a hallucinatory quality and the poem is full of dreams and half-recollections, presenting a disjointed and confused view of events, punctuated by moments of awareness. The spatial focus of the poem shifts from dormitory to yard to padded cell, but the fear and guilt that haunt Maurice take time to abate. His feeling of being watched is acute, as though Clarke's process of exposure through autobiographical writing were being figured in the texture of the poem. The new visibility of the body yields a treatment of sexual imagery that is crude rather than expressive, and the body at once facilitates and impedes Maurice's journey to recovery. For Maurice, the recapturing of memory is crucial to his ultimate cure; it enables him to create a context for body and mind. His increasing awareness of his surroundings is his first move towards assessing his present environment as part of a continuum for which he may yet recover the codes of meaning. That these codes are to be found neither in the sensory nor in the purely intellectual emphasises the fact that the movement through extremes must result in eventual balance. In this way, *Mnemosyne Lay in Dust* prefigures the progress and final resolution of the late poems.

The memory of confinement and release, and its recapitulation in verse form, changed Clarke's treatment of both the personal and the cultural past. The final phase of his career reveals a new lightness to the poet's art, a capacity to fully assimilate – and thus to move on from – the dark themes and personal struggles that obliquely shaped his creative life. After *Mnemosyne Lay in Dust* Clarke returned to the satirical mode, and the best of these later poems exhibit a new dramatic precision. 'The Redemptorist', which is among Clarke's finest poems, is a powerful statement on the oppression of women by the tyranny of required childbirth. Here direct speech becomes a confrontational device, and the woman's deathly confinement (in both senses) is a powerful indictment of Catholic doctrine: 'Shutter became / Her coffin lid. She twisted her thin hands / And left the box' (*Collected Poems* 374).

Clarke's return, in the last decade of his life, to mythology as the basis of his inspiration offers the substance and structure that he needs to realise his new creative freedoms. Unlike his treatment of epic in the early years of his career, this final turn is towards the comic possibility of classical work. Both 'The Dilemma of Iphis' (1970) and *Tiresias* (1971) harness the narrative power of myth to tell the story of gender transformation, once again showing Clarke to be ahead of his time in pushing the boundaries of sexual identity and debate. The experience of Iphis in the body of a female, though she is being brought up as a male, reinforces the gulf between desire and physical fulfilment which has haunted many of Clarke's earlier poems: 'Why am I afflicted, / Alas, with so wicked, so unnatural a passion / As this? Can cow inflame cow? Mare burn for mare?' (*Collected Poems* 500–1). Clarke's return to mythic material culminates in two new versions of Irish myths. Both 'The Healing of Mis' and 'The Wooing of Becfola' feature a journey at their core, a significant metaphor for Clarke in his lifelong attempt to come to terms with stifling moral dilemmas. These poems display a more resolved attitude towards the erotic than any of Clarke's earlier poems, depicting sex in its most gentle and restorative role.

Clarke's own creative journey has involved a complex relationship between a variety of forms and genres. The range and dedication of his artistic engagement, through more than a half-century of writing, is a testament to his vision and tenacity as an artist and as a man. Always principled, Clarke could sometimes be inflexible in his approach to his art, but it was this very inflexibility that made his commitment to social justice and ethical enquiry so relentless. His poetry is not easy to assimilate, either for readers of his day or our own, but it articulates a public role for poetry during a time of great political and social change in Ireland and offers a model for such work into the future.

NOTES

1. Peter Denman, 'Austin Clarke: Tradition, Memory and Our Lot', in *Tradition and Influence in Anglo-Irish Poetry*, eds Terence Brown and Nicholas Grene, London: Macmillan, 1989, p. 63.
2. 'Austin Clarke's Notes on the Poems', *Collected Poems*, ed. R. Dardis Clarke, Manchester: Carcanet Press, 2008, p. 541.
3. Austin Clarke, 'Poetry in Ireland Today', in *Reviews and Essays of Austin Clarke*, ed. Gregory Schirmer, Gerrard's Cross: Colin Smythe, 1995, p. 105.
4. A. E. A. Smyth, review of *The Vengeance of Fionn*, *The Times Literary Supplement*, 17 January 1918, p. 30.
5. Alan Gillis, *Irish Poetry of the 1930s*, Oxford: Oxford University Press, 2005, p. 84.
6. Austin Clarke, 'Irish Poetry Today', in *Reviews and Essays of Austin Clarke*, p. 57.
7. Denis Donoghue, 'Austin Clarke', *We Irish*. Brighton: Harvester Press, 1986, p. 245.
8. Gillis, Irish Poetry of the 1930s, p. 87.
9. Reader reports on Clarke's fiction question the suitability of the material for an English market and see Irish readers as key to the commercial viability of the work. Unwin Papers, Archive of British Printing and Publishing, Reading University.
10. Clarke, 'Poetry in Ireland Today', p. 105.
11. Mavis Arnold and Heather Laskey, *The Children of the Poor Clares*, Belfast: Appletree Press, 1985, p. 28.
12. Robert F. Garratt, 'Austin Clarke in Transition' *Irish University Review*, vol. 4, no. 1 (Spring 1974), p. 100.
13. Of these poets, which included Thomas Kinsella, John Montague, Richard Murphy and Richard Weber, only Kinsella would highlight Clarke as an important precursor.
14. Charles Tomlinson, 'Poets and Mushrooms', *Poetry* (1962), p. 113.
15. Austin Clarke, *Flight to Africa and Other Poems*, Dublin: Dolmen Press, 1963, p. 125.

SELECTED FURTHER READING
Editions

Reviews and Essays of Austin Clarke, ed. Gregory Schirmer, Gerrards Cross: Colin Smythe, 1995.
Collected Poems, ed. R. Dardis Clarke, Manchester: Carcanet Press, 2008.

Secondary Works

Brown, Terence, 'Austin Clarke: Satirist', *Poetry Ireland Review*, nos. 22 & 23 (Summer 1988), pp. 110–21.
Donoghue, Denis, 'Austin Clarke', *We Irish*, Brighton: Harvester Press, 1986.
Garratt, Robert F., 'Austin Clarke in Transition', *Irish University Review*, vol. 4, no. 1 (Spring, 1974), pp. 100–16.
Gillis, Alan, *Irish Poetry of the 1930s*, Oxford: Oxford University Press, 2005.
Goodby, John, 'From Irish Mode to Modernisation': The Poetry of Austin Clarke, in *The Cambridge Companion to Contemporary Irish Poetry*, ed. Matthew Campbell, Cambridge: Cambridge University Press, pp. 21–41.
'"The Prouder Counsel of Her Throat": Towards a Feminist Reading of Austin Clarke', *Irish University Review*, vol. 29, no. 2 (Autumn–Winter 1999), pp. 321–40.
Harmon, Maurice, *Austin Clarke 1896–1974: A Critical Introduction*, Dublin: Wolfhound Press, 1989.
Tapping, G. Craig, *Austin Clarke: A Study of His Writings*, Dublin: Academy Press, 1981.

11

TOM WALKER

Patrick Kavanagh

In Ireland, Patrick Kavanagh is a beloved poet: a staple of school and university syllabi; a figure in the public consciousness; a poet liked by people who do not otherwise read much poetry. If the stories are to be believed and Moscow's taxi drivers really can quote reams of Pushkin at you, it would be worth wagering that at least some of Dublin's taxi drivers could quote some Kavanagh back. Yet in some ways Kavanagh's poems have proved quite difficult to read. A curious moment of non-reading, for instance, occurs in James Liddy's 1969 'Open Letter to the Young about Patrick Kavanagh'. Having dismissed W. B. Yeats's work as having 'nothing' to teach aspiring poets and, by contrast, recommended Kavanagh as offering 'a poetry in which real ideas from living come at us', Liddy explicitly eschews further description and analysis: 'It is not necessary for me to say much about the poetry of Kavanagh.'[1] Writing just two years after the poet's death, the oddly insubstantial nature of Liddy's advocacy partly anticipates the shape of Kavanagh's subsequent critical reception. He is often seen as constitutive of the Irish poetic present, but in the sense of offering pathways through various mid-century mires that are then more extensively and successively pursued by subsequent poets. Kit Fryatt, for instance, describes Kavanagh as having offered a 'service to Irish poetry in freeing it from the pieties of cultural nationalism and Yeatsian high-talk'. Except for 'a handful' of his own poems, however, she argues that 'It has been left to posterity – in Ireland, pre-eminently represented by Seamus Heaney and Paul Durcan – to explore possibilities revealed but not exploited by this extraordinary poetic personality.'[2] A similar sense of Kavanagh's importance primarily being a question of his 'benignly enabling influence' is also put forward by Stan Smith.[3]

Such an emphasis on the afterlife, though, has not always been balanced by a correspondingly detailed engagement with the unusual nature of Kavanagh's poetry. Echoing Kavanagh's self-deprecating opening to his author's note for *Collected Poems* (1964) – 'I have never been

much considered by the English critics' – Michael O'Loughlin perceptively observes that by 'standard English literary criticism' Kavanagh is
regarded as 'a minor poet', whereas 'in terms of modern Irish poetry, he
is a major figure'.[4] But beyond questions of canonical or geographical
importance, what may be lost in a slippage from the limited standard
critical evaluation of the work to a stress on the value of Kavanagh as a
figure in the ongoing history of Irish poetry is a sense of the complexity of
the work itself.

A further distraction from the business of attending to the poetry, it must
also be admitted, has sometimes been Kavanagh himself. In not saying much
about the work, Liddy rather points to Kavanagh's own pronouncements
and also to the poet's personality in his later years as being 'as commending
as a great saint'.[5] Yet Kavanagh was an idiosyncratic commentator on his
own work, by turns outlandishly boastful and witheringly dismissive, as he
sought to reshape his career according to current demands. In his late autobiographical prose piece *Self-Portrait* (1962), for instance, he repudiates his
work prior to 1955 as simply 'not poetry'.[6] As Oona Frawley wisely coun-
sels, 'While Kavanagh's journalism, essays and miscellaneous prose provide
insight into the writer's development and shifting ideologies, they cannot be
relied upon as maps by which his poetry, fiction and drama can be read.'[7]
Moreover, the contradictions of Kavanagh's character and his attitude
towards being cast as a character, whether as peasant poet or colourful
Dublin pub fixture, are legion. Having some sense of the different phases of
the poet's career is of course enlightening. What Heaney describes as the
'great documentary force' of *The Great Hunger* (1942) is more forcefully felt
if one understands that the objectivising realism Kavanagh pursued in the
early 1940s followed on from his own lyrical idealisation of the Irish peasant
at the start of his career.[8] His engagement in an often splenetic public agon
with the legacies of the Irish Literary Revival and the deficiencies of the
culture around him in 1940s and 1950s Dublin is reflected in the satirical
nature of much of the poetry he wrote during this period. It also informs the
tactical complexities of his shifting, self-dramatising public performances of
the roles of sage, fool and clown. Indeed, the turn towards insistently celebratory, comic and casual poetic modes from the mid-1950s on (and hence
his late identification of 1955 as the year of his true poetic birth) is partly a
self-reflexive response to the cost of the poet's preceding critical and satirical
tussles. Like many Irish writers in the decades following independence and
partition, Kavanagh's erratic and, at times, halting development bears the
traces of the pressures of the society into which he was writing. But in taking
due account of the man, the career and their broader contexts, the distinctive
character of the poetry should not be subsumed.

Born in rural County Monaghan in 1904, the son of a cobbler and small farmer with no formal education beyond the age of thirteen, Kavanagh as a young man put himself through an unusual kind of poetic self-education. 'With most other verse writers of whom I have read', he later noted, 'there was usually a literary background or some roots somewhere', but his roots were in school anthologies and the back pages of that farmhouse kitchen favourite *Old Moore's Almanac*.[9] New horizons were opened up when he was introduced to modern literature in chancing upon a copy of AE's *The Irish Statesman* in 1925; by the early 1930s, he was catching up on the origins of poetic modernism through reading back numbers of Chicago's *Poetry* magazine. He was also working out how to write by writing – toiling away night after night by candlelight after his days of hard labour among the fields. The poet's biographer and editor Antoinette Quinn has labelled as 'low-grade apprentice verses' most of the hundreds of poems (many of which remained unpublished at the time or, even if making it into print then, have gone uncollected since) that Kavanagh wrote before the appearance of his first collection *Ploughman and Other Poems* (1936) in his early thirties.[10] Even in attaining competence, he had to contend with the problem of originality. Writing in 1954, Kavanagh stresses that imitation is the natural mode of the naive country poet: 'when a country body begins to progress into the world of print he does not write out of his rural innocence – he writes out of Palgrave's *Golden Treasury*'.[11] The late romanticism promoted by AE and pursued by many prominent Irish poets of the early twentieth century (Padraic Colum, James Stephens, Joseph Campbell, Monk Gibbon) was also clearly a strong early model – followed with considerable accomplishment in 'Ploughman', the poem that became his gateway to literary Dublin on first being published in *The Irish Statesman* in 1930.

Yet aside from his unusual origins and various developmental struggles, right from near the beginning of his writing life there are intimations of a distinctive poetic voice to be found – or, perhaps to put it more accurately, a distinctive use of various poetic voices. 'Address to an Old Wooden Gate' which now opens the *Collected Poems* was first published in the *Dundalk Democrat* in 1929.[12] Quinn sees this local publishing outlet as indicative of Kavanagh's low judgement at the time of the poem's comic tone and focus on ostensibly 'unpoetic' and local subject matter; his more serious poems were appearing in the national *Irish Weekly Independent*. She also sees the poem as trying but not altogether succeeding in imitating the heroic couplets and 'tonal blend of elegy and whimsy' of Oliver Goldsmith's 'The Deserted Village', and attributes its inclusion of local dialect to the 'exigencies of rhyme' rather than any conscious skill on the poet's part.[13] The poem's handling of the demands of rhyme in consort with a range of rhythmical and other sound effects, though, suggests that, whether by design or not, a subtle kind of poetic craft is very much at work:

> Battered by time and weather, scarcely fit
> For firewood; there's not a single bit
> Of paint to hid those wrinkles, and such scringes
> Break hoarsely on the silence – rusty hinges:

The opening line and a half's emphatic judgement of the gate as defunct is aligned to a use of strong beats and heavy alliteration. But such certainty starts to be complicated just as a more meditative rhythmic feel briefly interposes after the semicolon and resulting caesura. Visual markers ('wrinkles') are joined by aural ones ('scringes / Break hoarsely'), as the gate noisily (in both literal and poetic terms) starts to articulate itself beyond the realm of utility. The onomatopoeic dialect word 'scringes' (meaning a scraping or grating sound) is partly glossed by the descriptor with which it rhymes, 'rusty hinges': such hinges make such sounds. However, the distance between the terms, connected by the fragmented grammar and syntax that effect the rhyme within the exigencies of the form, also seem to mark the difference between the commonplace fact of the degraded hinges and the categories of experience (not beautiful as such but certainly aesthetic) that the gate might offer if perceived in other terms (tellingly evoked through dialect). The unprepossessing pleasures of actuality are come to not only through a mimetic attention to the particular, but also through the drama of poetic form itself, somewhat according to John Hollander's sense of the traffic between the real and the workings of fictive pattern in verse: 'poetry gets to the poetry of life by successfully becoming first the poetry of poetry'.[14]

Part of 'the poetry of poetry' in 'Address to an Old Wooden Gate' is also present in Kavanagh's comic handling of rhyme in parallel to the development of the poem's conceit – whereby, in self-pitying fashion, the gate's looming failure as a gate is likened to the poet's failure as a lover. In the opening four lines the couplet is somewhat obscured by enjambment. But in the end-stopped couplets that mostly follow, the rhymes so emphasised often wittily undercut the aggrandisement of the speaking voice: 'But Time's long silver hand has touched our brows, / And I'm the scorned of women – you of cows.' The passing of personified Time is evoked as what joins poet and gate together. Yet in the following line similarity gives way to difference and bathos in the equation of 'women' and 'cows'. The pattern's completion, with the rhyme of 'brows' and 'cows', involves not only the congruence of sound but also a straining of sense and register. Such a bending of language and decorum to fit the form, or conversely of the form to maintain the conceit, are also a more general feature of the poem's playful use of rhyme: 'rotten'/ 'forgotten', 'sentry'/ 'country', 'rise'/ 'heaven-wise'. The poem does not so much maintain its ostensible proposition that the poet and gate are 'kindred' as manage to imply more complex truths through the dramatic interplay of poetic form and voice. The loneliness of the speaker's actual situation is clear. Also represented are the consolations of a close attention to the world as it is, including the ostensibly ugly and unpoetic. The poem performs too the workings of the poetic imagination on that world through the idiomatic linguistic resources of a farmer from Monaghan and an embrace of what might conventionally be thought of as a loose or indecorous use of poetic tone and form. Within what is a characteristically solipsistic and auto-erotic love poem (for Kavanagh is often only a love poet in the abstract, whose ardour is generally not directed at any particular individual and so goes unrequited at a rather general level), a cause of pleasure is the workings of poetry itself – even, or perhaps especially, when operating in a somewhat dilapidated manner.

Reflecting on the effect of outside influences on the budding country poet, Kavanagh jokes that: 'The Assyrian has come down like a wolf on the fold of much Irish balladry.'[15] Alluding to the opening line of 'The Destruction of Sennacherib', one of Byron's *Hebrew Melodies* (1815), the comment signals Kavanagh's later sense of his struggle towards originality and his repeated emphasis on the importance of poetic authenticity. However, such stylistic incongruity is also a more positive feature of Kavanagh's work. In perceptively querying previous critics' assumption that Kavanagh's 'looseness' constitutes a 'weakness' rather than 'part of the meaning of Kavanagh, and even, up to a point, a kind of strength', John Goodby persuasively points to the combination of 'radical heterogenity' and 'a poetics of the casual, informed but not bound by a regard for inherited form' in the late work. Even in *The Ploughman and Other Poems* romantic and symbolist modes lie alongside poems that might be described as imagist or objectivist, and, as Goodby argues, 'It is crucial to an understanding of Kavanagh's later poems, that we grasp his unwillingness to completely abandon these styles, including the romantic, conventionally poetic one, even as he denounced them.'[16] From moment to moment, earlier poems also playfully blend the high and the low, the local and the literary, the real and the affected, the formal and the informal. For instance, the underrated early sonnet 'After May' (and Kavanagh is a notable sonneteer) plays the mythic off against the humdrum in its opening line's somewhat informal description of the 'phoenix' as 'shabby'.[17] Its closing couplet also places particular emphasis on the word 'croon': 'Sweet May is gone, and now must poets croon / The praises of a rather stupid June.' In doing so the poet, who as Edna Longley reminds us 'grew up inside the border of Scottish influence on both languages in Ireland', catches the retreat from the possibility of poetic singing as the passing on of a prelapsarian mystical vision to it being a more servile form of entertainment via a word that by the mid-1930s had shifted from its origins in Scots dialect to being a term of globalised slang used to describe the close to the microphone singing style of Bing Crosby.[18] Comically framed by the overt rhyme and the shift in tone from a poetic cliché ('Sweet May') to a conversational gripe ('rather stupid'), such telling diction evokes how both the poet as grand visionary and as humble folksinger, like language itself, now live in a fallen, irremediably modern world. Yet poetry in such circumstances still offers scope too for the sensual and self-conscious consolations of imaginative and linguistic play.

O'Loughlin illuminates how Irish balladry 'bequeathed an attitude to language that is both ludic and confident' in Kavanagh's poems.[19] Such confidence stands in contrast to the manner in which many other Irish poets through much of the nineteenth and twentieth centuries were somewhat haunted by folksong as a remnant of a past (that might become a future) in which Irish poetry not only operated in a different language but also held a more socially integrated and empowered position. However, the example of Byron himself is also useful in highlighting aspects of the poet's varied voice that lie beyond the revivalist versus modernist and/or realist dichotomies that have often framed not only Kavanagh's critical reception but also accounts of mid-twentieth-century Irish literary history more generally. Peter McDonald describes how in contrast to Wordsworth's and Tennyson's sense of the profound, meditative creative possibilities and liabilities of rhyme, Byron's voice in *Don Juan* (1819–1823) 'takes the meaning of rhyme in poetry to be essentially transparent, that of a device only, which may be owned up to as part of a witty stylistic *sprezzatura*'.[20] Much the same might be said of a Kavanagh who in the 1940 poem 'Stony Grey Soil' frames a line invoking Apollo by rhyming 'stumble' with 'mumble':[21]

> You clogged the feet of my boyhood,
> And I believed that my stumble
> Had the poise and stride of Apollo
> And his voice my thick-tongued mumble.

Rhyme is simply used for momentary comic effect, rather than offering Wordsworthian intimations of immortality. Quoting stanza twenty from canto fifteen of *Don Juan*, which foregrounds its pretence of rhyme being improvised in the course of speech, McDonald describes Byron as offering 'a late culmination of the tradition of Dryden and Pope which seeks to reconcile the manifest artificiality of rhyme with an appearance of the "natural" in expression and argument'.[22] Kavanagh, as Goodby notes, displays a 'marked taste for eighteenth-century models' and has also been justly hailed by Paul Durcan as a 'maestro of the improvised line ... a great tenor sax'.[23] Yet his poetic voice and use of rhyme, as is suggested by the lines quoted above, lie at a distance from the smooth rhetorical fluency that often seems to be equated with reconciling the artificial and the natural – not only in Augustan verse, but also, say, in the poetry of Philip Larkin. Insouciance without polish is a key aspect of Kavanagh's aesthetic.

However, while Kavanagh's poetry might treat poetic form and voice in a casual, roughed up version of the late Byronic manner, it curiously still often posits a kind of visionary mysticism. This tension is dramatised in the self-questioning, provisional opening to the 1951 poem 'Auditors In':[24]

> The problem that confronts me here
> Is to be eloquent yet sincere;
> Let myself rip and not go phoney
> In an inflated testimony.
> Is verse an entertainment only?
> Or is it a profound and holy
> Faith that cries the inner history
> Of the failure of man's mission?
> Should it be my job to mention
> Precisely how I chanced to fail
> Through a cursed ideal?

These questions are answered in what follows by the abandonment of idealism (in turn poetically manifest in the dissatisfactions of satire) and a willed turn towards a humble, celebratory affirmation of poetry as faith and of a faith in poetry. 'Love' in the poem is 'experience' itself, 'the Real / Poised in the poet's commonweal'. Finding faith and love (near cognates in the poem) is not a question of returning to memory or to specific 'roots', but rather of turning in upon 'where the Self reposes, / The placeless Heaven that's under all our noses'. Vision, rather fragilely, seems to rest on the self and its faithful praise of the particularities of one's present existence; failure, in the sense of resisting the lure of the ideal, would seem to be a condition of this cataphatic apprehension of the divine. The drama of form again runs parallel to this developing sense of the mystic. In the opening lines, the entertainment of the end-stopped couplets' rhythmic kick and ringing use of rhyme gives way to a more reflective tone through the use of enjambment and breaking of the couplet, with the extra half-rhyme of 'history', which then leads into a series of muted half-rhymes and a near dissipation of poetic rhythm altogether in the line 'Through a cursed ideal'. More broadly, Quinn sees a 'move from self-exhortation to an evocation of the benevolent psychic state most conducive to verse enacted in a change from couplets to a sonnet sequence' in the poem's second section.[25] But the assent to a truer or more complete poetic is also finally enacted, ironically, in the flat conversational tone of the poem's closing lines:

> I am so glad
> To come so accidently upon
> My Self at the end of a tortuous road
> And have learned with surprise that God
> Unworshipped withers to the Futile One.

The poetic condition, in spiritual terms, can paradoxically be approached through a near abandonment of poetry's formal procedures; pride is to be resisted, even at the level of the poetic voice.

Heaney describes the final lines of the 1936 poem 'Inniskeen Road, July Evening' ('A road, a mile of kingdom, I am king / Of banks and stones and every blooming thing') as tending from the present towards 'the status of memory': 'The poet's stance becomes Wordsworth's over Tintern Abbey, attached by present feelings but conscious that the real value of the moment lies in its potential flowering, its blooming, in the imagination.'[26] But even in this early poem, what might be described as Kavanagh's reverse-engineered form of romanticism is at work. Value is willed on the present through a moment of mere affirmation. The word 'blooming', for instance, moves not so much towards the past but outside of temporality altogether, in what Terence Brown describes as the recurrent summoning in Kavanagh's work of 'an eternal present tense which serves as a magnetic charge, attracting past and future to the still point of the poems' weightless immediacy'.[27] Unlike Wordsworth's discursive and grandiose poetic assent in imagining (via his past experiences) the restorative value, in the case of his likely future loneliness, of the impact upon his body and soul of his walk along the River Wye with his sister, Kavanagh offers only the delight of a moment of linguistic audacity, in uttering a curse that is also a prayer ('blooming'), as a counterweight to the poem's evocation of the banal and lonely present. Moreover, within a more conventional body of poetry, this word choice might well be viewed as stylistically and tonally teetering on the brink of bathos. As Goodby describes, much of Kavanagh's poetry stands at a significant remove 'from the standard model of lyric, which modulates in a gradual way from empirical observation to symbolic closure'.[28] By contrast, Kavanagh's poetic consciousness is not so much transformative as at once static and playful: the mystical resides in the mediation of reality and the nature of being by the shifting, pleasurable deployment of language and form. The snatching of 'the passionate transitory' out of time advocated in the closing lines of the 1956 sonnet 'The Hospital' is effected not only by the recording of 'love's mystery without claptrap', but also paralleled by the associative sonic intrigue of assonance and consonance brought into play by the very use of the word 'claptrap': 'For we must record love's mystery without claptrap / Snatch out of time the passionate transitory'.[29]

The Great Hunger – Kavanagh's most sustained poetic achievement and a strong contender for the greatest long poem written by an Irish poet in the twentieth century – offers an extraordinarily unflinching portrait and analysis of the sociological, demographic, psychological and spiritual realities of Irish rural life at mid-century, and has rightly been much praised in such terms. Brown even suggests that it is a poem prophetic of the changes that would see further mass emigration from the Irish countryside reach crisis levels in the post-war period: 'if there is a case for viewing a major work of art as an antenna that sensitively detects the shifts of consciousness that determine a people's future, *The Great Hunger* is that work. Maguire's life and the dismal fate that befell countless Maguires in the hundred years following the Famine, were no longer acceptable.'[30] It was also tellingly written into a culture in which Irish rural life had been idealised and romanticised on a number of fronts, going back to the early days of the Literary Revival and finding a prominent political outlet in the policies and pronouncements of the Fianna Fáil government of the day. However, the poem's documentary force and intellectual insights are informed by the manner in which, as Heaney describes, 'the art of the poem is replete with fulfilments and insights for which the protagonist is famished'.[31]

Modulations of tone, voice, form and genre, together with allusion's ironies, work to anatomise and dramatise Maguire's tragic fate. The cinematic, wide-angle opening's use of biblical allusion ('Clay is the word and clay is the flesh' – reworking the opening of John's Gospel) and T. S. Eliot-like free blank verse (as used, for instance, in *The Waste Land* [1922] in the 'What the Thunder Said' section) starts the poem off in a high register. As the opening shot zooms in, this decidedly poetic language use is pitched against Maguire's reported speech. His commands start off in banal, utilitarian mode. But soon linguistic riches are revealed that work in distinct counterpoint to Maguire's sense of his own language: 'The wind's over Brannagan's, now that means rain. / Graip up some withered stalks and see that no potato falls / Over the tail-board going down the ruckety pass'.[32] The eloquence of Maguire's use of the vernacular might pass him by, but the descriptive and onomatopoeic aptness of 'graip', 'withered' and 'ruckety' offer the attentive reader a glimpse of an edenic natural language that marries sign and object – a moment of linguistic being at one with the particular outside of the exigencies of time. This soon gives way not only to the imperatives of

Maguire's labour and growing psychological doubts, but also to the further formal drama of the second section's employment of jaunty doggerel ('O he loved his ploughs / And he loved his cows') to satirise the very mindsets that have cut Maguire off from the divinity of life.[33] Writing in response to a prevailing critical stress on Kavanagh's sociological realism, Terence Brown insightfully suggests that the poet is also 'a profoundly religious thinker whose analysis of Irish society proceeded from an instinctive yet seriously considered view of life rooted in his own deeply spiritual nature'.[34] But it should also be more widely perceived that Kavanagh's modes of thought and representation happen through and within the distinctive formal and linguistic modes that his verse pursues and embodies. Indeed, in pursuing what the closing section of *The Great Hunger* describes as 'a music as flightily tangent / As a tune on an oboe', Kavanagh might be seen as occasionally pulling off what W. H. Auden (one of the few contemporary poets to meet with Kavanagh's unqualified praise) described as an impossibility in his introduction to *The Oxford Book of Light Verse* (1938), by writing 'poetry which is at the same time light and adult' in a society that was by no means 'integrated' or 'free'.[35]

NOTES

1. James Liddy, 'Open Letter to the Young about Patrick Kavanagh', *The Lace Curtain: A Magazine of Poetry and Criticism* 1 (1969), pp. 55–7.
2. Kit Fryatt, 'Patrick Kavanagh's "Potentialities"', in Fran Brearton and Alan Gillis, eds, *The Oxford Handbook of Modern Irish Poetry* (Oxford: Oxford University Press, 2012), p. 195.
3. Stan Smith, 'Introduction: "Important Places, Times"', in Stan Smith, ed., *Patrick Kavanagh* (Dublin: Irish Academic Press, 2009), p. 2.
4. Patrick Kavanagh, '*Collected Poems*: Author's Note', in *A Poet's Country: Selected Prose*, ed. Antoinette Quinn (Dublin: Lilliput Press, 2003), p. 302; Michael O'Loughlin, *After Kavanagh: Patrick Kavanagh and the Discourse of Contemporary Irish Poetry* (Dublin: Raven Arts Press, 1985), p. 7.
5. Liddy, 'Open Letter to the Young about Patrick Kavanagh', p. 56.
6. Patrick Kavanagh, 'Self-Portrait' (1962), *A Poet's Country: Selected Prose*, ed. Antoinette Quinn (Dublin: Lilliput Press, 2003), p. 314.
7. Oona Frawley, 'Kavanagh and the Irish Pastoral Tradition', in Smith, ed., *Patrick Kavanagh*, p. 75.
8. Seamus Heaney, 'From Monaghan to the Grand Canal: The Poetry of Patrick Kavanagh', *Preoccupations: Selected Prose 1968–1978* (London: Faber and Faber, 1980), p. 122.
9. Patrick Kavanagh, 'School Book Poetry' (1952), *A Poet's Country*, p. 270; Patrick Kavanagh, 'Old Moore's Poets' (1939), *A Poet's Country*, pp. 157–62.
10. Antoinette Quinn, 'Editorial Note', in Patrick Kavanagh, *Collected Poems*, ed. Antoinette Quinn (London: Allen Lane, 2004), p. xxxv.
11. Patrick Kavanagh, 'Return to Harvest' (1954), *A Poet's Country*, p. 106.
12. Kavanagh, *Collected Poems*, p. 5.

13. Antoinette Quinn, *Patrick Kavanagh: A Biography* (Dublin: Gill and Macmillan, 2001), pp. 53–4.
14. John Hollander, *Melodious Guile: Fictive Pattern in Poetic Language* (New Haven, Yale University Press, 1988), p. 15.
15. Kavanagh, 'Return to Harvest', p. 106.
16. John Goodby, 'The Later Poetry and Its Critical Reception', in Smith, ed., *Patrick Kavanagh*, pp. 125–6.
17. Kavanagh, *Collected Poems*, p. 13.
18. Edna Longley, 'Poetic Forms and Social Malformations', *The Living Stream: Literature and Revisionism in Ireland* (Newcastle: Bloodaxe, 1994), p. 207.
19. O'Loughlin, *After Kavanagh*, pp. 16–17. Also see: Goodby, 'The Later Poetry and Its Critical Reception', pp. 136–41.
20. Peter McDonald, *Sound Intentions: The Workings of Rhyme in Nineteenth-Century Poetry* (Oxford: Oxford University Press, 2012), p. 22.
21. Kavanagh, *Collected Poems*, p. 38.
22. McDonald, *Sound Intentions*, p. 23.
23. Goodby, 'The Later Poetry and its Critical Reception', p. 131; Paul Durcan, 'The Drumshanbo Hustler: A Celebration of Van Morrison', *Magill* (May 1988), p. 56, as quoted in Smith, 'Introduction: "Important Places, Times"', p. 3.
24. Kavanagh, *Collected Poems*, pp. 179–83.
25. Quinn, *Patrick Kavanagh: A Biography*, p. 304.
26. Heaney, 'From Monaghan to the Grand Canal: The Poetry of Patrick Kavanagh', p. 117; Kavanagh, *Collected Poems*, p. 15.
27. Terence Brown, 'Patrick Kavanagh: Religious Poet', *The Literature of Ireland: Culture and Criticism* (Cambridge: Cambridge University Press, 2010), p. 124.
28. Goodby, 'The Later Poetry and Its Critical Reception', p. 135.
29. Kavanagh, *Collected Poems*, p. 217
30. Terence Brown, *Ireland: A Social and Cultural History, 1922–2002* (London: Harper Perennial, 2004), p. 175.
31. Heaney, 'From Monaghan to the Grand Canal: The Poetry of Patrick Kavanagh', p. 122.
32. Kavanagh, *Collected Poems*, pp. 63–4.
33. Kavanagh, *Collected Poems*, p. 67.
34. Brown, 'Patrick Kavanagh: Religious Poet', p. 122.
35. Kavanagh, *Collected Poems*, pp. 88–9.

SELECTED FURTHER READING

Editions

The Green Fool (1938; London: Penguin, 2001).
Tarry Flynn (1948; London: Penguin, 2000).
Lapped Furrows. Correspondence 1933–1967 between Patrick and Peter Kavanagh: with Other Documents, ed. Peter Kavanagh (New York: The Peter Kavanagh Hand Press, 1969).
Selected Poems, ed. Antoinette Quinn (London: Penguin, 1996, 2000).

A Poet's Country: Selected Prose, ed. Antoinette Quinn (Dublin: Lilliput Press, 2003).
Collected Poems, ed. Antoinette Quinn (London: Allen Lane, 2004).

Secondary Works

Allison, Jonathan, 'Patrick Kavanagh and Antipastoral', in Matthew Campbell, ed., *The Cambridge Companion to Contemporary Irish Poetry* (Cambridge: Cambridge University Press, 2003).

Brown, Terence, 'After the Revival: Seán O Faoláin and Patrick Kavanagh', *Ireland's Literature: Selected Essays* (Dublin: Lilliput Press, 1988).

'Patrick Kavanagh: Religious Poet', *The Literature of Ireland: Culture and Criticism* (Cambridge: Cambridge University Press, 2010).

Foster, John Wilson, 'The Poetry of Patrick Kavanagh', *Colonial Consequences* (Dublin: Lilliput Press, 1991).

Fryatt, Kit, 'Patrick Kavanagh's "Potentialities"', in Fran Brearton and Alan Gillis, eds, *The Oxford Handbook of Modern Irish Poetry* (Oxford: Oxford University Press, 2012).

Heaney, Seamus, 'From Monaghan to the Grand Canal: The Poetry of Patrick Kavanagh', *Preoccupations: Selected Prose 1968 – 1978* (London: Faber and Faber, 1980).

'The Placeless Heaven: Another Look at Kavanagh', *The Government of the Tongue: The 1986 T. S. Eliot Memorial Lectures and Other Critical Writings* (London: Faber and Faber, 1988).

Kiberd, Declan, 'Underdeveloped Comedy: Patrick Kavanagh', *Irish Classics* (London: Granta, 2000).

Longley, Edna, 'Poetic Forms and Social Malformations', *The Living Stream: Literature and Revisionism in Ireland* (Newcastle: Bloodaxe, 1994).

'"It Is Time that I Wrote my Will": Anxieties of Influence and Succession', in Warwick Gould and Edna Longley, eds, *Yeats Annual 12. That Accusing Eye: Yeats and His Irish Readers* (Basingstoke: Macmillan, 1996).

'Pastoral Theologies', *Poetry and Posterity* (Newcastle: Bloodaxe, 2000).

O'Loughlin, Michael, *After Kavanagh: Patrick Kavanagh and the Discourse of Contemporary Irish Poetry* (Dublin: Raven Arts Press, 1985).

Quinn, Antoinette, *Patrick Kavanagh: Born-Again Romantic* (Dublin: Gill and Macmillan, 1991).

Patrick Kavanagh: A Biography (Dublin: Gill and Macmillan, 2001).

Smith, Stan, ed., *Patrick Kavanagh* (Dublin: Irish Academic Press, 2008).

12

GERALD DAWE

Samuel Beckett

I

In her fascinating portrait, *How It Was: A Memoir of Samuel Beckett* (2001), Anne Atik recalls the extent to which the world-renowned playwright and novelist could recite poetry from memory, even in his later years, with his health fading. Discussing the final lines of W. B. Yeats's poem 'Under Ben Bulben' and which version of the epigraph he preferred, Beckett 'gave examples of the *suste viator* ("Halt, traveller") genre, from Swift, to Yeats's lines on Synge, and so on'. Where this all leads is indicative of just how Beckett's imagination was fired with the poetry of other writers across the history of different literatures and languages: 'This in turn led him to discuss – with immense gusto, scholar that he was, in spite of himself – the *ubu sunt* topos ("where are they now, those dead and gone"), which led inevitably to Thomas Nashe's *Summer's Last Will and Testament* in the same vein: Brightness falls from the air / Queens have died young and fair'. The scene continues with the friends 'chanting together, [Beckett] stressing a pause after each line, followed by a momentary silence pregnant with feeling, sometimes followed by a predictable reference to Villon ('*Mais ou sont les neiges d'antan?*'):

> 'But where are the snows of yesteryear?'; then both he and A.[her husband Avigdor Arikha] invariably proceeded to Holderlin's Die Titanen, standing up in their emotion when they got to the lines: Viele sin gestorben, Feldherrn in alter Zeit/ Und schöne Frauen und Dichter/ Und in neuer/ Der Männer viel,/ Ich aber bin allein.[1]

And on the evenings would go, Beckett reciting lines from Yeats' 'Friends' when he would 'stand up and repeat them … in amazement' and on to Goethe, among others. It is a very telling reminiscence because it reveals how for Beckett poetry was a *spoken* art, first and foremost. His obsession with language – English, French, German, Spanish, Irish-English – and the inner sound system of words and how this conveyed almost physically an emotional charge, it all mattered hugely to him. It was, in effect, his reason for writing. The meanings of words would alter across all these various soundscapes but Beckett's fascination, as this scene recounts, is with the dramatic value of the voice 'saying poems' as it is called in vernacular English in Ireland.

As a young Irish poet – born in Dublin in April 1906 – in the late 1920s and early '30s to his final years in his adopted home of Paris (where he died in December 1989), Beckett would remain fixated upon the *voice*. Of those, like Anne Atik and her husband, the artist Avignor Arikha, who knew Beckett very well from the 1950s and were part of his inner circle, one thing is clear: like so many of his generation in Ireland, poetry was still considered to be fundamentally a spoken art, notwithstanding, in Beckett's case, his academic scholarship and extensive knowledge of European literatures and continental philosophy.

So it comes as little surprise that when he started to publish his poems and to take himself seriously as a poet in the 1930s, Beckett should produce poems that were defiantly aural and which, to the 'conventional' reader, would seem belligerently uninterested in common sense. In 'Whoroscope' (1930), described by Seán Lawlor and John Pilling, the editors of *Samuel Beckett Collected Poems* (2012) as 'unique in SB's *oeuvre* as his only attempt at writing a sustained Browningesque poem *in persona*',[2] the erudite young man provocatively shows off his learning – his reading of Descartes is the source of the poem – in a (successful) attempt to win a poetry prize on the subject of Time. Sponsored by Nancy Cunard, the heiress, art patron and, among many other talents, owner of Hours Press who published the winning poem, 'Whoroscope' takes some time to get used to:

> The little grey flayed epidermis and scarlet tonsils!
> My one child
> scourged by a fever to stagnant blood,
> murky blood,
> blood!   (*CPSB* 41)

In the years that followed the appearance of 'Whoroscope' and the publication of his first (and only) single collection of poetry, *Echo's Bones and Other Precipates* (1935), Beckett established a name for himself among the avante garde based in Paris and London, clustered around experimental magazines such as the Joyce-inspired *transition* and *This Quarter* while retaining contact with Dublin journals, including *Dublin Magazine* where he published some early poems, on occasion under the name 'Sam Beckett'. The journey to see his poetry published was a very rocky one as even a brief sample of some correspondence of the time plainly shows.

According to the editors of *The Letters of Samuel Beckett 1929–1940*, Beckett had sent 'a group of his poems to Chatto and Windus (rejected 27 July 1932), to the Hogarth Press (rejected mid-August 1932), then to Rickwood (mid-August 1932 with no reply), and possibly to The Bookman (16 August 1934, which rejected a poem by 27 August 1934'[3] (*Letters* 235). The slim volume of *Echo's Bones*, when it was finally published 'depended upon subscriptions to underwrite the costs of printing' (*Letters* 286). It appeared in December 1935 and, like most every young poet before and since, Beckett fretted over the book and its reception. Though mentioned as forthcoming in the *Irish Times* (*Letters* 297), Beckett's letters to friends such as Thomas MacGreevy and others bemoan 'not a word about the poems' (*Letters* 305); somewhat later he comments that *Echo's Bones* 'had not been reviewed or distributed in Ireland' and was unavailable even on order, according to what he had been told:

> I was at the Salkeld's last night, when Blanaid [Salkeld] told me she had been in 5 or 6 times to Combridge [stationers and bookshop, Grafton Street, Dublin] for my poems and that they had written for them to [George] Reavey [the publisher] as often in vain. He says he has sent out copies for review. I don't believe him. (Letters 325)

As the editors of *Letters* make clear, George Reavey had indeed sent review copies of *Echo's Bones* to various literary journals in Britain and Ireland (*Letters* 327, n.10) but Beckett was unconvinced. Writing to MacGreevy he remarks: 'I met a man from the I.T. [*Irish Times*] I knew, one day by chance in the street, & he said no copy of the Bones had reached them for review. Though I gave Reavey the name of who to send it to. I sent him a copy, but no review so far' (*Letters* 341). The man from the *Irish Times* was Lionel Fleming, a contemporary of Beckett's at Trinity College Dublin. Like a dog with a bone, Beckett returns to the matter in his correspondence with MacGreevy: 'Fleming of the Irish Times, when he asked for *Echo's Bones*, said: "A good review or none". That was 3 weeks ago. No review has appeared' (*Letters* 346), although the book was flagged by the *Irish Times* in a column signed by M. C.: 'Transition, a Very Modern Magazine, The Artistic Left Wing' and comments on three of Beckett's poems reproduced in the issue from *Echo's Bones*: 'They are "difficult" but no more so than the poems of many modern authors' (*Letters* 348).

It's clear that Beckett had invested a great deal in *Echo's Bones*. The mixed review of the book in, for instance, *The Dublin Magazine* is characteristic and may well have added to Beckett's growing disenchantment: 'I am somewhat bewildered by Samuel Beckett. Bewildered but impressed'. Singling out several poems, including 'The Vulture', 'Enueg I', 'Enueg II' and 'Alba', in which 'Mr Beckett finds himself', the reviewer responds less positively to other poems because of Beckett's idiom – 'a very private, personal idiom': 'There is a confusion of accidental phenomena that leaves me adrift. Adrift; but, in spite of myself, impressed'.[4] It was a telling response that would remain in place for decades to come. But for Beckett the thirties were also a period of unrelenting difficulty and, indeed, tragedy, some of which is etched under the bravado and bravura of the poems he published. To understand this period of his life is to understand the writer he became.

II

Coming from a solid upper-middle-class protestant family with strong religious, business and cultural roots in the lifestyle and expectations of a prosperous south county Dublin, Samuel Barclay Beckett followed a fairly traditional pathway through local private schooling to the well-established Portora Grammar School in Enniskillen, county Fermanagh, in the north west of the country (and noted for an earlier Dublin writer, Oscar Wide who had also attended the school (1864/71)). Beckett, like Wilde again, went on to Trinity College Dublin (1923/27) where he would perform very well academically, graduating first in his BA in Modern Languages (First Class), and, after a two-year stint in Paris as a visiting lecturer, was appointed junior lecturer in French in 1929.

His experience of life in Paris – where he had been a visiting lecturer at the Ecole Normale Supérieure and where he originally met James Joyce, through the good offices of his fellow lecturer and poet, Thomas MacGreevy and with an introductory letter from his uncle, Harry Sinclair who had known Joyce before he left Dublin – altered Beckett's life, having a powerful transformative effect upon his sense of himself and, most significantly, upon what was achievable *in* Ireland. At best a reluctant teacher, and though it caused great consternation at home, Beckett resigned his Trinity teaching post in 1932 and sought out other ways to support himself as a writer.

The achievements and public recognition of the Irish literary revival in the newly fledged Irish Free State was viewed by many of Beckett's generation in their late twenties and early thirties, and seeking to publish their own first books, as 'history'. The international recognition of Yeats (awarded the Nobel Prize in 1926), who would remain such a powerfully eminent presence throughout Dublin (he died in 1939), was for Beckett a symptom of a much deeper malaise at the heart of Irish literary culture. Beckett published some caustic reviews of the Yeatsian revolution and dismissively compared many of its (once) leading lights as 'antiquarians' who had been writing the same kind of material since Victorian times.

These Irish contemporaries were unaware of the profound changes taking place in modern poetry in English and other languages: 'the new thing that has happened or the old thing that has happened again, namely, the breakdown of the object, whether current, historical, mythical or spook'. Rising to his topic, the twenty-eight-year-old Beckett, having identified this breakdown as 'a rupture of the lines of communication', continues that the artist 'who is aware of this may state the space that intervenes between him and the world of objects; he may state it as a no-man's-land, Hellespont or vacuum, according as he happens to be feeling resentful, nostalgia or merely depressed'. Beckett identifies as two such 'notable statements of this kind': 'A picture by Mr Jack Yeats' and 'Mr Eliot's Waste Land'.[5]

By 1934, when he published the article 'Recent Irish Poetry', Beckett had spent periods in hospital for surgery for a recalcitrant cyst on his neck and underwent foot surgery. While recovering from the former in 1933, he discovered that his cousin Peggy Sinclair, with whom he had a strong emotional bond, had in May of that year died in Germany of TB. Her death was followed in June by the death of his much beloved father:

> thrice he came
> the undertaker's man
> impassible behind his scutal bowler
>
> to measure   (CPSB 21)

The notion of 'breakdown' that Beckett registers in 'Recent Irish Poetry' had powerful subjective roots as well as relating to his increasing hostility to the Dublin literary world mercilessly satirised in his collection of stories, *More Pricks than Kicks* (1934), and his novel, *Murphy* (1938). When one considers the unfolding plight of Beckett's personal situation in the years leading up to and subsequent to the publication of *Echo's Bones* and the declaration of World War II in 1939, it is precious wonder that the poems are marked by a profound sense of aloneness, anguish and disconnection from the sonorities and thematic conventions of mainstream Irish poetry as it was perceived in the early decades of the twentieth century. The abiding emotional tone of these early Beckett poems conveys an oppressive and claustrophobic pressure and the enduring presence of a journey without motivation or a sense of destination:

> Above the mansions the algum-trees
> the mountains
> my skull sullenly
> clot of anger
> skewered aloft strangled in the cang of the wind
> bites like a dog against its chastisement.

> I trundle along rapidly now on my ruined feet
> flush with the livid canal   (CPSB 6)

The landscape, even when it is seen as 'livid', provides no respite or distraction from the 'cang of the wind', the nagging 'chastisement' that brings to mind a dog's snapping against reproach or instruction.

Notwithstanding his having been an athletic young man, playing cricket, rugby and golf, as well as swimming in the famous Forty Foot bathing area in Sandymount, nearby his Foxrock home, Beckett's health deteriorated and he was afflicted with an extraordinary list of physical ailments and psychological conditions that included panic attacks, tachycardia, boils, cysts, psoriasis, eczema, pleurisy, night sweats and insomnia. The culmination of these problems necessitated attendance at a clinic in London, paid for by his bewildered mother. Beckett' short poem 'Gnome' gives a clear idea of what he was going through:

> Spend the years of learning squandering
> Courage for the years of wandering
> Through the world politely turning
> From the loutishness of learning.   (CPSB 55)

It was becoming increasingly difficult, after his father's death and minding his mother's inconsolable grief, for Beckett to function in Dublin while remaining at home – jobless and effectively penniless and without much prospects of improvement in spite of the numerous job applications which he half-heartedly submitted for positions in Ireland, South Africa and the Soviet Union. The new Irish state, with its deeply conservative and catholic ethos, had enacted censorship laws which banned any art form – literature, theatre, cinema, dance – considered salacious or indecent. In such a hostile environment it is hardly surprising that Beckett's collection of short stories, *More Pricks than Kicks*, was placed a mere five months after publication on the 'Index of Forbidden Books in Ireland'. Things literally were going from bad to worse. He was involved in a libel court case involving his Sinclair in-laws and Yeats's old friend Oliver St John Gogarty, where he was mocked in court by the defence lawyer and his testimony reported in the national newspaper, much to the chagrin of his mother. Gogarty (who lost the case) encouraged Austin Clarke to bring a separate action against Beckett for his portrayal of Clarke as Austin Ticklepenny in his novel *Murphy*. Clarke wisely demurred. There was a further court case concerning a car accident with a lorry, the suggestion being that Beckett was drinking and not in control of the car. He hadn't been drinking, but he lost the case.

So, by his early thirties, Beckett the poet and translator, writer of short fiction and a novel, had reached an impasse, recalled by Morris

Sinclair – Peggy's brother, son of Beckett's uncle 'Boss' Sinclair – in a letter to Beckett's biographer, James Knowlson:

> Living in Ireland was confinement for Sam. He came up against Irish censorship. He could not swim in the Irish literary scene or in the Free State politics the way W B Yeats did . . . But the big city, the larger horizon, offered the freedom of comparative anonymity . . . and stimulation instead of Dublin oppression, jealousy, intrigue and gossip.[6]

Even in Paris, Beckett's change of residence did not initially bring good fortune as he was stabbed in the street by a pimp in 1938, and barely two years later the Cultural Capital of Europe was occupied by the Nazi regime of Hitler's Germany in 1940. Luckily for himself and his partner, Suzanne, after working for the French resistance, they got out in time and went on the run before securing a safe house in Rousillon in Vichy, France, in 1942, where Beckett rebuilt himself and his writing life as best as he could in the straightened circumstances.

This experience of living somewhat furtively, as it were, 'on the run' during 1942–5, unlike several of his Parisian friends, yet surviving some of the worst of the Nazi occupation elsewhere in France, was to prove crucial. For Beckett would eventually be confronted with the grim realities of war when, for a short period, he served with the Irish Red Cross, setting up a hospital in the destroyed town of Saint-Lo, through which the River Vire flows in his poem of the same name.

The quatrain he wrote not only conveys what he had witnessed, but also reveals a sense of abandonment, particularly in the unrelenting power of the final word – the lasting damage that war inflicts as aftermath as much as during the actual Allied bombardment:

> Saint-Lô
>
> Vire will wind in other shadows
> unborn through the bright ways tremble
> and the old mind ghost-forsaken
> sink into its havoc   (*CPSB* 105)

III

In Beckett's one-act play *Krapp's Last Tape* (1958), Krapp's self-reflections about his achievement as a writer of sorts are both mordant and comically acerbic:

> Seventeen copies sold, of which eleven at trade price to free circulatory libraries beyond the seas. Getting known. (*Pause.*) One pound six and something, eight

I have little doubt. (*Pause.*) Crawled out once or twice, before the summer was cold, sat shivering in the park, drowned in dreams and burning to be gone. Not a soul.[7]

Beckett was indeed 'getting known' by the time *Krapp's Last Tape* was performed. He had produced in the preceding decade a frenzy of writing in prose and drama, including the trilogy of novels – *Molloy, Malone Dies, The Unnamable* – and *Waiting for Godot* (1953). In 1959 his alma mater, Trinity College Dublin, conferred upon him an honorary doctorate, and ten years later Beckett was awarded the Nobel Prize for Literature (1969), following in the footsteps of fellow Dubliners George Bernard Shaw (1925) and W. B. Yeats. But what place did poetry play in these substantial post-war developments?

Beckett had been 'known' to a very small coterie of writers, his one and only poetry collection, *Echo's Bones*, having been published by George Reavey's auteur Europa Press in, as James Knowlson reminds us, 'a slim edition of 327 copies, of which 25 copies were signed by the author'.[8] While he had continued to contribute translations of European poetry to various magazines, his reputation as a poet seemed to have stalled; certainly, the (re)publication of his poetry post-war suggests as much. From 1935 no single volume appeared in English until John Calder published *Poems in English* in 1961, followed ten years later by a second edition, and further supplements in 1977 with *Collected Poems in English and French*. Calder would manfully continue publishing Beckett's poetry in different formats and under various titles until the appearance of *Poems 1930–1989* in 2002 – an edition which met with stern and uncompromising rejection by leading Beckett scholars. Writing in *The Guardian*, for example, Christopher Ricks dismissed the collection as 'this squalid edition ... the whole thing is peppered with errors',[9] and proceeded to enumerate the shaky editorial foundations of Calder's loyal efforts, over many decades, making Beckett's poetry (and fiction) available in affordable English language editions. David Wheatley remarked more in sadness than anger that *Poems 1930–1989* 'has been a long time coming, but is sadly far from perfect', before concluding 'Beckett's poetry remains overshadowed. Now would be a very good time for a reassessment. One logical outcome of such a process would be a *Complete Poems*, tidying up the unfinished business still on show in *Poems 1930–1989*.'[10] The 'process' of rehabilitating Beckett the poet had begun. In 2009 Wheatley published a clarifying *Selected Poems*[11] based around *Echo's Bones* but which included, along with the lucid Preface and unfussy notes, some of Beckett's finest translations. It is a perfect introduction to Beckett's poetry as a whole. *Selected Poems* was followed in 2012 by the magisterial *Samuel Beckett Collected Poems*, previously referred to here; a magnificent edition, accessible, well presented and with the kind of elucidatory material of commentary and notes from which the general reader and specialist can greatly benefit. The edition finally established Beckett's value as a poet and the not inconsiderable challenges some of his early poems present to a twenty-first-century audience. It is clear that Beckett flies in the face of much contemporary fashion in poetry in English: entertainment, accessibility, social concerns, historical engagements were *not* his concerns. The poems at times read as anti-poems, shorn of the sonorities and consolations of what we expect to find in an Irish poem written in either English or Irish. It is precisely this contrary strain in Beckett's writing that attracted many playwrights, poets, artists and theatre practitioners from all over the world into his orbit, a subject all to itself, in fact. But the influence and legacy of Beckett's poetry has a definite trajectory as far as *Irish* poets are concerned. His support and critical responses to a generation of thirties poets – Denis Devlin and Brian Coffey, among them – and his enduring friendship with many others who became long-time correspondents, including Thomas MacGreevy and George Reavey, publisher at Europa Press of *Echo's Bones and Other Precipitates*, is an important human quality to note in Beckett the man as much as Beckett the writer.

These relationships have been charted in several recent studies,[12] but the significance of Beckett's poetry can be misconstrued when placed exclusively into an historical framework of the thirties poets in Ireland. For Beckett's influence as a poet skipped a generation and had the greater impact upon post-World War II poets who started to publish in the late 1950s and early '60s; in particular, poets who learnt from Beckett the value of translation as a vital form of poetic expression, not only a mechanical exercise – a necessary job of work. Translating French or Mexican or German poetry into English was, for Beckett, not only an effort to bolster his paltry income during the thirties and later. He continued throughout his writing life to make translations; it was a fundamental aspect of his art. Crossing back and forth across French and English, writing in one language and translating into another, reading and absorbing an immense range of non-English literature, places Beckett at the very centre of European culture. This is well attested in the many critical studies devoted to Beckett's writing for stage and in his novels, and, as we have seen, even in old age he retained the facility of being able ('by heart' was the phrase once used) to recite and write out from memory examples from various literatures in different languages.

Beckett's imaginative and cultural engagement with European literature and art was a powerful influence on many leading Irish writers: for example, the novelist Aidan Higgins, and poets John Montague and Derek Mahon, both of whom have followed Beckett's example as masterly translators of French poetry into English. Montague has written movingly about his friendship with Beckett,[13] while Mahon from an early stage in his career has followed somewhat in Beckett's footsteps. As Mahon remarked in an interview in 1985 with fellow Trinity College Dublin contemporary Terence Brown, Beckett was 'a friendlier, a matier kind of voice speaking in my ear . . . hilariously funny'.[14] In his own literary criticism Mahon has explored Beckett's poetic oeuvre to telling effect, identifying what he (Mahon) considers to be the essential poems while acknowledging in a review of Beckett's *Collected Poems in English and French* (1977) the wider achievement of Beckett's extending 'the possibilities of English poetry, the more so since his work owes its beginning to a quite different set of premises from that to which the English poet is accustomed'.[15]

In the context of Irish poetry, Beckett's influence[16] in some ways recalls that of Patrick Kavanagh – Kavanagh's well-studied confirmatory role in the early development of poets such as Seamus Heaney and Paul Durcan is paralleled by the example Beckett offered to Mahon, his main poetic heir, and Paul Muldoon, whose language games are Beckettian at times, although much less introverted and sealed off from the reader than Beckett's earliest poems are generally viewed to be. As Lawrence E. Harvey stated in *Samuel Beckett, Poet and Critic* (1970), an authoritative and still the most valuable of studies, Beckett's poems 'are difficult if not hermetic, primarily because they are filled with illusions to worlds beyond the world of poetry – to literature and philosophy, to Ireland and France and especially to the Dublin and Paris that Beckett knew as a young man, to the events in the life of the poet'.[17]

IV

By the time Beckett had purged himself of the excessive playful and mocking allusiveness of 'Casket of Pralinen for a Daughter of a Dissipated Mandarin' (*CPSB* 32 – 4) or 'Whorosope' (*CPSB* 40–3), for instance, he had found a definitive voice to utter his thoughts; spare and as stretched as we hear it in 'Dieppe' in both of the languages to which Beckett had turned: 'again the last ebb / the dead shingle / the turning then the steps / towards the lights of old' (*CPSB* 99). In other similarly 'voiced' poems, Beckett had found a way to reconnect his poetic priorities with the dramatic monologues of his drama and the ceaseless story-telling of the narrators of his fiction. These poems, often in his favourite form of quatrains, and reproducing the guiding voices in his translations of major French poems such as Rimbaud's *Drunken Boat* (*CPSB* 64 – 7) and Apollinaire's *Zone* (*CPSB* 145 – 9), remind us of how versatile Beckett actually was as a poet; how exact and exacting his inner ear was for nuance and inflection, as in this brief extract from his version of *Zone*:

> This morning I saw a pretty street whose name is gone
> Clean and shining clarion of the sun
> Where from Monday morning to Saturday evening four times a day
> Directors workers and beautiful typists go their way   (*CPSB* 145)

The later poems of the 1970s, such as the translations of the eighteenth-century French writer Nicholas-Sebastien Roch Chamfort, alongside Beckett's sequence of *Mirlitonnades* ('doggerel or trashy verse' which Beckett wrote 'on scraps of paper and cardboard – and even a beer mat!', *CPSB* 447), build towards the lambency of the last poem it is believed he wrote, 'what is the word', with its liturgical refrain of seeking to find what is not actually there but forever sought after, like a vision:

> what is the word –
> see –
> glimpse –
> seem to glimpse –
> need to seem to glimpse –
> folly for to need to seem to glimpse –
> what –   (*CPSB* 228)

In *Beckett's Friendship 1979–1989*, Andre Bernoldin tells of an encounter with Beckett three years before his death:

> The calendar would wind on and, thin as a thread, traverse the years intact, weaving together the moments we spent in each other's company; on it would be inscribed friendly names, the cogs of correspondence, a gesture, a piece of clothing, a recurrent intonation, nocturnal dreams. His were composed of images, he used to say: 'Oh, there are no words, there are only images, a lot of images [.']¹⁸

Beckett's poetry is nothing more nor less than an orchestration of images that are presented in the unmistakeable voice of a man (mostly) talking about what he glimpses of the world around and within himself. As the American visual artist Ellsworth Kelly remarked about his own artistic life spanning seven decades, going back to when he had served in the US Army stationed in liberated Paris where he lived for several years, particularly impressed by the sculpture of Beckett's friend, Alberto Giacometti: 'I think what we all want from art is a sense of fixity, a sense of opposing the chaos of daily living. This is an illusion, of course. What I've tried to capture is the reality of flux, to keep art an open, incomplete situation, to get at the

rapture of seeing.'[19] In Beckett's case this 'rapture of seeing' was a delicate
balance – a no-man's-land, as the young poet had presciently put it in 1934
as he was about to leave home for good, unaware that it would take almost
seventy years before his poetry and his translations, caught between the
lyrical and the mocking, would finally reach the wider audience they so
richly deserve:

> on the Bootersgrad breakwind and water
> the tide making the dun gulls in a panic
> the sands quicken in your hot heart
> hide yourself not in the Rock keep on the move
> keep on the move   (*CPSB* 20)

NOTES

1. Anne Atik, *How It Was: A Memoir of Samuel Beckett* (London: Faber and Faber, 2001), p. 61.
2. *The Collected Poems of Samuel Beckett, A Critical Edition*, edited by Seán Lawlor and John Pilling (London: Faber and Faber, 2012), p. 320. Hereafter *CPSB*.
3. *The Letters of Samuel Beckett 1929–1940*, edited by Martha Dow Fehsenfeld and Lois More Overbeck (Cambridge: Cambridge University Press, 2009), p. 235. Hereafter *Letters*.
4. *The Dublin Magazine* (April–June 1936), p. 78.
5. 'Recent Irish Poetry', *The Bookman* (August 1834), p. 235. Republished in Samuel Beckett, *Disjecta: Miscellaneous Writings and a Dramatic Fragment*, edited with a foreword by Ruby Cohn (London: John Calder 1983), p. 70.
6. James Knowlson, *Damned to Fame: The Life of Samuel Beckett* (London: Bloomsbury, 1996), p. 274.
7. Samuel Beckett, 'Krapp's Last Tape', *Samuel Beckett: The Complete Dramatic Works* (London: Faber and Faber, 1986), p. 222.
8. *Damned to Fame*, p. 22.
9. Christopher Ricks 'Imagine Dead Imagine', *The Guardian* (1 June 2002).
10. David Wheatley 'Labours Unfinished: *Samuel Beckett Poems 1930–1989*', *The Irish Times* (27 April 2002).
11. Samuel Beckett, *Selected Poems*, edited by David Wheatley (London: Faber and Faber 2009).
12. See, for instance, Alex Davis, *A Broken Line: Denis Devlin and Irish Poetic Modernism* (Dublin: UCD Press 2000) and Roger Little, 'Beckett's poems and verse translations or: Beckett and the limits of poetry', *The Cambridge Companion to Beckett*, edited by John Pilling (Cambridge: Cambridge University Press, 2994), pp. 184–95.
13. John Montague, *The Pear Is Ripe* (Dublin: Liberties Press 2007), p. x.
14. Terence Brown, 'An Interview with Derek Mahon', *Poetry Ireland Review* 14 (Autumn 1985), p. 18.

15. Derek Mahon, 'A Noise Like Wings: Beckett's Poetry' and 'The Existential Lyric', in *Journalism: Selected Prose 1970–1995*, edited by Terence Brown (Oldcastle: The Gallery Press 1996) pp. 50–5 and 55–7.
16. For a more detailed reading of Beckett's influence on Irish writing, and poetry in particular, see Stephen Watt, *Beckett and Contemporary Irish Writing* (Cambridge: Cambridge University Press, 2009); Mark Nixon, '"A brief glow in the dark": Samuel Beckett's Presence in Modern Irish Poetry', *The Yearbook of English Studies* (1/1/2005, vol. 35), 43–57, and Gerald Dawe 'The Opposing Self: Derek Mahon', *The Proper Word: Collected Criticism* (Omaha, Nebraska: Creighton University Press, 2007), 269–75.
17. Lawrence E. Harvey, *Samuel Beckett, Poet and Critic* (New Jersey: Princeton University Press, 1970).
18. Andre Bernold, *Beckett's Friendship 1979–1989* (Dublin: Lilliput Press, 2015), p. 23. Readers might be interested in a fictionalised account of Beckett's life a little earlier in Jo Baker, *A Country Road, A Tree* (London: Doubleday/Transworld Publishers, 2016).
19. 'Ellsworth Kelly, art visionary, dies at 92', *International New York Times* (29 December 2015), p. 3.

SELECTED FURTHER READING

Editions

Samuel Beckett Selected Poems 1930–1989, edited by David Wheatley (London: Faber and Faber, 2009).
The Letters of Samuel Beckett, edited by Martha Dow Fehsenfeld and Louis More Overbeck (Cambridge: Cambridge University Press, 2009–2014).
Collected Poems of Samuel Beckett, edited by Seán Lawlor and John Pilling (London: Faber and Faber, 2012).

Biography

Atik, Anne. *How It Was: A Memoir of Samuel Beckett* (London: Thames and Hudson, 2001).
Cronin, Anthony. *Samuel Beckett, The Last Modernist* (London: HarperCollins, 1996).
Gaffney, Phyllis. *Healing Amid the Ruins: The Irish Hospital at Saint-Lo (1945–46)* (Dublin: A & A Farmar, 1999).
Knowlson, James. *Damned to Fame: The Life of Samuel Beckett* (London: Bloomsbury, 1996).

Critical

Brater Enoch. *Why Beckett* (London: Thames and Hudson, 1989).
Kennedy, Sean, ed. *Beckett and Ireland* (Cambridge: Cambridge University Press, 2010).

Pilling, John, ed. *The Cambridge Companion to Beckett* (Cambridge: Cambridge University Press, 1994).

Mooney, Sinead. *A Tongue Not Mine: Beckett and Translation* (Oxford: Oxford University Press, 2011).

Watt, Stephen. *Beckett and Contemporary Irish Writing* (Cambridge: Cambridge University Press, 2009).

13

CHRIS MORASH

Louis MacNeice

There was a time – particularly during his own lifetime – when the inclusion of Louis MacNeice in a *Cambridge Companion to Irish Poets* would have been hedged with qualifications. Writing in *The Bell* in 1943, Belfast poet Roy McFadden provocatively declared him 'irretrievably lost to this country': 'MacNeice was never Irish, and it is mere sentiment to imagine him so'.[1] McFadden's case was, in some respects, easy enough to make. Although born in Belfast and raised in Carrickfergus, MacNeice was sent in 1917 to boarding school at Sherborne in Devon, England, and went from there to Marlborough, where his classmates included John Betjeman and the art historian (and later Soviet spy) Anthony Blunt; he went on to Oxford (where he met W. H. Auden), later taking up university posts in Birmingham and London. By the mid-1930s, he was being published by T. S. Eliot at Faber and in *The Criterion*, as well as having his plays performed by the Group Theatre in London. By the time he co-authored *Letters from Iceland* with Auden in 1937 ('Three months ago or so / Wystan said that he was planning to go / To Iceland to write a book and would I come too'),[2] he was very much an insider in London literary and media culture. This position was consolidated further when he joined the BBC in 1941, where he collaborated with figures such as the composer William Walton, William Empson and Laurence Olivier. MacNeice continued to be very much part of that world in the post-war years, writing the screenplay, for instance, for the film which, arguably more than any other of its time, defines a certain iconic moment of British post-War endeavour, *The Conquest of Everest* (1953).[3] Awarded a CBE in 1958, given the company he kept it was a wonder he escaped knighthood.

The argument for reading MacNeice's poetry in the context of English culture is more than simply biographical. A prolific literary critic from an early point, MacNeice began defining his own place in literary history almost as soon as his second collection, *Poems*, appeared in 1935. In an essay published shortly after, 'Subject in Modern Poetry' (1936, which later became part of his influential book, *Modern Poetry: A Personal Essay*, in 1938), he begins by acknowledging that 'it is notoriously difficult to write a history of one's own times'. Nevertheless, he maps out the poetic terrain he inhabits. Dismissive of the 'Art for Art's Sake' poets ('for some time foundering'), the Georgians (such as Rupert Brooke and John Masefield) and Surrealism ('an extreme fashion'), carefully critical of T. S. Eliot ('the arch high-brow'), and steering an appreciative but cautious course around Yeats (like Eliot, a poet to admire, but 'not a poet to imitate'), MacNeice clearly aligns himself with what he calls 'the nineteen-thirty school of English poets, represented by Mr. Auden and Mr. [Stephen] Spender'. They are, he announces, 'essentially young poets', 'almost blatant in their loves and hates', whose poetry implicitly asserts that 'every man lives in a contemporary context which is of value and interest.'[4]

More than just a public school education and Oxford linked MacNeice with Auden and Spender, as much as Spender would later claim that the association was more apparent than real. Instead, MacNeice makes the case for a commonality in their work in terms of poetic form. 'The Auden-Spender school of poets', he maintains, in an argument with echoes of Burkean conservatism, is upholding 'the English tradition of freedom in that it walks a middle course'. This 'middle course' was not only philosophical or political: it shaped a distinctive poetic practice, which MacNeice defines as not 'over-revolutionary in form', and 'having a mixed content'. The touchstone of an 'English tradition' here, of course, is Shakespeare, whose 'mixed content' was traditionally seen as distinctively English when contrasted with the rule-governed – and equally typically French – neo-classicism of Racine. Such poetry 'develops itself instinctively but with a reasonable amount of self-consciousness and self-criticism'[5] – in other words, it is not governed by a manifesto. Summing up this aesthetic later in terms of subject matter, MacNeice would declare: 'My own prejudice, therefore, is in favour of poets whose worlds are not too esoteric.'[6] Consequently, when compared to contemporaries such as Pound or Eliot (aspects of whose poetic practice he labels as 'vicious'[7]), MacNeice's poetry has a studied formal conservatism. This is typically combined with determinedly modern, and often determinedly pedestrian, subject matter. His early 'Ecologue for Christmas' (1933), for instance, is indeed an ecologue (a classical form, as one might expect from a writer who taught classical literature for many years); however, it is an ecologue for a world in which 'the street is up again, gas, electricity and drains / Ever-changing conveniences, nothing comfortable remains / Un-improved, as flagging Rome improved villa and sewer.'[8] By the same token, even the casual reader of MacNeice cannot but notice his penchant for arguably the most conventional of poetic conventions: rhyme.

'As for rhyme', he writes in *Modern Poetry*, 'rhyme is also returning'. Among the 'younger poets' with whom he aligns himself, a new kind of engagement with the realities of the modern world of 'gas, electricity and drains' made it possible once again to use conventional verse forms, because 'conventionality does not kill their content'.[9]

Given MacNeice's understanding of the relationship between poetic form and content, the kind of poetry he wrote can be understood as a response, tinged with a sense of impending catastrophe, to modernity – and specifically to an English modernity. 'Close and slow, summer is ending in Hampshire, / Ebbing away down ramps of shaven lawn where close-clipped yew / Insulates the lives of retired generals and admirals', he writes at the beginning of his long major work, *Autumn Journal* (1939),[10] evoking a world that will be consumed in fire. The twenty-four canto *Autumn Journal*, along with poems such as 'Prayer Before Birth' (1944) and 'Brother Fire' (1942) are among the most powerful literary responses to the British civilian experience of World War II. These are works not simply about war, but about this particular war as a kind of aggressively accelerated modernity, in which 'our brother Fire was having his dog's day / Jumping the London streets with his millions of tin cans'.[11] In the final years of MacNeice's life, these images of London on fire still haunted him. In 'Homage to Wren (a memory of 1941)' (published in *Solstices* from 1961, two years before his death), MacNeice conjures up a nightmare image of 'the dome of St. Paul's / Riding the firefull night'. Words from that time drift to mind, and dissipate: 'London expects – but the rest of the string was vague, / Ambiguous rather and London was rolling away / Three hundred years to the aftermath of the plague.'[12] When the world is burning – and, as Edna Longley and Peter McDonald have both pointed out, by the early 1960s the possibility of a global nuclear conflagration had made the firebombs of the Blitz seem tame by comparison – surrealist cut-up techniques were hardly needed to make the world seem strange. A distinctively English poetics of 'the middle course' was a more than adequate response to a world on fire.

The difficulty with the argument for MacNeice as an English poet is that we can make an equally plausible case for an Irish MacNeice, not least from his own account of himself. 'Don't you know that informal letter-writing is the only genre in which the English excel. & you are English', he wrote to Anthony Blunt in 1935. 'Not so me, thank God. I have nothing in common with Cowper, Lord Chesterfield or Queen Victoria.'[13] A few years later, in his 1941 book on Yeats, MacNeice was to claim that when he 'read Yeats's account of his childhood, I find many things which are echoed in my own or in that of other Irish people I know'. 'Yeats was always conscious', MacNeice continues, in terms that suggests he is writing about himself as much as he is about Yeats, 'that the English were foreigners or, to put the emphasis more correctly, that he was a foreigner among the English'. Indeed, he recalls that 'when the Great War broke out in 1914 (I was then nearly seven) it was some time before I could make out whether it was the English or the Germans who were the enemy'.[14] At times, MacNeice's insistence that he was Irish might suggest that he was performing a kind of Irishness, like a sober-suited Oscar Wilde, particularly when he was working for the BBC in the 1940s and 1950s, where, it has been noted, there was a 'radio Irishman culture at large'.[15] However, this argument cannot really account for the imaginative geography of Ireland that runs through his poetry, forming a kind of counter-world to his imagined England. Nor can it account for the fact that he never allows himself to fall into any easy 'identification of Ireland with the spirit and of England with crass materialism', which he notes in the Yeats book as being part of the Irish inheritance he shares with the older poet.[16] In the end, MacNeice would claim his connections with Ireland as firmly as he would claim his place with Auden and Spender – sometimes on the same page. So, for instance, he writes in 'Auden and MacNeice: Their Last Will and Testament' (in the co-authored *Letters from Iceland*), of 'My own [ancestors]', 'whose rooms / Were whitewashed, small, smooth with the smoke of peat,/ Looking out to the Atlantic's gleams and glooms'.[17]

This Ireland of the mind (and of his ancestors) runs throughout MacNeice's poetry. 'I was born in Belfast between the mountain and the gantries', he writes in 'Carrickfergus' (1937), 'To the hooting of lost sirens and the clang of trams: / Thence to Smoky Carrick in the County Antrim'.[18] Elsewhere, he writes in 'Belfast' of the city 'Down there at the end of the melancholy lough / Against the lurid sky over the stained water.'[19] The Irish geography that takes shape in MacNeice's poetry, however, is by no means confined to Northern Ireland, and this makes it difficult to claim him simply as an Ulster poet (and hence Roy McFadden's difficulties with him). There is 'Train to Dublin' (1934), which may include 'the vivid chequer of the Antrim hills', but takes in a circuitous route covering 'the laughter of the Galway sea', 'the toy Liffey' and 'the red bog-grass' of the West of Ireland.[20] And, of course, there is 'Dublin' itself, which in 2015 was voted onto a shortlist of Ireland's favourite poems, chosen in an audience competition by the Irish broadcaster, RTÉ:[21] 'This was never my town, / I was not born nor bred / Nor schooled here and she will not / Have me alive or dead / But yet she holds my mind'.[22] In spite of having spent only brief periods in Dublin when compared to the years living and working in London, MacNeice never renounces Dublin (or, indeed, Ireland) so fully as he does London in the late poem 'Goodbye to London' (from *The Burning Perch*, 1963), in which the English capital has become 'only some meaningless / Buildings and the people once more were strangers'.[23]

Whatever about his claim on Dublin (or its claim on him), MacNeice did have family ties further west. His father, Frederick MacNeice (for whom a fascinating biography exists by David Fitzpatrick),[24] was born on the island of Omey, off the western edge of Connemara, where MacNeice's paternal grandfather had served the Irish Church Missions, an evangelical (and millenarian) group within the Church of Ireland founded by the Rev. Alexander R. C. Dallas in 1843 to convert Irish Catholics before they were overtaken by the Last Judgement (at one point predicted for 1848). For Dallas, 'Ireland was England's chastisement. England has made an unrestful bed for herself, and she must lie upon it.'[25] The MacNeice family were thus only a generation removed (as was the family of Yeats) from a landscape that may have been the periphery of Europe, but was the epicentre of the geographical imaginary for so many Irish writers of the first half of the twentieth century (and beyond). Equally, it might be tempting to read the apocalyptic sense of history (albeit a secular apocalyptic sense) in MacNeice's war poetry not only in the context of Yeats's catastrophic understanding of history, most fully worked out in *A Vision* (as Tom Walker has convincingly argued),[26] but also as a kind of atavistic reworking of his grandfather's millenarian theology. It is even more tempting to argue that for Louis MacNeice, as for the founders of the Irish Church Missions (again, on determinedly secular rather than religious grounds), 'Ireland was England's chastisement' – with the proviso that for MacNeice, the reverse was also true.

'I come from an island, Ireland', announces the character of Ryan in 'Ecologue from Iceland' in *Letters from Iceland*, 'a nation / Built upon violence and morose vendettas'.[27] On the same note, MacNeice asks two years later in a particularly bitter passage in *Autumn Journal*: 'Why should I want to go back / To you, Ireland, my Ireland?/ The blots on the page are so black / That they cannot be covered with shamrock.' On the one hand, Ireland – tellingly, 'my Ireland' – is a place where it is still possible to believe in an individuality being crushed elsewhere, 'because one feels that here at least one can / Do local work which is not at the world's mercy / And that on this tiny stage with luck a man / Might see the end of a particular action.' A line later, this hope is dismissed: 'It is self-deception, of course.'[28] This ambivalent writing of Ireland as a site of hope and deception needs to be framed by the poems written during World War II that accompany *Autumn Journal*. 'Neutrality' (1942), for instance, written after the death at sea of his friend Graham Shepard in a U-boat attack, is both an Irish poem and part of a larger constellation of war poems that includes 'Prayer Before Birth' and 'Brother Fire'. 'Even the Ireland of "Carrickfergus"', as Edna Longley reminds us, 'also belongs to a wider British and European context, to a time of new wars mapped by "flags on pins moving across and across"'.[29] This aspect of MacNeice's unease in relation to Ireland has been the subject of much recent work by Clair Wills, Richard Danson Brown, Christopher Fauske and others. MacNeice 'often finds it hard to resist the spell of Ireland's solipsism and self-romanticizing', observes Wills, 'even as he chides her for failing to come to terms with the demands of maturity and the modern world'.[30] So, while it is possible to construct from the poetry and the letters a MacNeice profoundly disenchanted with Ireland (and particularly with Northern Ireland – one letter refers to 'Orangemen' as 'Ulster's own brand of fascist'[31]), there is equally ample evidence that for MacNeice, Ireland – or at least some shifting idea of Ireland – was both inescapable and necessary, even if it was by no means exclusively so. 'Ireland meant to Yeats something very specialized', he notes. 'It is not Ireland as the ordinary person knows it, yet it is something distilled from Ireland'[32] – an argument that, with different specifics, could equally apply to MacNeice himself.

By the 1960s, as Edna Longley points out, MacNeice's influence on the remarkable generation of Irish (and, more specifically, Northern Irish) poets emerging at the time – notably Derek Mahon and Paul Muldoon – would begin a long act of reputational repatriation. Within a few years of his death, MacNeice would, as Mahon puts it, provide a 'frame of reference for a number of younger poets',[33] not least for those anxious to escape the constraints of a geographically bounded poetic imagination, while still maintaining some kind of tie to the Irish landscape. In terms of Irish literary history, this made it possible to see MacNeice as the intermediary between Yeats (with whom MacNeice had a complex engagement[34]) and the poets who emerged in the 1960s. When two of the most influential literary critics of their generation from Northern Ireland, Longley and Terence Brown (whose *Louis MacNeice: Sceptical Vision* appeared in 1975), published books on MacNeice, it provided further testimony that MacNeice mattered (and belonged) in a wider Irish context. This was helped by neither of them claiming MacNeice for Irish (or even Northern Irish) poetry in any unproblematic way. Longley, for instance, would simply state in 1988: 'Louis MacNeice is a central poet of the twentieth century.'[35] In an essay published in 1987, Peter MacDonald suggested that the fact that MacNeice did not fit easily into any national tradition 'may itself yet turn out to be exemplary as far as criticism is concerned, forcing as it does a confrontation with those differences upon which an "Irish" culture will have to be built'[36] – a view Longley endorsed in the Belfast magazine *Fortnight*.[37] We can frame this flurry of interest in MacNeice in the late 1980s (Michael Longley also edited MacNeice's *Selected Poems* in 1988) by noting that it coincided with the publication of one of the most influential works of Irish cultural criticism of its time, David Cairns and Shaun Richards' *Writing Ireland*, which opens with Macmorris' oft-quoted question from *Henry V*: 'What ish my nation?'[38] In some respects, as far as understanding MacNeice's work was concerned, this was the central question.

It may well have been the wrong question (or, at least, was eliciting the wrong answers). In *Autumn Journal*, Louis MacNeice provides us with an altogether more complex answer to the question that shifts our understanding of his work away from questions of nationality. 'Time is a country, the present moment / A spotlight roving round the scene; / We need not chase the spotlight, / The future is the bride of what has been.'[39] Indeed, we might go further and say that by the time he wrote *Autumn Journal* in 1939, time was not only 'a country'; it was *his* country. If we consider both MacNeice's Irishness and his Englishness as performances of identity, the unstable frames for an understanding of self and world, he begins to appear closer to his equally displaced near-contemporary Samuel Beckett (Beckett was born in 1906, MacNeice in 1907). From this perspective, it could be argued that both writers had the good misfortune of precocity, identifying far too clearly and too early the problematic of their art; and both spent the rest of their lives struggling within the impasse in which they found themselves. For Beckett, the problem is alarmingly simple: 'There is no escape from the hours and the days,' he writes in his 1931 essay on Proust. 'We are not merely weary because of yesterday, we are other, no longer what we were before the calamity of yesterday.' For Beckett, this was something more than an acknowledgement of time passing; it is the anguished recognition that both the writer's and the world's 'permanent reality, if any, can only be apprehended as a retrospective hypothesis'.[40] With both subject and object continually transformed by the 'poisonous ingenuity of Time', the relation between the writer and the world collapses. It was principally this recognition that distanced Beckett from most other Irish writers of his time, as he makes clear writing in 'Recent Irish Poetry' in 1934 that his contemporaries in Ireland, caught up within a national paradigm, were unable to acknowledge 'this new thing ... the breakdown of the object'.[41] But then, in 1934, MacNeice's *Poems* was still a year away, where he would write 'Soundlessly collateral and incompatible; / World is suddener than we fancy it.'[42]

This is not to say that MacNeice and Beckett paid much attention to one another over the years. MacNeice only appears in Beckett's correspondence when he dies in 1963; MacNeice is a bit more attentive, writing about Beckett in *Varieties of Parable* (1963), and attending the first London production of *Waiting for Godot* in 1956 – both of which would be expected of an active literary critic and journalist at the time.[43] However, thinking about MacNeice and Beckett as contemporaries may help us to frame questions of geography in MacNeice's work. It might be objected that MacNeice's poetic attention is drawn to events in the world, as well as to his own complex romantic life, in ways that we do not find (at least as overtly) with Beckett. However, even if MacNeice did not define the problematic of time with quite the same relentless precision as Beckett, it runs throughout his work. 'Stop the clock, nurse, stop the clock' is the anguished plea at the end of 'Child's Terror'[44] early in *Blind Fireworks* from 1929. In the same collection, in 'A Lame Idyll' (the title of which suggests the inadequacy of the poem as a point of stillness), the figure of Pythagoras sits, 'Telling his counters, thinking on what was, / Dropping impartially the minutes from his finger-tips', until, in the closing lines, 'The universe fades in the upper distance; / It is no more, though it was once.' Pythagoras, MacNeice explains to his readers in a prefatory note (with a parodic nod to Eliot's notes to *The Wasteland*), he associates with 'Thor the Time-God'.[45] In *Poems* (1935) we find 'Train to Dublin': 'The train's rhythm never relents, the telephone posts / Go striding backwards like the legs of time', as the poet drinks toasts to things that go rushing by him. 'I would like to give you more but I cannot hold / This stuff within my hands and the train goes on.'[46] As was the case with Beckett, this sudden awareness of temporality leads to the loss of the object, and this is nowhere more true than in one of MacNeice's finest poems, 'Snow', also from *Poems*. 'World is crazier and more of it than we think, / Incorrigibly plural. I peel and portion / A tangerine and spit the pips and feel / The drunkenness of things being various.' As the enjambment of the lines suggests, 'things' are not just 'various' when compared to one another; each thing is 'incorrigibly plural' in and of itself. And so the poem concludes: 'There is more than glass between the snow and the huge roses.'[47]

MacNeice was only twenty-eight when he published 'Snow'; but it will define what is arguably the corrosive counterpoint to his determined engagement with the world of people and things. 'The taut and ticking fear / That hides in all the clocks / And creeps inside my skull' continues in 'The Heated Minutes' from *The Earth Compels* (1938), and by the time he writes *Autumn Journal* (1939) an awareness of time as destructive has been fused with an intimation of time ending, spurred by the cataclysm of the War. This will be the dominant trope in the work published in the prolific period of the late 1930s and early 1940s, in the collections *Plant and Phantom* (1941), *Springboard* (1944) and *Holes in the Sky* (1948). Glimpsed through the interstices are brief moments of respite, most powerfully in 'Meeting Point' (from *Plant and Phantom*) with its refrain 'Time was away and somewhere else.'[48] In the 1950s, a period that many critics find the least interesting in MacNeice's career, the concern is less with the effects of time on the world, than on the instability of the self in the face of temporal change. 'Purged of flowers that shone before me', he writes in 'Day of Renewal' from *Ten Burnt Offerings* (1952), 'I find in roots beyond me, past / Or future, something that outlasts me / Through which a different I shall last.'[49] The anxiety of temporality here is, if anything, more intense than in the earlier work because more focused on the self, whose instability robs both subject and object of any fixity. 'Yet sometimes, even now', he writes in 'Day of Returning' from *Ten Burnt Offerings*, 'I have a nightmare':

> Always the same, that the challenge has come again
> In a stony place, in ultimate darkness,
> And I feel my sinews crack in advance
> And, because this time I know my opponent,
> I know that this time I have no chance
> Of holding my own. My own is nowhere[50]

Places, things and people matter in MacNeice's poetry, and so they must be articulated clearly and directly. At the same time, they are never fully themselves, and are always in the process of fading, or, at the very least, of becoming something else. Everywhere is always in the process of becoming 'nowhere' as 'a different I' observes them, as if from windows in a moving train. Far from being a poet of place, MacNeice is a poet whose 'own is nowhere'.

The nightmare of 'the poisonous ingenuity of Time' persists until the end in MacNeice's work, coming into a final focus in *The Burning Perch*, which appeared ten days after his death on 3 September 1963. Jon Stallworthy records a postcard that the twelve-year-old MacNeice sent home to his parents in Carrickfergus from boarding school in 1919: 'saw stars in train from Sherborne'.[51] Twenty-one years later, in his autobiography, *The Strings are False*, MacNeice recalls this moment, glimpsing 'bagfuls and bucketfuls of stars' from the moving train: 'I ran from side to side of the carriage checking out the constellations as the train changed its direction.'[52] By 1963, the memory has coalesced into its full shape and meaning in 'Star-Gazer', written in January 1963:

> Light was leaving some of them at least then,
> Forty-two years ago, will never arrive
> In time for me to catch it, which light when
> It does get here may find that there is not
> Anyone left alive.[53]

From the perspective of a poem like 'Star-Gazer', the question as to whether MacNeice should be understood primarily as an Irish or an English poet recedes. This in turn opens up new ways of reading poems that we might otherwise be inclined to try to pin to a national tradition, including the poem for which he is arguably best known in Ireland: 'Dublin'. 'Dublin' was written between August and September of 1939, and first published in Dublin the following year by the Yeats sisters' Cuala Press as part of a longer sequence, 'The Coming of War', in a small volume called *The Last Ditch*; it later appeared as part of a sequence called 'The Closing Album' in *Plant and Phantom*, a collection deeply engaged with the experience of World War II. From the outset, then, the publication history of the poem positions 'Dublin' within the narratives both of the English MacNeice, and of the Irish MacNeice. Likewise, it is suspended between a place (Dublin) and an occasion in the start of the War, in which Ireland was neutral – 'the war came down on us here', a later section of the sequence reminds us.[54] However, the poem is framed around a question (in much the same way that Yeats employed questions to such powerful effect in his poetry) in its second stanza: how is it that this town, in which the poet admits he was not born, bred or schooled, and which wants no part of him ('alive or dead') 'hold[s] my mind'? An answer, of sorts, appears in the final stanza:

> Fort of the Dane,
> Garrison of the Saxon,
> Augustan capital,
> Of a Gaelic nation,
> Appropriating all
> The alien brought,
> You give me time for thought
> And by a juggler's trick
> You poise the toppling hour –
> O greyness run to flower,
> Grey stone, grey water,
> And brick upon grey brick.[55]

On one level, 'Dublin' could be read as an inscription of place as sedimentary memory, writing neutral Ireland as the product of waves of invaders, capable of accommodating 'all / The alien brought'. However, in the poem's closing lines, in a series of almost throw-away lines, the city not only gives the poet 'time for thought'; it also gives him thought for time. The repetition of the word 'grey' here is not simply social commentary on Dublin in the 1930s; grey will recur throughout MacNeice's work as an image of an inescapable presentness. It is there in 1936 in 'Passage Steamer', in which a trans-Atlantic journey ends with the lines 'The sea looks nothing more nor less than a grave / And the world and the day are grey and that is all'.[56] Almost three decades later, in 'The Grey Ones', from *The Burning Perch* (a collection which also includes 'Greyness is All'), MacNeice evokes the Graeae of Greek mythology, 'three grey sisters' who 'share an eye' can see: 'No past, no future, and no fall'.[57]

Dublin, with its greying monuments to waves of invaders who have vanished into the grey brick of the present moment, is 'by a juggler's trick' able to 'poise the toppling hour'. The key word here is 'poise', two discrete senses of which are held in balance, accentuated by the balancing act of rhyme: 'to poise' means both 'to weigh', but also 'to keep in balance or equilibrium'.[58] Etymologically, the link between the two can be imagined through the idea of weighing with a set of balances. However, in the phrase 'poise the toppling hour', the word 'toppling' upsets this consonance, so that the phrase may mean both to weigh (or to see clearly) the destructive effects of time, and, simultaneously, to hold 'the toppling hour' in equilibrium with some kind of counterweight – the counterweight of a world secured through poetic language. We should also recall that when the poem first appeared in *The Last Ditch*, it was followed by the poem in which this fragile point of equilibrium is most fully achieved in MacNeice's work, 'Meeting Point': 'Time was away and somewhere else'.[59] Here, we glimpse a third kind of 'poise' – 'poise' as a kind of level-headedness in the face of adversity – and this perhaps best defines MacNeice's poetic style: utterly assured, precise and yet unfussy, almost casual in its delivery. Places, events and people are real in MacNeice's writing, and as such are owed a debt of accuracy in language. Poised against the reality of the world is the precariousness of 'the toppling hour', the corrosive awareness of which gives even the seemingly solid stones of an historic city the grey sheen of the incorrigibly plural.

NOTES

1. Roy McFadden and Geoffrey Taylor, 'Poetry in Ireland: A Discussion', *The Bell* IV:6 (April 1943), pp. 338–46; p. 344.
2. W. H. Auden and Louis MacNeice, *Letters from Iceland* (London: Faber, 1937), p. 31.
3. The Conquest of Everest, dir. George Lowe; screenplay, Louis MacNeice (England, 1953).
4. Louis MacNeice, 'Subject in Modern Poetry', in *Selected Literary Criticism of Louis MacNeice*, ed. Alan Heuser (Oxford: Clarendon, 1987), pp. 57, 63, 64, 71, 74.
5. MacNeice, *Selected Literary Criticism*, p. 70.
6. Louis MacNeice, *Modern Poetry: A Personal Essay* (Oxford: Clarendon, 1938), p. 198.
7. MacNeice, *Modern Poetry*, p. 165.

8. Louis MacNeice, *Collected Poems*, ed. Peter McDonald (London: Faber and Faber, 2007), p. 5. This is the standard edition of MacNeice's poetry, and all subsequent references are to this edition. There is an earlier *Collected Poems*, ed. E. R. Dodds (London: Faber and Faber, 1966); there is also a useful *Selected Poems*, ed. Michael Longley (London: Faber, 1988).
9. MacNeice, *Modern Poetry*, p. 130.
10. MacNeice, *Collected Poems*, p. 101.
11. MacNeice, *Collected*, p. 216.
12. MacNeice, *Collected Poems*, p. 536.
13. Louis MacNeice to Anthony Blunt, 11 June 1935; in *Letters of Louis MacNeice*, ed. Jonathan Allison (London: Faber, 2010), p. 254.
14. Louis MacNeice, *The Poetry of W. B. Yeats* (Oxford: Oxford University Press, 1941), p. 47.
15. Tom Walker, *Louis MacNeice and the Irish Poetry of His Time* (Oxford: Oxford University Press, 2015), p. 120.
16. MacNeice, *Yeats*, p. 47.
17. MacNeice, *Letters from Iceland*, p. 229; also *Collected Poems*, p. 731.
18. MacNeice, *Collected Poems*, p. 55.
19. MacNeice, *Collected Poems*, p. 25.
20. MacNeice, *Collected Poems*, pp. 17–8.
21. See: http://apoemforireland.rte.ie/shortlist/dublin/ (accessed 12 Jan. 2016).
22. MacNeice, *Collected Poems*, p. 179.
23. MacNeice, *Collected Poems*, p. 609.
24. David Fitzpatrick, *'Solitary and Wild': Frederick MacNeice and the Salvation of Ireland* (Dublin: Lilliput, 2011).
25. Alexander Dallas, *The Story of the Irish Church Missions* (London: Society for Irish Church Missions, 1867), p. 1.
26. Tom Walker, *Louis MacNeice and the Irish Poetry of His Time* (Oxford: Oxford University Press, 2015), pp. 158–162.
27. MacNeice, *Letters from Iceland*, p. 124.
28. MacNeice, *Collected Poems*, pp. 140, 139.
29. Edna Longley, *Louis MacNeice: A Study* (London: Faber, 1988), p. 19. The line from 'Carrickfergus' is from MacNeice, *Collected Poems*, p. 56.
30. Clair Wills, 'The Aesthetics of Irish Neutrality During the Second World War', *boundary* 2 31:1 (Spring 2004), p. 119. See also: Richard Danson Brown 'Neutrality and Commitment: MacNeice, Yeats, Ireland and the Second World War', *Journal of Modern Literature* 28: 3 (Spring, 2005), pp. 109–129; see also: Christopher Fauske, *Louis MacNeice* (Dublin: Irish Academic Press, 2016).
31. MacNeice to Eleanor Clark (8 May, 1938), *Letters*, p. 328.
32. Louis MacNeice, *The Poetry of W. B. Yeats* (Oxford: Oxford University Press, 1941), p. 39.
33. Longley, *Louis MacNeice*, p. xiii.
34. See Walker, *MacNeice and Irish Poetry*, pp. 11–46.
35. Longley, *MacNeice*, p. ix.
36. McDonald, 'Ireland's MacNeice,' p. 64.
37. Edna Longley, 'Opening up: A New Pluralism', *Fortnight*, No. 256 (Nov., 1987), pp. 24–25.

38. David Cairns and Shaun Richards, *Writing Ireland: Colonialism, Nationalism and Culture* (Manchester: Manchester University Press, 1988), pp. 1, 10.
39. Louis MacNeice, *Collected Poems*, p. 162.
40. Samuel Beckett, *Proust and Three Dialogues with Georges Duthuit* (1931; London: John Calder, 1965), pp. 12–13, 17, 15
41. Samuel Beckett, 'Recent Irish Poetry', *Disjecta: Miscellaneous Writings and A Dramatic Fragment*, ed. Ruby Cohn (London: John Calder, 1983), p. 70.
42. MacNeice, *Collected Poems*, p. 24.
43. MacNeice, *Collected Letters*, p. 634 n2.
44. MacNeice, *Collected Poems*, p. 617.
45. MacNeice, *Collected Poems*, pp. 631–2, 613.
46. MacNeice, *Collected Poems*, pp. 18.
47. MacNeice, *Collected Poems*, p. 24.
48. MacNeice, *Collected Poems*, p. 183.
49. MacNeice, *Collected Poems*, pp. 353–4.
50. MacNeice, *Collected Poems*, p. 359.
51. Jon Stallworthy, *Louis MacNeice* (London: Faber and Faber, 1995), p. 64.
52. Louis MacNeice, *The Strings Are False: An Unfinished Autobiography* (1966; London: Faber and Faber, 2007), p. 78.
53. MacNeice, *Collected Poems*, p. 607.
54. MacNeice, *Collected Poems*, p. 685.
55. MacNeice, *Collected Poems*, pp. 178–80; also pp. 680–2.
56. MacNeice, *Collected Poems*, p. 63.
57. MacNeice, *Collected Poems*, p. 584.
58. *s.v.* 'poise', *OED*.
59. MacNeice, *Collected Poems*, pp. 686–7.

SELECTED FURTHER READING

Editions: MacNeice was not given to revising published work and published almost all of his poetry with the same publisher, Faber and Faber; he also had a literary executor in E. R. Dodds who assembled a reliable *Collected Poems* (London: Faber and Faber, 1966) shortly after his death. Hence, there are few thorny textual issues with his poetry; by contrast, his prose and his more than twenty years of writing for BBC radio pose more considerable bibliographic challenges.

Works by Louis MacNeice

MacNeice, Louis. *The Poetry of W. B. Yeats* (Oxford: Oxford University Press, 1941).
The Strings Are False: An Unfinished Autobiography (1965; London: Faber and Faber, 1982).
Selected Literary Criticism of Louis MacNeice. Ed. Alan Heuser (Oxford: Clarendon, 1987).

Selected Plays of Louis MacNeice. Ed. Alan Heuser and Peter McDonald (Oxford: Clarendon, 1993).

Selected Prose of Louis MacNeice. Ed. Alan Heuser (Oxford: Clarendon, 1990).

Collected Poems. Ed. Peter McDonald (London: Faber and Faber, 2007).

Letters of Louis MacNeice. Ed. Jonathan Allison (London: Faber, and Faber, 2010).

The Classical Radio Plays. Ed. Amanda Wrigley and S. J. Harrison (Oxford: Oxford University Press, 2013).

MacNeice, Louis and W. H. Auden. *Letters from Iceland* (London: Faber and Faber, 1937).

Selected Critical Bibliography

Brearton, Fran and Edna Longley, Eds. *Incorrigibly Plural: Louis MacNeice and His Legacy* (Manchester: Carcanet Press, 2012).

Brown, Terence. *Louis MacNeice: Sceptical Vision* (Dublin: Gill and Macmillan, 1975).

Fauske, Christopher J. *Louis MacNeice: In a Between World.* (Dublin: Irish Academic Press, 2016).

Longley, Edna. *Louis MacNeice: A Study* (London: Faber and Faber, 1988).

McDonald, Peter. *Louis MacNeice: The Poet in His Contexts* (Oxford: Clarendon, 1991).

Stallworthy, Jon. *Louis MacNeice* (London: Faber and Faber, 1995).

Walker, Tom. *Louis MacNeice and the Irish Poetry of His Time* (Oxford: Oxford University Press, 2015).

14

GUY WOODWARD

John Hewitt

Land, roots and territory: these are the things to which so much of John Hewitt's poetry gravitates. The poems address the physical features of the land, the roots, both real and metaphorical, embedded in it, and also seek to chart the way that land was inhabited, divided and colonised. In 1945 he wrote that the Ulster writer 'must be a rooted man, must carry the native tang of his idiom like the native dust on his sleeve; otherwise he is an airy internationalist, thistledown, a twig in a stream'.[1] Hewitt's most celebrated works – the long poems 'Conacre' and 'Freehold', and the much-anthologised, often-quoted shorter poems 'Ireland', 'The Colony' and 'An Irishman in Coventry' – duly emphasise the burdens and pressures of inherited histories and valorise fidelity to the land. The lesser-known 'Overture for Ulster Regionalism' (1948) conceded that 'Our speech is a narrow speech' before affirming that 'even this starved thing will serve our purpose / if we're obedient to the shape of the land', and stating confidently that 'We can make something of it, something hard / and clean and honest as the basalt cliffs', identifying creative expression with the physical terrain of the province.[2] Gerald Dawe has discerned in Hewitt's poetry 'the struggle against art's enticement, the lure of the imagination, distant horizons, the unknown – and the need to resist this in both poetic and political terms'.[3] Hewitt's resistance to these various attractions was anchored in the land of his birth, but those 'distant horizons', which drew much closer, of course, during World War II, are important to an understanding of this writer. Often remembered as an earnest regionalist, his poetry and prose are more fruitfully understood in the light of tensions and contradictions between his local and international preoccupations.

Hewitt's use of a public first-person plural in an 'Overture for Ulster Regionalism' and elsewhere in his work speaks of his belief in collective action and of a desire to be part of, rather than to lead, a distinctive literary movement in Ulster. Neither of these yearnings were to be satisfied: brief flutters of socialist promise in Northern Ireland during and after World War II were swiftly displaced, first by unionist retrenchment, and then by the flaring of violence in the province towards the end of the 1960s. The cultural renewal initiated by the war years also quickly dissipated, and from 1948 it would be two decades before the publication of work by Seamus Heaney, Michael Longley and Derek Mahon provided evidence of a successful group of Northern poets. In 2009 John Wilson Foster published an essay ironically entitled 'Was there Ulster literary life before Heaney?', noting that many students of Irish literature seem unaware of any Northern writing before the much-garlanded Nobel laureate, and sensing a danger that Heaney could become as synonymous with Northern Ireland as W. B. Yeats is with the southern state.[4] Re-examining John Hewitt's career and writings enables the recovery of an often overlooked period in the literary and cultural life of Ulster during the 1930s, '40s and '50s, a period that followed partition and the creation of Northern Ireland in 1921, and that preceded the rise to international prominence of Heaney and his contemporaries, against a background of renewed political violence, by the late 1960s.

Heaney himself observed that 'the continuous process in Hewitt's work has been one of coming to terms, of measuring the self against circumstances'; while for Eavan Boland, Hewitt was 'happiest when he can explicate his public places in terms of his private world'.[5] The circumstances to which Heaney refers were unavoidable: Hewitt was born in North Belfast in 1907 and so came of age in the early years of the new political arrangements that followed the partition of Ireland into Northern Ireland and the independent southern state in 1921. His childhood is the subject of *Kites in Spring: A Belfast Boyhood* (1980), a collection of 107 autobiographical sonnets which locate his upbringing against this historical context. 'Carson at Six Road Ends' tells of being taken at the age of six to a public address by the eponymous unionist leader. 'The YCVs and the Ulster Division' recalls the return to Belfast during World War I of soldiers who 'would tell us stories from / the shell-ploughed fields of Passchendaele and Somme.'[6] In 'Bangor, Spring 1916', Hewitt recalls the headmaster of his school returning from a 'ruined holiday' in Dublin in Easter week of that year, telling of 'dead horses and abandoned cars' but remaining silent on 'the politics of that affray'.[7] And 'After the Fire' describes the burning of Catholic-owned public houses in the city in the early 1920s, and Hewitt's feelings of solidarity with his Catholic next door neighbour. *Kites in Spring* is a valuable record of a city undergoing enormous change, refracted through the perspective of a single child observer. In Hewitt's draft foreword for the collection, he writes that he packed the sonnets 'with what I believe are factual statements or references, or accurate, so far as I know, undoctored memories, a highly [constricting] exercise'.[8] Constricting this might have been, but much of Hewitt's poetry is autobiographical, or at least dependent on direct experience and observation (the 1965 poem 'Poetry, Then . . . ' affirms that 'Poetry's an exercise, a way, / an attitude, a holding of the mind / like a vast radar-dish alert to life').[9] The 1940 poem 'The Mask' is insistently literal in its use of the eponymous metaphor, describing 'the old creased shiny mask with sagging jowl / lifted from peg beside the torn tweed coat', but otherwise Hewitt's work involves little apparent donning of masks or personae and it is difficult to separate the first person which pervades his work from Hewitt himself.[10]

Hewitt's parents were Methodist, a small and dissenting minority within the Protestant majority in the city: dissent, and fiercely guarded independence of mind, would animate much of Hewitt's career. His father's family were of Planter stock who had left England in the seventeenth century, settling in Kilmore, County Armagh, where both paternal grandparents were born in the mid-nineteenth century. In 1953 Hewitt would identify the 'Planter's Gothic' church at Kilmore, where the seventeenth-century square tower encloses the stump of a medieval round tower, as 'the best symbol I have yet found for the strange textures of my response to this island of which I am a native'.[11] Hewitt was educated at the Methodist elementary school on Agnes Street where his father was principal, before attending the Royal Belfast Academical Institution and then the Methodist College in the city. He was a studious child who read voraciously from his early years, later finding on his father's bookshelves works of literature and books on art, but also writings by Thomas Paine, William Cobbett and William Morris, as the younger Hewitt inherited the elder's socialism and affinity with the English radical tradition.[12] These allegiances endured, but were complicated by other preoccupations. In his long poem 'Freehold' he described his father's identity 'so tethered to antinomies it rocks / in seesaw straddle of a paradox': this was a man who had inherited memories of the Great Famine, yet was suspicious of Catholicism, prone to romanticising the 1798 Rebellion but proud of the British Empire, despising royal or papal pageantry yet in love with the 'sashes, banners, fife and drum' of the Orange Order.[13] Hewitt inherited some of these contradictions, and, in response to a range of mid-twentieth-century cultural and political conflicts, developed some of his own.

His early writing years were prolific, as he filled notebooks with exercises and experiments in many forms of verse-making, often expressing his commitment to socialist orthodoxy. Much of this early work is poor – perhaps most notorious is 'Chant for the Five-Year Plan' (1930), which included the lines 'Marx was a man with a big black beard, / he's dead many years, but his name is feared' and the refrain 'Shoulder to shoulder, woman and man, / another heave for the five-year plan'.[14] A poem published in 1928, 'To a Modern Irish Poet', adopts an accusatory tone to announce a rejection of Celtic Twilightery as inadequate to present socio-economic pressures:

You came with your strange, wistful, trembling verse,
    beguiled me for a while in quaint deceit;
and I forgot th'oppressor's blow and curse,
    the muffled tread of workless in the street.[15]

From 1924 to 30 he attended Queen's University, where he read for an English degree. He also trained to be a teacher at Stranmillis College, but instead of following this path applied to become an art assistant at the Belfast Museum and Art Gallery. He was appointed in November 1930 and would remain there until 1957. His memoir *A North Light*, which remained unpublished until 2013, is an engaging account of these years.

Hewitt seemed to date his own poetic maturity from the 1932 poem 'Ireland', which he placed very deliberately at the beginning of the *Collected Poems 1932–1967* (1968). Over four stanzas this poem repeatedly asserts the first-person plural to lament the folly of 'We Irish', content 'to spend our wit and love and poetry / on half a dozen peat and a black bog.'[16] In the second half of the poem Hewitt employs a tidal metaphor, describing a 'Keltic wave that broke over Europe', running up a beach only to be left stranded:

in crevices, and ledge-protected pools
that have grown salter with the drying up
of the great common flow that kept us sweet
with fresh cold draughts from deep down in the ocean.[17]

The acknowledgement of rootedness in soil, followed by a bitter yearning for revivification through a 'common flow', illustrates the tensions in Hewitt's work between local, national and international impulses. An attempt to resolve these in the poem's conclusion, which suggests that what is thought to be 'love of usual rock' instead 'is but forgotten longing for the sea', may fail to convince, but seems to establish a context against which Hewitt could make further and repeated attempts to reconcile rootedness with European and global currents.[18] The younger Belfast poet Roy McFadden recalled Hewitt murmuring 'pentametrically' over his pipe that 'Definition ... means comparison'.[19]

The thirty-six-year gap between the composition of 'Ireland' and its eventual appearance in a book of Hewitt's own (the poem had appeared in *The Listener* in 1932, and in various anthologies over the course of the intervening period) is not anomalous, and Hewitt's composition and publication history frequently followed radically different chronologies. His first collection of poems, *No Rebel Word*, was not published until 1948 when he was forty-one years old, but featured poems written as early as 1932, while the final collection published during his lifetime, *Freehold and other Poems* (1986) featured a title poem conceived in the mid-1940s together with the verse drama *The Bloody Brae*, which had been written in 1936. In addition, some of Hewitt's volumes (*An Ulster Reckoning* (1971) and *The Chinese Fluteplayer* (1974)) were privately printed, remaining elusive until Frank Ormsby's *Collected Poems* of 1991. As a result of these delays and irregularities, this most politically committed of poets can seem, on occasion, unresponsive or outpaced by events: as Hewitt's biographer W. J. McCormack has observed, the growing discontent in Northern Ireland was 'invisible' to readers of the 1968 *Collected Poems* upon their publication.[20]

The year 1932 also brought Hewitt's meeting with Roberta Black, whom he encountered while guiding visitors around a Rodin exhibition at the gallery; they married two years later, and her presence by the poet's side is registered by the use of 'we' and 'you' in many subsequent poems. As members of the Belfast Peace League and the National Council for Civil Liberties, the Hewitts were active together in left-wing circles, as far as John Hewitt's politically neutral occupation would permit. They attended socialist summer schools in England in 1933 and 1936, where they encountered John Middleton Murry and George Orwell, among others. Hewitt recalled Orwell as the first man of the Left he had encountered who voiced misgivings about the Soviet Union; following the Spanish Civil War, the Hewitts became more equivocal in their communist leanings, and there would be no more panegyrics to Soviet industrial policy.[21]

The war years, as he experienced them at home and apprehended their significance abroad, were crucial to Hewitt's career and development as critic and poet. Attempting to join the British Army in the autumn of 1939, Hewitt was variously turned down and ignored by recruiting officers due to his reserved status as a local government employee. He subsequently admitted to feeling 'a recurring sense of guilt' at his inability to become directly involved, and writes in *A North Light* of his regret at not being able 'to take any part in what I realised must have been the greatest imaginative experience of my generation; and maybe in that loss I have suffered a serious deprivation which has left me perhaps less adult than my years require'.[22] Nevertheless, Hewitt had a busy war, lecturing on art and literature in British army camps around Northern Ireland in addition to his duties at the museum, where he organised several exhibitions of works by overseas artists.

Hewitt produced relatively few poems directly addressing the conflict, preferring to explore the landscape and cultural history of Ulster in works of this period, as the Hewitts holidayed at home in the Glens of Antrim and the Rosses of Donegal. Wartime travel restrictions prevented travel to Britain or Europe but also served to concentrate his mind at a time of cultural stimulation. Hewitt recalled that 1943 was the year in which Belfast entered 'an unusually vigorous phase in the creative arts', citing 'small exhibitions in dingy rooms down-town' and the appearance of 'a new generation of writers' in the little magazine *Lagan*, and suggesting that 'While the basic causes for this wide striving are not readily teased out, the wartime isolation of Northern Ireland was certainly a factor, compelling us to till our own gardens.'[23]

That year saw Hewitt's promotion to chief assistant in the gallery and the publication of the long poem 'Conacre' in pamphlet form, beginning what Hewitt saw as a trilogy completed by 'Freehold' (1946) and 'Homestead' (1949). The poem was preceded by the *Oxford English Dictionary* definition of the word taken for its title: 'in Irish land system: the letting by a tenant for a season, of small portions of land ready ploughed and prepared for a crop'. Arising from Hewitt's wartime visits to the Glens of Antrim, the poem duly addresses the poet's quasi-mystical relationship with soil and with plotted and divided land and landscape, as it describes an urban-dweller's discovery of the textures of rural life. Written in the first person, like much of Hewitt's poetry it is characterised by didactic certainty, and proclaims several statements of intent:

> I would not raise a hand to bring a state
> magnificent in art, in commerce great,
> with the smooth comfort of its concrete squares
> superbly measured out in equal shares,
> where there was left no single ragged line
> of twisted thorn or resin-oozing pine
> where boys may light a fire, and for a day
> slough off two thousand years in naked play.[24]

The distinct and paradoxical atmosphere of the war years, where Northern Ireland was literally isolated but culturally and socially invigorated by the presence of many thousands of outsiders, encouraged Hewitt to formulate his theory of regionalism, inspired in part by his reading of Lewis Mumford's *The Culture of Cities* (1938). An outline of his resulting ideas appears in an article entitled 'Regionalism: The Last Chance' published in 1947. Here, he advocates breaking up national government organisations into smaller regional bodies to tackle specific problems, and describes a devolutionary process beginning with the stimulation of local culture.[25] Arguing that strongly held and defended regional identities 'do[] not preclude, rather [they] require[]' membership of a larger cultural and political association, he makes the radically subversive and impractical suggestion that for Ulster this could take the form of participation in a federal Ireland or federated British Isles.[26]

186

During the war, Charles Monteith, later commissioning editor and subse-quently chairman of Faber and Faber, but then serving in the Royal Inniskilling Fusiliers in Northern Ireland, observed that 'all our writers are caught in a lethal dilemma, from which they must escape or die – London or Dublin, which?'[27] Hewitt's regionalism attempted to resolve this post-parti-tion Northern dilemma, and in this respect it complemented his socialism, which, as Wilson Foster has observed, with reference to Hewitt, Sam Hanna Bell and Robert Greacen, offered a means by which Northern writers could escape 'prior and largely involuntary primary identities . . . and take part, first and foremost, in an unpartitioned and recognizable intellectual and artistic community'.[28] As such, the ideas gained little political traction, as Heather Clark observes: 'ultimately, regionalism could not accommodate the increas-ingly grim realities of life in Northern Ireland, for how could the region open up a conciliatory space when that very space was contested?'[29]

The impact on Hewitt's own output is harder to gauge, but it is questionable whether regionalism offered a coherent aesthetic or artistic programme for Hewitt or others to follow, other than the prospect of writing repeatedly about their locality. Hewitt's regionalist ideas and cultural historical excavations failed to inspire succeeding generations. Fourteen years younger than Hewitt, Roy McFadden recalled in 1961 that:

> Attempts were made to conjure up some inoffensive shoemakers, clergymen, mechanics who had happened to toss off the odd poem in their youth, were exhumed from their century-old graves and held up as our literary ancestors. But we shook our heads. They remained shoemakers, clergymen and mechanics. Ulster horseshoes have an extra nail hole. We remained uninspired.[30]

Earnestness and didacticism do not go unpunished in Irish literature on either side of the border, and Hewitt's efforts to inspire interest in the radical potential of the eighteenth-century weaver poets of Antrim and Down, for example, are easily shrugged off and belittled. However, his role as organiser and instigator in the decades before the move to Coventry in 1957 should not be underestimated. Regionalism sprang not only from a desire to resolve local difficulties, but also to promote the importance of the province to the outside world. In 1949 the Hewitts travelled to Venice, attending the PEN Conference to which Hewitt was a delegate. In a BBC talk he describes an encounter with a Venetian passer-by who was unable to understand his accent, and hearing only the word 'Irish' when Hewitt referred to himself as 'Northern Irish' responded 'Ah! Irlandese! De Valera!' Hewitt comments that 'Ireland for millions outside this island is represented by Irish horses, Irish whiskey and by the name De Valera. . . . But Northern Ireland – Ulster certainly on the continent, is, as far as I know, an utterly unheard-of place.' To combat this misapprehension, Hewitt argues that Northern Ireland must be better represented (and, we might infer, defined) by its art and culture, the international exposure of which suffers from a lack of state support.[31] Hewitt's attempts to square the relationship between Northern Ireland and 'Ulster certainly' remained unresolved, but his efforts to promote art and literature from the north-east part of Ireland are of enduring importance.

These efforts are present in the waspish caricature of Hewitt as the art dealer Griffin in F. L. Green's 1945 novel *Odd Man Out*, which satirises Hewitt's centrality to mid-century Belfast cultural life:

> There was hardly a platform which he could prevent himself from taking, and from which he theorized in a robust, crisp fashion. There was scarcely a stranger to the city who, coming to the North for information regarding its history, literature, drama, painting, politics, commerce, hopes, was not swiftly and adroitly contacted by Griffin and as swiftly loaded with facts. And similarly, when a new artist or novelist, poet, politician, playwright appeared from amongst the population, Griffin was there to study him from some vantage point and thereafter applaud him or dismiss him in a few theorizing remarks.[32]

Green's caricature, which to Hewitt's credit is quoted at length in *A North Light*, identifies Hewitt's role as conduit between Belfast or Ulster literary life and the outside world. During World War II, Roberta and he welcomed artists and writers of many nationalities to their house at 18 Mount Charles, including writers stationed in Northern Ireland with the British armed forces, such as Hamish Henderson, Rayner Heppenstall, Emmanuel Litvinoff and John Manifold. As a delegate to PEN, he attended conferences in Glasgow, Venice, Amsterdam and Vienna. Hewitt himself was aware of his role as an intermediary or facilitator, casting himself as a 'middleman' in the 1960 poem 'A Country Walk in May': 'For nearly thirty years my chosen part / has been to play the middleman in art ... between the man whose blessed privilege / is to be born an artist and the rest / born uncreative'.[33] As these lines suggest, he was not a vain or presumptuous man: W. J. McCormack notes that professionally Hewitt was careful to describe himself as 'gallery man' rather than 'art historian': such self-deprecation and self-examination are pervasive in Hewitt's poems which, notwithstanding his selective use of the first-person plural, frequently read as attempts to work things out for himself rather than to speak for others.[34] The 1975 poem 'Below the Mournes in May' describes an inner conflict between contradictory impulses as 'nature-poet' and Marxist:

> Then I remembered that the nature-poet
> has no easy prosody for

class or property relationships,
for the social dialectic,
the stubborn tenure of the small farm,
the billowed hillsides or timber
brimming the high-walled demesnes.[35]

In the 1975 poem 'A Local Poet', a version of the 1955 'Poet in Ulster' revised following Roberta's death in 1975 to register in sharper relief a sense of isolation, Hewitt again addresses himself in the third person:

And so, with luck, for a decade
down the widowed years ahead,
the pension which crippled his courage
will keep him in daily bread,
while he mourns for his mannerly verses
that had left so much unsaid.[36]

The mourning here for 'mannerly verses' indicates an awareness that formal conservatism had not always succeeded. Hewitt's early appetite for High Modernism and experimental art and literature is clear: in the early 1930s he smuggled a copy of *Ulysses* from Paris through British customs hidden in the seat of his plus fours.[37] Assembled over half a century, his library at Ulster University, Coleraine, is that of an autodidact, intellectually curious, with cosmopolitan interests ranging far beyond the regionalist caricature that has often been applied to him. In 1934 he acted as secretary to the short-lived Ulster Unit collective of artists, proclaiming in the exhibition catalogue that 'Ulster has for the first time a body of artists alert to continental influence while that influence is still real and vital ... working on experimental lines and no longer in an archaic dialectic'.[38] The unpublished 1940 poem 'I Talked and Raged and Planned ...' articulates some frustration with modern movements, however, as he writes with Miltonic disdain that 'I tried to understand / the scrannel modern crew, / till with the years I grew / a stranger in the land', but as gallery man in Belfast and Coventry, Hewitt was supportive of exhibitions of avant-garde and experimental work, even if the acquisitions for which he was responsible were relatively conservative.[39] In his poetry, however, he clove to his understated and controlled approach, so often reliant on regular iambs and couplets, throughout his career. In this respect his work contrasts with that of his friend and contemporary W. R. Rodgers, whose loud gusts of New Apocalypticism also contributed to the brief invigoration of Northern verse-making during the 1940s. Hewitt saw himself as a craftsman, writing in 'Ars Poetica' (1949) that 'With what I made I have been satisfied / as country joiner with a country cart / ... My symbol's master was that solid man, / that slow and independent carpenter'.[40] As a child Hewitt had followed the painter William Conor along the street, and there are occasions too when painterly metaphors or turns of phrase suggest a yearning to express himself visually, to produce pictures, rather than poems. The opening of 'Below the Mournes in May' describes how:

> The landscape's upper frame was bounded by
> the sinuous edge of the dark mountains:
> the middle distance, foothill-filled,
> in rough places gay mounds of whin
> yolk-yellow on the turf;[41]

The 1953 poem 'The Glens of Antrim' records that he has 'drawn this landscape now for thirty years' and has 'drilled my pen to draw each sign / which peoples time and place within this frame'.[42]

In 1953 Hewitt applied for the position of director of the Belfast Museum and Art Gallery, but was rejected due to his associations with socialism and his friendships with Catholics. His disappointment and anger at this setback and his feelings towards those who conspired against him are recorded in *A North Light* and in the poem 'Elegy for an Enemy', published in *The Honest Ulsterman* journal in 1968. In 1957 his application to become art director of the Herbert Art Gallery in Coventry was successful, and the Hewitts moved to England, where they would remain for the next fifteen years. The civic and cultural life of Coventry suited Hewitt well. Heavily bombed during the war, the city was undergoing a process of reconstruction and renewal under a Labour council which had forged links with several other European cities through town-twinning programmes and other cultural connections, offering Hewitt numerous opportunities to travel over the coming decade. The much-anthologised 'An Irishman in Coventry' articulates Hewitt's pleasure at this atmosphere, lauding 'the tolerance that laced its blatant roar ... image of the state hope argued for', before articulating rage and pity for Ireland from the home of its colonists, as a night in an Irish pub conjures up:

> a people endlessly betrayed
> by our own weakness, by the wrongs we suffered
> in that long twilight over bog and glen,
> by force, by famine and by glittering fables[43]

His most successful poetic engagements with contemporary politics in Northern Ireland were written from England. A series of poems in *An Ulster Reckoning* (1971) describe a shift in class authority in the mid-twentieth century, thrown into sharp relief by the escalation in sectarian violence at the end of the 1960s. 'An Ulster Landowner's Song' is an imagined lament of sorts for the decline in the status and influence of the aristocracy, in which a jaunty Betjemanesque register ('I'm Major This or Captain That / MC and DSO') and use of common metre is deliberately jolted by the final two stanzas, in which the speaker's tenants 'start a small affray':

> They stirred up an unwelcome noise,
> it set my nerves on edge,
> that day they beat those girls and boys
> across Burntollet Bridge,
>
> with journalists and cameras there
> to send in their reports.
> The world no longer seems to care
> for healthy country sports.[44]

Here, a sense of shock is articulated by the sudden contemporary specificity of the attack on the People's Democracy March at Burntollet on 4 January 1969. The poem is succeeded later in the collection by 'The Coasters' – a searing indictment of bourgeois complacency in Northern Ireland, of those who 'coasted along / to larger houses, gadgets, more machines, / to golf and weekend bungalows', who 'showed a sense of responsibility / with subscriptions to worthwhile causes', who 'even had a friend or two of the other sort' but who expressed sympathy 'when that noisy preacher started' and now, as 'the fever is high and raging', are threatened themselves:

> The cloud of infection hangs over the city,
> a quick change of wind and it
> might spill over the leafy suburbs.
> You coasted too long.[45]

A further series of four sonnets in *An Ulster Reckoning* – 'Prime Minister', 'Demagogue', 'Minister' and 'Agitator' – were published originally in the radical *Hibernia* magazine in October 1969, and address in turn Chichester-Clark, Ian Paisley (the 'noisy preacher' referred to in 'The Coasters'), Brian Faulkner and Bernadette Devlin. Following retirement in Coventry, the Hewitts returned to Belfast in October 1972, the year of the Troubles in which the greatest number of people lost their lives. Four months before they travelled, on 29 May, Hewitt's poem 'Neither an Elegy nor a Manifesto' was published in the top left hand corner of page 8 of the *Irish Times*, a page otherwise entirely filled by news of sectarian shootings, loyalist marches, political deadlock and a prison strike. Powerfully and irrevocably contextualised by this placement, the poem is preceded by a dedication 'for the people of my province and the rest of Ireland', and opens 'Bear in mind these dead: I can find no plainer words'. In it, Hewitt 'propose[s] no more than thoughtful response' and insists that there must be no differentiation 'between / deliberately gunned down / and those caught by unaddressed bullets: / such distinctions are not relevant.'[46]

In October 1975, a month after the Hewitts' fortnight-long visit to the Soviet Union, Roberta Hewitt died at the age of 70. John Hewitt remained in Belfast for the rest of his life, where his late career brought a flurry of official honours and awards from universities and cultural institutions, although he turned down an OBE in 1979. These were prolific years: for the first time Hewitt found a regular outlet for his work in Belfast's Blackstaff Press, who published several volumes of new and revised poems throughout the 1970s and '80s. He died in 1987, four months short of his eightieth birthday.

Hewitt himself was uncertain of what his legacy might consist. At the conclusion of 'A Country Walk in March' (1953) the poet wonders:

> if in any place
> my passing leaves a more enduring trace,
> and if the verses that I rush to print
> are worth as much as these stray wisps of lint.[47]

Wispiness need not constitute failure, however: the eight-line 1945 poem 'I Write For . . .' asserts that the quietness of his verses should be matched by the thoughtfulness of his readers, his 'own kind':

> their quality of mind
> must be withdrawn and still,
> as moth that answers moth
> across a roaring hill.[48]

Hewitt's prolific output did not always pay dividends. Ormsby's *Collected Poems* of 1991 is magisterially assembled but features too much pedestrian and literal material for the casual reader, for whom Ormsby and Michael Longley's 2007 edition of the *Selected Poems* provides a more stimulating introduction to Hewitt's work. Ambitious attempts at the big subjects sometimes fall flat: 'The Child, The Chair, The Leaf' (1953) is a ponderous attempt to address Newtonian physics. Clumsy but well-meaning liberal efforts in the 1970s to address the suffering of Jews ('Strangers and Neighbours') and gay rights ('As You Like It') have not worn well. Writing in 1986, following the exclusion of Hewitt's work from two major anthologies, Paul Muldoon's *Faber Contemporary Irish Poetry* (1984) and Thomas Kinsella's *New Oxford Book of Irish Verse* (1986), Eavan Boland despaired of the critical tendency to grant Hewitt, at best, 'a few polite paragraphs', and suggested that 'John Hewitt's poetry has been wished away at times because it seems to cling to old political positions which do not suit the new critical programme.'[49] The worthiness and earnestness have dismayed some, while the suspicion of Catholicism has alarmed others; although Hewitt has been defended on this point by McCormack and Clyde.

Responding to the quotation with which this essay began, Derek Mahon expressed such unease when he observed 'This is a bit tough on thistledown; and, speaking as a twig in a stream, I feel there's a certain harshness, a dogmatism, at work there.'[50] And yet Hewitt's presence in Belfast (before the departure for Coventry in 1957 and after his return in 1972), and his encouragement of generations of younger Northern poets, over nearly half a century, were important. In 1974 James Simmons described Hewitt affectionately as 'the daddy of us all' in his poem 'Flight of the Earls Now Leaving'.[51] Elmer Kennedy-Andrews suggests that 'nearly all subsequent Ulster poets have looked up to him as a moral exemplar and pioneering figure'; W. J. McCormack argues that his 'father-figure-hood' was important for the generation of Seamus Heaney, Michael Longley, Derek Mahon and Simmons 'partly because the only alternative, Louis MacNeice, had died in 1963 when Northern Ireland seemed beyond change'.[52] Tom Clyde concludes that regionalist ideas formulated by Hewitt during the war were taken on by the cultural institutions of the province – the BBC, CEMA (NI), Queen's University and the Ulster Museum – and claims that, as a result, 'no Ulster poet since that time has found his or her self so confused, isolated and burdened by cultural cringe as Hewitt and his predecessors did'.[53] These various tributes and assessments all suggest that Hewitt's activities as an organiser, a promoter, a mentor and a general one-man advance party for twentieth-century Ulster writing are of enduring importance.

NOTES

1. John Hewitt, 'The Bitter Gourd: Some Problems of the Ulster Writer', *Lagan*, 3 (1945), pp. 93–105 (p. 99).
2. John Hewitt, 'Overture for an Ulster Literature', in *The Collected Poems of John Hewitt*, ed. Frank Ormsby (Belfast: Blackstaff Press, 1991), pp. 511–12 (p. 512). All subsequent quotations from Hewitt's poetry are from this volume, and dates cited are to the date of composition, as recorded in this volume.
3. Gerald Dawe, 'Against piety: a reading of John Hewitt's poetry', in *The Poet's Place: Ulster Literature and Society Essays in honour of John Hewitt, 1907–87*, ed. by Gerald Dawe and John Wilson Foster (Belfast: Institute of Irish Studies, 1991), pp. 209–24 (p. 218).
4. John Wilson Foster, 'Was there Ulster literary life before Heaney?', in *Between Shadows: Modern Irish Writing and Culture* (Dublin, Portland, Oregon: Irish Academic Press, 2009), pp. 205–18 (p. 205).
5. Seamus Heaney, review of John Hewitt, *Collected Poems, 1932–67*, in *Threshold* (Summer 1969), pp. 73–7, p. 76; Eavan Boland, 'Hewitt the Outsider', *Irish Times*, 26 July 1986, 'Weekend' section, p. 10.
6. Hewitt, 'The YCVs and the Ulster Division' in *Collected Poems*, p. 296.

7. Hewitt, 'Bangor, Spring 1916', in *Collected Poems*, p. 296.
8. Reproduced in notes to Ormsby (ed.), *Collected Poems*, p. 617.
9. Hewitt, 'Poetry, Then...', in *Collected Poems*, pp. 226–7 (p. 227).
10. Hewitt, 'The Mask', in *Collected Poems*, p. 41.
11. John Hewitt, 'Planter's Gothic', in *Ancestral Voices: The Selected Prose of John Hewitt*, ed. by Tom Clyde (Belfast: Blackstaff Press, 1987), pp. 1–33 (p. 9).
12. Frank Ormsby, 'Introduction' in *Collected Poems*, pp. xli–lxxiv (pp. xlii–xliii).
13. Hewitt, 'Freehold', in *Collected Poems*, p. 369–86 (p. 377).
14. Hewitt, 'Chant for the Five-Year Plan', in *Collected Poems*, pp. 468–9 (p. 469).
15. Hewitt, 'To a Modern Irish Poet', in *Collected Poems*, p. 443.
16. Hewitt, 'Ireland', in *Collected Poems*, p. 58.
17. Hewitt, 'Ireland', in *Collected Poems*, p. 58.
18. Hewitt, 'Ireland', in *Collected Poems*, p. 58.
19. Roy McFadden, 'The Dogged Hare', McFadden Papers, Special Collections Department, Queen's University Belfast, MP35 (vii).
20. W. J. McCormack, *Northman: John Hewitt (1907–87): An Irish Writer, His World, and His Times* (Oxford: Oxford University Press, 2015), p. 195.
21. John Hewitt, *A North Light: Twenty-five Years in a Municipal Art Gallery*, eds Frank Ferguson and Kathryn White (Dublin, Four Courts Press, 2013) pp. 106–7.
22. Hewitt, *North Light*, pp. 127–8
23. John Hewitt, *Colin Middleton* (Belfast and Dublin: Arts Council of Northern Ireland, and An Chormhairle Ealaion, 1976), p. 18.
24. John Hewitt, 'Conacre', in *Collected Poems*, pp. 3–12 (p. 8).
25. John Hewitt, 'Regionalism: The Last Chance' in *Ancestral Voices: The Selected Prose of John Hewitt*, ed. by Tom Clyde (Belfast: Blackstaff Press, 1987), p. 123.
26. Hewitt, 'Regionalism: The Last Chance' in *Ancestral Voices*, p. 125.
27. Charles M. Monteith, 'Letter to the Editor', *New Northman*, IX.2 (Summer 1941), p. 31.
28. Wilson Foster, 'Was there Ulster literary life before Heaney?', in *Between Shadows*, p. 213.
29. Heather Clark, *The Ulster Renaissance: Poetry in Belfast 1962–1972* (Oxford: Oxford University Press, 2006), p. 127.
30. Roy McFadden, 'Reflections on Megarrity', *Threshold*, 5.1 (Spring/Summer 1961), 25–34 (p. 32).
31. John Hewitt, '*Ulster Commentary*', radio broadcast on BBC NIHS, Friday 7 November 1949, John Hewitt Collection, Ulster University, Coleraine.
32. F. L. Green, *Odd Man Out* (London: Michael Joseph, 1945), pp. 187–8.
33. Hewitt, 'A Country Walk in May', in *Collected Poems*, pp. 516–30 (p. 517).
34. McCormack, *Northman*, p. 94.
35. Hewitt, 'Below the Mournes in May', in *Collected Poems*, pp. 244–5 (p. 245).
36. Hewitt, 'A Local Poet', in *Collected Poems*, pp. 219–20 (p. 220).
37. Hewitt, *North Light*, p. 75.
38. John Hewitt, 'Preface', *Ulster Unit* (unpaginated exhibition catalogue, Belfast: 1934).
39. Hewitt, 'I Talked and Raged and Planned ...', in *Collected Poems*, pp. 425–6.
40. Hewitt, 'Ars Poetica', in *Collected Poems*, pp. 227–9 (p. 228).
41. Hewitt, 'Below the Mournes in May', in *Collected Poems*, p. 244.
42. Hewitt, 'The Glens of Antrim', in *Collected Poems*, p. 231.

43. Hewitt, 'An Irishman in Coventry', in *Collected Poems*, pp. 97–8.
44. Hewitt, 'An Ulster Landowner's Song', in *Collected Poems*, pp. 134–5.
45. Hewitt, 'The Coasters', in *Collected Poems*, pp. 135–7.
46. John Hewitt, 'Neither an Elegy nor a Manifesto', *Irish Times*, 29 May 1972, p. 8.
47. Hewitt, 'A Country Walk in March', in *Collected Poems*, pp. 84–6 (p. 86).
48. Hewitt, 'I Write For . . .', in *Collected Poems*, p. 159.
49. Boland, 'Hewitt the Outsider', *Irish Times*, 26 July 1986.
50. Derek Mahon, review of *Ancestral Voices: Selected Prose of John Hewitt*, ed. Tom Clyde, in *Journalism: Selected Prose 1970–1995* (Dublin: Gallery Press, 1996), pp. 92–4 (p. 94).
51. James Simmons, 'Flight of the Earls Now Leaving', *Judy Garland and the Cold War* (Belfast: Blackstaff Press, 1976), p. 3.
52. Elmer Kennedy-Andrews, *Writing Home: Poetry and Place in Northern Ireland, 1968–2008* (Cambridge: D. S. Brewer, 2008), p. 21; McCormack, *Northman*, p. 251.
53. Tom Clyde, 'A Stirring in the Dry Bones: John Hewitt's Regionalism', in Gerald Dawe and Wilson Foster (eds.), *The Poet's Place*, pp. 249–58 (p. 258).

SELECTED FURTHER READING

Editions

Ancestral Voices: The Selected Prose of John Hewitt, ed. Tom Clyde, Belfast: Blackstaff Press, 1987.

The Collected Poems of John Hewitt, ed. Frank Ormsby, Belfast: Blackstaff Press, 1991.

Selected Poems, eds Michael Longley and Frank Ormsby, Belfast: Blackstaff Press, 2007.

A North Light: Twenty-five Years in a Municipal Art Gallery, eds Frank Ferguson and Kathryn White, Dublin: Four Courts Press, 2013.

Secondary works

Brown, Terence, 'John Hewitt and memory: a reflection', in *The Literature of Ireland: Culture and Criticism*, Cambridge: Cambridge University Press, 2010.

Dawe, Gerald, and John Wilson Foster (eds.), *The Poet's Place: Ulster Literature and Society. Essays in Honour of John Hewitt, 1907–87*, Belfast: Institute of Irish Studies, 1991.

Greacen, Robert, 'John Hewitt', in *Rooted in Ulster: Nine Northern Writers*, Belfast: Lagan Press, 2000.

Heaney, Seamus, 'The Poetry of John Hewitt', in *Preoccupations: Selected Prose, 1968–1978*, London: Faber and Faber, 1980.

Kennedy-Andrews, Elmer, 'Paradigms and Precursors: Rooted Men and Nomads (John Hewitt, Patrick Kavanagh and Louis MacNeice', in

Writing Home: Poetry and Place in Northern Ireland, 1968–2008, Cambridge: D. S. Brewer, 2008.

Longley, Edna. 'Progressive Bookmen, Politics and Northern Protestant Writers since the 1930s', in *The Living Stream*, Newcastle Upon Tyne: Bloodaxe Books, 1994.

McCormack, W. J., *Northman: John Hewitt (1907–87): An Irish Writer, His World, and His Times*. Oxford: Oxford University Press, 2015.

McDonald, Peter, 'The Fate of Identity: John Hewitt, W. R. Rodgers, and Louis MacNeice', in *Mistaken Identities: Poetry and Northern Ireland*, Oxford: Oxford University Press, 1997.

Patten, Eve, (ed.), *Returning to Ourselves: Second Volume of Papers from the John Hewitt International Summer School*, Belfast: Lagan Press, 1995.

Woodward, Guy, '"We must know more than Ireland": John Hewitt and Eastern Europe', in *Ireland, West to East: Irish Cultural Interactions with Central and Eastern Europe*, eds Aidan O'Malley and Eve Patten, Oxford, Bern and New York: Peter Lang, 2014.

15

LOUIS DE PAOR

Seán Ó Ríordáin

In a biographical note published in 1966, Seán Ó Ríordáin described himself as 'neamh-fhile ag scríobh neamh-fhilíochta i neamh-Ghaeilge do neamh-dhaoine' [a non-poet writing non-poetry in non-Irish for non-people].[1] This self-deprecation, bordering on self-abasement, is not uncharacteristic of Ó Ríordáin, but there is more at issue here than modesty or inverted vanity. It is not only the poet himself and his work which are considered null and void; the language in which he wrote and his imagined audience are also nullified. In a 1974 column in the *Irish Times*, the poet identified 1966 as the year in which Ireland exhausted whatever national philosophy had sustained it until then, becoming a satellite culture, content with dominion status in politics, language and culture: 'Stopamar i lár abairte i 1966 nó mar sin. Ba léir athrú mór ar mheon an phobail as sin amach' [We stopped mid-sentence in 1966 or thereabouts. From then on there was a clear change in public attitude].[2] This (1966) was also the year in which Thomas Kinsella argued that the discontinuities of Irish history made a return to Irish impossible for him, but that recognition of his own cultural disinheritance might provide a basis for discovering forms of English adequate to a divided imagination.[3] Ó Ríordáin struggled with the same colonial history as Kinsella, committing himself to Irish rather than English without ever finally resolving the linguistic uncertainty confronted by both poets half a century after the cultural revolution of the early twentieth century which had attempted 'to make the present a rational continuation of the past'.[4]

Ó Ríordáin was born on 3 December 1916, the eldest of the three children of Seán Ó Ríordáin, a cobbler, and Máiréad Ní Luineacháin, in the village of Baile Bhúirne, twenty miles from Cork. In 1932, six years after his father's death from tuberculosis, the family moved to the rural community of Inis Cara, five miles from the city where the poet lived until his death in 1977. He attended school in the North Monastery, where his classmates included Jack Lynch, who would later become Taoiseach and one of the principal architects of the new liberal consensus against which the poet railed in the newspaper columns he contributed to the *Irish Times* between 1967 and 1975. He was appointed to a position as a clerk in Cork City Hall, where he worked in the Motor Taxation Office until his early retirement due to ill-health in 1965. Having been diagnosed with tuberculosis shortly after his appointment, Ó Ríordáin spent a considerable amount of time in hospital and in the sanatorium at Heatherside in north Cork. Prior to the introduction of the drug Streptomycin, the treatment prescribed for TB favoured bed rest and isolation, often in rural locations which were considered conducive to patients' recuperation but also prevented the spread of contagious diseases. 'Ní chun tú a leigheas a cuireadh isteach tú – ach chun an pobal a chosaint ort' [You were not sent in to be cured – but to protect the community from you].[5]

The living death of tuberculosis, the sense of physical disintegration and imminent annihilation that accompanied an incurable disease, aggravated the instability which is a central feature of the existential crisis at the heart of Ó Ríordáin's work. The relentless search for a unitary self that would provide a more secure basis for certainty and authenticity is a defining element of his poetry and prose, continuing until the final entries in his diary just days before his death. While illness deepened his sense of insecurity, the cultural and linguistic confusion arising from his upbringing in a family and community in which the cultural authority of Irish was being gradually eroded by the infiltration of English is a key factor also in Ó Ríordáin's conflicted imagination: 'Duine gan rútaí á stracadh idir dhá theanga ab ea mise riamh' [I was always a person without roots, torn between two languages].[6] The poet's experience of bilingualism was not an expansive pluralist one where two languages offered alternative possibilities of articulation and signification, but a colonial one where one language gradually suppressed and replaced the other. For Ó Ríordáin, Irish and English represented alternative worlds:

Bóthar Béarla is ea an bóthar so. Bóthar Gaeilge ab ea bóthar Bhaile Bhuirne agus sinn óg. Ba ghaláinte an bóthar Béarla. Baineann an bóthar so ó Inis Cara go Carraig an Droichid le William O'Brien agus amhráin Tom Moore agus leis an Mardyke agus 'The Banks of My Own Lovely Lee'. Baineann an bóthar eile ó Mhaigh Chromtha siar go Baile Bhuirne leis an Ath Peadar agus le Séadna agus le Daingean na Saileach, le Lá Bealtaine agus le lucht na bpiseog, le Reilig Ghobnatan agus le Dámhscoil Mhúscraí, le hEibhlín Dubh Ní Chonaill agus lem athair féin. Arraing trím chroí na bóithre seo agus mothaím ag comhrac iad im aigne. Tuigtear dom ar uairibh gur éirigh liom babhtaí iad a bhá i mbóthar eile – bóthar Chinn Sléibhe siar go Dún Chaoin.[7]

This road is an English language road. The Baile Bhúirne road was an Irish language road when we were young. The English road was more refined. This road from Inis Cara to Carraig an Droichid belongs to William O'Brien and the songs of Tom Moore and the Mardyke and 'The Banks of My Own Lovely

Lee'. The other road from Macroom back to Baile Bhúirne belongs to An tAth Peadar and Séadna and Daingean na Saileach, to Mayday and the piseog people, to Gobnait's Cemetery and Dámhscoil Mhúscraí, to Eibhlín Dubh Ní Chonaill and my own father. These roads pierce my heart and I feel them struggling with each other in my mind. I think sometimes that I have drowned them both from time to time in another road – the road west from Slea Head to Dún Chaoin.

The sense of what has been lost in the transition from Irish to English is particularly acute in some of Ó Ríordáin's later prose writings where Hiberno-English is associated with stagnation and atrophy:

Tá *hiatus* mór idir Thrá Lí agus an Daingean .i. Gleann na nGealt – gleann gann gortach, gleann fairsing folamh. Ní fhaca an gleann so riamh gan faitíos agus éadóchas a theacht orm. Tuigtí dom ná baineadh sé le spás ná le ham. Is leis an ngleann so a dhealraím intinn na dúthaí timpeall agus na coda san d'Éirinn go bhfuil an Ghaeilge imithe aisti. Níl bás ná beatha ann. Níl ann ach stad. Tá an Ghaeilge imithe agus níl á labhairt ann ach Béarla briste. Aicme mhaolchluasach atá bunaithe ann. Tá uirlisí na hintinne creachta. Tá an intinn ann ach tá sí ina stad.[8]

There is a large hiatus between Tralee and Dingle i.e. Gleann na nGealt [the Valley of the Mad] – a poor bare valley, wide and empty. Every time I have seen this valley, I have felt fear and despair. It seemed to me that it had nothing to do with space or time. I associate this valley with the mind of the surrounding area and the mind of those parts of Ireland where Irish has gone. There is neither birth nor death there. There is nothing except a full stop. Irish is gone and only broken English is spoken there. The people who live there are awkward. The equipment of the mind is destroyed. The mind is there but it is at a standstill.

The unequal power relations operating in the colonial encounter between the two languages is foregrounded in Ó Ríordáin's journalism:

Cad é mar umhlaíocht, cad é mar éadóchas, cad é mar mhisneach, cad é mar náire, a dteanga féin a chur uathu agus dul ar an mBéarla gan oiliúint dá laighead acu chuige agus ansan an Béarla briste sin a labhairt breallach lena máistrí iasachta a bhí chomh teann as a mBéarla féin, as a gcéim, as a gcumhacht. [...] Níl dlí le riachtanas. Chaitheadar a dhéanamh. Chaitheadar labhairt suarach i measc daoine d'ainneoinn friotal uasal a bheith ar a gcumas. Thógadar a gclann balbh mar mhaithe le bheith beo. Cuimhnigh ar an oidhreacht a cheileadar orthu. Níorbh oiriúnú go dtí é. Thugadar na cosa leo ach arbh fhiú é? Níorbh aon iontas é dá mbeadh coimpléasc ísleachta acusan agus againne.[9]

Such self-abasement, such despair, such courage, such shame, to abandon their own language and depend on English without any training in it and then to speak that broken English badly to their foreign masters who were so confident of their own English, their status, their power. [...] Needs must. They had to do it. They had to speak poorly among people despite being proficient in more dignified speech. They raised their children mute in order to survive. Think of the inheritance they concealed from them. The ultimate accommodation. They survived but was it worth it? It would hardly be surprising if they and we had an inferiority complex.

The hardening of Ó Ríordáin's public attitude to Ireland's skewed bilingualism was a reaction to what he perceived as the State's abandonment of its responsibility to those aspects of Irish cultural history and identity that survived in the language itself and in the traditional community life of the Gaeltacht. As the rhetoric of economic progress came to dominate State policy from the mid-1960s onwards, the poet identified the emergence of a new ideology that justified the rejection of Irish by charging language revivalists with a reactionary form of cultural exclusivity.[10] In the new dispensation, the Irish language was a form of 'ethnocentric arrogance', an insult to liberalism. In responding to the charge, Ó Ríordáin insisted that Irish represented an alternative perspective and understanding, a distinctive humanity and civilisation:[11]

Doras is ea gach teanga. Doras is ea an Ghaeilge a osclaíonn dúinn an saol a caitheadh agus atá á chaitheamh tríthi. Ina theannta san tá a leithéid de rud agus aigne na Gaeilge ann. Tá sí le tuiscint as an dteanga féin. Tá gach teanga ar tinneall lena haigne féin. Sin ceann des na fáthanna go bhfoghlaimítear teanga iasachta – chun teagmháil le haigne na teangan san .... Sórt ionad faire nua is ea é. Is tábhachtaí ná sin é nuair is í ár n-aigne féin atá i gceist – aigne go mbímid ar deighilt uaithi de ghnáth.[12]

Every language is a doorway. Irish is a doorway that opens up to us the life that has been lived and continues to be lived in it. There is also such a thing as the mind of Irish. That mind is implicit in the language itself. Every language reverberates with its own intelligence. That is one of the reasons we learn foreign languages – to come in contact with the mind of that language ... It's a kind of new vantage point. This is even more important when it is our own mind that is at issue – a mind we are separated from for the most part.

Ó Ríordáin's polemical writings are a response to the post-colonial crisis of identity he associated with the extraordinary changes that took place in Irish politics and culture during the final decade of his life. The degree of conviction necessary in such a confrontation is at odds, however, with the deep scepticism and wariness of all ideologies that characterise his poetry. In fact, it is the instability of his conflicted imagination and fractured identity that provides the basis for his most accomplished poems. From his earliest writing, he adopts an adversarial role in opposition to structures of authority he considers hostile to individual freedom, to the discovery and articulation of the unmitigated self. For Ó Ríordáin, the true self, 'an mise ceart', which might provide the basis for an ethical approach to life and art, is at odds with the established authority of the Catholic Church, the social pressure of community, the Gaelic literary tradition, the inherited patterns of the language itself. The difficulty for the poet is that absolute freedom is a form of madness, and the retreat to orthodoxy a relief from the overwhelming responsibility of uncompromised selfhood:

Gealt iseadh duine a tuisligheadh agus a thuit isteach ann féin agus nár fhéad teacht aníos cosamhail leis an leanbh ins na Stáit Aontuighthe a thuit isteach san tobar an lá fé dheire. Agus gealt iseadh duine a tuisligheadh agus a thuit isteach i mbuidéal agus nár fhéad teacht aníos. Sin é é. 'No loitering'. Ní mór do dhuine bheith ag síorthaisteal ó mhise go mise.[13]

A lunatic is a person who was tripped and fell into himself and couldn't get back out like the child in the United States who fell into the well the other day. And the person who was tripped and fell into a bottle and couldn't get out is also a lunatic. That's it. No loitering. A person has to keep travelling from self to self.

The solution was through an act of self-negation and immersion in the non-self.

Féachaim ar bhuidéal agus buidéalaítear mé. Smaoiním ar mhnaoi agus beanaítear mé. 'Sé sin, ardaíonn an buidéal agus an bhean asam féin mé. Bainid díom an t-ualach 'misiúil' atá 'om bhrú. Deintear buidéal díom – deintear bean díom, ach smaoineamh orthu. Sórt slaitín draíochta smaoineamh. Tá an teitheadh seo riachtanach. Do raghfá as do mheabhair dá mbeifeá id thusa i gcónaí.[14]

I look at a bottle and I am bottled. I think of a woman and I am womaned. That is to say that the bottle and the woman lift me out of myself. They relieve me of the burden of myself that oppresses me. I become a bottle – I become a woman just by thinking about them ... The escape is necessary. You would go out of your mind if you were yourself all the time.

Ó Ríordáin's poetic credo is outlined in the introduction to his first collection *Eireaball Spideoige* [A Robin's Tail] (1952), where he proposes that the responsibility of the poet is to discover the integrity of the poem's subject in language capable of giving utterance to its inalienable essence. In 'Siollabadh' [Syllabling], the pulses measured by a nurse in a hospital ward determine not only the rhythm of the poem but the essence of a world in which human beings are reduced to heartbeats that gradually infect everything around them, from the nurse 'syllabling out / The door most rhythmically', to the Angelus 'syllable- / Shaking each lip', to the patients praying, their pulses 'like monks / Syllabling their nones' (trans. David Wheatley). In 'Adhlacadh mo Mháthar' [My Mother's Burial], remembered details from the day of the funeral are excavated to articulate the guilt and delayed grief of a son six months after his mother's death. By a chain of association, the snow is connected to a letter from the poet's mother, to her hands, to her essential goodness:

> Gile gearrachaile lá a céad chomaoine,
> Gile abhlainne Dé Domhnaigh ar altóir,
> Gile bainne ag sreangtheitheadh as na cíochaibh,
> Nuair a chuireadar mo mháthair, gile an fhóid.

> *The white of a girlchild at her First Communion,*
> *The white of the Eucharist, Sundays on the altar,*
> *The white of milkwires running from the breast,*
> *When they buried my mother, the white of the earth.*
> [trans. Louis de Paor]

As often as not, the poet's subject is himself, his physical and spiritual crises, moments when the self is on the brink of extinction and writing a temporary stay against disintegration. The necessity and the impossibility of discovering a fully integrated unalienated self are central to Ó Ríordáin's poetics, which identifies the tension between irreconcilable contradictions as the dynamic element in a conflicted imagination. The precarious equilibrium proposed by the poet, based on relentless fluctuation between opposites, an uneasy lurching between one extreme and another, provides the contrapuntal structure and rhythm of his own thought and writing. In the dispute with organised religion and with God, with his own geographical community and the inherited traditions of Irish language and literature, he vacillates between competing pressures, occasionally discovering a momentary respite from uncertainty and instability.

While reaction to *Eireaball Spideoige* was generally favourable, more negative criticism focussed on the extent to which Ó Ríordáin's poetic dialect and metrical procedures betrayed the influence of English and his failure to defer to the authority of traditional precedents. The most trenchant criticism came from Máire Mhac an tSaoi who accused him of lack of mastery of the language itself and lack of understanding of Irish prosody. Her critique was predicated on a conviction that the poet in a minority language has a responsibility to preserve cultural patterns which are particular to that language as a stay against the homogenising tendencies of a global culture hostile to difference.[15] The terms of the critique as much as its vehemence had a considerable impact on Ó Ríordáin, confirming his own anxiety that his poetic practice was culturally and artistically illegitimate.

Ó Ríordáin's struggle with the inherited traditions of Irish language poetry was also an argument with his mentor Daniel Corkery (1878–1964) which persisted until the final years of his life:

> Dúirt Ó Corcora liom uair gan aon líne a scríobh ná beadh bunaithe ar líne as an seanfhilíocht. Ach cad tá le déanamh nuair a bhíonn nithe lasmuigh den dtraidisiún dulta i nduine – nuair a bhíonn an duine níos fairsinge ná an traidisiún? (Gan dabht bíonn sé níos cúinge leis.) Tá sé ceart go leor fanúint laistigh de thuiscint na Gaeilge ach rud eile is ea é cuid díot féin a fhágaint as an áireamh. Ní foláir an dúchas d'fhairsingiú dá dhainséaraí é. Tá fairsingiú déanta ag Ó Direáin agus fós tá sé istigh.[16]

> *Corkery once told me not to write a single line that was not based on a line from the older poetry. But what is to be done when things outside the tradition have entered a person – when the person is broader than the tradition? (Of course he is narrower than the tradition as well.) It's alright to stay within the mind of Irish but it is another thing to discount a part of yourself. The inherited element must be extended however dangerous that may be. Ó Direáin has extended it and yet he is still inside.*

In the argument with Corkery and himself, Joyce seemed to provide an enabling alternative to the stifling authority of tradition:

> Is mó de dhraíocht atá ag baint le Béarla frith-Ghaeilge ná le Béarla atá díreach ina Bhéarla nó Gaeilge atá díreach ina Gaeilge ... sin é a thug doimhneas do leithéid Joyce – an teanga a bhí séanta acu a bheith ar chúlaibh a gcuid focal. Dhein san a mBéarla débhríoch, frithbhríoch. Bhí níos mó á rá acu ná bhí siad a rá ... is saibhre frithchultúr ná díreach cultúr.[17]

> *There is more magic in an English that is counter-Irish than an English that is simply English or an Irish that is simply Irish ... that is what gave depth to the likes of Joyce – the language they had denied was behind their words. That made their English ambiguous, contradictory in its meaning. They said more than they were saying ... a counter-culture is richer than simply culture.*

The dynamic operating in the work of Joyce and other Anglophone Irish writers, however, did not function in the opposite direction: 'Níor oibrigh an draíocht seo droim ar ais. San áit a raibh rian an Bhéarla ar an nGaeilge ní raibh an Ghaeilge os cionn a cumais. DrochGhaeilge ab ea í – rud ciotach, ní draíochtúil' [This magic did not work in reverse. Where Irish carried the trace of English, Irish was deficient. It was bad Irish – a clumsy thing rather than a magical thing]. Nevertheless, if Anglicised Irish was a form of post-colonial treachery, it might also be a form of inspiration: 'údar ionspioráide is ea feall – go h-áirithe ar do thigh agus do threabh. Fuascailt ó cheangal is ea é agus cabhair mhór don scríbhneoir' [treachery is a source of inspiration – especially against your home and your people. It is a release from restriction and a great boon to the writer].[18]

Ó Ríordáin's 'treacherous' use of Irish is evident throughout his first collection. Despite occasional lapses, his poetic voice has its own idiosyncratic authority that challenges established modes of reading and writing Irish. His poetic dialect is a legitimate response to the poet's anguished search for a language that would be adequate to a divided imagination not entirely at home in the received patterns of either Irish or English. The startling imagery, the incongruous metaphors, the strange juxtapositions and compound words, at odds with the received conventions of Irish language poetry, challenged contemporary readers who encountered Ó Ríordáin's iconoclastic voice for the first time in the 1940s and '50s:

Gur ghíosc geataí comharsan mar gho-gallach gé,	While the neighbours' gate gaggle-
Gur bhúir abhainn shlaghdánach mar tharbh	Of-geesily groaned, the hoarse river roared like a bull
('Oíche Nollaig na mBan')	[trans. David Wheatley]

Mar scríbhinn breacaithe ar phár	Like writing blackening a page
Is scríbhinn eile trasna air	Criss-crossed with other words
Chonac geanc is glún is cruit is spág,	I saw gimp and knee and hump and hoof,
Fá dheoidh chonach dealramh Gandhi.	Finally, I saw the face of Gandhi.
	('Oileán agus Oileán eile')

The best of the shorter poems in *Eireaball Spideoige* give effect to Ó Ríordáin's poetics by discovering a register of language that contains the essence of the poem's subject: the sensuality and vanity of a blind man sitting for his portrait ('An Dall sa Studio'), the reciprocal empathy and shared sadness of a man and a horse ('Malairt'), the benign confusion of discarded things in a backyard ('Cúl an Tí'), a winter storm ('Oíche Nollaig na mBan'), a hospital ward ('Siollabadh'), his own death imagined as a form of sexual seduction ('An Bás'):

An Bás	Death
Bhí an bás lem ais,	Death alongside me,
D'aontaíos dul	I agreed to go,
Gan mhoill gan ghol,	No crying, no delaying,
Bhíos am fhéinmheas	Just appraising myself,
Le hionadh:	Surprised,
A dúrtsa	Saying:
'Agus b'shin mise	'And so that was

Go hiomlán,	All I was.
Mhuise slán	Goodbye, then,
Leat, a dhuine.'	Mister.'
Ag féachaint siar dom anois	Now looking back
Ar an dtráth	To the time
Go dtáinig an bás	Death hustled
Chugham fé dheithneas,	Up for me,
Is go mb'éigean	And I had to
Domsa géilleadh,	Give in,
Measaim go dtuigim	I think I can gather,
Lúcháir béithe	Even though I'm a man,
Ag súil le céile,	The joy of a woman
Cé ná fuilim baineann.	Waiting on her lover.
	[trans. Mary O'Donoghue]

The collection also includes a series of longer philosophical poems in which the poet confronts his own religious doubt. 'Cnoc Mellerí' contrasts the orderly life and the suppression of sexuality in the lives of monks in a monastery with the disorderly sinfulness of penitents on retreat. 'Oileán agus Oileán eile' attempts to discover the essence of St Finbarr's rejection of the carnal, material world on the island sanctuary of Guagán Barra. The paradox that freedom might be achieved through voluntary surrender to the constraints of religion and community is developed further in 'Saoirse', where the poet resolves to abandon 'freedom's fruits and all unfettered / Independence' in favour of 'rule and discipline and crowded churches', discovering a form of grace in the quotidian and the banal, 'the cheapest / Petty cash of thought and easy / Current coin' (trans. Coslett Quinn).

In his second collection *Brosna* [Kindling] (1964), Ó Ríordáin achieved a temporary equilibrium between his own recalcitrant imagination and the established protocols of the Irish language. 'Fiabhras' outlines the distorted cartography of illness as the fevered brain struggles to stabilise the physical co-ordinates of a world on the verge of dissolution. A moth drawn to and destroyed by the light in 'Na Leamhain' seems to symbolise his own precarious virility:

Oíche eile i dtaibhreamh bhraitheas-sa	Another night I felt the touch
Peidhre leamhan-sciathán,	In a dream of gauzy wings,
Mar sciatháin aingil iad le fairsingeacht	Angelic in their outstretched
Is bhíodar leochaileach mar mhná.	Span but tender and feminine.
. . .	

Ach dhoirteas-sa an púdar beannaithe	But I spilled the magic powder
'Bhí spréite ar gach sciathán,	Scattered on each wing-tip,
Is tuigeadh dom go rabhas gan	And saw I was innumerate
uimhreacha,	In the ways of manhood forever.
Gan uimhreacha na fearúlachta go	[trans. David Wheatley]
brách.	

In 'Claustrophobia', the short lines and repeated end-rhymes mimic the sense of suffocation and restriction that is the poem's subject. The language of religious belief is emptied of the consolation usually associated with the Christian imagery of candles and wine, extinguished by the apocalyptic sense of imminent annihilation and capitulation to political tyranny.

In 'An Gealt' [The Madwoman], the obsessive behaviour of a woman on the brink of mental collapse is captured in the long slender vowel sound 'é' and the multiple meanings of the verb 'géaraigh' [to sharpen, accelerate, intensify], while the blunting of intelligence following her treatment in the asylum is matched by the switch to the broad vowel sound of its opposite 'maolaigh' [to blunt, decelerate, relax]:

An Gealt

Tá ag géarú ar a fuadar ó iarnóin,
Is go bpléascfaidh sí a haigne géaróidh,
Tá an seomra ina timpeall ag géarú maille léi,
Is na freagraí atá faighte aici, táid géaraithe dá réir,
Ach cuirfear í go teach na ngealt le hamhscarnach an lae,
Chun go maolófaí an seomra is na freagraí is í féin.

The Madwoman

Since afternoon her fussing is worse,
At worst enough to burst her head,
The room around her is worsening with her,
And the answers she's found are worse again,
But she'll be sent to the madhouse at dusk,
And the room and the answers and the woman blunted.

[trans. Mary O'Donoghue]

The collection hinges on three poems strategically placed at the beginning, middle, and end of the book. The opening poem, 'A Ghaeilge im Pheannsa' [To the Irish in my Pen], addresses the poet's own idiolect as an illegitimate child, a potential source of sin despite its indeterminate sex. The poet is mother to this strange progeny whom is suckled by another language, a foreign prostitute from whom the poet steals thoughts to feed his own offspring. There is a sense of latent sexual violence in 'A Theanga seo Leath-liom' [Language that is Half-mine], in which Irish is imagined as feminine and the poet, torn between two languages, one resistant, the other solicitous, determines that he must enter and be submerged in her:

Ní mheileann riamh leath-aigne	A half-mind cannot grind
Caithfeam dul ionat;	We must enter you;
Cé nach bog féd chuid a bhraithim tú,	Although you seem tight with your
A theanga seo leath-liom.	favours
	Language that is half-mine.

The final poem, 'Fill Arís' [Go Back Again] offers its own resolution to the mutilations of colonial history, proposing a rejection of English and a return to a language and community that remains intact and accessible in the Gaeltacht village of Dún Chaoin.

Dún d'intinn ar ar tharla
Ó buaileadh Cath Chionn tSáile,
Is ón uair go bhfuil an t-ualach trom
Is an bóthar fada, bain ded mheabhair
Srathar shibhialtacht an Bhéarla,
Shelley, Keats is Shakespeare:
Fill arís ar do chuid,
Nigh d'intinn is nigh
Do theanga a chuaigh ceangailte i gcomhréiribh
'Bhí bunoscionn le d'éirim:
Dein d'fhaoistin is dein
Síocháin led ghiniúin féinig
Is led thigh-se féin is ná tréig iad,
Ní dual do neach a thigh ná a threabh a thréigean.

Close your mind on all that has happened
Since the Battle of Kinsale was lost,
And since the load is heavy
And the road is long, free your mind
From the yoke of English civilization,
Shelley, Keats and Shakespeare:
Go back again to what is yours,
Rinse your mind and your tongue
That has been fouled in syntax
Unsuited to your thoughts:
Make your confession and make
Peace with your own seed
And your own home and do not desert them.
One should not desert one's home or people.

[trans. Louis de Paor]

For Ó Ríordáin, Dún Chaoin represented Gaelic Irish civilisation before colonialism reduced Anglophone Ireland to a provincial sub-culture. It was also Baile Bhúirne during his father's time, before a disabling bilingualism replaced the cultural certainty of a unitary identity grounded in a single stable language. 'Fill Arís' proposes that a return to the sanctuary of an undivided self was still possible:

Sin é do dhoras,	That is your door,
Dún Chaoin fé sholas an tráthnóna,	Dún Chaoin in the evening light,
Buail is osclófar	Knock and your own mind
D'intinn féin is do chló ceart.	And true self will be opened.

It is a disturbing poem which as Seán Ó Tuama has argued, 'ignores the extent of what his "real self" owes to English civility, how impossible it is for him to disencumber himself of Shelley, Keats and Shakespeare'.[19]

Six months before his death, Ó Ríordáin acknowledged that his own inspiration had waned after the publication of *Eireaball Spideoige*. 'Nuair a thosnaíos ag scríobh ar dtúis ní rabhas ag cuimhneamh ar an nGaeilge in aon chor, bhíos ag cuimhneamh ar an bhfilíocht' [When I started writing I wasn't thinking of Irish at all, I was thinking of the poetry].[20] There is little in *Línte Liombó* [Limbo Lines] (1971) and *Tar éis mo Bháis* [After my Death] (1978) to match the startling iconoclasm of *Eireaball Spideoige* or the integrity of language, form, and feeling in *Brosna*, despite the mastery of language and form and occasional flickers of Ó Ríordáin's ability to give concrete expression to philosophical abstractions.

The best of Ó Ríordáin's work derives from the relentless and finally unresolved quarrel with himself that is manifest in the conflict with religion, community, language and tradition. It is a measure of his integrity in a life blighted by illness, isolation, religious doubt, linguistic uncertainty and cultural instability that the search for meaning and unrelenting self-interrogation continued until the final days before his death on 21 February 1977:

Ní fheadar an bhfaca riamh go dtí anocht chomh mór agus a chuas amú i gcaitheamh mo shaoil. B'fhéidir gur dul amú is ea an Ghaeilge seo go léir leis. B'fhéidir gurb é atá orm ná easpa carthanachta. Ba mhó liom focail ná daoine agus anois táim fágtha ar an dtráigh folamh. Is féidir leo déanamh dem cheal. (January 1977)

Bhfuil Íosa Críost ann? Cá bhfuil sé? Cad ina thaobh ná cabhraíonn sé liom. Cabhraigh liom. Níl aoinne eile. Táim i gcruachás. Níl cara beo. Tá pian im chliabh. Giorranáil. (14 February 1977)

A leithéid d'oíche. Banaltra speisialta agam, Mrs Holly. Ola dhéanach orm. Léacht ón dochtúir [X] ar chúrsaí creidimh. Ní chreideann sa tsíoraíocht. Mar

sin féin ní miste leis bheith á choisreacan féin. Gliondar a chuir tuairisc mo
bháis orm, ní a mhalairt.   (16 February 1977)[21]

I don't know if I ever realised until tonight how much I was mistaken throughout my life. Maybe this Irish is a mistake as well. Maybe I suffer from a lack of
charity. I preferred words to people and now I'm stranded. They can do without me.

Does Jesus Christ exist? Where is he. Why does he not help me. Help me.
There's no one else. I'm in trouble. No living friend. There's a pain in my chest.
Breathlessness.

Such a night. I have a special nurse. Mrs Holly. Received extreme unction. A
lecture from Dr X on religious belief. He doesn't believe in eternity. Still he
doesn't mind blessing himself. News of my death made be happy, not sad.

NOTES

1. Breandán S. Mac Aodha, *Cnuasach*. Dublin: Scepter, 1966.
2. Seán Ó Ríordáin, 'An Cliché Crús?', *Irish Times*, 13 July 1974.
3. Thomas Kinsella, 'The Irish Writer', in *Davis, Mangan, Ferguson?: Tradition
   and the Irish Writer; Writings by W. B. Yeats and by Thomas Kinsella*. Dublin:
   The Dolmen Press, 1970, pp. 57–70.
4. Douglas Hyde, *A Literary History of Ireland*. London: E. Benn, 1967.
5. Seán Ó Ríordáin, 'Aicme Íseal', *Irish Times*, 13 February 1971.
6. Seán Ó Ríordáin, Unpublished Diary, Ó Ríordáin Archive, UCD Library,
   7 September 1964.
7. Ibid., 5 June 1962.
8. Cited in Seán Ó Coileáin, *Seán Ó Ríordáin: Beatha agus Saothar*. Baile Átha
   Cliath, An Clóchomhar Tta, 1982, p. 192.
9. Seán Ó Ríordáin, 'Laethanta Breátha', *Irish Times*, 16 September 1972.
10. Stiofán Ó Cadhla, *Cá bhfuil Éire?: Guth an Ghaisce i bPrós Sheáin Uí Ríordáin*,
    Baile Átha Cliath, An Clóchomhar Tta, 1998, 117.
11. Ibid., 101–31.
12. Seán Ó Ríordáin, 'Aigne an Taibhrimh', *Irish Times*, 22 May 1971.
13. Seán Ó Ríordáin, Unpublished Diary, 12 April 1949.
14. Diary 12 April 1949, cited in Ó Coileáin, Seán Ó Ríordáin, p. 155.
15. Mhac an tSaoi Máire, 'Filíocht Sheáin Uí Ríordáin'. *Feasta*, Márta 1953,
    pp. 17–19; and 'Scríbhneoireacht sa Ghaeilge inniu', *Studies*, Spring 1955,
    pp. 86–91.
16. Seán Ó Ríordáin, 'Má Nuad', *Irish Times*, 12 August 1972.
17. Seán Ó Ríordáin, 'Cá bhFuil ár dTriall?', *Irish Times*, 22 September 1972.
18. Ibid.
19. Seán Ó Tuama, 'Seán Ó Ríordáin: Modern Poet', in *Repossessions: Selected
    Essays on the Irish Literary Heritage*, Cork: Cork University Press, 1995, p. 29.
20. Seán Ó Mórdha, 'Seán Ó Ríordáin ag Caint le Seán Ó Mórdha', *Scríobh* 3,
    S. Ó Mórdha ed. Baile Átha Cliath: An Clóchomhar Tta, p. 174.
21. Diary cited in Ó Coileáin, *Seán Ó Ríordáin*, pp. 404, 405

SELECTED FURTHER READING

Editions

Eireaball Spideoige, Baile Átha Cliath: Sáirséal agus Dill, 1952.
Brosna, Baile Átha Cliath: Sáirséal agus Dill, 1964.
Rí na nUile, with Seán S. Ó Conghaile, Baile Átha Cliath: Sáirséal agus Dill, 1967.
Línte Liombó, Baile Átha Cliath: Sáirséal agus Dill, 1971.
Tar éis mo Bháis, Baile Átha Cliath: Sáirséal agus Dill, 1978.
Na Dánta, Indreabhán: Cló Iar-Chonnacht, 2011.
Selected Poems/Rogha Dánta, ed. Frank Sewell, New Haven & London: Yale University Press, in association with Clo Iar-Chonnacht, Indreabhán, 2014.
Anamlón Bliana ó Dhialanna an Ríordánaigh, ed. Tadhg Ó Dúshláine, Indreabhán: Cló Iar-Chonnacht, 2015.
Leabhar na hAthghabhála/Poems of Repossession: Twentieth-century Poetry in Irish, ed. Louis De Paor, Newcastle: Bloodaxe, in association with Cló Iar-Chonnacht, Indreabhán, 2016.

Secondary Works

De Paor, Louis, '"Adhlacadh mo mháthar", Seán Ó Ríordáin', *Irish University Review: Poems that Matter 1950–2000*, vol. 39, no. 2, 2009.
Mc Crea, Barry, *Languages of the Night: Minor Languages and the Literary Imagination in Twentieth-century Ireland and Europe*, New Haven: Yale University Press, 2015.
Nic Ghearailt, Eibhlín, *Seán Ó Ríordáin agus 'An Striapach Allúrach'*, Baile Átha Cliath: An Clóchomhar Tta, 1988.
Ó Cadhla, Stiofán, *Cá bhfuil Éire?: Guth an Ghaisce i bPrós Sheáin Uí Ríordáin*. Baile Átha Cliath: An Clóchomhar Tta, 1998.
Ó Coileáin, Seán, *Seán Ó Ríordáin: Beatha agus Saothar*. Baile Átha Cliath: An Clóchomhar Tta, 1982.
Ó Mórdha, Seán, ed. *An Duine is Dual: Aistí ar Sheán Ó Ríordáin*, Baile Átha Cliath: An Clóchomhar Tta, 1980.
'Seán Ó Ríordáin ag Caint le Seán Ó Mórdha', *Scríobh 3*, S. Ó Mórdha ed. Baile Átha Cliath: An Clóchomhar Tta. 1978
Ó Tuama, Seán, 'Seán Ó Ríordáin: Modern Poet', in *Repossessions: Selected Essays on the Irish Literary Heritage*. Cork: Cork University Press, 1995.
"Seán Ó Ríordáin', *Filí faoi Sceimhle*, Baile Átha Cliath: An Clóchomhar Tta, 1978.
Sewell, Frank, 'Seán Ó Ríordáin: Between Corkery and Joycery', in *Modern Irish Poetry: A New Alhambra*. London: Oxford University Press, 2000.
Welch, Robert, 'Seán Ó Ríordáin: 'Renewing the Basic Pattern', *Changing States: Transformations in Modern Irish Writing*, London & New York: Routledge, 1993.

16

BENJAMIN KEATINGE

Richard Murphy

Despite publishing four landmark collections in twentieth-century Irish poetry – *Sailing to an Island* (Faber, 1963), *The Battle of Aughrim* (Knopf and Faber, 1968), *High Island* (Faber, 1974) and *The Price of Stone* (Faber, 1985) – Richard Murphy's critical reputation has faded somewhat in the new century. Since 2007, he has lived in retirement near Kandy, Sri Lanka, maintaining an association with the outposts of the British Empire which is a signature in his life and poetry. The publication, in 2002, of his highly acclaimed memoir *The Kick: A Life Among Writers* (Granta, 2002) has served to underscore Murphy's postcolonial consciousness, by which he has served as poet of 'two traditions': Anglo and native Irish. This latter perception, of Murphy as a poet of two traditions, served as point of departure for the *Irish University Review* special issue of 1977 and the subsequent volume, *Richard Murphy: Poet of Two Traditions*, edited by Maurice Harmon (Wolfhound Press, 1978). These volumes may have marked the high-point of Murphy's reputation, and they usefully underscore some core critical issues in the assessment of Murphy's poetic legacy.

Issues of poetic legacy and achievement should not, however, be confounded with passing matters of momentary visibility or fame. John Burnside does justice to the true value of Richard Murphy's contribution to Irish letters in his assessment of Murphy's *The Pleasure Ground: Poems 1952–2012* in his Special Commendation for the 2013 Poetry Book Society bulletin, where Burnside writes:

> Certainly his work has enjoyed less of a reputation than it has deserved, partly because of his cool classicism, and partly because most of the attention paid to Irish poetry has been directed at those whose work emerged from, or dealt with 'the Troubles' . . . As a body of work, *The Pleasure Ground* is not only a unique poetic achievement, but also the gorgeous repository of a live tradition, embodied in poem after poem of magisterial command and attentiveness to the textures of the real.[1]

Central to this poetic achievement has been his attempt 'to cure' the 'impossible wrong' of the British imperial project.[2] Not only was Murphy a child of the British empire, spending part of his childhood in Ceylon (modern-day Sri Lanka) where his father was the last British Mayor of Colombo, but also, his engagement with Irish history and Irish society has been through the lens of a Protestant, Anglo-Irish inheritance. This has prompted Murphy to explore the agonistic poles of inheritance/disinheritance, Protestant/Catholic identities, colonialist/native social positions, ownership and dispossession, the discussion of which has pivoted around Richard Murphy's acute self-perception of his divided Anglo-Irish heritage.

His landmark long poem 'The Battle of Aughrim', published in 1968, is subtitled in his most recent collected volume, *The Pleasure Ground: Poems 1952–2012*, as 'A meditation on colonial war and its consequence in Ireland written in Connemara between 1962 and 1967'.[3] Narrowly pre-dating the eruption of the Troubles in Northern Ireland, the poem takes a long view of the tensions inherent in Ireland by offering a panoramic view of Irish history through the fateful military encounter between a French-led Irish Jacobite army loyal to the deposed King James II and a Dutch-led Williamite army defending the Protestant and English interest of William of Orange who had claimed the English throne in the Glorious Revolution of 1688. The defeat of the Jacobite cause led to the severities of the Penal Laws and the confirmation of the Cromwellian and Elizabethan land settlements in Ireland and to the further marginalisation of the remnants of the older Gaelic social order. Murphy's opening question: 'Who owns the land. . . ?' (60) is one which has haunted Irish politics ever since. As well as being a carefully researched foray into early-modern military history, the poem deftly connects past and present in a way which speaks to an Irish readership of the 1960s and to a contemporary audience, so that Murphy's rhetorical insistence that 'The past is happening today' (69) rings true then and now.

The poem is projected outwards to a readership whose own inheritance may be mixed up in the Battle of Aughrim and its aftermath. But the poem is also projected inwards in being a very personal meditation by Murphy on his own family inheritance. As he explains in his memoir, *The Kick*:

> I recalled that one of my mother's ancestors, Robert Miller, had acquired from a dispossessed Catholic the land and house he called Milford [family demesne of Richard Murphy's maternal ancestors]. I had written enough externally about boats and the sea in *Sailing to an Island*. Now I wanted to look inward at the divisions and devastations in myself as well as in Ireland: the conflicts, legends, rituals, myths and histories arising from possession of the land – why we still had borders and bigotries.[4]

The poem thus reflects, as Seamus Heaney has remarked, 'Murphy's shaping of his inheritance into a poetic theme: his quarrel with himself.'[5] This quarrel, however, achieves, in the words of Ted Hughes, an 'epic objectivity' in 'The Battle of Aughrim', so that, arguably, Murphy's personal view implicates us all in imperial injustice and 'colonial war and its consequence'.[6] The fact that 'The Battle of Aughrim' was published alongside 'The God Who Eats Corn', an even more explicitly anti-colonial meditation on Murphy's father's life in retirement on a farm in Southern Rhodesia (now Zimbabwe), makes it surprising that Murphy's work should be almost completely ignored in ongoing postcolonial debates in Ireland showing, as John Goodby suggests, 'the narrowness of the field of discussion'.[7]

Richard Murphy's inheritance is perhaps not typical of a twentieth-century Irish poet. He was born in 1927 at Milford, near Kilmaine, Co. Mayo, in a house rich in familial and historical associations which feature in Murphy's poetry. More than most, Murphy dwells on his ancestry: Anglo-Irish on his mother's side while his father's family were of Co. Carlow Irish origin. Murphy was educated first at preparatory school in Dublin followed by Canterbury Cathedral School and Wellington College, England. This splicing of his life between England and Ireland thus began early and would continue. Murphy took an English degree at Magdalen College, Oxford, where he briefly broke off his studies, in 1946, to escape to Connemara, before being persuaded to return and complete his degree. Murphy's gradual development as an aspiring poet is wonderfully charted in *The Kick*, which traces Murphy's adventures and youthful indiscretions in London, Paris and Dublin (with interludes in the Bahamas and Crete) leading to marriage to Patricia Avis in 1955 and the publication of his first volume of poems, *The Archaeology of Love* (Dolmen Press, 1955), in the same year.

These early poems are marked by some of Murphy's key concerns: 'Auction' describes the imagined dispersal of the contents of Milford,[8] Murphy's ancestral home, and thus evokes the decline and decay of Anglo-Ireland more generally:

> I come,
> To bid for damp etchings,
> My grandaunt's chair...
> With what shall I buy
> From time's auctioneers
> This old property
> Before it disappears? (27)

Murphy's nature poetry of *High Island* (1974) is anticipated in the poem 'Living with Animals', written at Rosroe, Leenane, Co. Mayo, where

Murphy spent several months writing feverishly in 1951–2 after receiving £100 in prize money for the AE Memorial Award in April 1951:

> You were laughing through hazel
> In level sun
> Cast on a pool
> Of waiting salmon,
>
> Kittiwakes were circling
> Around your head
> As I heard you sing[9]

Meanwhile, a poem written at the same location vividly recounts the sojourn of Austrian philosopher Ludwig Wittgenstein (1889–1951) in the very same cottage which Murphy had rented. In 'Wittgenstein and the Birds', Wittgenstein is presented as the 'stone' amidst 'a tenebrous epoch', clipping away at the '[m]etaphysical foliage … beginning with words' (22). But Murphy also portrays him as an eccentric castaway in a remote part of Ireland referred to by the philosopher as 'one of the last pools of darkness in Europe'.[10] Here, enlightenment occupies a 'tenebrous' space ('I can only think clearly in the dark', wrote Wittgenstein) and when Wittgenstein leaves, in Murphy's poem, 'hordes / Of village cats' massacre 'his birds' (22). This poem anticipates a number of others Murphy would write about well-known writers, thinkers and actors who stayed in Connemara during Murphy's time on the western seaboard, including 'Theodore Roethke at Inishbofin, 1960', 'Mary Ure' and 'Tony White at Inishbofin'. Finally, the 1955 volume concludes with a love poem 'The Archaeology of Love' written '[h]igh up at Phaestos', Crete, in 'gratitude' to Patricia Avis 'for her … restoration of my heart', as Murphy writes in *The Kick*.[11] This lyric would be one of several hetero- and homosexual love lyrics by which Murphy would explore the ambiguities, tensions and fulfilment of Eros.

Following the break-up of his marriage, Murphy would base himself in Cleggan, Connemara, from 1959 to 1979, while continuing to visit Dublin and London regularly. His first Faber volume *Sailing to an Island* (1963) reflected his interest in sailing, begun at Rosroe and developed further when he acquired and refurbished a Galway hooker called the *Ave Maria* and ran her, during the summer months, as a tourist vessel between Cleggan and nearby Inishbofin. His first and best-known poem of the sea, 'Sailing to an Island', recalls a voyage taken in another traditional Irish vessel, a pookaun, from Rosroe in 1952, when Murphy and his brother Chris, along with a local man Padraic O'Malley, attempted and failed to reach Clare Island, instead being blown off course in a gale to finally reach the safety of Inishbofin harbour. The poem is one of action and endurance written in a metre which uses an Anglo-Saxon half-line and is heavily alliterative:

She luffs to a squall; is struck; and shudders.
Someone is shouting. The boom, weak as scissors,
Has snapped. The boatman is praying.
Orders thunder and canvas cannonades. (20)

But the poem's conclusion reminds us that this is not Richard Murphy's customary environment and that he is beholden to the local boatmen whose expertise he needs to acquire. Murphy is the self-conscious outsider greeted by the 'courteous fishermen' who know the sea '[i]ntimately' (20). The sea journey is thus also a traversal of the social space which separates the Anglo-Irish Murphy from the local fishermen with whom he converses somewhat uneasily. He would go on to celebrate their maritime exploits in such poems as 'The Cleggan Disaster' and 'The Last Galway Hooker' and, in the figure of Pat Concannon, survivor of the Cleggan Disaster of 1927, Murphy finds an heroic figure, a survivor of the 'hungry soil and woeful sea' (55) and thus a representative of the sufferings and deprivations through history of a local community of which Murphy can, in the final analysis, never fully belong.

One can readily see how this story of 'two traditions' leads logically to Murphy's major poem 'The Battle of Aughrim', with its opposition of Gaelic/Jacobite and English/Williamite forces. In the first section 'Now' (one of four temporal sections: 'Now', 'Before', 'During' and 'After') we even have opposing sectarian lyrics: 'Green Martyrs' and 'Orange March'. But what marks the poem most forcefully is its sense of aftermath, both the precise aftermath of the battle itself – execution of prisoners, retreating cavalry, butchery on all sides, the flight of the Wild Geese – but also the long aftermath up to the mid-1960s moment and beyond. Murphy deploys very powerful images from this longer view of Irish history: 'heretics . . . burnt at stakes for what they said' (80); '[l]andlords correspond[ing] with landlords across bogs' (80); 'the great hunger and the exodus' (99); 'beggars howl[ing] on every street' (94). Ted Hughes' claim, reproduced most recently in the blurb of *The Pleasure Ground: Poems 1952–2012*, that Murphy allows us to feel 'not the assertion of his personality, but the actuality of events, the facts and sufferings of history' is surely an acute judgement. The poem is a combined act of empathy, self-definition and deliberate historical reclamation for a battle often overshadowed by the Battle of Boyne of 1690; the documentary quality of the poem, its unflinching attention to detail, serves to heighten the overall pathos of those 'facts and sufferings of history'.

In an article titled 'The Lost Link: Richard Murphy's Early Poetry', Bernard O'Donoghue reminds us that Murphy's 1974 volume *High Island* 'was greeted as eagerly as any volume of its time' and that 'in 1970 only Larkin and Hughes enjoyed such prominence in English poetry in Britain and Ireland.'[12] The poems of *High Island* bring together a number of different strands of

Murphy's spectrum of interests: islands, and the sea; nature and ecology; sexuality and spirituality; structures and built heritage; as well as historical themes. Murphy had acquired ownership of this uninhabited island in April 1969 and he was to use it as a sanctuary for solitary meditation in the early seventies, using a converted miners' hut for short stays on the island. His acquisition of this domain of solitude and spirituality posed its own dilemmas, as Murphy noted in a journal entry for 1 April 1969 reproduced in *The Kick*:

> Buying an island, even with the intention of creating a wild life sanctuary, is a predatory act among predators, much easier than writing a book. Once you become the owner, your view of the island alters: you turn possessive and protective. People regard you as a different person – a man who owns an island must be rich. But I know that High Island can never be possessed because it will always remain in the possession of the sea. Its virtue will grow from its contemplation, not its use, from feelings and ideas evoked by its wild life, and its end of the world terrain.[13]

In a certain sense, the purchase of High Island completed a journey which Murphy had begun much earlier and which he describes in an essay 'The Pleasure Ground', first published in 1963, an essay which charts the decay of the carefully manicured, enclosed space of the 'pleasure garden' at Milford. Revised for publication as the Preface to Murphy's *The Pleasure Ground: Poems 1952–2012*, Murphy uses the essay to illustrate his metaphorical and literal progress from the proprieties of his upbringing to the more unkempt domain of the Atlantic seaboard: 'As I grew older the Pleasure Ground sank through decay into oblivion, as the old people died and the young left the country. So I searched for grounds of pleasure that excluded nobody, till I found them by living with friends I loved among people on or near the sea' (16). High Island represents the apotheosis of this progress. Murphy is able to enjoy an unmediated encounter with 'rock, sea and star' (135) as the poem 'High Island' describes and he joins his poetic project to the ancient spiritual asceticism of medieval Christianity in Ireland manifest in the monastery founded by St Féichín on the island in the seventh century.

The dialectic of freedom and containment is also captured in 'The Reading Lesson', a poem about teaching a boy from a Traveller family how to read:

> If books resembled roads, he'd quickly read:
> But they're small farms to him, fenced by the page,
> Ploughed into lines, with letters drilled like oats:
> A field of tasks he'll always be outside. (124)

The poem's imagery suggests that the taming of the boy into husbandry and the settled community is futile, 'a field of tasks' he will evade. The idea of 'a small safe paddock' (158), as the later poem 'Husbandry' puts it, is anathema.

By analogy, just as the island cannot be owned or 'possessed', nor can it be 'fenced' or contained. Thus, the title poem of the collection, 'High Island', evokes a boundlessness, suggesting that the island is at one with the sea from which it rises: 'A shoulder of rock /. . . Fissile and stark' (135). In his quest to be at one with the island, Murphy adheres to the island's lesson, expressed in 'Brian Boru's Well' as 'Don't interfere!' (136). If 'The Battle of Aughrim, 1691' had been a poem about ownership and conquest, the poems of *High Island* are about how to disavow such social and historical conventions.

All of this may lead us to question the dialectical terms of the 'two traditions' through which Richard Murphy's poetry has often been viewed. Of course, the Anglo-Irish tradition and situation is anything but simple since the term 'Anglo-Irish' denotes a class in Irish society whose identity is neither English nor Irish and whose presence has been all but occluded in the second half of the twentieth century. If Murphy's preoccupation with his own origins appears belated, one may also suggest that *High Island* is the volume which transcends those concerns, overcoming the containment of social identity. We see Murphy as an ecological poet with poems like 'Corncrake', 'Song for a Corncrake', 'Stormpetrel' and others lending themselves to contemporary eco-criticism while also encompassing themes of love, longing and sexuality. In such poems as 'Little Hunger' and 'Omey Island', we see Murphy the builder of poetic and stone structures using 'pink stone' from deserted 'cabins' to build a new structure (111), the Hexagon on Omey Island, where Murphy would live during the mid-1970s. He explores more openly themes of sexuality, love and loss, including gender ambiguity and bisexuality, in such poems as 'Seals at High Island' and 'Sunup'.

Some of these concerns resurface in four remarkable poems – 'Tony White 1930–1976', 'Tony White at Inishbofin', 'Circles' and 'The Afterlife' – published in 'Part 4: *Care* and Poems of 1974–1984' in *The Pleasure Ground* and written as elegies to Murphy's close friend Tony White who died suddenly in January 1976. The poem 'Tony White 1930–1976' begins:

> Growing, he saw his friends increase
> Their incomes, houses, families,
> And saw this growth as a disease
> Nothing but unpossessive love could cure.
> Possessing nothing, he was not possessed
> By things or people, as we are.   (160)

Indeed, it was Tony White who had cautioned Richard Murphy about the dangers of owning High Island and White himself had 'sacrificed a plausible career' on the London stage in order to live a life '[r]eborn as a fisherman', as we learn in 'Tony White at Inishbofin' (161). In another poem of this period,

Murphy accuses himself of 'Stone Mania', by which his 'mad obsession of building more rooms' has only kept him 'entirely apart' from those he loves most (157). Murphy had made this mistake once already in his life by energetically renovating a Georgian house, Lake Park in County Wicklow, where he had lived with Patricia Avis and their daughter Emily. In the sonnet sequence *The Price of Stone* (1985), Murphy would use the poem 'Roof-tree' to conclude that he had 'flawed the tenderest movement of three lives' in the 'hackwork' and 'dull, stupefying knocks' of these renovations (187).

The emotional cost of these mistakes, Murphy calculates, is far greater than any financial cost. *The Price of Stone*, a sequence of fifty sonnets written in Dublin between 1981 and 1984, uses what Murphy calls 'sonnet houses' to revisit aspects of the poet's life by using buildings and monuments to give voice to the poet's own autobiographical self.[14] This method of occluding the poet's own voice enables him to broach sensitive subjects and to assess the emotional reversals of his life while avoiding a confessional mode of address. The sonnet sequence has sometimes been criticised as being stilted or mannered (one critic used the term 'ponderously contrived');[15] nevertheless, behind the sequence, we can discern the same emotional candour of the poems to Tony White and of Murphy's actual autobiography, *The Kick*.

In *The Kick*, Richard Murphy admits that: 'To me poetry would never come naturally, as a gift. It would have to be made.'[16] In order to assist this process, Murphy has kept, since his stay in Paris in 1954, voluminous prose notebooks, a 'mesh of vertical and horizontal lines' in which he can 'fish' for poems that may be 'lured to the surface' from the prose reflections in these notebooks.[17] We get a glimpse of this process in three extracts from an unpublished longer work – 'Transgressing into Poetry' – published in *Poetry Ireland Review* which trace the development of individual sonnets in *The Price of Stone* from prose meditations to publishable poems. For example, some notes on the poem 'Wellington Testimonial', recalling Murphy's unhappy period as a schoolboy at Wellington College, make a link between the poet's own experience and the symbolic status of the Wellington monument in Dublin's Phoenix Park. Murphy recalls '[e]ntering Wellington College reluctantly at fifteen' and being 'placed in a house' with 'a dozen hearty athletic boys of my age destined for careers in the forces' and being 'mocked' by these same school contemporaries.[18] The militaristic ethos of the school and its petty barbarities ('cold baths summer and winter')[19] are the unspoken background to a poem which dwells on the redundancy of the 'Wellington Testimonial', its belatedness and incongruity in modern Dublin, as he also describes in the notebooks: 'a monument in a country and a century that have changed ... celebrating things or people that nobody remembers ... in a form now regarded as too rigid ... on behalf of a foreign power'.[20] All of this material is condensed in the published text. Wellington speaks from atop the plinth, as if commanding 'an obsolete parade' asking the question: 'what good I've done?' (181). Murphy concludes that that 'sole point' of Wellington's militaristic demeanour, 'in this evergreen oak aisle' in Phoenix Park, '[i]s to maintain a clean laconic style' (181).

Here, as elsewhere in *The Price of Stone*, phallic imagery acts as a kind of empty signifier for the redundant colonial vision of the past. Wellington is '[n]eedling' the sky 'over Phoenix Park' but has lost his 'nosey flair' (181). Likewise, 'Nelson's Pillar' (since replaced by another empty signifier, the Spire, on Dublin's central thoroughfare, O'Connell Street), 'rose as a Doric column / Far from at home' (180) before being blown up by the IRA in 1966. He is thus '[d]ismasted and dismissed' (180), like soldiers on the parade ground, with his brand of tumescent conquest no longer relevant. 'Lead Mine Chimney' is yet another phallic monument '[p]ointlessly standing up' with 'a sooty chill of hollowness' (178). Previously used to smelt ore, the disused chimney is a remnant which now lacks '[t]he guts to pour out sulphur and hot air' (178), further suggesting that the rhetoric of Empire was simply a verbal trick, sulphurous 'hot air'.

The Price of Stone reflects what Murphy refers to in *The Kick* as his 'split-level life' that he was leading in the early 1980s, living at his house Knockbrack in Killiney, County Dublin. The final sonnet of the volume celebrates the birth of Murphy's 'Natural Son', Richard William in January 1982, from his relationship with Anya Barnett, and it has justly been celebrated, by Joseph Sendry, as 'among the greatest sonnets in the language'.[21] Breaking with the careful ventriloquism of the earlier sonnets, Murphy speaks in his own voice. The shelter or habitation of the poem is the womb from which a new life emerges '[t]o share our loneliness', the security of a 'fluid home' exchanged for the uncertainties of life (226). The final poem echoes many of these sonnets in suggesting a certain provisionality in the habitations they describe. For example, the poem 'Family Seat' depicts the apparent solidity of a family demesne, with the phallic superiority of a ruling elite: 'a trout river talking with propriety / Through cockshoot woods, bailiffed by underlings' (195). However, we learn in the final couplet that the family members have 'all been buried in their name-proud vaults' and that 'Paraplegics live here now' (195). Another poem, 'Liner', evokes the 'split-level' nature of Murphy's own upbringing, divided not just between Ireland and England, but also between Europe and Ceylon (Sri Lanka) where Murphy spent some of his earliest years. The liner of the poem bears testimony to these dislocations:

> Child, when you've sailed half way around the world
> And found that home is like a foreign country,

Think how I've had to keep an ironclad hold
On your belongings, not to lose heart at sea.   (193)

One senses, therefore, that part of the 'point' of these poems is to make sense of these displacements and, in a kind of limp echo of imperial fortitude, 'not to lose heart at sea'.

The 'split-level' nature of *The Price of Stone* is also borne out in poems which meditate on 'queer' encounters. The phallic emptiness of 'Wellington Testimonial' and 'Nelson's Pillar' may be equated with the homosocial sterility of imperial institutions: public schools, the army and navy, London clubs. But Murphy 'transgresses into poetry' in a number of poems with frankly 'queer' subject matter. The sonnet 'Portico' evokes a monument on a 'dark headland' where 'solitary shadows of men cruise' like 'hooded devotees' of an alternative cult (179). Meanwhile, 'Gym' presents the 'body culture' of a gay sauna where '[n]ude club members, immune from women, bask' and enjoy 'skin-deep masquerades' (183). It would be easy to contrast this 'ithyphallic art' (179) of gay subject matter with the heterosexual poems of birth, such as 'Natural Son', 'Beehive Cell' and 'Birth Place', by privileging the latter against the former. But in reality, both reflect the constellation of 'split-level' experiences which Murphy brings together, in masterly fashion, in *The Price of Stone*.

Much of Murphy's subsequent poetic output has been connected with Sri Lanka, an island to which he returned in November 1984 in a visit which would reconnect Murphy with some of the childhood memories he had described in poems published in *High Island* (1974), among them 'Coppersmith', 'Firebug' and 'Traveller's Palm'. In *The Kick*, Murphy vividly describes his return as a kind of homecoming saying that a 'wave of euphoria' washed over him on arrival at Colombo airport.[22] Murphy charts his adult re-engagement with an island nation greatly changed from the early 1930s, when Murphy had lived there as a child. In the early pages of *The Kick* we read about the colonial attitudes which Murphy (and other children of empire) absorbed in their upbringing:

> The key to it all seemed to be that we spoke English, through which we had direct access to God through our prayers ... It seemed obvious that praying in Sinhala or Tamil achieved poorer results. On a little globe that Nanny had given me, she pointed out that we ruled a third of the world. In return for our privilege, God expected us to behave well, work hard, do our duty and set a good example. The natives of Ceylon ... ought to have been grateful to us for having brought them the benefit of our language and civilization ... we children were taught nothing about the resplendent island's ancient Buddhist culture.[23]

Murphy's poetic and personal project of the later 1980s and beyond has been to explore that culture. The translations or versions he published in *The*

Mirror Wall (1989) are adaptations from ancient Sinhalese inscriptions written on the rock face of Sigiriya, an ancient fortress in central Sri Lanka; the inscriptions are themselves graffiti which eulogise, in differing modes, the 'cloud nymphs'[24] or 'golden girls'[25] erotically painted on the rock face at Sigirya in what is now a UNESCO World Heritage site and symbol of Sri Lankan culture and independence. In an interview with Dennis O'Driscoll in 1987, Murphy commented: 'It's a pluralists dream of different levels, ranging from light erotic witticism to heavy moralising, or from mystical devotion to mundane scorn.'[26] One senses, again, Murphy responding to the ventriloquistic possibilities of his source material.

By describing Sigiriya as 'a Sri Lankan Aughrim',[27] in her review of *The Mirror Wall*, Antoinette Quinn makes the not immediately obvious connection in Murphy's poetic process between Irish and Sri Lankan experience: engagement with a site of cultural and historical significance, an oblique linkage to the poet's own autobiography and a painstaking act of poetic reclamation which makes a larger statement about post-imperial spaces. The great and abiding value of Richard Murphy's poetry lies not only within an Irish tradition, or Anglo-Irish tradition, but, more importantly, as a poet who has traced the aftermath of great historical transitions: Ireland after Aughrim, Ireland after independence and, more generally, a world in which the hypocrisies of the British imperial project are entirely discredited.

NOTES

1. John Burnside, 'Special Commendation', *The Poetry Book Society Bulletin* (Summer 2013), p. 17.
2. Richard Murphy, 'The Woman of the House', in *The Pleasure Ground: Poems 1952–2012*, Tarset: Bloodaxe, 2013, p. 30. All references are to this edition, unless otherwise indicated, and are given in parentheses. It should be noted that Richard Murphy's collected poems have been published in Ireland by Lilliput Press as *Poems 1952–2012*, in the United Kingdom by Bloodaxe as *The Pleasure Ground: Poems 1952–2012* and under the same title by Wake Forest University Press in the United States. The typesetting is identical for all three editions and thus the page references given here are valid for all three.
3. Richard Murphy, 'The Battle of Aughrim, 1691', in *The Pleasure Ground: Poems 1952–2012*, Tarset, Bloodaxe, 2013, p. 59. All references are to this edition, unless otherwise indicated, and all given in parentheses.
4. Richard Murphy, *The Kick: A Life Among Writers*, London: Granta, 2002, p. 217.
5. Seamus Heaney, 'The Poetry of Richard Murphy', in *Richard Murphy: A Poet of Two Traditions*, ed. Maurice Harmon, Dublin: Wolfhound Press, 1977, p. 25.
6. Ted Hughes' well-known comments on Richard Murphy were reprinted in the blurb for Murphy's *Collected Poems* (Oldcastle: Gallery Press, 2000) and, most recently, on the back cover of *The Pleasure Ground*.

7. John Goodby, 'Richard Murphy: Last of the Anglo-Irish?', in *Irish Poetry since 1950: From Stillness into History*, Manchester: Manchester University Press, 2000, p. 84.

8. The poem was occasioned by a dream since there was no real firesale of the contents of Richard Murphy's ancestral home, Milford. Richard Murphy, personal communication with the author, 18 June 2016.

9. Richard Murphy, 'Living with Animals', *The Archaeology of Love*, Dublin: Dolmen Press, 1955, p. 9.

10. Tim Robinson, *Connemara: The Last Pool of Darkness*, London: Penguin, 2008, p. 1.

11. Murphy, *The Kick*, p. 159.

12. Bernard O'Donoghue, 'The Lost Link: Richard Murphy's Early Poetry', *Metre* 10 (2001), p. 138.

13. *The Kick*, p. 277.

14. Richard Murphy, 'Transgressing into Poetry', in *Poetry Ireland Review* 107, p. 26.

15. Antionette Quinn, 'Aughrim in Sri Lanka', *The New Nation* 7 (1989), p. 20.

16. *The Kick*, p. 95.

17. Ibid., p. 154.

18. Richard Murphy, 'Notes for Sonnets', in *Poetry Ireland Review* 104, p. 100.

19. Ibid.

20. Ibid.

21. Joseph Sendry, 'The Poet as Builder: Richard Murphy's *The Price of Stone*', in *Irish University Review* 15 (1985), p. 42.

22. *The Kick*, p. 340.

23. Ibid., p. 35.

24. Richard Murphy, *The Mirror Wall*, Dublin: Wolfhound Press, 1989, p. xiv.

25. Ibid., p. 5.

26. Richard Murphy and Dennis O'Driscoll, 'Richard Murphy at Sixty', in *Poetry Ireland Review* 21 (1988), p. 18

27. Quinn, 'Aughrim in Sri Lanka', p. 20.

SELECTED FURTHER READING

Editions

Sailing to an Island, London: Faber and Faber, 1963.

The Battle of Aughrim and The God Who Eats Corn, London: Faber and Faber, 1968.

High Island, London: Faber and Faber, 1974.

Selected Poems, London: Faber and Faber, 1979.

The Price of Stone, London: Faber and Faber, 1985.

New Selected Poems, London: Faber and Faber, 1989.

The Mirror Wall, Tarset: Bloodaxe, 1989.

Collected Poems, Oldcastle: The Gallery Press, 2000.

The Kick: A Life Among Writers, London: Granta, 2002.

The Pleasure Ground: Poems 1952–2012, Tarset: Bloodaxe, 2013.

Secondary Works

Biographical

Murphy, Richard and David Wheatley, 'Richard Murphy: Interview', in *Metre* 10 (2001), 141–55.

Murphy, Richard and John Haffenden, 'Richard Murphy', in *Viewpoints: Poets in Conversation with John Haffenden*, London: Faber and Faber, 1981.

Critical

Brown, Terence, 'Poets and Patrimony: Richard Murphy and James Simmons', in *Ireland's Literature: Selected Essays*, Dublin: Lilliput Press, 1988.

Deane, John F. (ed.), *The Snow Path: Tracks 10: 'Richard Murphy Feature'*, Dublin: Dedalus Press, 1994.

Goodby, John, 'Richard Murphy: Last of the Anglo-Irish?', in *Irish Poetry since 1950: From Stillness into History*, Manchester: Manchester University Press, 2000.

Keatinge, Ben, '"My Form Is Epicene": Sexual Ambiguity in the Poetry of Richard Murphy', in *Essays in Irish Literary Criticism: Themes of Gender, Sexuality, and Corporeality*, ed. Deirdre Quinn and Sharon Tighe-Mooney, Lampeter: Edwin Mellen Press, 2008.

Harmon, Maurice (ed.), *Richard Murphy: A Poet of Two Traditions*. Dublin: Wolfhound Press, 1977.

O'Donoghue, Bernard, '"Pat Cloherty's Version of *The Maisie*" by Richard Murphy', in *Irish University Review* 39.2 (Autumn/Winter, 2009), 239–45.

17

ANDREW FITZSIMONS

Thomas Kinsella

According to Michael Schmidt, 'When I first came to Britain in the late 1960s, the best-known Irish poet of the newer generation was Thomas Kinsella, whose volume *Nightwalker and Other Poems* (1968) was widely admired, if not understood.'[1] As Schmidt implies, that key volume presented difficulties that Kinsella's previous work had not. Not only did the poems depart from strict adherence to the traditional lyric forms and regular rhythms of his first volumes, *Another September* ('As I roved out impatiently / Good Friday with my bride / To drink in the rivered Ringwood / The draughty season's pride', p. 16)[2] and *Downstream* ('Her chair drawn to the door, / A basket at her feet, / She sat against the sun / And stitched a linen sheet. / Over harrowed Flanders / August moved the wheat', p. 31), but Kinsella in the volume's title poem was taking Irish poetry into 'uncharted territory'.[3] That poem's extended, insider exploration of the economic and cultural carving up of Ireland in the 1960s (Kinsella worked in the Department of Finance, and at one time served as private secretary to T. K. Whitaker, the architect of Irish economic expansion) has tended to overshadow the range of a collection that deepens and extends Kinsella's examination of his perennial themes: love, death and the artistic act. As central as the matter of Ireland to Kinsella's work are the Darwinian, post-Christian quandaries of 'Ballydavid Pier': 'The line of life creeps upward / Replacing one world with another' (p. 57); and the evocative, pained poems of marriage and parenthood of the 'Wormwood' sequence:

> Upstairs a whimper or sigh
> Comes from an open bedroom door
> And lengthens to an ugly wail
> – A child enduring a dream
> That grows, at the first touch of day,
> Unendurable.   (p. 65)

The claim on Kinsella's work of the Irish social realities evident in 'Nightwalker' runs in tandem with the profoundly contingent view of the claims of place visible elsewhere in the collection: 'I am sure that there are no places for poets, / Only changing habitations for verse to outlast' ('Magnanimity', p. 73). In a later poem, 'Brothers in the Craft' (1990), Kinsella captures this tension between contingency and design when he refers to 'the early accidental particulars' that remain 'a part of the lasting colour of the work' (p. 287).

'Accident', furthermore, is a propulsive force within Kinsella's thinking about the processes of life ('let accident / Complete our dreadful journey into being', p. 24) and is explicitly Darwinian in 'St Paul's Rocks: 16 February 1832', which re-writes a scene from *Voyage of the Beagle*[4] and resembles 'Ballydavid Pier' in the neutrality of its observational tone. After the Darwinian notation, however, the deduction the speaker makes from the evidence is quintessentially Kinsellian in its emphasis on violence, the good as accident ('Goodness is where you find it. / Abnormal', p. 214), and achievement against unfavourable odds:

> In squalor and killing and parasitic things
> life takes its first hold.
> Later the noble accident: the seed,
> dropped in some exhausted excrement,
> or bobbing like a matted skull into an inlet.   (p. 127)

Accident also guides Kinsella's thinking about the processes of art. In 'A Portrait of the Artist', Kinsella supplies his own definition of beauty, provoked by an encounter with the shades of the arguing Stephen Dedalus and Lynch: '*But what is beauty.* // A jewel of process. / The fugitive held fast, exact in its accident' (p. 293). In *The Good Fight*, John F. Kennedy describes the United States in Kinsella's Darwinian terms: 'The accident that brought our people together / out of blind necessities / – embrace it! – explosive – to our bodies' (p. 149).

Beginning with 'Nightwalker', and continuing into the series he has been publishing under his own Peppercanister Press imprint since 1972, Kinsella examines the 'accidental particulars' of the unfavourable environment of his upbringing in 1930s and 1940s Ireland, and his literary beginnings in postwar and early 1950s Dublin. Kinsella's 'first neighbourhood' (*Late Poems*, p. 87) of Inchicore and the Liberties area of central Dublin is the setting for much of the work in *New Poems 1973*, and throughout the Peppercanisters: in *One* ('38 Phoenix Street'; 'His Father's Hands'); in his elegy for his father, *The Messenger*; in *Songs of the Psyche* ('Model School, Inchicore'; 'Phoenix Street'; 'Bow Lane'); and in the exploration of the history, personal and public, of the Liberties area in *St Catherine's Clock*.[5] This work explores childhood memory, personal and communal isolation, frustrated ideals, waste, loss and political failure, but also, as much as Wallace Stevens's, Kinsella's poems are concerned with the making of their own meanings:

> We were a closed community.
> The young ones wore their sex tight
> in a slum without rest;
>> revelling in noise and gang,
>> spitting irresponsible.
>
> The soul confined,
>> her face pressed against the lattice.
> Looking out at the day and the bright details
>> descending, selecting themselves
>> and settling in their own light.
>
> ('Songs of Exile', *Late Poems*, p. 26)

The Peppercanister project begins with a poem of incandescent fury, *Butcher's Dozen* (1972), a visceral, defiant response to the Widgery Tribunal's exoneration of the British Paratroop Regiment's killing of thirteen unarmed demonstrators on Bloody Sunday (30 January 1972). That poem's occasion and the 'pulse of doggerel ease' in which it was written ('I went with Anger at my heel / Through Bogside of the bitter zeal', p. 133) is uncharacteristic of the way the Peppercanister series eventually developed. The name of the imprint derives from the local nickname for St Stephen's Church, near Percy Place in Dublin where the Kinsellas lived in the 1970s and 1980s. Kinsella initially envisioned the press as an alternative form of draft publication, partly due to dissatisfaction with magazine printings of poetry. The 'ongoing dynamic' (*Late Poems*, p. 28) of his poetry, however, saw Peppercanister develop into a venue for the publication of the interrelated sequences excavating the foundations of self and society and art that Kinsella had begun to write as an extended sequel to 'Nightwalker' and 'Phoenix Park' (*Nightwalker and Other Poems*).[6]

A brief overview of some of the subjects and sources of the Peppercanister series from 1972 to the publication of *Fat Master* and *Love Joy Peace* in 2011 gives a sense of Kinsella as, in William Blake's lines, 'A self-contemplating shadow / In enormous labours occupied':[7] the mythological founding of Ireland, *Lebor Gabála Érenn* (the *Book of Invasions*), patrilineal inheritance, the industrial preparation of meat, cartography, taxonomy, the *Encyclopédistes*, Diderot, Voltaire, Jonathan Swift, Mahler, the letters of Thomas Mann, the 'muttonchop slaughter' of World War I, the 'enabling feminine', the life and work of Carl Jung, Eriugena, Giraldus Cambrensis, the origins of musical polyphony, the diaries of Albert Speer, the life of Oliver

Goldsmith, the history of the early church, St Augustine, Martin Luther, the origins and history of war, the *Book of Job*, the *Iliad*, entomology and the music of Bach. As can be seen even from this bald and incomplete catalogue, the range and reach of Kinsella's work is among the most extraordinary in contemporary poetry.

Kinsella's work before *Nightwalker and Other Poems* and the Peppercanisters resembles, at least superficially, the well-made poems of his English contemporaries in the Movement. Indeed, *Another September* (1958) and *Downstream* (1962) had found an audience in England, and both had been Poetry Book Society Choices. Kinsella was included in Robert Conquest's *New Lines II* (1963), the only Irish poet alongside, among others, Ted Hughes, Edward Lucie-Smith and Anthony Thwaite. There is even, in the '*I wonder whether one expects*', the prologue poem to *Downstream*, a very Movement-like reflection on the humdrum suburban sobriety of the contemporary poet: '*I wonder whether one expects / Flowing tie or expert sex / Or even absent-mindedness / Of poets any longer*' (p. 29; italics in the original).

Kinsella's rhythms and diction in his first work find their source in the English literary tradition more than in the Irish-language literary tradition or the Hiberno-English variety of the English language Kinsella actually heard around him growing up in working-class central Dublin in the 1930s and 1940s. 'A Lady of Quality' models its rhyme scheme and stanza form on W. H. Auden's 'A Summer Night':

> In hospital where windows meet
> With sunlight in a pleasing feat
>   Of airy architecture
> My love has sweets and grapes to eat,
> The air is like a laundered sheet,
>   The world's a varnished picture.   (p. 6)

The 'varnished' literariness of Kinsella's first style was a deliberate turning aside from the available but discredited forms of post-Revival Irish writing. This stance was generational; in the preface to the *Dolmen Miscellany of Irish Writing* (1962), the editors, John Montague and Kinsella, wrote that the contributors, among them John McGahern, Aidan Higgins and Richard Murphy, did not form in any coherent sense a 'movement' but more 'a general change in sensibility', distancing themselves from the 'forms of "Irishism" (whether leprechaun or garrulous rebel) ... so profitably exploited in the past'.[8]

Kinsella's first books, along with those of other poets representing this change of sensibility, were published by Dolmen Press, a relationship that started for Kinsella with single poem pamphlets and chapbooks: *The Starlit*

Eye (1952), *Three Legendary Sonnets* (1952) and *Per Imaginem* (1953; re-published as *Echoes, CP* 1–2); as well as translations from the Irish: *The Breastplate of St. Patrick* (1954) and *The Sons of Usnech* (1954), commissioned by the founder/Director of Dolmen, Liam Miller. Kinsella published with Dolmen until Miller's death in 1987. (*Downstream* and subsequent collections were published in Britain in association with Oxford University Press, and later Carcanet Press; in the United States Knopf, and later Wake Forest, published Kinsella's work.) The founding of Dolmen marks the initial stage of the 'confused awakening' in Ireland that Kinsella dates to the mid-1950s: 'Up to 1955 or so the feeling is one of isolation – isolation from war and then from the dynamic post-war phenomena in literature, economics and everything else: an Ireland hardly aware of what modern men and nations were demanding of themselves'.[9] The success of Dolmen's publications, Kinsella's chief among them, led to the publisher being a centripetal force in the re-appearance of Irish writers as prominent figures at home and internationally. Not only did Kinsella, Montague and Richard Murphy publish with Dolmen, the press also played a significant part in the rejuvenation of Austin Clarke's writing. The significance of Clarke in Kinsella's development, as monitoring and mentoring presence, is remembered in 'Brothers in the Craft': 'Again and again, in the Fifties, "we" attended / Austin Clarke. He murmured in mild malice / and directed his knife-glance curiously amongst us' (p. 287). The example of Clarke's Bridge Press also feeds into Kinsella's practice in publishing with his own Peppercanister imprint.

In the early pamphlets *The Starlit Eye* and *Per Imaginem*, love and art are mirrors of each other ('Love I consider a difficult, scrupulous art', p. 1), and Kinsella has written of the momentum given to his vocation by the key relationship of his life: 'I think it was meeting the particular woman whom I eventually married that got me seriously writing love poetry, which was the first poetry I now regard as valid.'[10] Eleanor Kinsella is the 'unspeaking daughter, growing less / Familiar where we fell asleep together' of 'Another September' (p. 19), a trope elaborated upon in the sequence *The Familiar* (1999), which revisits 'the Ringwood' and 'St John's', the sites of both their courtship and his early love poems. She is 'unspeaking' because asleep, but a coded reference also to the illness that for many years affected her voice. This illness occasions the hospital visit of 'A Lady of Quality', and 'the hells of circumstance' (p. 66) of 'Wormwood' and 'Traveller':

> Behind me my children vanish, left asleep
> In their strange bed, in apple-tasted night.
> I drive from worry to worry, to where my wife
> Struggles for her breath in a private room.　　　　(p. 59)

'Traveller' clearly shows the gathering influence of American poetry, here Robert Lowell, on Kinsella's language, an influence accelerated by a year spent on an exchange scholarship to the United States in 1963, and his eventual move there in 1965, to take up a position as Writer-in-Residence at Southern Illinois University. In 1970, Kinsella would move on to Philadelphia, and a professorship at Temple University, and begin a permanently bi-located existence between that city and Ireland (Kinsella's poetry is full of migrations and dispersals, landfalls and departures). Not only the prospect of more time devoted to the practice and study of poetry, but also finding treatment (eventually successful) for his wife's illness, contributed to the decision to resign from his position as an assistant Principal Officer in the Department of Finance and move to the United States.

The plain-spoken, 'confessional' directness of 'Traveller' contrasts with the decorativeness of 'Soft, to your Places' (*Another September*), which also illustrates that for all the recourse to non-Irish exemplars as a means to avoid 'Irishism', Kinsella was unafraid to sound at times a Yeatsian note; as Donald Davie remarked: 'stanzas out of Auden, refrains out of Yeats':[11]

> Soft, to your places, animals.
> Your legendary duty calls.
>   It is, to be
> Lucky for my love and me
>   *And yet we have seen that all's*
> *A fiction that is heard of love's difficulty.*   (p. 6)

Despite the poem's derivative élan, the co-option of the animals into 'legendary duty' is a marker of Kinsella's individuality, visible also in the final lines of '*I wonder whether one expects*':

> *And so my bored menagerie*
> *Once more emerges: Energy,*
> *Blinking, only half awake,*
> *Gives its tiny frame a shake;*
> *Fouling itself, a giantess,*
> *The bloodshot bulk of Laziness*
> *Obscures the vision; Discipline*
> *Limps after them with jutting chin,*
> *Bleeding badly from the calf;*
> *Old Jaws-of-Death gives laugh for laugh*
> *With Error as they amble past;*
> *And there as usual, lying last,*
> *Helped along by blind Routine,*
> *Futility flogs a tambourine*   (p. 30)

The animals in 'Soft, to your Places' have been coralled to perform a 'legendary' function; here, the animals have been so domesticated the mentality they inhabit has the torpor of a zoological danse macabre. Davie saw this allegorical turn of mind, and his persistence with this mode – see 'The Last Round: an Allegory', *Fat Master* (2011) – as virtually unique among Kinsella's contemporaries.[12] In 'Ballydavid Pier' allegory is something which 'forms of itself' (p. 57), the evanescent meaning that 'glistens like quicksilver' (p. 57) as it emanates out of significant, if often brutal, event and habitual action.[13]

This allegorical mode feeds into Kinsella's concern with custom and ceremony, and the public and private rituals so prominent in his poetry are part of the deep continuities within his work, belying the apparent division between the formality of the early work and the exploratory forms of the later. Forty years may divide 'Wedding Morning' (p. 32) from 'Wedding Evening' (p. 333), and the funerals of 'Cover Her Face' (p. 37) and 'The Body Brought to the Church' (p. 357), but, both early and late, Kinsella is concerned with the forms and rituals of individual and collective behaviour. In *The Familiar*, even the preparation of breakfast can be infused with eucharistic significance:

> I sliced the tomatoes in thin discs
> in damp sequence into their dish;
> scalded the kettle; made the tea,
>
> and rang the little brazen bell.
> And saved the toast.
>   Arranged the pieces
>
> in slight disorder around the basket.
> Fixed our places, one with the fruit
> and one with the plate of sharp cheese.
>
> *
>
> And stood in my dressing gown
> with arms extended
> over the sweetness of the sacrifice.
>
> Her shade showed in the door.
> Her voice responded:
> 'You are very good. You always made it nice.'   (p. 332)

In the preface to *Prose Occasions*, Kinsella says '1965 was the year of change' (p. 1), citing his resignation from the civil service and his move to the United States. His contemporaneous statements about American poetry, Lowell and Carlos Williams in particular, shed light on the re-orientation he was initiating on his own poetry at this time: 'The scene has the groping characteristics of growth' (*PO*, p. 18). The phrase is echoed in the exploratory turn figured in 'Leaf Eater' (*Nightwalker and Other Poems*), a poem with antecedents in the glosses of early Irish monastic poetry:

> On a shrub in the heart of the garden,
> On an outer leaf, a grub twists
> Half its body, a tendril,
> This way and that in blind
> Space: no leaf or twig
> Anywhere in reach; then gropes
> Back on itself and begins
> To eat its own leaf. (p. 76)

This is another of Kinsella's figures for the dialectic between destruction and growth, growth achieved through forms of mutilation and self-harm: the trees of 'Mirror in February' have been '[h]acked clean for better bearing', the about-to-be shaved face is an 'untiring, crumbling place of growth' (p. 53). 'He must progress / Who fabricates a path' (p. 26), Kinsella says, but advancement comes at a price: 'A step forward and a lesser / step back' (p. 247). Similarly, although in 'Hen Woman' the accidental breaking of the egg means that the physical nourishment it could have provided has been lost, the imaginative nutrition of the event is lifelong: 'I feed upon it still' (p. 99).

If the encounter with America and American poetry initiated a 'step forward' into a poetic practice displaying 'the groping characteristics of growth', there was an equally important move in a different direction. Denis Donoghue has written of Kinsella *becoming* an Irish poet: 'he has become an Irish poet by taking full responsibility for everything that phrase entails'.[14] Yet it would be wrong to see Kinsella's 'groping back' towards the matter of Ireland, and the increasing influence of the Irish-language tradition, in exclusively national or nationalistic terms. The function of the artist, Kinsella says, is to find an adequate response to actuality, to what he calls 'the facts',[15] 'the particulars' of the time and place in which, as a result of 'accident', the artist happens to find him or herself.[16] This response to the 'facts' of his own circumstance includes, for Kinsella, the historical dimension: 'that body of interlocking accident'.[17] But, the dimensions of the 'leaf' in 'Leaf Eater' are wider than Ireland. Though the economic and political ferment of the 1960s, both in the Republic and in Northern Ireland, is part of the story, Kinsella's turn is also of a piece with his thoughts concerning the imaginative and spiritual consequences of the events of World War II: '[i]n the poetic voice, once religion disappears, you're in trouble, you're on your own and you're really forced back on your own depths then'.[18] In the post-Holocaust, post-Atomic age, after the actualisation of Yeats's

Second Coming ('Downstream' portrays a Dantesque vision of the death camps; 'Old Harry' concerns the decision to drop the atomic bomb on Hiroshima), the isolation of the poet is no longer unique: 'After the catastrophe the poet is still isolated, of course; but so now is every man' (*PO*, p. 37).

Images of isolation and mutilation pervade Kinsella's poetry from the beginning: 'Alone we make symbols of love' (p. 1); 'I nonetheless, inflict, endure, / Tedium, intracordal hurt' (p. 13); 'Pitiless, again I ply the knife' (p.19); 'And how should the flesh not quail that span for span / Is mutilated more?' (p. 53). Mutilation is physical and psychic, and, as in 'Mirror in February', a part of the 'brute necessities' of both the natural and human worlds. As with isolation, mutilation is also a marker of modernity: 'In this slight mutilation of the spirit, he seems most modern of all',[19] Kinsella writes, approvingly, of the Anglo-Welsh poet, R. S. Thomas. The imagery of self-scrutiny in the poems bleeds into Kinsella's discussion of the Irish tradition and his relationship with the past: 'I am certain that a great part of the significance of my own past, as I try to write my poetry, is that that past *is* mutilated' ('The Irish Writer', p 66).[20] In 'The Divided Mind' he writes of 'the special mutilations which are a part of the Irish experience' (*PO*, p. 37); in *The Dual Tradition* he writes that 'Yeats stands for the Irish tradition as broken, and Joyce stands for it as healed – or healing – from its mutilation' (p. 91). Joyce's tutelary presence in 'Nightwalker' as 'Father of Authors' derives from his being the 'first major Irish voice to speak for Irish reality since the death-blow to the Irish language' (*The Dual Tradition*, p. 90). Buck Mulligan's nickname for Joyce's alter ego Stephen, Kinch the knife-blade, is apposite here. In *A Technical Supplement* (1976), Kinsella writes of the mutilating knife as bringer of a bodily knowledge, both of reality and of its counterfeit forms, which acts as a yardstick with which everything subsequent has been measured:

> That day when I woke
> a great private blade
> was planted in me from bowels to brain. . . .
>
> From that day forth I knew
> what it was to taste reality
> and not to [.]   (p. 192)

In Kinsella, the knife and the pen are analogues of each other, as is the needle of the intravenous drug user in *St Catherine's Clock*, bent over in the classic Kinsella *incurvatus in se* posture of self-contemplation/self-mutilation:

> In a corner, a half stooped image
> focused on the intimacy
> of the flesh of the left arm.

> The fingers of the right hand are set
> in a scribal act on the skin:
> a gloss, simple and swift as thought,
> is planted there.   (p. 261)

This image of the Irish tradition, the orchestration of the varied registers of reality, from monk in the act of composing the beginnings of Irish poetry in a marginal 'gloss' on calfskin parchment, to the 'gloss' of blood of the drug addict in the act of intravenous injection, is an even more extraordinary yoking together of past and present than Kinsella's most well-known modulation, of Yeats's 'Easter, 1916' in 'A Country Walk':

> Around the corner, in the Market Square,
> I came upon the sombre monuments
> That bear their names: MacDonagh and McBride,
> Merchants; Connolly's Commercial Arms   (p. 46)

The interrogation of self implied by the *incurvatus in se* posture frequently adopted by the Kinsella speaker: the worker bent over his work, the writer 'bent like a feeding thing / over my own source' ('Minstrel', p. 170), even the Godhead: 'Father, bent above Thyself, / still as at the beginning; / reflecting on Thine own image / – not yet perfect. Lost in the work' (*Godhead*, p. 336); and the interrogation of place figured in 'Leaf Eater', ramifies into the three main strands of Kinsella's work: as poet, as critic and as translator. As with T. S. Eliot, Kinsella's literary criticism is a 'by-product of his creative activity'[21] – and this is equally true of his translations, of *The Táin* (1969), *An Duanaire* (1981) and of the anthology, the *New Oxford Book of Irish Verse* (1986) – and the concerns of his poetry unfold in his criticism, and vice versa. 'The Irish Writer' (1966), which in expanded form became *The Dual Tradition* (1995), takes its cue from 'Tradition and the Individual Talent' and the work of the cultural nationalist critic Daniel Corkery, and derives impetus from a preoccupation, shared with Eliot and Corkery, and visible in 'Baggot Street Deserta' (1958), with the past as a living pressure.

'Baggot Street Deserta' figures the discontinuity of the Irish tradition in terms of the relationship of the individual to the past. The speaker conflates poetry with 'exile': 'Versing, like an exile, makes / A virtuoso of the heart'; this exile, though, is a temporal displacement that affects the sense of place: the speaker looks back and 'all is lost; / The Past becomes a fairy bog' (p. 12). The business of the past is unfinished (the poem was first published as 'Unfinished Business', a common phrase at the time to refer negatively to the Partition of Ireland in 1922), but also, and here Kinsella advances beyond the nationalist politics the poem invokes, unfinishable. Similarly, 'A Country Walk' (1962) offers a summary of the Irish story, from myth to history, and up to the provincial, mercantile early 1960s, while in 'Downstream' (1962), the ignorance of the self-accusing speaker – who had envisioned 'a formal drift of the dead / Stretched calm as effigies', but is forced to confront the 'actual mess' (p. 49) of a decaying body found in the woods – parallels Ireland's wilful avoidance of the modern world during the years of World War II, the 'Emergency'. At the end of the poem the speaker and his companion are left drifting downstream, an emblem of the dark flow of history: 'Searching the darkness for a landing place' (p. 50).

New Poems 1973 revealed in a more sustained way than 'Nightwalker' the poetic consequences of the 'groping back' and self-predation of 'Leaf Eater'. The aesthetic growth founded on the destruction of previous practice saw Kinsella move towards interweaved sequences, utilising clusters of related images and themes accumulating in resonance and power. 'Notes from the Land of the Dead' (re-arranged and retitled 'From the Land of the Dead' in *Collected Poems*) established the scheme and the procedures Kinsella would use in the Peppercanister series: sequences organised around related experiences and co-ordinated images. Jung's theories of the growth of the personality and of the archetype provided the thematic template and the governing narrative model for poems of seemingly ad hoc poetic forms. The sources in Jung, the use of the myths and pseudo-history of the mediaeval *Book of Invasions* as a frame narrative to parallel the foundations of the Jungian personality, and the borrowing of tropes from science fiction, can lead to forbidding density:

> *The sun tunnelled onward*
> *eating into the universe's thin dusts*
> *with the World waltzing after it*
>
> – Bith, a planetary pearl-blue
> *flushed with sheets of light,*
> *signed with a thin white wake,*
> the Voyage of the First Kindred   (p. 159)

But the same sequence, *One* (1974), builds towards the thrilling specificities of 'His Father's Hands', where the 'rude block' of the workbench of the speaker's grandfather impregnated with hundreds of nails driven into it by the young Kinsella and other children brings together the sequence's cluster of phallic images of standing stones, uprights and uncoiled snakes, the iterations and accidents of the evolutionary chain, in a final irreducible image of hoarded and released imaginative and sexual vitality:

> Extraordinary ... The big block – I found it
> years afterward in a corner of the yard

in sunlight after rain
and stood it up, wet and black:
it turned under my hands, an axis
of light flashing down its length,
and the wood's soft flesh broke open,
countless little nails
squirming and dropping out of it.   (p. 173)

In *St Catherine's Clock* the clusters of related experience include a sardonic examination of language and political rhetoric. 'From a non-contemporary nationalist artist's impression' conflates several versions of the rebel leader Robert Emmett's 1803 speech from the dock, and evinces Kinsella's distance from the limitations and rhetoric of nationalism:

The torch of friendship and the lamp of life
extinguished, his race finished,
the idol of his soul offered up,

sacrificed on the altar of truth and liberty,
awaiting the cold honours of the grave,
requiring only the charity of silence,
he has done.   (pp. 262–3)

There are also instances of bitter comedy in Kinsella's way with sardonic Dublinese and mastery of register. *One Fond Embrace* (1988) lays into the failings of Kinsella's contemporaries, the cultural and political elite who placed their 'bungled city' into the hands of 'Invisible speculators, urinal architects', in a Swiftian laceration of a 'generation / of positive disgrace' (p. 275):

A modest proposal:
Everything West of the Shannon,
women and children included,
to be declared fair game.
Helicopters, rifles and night-glasses permitted.

The natives to have explosive
and ambush and man-trap privileges.
Unparalleled sport

and in the tradition
– the contemporary manifestation
of an evolving reality.

And he said,

> Have love for one another
> as I have loved the lot of you.   (pp. 280–1)

The 'cross-weaving' (p. 157) of different orders of reality (JFK, Lee Harvey Oswald and Robert Frost in *The Good Fight*; the monastic scribe and the drug addict in *St Catherine's Clock*); and the manipulation of language register, are part of a dialectical vision of reality: 'You have to / wear them down against each other / to get any purchase' (*The Good Fight*, p. 157). The 'cross-weaving' of the contemporary world and the ancient in 'Marcus Aurelius' (*Marginal Economy*, 2006) combines a Cavafy-like portrait of the world of the Emperor-philosopher with an introductory section of late-Kinsella at his most gnomic, and Joycean:

> Gaspbegotten. In shockfuss.
> Out of nowhere.   (*Late Poems*, p. 22)

The brilliance of the poem lies in its distillation of the historical material, the way in which that material mischievously echoes affairs closer to home ('Threatened on the Northern border by brutal tribes / with no settled homes') and, ultimately, its completely achieved tone of 'baffled humaneness':

> Called upon for decisive positive action,
> at which he was more than averagely effective;
> but preferring to spend his time in abstract inquiry,
> for which he was essentially ungifted;
>
> he kept a private journal, in Greek, for which
> he is best remembered. Almost certainly
> because it engaged so much of the baffled humane
> in him, in his Imperial predicament[.]   (*Late Poems*, p. 23)

The poem adds to Kinsella's range, just as it also looks back to one of his earliest and most abiding influences, W. H. Auden:

> As to the early Christians, who might have helped
> with their simplicities, he took no interest,
> unsystematic in their persecution,
> permitting their martyrdoms to run their course.
>   (*Late Poems*, p. 24)

The pointed reference to 'Musée des Beaux Arts' ('They never forgot / That even the dreadful martyrdom must run its course') takes the equanimity of Auden's 'Old Masters' back into the realm of human action, and imperial inaction. The perspective is uniquely Kinsella's, removed yet involved, the

language goal is a denotation and clear-eyed accounting of the 'irresistible
/... movement and nature of things' (*Late Poems*, p. 23). For Kinsella, the
'nature of things' has required a language rinsed of rhetoric. Yet for all the
verbal rectitude, a poem such as 'Marginal Economy' mines the resources and
ambiguities of simple statement to offer the quintessential Kinsella goals of
response to actuality, personal growth and art as an offering to the future,
cross-weaved with the loss inherent in, and the cost of, such sacrifice:

> We accepted things as they were,
> with no thought of change.
> The only change was in ourselves:
> moving onward, leaving
> something more behind each time.   (*Late Poems*, p. 27)

NOTES

1. Michael Schmidt, *Lives of the Poets* (London: Phoenix, 1999), p. 838.
2. All page numbers, unless otherwise indicated, refer to Thomas Kinsella, *Collected Poems* (Manchester: Carcanet, 2001).
3. Gerald Dawe, 'In the Violent Zone: Thomas Kinsella's Nightwalker and Other Poems', *Thomas Kinsella, Special Issue of Tracks* 7 (1987), p. 31.
4. Charles Darwin, *Voyage of the Beagle*, ed. and abridged with an introduction by Janet Browne and Michael Neve (London: Penguin, 1989), pp. 47–9.
5. In 2007, Dublin City Council voted unanimously to grant Kinsella, and Louis le Brocquy, the Freedom of the City, in recognition of their 'enormous contribution to the city, in art and literature'.
6. The first collected trade edition of Peppercanister pamphlets, *Fifteen Dead* (Dolmem/Oxford, 1974) brought together *Butcher's Dozen* and three other elegies, two written for the composer and musician Seán Ó Riada, *A Selected Life* (1972) and *Vertical Man* (1973), and *The Good Fight* (1973), which marked the tenth anniversary of the death of John F. Kennedy. *One and Other Poems* (Dolmen/Oxford, 1979) collected Peppercanisters 4–7: *One* (1974), *A Technical Supplement* (1976) and *Song of the Night and Other Poems* (1978). *Blood and Family* (Oxford Poets, 1988) collected Peppercanisters 8–12: *The Messenger* (1978), *Songs of the Psyche* (1985), *Her Vertical Smile* (1985), *Out of Ireland* (1987) and *St Catherine's Clock* (1987). *From Centre City* (Oxford Poets, 1994) collected 13–17: *One Fond Embrace* (1988), *Personal Places* (1990), *Poems from Centre City* (1990), *Madonna and Other Poems* (1991) and *Open Court* (1991). The work of criticism *The Dual Tradition: An Essay on Poetry and Politics in Ireland* (Carcanet, 1995) is numbered Peppercanister 18. Peppercanisters 19–23: *The Pen Shop* (1997), *The Familiar* (1999), *Godhead* (1999), *Citizen of the World* (2000), and *Littlebody* (2000), appeared in *Collected Poems* (Carcanet, 2001). *Late Poems* (Carcanet 2013) collected Peppercanister 24, *Marginal Economy* (2006), and 26–29, *Man of War* (2007), *Belief and Unbelief* (2007), *Fat Master* (2011), *Love Joy Peace* (2011). Peppercanister 25 *Readings in Poetry* (2006) is a close reading of Shakespeare's Sonnets 29 and 30, Yeats's 'The Tower' and Eliot's 'The Love Song of J. Alfred Prufrock'.

7. David V. Erdman (ed.), *The Complete Poetry and Prose of William Blake*, rev. 2nd edn (Berkeley: University of California Press, 2008), p. 71.

8. John Montague and Thomas Kinsella (eds.) *The Dolmen Miscellany of Irish Writing* (Dublin: Dolmen Press, 1962), prefatory page.

9. *Prose Occasions 1951–2006*, ed. Andrew Fitzsimons, Manchester: Carcanet, 2009, p. 19; henceforward *PO*.

10. Kinsella, in *The Poet Speaks: Interviews with Contemporary Poets*, ed. Peter Orr (London: Routledge and Kegan Paul, 1966), p. 105.

11. Donald Davie, 'First Fruits: The Poetry of Thomas Kinsella', *Irish Writing* 37 (Autumn 1957), p. 49.

12. See 'Thomas Kinsella', *Under Briggflats: A History of Poetry in Great Britain 1960–1988* (Manchester: Carcanet Press, 1989), p. 68.

13. The procedure of Pound's *Cantos* is a clear influence on Kinsella's practice in the Peppercanisters, but the influence of his idea of 'luminous detail' is also evident here, as it is in the pun, and the allusion to Pound as exemplar, in 'Wyncote, Pennsylvania: a gloss': 'my papers seem luminous. / And over them I will take / ever more painstaking care' (p. 130).

14. Denis Donoghue, *We Irish: Essays on Irish Literature and Society* (Berkeley and Los Angeles: University of California Press, 1986), p. 16.

15. Kinsella, in *Viewpoints: Poets in Conversation with John Haffenden* (London: Faber, 1981), pp. 102–3.

16. Kinsella, '"Omphalos of Scraps", An Interview with Thomas Kinsella' by Philip Fried. *Manhattan Review* 4.2 (Spring 1988), p. 9.

17. Ibid.

18. Kinsella, 'An Interview with Thomas Kinsella' by Ian Flanagan, *Metre* 2.2 (Spring 1997), p. 113.

19. Kinsella, 'Review of *Poisoned Lands*, by John Montague; *Out of Bounds*, by Jon Stallworthy; and *The Bread of Truth*, by R. S. Thomas, *New York Times Book Review*, 12 April 1964, p. 41.

20. 'The Irish Writer', a lecture delivered as 'Literary Continuity', MLA (New York) Dec. 1966. In *Davis, Mangan, Ferguson? Tradition and The Irish Writer. Writings by W. B. Yeats and by Thomas Kinsella*. Tower Series of Anglo-Irish Studies, II, ed. Roger McHugh (Dublin: Dolmen Press, 1970), pp. 57–66.

21. Frank Kermode, ed. *Selected Prose of T. S. Eliot* (London: Faber, 1975), p. 11.

SELECTED FURTHER READING

Editions

The Táin, trans. Thomas Kinsella, Dublin: Dolmen, 1969.

An Duanaire 1600–1900: Poems of the Dispossessed, ed. Seán Ó Tuama, trans. Thomas Kinsella, Dublin: Dolmen Press, 1981.

New Oxford Book of Irish Verse, ed. and trans. Thomas Kinsella, Oxford: Oxford University Press, 1986.

The Dual Tradition: An Essay on Poetry and Politics in Ireland, Manchester: Carcanet, 1995.

Collected Poems, Manchester: Carcanet Press, 2001.
A Dublin Documentary, Dublin: O'Brien Press, 2006.
Selected Poems, Manchester: Carcanet Press, 2007.
Prose Occasions 1951–2006, ed. Andrew Fitzsimons, Manchester: Carcanet, 2009.
Late Poems, Manchester: Carcanet, 2013.

Secondary Works

Badin, Donatella Abbate, *Thomas Kinsella*, New York: Twayne, 1996.
Clutterbuck, Catriona, ed. *Thomas Kinsella* Special *Issue of Irish University Review* 31: 1 (Spring–Summer 2001).
Fitzsimons, Andrew, *The Sea of Disappointment: Thomas Kinsella's Pursuit of the Real*, Dublin: UCD Press, 2008.
Harmon, Maurice, *Thomas Kinsella: Designing for the Exact Needs*, Dublin: Portland OR, Irish Academic Press, 2008.
Jackson, Thomas H., *The Whole Matter: The Poetic Evolution of Thomas Kinsella*, Syracuse University Press; Dublin: Lilliput Press, 1995.
John, Brian, *Reading the Ground: The Poetry of Thomas Kinsella*, Washington, DC: Catholic University of America Press, 1996.
Johnston, Dillon, *Irish Poetry after Joyce*, 2nd edn., New York: Syracuse University Press, 1997.
Lynch, David, *Confronting Shadows: An Introduction to the Poetry of Thomas Kinsella*, Dublin: New Island Books, 2015.

18

MAURICE RIORDAN

John Montague

John Montague's earliest memories were of city streets, of playing on a tenement roof, laying nickels under subway trains, and going to see Mickey Mouse movies.[1] It is not the beginning one expects for a poet who represented the nationalist tradition of rural Northern Ireland. Born in Brooklyn in 1929 to Irish emigrant parents, he was brought to Ireland at age four, to the village of Garvaghey, Co Tyrone. He was fostered by his father's unmarried sisters, while his mother – who returned when he was seven – lived with his two older brothers in the nearby village of Fintona. His father remained in America. The experience of a disrupted childhood left him with an enduring sense of abandonment.

The pattern of exile and return continued. Montague retained his connection with America. He returned there on a Fulbright scholarship in his twenties. He met his first wife, Madeleine de Brauer, at the Iowa Writers' Workshop. Later he taught at Berkeley and befriended Gary Snyder and Allen Ginsberg, among other American poets. The Montagues lived in Dublin until 1961, when they moved to Paris. In 1972 he returned to Ireland to teach at UCC. He lived in Cork with his second wife, Evelyn Robson, with whom he had two daughters, until 1998. Thereafter, until his death in 2016, he lived in Nice with his third wife, the novelist Elizabeth Wassell, while also having a house in West Cork.

It is a life with cosmopolitan flavour, which left evident traces on his poetry. He absorbed French and especially American influences, and he was guided by a sense of the poet as an intellectual and cultivated presence in a modern society. At the same time, he remained essentially a poet of locality, who drew, in his own words, 'an artesian energy' from a 'submerged population'.[2] That 'population' was the community he knew as a child, the mainly – though not exclusively – Catholic people of the 'border' counties of Ulster.

Montague's three collections up to 1970 reflect both his rural upbringing and the cosmopolitan range of experience. In the pamphlet *Forms of Exile*

(1958), it is the outside world, mainly America, that dominates the subject
matter. With *Poisoned Lands* (1961), these poems are joined by more based
on his Tyrone childhood. That balance is maintained in *A Chosen Light*
(1967) and *Tides* (1970), two volumes that also established him as a love
poet.

The poems of rural life owe something to Patrick Kavanagh. In 'A Drink of
Milk' (200),[3] we see more than a hint of 'Paddy Maguire' (the bachelor
farmer of *The Great Hunger*) in the farm hand who 'lurches / to kick his
boots off / in the night-silent kitchen'. The early aesthetic is also shaped by
American influences, especially the spare diction and taut line of William
Carlos Williams. In this poem of rhyming quatrains, however, it is not
Williams's rhythmic influence we find, but a sturdy realism reminiscent
specifically of 'To Elsie' in its observation of a world at once modern – or
modernised, with its milking parlour – and culturally backward:

> A pounding transistor shakes
> the Virgin on her shelf
>
> as he dreams towards bed.
> A last glance at a magazine,
> he puts the mug to his head,
> grunts, and drains it clean.   (201)

In the most assured poems of Montague's early period, the assimilation of
influences crystallises in the attempt to be 'luminously exact', a phrase from
the title poem of *A Chosen Light* (240). 'A Bright Day', from the same
volume, also uses 'luminously' and proceeds to a fuller expression of stylistic
intent: 'a slow exactness // Which recreates experience / By ritualizing its
details' (236).

Ritual implies both attentiveness and ease of execution. Such are the
qualities of 'The Water Carrier' (197), one of Montague's most influential
poems, in its recollection of the childhood chore of fetching water from the
well:

> Twice daily I carried water from the spring,
> Morning before leaving for school, and evening:
> Balanced as a fulcrum between two buckets.

There is a polarity of morning and evening, of home and school, of the
homely 'buckets' opposed to the school word 'fulcrum'. This is in line with
an overall balance, the poem poised between the recollected source of
inspiration and the act of writing here and now. The verse lingers to attend
to such details as 'the slime-topped stones' and the 'rust-tinged water' (and
when Montague revised the poem, he restored a stanza that notes the water's

'manacles of ice on the wrists').[4] Simultaneously, the forward movement is surely co-ordinated, as it keeps one step in childhood memory, the other in adult composition:

> Recovering the scene, I had hoped to stylize it,
> Like the portrait of an Egyptian water-carrier:
> But halt, entranced by slight but memoried life.

The eye is partly focused on the remembered 'scene', partly concentrating on the actual drawing of inspiration from the memory. The poem maintains the equilibrium to the end: 'Some living source, half-imagined and half-real // Pulses in the fictive water that I feel.' That 'fictive' is a 'loan' word, fetched cunningly from Wallace Stevens to apply here with exemplary precision.

The same bi-focal effect is present – albeit more crudely – in another early poem, 'The Trout' (225). We have an equally vivid sense of 'memoried life', 'a photographic calm' in the realisation of images, as the boy hovers above the fish in the stream:

> As the curve of my hands
> Swung under his body
> He surged, with visible pleasure.
> . . .
> The two palms crossed in a cage
> Under the lightly pulsing gills.

Thus the poem builds with exactness to the climax, 'I gripped'. But then it steps away from recollection to end with an assertive gesture: 'To this day I can taste / His terror on my hands.' It is an instance of a tension that becomes characteristic of Montague's style – where the receptivity of the writing gives way to rhetorical statement.

Paul Muldoon, who read 'The Trout' as a school boy, observes its 'underlying sexuality', and comments ruefully on its 'autoeroticism'.[5] It is a mode Muldoon would adopt in his own first poems, such as 'Blowing Eggs'. The school was St Patrick's College, Armagh, a Diocesan Seminary where two decades before Montague had been a student. This is not a coincidence. Catholic boys from rural Ireland belonged, in those decades, to a homogenous culture: not only were they liable to go to the same schools, they learned the same prayers, played the same games, and were familiar with identical customs and routines of daily life. At the primary level of sensory experience, they had much the same stock of potential material for poems. In this context, for instance, one sees that 'The Water Carrier' anticipated Seamus Heaney's 'Personal Helicon'.

More generally, Montague's poems of 'memoried life' sketched out the terrain for the forming generation of poets in Northern Ireland in studies of rustic manners such as 'The Mummer Speaks', 'Forge', 'Clear the Way' and 'Like Dolmens Round My Childhood'. This last also uncovers the landscape as a trove of subject matter, as does – most memorably – 'The Wild Dog Rose', which activates the archetype of the *cailleach*, the hag or crone of tradition, in presenting a heartrending, scrupulous portrayal of rural loneliness. There is also an outward reach to America ('Bus-stop, Nevada') and France ('The Centenarian'), setting up a polarity between Ireland and 'abroad' that becomes familiar in the work of succeeding poets.

'The Trout' – as Muldoon notes – recalls the trout in Yeats's 'Song of Wandering Aengus' that turns into 'a glimmering girl', and thus becomes the muse of the poet's quest. As well as writing poems of childhood, Montague emerged as a love poet in *A Chosen Light* and its succeeding volume, *Tides*, a development consolidated in *The Great Cloak* (1978). As directed by the influence of Robert Graves's *The White Goddess*, he writes as a poet in service to the Muse.

The poems are typically set in North America or Paris, or in an unspecified modern cityscape, with 'all the superstructure / of the city outside' ('Talisman', 103). They form the transgressive axis of Montague's work and, cumulatively, they attain a polemical force. Rejecting the narrowness of Irish Catholicism, they welcome the tolerance of French culture, and likewise rejoice in the new-found freedoms of the sexual revolution. The poet-persona may be seen to embody the priapic male of the era, though in a more chivalric guise than one finds, say, in Updike or Mailer.

Insofar as these poems react against puritanical mores at home, Montague was following Austin Clarke, whose work dramatised the conflict between religion and the imagination, which the latter associated with apostasy and sexual freedom. Thus in Clarke's 'The Straying Student', the protagonist abandons his clerical studies to follow the errant Muse: 'Long had she lived in Rome when Popes were bad'.[6] The poem celebrates secular 'knowledge' and invokes, in a notional sense, a life-giving sensuality: 'for a summer [she] taught me all I know'. In Clarke's view, he was re-asserting a native, secular engagement with life in the face of a repressive Catholic Church.

Analogously, Montague's 'The First Invasion of Ireland', loosely based on an early Irish text, presents those remote ancestral invaders engaged in love-making (221). He also follows Clarke in uncovering (to use the latter's phrase) 'the lost treasure of Ireland'.[7] 'Life Class', which is spread over four pages in its first printing, graphically depicts and celebrates the female nude in anatomical detail and explicitly rejects the 'desert // father's dream of / sluttish nakedness' (262). 'Love, a Greeting' notes 'the honey sac / of the cunt' (104), while 'The Same Gesture' observes the lover's hand 'changing gears with / the same gesture / as eased your snow-bound / heart and flesh' (124).

The political implications of sexuality become overt in 'The Siege of Mullingar', where the young people at the music festival, or *fleadh*, are seen as ushering in – prematurely, it turned out – a new era of liberation: 'Puritan Ireland's dead and gone, / A myth of O'Connor and O'Faolain' (79). Elsewhere, Montague's love poems have personal focus. They address the difficulties of relationships, such as marital discord, or involve complexities of communication and mutual desire. Love is seen as a tense engagement, although a redeeming force in a hostile world, a human-centred activity that mitigates the impersonal forces of modern life.

These elements are active in 'All Legendary Obstacles' (229). The passing trains with their 'great flanged wheels' are at odds with human scale, as the lover waits 'nervously', separated from the beloved by seemingly inimical forces:

> All legendary obstacles lay between
> Us, the long imaginary plain,
> The monstrous ruck of mountains
> And, swinging across the night,
> Flooding the Sacramento, San Joaquim,
> The hissing drift of winter rain.

We see here an example of that stylistic tension whereby scrupulous meanness is overcome by lyric eloquence. As Patrick Crotty has pointed out, the plain is not 'imaginary', but imagined – and this inexactness is rhetorical.[8] There is also reliance on intensifiers: 'long' and, in the following stanza, 'great'. The fuller rhythm of the verse involves a more expansive use of phrase. But this is reined back – and severely – by rough enjambments ('between / Us'; and later 'sail / By'), and by effects of metrical hesitation, whereby the runs of lightly accented syllables alternate with three or four stresses per line.

The result, overall, is a stammering eloquence – an impeded speech that is matched by the emotional stress of reunion. We have a hint of Persephone being returned from the underworld ('pale / Above the negro porter's lamp'), as an ambiguous crone-like figure watches the couple move off into the night, 'Kissing, still unable to speak' (229).

*

While Montague was establishing a reputation for lyric poetry of a certain austerity, he was also following a different tack. Beginning with what he called a 'vision' in 1961, he embarked on a long poem centred on the historical Gaelic kingdom of the O'Neills.[9] He found his title in his own native place, Garvaghey – *Garbh Acaidh* in Irish, which translates as 'a rough field'. This resulted in a series of pamphlets. The first, 'Patriotic Suite', appeared in 1966 and marked the 50th anniversary of the Easter Rising.[10] It featured a woodcut from John Derricke's *The Image of Irelande* (1581) of a piper leading a contingent of 'woodkernes' on a raid. *The Image of Irelande* recorded Henry Sidney's (father of the poet Philip Sidney) brutal campaigns against Irish chieftains in the 1570s. When *The Rough Field* appeared in 1972, a handsomely produced volume, it deployed Derricke's woodcuts as an important component of the overall effect.[11]

The Rough Field is Montague's most audacious and most problematic work. Described by himself as an epic, it brings together strands of history and family history, using a variety of narrative and lyrical forms. The sequences contain many of the rural poems from the three existing collections. But it gives them a different orientation, whereby they gain political resonance in the new context. In form, it has some of the features of fragmentary modernist epics, such as Williams's *Paterson* and Hart Crane's *The Bridge*, though it is more dilute in style than either. Even so, it makes extensive use of collage, with marginalia and glosses of historical and contemporary quotations, and fragments of popular song.

The book's publication coincided with a high point of nationalist feeling in Ireland. It was the year of Bloody Sunday, the massacre in Derry that unleashed a tide of anti-British feeling among nationalists north and south. In the immediate aftermath, the British Embassy in Dublin was burned down. Conspicuous in the woodcut that accompanies 'A Severed Head' is the head of the wife of the rebel Rory Óg O'More. Such an image recalls in tribal memory the massacres of native chieftains, and specifically that at Mullaghmast in 1578. A woodcut of O'More himself, hunted in the forest, illustrates 'A Good Night'; the image of the outlawed chieftain evokes the lineage of Irish rebels, down to those involved – or soon to be – in the IRA campaign in Northern Ireland.

Montague's political stance put him at the centre of events at the time. In July 1970 the Taoiseach Jack Lynch began his 'two nation' broadcast to the country by quoting 'Old moulds are broken in the North', which stands at the start of the book. That same year Montague read 'A New Siege', dedicated to Bernadette Devlin, outside Armagh jail, where the civil rights leader was imprisoned. In keeping with the nationalist mood of the time, this section has a plangent rhetoric:

> Lines of leaving
>   lines of returning
> the long estuary of Lough Foyle
>   a ship motionless
> in wet darkness
>   mournfully hooting   (84–5)

The Rough Field, then, had something of the force of protest poetry. It was itself an intervention in the Civil Rights campaign in Northern Ireland. That aspect of the book made it controversial in the decades that followed. Its political implications are those of an unaccommodating nationalism, though this is somewhat blurred by a fatalist view of an impersonal historical process at work. It contrasts with the more circumspect approach of Seamus Heaney, whose *North* (1975) was then in progress.

Now at some distance from the Troubles, the work remains a curious hybrid between the innovative methods of 'modernist' epic and the emotive protest poetry of the 1960s. The book falters not for moments of rhetorical intemperance ('the vomit surge / of race hatred' (58)), but because of its simplistic 'vision'. Its ostensible view of history, as set out on the back cover, reads: 'the New Road I describe runs through Normandy as well as Tyrone. And experiences of agitations in Paris and Berkeley taught me that violence of disputing factions is more than a local phenomenon.' This is a shallow historical perspective, which the verse often strains to justify:

> I assert
> a civilization died here;
>   it trembles
> underfoot where I walk these
>   small, sad hills:
> it rears in my blood stream
>   when I hear
> a bleat of Saxon condescension,
>   Westminster
> to hell, it is less than these
>   strangely carved
> five-thousand year resisting stones,
>   that lonely cross.   (58)

Some poems, such as 'The Siege of Mullingar' and 'The Wild Dog Rose' (which forms the final section), are herded into the overall sequence – and they lose some of their individuality as a result, without adequately bolstering the flimsy structure. On purely formal grounds of *integritas*, as an 'epic' – whether 'modernist' or nationalist – *The Rough Field* falls apart into its component parts. It retains historical importance, however, as one of the few expressions, and the most eloquent and sustained, of the submerged nationalist culture of Northern Ireland.

That partisan stance is embedded in emotional experience, in the hereditary transmission of music and story, in the felt life of family and community. It should be understood that such organic nationalism was intensified in Northern Ireland by partition. The nationalist community was left adrift from the evolving Irish state and kept culturally, and materially, impoverished within the Northern enclave. As a consequence, an intimate attachment to the land acted as a guarantor of cultural identity, and indeed served as a record of territorial dispossession.

In 'Feeling Into Words' (1974), Seamus Heaney makes his view of the mythological dimension of this shared cultural exclusion explicit:

> There is an indigenous territorial numen, a tutelary of the whole island, call her Mother Ireland, Kathleen Ni Houlihan, the poor old woman, the Shan Van Vocht, whatever; and her sovereignty has been temporarily usurped or infringed by a new male cult whose founding fathers were Cromwell, William of Orange and Edward Carson and whose godhead is incarnate in a rex or Caesar resident in a palace in London.[12]

Such quasi-religious fealty to the island had consequences in the prolonged violence of the Troubles; and Northern poets responded variously to the complexity of a history where the competing myths – of Planter and Gael – are intertwined within the small divided communities. Heaney's own approach, appropriating a phrase from Yeats, was to seek 'befitting emblems of adversity'. For the nationalist imagination, even so, the landscape – with its Gaelic associations and reminders of the historical kingdoms – has retained the status of holy land, and thereby exerts something akin to an erotic force. The poems of *North* consciously resonate within Northern European myth, yet the avowal of 'The Tollund Man', as 'Bridegroom to the goddess', affirms an atavistic attachment to sacred ground.[13] The Irish bog, for Heaney, is feminine and yielding, 'kind, black butter, opening underfoot'.[14]

In Montague's poems, the 'tutelary' of the island is the Celtic (and pre-Celtic) goddess Anu. She has associations with the Clogher Valley in Tyrone, where her name is preserved in Knockmany – the Hill of Anu – the site of a Stone Age passage grave. This is the landscape evoked in his 1976 sequence, 'A Slow Dance', where he reanimates the *persona* of Sweeney, the bird-king of tradition who lived in the woods. He follows Robert Graves in portraying Sweeney as a poet dedicated to the White Goddess, represented here by the ancient fertility goddess.[15]

Sweeney is the type of poet alert to the natural world ('A nest of senses / stirring awake' (273)), who establishes an organic connection with the fecund land. In 'Message', this takes on erotic intimacy: 'ease your / hand into the / rot-smelling crotch // of a hollow / tree' (275); while 'Seskilgreen' acknowledges the 'still fragrant goddess' (276). To continue the quasi-religious import of the primitivist vision, 'For the Hill Mother' (277) adapts the form of the Marian litany:

Hidden cleft
speak to us
Portal of delight
inflame us

The sequence celebrates fertility, fecundity, sensuous pleasure. Other poems in this collection show a resourceful variety of tone in their celebration of the senses. 'Small Secrets' (281) can be read as a 'nature' poem in its description of the snail's progress on 'his singular / muscular foot'. But there is a subtle link to early Irish poetry. Its opening ('where I work / outdoors') echoes the ninth-century lyric 'The Scribe in the Woods'; then, with the use of 'habitation', it recalls Sweeney who, in a lyric from the same century, makes his habitation in the trees.

'Dowager' (284) gives the fertility goddess a surprising, and sprightly, incarnation as the chatelaine of a 'leaky Western castle':

Alone, I hum with satisfaction in the sun,
An old bitch, with a warm mouthful of game.

We have an allusion here to the 'old bitch gone in the teeth' of *Hugh Selwyn Mauberley*, for whom – in Pound's sequence – the dead of the Great War were sacrificed. The dowager in her Rolls speeding through the countryside does indeed represent another 'botched civilization': that of the Anglo-Irish Ascendancy.

The Irish landscape is perhaps the most variously fruitful source for Montague's imagination. Its 'restless whispering', in a phrase from 'Windharp' (288), can be heard in poems across the collections. *The Dead Kingdom* (1984) resumes and extends much of the matter of *The Rough Field*, although it lacks the splendid gestures of the earlier work as it interweaves, in narrative form, painful autobiographical subject matter – centred around the death of Montague's mother – with the cultural associations of the landscape. Its highlights are those poems that elude the confessional norm: 'The Well Dreams' (155), and two poems re-used from *Tides*, 'Last Journey' (178) and 'What a View' (179). The latter offers literally a gull's-eye view of terrain that is denuded of historical and religious associations – a scene in which *gairbh acaidh* is just that, a rough field of 'hillocky / Tyrone grassland'.

These poems belong in Montague's oeuvre to a sub-set of landscape poems that have a reflective impersonality that is reminiscent of the Franco-Breton poet Guillevic (whom Montague translated). The manner is continued in the title poem of *Mount Eagle* (1989), in which an eagle surveys the passing of the Gaelic world. It offers a valedictory parable when the bird sacrificially flies into Mount Eagle (located in the Kerry *Gaeltacht*) to become its guardian (340). As is suggested by the imperfect anagram, its destiny symbolises Montague's completed body of work.

Three further collections, however, followed *Mount Eagle*. There are notable poems of domestic life in *Smashing the Piano* (1999), such as the tender evocation of fatherhood in 'Guardians' (387); while 'Crossroads', from the same volume, gives an unflinching account of a childhood road fatality (384). Among the later reminiscences, 'Many Mansions' in *Speech Lessons* (2011) returns to the same sensory alertness of Montague's first period. In this proto-sexual experience, the boy exploring his grandfather's derelict shop finds some Edwardian mannequins:

> I tried to dance with them
> but the metal scraped and tangled
> in our slow stiff waltz
> so I toppled them over one by one
> until they lay still as the dicky bows on their shelf.　　　(506)

The bleak rehearsal of mechanical sexual activity not only portrays the child's loneliness, but intimates the proximity of *eros* and *thanatos*. It is a late-early encounter with the Muse, seen here as both bride and crone, that vibrates retroactively through the love poems.

Another strand surviving into the later work is the extended narrative. Both 'The Plain of Blood' (*Drunken Sailor*, 2004) and 'Border Sick Call' (*Collected Poems*, 1995) evoke the 'border country' as a region where the imagination slips beyond the here-and-now into another world, but one that is realised in particulars of place and people. The verse is prose-like, relaxed – at times slack – yet it achieves a cumulative narrative rhythm. 'The Plain of Blood' (471) – the second poem of that title in the oeuvre – recounts an afternoon drive in quest of the Crom Cruach, 'the crooked or dark one', an obscure figure in Irish mythology who has survived as a feared presence in folk memory. The poem reveals the Crom as a benign deity, 'an Irish Apollo' overthrown by the new Christian dispensation. Beyond the ostensible subject, it attends to contingencies of weather and countryside, and is adept in its sketches of country types. It achieves a quiet lyricism that outweighs the revelation, whose reliability, in any case, is put in doubt when the Montague-narrator wonders if it is a tale 'told by a doting man'.

The same scepticism frames the narrative of 'Border Sick Call', in which the Montague-narrator accompanies his doctor brother, Seamus, on his rounds (363). This ambulatory narrative, 'in memory of a journey in winter along the Fermanagh-Donegal border', takes us into a snow-bound borderland. The brothers are obliged to abandon their car and continue on foot to tend the sick. And so they pass into a semi-mythic realm. There is a Dantean motif of climbing Mount Purgatory, with the doctor as the poet's guide – but it is one that emerges on the return journey, when the Montague-narrator sees a boat on the frozen lake and recognises it as 'the small bark of my wit'. As the brothers are waved back through the border post, he wonders 'in what country have we been'. The success of the narrative is to have maintained that sense of a world that is at once liminal and robustly real.

This border country is the core of Montague's world. It is the 'ancient Ireland' of his childhood. Here lives the 'submerged population' he cites as his source of 'artesian energy from many silent centuries'. It is depicted as a chill remnant of the Ice Age, a region forgotten by the modern world. It seems, at first, to be solely a vale of tears, a land of sickness, pain and lonely death: 'stale urine and faeces – the old man on the grey bed'. And yet, in the face of suffering, it offers hospitality, and warmth, with a lively fire in the kitchen, where MacGurren, the host, is not only ancient but convivial. He rewards the brothers for braving the snow with a prescription bottle of 'the good stuff', that is *poitín*, which fires the imagination of the doctor as well as the poet.

The comradeship of brothers, of doctor and poet, suggests a perfection of role in relation to the community they came from. Together they embody a nobility of vocation, 'a stubborn devotion' (as the poem rather explicitly says) 'sustained by an ideal of service'. Here, then, is Montague's kingdom, that 'half-imagined' place that hearkens back to 'The Wild Dog Rose' and 'Like Dolmens Round My Childhood', which in 1961 set in motion *The Rough Field*. Its natives live beyond the norms of civic society, survivors who rely on patience, cunning, illicit trade, and draw on a pragmatic wisdom, none more so than the ex-smuggler MacGurren – who in his wry estimate of partition may well be speaking for several Northern poets: 'Border bedamned. It was a godsend'.

*

Writing over six decades, Montague accumulated an extensive body of work, including translations from French and early Irish verse. But it is poems of the 1960s and 1970s that are central to the dynamics of Irish poetry. Thereafter, developments in Ireland and internationally superseded his ongoing concerns. In particular, both the complexity of the Northern conflict and the arrival of gender politics challenged the assumptions that often underlie his poems. As Patrick Crotty observes: 'It may be Montague's tragedy, where the fortunes of his reputation are concerned, that the historical and amorous themes round which his ambitions for a major poetry began to crystallise became, within a decade or so of his adopting them, the most fiercely contested sites in Irish literary criticism.'[16]

Montague, however, remains pivotal in the Irish context as an enabling link between the antithetical mid-century poetries of Kavanagh and Clarke and the diversity of poetry, north and south of the border, in the 1970s. It is his inheritance from Kavanagh, and the manner in which he enriched it, that is foremost. He reinstates the Revival's concerns with national identity and builds on its understanding of the landscape as a repository of history and tradition. Not just 'stony grey soil' but layered and textured, it becomes 'a manuscript / We [have] lost the skill to read' (47).

This distinction forms the nub of Heaney's 1977 comparison of the two poets:

> although both Montague and Kavanagh look and listen with intensity inside their parishes, their eyes and ears seek and pick up different things. Kavanagh's eye has been used to bending over the ground before it ever bent over a book ... Kavanagh's place names ... are denuded of tribal and etymological implications ... but Montague's are rather sounding lines, rods to plumb the depths of a shared and diminished culture. They are redolent not just of his personal life but of the history of his people, disinherited and dispossessed.[17]

Heaney's stronger affinity is with Kavanagh. But his practice accords with that of Montague in bringing an educated eye, and a politicised and historical perspective, to bear on the Northern terrain. More generally, in opening up that imaginative territory, Montague introduced a broadly American poetic idiom to Irish verse, notably in his predilection for sequences and in his naturalised and resourceful use of free form.

It is also arguable that Montague's unguarded nationalism was helpful to his successors. Heaney's nationalist allegiance is explicit only in his prose. Similarly, the political anger that burns at the core of Muldoon's poetry is barely felt through the cordon of obliquity and ironic deflection. It may be that Montague's disposition to speak forthrightly for 'his people' allowed, or perhaps obliged, the major poets in his slipstream to be more circumspect.

Montague's achievement rests, of course, on poems. Sensitised by a troubled infancy, he was acutely responsive to the tremors and fractures of a society in a quiescent phase. His own stammering speech acted as a medium to voice that muted world even as political upheaval began. As he wrestled his demons, his imagination expanded to explore themes of difficult love and, in keeping with the intrepid trajectory of the life, he made a record of affection and varied attachment. Over the decades he produced poems that are decorous in phrase and line, musical in cumulative effect, which at their truest achieve a halting eloquence. They constitute a core of work that is moving, passionate, often funny and crafted to last.

NOTES

1. *Born in Brooklyn: John Montague's America*. Edited by David Lampe (Fredonia, New York: White Pine Press, 1991), p. 33.
2. *The Bag Apron, or, The Poet and his Community: Inaugural Lecture of the Ireland Chair of Poetry* (Belfast: Lagan Press, [1998?]), pp. 29–30.
3. Page references are to *New Collected Poems* (Oldcastle, Co Meath: Gallery Press, 2012).
4. Introduction, *Poisoned Lands* (Dublin: The Dolmen Press, 1977), p. 10.
5. *Chosen Lights: Poets on Poems by John Montague in Honour of His 80th Birthday*. Edited by Peter Fallon (Oldcastle, Co Meath: Gallery Press, 2009), p. 28.
6. *Collected Poems* (Dublin: The Dolmen Press, 1974), p. 188.
7. *The Bright Temptation* (Dublin: The Dolmen Press, 1965), p. 178.
8. 'Montague Bound: A Note on *Collected Poems*', *Well Dreams: Essays on John Montague*. Edited by Thomas Dillon Redshaw (Omaha, Nebraska: Creighton University Press, 2004), p. 383.
9. *The Figure in the Cave, and Other Essays*. Edited by Antoinette Quinn (Dublin: Lilliput Press, 1989), p. 55.
10. *Patriotic Suite* (Dublin: The Dolmen Press, 1966).
11. *The Rough Field* (Dublin: The Dolmen Press, 1972).
12. *Preoccupations* (London: Faber and Faber, 1980), p. 57.
13. 'The Tollund Man', *Wintering Out* (London: Faber and Faber, 1972), p. 47.
14. 'Bogland', *Door Into the Dark* (London: Faber and Faber, 1969), p. 55.
15. *The White Goddess* (London: Faber and Faber, 1961), p. 455.
16. 'Montague Bound', p. 381.
17. 'The Sense of Place', *Preoccupations*, p. 140.

SELECTED FURTHER READING

Death of a Chieftain, and Other Stories. London: Macgibbon & Kee, 1964.

The Lost Notebook. Cork: Mercier Press, 1987.

The Figure in the Cave, and Other Essays. Edited by Antoinette Quinn. Dublin: Lilliput Press, 1989.

Born in Brooklyn: John Montague's America. Edited by David Lampe. Fredonia, New York: White Pine Press, 1991.

A Love Present, and Other Stories. Dublin: Wolfhound Press, 1997.

Selected Poems / Francis Ponge. Edited by Margaret Guiton; translated by Margaret Guiton, John Montague and C. K. Williams. London: Faber and Faber, 1998.

Carnac / Guillevic. Translated by John Montague; introduction by Stephen Romer. Newcastle Upon Tyne: Bloodaxe Books, 1999.

Company: A Chosen Life. London: Duckworth: 2001.

The Pear Is Ripe: A Memoir. Dublin: Liberties, 2007.

A Smile Between the Stones / Sur La Dernière Lande by Claude Esteban. Translated by John Montague. Mayfield, East Sussex: Agenda Editions, 2005.

Criticism

Irish University Review. John Montague Special Issue. Edited by Christopher Murray. 19 (Spring, 1989).

Dillon Redshaw, Thomas, ed. *Well Dreams: Essays on John Montague.* Omaha, Nebraska: Creighton University Press, 2004.

Fallon, Peter, ed. *Chosen Lights: Poets on Poems by John Montague in Honour of His 80th Birthday.* Oldcastle, Co Meath: Gallery Press, 2009.

19

RICHARD PINE

Brendan Kennelly

A critic attempting to discuss a poet epitomises the unspeakable in pursuit of the unreachable. He can merely scratch in the margins of the work. And perhaps the margins are all we have to go on. The poet, too, pursues the unreachable, the unknowable, working through hope and despair towards an anticipated moment. It is a constant iteration and re-iteration in pursuit of a brief glimpse of the *merveilleux*, an image of love and light and the possibility of the word 'Yes!' But he lives *en marge*. Brendan Kennelly is the eye and voice of the voyeur, whose unique position encapsulates the visible and invisible, the known and unknown, the spoken and unspoken. A membrane of creative struggle that is fragile and permanent. This, he calls 'the struggling arena',[1] wherein he enacts an *agon* of observation and articulation.

This essay will address three central factors in Kennelly's poetry (which includes his verse dramas): first, the 'two villages' of Ballylongford (his birthplace) and Trinity College, Dublin (TCD, his place of work 1963–2006), between which his imagination commutes; second, his negotiation of the poetic gift, the task of defining love, and the dangers of language; third, the need for a critical writing of Ireland in the light of what Kennelly sees as its inhibitions, prejudices and taboos.

Life and Career

Brendan Kennelly was born in the village of Ballylongford, County Kerry, in 1936, and educated at TCD and Leeds, where he wrote a PhD thesis on Gaelic epic poetry. He began publishing poetry in 1959, with his first collection, *My Dark Fathers*, appearing in 1964. He worked as a bus conductor in London before returning to TCD as a lecturer in English in 1963; he became a Fellow of the college in 1967, and was appointed to a personal chair of modern literature in 1973.

His principal collections are *Moloney Up and At It* (1965/1985), *Love Cry* (1972), *A Kind of Trust* (1975), *The Boats are Home* (1980), *Cromwell*

(1987), *The Book of Judas* (1991), *Poetry My Arse* (1995) and *The Man Made of Rain* (1998), with five selected editions culminating in *The Essential Brendan Kennelly* in 2011.[2] He has also published two novels, *The Crooked Cross* (1963) and *The Florentines* (1967); three Greek tragedies in verse, *Antigone* (1986), *Medea* (1988) and *The Trojan Women* (1993); and a version of Lorca's *Blood Wedding* (1996). His collected essays were published as *Journey into Joy* (1994).

To say that Kennelly had an 'academic' career at TCD would be to question the nature of academe. His 'academic' work is the response of a poet to poetry. His teaching was inspirational, but entirely unacademic. Michael D. Higgins remarked that Kennelly 'has discarded the neat rational use of polarities that might suffice in the academy or in the shadowland where critical thought is reputed to live'.[3]

In the 1950s, a Catholic, rural student was atypical of the Trinity profile – Protestant, Anglo-Irish or English. Outside the walls of this un-Irish island in the midst of Dublin city, Kennelly, however, found a metropolitan *milieu* for poetry: 'a helplessly (one is tempted to say happily) incestuous city where we feed off each other's characters, marriage troubles, drink problems, money messes, sex cavortings, job catastrophes and other attractive forms of misfortune, distress, failure and crack'.[4]

He is at home within his family context and its larger hinterland, but stands at an oblique angle to many aspects of Irish society. As a winger in football, he played on the outside, a position allowing him certain latitude, a freedom from the mid-field melée – a freedom in which he displayed his capacity to behave with élan and cunning which the mid-fielder cannot know.

Kennelly brought to TCD a sense of the hedge-school, the traditional locus of alternative, unofficial, unorthodox instruction in the rhythm and periodicity of nature: an oral tradition of song finding its way into the lecture theatre. In this, Kennelly most closely resembles Patrick Kavanagh in his transitus from village to city, but he lacks Kavanagh's arrogance.

It would be difficult, and ill-advised, to label Kennelly as a postcolonial poet. His poetry, while it engages with aspects of colonialism, and also of the postmodern, does not lend itself to '-isms' as much as it does to the intensely personal and atavistically communal. But central to his personal *agon* are the issues of betrayal and the man–woman nexus, especially played out in his 'Greek' plays. When he asks 'Is Medea's crime also Medea's glory?',[5] the question is equally valid of his Antigone. In his professed 'attempt to be, imaginatively, a woman'[6] he encapsulates Antigone's question: 'What man / knows anything of woman? / If he did / He would change from being a man / As men recognise a man'.[7]

In one sense, Kennelly's increasingly public profile, with *Cromwell*, *The Book of Judas* and the 'Greek' plays, marks a sea-change in his work, moving from the more introverted, private considerations into an epiphany of shared grief, anger and bewilderment. The lack of certainty in *all* Kennelly's work, the permanent sense of impermanence, underlines the provisional nature of the self-imposed task, 'to define love', especially when it is associated with 'emotional maimings' (*WI* 141).

Two Villages

Every writer is a citizen of two worlds: the public world in which he or she functions as child, sibling, lover, parent, teacher, and the private world where the writing is done. And this ubiquitous writer is an alien in both worlds because he or she is never at home in public and becomes a stranger to themself. The writing is an attempt to reconcile the two, and to find for himself some place to call 'home' before the end. *Topos* is both space and place, the context and the location, and every *topos* has its hinterland of memory and atavism. Ballylongford is not merely a rural hamlet in County Kerry, it is a village of the mind which Kennelly has never left either in body or soul: however much the world tugs at his career, the first images are constant visitors, images in textures, smells, sounds, words, body language, signs both tangible and sensible.

Kennelly is unusual in that his private world is located somewhere between the public worlds, a *mesotopos*; he is always commuting between the real and the imagined, and never being entirely sure which is which. A 'virtual' *topos* located, perhaps exclusively, in the mind: a mindscape which draws on all contexts, an imaginative laboratory in which he tests established and new visitors to memory and context, and sculpts verbal images of their appearance. Perhaps only James Clarence Mangan (in the nineteenth century) and Máirtín Ó Cadhain (in the twentieth) were in a similar position: villagers who came to the bright city of learning, alien and yet absorbed into the collegiate fabric; not *oppidanus* but *paganus*.[8]

These two worlds are at one and the same time physical and metaphysical; both places exert a profoundly psychological affect while presenting a range of images to the poetic mind. It is the creative tension between the two villages that fuels the poet.

The two worlds might seem incompatible, or their occupant might seem schizophrenic, his work as a poet interfering with that of a professor, or vice versa. That that is not the case is evident if we examine Kennelly's work as a critic – his essays, on poets such as Yeats, Kavanagh, MacNeice, in the same light as his creative work as novelist, playwright and poet, a man of deep and compassionate creative power, attuned to his own and others' pain, suffering and joys.

Dark Fathers

Growing up in his father's public house introduced Kennelly to the culture of male drinking; as a youngster he had, as he puts it, to find his way through what seemed to him to be a dark forest of legs, pushing his way towards the light.[9] 'Poets are blind men groping for light', 'unravelling the fears, terrors, hopes and loves' of childhood (*WI* 135, 134). The sense of darkness and the ever-present memory of the dead are epitomised in his most anthologised poem, 'My Dark Fathers' (*EBK* 26–7). There are depths in this poem which are suggested, but not revealed, by the intensity of the images Kennelly evokes.

This 'memory of the dead' prints on Kennelly's earliest consciousness his knowledge of 'My Dark Fathers' who are 'committed always to the night of wrong' (*EBK* 26), a night of darkness which is not merely inescapable but necessary.

The celebration of ancestors inured in darkness is a striving towards integration, 'to find the unbroken man' ('I See You Dancing, Father', *EBK* 92); he is never unhaunted: in an untitled poem in *The Man Made of Rain* (*EBK* 144–45), he writes:

> It is part of me tonight,
> This high springtide of blood
> Lifting in its rising hands
> images
> I cannot hide.
> How much have I hidden?
> How much have I lied?

Memories are a 'living presence',[10] admonishing, compelling. The bewilderment of the child in their presence is explicit in the last line of 'Poem for a Three Year Old' (*EBK* 54–55): 'And why?' The need to find out, to swallow the whole world, makes the child a hostage to fortune: as late as 2001, in *Glimpses*, he says:

> Tiredness hits him, failure to snuggle in close,
> years of work stalk him; bleating
> and slipping. One thing he knows, one thing.
> Everything is still to be done. Everything.
>
> ('Still to be Done', *EBK* 150)

Experience can never be anything more than indeterminate; there is never a definitive moment which says 'now' and 'yes' and 'love', but only a provisional sense of temporary acquiescence and passing affection, however deeply they may be etched. When the poem 'Yes' opens with the lines 'I love the word / And know its long struggle with no' we are in the presence of a man whose doubts and longings stand in the way of love and trust. Kennelly longs, with a 'love cry', to say 'Yes!' but knows that so many 'no's' stand in his, and its, way. In his own words, 'love cry' is 'the cry of the inarticulate'.[11] It's a phrase he repeats: 'I / Serve / Your most inarticulate cry'.[12] He is not only revoicing the cry itself, but re-imagining the 'I' who makes that cry.

Kennelly's development as a poet may be described as a journey from darkness into light. The sense of movement towards light is constant: In 'Living Ghosts' 'I close my eyes and see them / Becoming song' (*EBK* 57). But 'all the songs are living ghosts' which 'long for a living voice' – as if it is the poet's fate and purpose to provide that voice for the inarticulate. In addition, when he confronts his 'other' in womanhood, 'There will be / womansongs in answer to the false songs of men'.[13]

Despite the darkness, Kennelly persists in recognising and greeting laughter, or at least the echo of laughter, before plunging back into dark despair. 'Hope is an achieved thing ... the one thing on which my poetry rests' (*WI* 134). The poems focus on an elusive paradise, where the ancestors may sing unspancelled in the light.

Kennelly's 'epic' poems (*Cromwell* and *The Book of Judas*) owe something perhaps to his PhD thesis: they allow him to embrace the gamut of emotions *in extenso*, the overarching condition of times past, present and the wished-for future all simultaneously summoning him in all directions.

But it is in the minute, aphoristic poems that we find his microscope applied most effectively to the lesions of both happiness and uncertainty. They are utterly economic, yet offer an *embarras de richesses*: intimately profligate with longing and disaster.

The Greek poet Odysseas Elytis wrote that 'you will come to learn a great deal if you study the insignificant in depth',[14] while his compatriot, the novelist Alexandros Papadiamandis, recorded 'the smaller the village, the bigger the evil'.[15] In the late poem 'Blasting Away', Kennelly succeeds them, alluding to the ubiquity of a 'Europoem' embracing 'Homer Goethe Dante Camões, Shakespeare Blake' – 'all the voices of obscure parishes burdened with universality' (*EBK* 136): this, too, is the village writ large. When he writes

> There is a loaf of bread on Derek's threshold
> And we will never know who put it there ('A Giving', *EBK* 41)

he is offering us a microcosm of mystery, surprise, bewilderment.

Defining Love

Kennelly's principal motive is 'to define love' by pursuing the integer of the self, but in doing so he encounters the impossibility of ever fulfilling his destiny.

'Love' is probably the word in his poetry with the most antonyms and synonyms, a labile sense of delicious uncertainty. It is both vocable and invocable.

There are 'four preparatory stages to love': confusion, contradiction, turmoil and vulnerability, and a great poet of love will transact these stages and arrive at 'lucidity', 'a moment of contact with love':[16]

> As far as I know
> Love always begins
> Like a white morning ('A Kind of Trust', *EBK* 47).

The poet must 'bitterly insist / On that white morning', and the insistence comes 'out of a kind of trust / In this beginning' – a trust that is fissile, a trust not to be trusted. It's another negotiable word, inextricably connected with 'love' and also with the poet's faith in the necessity of a continual beginning.

Apart from love, the principal themes are: violence, betrayal, joy and hope. The principal strategy is the only possible one: language. The images which empower the poetry are born of preternatural facts such as *river* (the relentless strength of the Shannon, in Kennelly's hinterland), *village* and *house*. 'We do not ever escape from a certain house' (*WI* 135). The house is childhood and therefore vulnerable. If, as Baudelaire believed, 'genius is ... childhood recovered at will',[17] then Kennelly had genius thrust upon him by these ever-present memories.

One of his most depressing poems is 'The Experiment', which concludes

> Theories of origins vary, yet all are agreed
> Somewhere along the line, for reasons hard to grasp
> The experiment went wrong   (*EBK* 114).

The experiment is 'life', 'love', 'trust' and inevitably it 'goes wrong'. But in 'poemprayer' which, like the poem 'bridge', is an attempted metaphor, he writes of his poem:

> it was made of moments of betrayal and wonder
> and mockery and slander and pain
> it was made of dead friends and enemies
> and stories of this man and that woman
> it was made of every defeat he had faced or ignored
> and hurts known and unknown   ('poemprayer', *EBK* 124)

Kennelly has omitted from this litany of the poet's creed 'love', 'joy', 'tenderness' – should we therefore expect a poet's prayer to exclude these? Is this litany a cry for release, for exculpation? He accepts that *fear* is 'a dynamizing factor ... that there are things one is afraid of and that they're everywhere' and is determined 'to turn things to good ... in the sense that you can make a poem out of your horror, that art is frequently transfigured horror and can be beautiful ... The roots of beauty ... can be frightening, and that is why I am attracted to an amoral situation' like that of *Medea* (*WI* 132–3). He sees violence in the tenderness of love (*WI* 143). 'Medea does kill hope, deliberately, in order to bring a man to the state of pained consciousness that she suffered' (*WI* 141).

Language and Poetry

As Louis Aragon observed, 'Life is a language; writing is a completely different one: their grammars are not mutually interchangeable'.[18] This is the arena where the poet struggles. As a birthright, poetry is a *datum*, thrust onto the child: 'it was a gift that took me unawares / And I accepted it' ('The Gift', *EBK* 20). Poetry, as his given métier, is a cruel mistress, relentless in its demands.

> Begin to the loneliness that cannot end
> since it perhaps is what makes us begin
> . . .

Though we live in a world that dreams of ending

> that always seems about to give in
> something that will not acknowledge conclusion
> insists that we forever begin   ('Begin', *EBK* 33)

Kennelly insists that the empowering of poetry is intricately connected with childhood, the unpredictable possibility of surprise, and he calls it 'wonder' (*DFL* 180). Making the invisible visible is not merely the disclosure of the vision, but also, at least for the poet himself, the discovery of joy and the joy of discovery. But the moment of the miracle is also the instant of disaster.

For any writer, language is both the means of survival and salvation, the way of expressing man's experience of the *merveilleux*, and the way of betraying it, getting it wrong, leading towards 'no' rather than 'yes'. In 'Word', Kennelly acknowledges the supremacy of language because it is his only means of communicating:

> If you call me anything
> Say I'm a maker of men.
> I was in the beginning
> I will be there at the end.[19]

Language is all we've got: 'The promise that keeps us all going, that words *can* do it ... There are moments ... when you are only scratching the skin of the darkness' (*DFL* 173). A means of communication that is also a cruel system, reflecting ambivalence, ambiguity and mendacity. Language is a way of saying 'I love you', but it is also the conduit of betrayal.

Is Kennelly making poetry out of the struggle with self, and rhetoric out of the struggle with the world (as Yeats suggested)?[20] There is also the problem of poetry as a bridge from the private to the public. As soon as it is uttered, the poem becomes a rhetoric. Private becomes public when a crisis in affection occurs. Kennelly's publications have the rhetoric of his privacy. Poetry seeks silence but can also murder it. Kennelly publishes a language both compassionately tender and introverted, and resolutely declamatory. This is especially true of *Cromwell* and *The Book of Judas*.

The best he can hope for is that 'hope must co-exist with hopelessness': but in 'the dark inadequacy of the whole enterprise' (*DFL* 174) there is the belief that 'Words are wild creatures. Fly them home' ('Poem', *EBK* 154). 'Poetry is a blind art, and is written with skill and faith. You have to believe in your blindness ... I'd like to become a poem, to become coherent and accomplished and singing and communicate and touch' (*DFL* 170). 'My best poem will be one line' ('Best' *EBK* 151). But his 'best poem' will in fact be one word: '*yes*'.

Irreverence

To write of such a senior poet as an *enfant terrible* of Irish poetry – and of Irish life – may seem bizarre, but a reader coming to the work of Brendan Kennelly with no previous knowledge of his age or context could very easily form the view that the poet is a character *méchant* and deviant from social, if not aesthetic, norms.

Even when Kennelly is at his most serious, he is also light of heart; even when he is breaking taboos and questioning shibboleths, he is faithful to his art. 'My attraction is to the boundary-breakers, the limit-smashers, both in myself and in society' (*WI* 141).

> An awful lot of my stuff is a genuine violation of inherited prejudices ... because prejudice to me is not unlike snobbery: it is basically a desire not to let others into your heart, a determination not to relate ... As you push towards your honesty, you can become honest enough not to bother with morality ... You have to create morality for your own life. (WI 136, 145)

How far did the Ireland of the 1940s and 1950s affect his poetry? 'The repression in the church – the suicides of girls, the schools, the brutal teacher ... the total lack of any sexual education – these are all in retrospect comic in a way, but at the time you're going through it as an intelligent child, it was very puzzling' (*WI* 134).

In the 1950s emigration afflicted many young Irish people. Kennelly celebrated this pain: 'Say something then, before / Leaving. A word or two. No more' ('Before Leaving', *EBK* 22) The 'no more' is Beckettian in its ambivalence, its ambiguous economy. As late as *Cromwell*, Kennelly is revisiting the exilic world:

> I am an emigrant in whose brain
> Ireland bleeds and cannot cease
> To bleed till I come home again
> To fields that are a parody of peace ('Am', *EBK* 88)

But it is more than the legacy of the 1950s or 1990s exodus: it is the exile of the writer in the hell of his own imagination, fighting within Joyce's nightmare of history,[21] only to find that the homecoming will be one of parody – an unreal reality.

'The nature of the Irish experience … has produced a deeply immoral people, where that special breed of corruption – rural, catholic, mindless and dynamic … is being questioned at last … As if to compensate for our inherited mindlessness, we are driven to make absolute claims on others. That is the thing we must stop – being possessors of truth, owning other people' (*DFL* 179, 184). His rebellion was also, therefore, against the labelling of people: 'I resisted, or resented, people beating you with labels and *assuming* all that to be true about you' (*DFL* 168).

As a controversialist, particularly in *Cromwell* and *The Book of Judas*, he emerges as an agent provocateur, whose mission is to encounter 'forbidden figures',[22] civilise uncivil beliefs and prejudices, to question received wisdom, to mock the unmockable. Within the poet, with his loyalties and adhesions, there is a traitor determined to go beyond the limits of decorum and *la politesse*.

His irreverence began early. In *Moloney Up and At It* the poet finds himself having sex on the grave of his newly buried mother and is thus vividly brought into collision – and collusion – with 'the memory of the dead … the unforgettable dead' ('Maloney Up and At It', *EBK* 23–5). So too in 'Bread', the sexual imagery of kneading dough is as powerful as anything in Marvell, but more subtle: 'I came to life at her finger-ends. / I will go back into her again' (*EBK* 39).

Kennelly remains an outlaw to propriety. Within the larger Ireland, he has rebelled against injustices, challenged conventions, questioned authority and put before his audience a language which is never entirely comfortable in the anglophone or hibernophone ear: a hybrid, stepchild of both learning and ignorance.

The iconoclastic humour comes to the fore not merely in the title of *Poetry My Arse* but in one of the protagonists, 'Ace de Horner', whose name is a play on *Aosdána*, the Irish self-regulating parliament of artists, while his dog, Kanooce, is named for the annual stipend or *cnuas* which members of *Aosdána* receive.

Kennelly's fusion of reverence and irreverence has raised eyebrows amid the niceties of criticism: the animal enjoyment of sex within the same frame of reference as the wonder at the dignity and ferocity of women is justified in the line 'Faith in a woman is all we need'.[23] For man, finding himself in woman, in the 'other', is a condition of *ecstasy*, of standing outside the self in order to locate the self.

The irreverent is predictable in *Judas*, when the poet asks whether Christ had a normal childhood:

> What was it like on a Saturday night
> In the Holy Family home?
> . . .. Did he ever get a kick in the balls
> From some frigger twice his size?
> . . . Did he wonder at times if Jesus
> Was out of his tree, or worse?
> ('My Mind of Questions', *EBK* 107–8)

The irreverence leads ultimately to a loss of self-respect or self-esteem: 'I feel like a battleground in which there is this fight between intelligent, enlightened surviving and loving, and a kind of black desire to fuck it up' (*WI* 135). 'There is a side to me that revels in ecstatic self-destruction . . . and loves to upset. *Cromwell* was the start of my upsettedness . . . Until your chaos is formed, it has no meaning – it's only to be suffered, not shared' (*WI* 140). Kennelly believes in the light but is also afraid of it. *Joy* can so easily be fucked up. And then we are back in the dark.

He locates himself in 'the struggling arena' in which the demons appear: 'I never knew a love that wasn't a running battle' ('A Running Battle', *EBK* 87). As in his own life, much of his poetry has been a struggle to prevent himself from fucking it up.

Perhaps Kennelly's 'fuck it up' is part of his refusal to submit to convention, to *politesse*. He is, at heart, a protestant, a man who will never take 'yes' for an answer and yet who craves for 'yes' and 'light' and 'silence' as beauty spots in a transience through paradise. But he does not know how to achieve it, knows only how to be a poet, a conduit of songs, of ideas, of visions, of sensations, a maker of icons. The 'struggling arena' is, in fact, at the heart of metaphor, the striving for dependable meaning which is labile, refusing to submit to the definition of love which Kennelly sees it as his mission to perform.

Fears and Joys

Kennelly's two demons have been alcohol and women – demons that have both delighted and abandoned him. His two angels have been language itself and the joy of people – neither of these has abandoned him, and both continue to delight him. 'Fear' is more obvious because it is more dependable. 'Love' remains the problematic, and from it descend the difficulties of light, place and 'yes'. Even the juxtaposition of the title words *Love Cry* indicates the simultaneous process of pain and excitement that drive both the lover and love itself. Fear and love are mutually reinforcing, just as trust and betrayal, or coloniser and colonised enjoy, or suffer, symbiosis.

His own demons are contained in the 'Black Fox' and 'The Visitor', while Ireland's demons are Cromwell and Judas. When the 'Black Fox' leaves him with a sense of fear, it is 'fear dispelled by what makes fear / the point of pure creation'. This must be one of the most cryptic lines in all his work. It is a fear which is innate in creation, but it is also fear which 'might have taught me / Mastery of myself' but doesn't ('Dream of a Black Fox', *EBK* 37–8).

One of his 'strangest' poems is 'The Visitor' (*EBK* 51–53): the revenant visitor is the embodiment of the surprise, the *merveilleux*. Later in the work the 'visitor' becomes Cromwell: 'I am the guest of your imagination' ('Measures', *EBK* 69). Invited into the self, 'Cromwell' becomes 'murderous syllables'; language itself, therefore, becomes the killer. The visitor is, ultimately, 'the stranger / shaping the self' ('Shaper', *EBK* 149).

Cromwell and Judas

Cromwell has a more local explanation than the desire to explain the historical figure. Kennelly wanted 'to illustrate in more coherent terms' some of the themes of his earlier work, especially the perception of outcast figures, 'excursions into the otherworld ... The imagination is the expansive soul that we have' (*DFL* 169, 171–2). The poem 'is an ordinary experiment in my own psyche ... I am giving voice to a man who made trees wither' (*WI* 136).

'I don't think any Irishman is complete as an Irishman until he becomes an Englishman, imaginatively speaking ... We can't solve our problems until Catholics become Protestants, and Protestants become Catholics, country people become Dubliners' (*WI* 136). The enigma is the same as the need to 'become, imaginatively, a woman'. Figures such as Cromwell or Judas are anti-icons of Irishness which must be negotiated if the complete picture is to be resolved.

The obsession with selfhood marks the poet as in thrall to otherness. 'Letting your imagination be enhanced by a *difference* . . . is my own attempt to know that this thing is in you . . . that turns your despair, your depression, your desire not to be, into vital forces of being' (*WI* 138–9). The title of his *New and Selected Poems, Familiar Strangers* (2004), underlines Kennelly's intimate recognition of the uncanny, the idea of an otherness which establishes (in Rimbaud's words) that *je est un autre*[24] [(I is an other)] and thereby reinforces one's sense of self as both stranger and habitué. 'I feel I'm not even writing for me, I'm writing for this person in myself that I want to apologise to, or get in touch with, or explain something to, or enter into a dialogue with' (*DFL* 177).

Judas loved Christ, 'loved him, admired him, studied him, pestered him and wanted to know certain things about him and, therefore, of himself, wanted to know if he could do certain things with him, and put himself to the test of his conscience and the limits of his consciousness; asked himself the questions "Dare I do this?" "Can I do this?"' (*WI* 143)

A kiss is a metaphor, yet it was the sign of Judas' betrayal; thus the most vital, silent word of meaning is also the roaring symbol of chaos. The betrayal of Christ by Judas is in fact an enabling act:

> If you had not betrayed me
> How could I ever have begun to know
> The sad heart of man?[25]

This is also the key to Kennelly's compassion for womenfolk: if Jason had not betrayed Medea, how could the poet have seen the rage at the heart of love?

The questions about the reality of Jesus become deeply caring questions about his humanity and his sense of destiny:

> At what moment did he know
> That home is not enough
> And he must scour the darkness
> To give and find love
> Among strangers
> . . .
> Was his life a preparation
> For what can never happen?
> ('My Mind of Questions', *EBK* 109)

– that is, for the joy of surprise which is promised to all men and given to none.

Judas is to be found in all our hearts and voices (*WI* 141). The kiss is the signal of both love and betrayal, of necessary duplicity. For Judas, 'this was the stroke of treachery ... Judas the *fingerer*' and the poet goes on to ask whether we 'fuck life, kiss it, finger it ... What does poetry do? ... What have I tried to do in my work? ... Have I betrayed myself?' (*WI* 143–4). Where Cromwell was a 'scapegoat ... in the political, historical world', Judas was his spiritual equivalent (*WI* 142). Kennelly saw him as the means of examining 'the Judas in myself, the Judas in my society, the Judas in Irish Christianity ... the Judas in the heart' who is the necessary traitor (*WI* 142).

Kennelly's poetry thus becomes an intimate transaction between himself, his society, and history, a set of simultaneous equations where village becomes world, where poetry becomes rhetoric becomes poetry, and private and public are engaged in a perennial *copula*. Kennelly becomes a metaphor of himself, and of those who populate his imagination.

NOTES

1. B. Kennelly, 'A Return', *Breathing Spaces* (Newcastle: Bloodaxe Books, 1992), p. 16.
2. All quotations from Kennelly's poetry are from *The Essential Brendan Kennelly: Selected Poems*, edited by Terence Brown and Michael Longley (Highgreen, Northumberland: Bloodaxe Books, 2011), cited parenthetically in the text as *EBK*, except where otherwise noted.
3. M. D. Higgins, 'Foreword', in R. Pine (ed.), *Dark Fathers into Light* (Newcastle: Bloodaxe Books, 1994), p. 9; Higgins, later elected president of Ireland, was Minister for Culture at the time he wrote this Foreword.
4. B. Kennelly, 'Acenote', *Poetry My Arse* (Newcastle: Bloodaxe Books, 1999), p. 13.
5. B. Kennelly, *Medea* in *When Then Is Now: Three Greek Tragedies* (Highgreen, Northumberland: Bloodaxe Books, 2006), p. 136; this volumes collects together Kennelly's *Antigone*, *Medea* and *The Trojan Women*, and in which the author emphasises that 'mythic drama is both immediate and distant ... These ancient plays are *then* illuminating *now* ... Listening to ancient voices can help us to confront, understand and express many problems of today': ibid., pp. 7–8.
6. R. Pine, 'Interview', with Brendan Kennelly, in James P. Myers Jr (ed.), *Writing Irish: Selected Interviews with Irish Writers from the Irish Literary Supplement* (Syracuse: Syracuse University Press, 1999) p. 138; further references to this interview will appear parenthetically in the text as *WI*.
7. B. Kennelly, *Antigone* in *When Then Is Now*, p. 41.
8. I am using *paganus* in the literal meaning, 'from a village'.
9. Conversation with the author, pre-1980.
10. Ciaran Carty, interview with Brendan Kennelly, Sunday Independent, 8 February 1981.
11. B. Kennelly, 'Love Cry', *A Time for Voices: Selected Poems 1960–1990* (Newcastle: Bloodaxe Books, 1990), p. 30.
12. B. Kennelly, 'Word', *Familiar Strangers: New and Selected Poems, 1960–2004* (Highgreen, Northumberland: Bloodaxe Books, 2004), p. 439.
13. B. Kennelly, *Medea*, in *When Then Is Now*, p. 98.

14. O. Elytis, *Axion Esti*, in *Collected Poems* (trans. J Carson and N Sarris; Baltimore: Johns Hopkins University Press, 2004), p. 127.
15. A. Papadiamandis, 'The Fey Folk', *The Boundless Garden: Selected Short Stories Volume 1* (ed. L. Kamperidis and D. Harvey; Euboea, Greece: Limni, 2007), p. 241.
16. R. Pine, 'The Roaring Storm of Your Words', interview with Brendan Kennelly, in R. Pine (ed.), *Dark Fathers into Light*, p. 176; further references to this interview appear parenthetically in the text as *DFL*.
17. C. Baudelaire, *The Painter of Modern Life*, quoted in Anne Jefferson, *Genius in France* (Princeton: Princeton University Press, 2014), p. 163.
18. Quoted in Renato Poggioli, *The Theory of the Avant-Garde* (Massachusetts: Harvard University Press, 1968), p. 197.
19. B. Kennelly, 'Word', *Familiar Strangers: New and Selected Poems,1960–2004* (Highgreen, Northumberland: Bloodaxe Books, 2004), p. 439.
20. W. B. Yeats, 'Anima Hominis' in *Mythologies* (London: Macmillan, 1962), p. 331.
21. Cf. J. Joyce, *Ulysses*: 'history is a nightmare from which I am trying to awake'. (Harmondsworth: Penguin Books, 1968), p. 40.
22. B. Kennelly, 'Introduction', *Breathing Spaces*, p. 11.
23. *Moloney Up and At It* (Cork: Mercier Press, 1984), p. 43.
24. A. Rimbaud, letter to Georges Izambard Charleville, 13 May 1871.
25. B. Kennelly, *The Book of Judas*, p. 156.

SELECTED FURTHER READING

Ferguson, Katelyn, *A Lesson in Presents: Social Change in the writing of Brendan Kennelly, 1980–2000* (TCD THESIS: 9884).

Pine, R. (ed.), *Dark Fathers Into Light* (Newcastle: Bloodaxe Books, 1994).

McDonagh, John, *Brendan Kennelly: A Host of Ghosts* (Dublin: Liffey Press, 2004).

Redmond, John, 'Engagements with the Public Sphere in the Poetry of Paul Durcan and Bredan Kennelly', in Fran Brearton and Alan Gillis (eds), *The Oxford Handbook of Modern Irish Poetry* (Oxford: Oxford University Press, 2013), 403–18.

20

TERENCE BROWN

Seamus Heaney

Seamus Heaney's first collection, *Death of a Naturalist*, was published to wide acclaim in 1966. Critics were immediately impressed by the poet's gift (which over the years would win him a large international readership) for realising in poems the palpable givenness of the natural world, held in Wordsworth-like recall of a rural Irish childhood. The opening poem of the collection, 'Digging', made farm labour seem fully present to the reader as lived experience, as sensation rather than thought. Rural work and crafts recur in Heaney's early work, often aligning the labour of poetic endeavour with the arduous work performed by his ancestors. This comparison of types of work was the main theme of 'Digging', which declared that Heaney as poet would employ his pen as instrument to the same efficient effect as his father and grand-father had wielded the spade on a turf-bog. 'Digging', which Heaney often recited as an opening poem at public readings from his work, and which he placed at the head of his selected poems, *Opened Ground* (1996), as well as being a vivid description of digging potato drills and cutting turf, also expresses what would become a life-long preoccupation of this poet, a concern about the significance and worth of poetry as a human activity. Indeed, 'Digging' is haunted by a telling sense that a poetic vocation may be deficient in masculinity, and unworthy of a mature adult: 'I've no spade to follow men like them'.[1]

And as if to counter such an apprehension, Heaney's early collections included poems about craftsmen and workers whose endeavours could be read as analogous with the poet's work, possessed of transformative, even shamanistic powers. In *Door into the Dark* (1969) a thatcher is seen at work, stitching 'all together / Into a sloped honeycomb'[2] that leaves observers 'gaping at his Midas touch'. In 'The Forge' in the same volume, a blacksmith 'expends himself in shape and music' to 'beat real iron out'.[3]

Events in the poet's native province following the outbreak of political violence in Northern Ireland in 1969 would test the mettle of the poet in very challenging ways. As early as 1966, in *Death of a Naturalist*, Heaney had signalled in 'Docker' that sectarian conflict 'could start again'.[4] When it did in 1969 and thereafter, the poet was confronted by a dilemma: how could poetry deal with a society experiencing almost daily horrors in a state of near-war? Eschewing overt partisanship of any kind, Heaney, in a body of verse that comprised his first four collections (*Wintering Out* appeared in 1971, *North* in 1975), offered to his readers an imaginative interpretation of the Irish past that served as the inspiration for some of his most powerful 'Troubles' poems. As befitted a poet who had associated poetic composition with digging, Heaney in these volumes invoked the Irish past, as though the very topography of Ireland itself were true metaphor of that past, carrying as it did a buried weight of historical memory. Bogland is made to seem analogous with the poet's personal memory and with Irish communal memory. Consequently, the characteristic Heaney poems of this period were those in which the poet brooded meditatively upon the past as if it were a bogland that had preserved the past intact, only for it to be repeated again and again.

Poems that gave mythic import to that interpretation of the past in *Wintering Out* and *North* depended on an idea of Ireland as a Nordic, even Icelandic, territorial space. In such poems as 'The Tollund Man', 'The Grauballe Man' and 'Punishment' which contemplated in awestruck reverence photographs of preserved bodies unearthed from a Jutland bog, the poet made ancient sacrificial rites seem to bear analogously on contemporary events in a violent Northern Ireland. The effect of these poems was to suggest that the poet was courageously determined to confront atrocious realities in his art. The tone was that of oracular utterance, as of one undertaking almost sacerdotal duties. Gone was the suspicion that had found expression in 'Digging' – that poetry was an unmanly avocation. Indeed, in 'Funeral Rites', one of the finest poems in *North*, the poet engages directly with the concept of masculinity when he confesses that he had only 'shouldered a kind of manhood'[5] when he had participated as pall bearer in the funeral rites of dead relations. By contrast with such feminised Catholic obsequies, with women 'hovering', the poet, in commanding voice, called for the megalithic tombs in the Boyne valley to be restored as fitting resting-places for the slain of Ulster's 'neighbourly murder'[6] victims. The poet imagined such an interment would involve in its pagan assertion of ritual from which women are excluded, left behind in 'emptied kitchens', Heaney sees a 'slow triumph'[7] of heroic, martial marching in contrast with the obeisance implicit in the evocations of Catholic ritual with which the poem began.

North, published in 1975, show-cased a poet in confident possession of his powers. It had thematic and mythic range and an impressive linguistic amplitude that gave no hint that the poet had ever doubted the purchase of poetry on the intractable problems of a province at war. Nonetheless this, authoritative volume concluded with two sequences that served notice that the poet had not fully shed his concern about the valency of poetry in pertaining conditions. In the third poem of 'Whatever You Say, Say Nothing', the poet confessed that he was afflicted by a sense of powerlessless: 'Yet for all this art and sedentary trade', he stated ruefully, he was 'incapable' of breaking a cultural habit of 'Northern reticence, the tight gag of place and times'.[8] The second sequence, entitled 'Singing School', with a nod to Yeats's 'Sailing to Byzantium', was a study of the times and places that had made Heaney a poet. The forces antithetical to art with which the poet had had to contend were identified in the sequence as a provincial cultural cringe, an all-pervasive sectarianism and a blood-soaked history akin to that of Lorca's Spain. A final poem, entitled 'Exposure', is set in County Wicklow, in Southern Ireland, to which the poet had moved with his family from Belfast in 1972. The season is winter, the month December; the dying year with imagery of a 'spent' life cycle and pervasive damp are the objective correlative of a self-doubting mood, which has the poet regretfully imagine 'a hero / on some muddy compound, / his gift like a slingstone / Whirled for the desperate'.[9] And the poet, by contrast, is one who sits 'weighing and weighing' his 'responsible *tristia*', 'neither internee nor informer', an 'inner émigré', 'escaped from the massacre'.[10] The poem seems to cast doubt on the very purpose of poetry itself.

As if to counter the depressed mood with which *North* concluded, Heaney's next volume, *Field Work* (1979) opened with a poem of opulent sensuousness. 'Oysters' celebrates the fruits of the sea and a moment of convivial indulgence, where 'Exposure' had contemplated 'the anvil brains' of some who hated the poet. The poem is not, however, free of the guilt that would become a recurrent emotion in the poems of Heaney's mid-career. For in 'Oysters', hedonistic pleasure is understood to depend on violation of nature and on the 'Glut of privilege'. The poem ends with the poet angry that his trust could not 'repose / In the clear light, like poetry or freedom / Leaning in from the sea'.[11] Consequently, the volume gives a distinct impression of a poet assuaging a sense of obligation and maintaining fidelity to a high sense of the poetic vocation. There are elegies for the American poet Robert Lowell, for victims of the Troubles and for the Irish musician and composer Seán Ó Riada. There are too poems that register the ongoing horrors of the Northern Irish Troubles. Nonetheless, *Field Work* represents an important development in Heaney's poetic. Where Heaney's early poetry had readily adopted mythopoeic perspectives on contemporary events, *Field Work*, although it concluded with a translated passage from Dante's *Inferno*, is notable for its direct engagement with social reality and everyday human relations. In

'Badgers', tellingly, Heaney asks 'How perilous is it to choose, / not to love the life we're shown?'[12] The life the poet is shown emerges as eminently worthy of love in tenderly lyrical poems in the volume. Music and song are invoked, as in 'Song', with its conjuring of a 'moment when the bird sings very close / To the music of what happens.'[13] In poem one of 'Triptych', the grim intensity of armed men is contrasted with the beneficent presence of a girl who walks home 'Carrying a basket full of new potatoes, / three tight green cabbages, and carrots / with the tops and mould still fresh on them'.[14] Perhaps most tellingly, for the first time in Heaney's oeuvre the erotic is frankly acknowledged in a number of poems. In 'The Otter' and 'The Skunk', for example, it is granted an elemental, almost comedic, energy.

Field Work has as a centre of gravity a sequence of ten pastoral poems which give to the collection as a whole a sense of balance. 'Glanmore Sonnets', in their orderly evocation of a rural retreat and place of familial refuge in County Wicklow, suggest a man maturely at ease with his medium and secure about his role as a poet: 'Each verse returning like the plough turned round'.[15] Yet despite the note of Wordsworthian rusticity struck in this sequence, the darker aspects of the poet's Northern Irish inheritance is not occluded by pastoral Glanmore. Poem VIII describes a thunderstorm in which the poet is gripped by disturbed imaginings:

> This morning when a magpie ...
> Inspected a horse asleep beside the wood
> I thought of dew on armour and carrion.
> What would I meet, blood-boultered on the road?[16]

In poem IX, in which a 'black rat / Sways on the briar like infected fruit', the poet asks himself 'What is my apology for poetry?' [17] The answer, perhaps implied in these two sonnets, is that poetry can summon powerful symbols of the destructive forces in human affairs with which a mature poetic must engage. The manner in which each of these poems shifts swiftly from natural description to a symbolic order of statement indicates that Heaney, despite the social and personal focus of much of *Field Work*, remained a poet for whom myth was an imaginative resource.

In 1982, in the forward to a collection of stories by Tom MacIntyre, Heaney wrote of the function of mythology in Irish literature:

> When Irish mythology began to become a literary currency at the end of the nineteenth century, it was used to vindicate a claim to national identity, historic culture, spiritual resource, A hundred years later the writer approaches it with less propagandist intent, with a primary hunger for form, in order to find a structure for unstructured potential within himself.[18]

In the same introduction Heaney wrote hauntingly of 'the shape-shifting, submarine half-light of myth'.[19] Undoubtedly, when Heaney wrote these words he was already at work on his English-language version of *Buile Suibhne*, which was published in 1983. A series of poems that comprised part three of Heaney's next published collection, *Station Island* (1984), was derivative of this translation. Of 'SWEENEY REDIVIVUS', Heaney wrote: 'The poems in this section are voiced for Sweeney, the seventh century Ulster king who was transformed into a bird-man and exiled to the trees by the curse of St Ronan ... I trust these glosses can survive without the support system of the original story.'[20] On first readings, these twenty mostly short poems can seem disturbingly obscure (half-lit). But an awareness that the poet is exploiting the myth of banishment to the wilderness as a resource that enables self-examination gives the series its purchase on personal meanings. For Sweeney as the poet's alter ego is understood to engage with forces antithetical to his right to be a free spirit, as Heaney the poet had felt he had been required to do. For example, in a poem entitled 'First Flight', Sweeney confesses: 'I was mired in attachment / until they began to pronounce me / a feeder of battlefields'.[21] Elsewhere in the series Sweeney forswears attachment to 'Old Icons' that read like a list of Catholic nationalist historical shibboleths: 'Why', he asks 'when it was all over, did I hang on to them?'[22]

It is understandable that in a work based on the Sweeney legend that dramatised 'a tension between the newly dominant Christian ethos and the older, recalcitrant Celtic temperament',[23] the issue of religion should surface as a theme. In 'The Cleric', this is at its most explicit as Sweeney scorns a religious man's 'Latin and blather of love'.[24] Heaney can be seen to be signalling a shift in his world-view towards a secular vision. For Sweeney claims of his religious antagonist: 'Give him his due. In the end / he opened my path to a kingdom / of such scope and neuter allegiance / my emptiness reigns at its whim'.[25] Hitherto in Heaney's oeuvre there had been persuasive indications that his was an imagination in which the images and rituals of the Catholic faith, into which he had been born, played a formative part. Indeed, there was a certain irony that it was in *Station Island* that this coded admission of loss of faith was made. For the title poem of the volume is a powerful account of participation in what can be seen as a quintessentially Irish Catholic ritual occasion, the annual Lough Derg Pilgrimage. This three day penitential pilgrimage takes place on an island in a lough in County Donegal known as St Patrick's Purgatory. It involves prayer, fasting and walking barefoot around stone circles believed to be the remains of early monastic cells. In *Station Island* (the pilgrimage is made up of units known as 'stations') the poet vividly describes his own experience as a young man

participating in such a ritual and uses the context of confession and examination of conscience this establishes to reflect upon his career to date as
citizen and poet. In the poem the poet, imagined as in his youth moving from
station to station (twelve of them, each warranting a separate poem) is joined
by ghosts who represent aspects of his experience as an Irish writer. Among
them are the nineteenth-century novelist William Carleton who had had to
deal as a writer with the same kind of sectarian imbroglio as Heaney had
been required to confront in his native province. The ghost of Carleton sagely
advises: 'but you have to try to make sense of what comes'.[26] Guilt feelings,
as we have seen, had been a marked aspect of Heaney's poetry find further
expression in *Station Island* inasmuch as the poet chooses among the ghosts
whom he imagines as haunting him at the stations, those of people who
unluckily died young, or of those who sacrificed their lives in a cause – a
missionary priest, a republican hunger-striker – and that of a victim of
sectarian murder who accuses the poet (his second cousin) of saccharining
his death in an elegiac poem included in *Field Work*: 'The Strand at Lough
Beg'. In contrast with such idealism and victimhood, the poet berates himself
for the circumspect life he has led with its good fortune denied to these
figures.

The final ghost whom Heaney imagines as haunting him on Station Island
is that of James Joyce, who advises the poet to abandon his sense of national
obligation as poet and to 'fill the element / with signatures on your own
frequency'.[27] *Station Island*, accordingly, in the title poem and in 'Sweeney
Redivivus', amounted to an aesthetic manifesto by the poet : that he would
thereafter write as an independent spirit, free of any prescribed national
narrative ('that subject people stuff is a cod's game' the ghost of Joyce insists)
and from a secular perspective.

The Haw Lantern, published three years later in 1987, served further
notice that the poet was engaging with the world in new ways, as a secular,
politically aware if non-partisan observer of the contemporary scene. There
is even a sense in 'The Mud Vision', for example, of the sociological, though
the poet maintained his almost Wordsworthian intimacy with Nature. An
engaged European political conscience finds expression in the volume in a
number of parable poems (reminiscent of the work of Mandelstam and
Holub) while a bleak 'secular' view of the world is admitted to in 'The
Song of the Bullets', which has those dealers of death claim that 'Mount
Olivet's beatitudes / The soul's cadenced desires / Cannot prevail against
us'.[28] Death is a ubiquitous presence in a volume in which grief is not
assuaged by any religious consolation. Poetic form, it is implied, must serve
as human recourse in face of inevitable mortality. This is suggested in the
centre piece of the book, in which the poet reflects on the life and recent death

of his mother in a sequence of eight tender sonnets entitled 'Clearances'. In this work, although a death-bed scene involves Catholic Last Rites, the absolute negation of death for the secular imagination is a principal apprehension. The death of a much-loved family member is like the felling of a long-standing tree that leaves only empty space: 'Its heft and hush become a bright nowhere, / A Soul ramifying and forever / Silent, beyond silence listened for.'[29]

'Clearances' in *The Haw Lantern* introduces a new note in Heaney's oeuvre which one might identify as one of philosophic reflection. In the same sonnet he wrote of how he 'thought of walking round and round a space / utterly empty, utterly a source'[30] as if nothingness, extinction could be an inspiration for poetry. For this reader it would be Seamus Heaney's capacity to write a visionary poetry while resolutely holding as a modern man to such a secular awareness which would largely account for his distinctive power as writer as he grew older. It was in a substantial single volume of 113 pages (*Seeing Things*, published 1991) that this would be displayed with signal force. The death of the poet's father in 1986 and the deaths of friends and fellow poets shadow this volume (there are memorial poems for John Hewitt, for Tom Delaney, who had appeared as a ghost in *Station Island*, and for Richard Ellmann). Death is a preoccupation in a volume which opens and closes with poems that summon to mind the classical underworld, the one a translation of a passage from Virgil, the other from Dante. The ineluctable finality of death for the secular mind is acknowledged when the poet, imagining an after-life 'particular judgement' (a concept derived from Catholic eschatology), warns: 'there is no next-time round'.[31] From the perspective enforced by such an awareness the phenomenal world which had been so important a feature of Heaney's earlier work was now perceived with a new intensity which does not preclude the visionary. *Seeing Things* is a book of sensations; of sounds, sight and touch. The material world is granted a full reality: 'Blessed be down-to earth!',[32] the poet affirms in one poem, 'Man and Boy', which honours his father's cautious predictability. In a poem in honour of Philip Larkin, who died in 1985, Heaney invokes 'the heartland of the ordinary',[33] which is present in various objects recalled in the course of the book. In apposition with this weighty materiality in the volume (key words are 'weight', 'heaviness', 'heft'), *Seeing Things* celebrates light, skies, unroofed rooms, air, free-flowing water, space, scope, moments of spiritual release when transcendence is allowed an imaginary, possible existence. In one poem ('Fosterlings'), Heaney expresses regret that he had waited until he was 'nearly fifty / to credit marvels'. The poet declares 'So long for air to brighten, Time to be dazzled and the heart to lighten'.[34] What the poet identifies in one poem as 'the journey of the soul' does not preclude the presence of the marvellous. True to the philosophic tenor of the book, it is in 'the heartland of the ordinary' that the poet experiences marvels. Tellingly, it is in the long sequence of poems entitled 'Squarings' which takes up much the latter part of the book that Heaney reflects on the mysterious, marvellous giveness of the world, available to the poet in memory as a kind of spiritual energy. It is striking that this encomium to materiality is a work of studied formality: forty-eight poems, as Helen Vendler has it, 'poems "square in shape, five beats wide and twelve lines long"'.[35] An art which honours phenomenal reality, in the knowledge of extinction, appropriately has its own crafted shape and bulk. In the book a reiterated trope is concerned with how the visible can become akin to painting. In 'A Retrospect', for example, 'everything ran into water-colour';[36] in another poem Heaney instructs: 'strike this scene in gold ... in relief,/Stable straw, Rembrandt-gleam and burnish'.[37]

For all *Seeing Things* credits marvels, most notably in poem eight of 'Squarings' with its heavenly ship snagging an altar rail at Clonmacnoise, it is in no way credulous. The questions it poses are those of an agnostic: 'Was music once a proof of God's existence?';[38] 'Where does spirit live? Inside or outside // Things remembered, made things, things unmade?'[39] Its visionary moments are those of consciousness exhilarated by motion, bodily passage though the given world.

Seamus Heaney was awarded the Nobel Prize for Literature in 1995. In his acceptance lecture, published the same year as *Crediting Poetry*, the laureate was much exercised by how problematic being a poet had been during the years of violence in his native Northern Ireland. These had seemed to draw to a conclusion when the IRA called a complete cessation to armed struggle in the autumn of 1994. In his lecture, Heaney admitted, as he recalled 'One of the most harrowing moments in the whole history of the harrowing of the heart in Northern Ireland': 'It is difficult to repress the thought that history is about as instructive as an abattoir'.[40] Given such feeling, it is not surprising that in the volume of poems he published as *The Spirit Level* in 1996 Heaney engaged with that violence and the political situation there as subjects in ways he had not done in *Seeing Things*. In 'The Flight Path', for example, he describes an encounter with a Republican activist who aggressively demands of him: 'When, for fuck's sake, are you going to write / Something for us?' 'The poet replies in the independent spirit of the concluding poem of *Station Island*: "If I do write something, whatever it is, I'll be writing for myself"'.[41] *The Spirit Level* does in fact admit to its pages more direct reference to the Troubles than any other of the poet's collections. Here we read of a bombing, of 'body bags', the 'dirty protest' in Long Kesh, assassination, roadblocks, a nightmare involvement in a proxy bombing (a gruesome tactic of the Provisional IRA).

A central work in the book is 'Mycenae Lookout', that exploits as its ur-text the *Agamemnon* of Aeschylus. This sequence of five poems takes a Watchman who remained at the palace in Mycenae during the Trojan war as a figure of the poet himself, his surrogate as it were, who had endured the emotional anguish of living through a turbulent period of Irish history (Helen Vendler has claimed that the value most esteemed in *The Spirit Level* is stoicism[42]). The watchman tells of how he had 'felt the beating of the huge time-wound / We lived inside',[43] as the poem does not flinch from representing the horrible facts of human cruelty. Poem four, 'Cassandra', makes the abducted raped girl of the play, in her fragile vulnerability, a symbol of war-time female victimage, while Agamemnon is masculinity and militarism run riot.

Despite the grim contents of some of the poems in *The Spirit Level*, the mood does lighten in ways that suggest that the positive perspectives attained in *Seeing Things* could be sustained even in the face of such horrors. Most notably, the fifth poem of 'Mycenae Lookout' ends with 'seers of fresh water / in the bountiful round mouths of iron pumps / and gushing taps',[44] an intimation of cleansing in a hoped-for future. In the concluding poem of the volume ('Postscript', the poem Heaney would choose to include as the final poem of his selected poems, *Opened Ground*), the poet experiences a West-of Ireland setting as a moment of emotional transport, when 'big soft batterings' of wind, 'catch the heart off guard and blow it open'.[45]

In the penultimate poem of *The Spirit Level* (entitled 'Tollund' and dated September 1994) the poet described how he had been visiting Jutland in the aftermath of the IRA's cessation, referred to above. The final lines of this poem refer to 'a new beginning' and to 'ourselves again, free-willed again'[46] The collection of poems which Heaney published as *Electric Light* in 2001 accordingly was the fruit of a new unburdened phase of the poet's career welcomed in 'Tollund', the title referring back to a key poem in *Wintering Out*. Where *The Spirit Level* had as its centrepiece a poem which confronted horrific, unmitigated violence, this new collection made but the one mention of murderous event. By contrast, child-birth and new life are celebrated, in such poems as 'Out of the Bag' and 'Red White and Blue'. In the collection, the poet's voice is that of the mature and renowned literary figure he had become, conversationally at ease with the poetic medium he had mastered. The range of poetic subjects is wider than in earlier volumes, including poems about travel in Serbia, Spain and Greece. For the book is unselfconsciously literary, with unforced reference to other writers, to Thomas Hardy and Gerard Manley Hopkins, for example. There is no sense that the poet doubts the worth of his calling as he had done at the outset of his career. Rather, his willingness to make the ancient classical eclogue a model for contemporary composition (there are four such poems in the book) bespeaks confidence in his powers, as do generous-spirited memorial poems for recently dead poets and friends. Heaney's deep respect for ancient literary texts had previously been evident in his 1999 translation of the Old-English epic, *Beowulf.*

A striking feature of this book is the way the poet, attentive as he is to developments on the international scene ('Known World' is set in strife-torn Macedonia) returns to memories of the primal Irish world of his childhood and youth which had been the inspiration of his early successes as a poet. Reprise indeed would be a characteristic of the volumes of poetry he would publish subsequently: *District and Circle* (2006) and *Human Chain* (2010).

Heaney's primal world returns in these volumes with all the vivid immediacy it had originally possessed. Poems such as 'Toomebridge', 'Perch' and 'Lupins' at the beginning of *Electric Light* inaugurate a period (the first decade of the twenty-first century), when Heaney in maturity wrote a poetry in which rapt remembrance of nature's effulgent abundance was a constant artistic resource. However, these late collections (Heaney died in 2013) are by no means pastoral or bucolic in intent or effect. For the phenomenal world is recognised as a dimension replete with very quotidian objects, substantial things. We read of a bookcase, a turnip shredder, a helmet, a harrrow-pin, an anvil, a scuttle, a stove lid, a baler, a coal house door, a loose box. The impression created is of a poet concerned to grant reality its ineluctable materiality, what he apprehends, quoting a poem by W. H. Auden, as the 'mass and majesty of this world'. This poem 'A Stove Lid for W. H. Auden' ends: 'Think of dark matter in the starlit coalhouse'.[47] Coal recurs as slack in a later poem with 'Its wet sand weight'.[48] When one associates such object and thing poems with others of this period which imagine acts of lifting, carrying, taking satisfaction in traction, and notes the poet confessing in 'A Herbal', 'Between oak tree and slated roof, / I had my existence. I was there. / Me in place and the place in me',[49] then one senses that Heaney was writing in confirmation of the essentially this-wordly, even materialist perspective which had inspired his poetry since the publication of *Station Island.*

This being said, it is important to recognise that Heaney as poet retained in the final period of his career a distinct respect for the Catholic religion of his youth and young manhood. In *The Spirit Level*, in a poem entitled 'Weighing In', he had pondered the validity of the Christian ethic of turning the other cheek in terms which suggested that it still possessed valency for the him: 'peace on earth, men of good will, all that'.[50] *District and Circle* included 'Out of this world', a poem in two parts in memory of Csezlaw Milosz. In the second of these Heaney recalled his youthful experience of acting as a Brancardier (a stretcher-bearer) at the Lourdes shrine. The tone is almost regretful for a time of faith: 'And always prayers out loud or under breath'.[51] Poem one of this poignant diptych describes the agnostic poet taking the sacrament at Mass, joining a congregation in the rite as if by deeply engrained custom. The poet tells us his loss of faith that it had 'occurred off stage' as he confesses in conclusion: 'And yet I cannot / disavow words like "thanksgiving" or "host"/ or "communion bread". They have an undying / tremor and draw, like well water far down'.[52]

It is such a poem that allows the critic John Wilson Foster to write of Heaney's 'residually Christian, even secular sensibility'.[53] Rather, I would argue that the emotion expressed in this poem is of a piece with the vital humanist spirit which made of Heaney throughout his career a conscientious, moving celebrant of the traditional in human culture: in the domestic sphere, in social relations (Heaney, like Yeats before him, was a true poet of friendship), in custom, craft and art, in love of place and country. In the final phase of his career the poet, who had remained faithful to his calling through the long years of the Northern Irish Troubles, made it clear that such a Virgilian *piatas* should not be allowed to disguise the fact that the early twenty-first century was also a time of trouble. In *District and Circle*, with its memories of how World War II had impinged on his childhood, the poet warns that in a world in which the 'tallest towers' can be overturned: 'anything can happen'.[54] A prevailing sombre gravity of tone in these last three collections gives to the moments of pure lyricism in them a special precision of utterance which makes one recall a passage in one of Geoffrey Hill's essays. There he wrote of how the poet Jon Stallworthy had written of Yeats's possession of 'almost perfect pitch', which Hill had glossed in words that seem apposite to Heaney's work as a whole as they do to these final volumes: 'a poet who possesses such near-perfect pitch is also able to sound out his own conceptual discursive intelligence ... He is hearing words in depth and is therefore hearing, or sounding history and morality in depth'.[55]

NOTES

1. Seamus Heaney, *Death of a Naturalist*, London: Faber and Faber, 1966, p. 14.
2. Seamus Heaney, *Door into the Dark*, London: Faber and Faber, 1969, p. 20.
3. Ibid, p. 19.
4. Heaney, *Death of a Naturalist*, p. 41
5. Seamus Heaney, *North*, London: Faber and Faber, 1975, p. 15.
6. Ibid., p. 16.
7. Ibid., p. 17.
8. Ibid., p. 59.
9. Ibid., p. 72.
10. Ibid.
11. Seamus Heaney, *Field Work*, London: Faber and Faber, 1979, p. 9.
12. Ibid., p. 26.
13. Ibid., p. 56.

14. Ibid., p. 12.
15. Ibid., p. 34.
16. Ibid., p. 40.
17. Ibid.
18. Seamus Heaney, 'Introduction', Tom MacIntyre, *The Harper's Turn*, Dublin: The Gallery Press, 1982, p. 9.
19. Ibid.
20. Seamus Heaney, *Station Island*, London: Faber and Faber, 1984, p. 123.
21. Ibid., p. 102.
22. Ibid., p. 117.
23. Seamus Heaney, *Sweeney Astray*, Derry: Field Day, 1983, p.vii
24. Heaney *Station Island*, p. 107.
25. Ibid., pp. 107–8
26. Heaney, *Station Island*, p. 66.
27. Ibid., p. 94.
28. Seamus Heaney, *The Haw Lantern*, London:Faber and Faber, 1987, p. 43.
29. Ibid. p. 32.
30. Ibid.
31. Seamus Heaney, *Seeing Things*, London:Faber and Faber, 1991, p. 55.
32. Ibid., p. 14.
33. Ibid., p. 7.
34. Ibid., p. 50.
35. Helen Vendler, *Seamus Heaney*, *Cambridge, Mass.*: Harvard University Press, 1998, p. 136.
36. Heaney, *Seeing Things*, p. 42.
37. Ibid., p. 71.
38. Ibid., p. 106.
39. Ibid., p. 78.
40. Seamus Heaney, *Crediting Poetry*, Oldcastle, County Meath: The Gallery Press, 1995, pp. 17–18.
41. Seamus Heaney, *The Spirit Level*, London: Faber and Faber, 1996, p. 25.
42. Vendler, *Seamus Heaney*, pp. 155–75.
43. Heaney, *The Spirit Level*, p. 34.
44. Ibid., p. 37.
45. Ibid., p. 70.
46. Ibid., p. 69.
47. Seamus Heaney, *District and Circle*, London: Faber and Faber, 2006, p. 71.
48. Seamus Heaney, *Human Chain*, London: Faber and Faber, 2010, p. 34.
49. Ibid., p. 43.
50. Heaney, *The Spirit Level*, p. 17.
51. Heaney, *District and Circle*, p. 48.
52. Ibid., p. 47.
53. John Wilson Foster, 'Crediting Marvels: Heaney After 50' in *The Cambridge Companion to Seamus Heaney*, ed. Bernard O'Donoghue, Cambridge: Cambridge University Press, 2009, p. 214.
54. Seamus Heaney, *District and Circle*, p. 13.
55. Kenneth Haynes, *Geoffrey Hill: Collected Critical Writings*, Oxford: Oxford University Press, 2008, p. 391.

SELECTED FURTHER READING

Andrews, Elmer, *Seamus Heaney: A Collection of Critical Essays*, Basingstoke: Macmillan, 1992.

Corcoran, Neil, *Seamus Heaney*, London: Faber and Faber, 1986.

Curtis, Tony, *The Art of Seamus Heaney*, Bridgend: Poetry Wales Press, 1982; 2nd edition: Bridgend: Seren Books, 2001.

Foster, John Wilson, *The Achievement of Seamus Heaney*, Dublin: The Lilliput Press, 1995.

Hart, Henry, *Seamus Heaney, Poet of Contrary Progressions*, New York: Syracuse University Press, 1992.

Morrison, Blake, *Seamus Heaney*, London: Methuen, 1982.

O'Donoghue, Bernard, *Seamus Heaney and the Language of Poetry*, Hemel Hempstead: Harvester Wheatsheaf, 1994.

O'Driscoll, Dennis, *Stepping Stones: Interviews with Seamus Heaney*, London: Faber and Faber, 2008.

Parker, Michael, *Seamus Heaney: The Making of the Poet*, Basingstoke: Macmillan, 1993.

21

FLORENCE IMPENS

Michael Longley

Michael Longley, in John Banville's words, has composed 'the most delicate lyrics of his time', and 'a nature poetry that is an exalted naming of things'.[1] For Dennis O'Driscoll, his war poetry is 'as poignant as the orphic waft of a harmonica',[2] while for Brendan Kennelly, he is 'a special Homer of Irish poetry'.[3] Writing those words of encomium in *Love Poet, Carpenter*, a festschrift published on the occasion of Longley's seventieth birthday in 2009, those three writers were among many key figures of contemporary Irish and Anglophone literature to praise the poet's achievements, and celebrate the variety of an oeuvre and poetic career started almost fifty years ago. The impressive list of contributors to the publication, including Seamus Heaney, Derek Mahon, Paul Muldoon, Fleur Adcock and Sinéad Morrissey, highlights Longley's importance in the Irish and Anglophone poetic landscape of the new millennium, revealing the extent to which his work and presence had influenced his contemporaries as well as younger poets.

Belonging to a prolific generation of poets hailing from Northern Ireland who started to publish in the late 1960s, Michael Longley has contributed to raising the profile of Irish poetry across the Anglophone world, and to what Heather Clark calls 'the Ulster Renaissance'.[4] With Heaney and Mahon, both of whom were lifelong friends of his, he is probably nowadays one of the most famous contemporary Irish poets in Ireland and abroad.

But his is also a singular voice, occupying a place of its own in the Irish poetic landscape. Marked by a dual Irish and English cultural heritage, Longley is a lyricist and humanist, whose work defies simple characterisations of Irish poetry, inviting us to reconsider the premises on which the latter has been read, and its links with other literatures in the British archipelago and Europe.

*

Michael Longley published his first full-length collection of poetry, *No Continuing City*, in 1969, three years after Seamus Heaney's *Death of a Naturalist*, and a year after Derek Mahon's *Night-Crossing*. The volume, which would soon be followed by *An Exploded View* (1973), *Man Lying on a Wall* (1976) and *The Echo Gate* (1979), is in many ways a collection of beginnings.

Gathering poems written between 1963 and 1968, it bears traces of Longley's years as a young adult and budding poet in Dublin. Born in 1939 and educated at the Royal Belfast Academical Institution, Longley had moved to the Republic in 1958 to undertake an undergraduate degree in Classics at Trinity College, Dublin. By his own admission not very dedicated to his studies, he had, after meeting Derek Mahon in 1960, devoted most of his time to poetry and creative writing. Together, they had 'inhaled with [their] untipped Sweet Afton cigarettes, MacNeice, Crane, Dylan Thomas, Yeats, Larkin, Lawrence, Graves, Ted Hughes, Stevens, Cummings, Richard Wilbur, Robert Lowell, as well as Rimbaud, Baudelaire, Brecht, Rilke – higgledepiggledy, in any order, [and] scanned the journals and newspapers for poems written yesterday'.[5]

The eclecticism of those readings finds its way into *No Continuing City*, in its many literary and cultural references, combining allusions and homages to, for example, Emily Dickinson, Dr Johnson, John Clare, Homer's *Odyssey* and James Joyce's *Ulysses*, as well as jazz music. At times, the poems may, in their forms and strict rhyming patterns, feel somewhat stilted, prompting Terence Brown to later comment that they 'read like the self-conscious, conventional experiments of the Classics student Longley had recently been at Trinity College, Dublin'.[6] But poems such as 'Epithalamion' and 'En Route', 'The Osprey' and 'The Ornithological Section', as well as 'In Memoriam', among many others, are also in hindsight extraordinary, for they encapsulate from a very early stage the main themes which would become hallmarks of Longley's singular oeuvre, whether it be love, nature or war. Throughout his career, those would be the main three directions he would explore in his poetry, under many guises.

In a distant echo of imagist poets, Longley's early love and nature poems in the 1970s derive their evocative power from detailed observations based on a precise vocabulary – of the landscape and its fauna, or of the female body and the lovers' intimacy. The poems celebrating the love of women, and of his wife in particular, paint sensual scenes, as in 'The Swim' (*Man Lying on a Wall*), where the lovers 'make love there and then' on the banks of a lake.[7] Often, they are not shy of describing the physicality of human sexuality, preferring the directness of precise and anatomical vocabulary to metaphors, and indeed seem at their best when they do so. While some explicitly sexual images might sound incongruous, as is the case in the opening line of 'Dead Man's Fingers' (*The Echo Gate*), 'A cat with a mouse's tail dangling out of its mouth / Flashes from between her legs and escapes into my head',[8] 'Love Poem',[9] on the other hand, epitomises the delicate and intimate voice that characterises Longley's best love poetry. Successively detailing imagined sensory experiences with his lover, the speaker expresses his love for the latter in his tender listing of ordinary parts of her body, whether her 'fingernails, toenails', or even her 'body's independent processes / lungs, heartbeats, intestines'. Conveying a sense of familiarity and ease between the lovers, those poems powerfully resonate in the private sphere, while they also, in their apparent simplicity, capture the reader's imagination.

Longley's voice thus emerged early on in his career as that of a lyricist with an attention to detail that was unique among his contemporaries. Combined with his early war poetry, it contributed to making his oeuvre a singular one in the Irish poetic landscape. If the poet was born in Belfast, where he still resides, his English parents had only emigrated to the city in 1927, prompting him to say later in life that he feels 'neither English nor Irish completely'.[10] This hyphenated identity is further reinforced by the fact that his father was a veteran of World War I, and had fought in the trenches with the London Scottish Regiment. At a time when the conflict was a contentious memory on the island of Ireland, whether largely side-lined in the history of the Irish Free State and Republic as collusion of some with the British imperial forces, or re-appropriated as a sign of loyalism, Longley began to write about the Great War, in the early 'In Memoriam', as well as in many other poems resurfacing throughout his career, in the 1970s and thereafter.

Sometimes inspired by his father's experiences ('Second Sight' and 'Last Requests'), sometimes by well-known British war poets (e.g. 'Edward Thomas's War Diary', 'Mole', 'War Poets' and 'Bog Cotton'), the poems remember the horror of the trenches, and of warfare. Often elegies for a father the poet had lost aged nineteen, they also resonate as attempts to imaginatively engage with a part of his family history that was the object of little discussion at home and in the public domain. 'Last Requests' (*The Echo Gate*), for example, is a two-part poem for his father who had died in 1958. Re-reading his last moments in the light of a near-death experience in the war, Longley suggests how much of his father's life had been shaped by the conflict, as well as his own inability to comprehend what the latter had gone through. He writes:

> I thought you blew a kiss before you died,
> But the bony fingers that waved to and fro
> Were asking for a Woodbine, the last request
> Of many soldiers in your company,
> ...
> I who brought peppermints and grapes only
> Couldn't reach you through your oxygen tent.[11]

Sometimes in the 1970s, those war poems also provided a framework with which to try and perceive the conflict that was rapidly developing in Northern Ireland in the decade. If *No Continuing City* had been written before violence erupted in the region, *An Exploded View, Man Lying on a Wall* and *The Echo Gate* had all been composed after the onset of the 'Troubles', and like much of the work published by his contemporaries in the period, they bear traces of the poet's struggle to address what was becoming a civil war. Reflecting on his work years later, Longley writes:

> Sometimes I listen to Owen and Rosenberg as though they were my dad's drinking companions, sharing a Woodbine between the lines during a lull. And sometimes I wonder what he would have to say about the 'Troubles'. ... These poets provided me with a map and compass when I began to contemplate our own little sordid conflict.[12]

'Wounds',[13] one of Longley's earliest poems about the 'Troubles', thus reads the sectarian murder of a bus conductor killed in his own home in the light of his father's experience in the Battle of the Somme, creating a link between the loss of life in World War I and in Northern Ireland. The connection is tentative, and stays clear of any attempt to make sense of the events. Listing the objects and people he would bury beside his father, Longley adds 'a bus conductor's uniform', almost as an afterthought – symbolised in the poem by the semi-colon separating the first list from this last item. Rather than a mark of indifference, the addition conveys the speaker's helpless resignation, when faced with the return of violence in yet a new context. No rationale can be given that might justify the sectarian murder, and the last seven lines of the poem narrate the latter, emphasising details of the domestic setting to highlight the atrocity of the event.

In its focus on individual lives shattered by the conflict, and on the domestic, 'Wounds' is in many ways exemplary of the poet's other elegies for victims of the 'Troubles' in the period. In 'Wreaths', the 'civil servant' dies in his kitchen, while 'preparing an Ulster Fry for breakfast', 'the greengrocer', while in his shop, 'behind the counter, organised / With holly wreaths for Christmas', and finally, of the 'ten linen workers' murdered during the Kingsmill massacre in January 1976, there remain on the road 'spectacles, / Wallets, small change, and a set of dentures', as many tokens of their daily lives.[14] Portraying ordinary lives cut short by the conflict, Longley wrote elegies conveying a non-sectarian message of peace – those were victims and surroundings with which anyone could identify. To some extent, this perspective, which also allowed him to stay clear of politics by focusing on the private sphere, echoes as well his attention to details, and his observation of minutiae in his nature and love poetry.

But Longley, like many of his contemporaries, also felt uncomfortable with public demands to have artists and poets comment on the 'Troubles' in their work. In 1971, a year after his appointment as Combined Arts Director at the Arts Council of Northern Ireland, where he would work over the next twenty years, he wrote in the introduction to *Causeway*, a panorama of contemporary arts in the region he edited:

> Too many critics seem to expect a harvest of paintings, poems, plays and novels to drop from the branches of civil discord. They fail to realise that the artist needs time in which to allow the raw material of experience to settle to an imaginative depth where he can transform it and possibly even suggest solutions to current and very urgent problems by reframing them according to the dictates of his particular discipline. He is not some sort of super-journalist commenting with unfaltering spontaneity on events immediately after they have happened.[15]

This tension between private and public, and the issue of the poet's social responsibility, are best expressed in poetic terms in Longley's rewritings of Latin love elegies in the 1970s. Re-appropriating Propertius, Tibullus and Sulpicia, all of whom he had read at Trinity College, Dublin, in 'Altera Cithera' (*An Exploded View*), 'Peace' and the eponymous 'Sulpicia' (both in *The Echo Gate*), Longley wrote texts that examine the tension between lyric and epic, and insist on the qualities of the former over the latter. Alluding to an elegy by Propertius (*Elegies* 2.10), 'Altera Cithera' thus negatively comments on the Latin poet's decision to abandon the topic of his lover Cynthia and instead focus his energy on military themes, concluding in the second stanza that the Latin poet is but 'the shadow / Of his former self'.[16] 'Peace', a poem composed in response to a request from the Peace People organisation in Belfast, rewrites Tibullus, and his lament in *Elegy* over the loss of the Golden Age destroyed by man's appetite for violence. Finally, 'Sulpicia' imagines the Latin poet rewriting hunting metaphors as images of seduction. To some extent, the poems form a miniature *ars poetica*, in which Longley defends the lyric mode, with which he feels great affinity, against the context of growing endemic violence. Symbolically, they also form a post-script to a first decade of writing, in which the private and lyric qualities of Longley's voice as well as his complex cultural heritage became under increasing pressure from social and political upheavals in Northern Ireland.

*

For most of the 1980s, Michael Longley indeed stopped publishing new volumes of poetry. If *Poems 1963–1983*, released in 1985, contains a small number of unpublished poems, the decade was a period of near-creative silence, the byproduct of a middle-age crisis caused by a combination of personal and professional factors, and heightened by the pressure on Northern Irish society at the time. In Longley's words, it was 'agony really. I thought I was finished. I didn't think I was going to write any more poetry and it was like having an enormous itch I couldn't scratch.'[17]

Coinciding with his early retirement from the Arts Council of Northern Ireland, the publication of *Gorse Fires* in 1991 marked the beginning of a new productive phase in the poet's career, who has since regularly published new work. Met with critical acclaim, it also signalled a change in the reception of Longley's work, whose importance for contemporary Irish and Anglophone literatures has since increasingly been recognised. Awarded the Whitbread Poetry Prize, *Gorse Fires* marked the start of a long series of institutional accolades the poet would receive over the next twenty-five years, including the T. S. Eliot Prize for *The Weather in Japan* in 2000, and the Griffin Poetry Prize for *The Stairwell* in 2015.

If Longley's role for the arts and for poetry received seals of official recognition both in Ireland and in the United Kingdom at the turn of the new millennium, when he was, for instance, appointed Ireland Professor of Poetry (2007–2010), and made Commander of the Order of the British Empire (2010), his growing success might, however, have more to do with a change in the reception of Irish poetry by critics and institutions in Ireland and abroad, than with a profound transformation of his work after a creative hiatus. Although 'his Irish-English heritage still proves a disrupting force, and ... causes, as does Yeats with his literary Anglo-Irishness, ideological unease in certain quarters', as Fran Brearton wrote in 2006 in the first monograph to be published on his work,[18] it may also be noted that those awards coincided with the beginnings of the Northern Irish peace process, and multiplied in a period which saw a growing acceptance by most of Ireland's cultural hybridity.[19] Longley's poetry, celebrating the West, particularly County Mayo, at the same time as it draws from British war poets, had long challenged narrow-minded definitions of Irish writing. Finally, it chimed with the growing tendency to acknowledge the intricate history linking Irish writers with their British counterparts, Ireland's with Great Britain's past.

Rather than a break from previous work, *Gorse Fires*, and the collections that have since followed – *The Ghost Orchid* (1995), *The Weather in Japan* (2000), *Snow Water* (2004), *A Hundred Doors* (2011) and *The Stairwell* (2014) – are indeed characterised by a new and sustained bout of creative energy bringing back many of the themes Longley had already explored in the 1970s. In what has been described as a 'widening gyre',[20] the poet has, while experimenting with new forms – from the long one-sentence poems of *Gorse Fires* playing with the tension between prosody and syntax, to the haikus of *The Weather in Japan* and thereafter, redeveloped his work along the three main concerns he had identified early on in his career: love, nature, and war.

The lovers may have aged, and the eroticism of the early poems been replaced with tenderness, as in 'The Scissors Ceremony', where the cutting of one's husband's nails is 'a way of making love'.[21] The speaker may also sometimes be looking back at the passionate poetry of his early years, as in 'The Couplet' ('When I was young I wrote that flowers are very slow flames / And you uncovered your breasts often among my images'),[22] remembering sensual moments rather than creating new memories. But despite the passing of time, those love poems, examples among many other similar ones, display the same attention to details and empathy for their subject that had been features of Longley's work in the 1970s, whereby love was expressed in seemingly simple and unadorned form.

This apparent simplicity Longley has also retained in his nature poems, building a rich inventory of Irish fauna and flora, and crisscrossing the same imaginative terrain over decades. After 'Remembering Carrigskeewaun' (*Gorse Fires*), an echo of the early 'Carrigskeewaun' (1973), with which it shares its snipe and the image of the homely cottage with smoke coming out of its chimney, the poet has kept returning to the small townland in County Mayo where he regularly sojourns, adding poems recording the landscape and its natural inhabitants. Many focus on an encounter with an animal or flower, such as 'The Lapwing', 'Snow Bunting', 'The Fox', 'The Hare', 'Marshmarigold', 'The Wren', 'Stonechat', 'Dipper', 'Robin', 'Snipe', 'Wheatear' and 'Another Wren'. But such poems are also more than descriptions of local birds, wild animals and flowers that can be observed in the region: often, they record the speaker's presence in nature, or use the natural element as an occasion to recall the memory of its discovery with a loved one. At times, they are also gifts offered as elegies for the dead, as in the recent 'Fragrant Orchid',[23] in memory of his friends' daughter, where the flowers of Carrigskeewaun are tentatively made into a poetic wreath, or on the contrary celebrate new births in the poet's family, as in 'The Wren', for his grandsons, which starts with the line 'I am writing too much about Carrigskeewaun'.[24]

Such poems are variations on recurring themes, each echoing previous work while also adding new elements to Longley's oeuvre. As well as love and nature, Longley has also developed his reflection on war, whether either world war, or the 'Troubles'. Revisiting memories of his father's experiences in World War I, he writes poems often inspired by the same anecdotes and details he has been able to recover from the past. The kilt, symbol of his father's enrolment with the London Scottish Regiment, briefly mentioned in 'Wounds', for instance resurfaces several times over the years: in the aptly-named 'The Kilt' (*The Ghost Orchid*), as well as more obliquely in 'Ronald Colman' (*The Stairwell*). Longley has also added to his poetry of World War II, with poems inspired by the experience of one of his friends, Helen Lewis, in concentration camps, as well as by war poets such as Keith Douglas. As in the poems of the 1970s, those often narrate stories where the ordinariness of human life is shattered by the arrival of war, as is the case in 'Ghetto' (*The Ghost Orchid*). The first section of the poem in particular powerfully conveys the destruction of domesticity in times of conflict, when it starkly shows that the careful selection of personal belongings one is accustomed to making before going away becomes nonsensical when leaving for an extermination camp. Addressing an anonymous 'you' that involves the reader into the experience of the poem, it opens with the lines 'Because you will suffer soon and die, your choices / Are neither right nor wrong', before reiterating the idea that reason is no more at the very end, in 'what you bring is the same as what you leave behind, / Your last belonging a list of your belongings'.[25]

If Longley's poetry, contrary to what has often been suggested, is thus characterised by forms of continuity after his creative silence in the 1980s, the poet has also engaged with a new material that has informed much of his output from *Gorse Fires* to *The Stairwell*, in what may be one of the most significant developments in his work in the last twenty-five years. Reviving his knowledge of Classics from his student days, Longley has since the 1990s indeed rewritten Greek and Latin literatures with unprecedented intensity, establishing his reputation as a poet-translator and 'lapsed classicist',[26] adapting authors as diverse as Homer, Ovid, Horace, Virgil, Sappho and lesser-known Greek lyric poets. Among those classical poems, some have been prompted by commissions, as is the case with the Ovidian rewritings in *The Ghost Orchid*,[27] but one author in particular, Homer, has really captured the poet's imagination, and remained a presence in his work for over two decades.

Longley rediscovered Homer in the late 1980s, during his mid-life crisis. This was a writer he had first read and enjoyed at school, but who until then had not played an active role in the poet's universe. Rediscovering the *Odyssey* in the late 1980s, Longley identified narratives that resonated with his crisis of identity and his coming to terms with middle age. Not only did the rewriting of selected passages in the *Odyssey* provide a source-text on which the poet could rely at a time when creativity was sometimes problematic, the passages chosen by Longley also created a safe distance from which to address personal issues while avoiding the pitfalls of confessional poetry. The Homeric poems of *Gorse Fires* thus retrace the final stages of Odysseus's journey home, from the moment he lands on Ithaca ('Homecoming'), to his reunion with members of his family: his wife in 'Tree-House', his father in 'Laertes', his mother in 'Anticleia',[28] his nurse in 'Eurycleia' and, finally, his dog in 'Argos'. Although focused on the classical narrative, their place within the collection, whereby they are paired with poems recalling family memories, discreetly courts autobiographical echoes, as metaphors of his own 'homecoming': of the reconquering of his own identity, as well as of his coming to terms with family deaths. Like Seamus Heaney's first rewritings of Book Six of Virgil's *Aeneid*, a text that had also fascinated the latter from a young age, in *Seeing Things* (1991), Homer's *Odyssey* provided Longley with 'a new emotional and psychological vocabulary', allowing the poet to 'give expression to sorrows'.[29]

But more than the *Odyssey*, it is the *Iliad*, this 'painful exploration of war [and] gigantic poem about death',[30] that has proved the most enduring presence in Longley's work, feeding into his war poetry and providing an imaginative framework in which to reflect on contemporary warfare. 'Ceasefire' in particular, a rewriting of Book XXIV, 477–670, captured the public's attention upon publication. For Longley, whose lyric poetry 'almost always makes its occasion in private', the poem 'was an exception'.[31]

The rewriting narrates the episode in which two of the main enemies of the Trojan War, Achilles and Priam, reconcile over the death of the latter's son, Hector, and highlights this moment of extraordinary reconciliation, when it reverses the chronological sequence of the original to conclude with a couplet voiced by Priam: 'I get down on my knees and do what must be done / And kiss Achilles' hand, the killer of my son'.[32] Not only is this the sole instance of direct speech in the poem, given prime position in the sonnet structure, the importance of Priam's forgiveness is also reinforced by the alliteration in /k/, linking 'kiss' and 'killer'. Published in *The Irish Times* a few days after the IRA had announced a ceasefire in August 1994, 'Ceasefire' powerfully echoed the growing sense of the need for reconciliation in Northern Ireland, and support of the peace process. As Longley recalls, 'priests and politicians quoted from it'. In her survey of Irish poetry in the 1990s for the anthology *Watching the River Flow* Nuala Ni Dhomhnaill says: 'Its effect was dynamic and rippled right through the community, both North and South'.[33]

Reprinted in *The Ghost Orchid* the following year, 'Ceasefire' became the climactic conclusion of a micro-sequence based on the *Iliad* (with 'The Camp-Fires', 'The Helmet' and 'The Parting') and focusing on the figure of Hector: in a stark contrast emphasising the tragedy of his death, the poems capture lively scenes portraying the warrior interacting with his closest relatives, with his son Astyanax in 'The Helmet', and his wife in 'The Parting'. With three intimate family scenes, juxtaposed with a poem of utter emotional desolation, the sequence radically revises the values of heroism and bravery associated with the epic, transforming the Homeric material into a pacifist text.

By the mid-1990s, the *Iliad* had become Longley's classical text of choice to reflect on warfare, and in particular on World War I. As suggested in 'A Poppy' (*The Weather in Japan*), the poet at the turn of the new millennium casts himself as belonging to a long and transnational tradition of war poetry, linking Homer and Virgil with John McCrae and other British war poets. Time and again, he has borrowed images and rewritten excerpts from the epic to give a new imaginative depth to his meditation on twentieth-century violence, and on the conflicts that have affected his family and friends. Most recently, the *Iliad* has provided images with which Longley can address the loss of his twin Peter in *The Stairwell*, exemplifying the continued importance of the epic for the poet in his late career.

*

Reading Michael Longley's poetry over his whole career, from the early experiments of *No Continuing City* to those recent poems where the poet hints at his own passing, is to witness the development of an imagination building a coherent body of work, all the while experimenting with new forms and refining its craft. In a recent interview, the poet compares his work to a braid, and in the braid, he says, 'are these strands, weaving in and out of each other: war, art, children, love, nature. And by the time I die it'll all add up to one long poem.'[34] Echoes and variations between poems within each collection as well as over time indeed chart the evolution of a poet influenced by lyricism and his Irish-English background as he grapples with personal events and contemporary history, making Longley's oeuvre an important testimony of the issues faced by Irish writers of his generation. Drawing from a wide range of sources, including Classics, English and Irish literature, his work also illustrates the fluidity of literary relations between the twin nations of Ireland and England, and beyond, and serves as a powerful reminder of the transnational and European nature of modern and contemporary Irish writing.

NOTES

1. John Banville, in *Love Poet, Carpenter: Michael Longley at Seventy*, ed. by Robin Robertson. London: Enitharmon Press, 2009, p. 16.
2. Dennis O'Driscoll in *Love Poet, Carpenter*, p. 99.
3. Brendan Kennelly in *Love Poet, Carpenter*, p. 76.

4. Heather Clark, *The Ulster Renaissance, Poetry in Belfast 1962–1972*. Oxford: Oxford University Press, 2006.

5. Michael Longley, *Tupenny Stung: Autobiographical Chapters*. Belfast: Lagan Press, 1994, pp. 36–7.

6. Terence Brown, 'Mahon and Longley: Place and Placelessness', in Matthew Campbell ed., *The Cambridge Companion to Contemporary Irish Poetry* (Cambridge: Cambridge University Press, 2003), p. 146.

7. *CP* 84.

8. Michael Longley, *Collected Poems*. London: Jonathan Cape, 2006, p. 145. Thereafter referred to as *CP*.

9. *CP* 87.

10. Michael Longley, 'Michael Longley interviewed by Dillon Johnston', *Writing Irish, Selected Interviews with Irish Writers from the Irish Literary Supplement*, ed. James P. Myers (Syracuse: Syracuse University Press, 1999) 54. The interview was first published in the *Irish Literary Supplement* 5 in Spring 1986.

11. *CP* 120.

12. Michael Longley, in John Brown (ed.), *In the Chair: Interviews with Poets from the North of Ireland*. Cliffs of Moher, Salmon Publishing, 2002, p. 94.

13. *CP* 62.

14. *CP* 118–19.

15. Michael Longley (ed.), *Causeway: The Arts in Ulster* (Belfast: Arts Council of Northern Ireland, 1971), p. 8.

16. *CP* 137.

17. Michael Longley, in Clive Wilmer, *Poets Talking: Poet of the Month Interviews from BBC Radio 3*. Manchester: Carcanet Press, 1994, p. 117.

18. Fran Brearton, *Reading Michael Longley*. Newcastle: Bloodaxe, 2006, p. 11.

19. For instance, in 1998, the Republic officially recognised Irish participation in World War I, in a joint ceremony at Messines with then president of Ireland Mary McAleese and Queen Elizabeth II. This may have facilitated a more open discussion of Longley's poems about his father's experiences as a Tommy.

20. Fran Brearton, *Reading Michael Longley*, p. 162.

21. *CP* 217.

22. *CP* 217.

23. Michael Longley, *The Stairwell*. London: Jonathan Cape, 2014, p. 21.

24. Michael Longley, *A Hundred Doors*. London: Jonathan Cape, 2011, p. 7.

25. *CP* 187.

26. Michael Longley, 'Lapsed Classicist,' in S. J. Harrison (ed.), *Living Classics: Greece and Rome in Contemporary Poetry*. Oxford: Oxford University Press, 2009, p. 97–113.

27. Michael Longley began by translating 'Baucis and Philemon' as a commission for *After Ovid: New Metamorphoses*, edited by Michael Hofmann and James Lasdun, and quickly became fascinated with the Ovidian poem, leading to another six rewritings. See Longley, in *Living Classics*, p. 108.

28. The poem is based on an earlier episode, before Odysseus arrives back on the island, when the hero encounters the ghost of his mother who has died in his absence (Books X, 513–37 and XI, 23–50).

29. Michael Longley, in Peter McDonald, 'An Interview with Michael Longley, "Au Revoir, Oeuvre".' *Thumbscrew* 12 (Winter 1998/99): 10.

30. Michael Longley, 'Interview with Michael Longley by Sarah Broom', *Metre* 4 (Spring/ Summer 1998), 20.
31. Michael Longley, 'Lapsed Classicist', p. 104.
32. *CP* 225.
33. Michael Longley, 'Lapsed Classicist', p. 104.
34. Michael Longley, interviewed by James Meredith for *Culture Northern Ireland*, 21 April 2011. www.culturenorthernireland.org/features/literature/cqaf-michael-longley, last accessed 5 Feb. 2016.

SELECTED FURTHER READING

Essays by Michael Longley

Longley, Michael, *Causeway: The Arts in Ulster*. Belfast: Arts Council of Northern Ireland, 1971.
Tupenny Stung: Autobiographical Chapters. Belfast: Lagan Press, 1994.
'Lapsed Classicist,' in S. J. Harrison (ed.), *Living Classics: Greece and Rome in Contemporary Poetry*. Oxford: Oxford University Press, 2009, pp. 97–113.

Interviews

Brown, John, (ed.), *In the Chair: Interviews with Poets from the North of Ireland. Cliffs of Moher*, Salmon Publishing, 2002.
Longley, Michael, 'Michael Longley interviewed by Dillon Johnston', *Writing Irish, Selected Interviews with Irish Writers from the Irish Literary Supplement*, ed. James P. Myers. Syracuse: Syracuse University Press, 1999, pp. 51–64.
'Interview with Michael Longley by Sarah Broom', *Metre* 4 (Spring/ Summer 1998), pp. 17–26.
interviewed by James Meredith for Culture Northern Ireland, 21 April 2011. www.culturenorthernireland.org/features/literature/cqaf-michael-longley, last accessed 5 Feb. 2016.
McDonald, Peter, 'An Interview with Michael Longley, "Au Revoir, Oeuvre".' *Thumbscrew* 12 (Winter 1998/99), pp. 5–14.
Wilmer, Clive, *Poets Talking: Poet of the Month Interviews from BBC Radio 3*. Manchester: Carcanet Press, 1994.

Critical

Brearton, Fran, *Reading Michael Longley*. Newcastle: Bloodaxe, 2006.
Brown, Terence, 'Mahon and Longley: Place and Placelessness', in Matthew Campbell ed., *The Cambridge Companion to Contemporary Irish Poetry*. Cambridge: Cambridge University Press, 2003, pp. 133–48.

Clark, Heather, *The Ulster Renaissance, Poetry in Belfast 1962–1972*. Oxford: Oxford University Press, 2006.

Hardwick, Lorna, 'Degrees of Intimacy: Michael Longley's Poetic Relationship with Homer.' (2007): http://www2.open.ac.uk/ClassicalStudies/GreekPlays/PoetryDB/longley/poetrylongleyintro.htm.

Peacock, Alan, 'Prolegomena to Michael Longley's Peace Poem.' *Eire-Ireland* 23 (Spring 1988): pp. 60–74.

Peacock, Alan and Kathleen Devine (eds.), *The Poetry of Michael Longley*. Gerrards Cross: Colin Smythe, 2000.

Robertson, Robin (ed.), *Love Poet, Carpenter, Michael Longley at Seventy*, London: Enitharmon Press, 2009.

22

PETER SIRR

Michael Hartnett

Michael Hartnett's variety as a poet – balladeer, satirist, love poet, translator, poet in Irish as well as English – and his complicated bibliography, with numerous compilations, collections and selections, as well as individual volumes from several different publishers, had the effect of obscuring his achievement or hiding its core elements. The resultant confusion or uncertainty with respect to his reputation might also function as an indicator of his central condition and theme: a profound sense of displacement in constant search of a cultural, emotional and spiritual home. The shift from English to Irish and back again, the centrality of translation and the liminal world where translation meets original creation, the physical shifts from city to country and back all point to the kind of creative restlessness that fed Hartnett as a poet but that sometimes made critics scratch their heads. Where is the real Michael Hartnett, or Micheál Ó hAirtnéide? Is it the Hartnett of the precocious early poetry, with all its bravura posturing? The Hartnett in the skin of the *Tao* or the brilliant refiguring of Lorca's *Gypsy Ballads*? The Hartnett reaching his maturity just at the point when he was about to make a theatrical exit from the English language? The Ó hAirtnéide of *Adharca Broic* (1978), *An Phurgóid* (1983), *Do Nuala: Foighne Chrainn* (1984)? The poet who came down from the mountain and into a working class suburb of Dublin to write an extended haiku sequence in English? The Hartnett of the lampoons, satires, and the defiant localism of 'Maiden Street Ballad' or 'The Ballad of Salad Sunday'? The Hartnett of the striking engagement over three volumes with seventeenth-century precursors Aodhagán Ó Rathaille, Dáibhí Ó Bruadair and Pádraigín Haicéad? The Hartnett who seemed to make yet another new beginning with *Poems to Younger Women* (1988)? The poet of the late long poems such as 'Sibelius in Silence' or 'The Man who Wrote Yeats, the Man who Wrote Mozart'?

The truth, of course, is that he was all of these; he is the sum of all of these identity shifts, and to consider any one of these aspects is isolation is to miss the overall picture of a complex, restless and rewarding poet.

The poem that opens the 2001 *Collected Poems* (actually his collected English poems) is 'A Small Farm', and strikes an entirely characteristic note. On one level it seems the classic Irish rural poem of bleak memory, but the manner is more Lorca than Patrick Kavanagh:

> All the perversions of the soul
> I learnt on a small farm,
> how to do the neighbours harm
> by magic, how to hate.[1]   (*Collected Poems* 15)

It conjures up a rural Ireland of poverty, piety and emotional chill, a small, bare place whose negatively charged atmosphere is too powerful to be escaped. The soul-destroying perversions, once learnt, tend to dwell in the spirit. Another early poem seems to relish the inherited ferocities:

> So do not talk
> of death or love.
> Do not even talk;
> for I as a hawk
> will know the haunt
> of the ring-toed dove
> and will decide whether
> to gash the neck
> or cripple the wingfeather.
>   ('I will rise with the hawk . . . ', CP 23)

These poems are written in a stripped language and deploy an essentialist stock of images – birds, old women, the poet and his craft – a sort of abstract lyric pack. The country they inhabit is partly a recognisable rural Ireland, unsentimentally depicted, but also a private terrain of loss, a temporal zone somewhere between the seventeenth and twentieth centuries, haunted by the ghost of Irish, by the sense of a culture drained of what had made it vital and meaningful. Hartnett patrols this terrain registering the loss with anger, as in 'Visit to Croom, 1745': 'I had walked a long time / now to hear a Gaelic court / talk broken English of an English king. / It was a long way / to come for nothing' (CP 140). The road that would take him to abandoning English is already mapped out in the early poems. His tone of voice, especially in the earlier poems, has a disconcertingly magisterial self-assurance, but often it is shattered by the end of the poem into something nervier, more hesitant, as in the progression from 'I have exhausted the delighted range / of small birds' to the painful breakages in the rest of that poem.

Formally, the early poems are characterised by a terse well-made-ness that emphasises short lines, rhyme, spare vocabulary, spare gestures. In some respects they are curiously old-fashioned, with what can seem like an overly self-preoccupied and self-satisfied interiority. They're literary, highly self-conscious, unashamedly rhetorical:

> There will be a talking of lovely things,
> there will be cognisance of the seasons.
>
> ('There will be a talking ... ', *CP* 45)

On the other hand, they can have the attractive simplicity of this short lyric from 'Short Mass', for the poet and *sean-nós* singer Caitlín Maude:

> Listen,
> if I came to you, out of the wind
> with only my blown dream clothing me,
> would you give me shelter?   (*CP* 21)

Equally, the poems that seem to be from early childhood experiences make a strong impression, such as 'How goes the night, boy? ... ' (*CP* 51), in which the poet supplies words for his father on the night before his three-year-old daughter's funeral:

> She was my three-years child,
> her honey hair, her eyes
> small ovals of thrush-eggs
>
> ('How goes the night, boy? ... ', *CP* 51)

Or 'For Edward Hartnett', for his brother who died in infancy. One of the most powerful early poems is 'For My Grandmother, Bridget Halpin', the same woman evoked in the later, much-anthologised 'Death of an Irishwoman'. The poem is unflinchingly bleak:

> You died in utter loneliness,
> your acres left to the childless.
> You never saw the animals
> of God, and the flowers under
> your feet   (*CP* 52)

It's easy to see why Seamus Heaney could say of the early work 'I'll never forget reading his first short poems in the early sixties; they had a kind of hypnotic power, as if a new Orpheus had emerged from Newcastle West. He was Limerick's Lorca.'[2]

The Lorca reference reminds us of another aspect of early Hartnett that's easy to miss because it has always been hived off into other publications, such as the 1987 *Collected Poems, Vol. 2* (Raven Arts Press) or the 2003 Gallery volume, *Translations*. This is, apparently, how the poet himself wished it,[3] but translation nonetheless lies near the heart of Hartnett's achievement and he was active as a translator or mediator of poetry from other cultures right from the beginning, and in many important respects it's true to say that he found his way into poetry by way of translation. One of the most impressive of the early translations is his version of the *Tao Te Ching*, a nineteenth-century prose translation which he came across as a young man when he worked as curator of the Joyce Tower in Sandycove, Dublin. This is a nicely modernist connection – the young poet in the Martello towers where Joyce set the opening of *Ulysses*, entering upon the very Poundian task of converting a classic Chinese text into English – and it alerts us to one of the strongest patterns of Hartnett's life as a writer: the movement between cultures that allows a fluid shifting of identity out of which new work is created. There's no real sense in which his *Tao* is a mimetic translation. Nor could it be, since Hartnett spoke no Chinese; rather, it's mined from what the poet in his note on the poem calls the 'ugly prose' of a Victorian translation. The result, with its unusual and often abrupt juxtapositions and transitions, its concentration on image and the primacy of the line, is striking, though perhaps more a fruitfully displaced Hartnett than a text attributable to Lao-Tau:

> On lax velvet under aspen wood
> I have no jade; I do not encourage thieves.
> I hide from the people
> the pelt of the sea-lynx:
> I wish my friends to be humble.   (*Translations* 11)

This has the typical sonic patterning and the tone of the early work. Similarly, with their short, staccato lines and sense of the poem as ritual gesture, the translations of Lorca's *Gypsy Ballads* come from the same recognisable sensibility that produced the poems of Irish rural life. In any case, it makes more sense to read his translation work side by side with the original poetry rather than seeing it as a disconnected afterthought. Hartnett went to Spain in 1964 with the intention of learning Spanish so that he could translate Lorca; his engagement was real.

It's tempting to see a line from Hartnett's adventurous translation work to the felicity of a poem like 'Bread':

> Her iron beats
> the smell of bread
> from damp linen,
> silver, crystal,
> and warm white things   (*CP* 53)

Hartnett's self-assuredness didn't always lead to good results. The love poems gathered in the 1968 *Anatomy of a Cliché*, though often lit by brilliant flashes – 'Some white academy of grace / taught her to dance in perfect ways'

('Hands', *CP* 77) – are never entirely convincing and nor, for the most part, are the group of thirteen sonnets from the same period. In an odd way, the reason they fail is very much connected with Hartnett's positioning of himself as a poet, the very clear sense of his gift and role that makes itself felt from the outset. The rhetorical gestures and diction of the early work are not merely indications of apprenticeship but part of his determination to see himself as a representative poet, a spokesman for his tribe, a voice out of his immediate experience and region; they also function as a self-conscious alignment with the spirit of the eighteenth-century Irish-language poets from Limerick, whom he saw as important exemplars for his own work, Seán Ó Tuama and Aindrias MacCraith: 'When I was quite young, I became very conscious of these poets and, so, read them very closely indeed. Through them, without going into their elaborate syntax, I became unafraid of rhetoric as such.'[4] Those poets would come back to haunt him later, but they serve to remind us of Hartnett's keenness to situate himself in a context and tradition. Nor was it just the past he measured himself against – he was also very aware of his own immediate literary context, a world of rivalry as well as friendship, full of the cordial hatred Shaw deemed necessary for a literary movement. In 'Notes on My Contemporaries' (1969), Hartnett locates himself in the literary company of his own time, dedicating poems to Thomas Kinsella, Paul Durcan, Macdara Wood and Caitlín Maude, among others. These are watchful, uneasy pieces, full of the sense of Hartnett as a poet surrounded by other poets, observing and recoiling from the literary world's fraught and rivalrous atmosphere, where dead poets are more likely to be honoured than living ones, as in a poem dedicated to Patrick Kavanagh:

> they love the dead, the living man they hate.
> They were designing monuments – in case –
> and making furtive sketches of his face,
> and he could hear, above their straining laughs,
> the rustling foolscap of their epitaphs.
>
> ('The Poet Down', *CP* 93)

The figure of the poet is always outcast, exiled or haunted, prey to demons, trying to lock himself away from temptation 'in some suburban house'.

Some of the most sharply focussed of Hartnett's poems of this or any period come from his attention to the 'perversions of the soul' that are central to his vision of Irish rural life. This is strikingly evident in an intensely imagined poem such as 'The Retreat of Ita Cagney' (1975), where a widow's enjoyment of sexuality and subsequent childbirth are the subject of ferocious hatred:

> In rhythmic dance the neighbours move
> outside the door, become dumb dolls

as venom breaks in strident fragments
on the glass; broken insults clatter
on the slates.   (*CP* 114)

With its shifting perspectives, claustrophobic atmosphere and narrative energy,
the poem remains a high point of Hartnett's achievement. It also comes at a time
when Hartnett was struggling between Irish and English; he found, as he wrote
the poem, that one line would come out in English and the next in Irish; he
would go on to publish a version in Irish, 'Cúlú Íde', which is effectively a
reconfiguring of the material, a distinct poem in its own right. The skill of 'The
Retreat' and other poems of this period show a poet edging towards a mastery
of his craft, yet it is precisely at this time that he makes his most theatrical
gesture. In 1974, Hartnett made the decision, announced on the stage of the
Peacock Theatre during a reading with the poet Máirtín Ó Direáin, to take his
leave of English and from then on to write in Irish only. Or did he? Well, he
wouldn't necessarily stop writing in English – if a poem presented itself in that
language it would have to be accommodated. But he wouldn't publish any more
English poems. A number of things are at play here: on the one hand a decision –
complicated, emotional, theatrical – to effectively abandon not just a language,
but his achievement and potential development as a poet in that language, and
to attempt to recreate himself as a poet in Irish, a language he would have to
study hard to master. To have announced an intention to become a bilingual
poet would have fulfilled the need to pay due homage to the Gaelic tradition and
the side of his own sensibility that was enmeshed in the Irish language, but the
unequal relationship between the two languages and cultures don't easily
accommodate such to-ing and fro-ing. Eoghan Ó Tuairisc, who wrote in
English as Eugene Watters, ultimately made the quiet decision to stick to one
side of the 'psychic partition' and dedicate himself to Irish. Others worked
happily in both – Conleth Ellis comes to mind, or Rita Kelly or Pearse
Hutchinson, or, more recently, Gréagóir Ó Dúill. And it can, though more
rarely, work the other way: Micheal O Siadhail began as a poet in Irish but now
writes solely in English. A great many of the leading Irish-language poets came
and continue to come to Irish from English, making a conscious decision to
work as writers in that language. Yet, even allowing for the tug of love or war
that bilingualism can entail, the apparently absolute nature of Hartnett's decision, precisely because it seemed so hard to account for, was what puzzled his
admirers and maybe undermined its seriousness. There was something willed
and wilful about it, something quixotic – and something of the publicist's wish
to create the maximum effect. It was, after all, announced from a stage.

To further consolidate the decision Hartnett made a strategic decision to
withdraw from the city and returned not to his native Newcastle West but to

the countryside beyond it, a monkish isolation in which to conduct his study of his adopted language. His language shift was therefore also a life shift, an escape from the urban, a refocusing, a re-creation, the various impulses all coalescing in the move. A television documentary of the time shows the poet immersed in country life and lore, looking fondly at the pig that will sustain him through the winter. Interestingly, Hartnett did not remove himself to a Gaeltacht, like Seán Ó Riada, but to his own part of the world. He was going back to his roots, roots with strong Gaelic associations – with Croom's Aindrias MacCraith and Seán Ó Tuama, filí na Máighe – but firmly lodged in the past. The absence of an Irish-speaking community meant that his cultivation of Irish was an affair of private study. In a way this suited him. His feeling for Irish had a good deal of the scholarly about it; it was a repossession of a tradition, a conversation with the past more than an engagement with the present; most of all, it was a conversation with himself.

The first book to come out of his self-imposed exile was the book that announced his intent. There's an irony in the fact that the leavetaking should have been articulated in a book that in its own achievement argued against its declared position. *A Farewell to English* (Gallery, 1975) is, like all of Hartnett's work, uneven, a mix of the real and the rhetorical, but it contains some of his finest work – 'Struts', 'Death of an Irishwoman', 'A Visit to Croom, 1745'. The title poem is somewhat overblown, never escaping the kind of portentous self-importance that Hartnett was prone to:

> What was I doing with these foreign words?
> I, the polisher of complex clause,
> wizard of grasses and warlock of birds,
> midnight-oiled in the metric laws? (CP 141)

It's undermined by dubious arguments, a sentimental view of language and a kind of extremism that announced his withdrawal not just from the writing of English poems but from reading Wyatt or Browning or Hopkins or poets in English translation like Lorca or Pasternak.

There is a social and political context for this. Hartnett wasn't narrowly nationalistic, but he was certainly influenced by events in Northern Ireland and he reacted strongly to what he felt was the official belittlement of the Irish language. None of this, though, really explains his decision to abandon English. Many of his contemporaries would have shared his political views as well as his interest in the Gaelic heritage but none found it necessary to stop writing in English.

The real clue to Hartnett's 'rebel act' lies in the fact that he needed a book to express it; he had a highly literary, self-conscious and self-aware sensibility, and the decision was an expression of his aesthetic, an extension of the imaginative homeland his poems constructed. There was also the fact that he had already started to write in Irish, and no doubt felt that if he was to continue to do so successfully he had to embrace what was in fact an enabling identity as an Irish-language poet. His self-creation of himself as a poet in Irish is akin to his inhabiting of the skin of the Tao Te Ching or Lorca's *Gypsy Ballads*; his poetry is located in these shifts, in precisely the refusal of a single absolute linguistic or cultural identity. The theatrical announcement made the decision more absolute than it really was. The road that would take him to abandoning English is already implicit in the early poems, but like all aesthetic strategies it was provisional, equivocal, as the grammar of the title poem suggests, an indefinite rather than a definitive leavetaking. 'A Farewell to English' ends with the now well-known lines

> I have made my choice
> and leave with little weeping:
> I have come with meagre voice
> to court the language of my people.

This is less a forthright declaration of purpose than an acknowledgement of the task that lay before the poet – the meagreness of a resource that might take years to master, the act of courting rather than possession and the emphasis on 'my people'. One of the oddities of Hartnett's publishing history is that in the Gallery Press *Collected Poems* the announcement of the decision to court the language of his people is immediately followed by his return to English in 'Inchicore Haiku', whose last three sections echo the more dramatic conclusion of 'A Farewell to English':

> 85
> The empty pockets,
> old bills pounding on the door.
> Are these my people?

> 86
> All divided up,
> all taught to hate each other.
> Are these my people?

> 87
> My dead father shouts
> from his eternal Labour:
> 'These are your people!'   (*CP* 164–5)

What of the work in Irish produced in the interval between those two poems? No useful assessment of Hartnett can fail to take account of the work he produced mainly in the decade from 1975 to 1985. Once he had made the decision to write in Irish, Hartnett was freed from the rhetoric that attended his departure from English. The poems of *Adharca Broic* ('Badger's Horns', 1978)[5] set in the rural Co. Limerick where he was now living, enact his new beginning: poems of the natural world of badgers, otters, hares, of planting potatoes, dancing in the snow and 'praising a rook's nest', poems dedicated to his children at play in the country. It contains many fine poems, not least 'An Muince Dreoilíní' ('A Necklace of Wrens') with its memorable image of the wrens' gift of the craft of poetry, and the poems to his two children are among the best he wrote.

Yet it's a slightly anxious idyll. A poem for his wife Rosemary, not republished in *A Necklace of Wrens*, apologises for the lack of comfort and money, the time spent in the pub, though there's real energy too, wonderful achieved lyrics such as 'Domhan Fliuch', another poem not represented in the Gallery bilingual edition, with its brilliantly onomatopoeic rendering of a wet country Sunday:

> Láib, leac, linn is slaparnach
> slinn, screamh, scaird is siosarnach[6]
> [muck, flag, pond, splash, slate, scum, gush and hiss]

Even his own translations don't necessarily do justice to this work. In one of the best poems in the book, 'Fís Dheireanach Eoghain Rua Uí Shúilleabháin' (The Last Vision of Eoghan Rua Ó Shúilleabháin), the resonant 'mo spailpíní fánacha' becomes the flat and unevocative 'my fellow workers'. One of the real problems in assessing the full trajectory of Hartnett's career is that there is still no collected volume of his work in Irish. A Collected Irish Poems would greatly help to see him whole.

Hartnett wrote a number of long poems in Irish. The most substantial poem in *Adharca Broic* is the reimagining of 'The Retreat of Ita Cagney' as 'Cúlú Íde'. As Hartnett suggested, it is in fact a different poem from 'The Retreat of Ita Cagney' and to read them side by side in *The Necklace of Wrens* is somewhat disorientating as it is precisely the differences that are foregrounded. Taken on its own terms, 'Cúlú Íde' is powerful and successful and shows that Hartnett's shift into Irish had a real imaginative as well as linguistic basis.

The signs that the rural retreat was not proving entirely fruitful is most evident in the second long poem he produced: 'An Phurgóid' ('The Purge'), published in a later pamphlet, which addresses the poet's drought – 'For ages not one scrap of verse'. The truth is that Hartnett's commitment to Irish never really yielded the poetic achievement he wanted, and 'An Phurgóid' is an agonised interrogation after long silence of the worth of poetry brought on by his own self-isolation. The poem is a series of strictures, as if a poem might be made out sheer self-goading, but ultimately concluding that force of will and purgatorial endurance might not be enough.

Reading the poems of this period is to feel that the poet has become too much his own subject, too constrictedly self-aware; there's none of the free-spiritedness of, say, the Irish-language poets of the *Innti* generation. The last long poem Hartnett wrote in Irish, 'An Lia Nocht' ('The Naked Surgeon') is of a different order: a densely imagined poem which partly addresses the recent death of his father but also enacts a more abstract struggle between hope and despair. Deploying a richly symbolic language, it displays an ease and sureness in its rhythms and language that suggest the poet is beginning to settle into his chosen language, but, as often is the case with Hartnett, achievement is the precursor to change. His personal circumstances changed, and after his marriage ended he moved from rural Limerick to a working class quarter of Dublin, and it became clear to him that English had a greater claim on him than he thought:

> My English dam bursts
> and out stroll all my bastards.
> Irish shakes its head.   ('Inchicore Haiku', CP 149)

'Inchicore Haiku' is one of Hartnett's most attractive achievements. In one sense it's a return to the compressed urgency of the best of the early work but it's also characterised by a vein of chastened wit that's welcome after the relative solemnity of his Irish period.

> I push in a plug.
> Mozart comes into the room
> riding a cello.   (18, CP 151)

> From St Michael's Church
> the electric angelus –
> another job gone.   (25, CP 152)

If the poem marks an edgy comeback to English, it also does what Hartnett's poems consistently try to achieve: to locate a place, a community, a people to whom they can pledge themselves. As it happens, Hartnett had already broken his English fast during his time in Limerick to write a poem for a very specific community, the people of Newcastle West. Now published in *A Book of Strays* (Gallery, 2002) 'Maiden Street Ballad', initially written as a birthday present for his father, is a memorial to the poet's childhood street before its occupants were moved to a new housing estate. Its mischief, detail, comedy, satire and general flavour are all resolutely local – this is a poem that knows its audience. It also celebrates Hartnett's conviction that 'a poet's not a poet until the day he can write a few songs for his people'.[7] The responsibility is to instruct and amuse without leaving out the 'hunger, bad sanitation and child neglect' and being free to speak ill of the dead. The poem recalls street fights, games of pitch and toss, fleeing the wrath of the priest, and aligns itself cheerfully with a venerable ballad tradition – it is written to the tune of 'The Limerick Rake'. This and the other ballads, lampoons, satires and occasional poems add a further note to Hartnett's range and allowed him to savour the kind of direct local response not usually available to a poet, such as the headline on the front page of the *Limerick Echo and Shannon News* for 6 August 1993, referring to 'The Ballad of Salad Sunday': POET CAUSES MAYHEM WITH SALAD SAGA!

As well as chronicling the small incidents of town life, these poems provided outlets for political address ('Who Killed Bobby Sands') and a more personal confessionalism that sees him record his struggle with alcoholism or his love for his partner Angela Liston. Their fidelity to the local also links Hartnett again to his eighteenth-century Gaelic precursors.

After 'Inchicore Haiku', Hartnett continued to write and publish in English in the 1980s. Now that the complicating self-dramatisation has dimmed, we don't need to see a psychically divided Hartnett, but a poet who wrote in both languages, and also one who worked both traditions fruitfully. Nowhere is this more evident than in the interpretations of the work of three cranky, forceful, angry Gaelic poets at the end of the old order: Aodhagán Ó Rathaille, Dáibhí Ó Bruadair and Pádraigín Haicéad.[8] For all their hauteur and contempt for the uneducated commoners, these were kindred spirits for Hartnett, poets adrift in a world which had little time for them or their art:

> The once proud men of this land have swapped
> giving for gaming, culture for crap:
> no tunes on the pipes, no music on harps –
> we *ourselves* have buried the summer at last.[9]

With 'their immense dignity and immense bitterness',[10] they nonetheless clung to their own faith in poetry. Michael Hartnett's carefully crafted translations retain the slightly dogged and cantankerous tone of the originals, but the vigorous colloquial idiom he finds for them also superbly conveys their lucid energy. One of the most forceful, and most sadly resonant of these poems is the bleak yet defiant piece which closes,[11] 'On hearing that it was ordered by the Irish clergy that a brother may not compose Gaelic poetry'. His obeisance has all the humility of a punch in the jaw:

> I will sew up my lips with plaited cross-stitching
> and not speak of their niggardly pettiness,
> but I denounce this pack and their censoring
> and their hate, O God, for my fellow-countrymen.[12]

Hartnett's own imaginative terrain borders theirs. 'He would not have liked our Ireland', Hartnett wrote of Ó Bruadair, and likewise Hartnett himself lodged his poetry, in all the forms it took, in not being quite at home in the world.

Hartnett's final years saw more translation work – Catullus, Horace, Heine – as well the ambitious long poems, 'The Man who Wrote Yeats, the Man who Wrote Mozart', 'Sibelius in Silence' and 'He'll to the Moors', in the voice of Ramon Llull, the Mallorcan poet and visionary, but, interesting as these are, they don't have the compressed force of 'That Actor Kiss', about his dying father, or the best of the earlier work. For a poet so taken with translation, maybe it's fitting that one of his last poems should echo Salvatore Quasimodo's 'Ed è subito sera' ('And suddenly it's evening')

> I see the Morning Star
> through my childhood skylight
> and close my eyes and dream for fifty years,
> reliving every set-back, every high-light
>
> I open my eyes and there's the Evening Star.
> And suddenly it's twilight. (CP 242)

'Michael Hartnett's inspirations affected Irish poetry the way a power surge affects the grid: things quickened and shone when he published', Seamus Heaney wrote,[13] and his remark matched perfectly the quality in Michael Hartnett that is, more than any single achievement, a sense of the unmissable shadow cast by the poet's spirit on the landscape of Irish poetry in the twentieth century and which is, maybe, best caught in the famous conclusion to 'Death of an Irishwoman':

> She was a summer dance at the crossroads.
> She was a card game where a nose was broken.
> She was a song that nobody sings.
> She was a house ransacked by soldiers.
> She was a language seldom spoken.
> She was a child's purse, full of useless things. (CP 139)

NOTES

1. Quotations from the works of Michael Hartnett appear by kind permission of the Estate of Michael Hartnett and The Gallery Press, Loughcrew, Oldcastle, County Meath, Ireland.
2. In a memorial speech after the poet's death in 1999.
3. As described by Peter Fallon in the Afterword to *Translations*, Loughcrew: The Gallery Press, 2003, p. 126.
4. In an interview with Dennis O'Driscoll, *Poetry Ireland Review* no. 20, Autumn 1987, pp. 16–21.
5. A generous selection of Hartnett's Irish-language poems, along with his own translations, is collected in *The Necklace of Wrens*, Loughcrew: Gallery Press, 1987.
6. *Adharca Broic*, Loughcrew: Gallery Press, 1978, p. 21.

7. *A Book of Strays* (ed. Peter Fallon, Loughcrew: The Gallery Press, 2002), 'Maiden Street Ballad', first stanza.

8. Published in the individual Gallery volumes *O Bruadair* (1985), *Haicéad* (1993) and *O Rathaille* (1998).

9. *O Bruadair*, Loughcrew: Gallery Press, 1985, p. 26.

10. *O Bruadair*, p. 15.

11. Haicéad, Loughcrew: Gallery Press, 1993.

12. *Haicéad*, p. 87.

13. Introduction to John McDonagh and Stephen Newman, eds, *Remembering Michael Hartnett: A Language Seldom Spoken*, Dublin: Four Courts Press, 2006.

SELECTED FURTHER READING

Editions

Hartnett, Michael [Ó hAirtnéide, Micheál], *Adharca Broic*, Loughcrew: The Gallery Press, 1978.

A Necklace of Wrens: Selected Poems in Irish with English Translations by the Author, Loughcrew: The Gallery Press, 1987.

Collected Poems, ed. Peter Fallon, Loughcrew: The Gallery Press, 2001.

Michael Hartnett, A Book of Strays, ed. Peter Fallon, Loughcrew: The Gallery Press, 2002.

Michael Hartnett, Translations: A Selection, ed. Peter Fallon, Loughcrew: The Gallery Press 2003.

Ó hAirtnéide, Micheál, *An Phurgóid*, Baile Átha Cliath: Coiscéim, 1983.

Do Nuala, Foidhne Chuainn, Baile Átha Cliath: Coiscéim, 1984.

Haicéad, Loughcrew: The Gallery Press, 1993.

O Bruadair: Selected poems of Dáibhí O Bruadair, Loughcrew: The Gallery Press, 1985.

O Rathaille, Loughcrew: The Gallery Press, 1998.

Secondary Works

Hartnett, Niall, *Notes From His Contemporaries: A Tribute to Michael Hartnett*, self-published, 2009.

Lawlor, James, ed., *I Live in Michael Hartnett*, Limerick: Revival Press and Limerick County Arts Office, 2013.

McDonagh, John and Newman, Stephen, eds, *Remembering Michael Hartnett: A Language Seldom Spoken*, Dublin: Four Courts Press, 2006.

O'Driscoll, Dennis, 'Michael Hartnett' in *The Outnumbered Poet*, Loughcrew: The Gallery Press, 2013.

Walsh, Pat, *A Rebel Act: Michael Hartnett's Farewell to English*, Cork: Mercier Press, 2012.

23

MATTHEW CAMPBELL

Derek Mahon

It is a critical truism that Derek Mahon's poetry would be best served if the author left his poems alone. Publishing a succession of acclaimed single volume collections from the 1960s to the present day, Mahon made a convincing case for his reputation as a major poet. But as his career continued, he also proved to be an addicted collector and selector of his own work: the 1979 *Poems, 1962–1978* was followed by further selected editions in 1991, 2000 and 2006, a *Collected* in 1999, a *New Collected* in 2011 and a *New Selected* in 2016. All of these editions lifted the poems out of their individual collections, omitted dating and continued dropping whole stanzas, changing titles and swapping words in and out of striking lines with what can appear to be caprice, and sometimes even censorship.[1] The Mahon 'canon' is continuously buffeted by its author's restless, self-critical – some have said self-destructive[2] – eye. This chapter is not the place to think much about what is in and out of Mahon's canon, nor to yearn for a 'Complete Poems'. Neither will it spend much time on the justice of certain revisions (although in what follows I will refer to the first and last published titles of poems when relevant). But suffice to say here that Derek Mahon works in an international tradition of restlessly revisionary poets. The critic Hugh Haughton places him alongside Yeats and Coleridge, Marianne Moore and Auden, poets for whom, as Haughton says, 'vision and revision are intimately allied'.[3] To these we might add unlikely bedfellows Wordsworth and Whitman, where multiple versions of a single text can appear like multiple versions of the self; and fellow world-travellers, like Bowen and Beckett, who lived in and out of class and nationality and language.

For the reader new to Mahon, to approach the text of the poems with confidence in stable 'intentions' is one challenge, but approaching the author with stable intentions vis-à-vis word and world is maybe greater. For any poet writing primarily in English in the style of late modernism – that is, a poet writing after Eliot or Beckett or Rachel Carson or Elvis – the connection between the authenticities of the poet's attachment to the right word in a consumerist, pop-cultural, bomb-haunted, globally warming world, can be in a relation of seeming continuous crisis with what Mahon has memorably called the poet's 'eddy of semantic scruple / In an unstructurable sea'.[4] The desire of some readers for what Peter Denman calls the 'fixed and steady state in the text'[5] seems small matter for all that the writing of the poet so minutely adjusts and readjusts itself to its structure and forms, as well as a teleology (where are we going?) born so uncertainly out of its inheritance (where have we been?).

Mahon has been frequently drawn into bursts of autobiography, and many short memoirs have been collected from his extensive journalism and poems about his 'home' place, the place of his birth and youth, the environs of the city of Belfast. More unusually among his living contemporaries, Mahon has been the subject of an extensive 'authorised' biography by Stephen Enniss, *After the Titanic*.[6] The picture Enniss gives is of an author living the difficult life of the unsettled professional writer, living as much by necessity and accident as by choice in the many places which are remembered with varying degrees of unhappiness in his poetry. These are not just the Irish locations of Glengormley, Belfast or Portrush, but London, Paris, New York. 'Death in Bangor' / 'Bangor Requiem' (Section XVIII of the 1997 *Yellow Book / Decadence*) returns from the burial of the poet's mother in the quintessential Mahonian suburban resort town, and ends with an irony improvised around a favourite piece of Ulster graffiti: 'We shall never forsake the blue skies of our Ulster for the grey skies of an Irish Republic.' *The Yellow Book* settles in – and settles for – what has been Mahon's location for the last twenty or so years, 'the blue skies of the Republic',[7] in Kinsale in County Cork.

*

Along with Seamus Heaney, Michael Longley and James Simmons, Mahon first attracted British and then wider international attention as one of the 'Belfast poets', writers whose keynote semantic scruple was forged in an extraordinary set of volumes published from late '60s and early '70s Northern Ireland. Mahon was born into a Protestant family in 1941, and educated at the Royal Belfast Academical Institute and Trinity College Dublin. He read French, and the influence of French literature from the modern and classical periods is strong in his work: along with versions of Valéry and Jaccottet he has published translations of Racine and Rostand, and one of his last published poems is called 'Montaigne', a monologue spoken in the great sceptic's voice. His relation to his home city is ambivalent. Unlike Heaney or his fellow Trinity-educated Belfast-domiciled contemporary, Longley, Mahon was never a member of Philip Hobsbaum's celebrated writing workshop at Queen's University in the 1960s, the 'Belfast Group'. His friendships with those writers could be played out in his writing with some edge: when Longley published a poem dedicated to Mahon in 1971 in the London *New Statesman*, and referred to 'the Catholics we scarcely loved', calling their friendship that of 'Two poetic conservatives', Mahon was to object in the next issue of the magazine.[8]

Initially at least, this looked like a coterie of poets, and if Mahon would very quickly seek to escape such close company, there were shared aesthetic concerns which have proved a powerful example for ensuing Irish poetic generations. Key features were a continued preoccupation with technique, syntactic clarity, *le mot juste*, formal precision. By the latter, we might mean poems which count regular syllables and rhyme, in which sound and the sentence occupy stanzas of the same length, and the syntax seeks clarity of expression adjusted to the difficulties of thought, image and symbol. If Mahon is not a writer of sonnets, like Longley or Heaney or their follower Paul Muldoon, he is not afraid to take on the big stanza, and, like Muldoon, that involves trying out the models offered by Yeats and Auden – in what Muldoon has called the 'stadium stanza' – which address difficult contemporary subject-matter that is seemingly inimical to the idea of structure itself.

An early success is the 1965 'In Carrowdore Churchyard' / 'Carrowdore', victor in a mythical contest between Mahon, Longley and Heaney to compose a poem after a day trip to the grave of Louis MacNeice.[9] At the end of the poem, the sentence is run over the end of a stanza, to clinch a conclusion which must accommodate an ethic of ambiguity in the post-war British poem: irony, reconstruction and hope as much as faith in a continuity of the forms of culture.

> This, you implied, is how we ought to live –
> The ironical, loving crush of roses against snow,
> Each fragile, solving ambiguity. So,
> From the pneumonia of the ditch, from the ague
> Of the blind poet and the bombed-out town you bring
> The all-clear to the empty holes of spring,
> Rinsing the choked mud, keeping the colours new. (*NCP* 19)

Mahon was twenty-four when he published this poem of aftermath and the new in a little pamphlet of Queen's University Festival poems in 1965,[10] but the technique was entirely in place. The six-line stanzas of the rest of the poem have allowed rhymes which are now and again startling, flashy even: 'lie / peninsula', 'reverend trees' / 'Euripides', 'human perspective' / 'ought to live'. Those rhymes are posed in the ironic medium of their exemplar MacNeice, between clarity of syntax and ambiguity of import, where rhyme is both inevitable and random, rare and commonplace, as here: 'ague' / 'new'. Between the rhyme words Mahon pushes at the limits of both ethics and meaning. Semantically, 'how we ought to live' lands not just in the great apologia for not needing to make immediate sense in art that is Empsonian 'ambiguity', but further, in *solving* ambiguity'. It is paradox absolved from the accusation of the arbitrary, or worse, the formalist, even if the sound of the words is allowed to fuel their sense. The precision of elocution required in the play of consonant and vowel in the word 'ambiguity' is picked up again in the archaic, 'ague / Of the blind Poet' (an ague is a fever; for the blind poet, Haughton suggests Homer and Raftery, and Milton after the Commonwealth must be in the mix[11]). The word 'ague' is allowed a slow delayed rhyme after four lines, with the word 'new', which is both the Spring of the poem's setting and the potentialities of the example of MacNeice's writing for this poet – for these poets.

The rinsing mud and empty holes also suggest the twentieth-century battlefield. As they moved from their twenties into their thirties, these poets were faced with the political and humanitarian crisis of the Northern Irish Troubles. Poetry might seem like a mere detail beside political violence, but that brought with it the requirement that the poets not only be heard, but that they should have something to say. This was a moment coincident with campaigns for civil rights across many parts of the world in the 1960s, and, as in a number of those places (the Southern states of the United States, Algeria, South Africa), the executive (in this case the Northern Irish and then the British government) lost control. The situation was more than just a matter of revolution in the air: in Northern Ireland, the result was prolonged campaigns of bombing, assassination and sectarian murder, matched by frequently ruthless counter-reaction by the forces of law and order. It seemed a longer history was to blame, and the artists – among them the lyric poets – were expected to offer a digestible version of that historical blame. The Dublin poet Thomas Kinsella termed this recourse to the view of the Belfast poets as 'largely a journalistic entity'. His *Butcher's Dozen*, a poem about the 1972 Bloody Sunday shootings (and subsequent botched inquiry) by the British, adopted not lyric but Swiftian satire.[12] The varying responses of the 'Ulster' writers adopted other tonal resources, pitched in a key which weighed semantic scruples against the unstructurable sea of political impasse.

Mahon in particular revolted against his own suburban Protestant background, against a political and sectarian inheritance which seemed to be dragged back to the colonial origins of the violence between 'two communities'. The typical Mahon poem of this period will pit a refined aestheticism against uncontrollable hatred or manage exquisitely poised irony against the consolations offered by historical or scientific inquiry – the anthropologist, the journalist, the painter, or indeed the poet. Poems such as 'The Early Anthropologists', 'The Archaeologist' / 'A Stone Age Figure Far Below', 'What Will Remain' / 'The Golden Bough', 'Lives', 'Last of the Fire Kings', 'The Banished Gods', 'A Disused Shed in Co. Wexford' – look back to Eliot's appropriation of Weston and Fraser in *The Waste Land*. But the poems are also inevitably engaged in dialogue with those by John Montague and Seamus Heaney, immersed as they were in these years in the possibilities of symbolic redress for violence. Both were drawn to the long archaeological histories of Celticism, and in Heaney's case the bog people discovered by P. V. Glob in Denmark. They also gathered together the forms of Gaelic lament and the long, still-bloody aftermath of English colonisation.

Not for Mahon the paralleling of allegory or symbol or seeking for comparison in the manner of his friend Heaney. When Mahon's poetry offers 'civilisation' by invoking the Golden Age of Netherlands art or the haiku of Japanese poetry, it also offers inexplicably violent wars of conquest and ethnic cleansing, the sublime documents of 'barbarism' writ large alongside the exquisite and the small-scale. As Mahon said in a searching and always-illuminating interview with fellow poet Eamonn Grennan carried out in 1991, as he looked back to his writing of the 1970s:

> I've never been able to write directly about it [the Troubles]. In *Crane Bag* they'd call it 'colonial aphasia.' Perhaps, in fact, that's what it is. I was not prepared for what happened. What happened was that myself and all of our generation (particularly in the North) were presented with a horror, something that demanded our serious, grown-up attention. But, as I say, I was not able to deal with it directly.[13]

(*The Crane Bag* was a journal which initiated the Irish cultural criticism of the 1970s and '80s carried on by the *Field Day* project, seeking for an Irish understanding of the broader patterns of global cultural studies and post-colonialism from which Mahon's sense of indirectness could only demur.)

'The Snow Party' (1975) and 'Courtyards in Delft' (1981) point to the unknowing and unknowable where a poet like Heaney is compelled to seek understanding, no matter how uncomfortable that understanding might be. Where in the poem 'Punishment' (1975), Heaney allowed himself the socially and culturally specific, and said that 'I . . . understand the exact / and tribal intimate revenge',[14] it was an honest, if risky, adoption of the understanding of the perpetrator. Whether or not Mahon's poetry demonstrates 'colonial aphasia', he repudiates such intimacy and simply holds up 'elsewhere' and 'meanwhile'. By that I mean his procedure is not to flinch from atrocity, imperialism or holy wars, but to offer them as concurrence or coincidence, ever wary of the certainties of historical knowing. As regards the formulae of historical causality, '*That* happened because of *this*', for Mahon 'that' and 'this' can typically be just two things going on at the same time, neither offering understanding of each other, often at a long temporal or geographical remove, phrased as conditional and not necessary: 'Even now there are places a thought might grow' ('A Disused Shed in Co. Wexford'); 'We might be anywhere but are in one place only' ('A Garage in Co. Cork', 1999 revision); 'It might be anywhere, that ivory tower' ('A Lighthouse in Maine', as rewritten in 2006); 'A long time since the last scream cut short ... Bombs doze in the housing estates / But here they are through with history' ('Rathlin'); 'Elsewhere, they are burning / witches and heretics / in the boiling squares' ('The Snow Party');

> Era-provincial self-regard
> Finds us, as ever, unprepared
> For the odd shifts in emphasis
> Time regularly throws up to us.
>
> Here, as elsewhere, I recognise
> A wood invisible for its trees
> ('The Globe in North Carolina', 1982 version[15])

Of the rain in 'Derry Morning' / 'Derry' (1981), a 'boom town' (Mahon's ghastly pun) for the 'drizzling screen' of 1970s television news, Mahon writes:

> What of the change envisioned here
> the quantum leap from fear to fire?
> Smoke from a thousand chimneys strains
> one way beneath the returning rains
> that shroud the bomb-sites, while the fog
> of time receives the ideologue.   (*NCP* 99)

This poem was included in Declan Kiberd's collection of contemporary Irish poetry in the 1991 *Field Day Anthology of Irish Writing*. For Kiberd, Mahon holds 'the Northern violence at a chaste remove, or at least sets it against a wider pattern of universal history'.[16] Neither universal history nor pattern is Mahon's concern here. Such epistemological chastity as these lines show, is focussed on the meaning of the word 'change', the fire which has patently not given deliverance from fear, regardless of the irony of the assonance achieved by the mere swapping in and out of vowels, fear to fire.

What follows is the forgetting of atrocity, or rather the forgetting of exactly why it *might* have happened, the slinking away of ideology into something that is not called history (nor colonial aphasia) but has shown itself in Derry as 'the fog of time'. In 'Courtyards in Delft', published in the same year as 'Derry Morning', the elsewhere is global, even if the history resists universality. Sixteenth-century Holland and Cromwellian and then Williamite Ireland and South Africa are placed in the same poem, but the inevitability of the colour orange (William of Orange, The Orange Order, the Orange Free State) is never explicitly offered as point of contact. The speaker is lying low, and others are making history:

> I must be lying low in a room there,
> A strange child with a taste for verse,
> While my hard-nosed companions dream of war
> On parched veldt and fields of rainswept gorse.[17]

A major revision – or rather excision – is contentious, but justified: a subsequent and final stanza was printed by Kiberd but had appeared only in the 1982 Gallery Press *Hunt by Night* collection. It remembers Johann Vermeer's picture *The Art of Painting*, and offers a rare explanation (thus subsequently retracted) of art and its relation to holy war and a Christian theocracy here caught in the act of mapping its Empire.

> For the pale light of that provincial town
> Will spread itself, like ink or oil,
> Over the not yet accurate linen
> Map of the world which occupies one wall
> And punish nature in the name of God.[18]

'Even now', 'might be anywhere', 'But here', 'Elsewhere', 'Here, as elsewhere', 'While': these places, events, aesthetics, are 'civilisations' in minimal epistemological contact with what is going on 'elsewhere' – history, war, Empire. Grasping at one offers little elucidation of the other. Agreement would not offer radical consolation, or even the consolation of radicalism.

In the circumstances in which these poems were written, such thinking would be reductive, too simple. Seamus Deane has said of Mahon's 'companionship' with Montague, Heaney and Kinsella, that 'The subject of the meditation is the relationship between civility and barbarity, the thin partitions which divide them, the deep bonds which conjoin them.' But Mahon's poems of this period describe a process in which their author seeks division from that division, to be free of the rhetoric as much as the actuality of conceptual equivalence. Deane is not entirely praising Mahon when he goes on to say, 'His only loyalty is to the abandoned, the community which poses no threat to independence but which indeed liberates it'.[19] Elsewhere, in a provocative *Field Day* essay called 'Civilians and Barbarians', Deane has said that 'Political languages fade more slowly than literary languages', with which Mahon might agree. It is moot whether Mahon could go on to agree with Deane that the eventual fading of political languages heralds 'a deep structural alteration in the attitudes which sustain a crisis'.[20] For Mahon, the fading of the distinction between barbarian and civilian following on from the crisis in which he and Deane were writing in 1985 seemed a long way off. In the Grennan interview, Mahon assents to Shelley's formulation that, '"The great instrument of moral good is the imagination ... Poetry contributes to the effect by acting upon the cause."' He goes on to say,

> It's my observation that not just poetry, but art in any shape or form can tutor the imagination – the imagination can feed and strengthen itself on art, on poetry, in such a way that the sum of goodness and wisdom in the world is infinitesimally increased.[21]

Such official positions, perhaps the positions of hindsight (the end of art is peace?), are at a slight remove from the actualities of the control of concept, irony, tone and pitch in these poems facing the unstructurable, seeking not just 'loyalty to the abandoned' but the sympathy of the outcast, sympathy with those beyond the sympathies of the human and natural worlds. The fate of 'the lost people', from 'Treblinka and Pompeii' in Mahon's masterpiece first published in 1973, 'A Disused Shed in Co. Wexford', is that of the undifferentiated anonymous victims of human atrocity and geographical disaster. But this is writing at the verge of a possible humanism – humans, after all, created Treblinka, and not Vesuvius. One of Mahon's speakers in 'The Last of the Fire Kings' puts it this way, in what is as close as we can get to a statement of the Mahonesque:

> Either way, I am
> through with history –
> who lives by the sword
>
> dies by the sword.
> Last of the fire kings, I shall
> break with tradition and
>
> die by own hand
> rather than perpetuate
> the barbarous cycle.   (NCP 63)

If the fire king abdicates, will the barbarous cycle cease? The last line of 'A Disused Shed' allows the dumb victims of history to speak only as an unanswered plea to their enlightened visitors (the archaeologist, the cartographer, the tourist), 'let not our naïve labours have been in vain!' (NCP 82).

In a strong re-reading of 'A Disused Shed' in 2015, given a forty-year interpretative history of what has become a most unMahonian thing, a 'classic', Eric Falci excavates the historical moment in which this and other poems by Longley and Heaney were written. He returns to a recurrent criticism of Mahon, his 'deep scepticism about the poet's public role', an attempt 'to locate a place for poetry apart from the urgencies of history'. Falci seeks an allegorical reading of 'A Disused Shed', and when he finds that allegory won't work, he suggests that the poetry might then be 'unreadable as such'.[22] It is not clear whether this is a good thing, but the sense that Mahon is not-Heaney or not-Deane is strong here. Edna Longley, college contemporary of Mahon's, as well as prime advocate of the idea of a coterie of Northern poets, has long sought to present the delicacy of the way Mahon handles ideology as his prime political virtue. As Mahon himself wrote, early in these debates, in 1970, 'A good poem is a paradigm of good politics'.[23] This has been taken as credo (if he could be said to have such a thing) and used as ethical and poetic example by at least two generations of Irish poetic followers, from Belfast and Dublin: Muldoon, Ciaran Carson, and a later generation, Alan Gillis, Leontia Flynn, David Wheatley, Conor O'Callaghan and Justin Quinn. For Longley, the good of Mahon's poetry gives voice to, and provides a shelter for, the lost in history: 'Mahon does more than "translate a defeated community into the narrative of history", or even a "lost people" into symbolic salvation. (The resonance of Mahon's "lost" stretches from bewildered, to damned, to doomed.) He receives a defenceless spirit into the protectorate of poetry.'[24] These are high claims indeed, for poet and for poetry.

*

Such debates about Mahon's achievement and importance do tend to stay in the heated surroundings of 1960s to 1980s Ireland. But of course there are thirty or more years of writing. That career is by turns exilic and settled, traversing the urban world and contemplating an ongoing ecologic disaster in a tone not that removed from the one honed in contemplation of the Irish and global human disaster of the mid to late twentieth century. I say 'exilic' – that is, Mahon's later writing is as much about exile and its potential as it is about actually undergoing that state. That could include a sense of internal exile: the experience as Writer in Residence at the then University of Coleraine appears to have been deeply unhappy. A 1979 essay describes his time there as in the 'Coleraine Triangle', another ghastly Mahon joke, as if invoking the Bermuda Triangle, into which ships and planes disappear forever. The essay ends wishfully imagining the complete depopulation of the area.[25]

'Ovid in Tomis', the place of Ovid's internal exile, dates from this period, and the Ovidian has been a consistent mode in Northern Irish poetry.[26] As early as 1975, in 'Exposure', Heaney had invoked the *Tristia* of Ovid and described himself as an 'inner émigré'.[27] Mahon's version provoked, and was provoked by, a crisis – both personal and in his writing. The refusal to make easy or simplifying connections, as discussed earlier, brings with it the terror of artistic disconnectedness:

> The Muse is somewhere
> Else, not here
> By this frozen lake –
>
> Or, if here, then I am
> Not poet enough
> To make the connection.   (NCP 144)

Hugh Haughton says of this poem that it ultimately 'voices Mahon's redemptive pantheistic poetry of inanimate things, though with a certain desperation'.[28] In its way, this recourse to the inanimate is the counter to reading Mahon as a sceptic in epistemology or a stoic in ethics. For certain readers, aligning Vesuvius with the Holocaust, as he does by setting Treblinka and Pompeii alongside each other, looks like it obviates responsibility in the human, equalling the two events, while never allowing himself 'To make the connection'. But Mahon's 'Earth' has become a source of belief, a stay against the cynicism or even nihilism to which, in certain moods of despair, his poetry can seem tempted. In an interview of this period, in 1981, Mahon said,

> I think there is a sense in which the human race flatters itself, takes too much for granted its own status as the articulate centre of the universe. But I don't think the inanimate world has had its due ... I don't think I have a consciousness of things over and above, beside and below human life. I am deprived of belief in God, if deprivation it is, by my own rationalistic habits of mind, my own education, and yet there is ... I make room for the numinous, for the unexplained.[29]

Both Haughton and Bruce Stewart have invoked the idea of 'secular mysticism' that Mahon attributes to the poetry of Phillipe Jaccottet, which he translated in 1986. For Stewart, this is a counterweight or necessary anatomical companion to Mahon's much-vaunted 'scepticism': 'a *systole* requiring the *diastole* of visionary thought'.[30]

In Mahon's writing after the 1980s, making room for the numinous required a loosening of style, in some ways a repudiation of the finely controlled stanza, just as it required a repudiation of a certain formalism.

Mahon has turned to long sequences of loosely rhyming verse letters, and then to ecology, in a poetry involved in what the English geographer of western Irish natural and human spaces Tim Robinson has called 'geophany ... the showing forth of the earth'.[31] To take the verse letters first, two long sequences were published in the 1990s: *The Hudson Letter* (retitled in 2011 as *New York Time*) and *The Yellow Book* (later *Decadence*). These sequences have had their detractors, most notably the Irish poet and critic Peter McDonald, who found them at best 'millennium-gabble' and at worst playing to the cynicism of 'educated circles in the Irish Republic'.[32] Indeed, with the loosening of the line it appeared there was a loosening of control of the tone, appearing to reach a point where leaving places like Coleraine or Bangor behind is betrayed by the writer into a facile cosmopolitanism. At a remove from millennium gabble, it is now apparent that these sequences are part-memoir, part-reaction to the quotidian, part-reading diary, part-creative translation. At times it seems that these sequences are in whole a sort of therapeutic process, an addict's journal, a self in process relocating to the world, now and again succeeding, now and again failing. Take, for instance, the ending of the tenth section of *The Yellow Book* / *Decadence*, a poem which is based on Juvenal's tenth satire, the title of which is commonly translated as 'The Vanity of Human Wishes'. Here Mahon pulls no punches, calling it 'The Idiocy of Human Aspiration'. The poem ends,

> Ask for a sound mind in a sound body
> unfrightened of the grave and not demented
> by grief at natural declension; study
> acceptance in the face of fate; and if
> you want to worship mere materialism,
> that modern god we have ourselves invented,
> I leave you to the delights of modern life.

There is a fine line between satire and sarcasm.

Both sequences end in a call to be reprieved of their exile, and it is a Mahonian version of the quotidian which has effected that reprieve – at least for the disintegrating, degenerate self of the letter-writing and the ecological lyricist who has regenerated that self in subsequent collections. *The Hudson Letter* ends with the cry of the homeless, of other defenceless spirits seeking admission to the protectorate of poetry: 'We have been too long in the cold – Take us in; take us in!' 'Christmas in Kinsale', at the end of *The Yellow Book* / *Decadence* sequence, closes with the slightly more ambiguous cry of a dream to retire to 'the white islands' of Tír na nÓg or Hy Brasil: '"Come on; come on!" ... ' Inexplicably omitted from the 2016 *New Selected Poems*, 'Christmas in Kinsale' demonstrates that the virtuoso technique of Mahon had not been lost in the dark days of alcoholic exile or extinguished at its own self-conscious *fin de siècle*, no matter how it can be turned on the utterly unpoetic:

> Holed up here in the cold gardens of the west
> I take out at mid-morning my Christmas rubbish.
> Sphere-music, the morning stars consort together
> in a fine blaze of anticyclone weather
> hallowing the calm inner and the rough outer harbour,
> the silence of frost and crow on telephone lines,
> the wet and dry, the garbage and the trash,
> remains of rib and chop, warm cinders, ash,
> bags, boxes, bulbs and batteries, bathroom waste,
> carcases, tinfoil, leaves, crumbs, scraps and bones –
> if this were summer there would be clouds of flies
> buzzing for joy around the rubbish bins.   (NCP 228)

The long view of the beauties of an unseasonably fine Christmas morning, with its remembrance in poetry and song, and the stars, sky and harbour coming together into the picturesque, gives way to the close view of the detritus of the human, the remains of dead animals, the joy of flies in waste. The passage might appear to decline into a bare list, but it is in its way a sort of recycling of the quotidian and its obverse – waste, a happy business if you are a summer fly.

It might be thought that this is a sort of end of poetry at end of century: as Mahon asks in this poem, 'Does history exhausted come full cycle?' Haughton shows that the poem goes on to allude to birds in both Eliot and Yeats, poetry from the beginning of a century which is now in its 'post-historical phase'.[33] Subsequent volumes have brought together the waste of human cultures into their animal and inanimate environment, continuing to make room for the numinous and the unexplained. Many of these poems have tended to stay at the seaside, in versions inspired by or translating Homer and Valéry and Coleridge (in the magnificently controlled stanzaic poems 'Calypso', 'The Seaside Cemetery' and 'Biographia Literaria'). The long Kinsale poem 'Dreams of a Summer Night' replays Coleridge's 'Frost at Midnight' as a post-Celtic-Tiger conversation poem, accepting 'the lives we live' in a sort of quietistic farewell to poetry. These later poems also continue to seek companion figures from the past who are perhaps a little more forgiving of humanity than Juvenal: late poems include monologues spoken by Palinurus and Montaigne. 'Montaigne' is part-homage to the unfulfilled literary life of Cyril Connolly,[34] and part-elegy for Seamus Heaney. Alluding to 'Known World' a poem published by Heaney in 2011, in which Heaney had acknowledged his failure to read allegory, Mahon pictures himself as Montaigne, both sceptic and mystic: 'unknowing to the last, in the known world'.[35] It is a typical poised conclusion, if not quite a solving ambiguity, yet still eventually drawn back to everything that makes up – to quote from the title of his most recent Gallery collection – *Life on Earth*.

NOTES

1. The phrase 'middle class cunts' in the poem 'Afterlives' has found itself revised to 'middle-class shits', 'twits' and then 'shits' again during its publishing history.
2. See, e.g., Neil Corcoran, *Poets of Modern Ireland* (Carbondale: Southern Illinois University Press, 1999), p. 207: 'I myself find [Mahon's revisions] deeply irritating and usually disadvantageous.'
3. Hugh Haughton, *The Poetry of Derek Mahon* (Oxford: Oxford University Press, 2007). p. 126.
4. Derek Mahon, 'Rage for Order' in *New Collected Poems* (Oldcastle: Gallery, 2011), p. 47. This is currently the authorised edition. I will state when I am quoting from an edition other than this one.
5. Peter Denman, 'Know the One? Insolent Ontology and Mahon's Revisions', *Irish University Review* 24.1 (1994), pp. 27–37.
6. Stephen Enniss, *After the Titanic: A Life of Derek Mahon* (Dublin: Gill and Macmillan, 2014). The biography was written with the co-operation of Mahon, but as the book makes clear, that co-operation was subsequently withdrawn.
7. See 'The Coleraine Triangle', in Derek Mahon, *Journalism*, ed. Terence Brown (Oldcastle: Gallery, 1996), p. 218. Authorship of the sentiment has long been attributed to Ian Paisley.
8. Letter to the *New Statesman*, 1971, quoted in Heather Clark, *The Ulster Literary Renaissance, 1962–1972* (Oxford: Oxford University Press, 2006), pp. 183–8. The poem was called 'To Derek Mahon'. See Michael Longley, *Collected Poems* (London: Cape, 2006), pp. 53–61. Despite Mahon's requests, as detailed by Clark, the poem has not been revised.
9. Enniss, *After the Titanic*, pp. 60–1.
10. Derek Mahon, *Twelve Poems* (Belfast: Festival Publications, 1965).
11. Haughton, *The Poetry of Derek Mahon*, p. 39.
12. See Thomas Kinsella, ed., *The New Oxford Book of Irish Verse* (Oxford: Oxford University Press, 1973), p. xxx. And 'Butcher's Dozen', in *Collected Poems* (Manchester: Carcanet, 2001).
13. Eamonn Grennan, 'Derek Mahon, The Art of Poetry No. 82', *Paris Review*, 154 (Spring, 2000). www.theparisreview.org/interviews/732/the-art-of-poetry-no-82-derek-mahon.
14. Seamus Heaney, *North* (London: Faber, 1975), p. 38.
15. Derek Mahon, *The Hunt By Night* (Oxford: Oxford University Press, 1982), p. 62.
16. *The Field Day Anthology of Irish Literature*, ed. Seamus Deane et al. (Derry: Field Day, 1991), vol III, p. 1315.
17. Mahon, *The Hunt by Night*, p. 10.
18. Ibid.

19. Seamus Deane, *Celtic Revivals* (London: Faber, 1985), pp. 161&162.
20. Seamus Deane, 'Civilians and Barbarians' in *Ireland's Field Day* (London: Hutchinson, 1985), p. 42.
21. Grennan, 'Derek Mahon'.
22. Eric Falci, *The Cambridge Introduction to British Poetry, 1945–2010* (Cambridge: Cambridge University Press, 2015), p. 141.
23. Derek Mahon, 'Poetry in Northern Ireland', *Twentieth Century Studies*, 4 (Nov. 1970).
24. Edna Longley, *Poetry in the Wars* (Newcastle: Bloodaxe, 1986), p. 206.
25. See note 7.
26. See John Kerrigan, 'Ulster Ovids', in *The Chosen Ground: Essays on the Contemporary Poetry of Northern Ireland*, ed. Neil Corcoran (Bridgend: Seren, 1992), pp. 237–69.
27. Heaney, *North*, p. 73.
28. Haughton, The Poetry of Derek Mahon, p. 172.
29. Derek Mahon and Willie Kelly, 'Each Poem for me is a New Beginning', *The Cork Review*, vol. 2, No. 3 (June 1981), pp. 10–12; p. 11.
30. Bruce Stewart, '"Solving Ambiguity": The Secular Mysticism of Derek Mahon', in Elmer Kennedy-Andrews, ed. *The Poetry of Derek Mahon* (Gerrards Cross: Colin Smythe, 2002), p. 66.
31. Tim Robinson, 'Listening to the Landscape', in *Setting Foot on the Shores of Connemara* (Dublin: Lilliput, 2007), p. 164.
32. Peter MacDonald, 'Incurable Ache', *Poetry Ireland Review*, 56 (1998): 117–19.
33. Haughton, The Poetry of Derek Mahon, p. 311.
34. See the essay 'Montaigne Redivivus', in *Red Sails* (Oldcastle, Gallery, 2014), pp. 58–64.
35. Derek Mahon, *New Selected Poems* (Oldcastle: Gallery, 2016), p. 116; Seamus Heaney, 'Known World' in *Electric Light* (London: Faber, 2001), pp. 19–23.

SELECTED FURTHER READING

Clark, Heather, *The Ulster Literary Renaissance, 1962–1972* (Oxford: Oxford University Press, 2006).

Corcoran, Neil, ed. *The Chosen Ground: Essays on the Contemporary Poetry of Northern Ireland*, ed. Neil Corcoran (Bridgend: Seren, 1992).

Poets of Modern Ireland (Carbondale: Southern Illinois University Press, 1999).

Deane, Seamus, *Celtic* Revivals (London: Faber, 1985).

'Civilians and Barbarians' in *Ireland's Field Day* (London: Hutchinson, 1985).

Denman, Peter, 'Know the One? Insolent Ontology and Mahon's Revisions', *Irish University Review* 24.1 (1994).

Enniss, Stephen, *After the Titanic: A Life of Derek Mahon* (Dublin: Gill and Macmillan, 2014).

Falci, Eric, *The Cambridge Introduction to British Poetry, 1945–2010* (Cambridge: Cambridge University Press, 2015).

Deane, Seamus, et al., eds. *The Field Day Anthology of Irish Literature*, 3 vols. (Derry: Field Day, 1991).

Grennan, Eamonn, 'Derek Mahon, The Art of Poetry No. 82', *Paris Review*, 154 (Spring, 2000).

Haughton, Hugh, *The Poetry of Derek Mahon* (Oxford: Oxford University Press, 2007)

Irish University Review 24.1 (1994) – Derek Mahon Special Issue.

Kennedy-Andrews, Elmer, ed. *The Poetry of Derek Mahon* (Gerrards Cross: Colin Smythe, 2002).

Kinsella, Thomas, ed., *The New Oxford Book of Irish Verse* (Oxford: Oxford University Press, 1973).

Longley, Edna, *Poetry in the Wars* (Newcastle: Bloodaxe, 1986).

MacDonald, Peter, 'Incurable Ache', *Poetry Ireland Review*, 56 (1998), pp. 117–19.

Mahon, Derek and Willie Kelly, 'Each Poem for me is a New Beginning', *The Cork Review*, vol. 2, No. 3 (June 1981), pp. 10–12.

The Hunt by Night (Oxford: Oxford University Press, 1982).

Journalism. ed. Terence Brown (Oldcastle: Gallery, 1996).

New Collected Poems (Oldcastle: Gallery, 2011).

New Selected Poems (Oldcastle: Gallery, 2016).

'Poetry in Northern Ireland', *Twentieth Century Studies*, 4 (Nov. 1970).

Red Sails (Oldcastle, Gallery, 2014).

Twelve Poems (Belfast: Festival Publications, 1965).

Robinson, Tim, 'Listening to the Landscape', in *Setting Foot on the Shores of Connemara* (Dublin: Lilliput, 2007).

24

HUGH HAUGHTON

Eiléan Ní Chuilleanáin

I

In 'Acts and Monuments of an Unelected Nation: The Cailleach writes about the Renaissance', Eiléan Ní Chuilleanáin speaks of 'an awareness of foreignness as a sea we are always starting to climb ashore from, a version of the human condition that demands we keep on trying to cross over'. [1] Crossing over etymologically suggests 'translation', a central preoccupation of Ní Chuilleanáin as a poet and critic, and in appealing to that metaphor of 'a sea we are always starting to climb ashore from', she puts the foreign at the heart of the familiar. She makes us wonder how we can *always* be *starting* climbing, whether 'awareness' or 'foreignness' is the sea we are climbing from, and whether we are ever anywhere else than at sea. In Ní Chuilleanáin's formulation, we are clearly in a world of fluid boundaries, permanently situated between the familiar and strange, the native and the foreign. We are in Ireland with 'the Cailleach', but confronted with a founding sense of 'foreignness' in the 'human condition' more generally. This is akin to Kristeva's claim that 'the foreigner lives within us: he is the hidden face of our identity'. [2] It also confirms Nuala Ní Dhomhnaill's claim that recent Irish poetry by women represents 'a genuinely new phenomenon, nothing less than an attempt to create an alternative Logos which is inclusive of the Feminine at a fundamental level'. [3]

The title of Ní Chuilleanáin's historical essay alludes to Foxe's *Actes and Monuments*, a monument of Tudor Protestant martyrology dedicated to Elizabeth as 'defendour of the faith' which also provided the title of her first collection of poems. In representing herself as *cailleach*, Ní Chuilleanáin takes up a role deeply opposed to both English Reformation colonists and male Irish society, while in foregrounding 'an unelected nation' she suggests not only a nation opposed to Calvinist 'election' but the failures of representative government in Ireland under the Union and after Independence in regard to women. She writes that 'In the early modern period, languages keep their sharp edges, their strangeness to one another' and that if she 'wants the alien to go on keeping its distance' she has to keep her distance from 'that blurred entity known in my hemisphere as "Anglo-Irish literature"'. More drastically, she admits to having, 'like an ancient Irish hero, a geas, a taboo that will allow me to continue writing verse only if I do not get sucked into that particular academic black hole'. She also concedes that even 'the reading of history and early literature' risks making the past 'too domestically familiar'.[4]

Putting the weight on such words as 'edges', 'strangeness, 'alien' and 'distance', this compelling account of her taboo on 'Anglo-Irish literature' tells us a lot about her filiations and dis-affiliations as an Irish writer, attempting to by-pass what she calls 'the blurred entity' or 'academic black hole'. In affirming the necessity of 'distance', she resists seeing the past (even her own, even her own 'people's') as 'domestically familiar'. As John Kerrigan suggests, this critique of the 'Anglo-Irish' harks back to Daniel Corkery's classic polemic against the Irish Revival, *Synge and Anglo-Irish Literature: A Study* (1931) and celebration of Munster Irish-language poets *The Hidden Ireland* (1924).[5] In a 1993 interview, Ní Chuilleanáin restates her position in different terms when she contrasts herself with Seamus Heaney as a writer reaching out through essays and lectures to a 'wider audience', saying 'I don't give lectures because I don't want to become involved in the academic study of Anglo-Irish literature', which would give her 'a kind of psychological double-bind'.[6]

In aligning herself with the Cailleach, Ní Chuilleanáin identifies herself with the mythical image of 'An cailleach Bheara', the speaker of the anonymous ninth-century Irish poem associated with the Westernmost peninsular of her native Co. Cork. Translating it in *The Boys of Bluehill* (2015), she has the speaker adopt one of her signature dramatis personae, affirming 'I am the nun of Beare'. She also, however, records the way 'my body craves / Homing to where it is known' and invokes 'The wave at high tide, then / The tide falling again'.[7] Once more with the Cailleach we are on the fluid rhythmic boundary between sea and land, the known and unknown, the liminal bodily space occupied by much of her finest work.[8]

A similar image recurs at the close of the earlier 'Early Recollections', where she reflects that her education 'Left out the sight of death', says that 'I was born in the war but never noticed', notes that her aunt Nora's 'best china' has not 'changed or broken' and observes that 'I know how things begin to happen / But never expect an end' (*SP* 24). This still-life vignette about her childhood in a Cork parlour is an equivalent of Derek Mahon's 'Courtyards in Delft' or Seamus Heaney's 'Sunlight', where she ponders 'the habits of moss' and 'Rust softly biting the hinges' that keep 'the door always open'. In it she comments on her inability to write 'goodbye' on 'the torn final sheet', and enjoins its addressee (an unnamed 'Dearest') to reflect on 'Where I started', the place where 'I became aware of truth / Like the tide helplessly rising and falling in one place.' Again the poem leaves us on a moving temporal threshold, both a familiar domestic place and somewhere the tide is 'helplessly rising and falling' (as in estuarial Cork), giving us a sense not only of her beginnings, but of the unfinished past bearing down on the present.

Like so many of her poems, it offers a tight focus on 'one place' while retrospectively noticing things not noticed at the time. In a more recent autobiographical poem, 'Youth', she says 'I might go back to the place / where I was young' but 'all I have done combines to excavate / a channelled maze where I am escaping home'. Moving unnervingly between time and place, the lines implicitly project a compelling vision of her oeuvre as a 'maze' (*BoB* 34). If so, the phrase 'escaping home' simultaneously suggests 'escaping *from* home' and 'escaping *to* home', leaving both poet and reader on the cusp between the two opposed readings of a word that is a key but also contested term in contemporary Irish poetry.[9]

No contemporary poet has brought such a complex time-sense to the vision of place which shapes and is shaped by modern Irish poetry. Her claim to know how things begin to happen but not how they end might make us think about how her expansively condensed lyrics begin and end. 'An Information' begins 'I returned to that narrow street / where I used to stand and listen / to the chat from kitchen and parlour', before counting the years and questions she now can't ask, about keeping back 'your whole story' and finding out where a woman brought the bread and duck eggs. It ends by enjoining the addressee to drop 'whatever you were holding' and 'not look back to see whose hand / finds it, or where it is hidden again when found' (*BoB* 11). With its evocations of beginnings and endings, hidings and seekings, and its enigmatic sense of specific but unspecified people and places focused on a room, a door and river, the poem brings us close to the Cork of 'Early Recollections', again leaving us with a tantalising sense of open-endedness, of things still going on ('now I see her climbing towards me / up the long flight of steps that winds / beside the fever hospital'). Such poems have the attributes she ascribes to Seamus Heaney: 'they come from a mind which has waited for sediment to settle, different layers of experience to define themselves, a clarity to emerge on some subjects while others remain occult.'[10] This combination of 'clarity' and 'the occult' (or occluded) hints at the uncanny otherness that sustains Ní Chuilleanáin's poetry, again recalling Kristeva with her claim that after reading Freud's *Das Unheimliche* essay, our 'self' is 'a strange land of borders and othernesses ceaselessly constructed and deconstructed'.[11]

II

Born in Cork in 1942 and educated at University College Cork, Ní Chuilleanáin was brought up in a literary and Republican family, where Irish was spoken in the home. Her father was a Professor of Irish at UCC and her mother, Eilis Dillon, an influential children's writer whose books drew on Irish history, literature and folklore. Both parents left a legacy for the poet, whose work combines often arcane scholarship with an instinct for mythical or uncanny narrative. In 'On Lacking the Killer Instinct' (a phrase she said a critic once applied to her), she combines a narrative of her father's 'running from a lorry-load of soldiers' during the war of independence and a later memory of seeing a hare when her father was dying in hospital, while in 'Gloss/Clós/Glas' she portrays a 'scholar', apparently modelled on him, 'raking the dictionaries' and coming up against the limits of language. Such poems subliminally align her with her academic, nationalist, Irish-speaking father. Three of her aunts were nuns, however, and she says that in her twenties she found 'the figure of a nun would be standing quietly in the middle of a poem', or 'hermit' or 'other recollected female figure', and explains that this preoccupation with nuns, with their 'strangeness and familiarity', provides 'the first syllable of an explanation of the world I grew up in'.[12] As a result, one crucial aspect of her public role in a period of institutional crisis for the Church has been to record in searching ways the charged imaginative life – or afterlife – of Catholicism in Ireland, without the element of anti-clerical critique we find in Austin Clarke's 'Mnemosyne lay in Dust' or the 'spilled religion' Patrick Kavanagh portrays in 'The Great Hunger'. Ní Chuilleanáin published her first poem in 1966 and her first collection *Acts and Monuments* in 1972, the year of John Montague's *The Rough Field*, Derek Mahon's *Lives* and Seamus Heaney's *Wintering Out*. Her second collection, *Site of Ambush*, followed in 1975, the year of *North* and *The Snow Party*, and its title poem inscribed historical violence as arrestingly as theirs, taking its cue from local monuments to the War of Independence and Civil War. By this time she had completed a doctorate in English Renaissance literature at Oxford and joined the English Department at Trinity College Dublin. She had also launched *Cyphers*, the literary journal she would co-edit for the next 40 years, thus establishing herself in her dual roles as a distinguished Renaissance scholar and a poet running a challenging 'little magazine' of new writing.

Since her launch on the Irish poetry scene, Ní Chuilleanáin has produced eight collections with Irish publishers and a *Selected Poems* (2009) with Faber. After *The Second Voyage* (1977) and *The Rose-Geranium* (1981), her work acquired a new depth and range with *The Magdalene Sermon*

(1989) and *The Brazen Serpent* (1994), before entering a period of technical experiment and emotional resonance with *The Girl Who Married a Reindeer* (2001), *The Sun-Fish* (2009) and *The Boys of Bluehill* (2015). Taken together, this is a body of work comparable in range and intellectual force to that of Northern contemporaries such as Heaney, Longley and Mahon, and in historical and lyric resonance to Eavan Boland and Thomas Kinsella.

Ní Chuilleanáin is also an important translator and commentator on translation. With Medbh McGuckian, she is responsible for *The Water Horse*, offering English versions of Irish poems by Nuala Ní Dhomnhaill that symbolically bring together the three most linguistically inventive contemporary women poets in Ireland. She also produced two books of translations of poems by another major contemporary woman poet, Ileana Mălăncioiu, having learnt Romanian to do so. *After the Raising of Lazarus* (2005) and *Legend of the Walled-Up Wife* (2010) are uniquely attuned to the strange dissident folkloric frequency of the Romanian poet, whose focus 'on rural life and folklore, on religious and literary icons' she shares, as well as 'focus ... on the trauma of history' and investment in a 'small language'.[13] As Anne Mulhall has argued, *Cyphers* reflects something of the same commitment to translation, with its regular hospitality to translated work. In addition, Ní Chuilleanáin has co-edited two scholarly volumes about translation, the first with Cormac Ó Cuilleanáin and Susana Bayó Belengu, *Translation and Censorship: Patterns of Communication and Interference* (2009), and the second, with Cormac Ó Cuilleanáin and David Parris, *Translation, Right or Wrong* (2013).[14]

All this represents a formidable double-life as poet and scholar. If it has taken longer for her to win critical recognition comparable to others of her generation, this is a measure of the intransigent complexity of her maze-like oeuvre as well as her refusal to act as a critical mediator of it along the lines of Seamus Heaney, Eavan Boland and Paul Muldoon. With the appearance of Patricia Haberstroh's *Women Creating Women: Contemporary Irish Women Poets* in 1996, however, and the landmark 2008 special issue of the Irish University Review dedicated to her work, things have begun to change,[15] as critics have begun to open up the cryptic and sensuous corpus of her poems that, as John Kerrigan has argued, represents, among other things, a modern equivalent of Daniel Corkery's 'Hidden Ireland', an everyday Ireland hidden in plain sight.[16]

In 'Small', Ní Chuilleanáin speaks of 'the small languages clustering / like swallows on wires' in Moscow, as well as imagining tapping out a message in Irish and seeing it caught 'like the birds / beating their wings madly against the cage / of the imperial tongue' (*BB* 43). The shadow of the 'small' Irish language falls everywhere across her oeuvre. *The Brazen Serpent*, for example, includes a mysterious, fable-like poem called 'Studying the Language', which recounts watching and listening to 'hermits coming out of their holes / Into the light' and, while set in an unnamed landscape and island, seems to draw on a visit to the Dingle peninsular to learn Irish, and ends: 'I call this my work, these decades and stations – / Because without these, I would be a stranger here' (*SP* 89). The poem speaks of 'studying the language' but doesn't specify which one. Nevertheless, in talking about her work in terms of 'decades and stations', she certainly aligns herself to Irish Catholic tradition while imagining being a 'stranger' to it. Ní Chuilleanáin has said that she writes 'English rather as if it were a foreign language into which I am constantly translating', adding that this has made her 'free – like many Irish poets – of the need to simply accept the traditional verse rhythms of English poetry, because there are always other languages pressing to be heard all the time'.[17] That sense of other languages 'pressing to be heard' gives a unique accent to Ní Chuilleanáin's work, which, with its slowly unwinding sentences, multiple time-signatures and elaborately architectural space, does indeed feel 'foreign' as well as colloquial.

If Ní Chuilleanáin imagines small languages like Irish 'beating their wings madly against the cage / of the imperial tongue', in her essay on 'Borderlands of Irish Poetry' she speaks of being part of a 'determined movement, which has existed since the 30s, to break out from the English-speaking world ... dominated by the culture of the English Home Counties'.[18] In 'The Cailleach write back', she observes that 'History has been particularly alive for me as for many Irish people ... like others who share my linguistic background, I am aware always of the presence of the past and of the strangeness, the untypical edge on the way I read history. We read with anger, anger forced through narrow passages created by minority languages and small audiences.'[19] 'Strangeness', like foreignness, establishes a defining note of linguistic alienation different from the proprietary licence James Joyce claims in *Station Island* when he tells Seamus Heaney 'The English language belongs to us.'[20] Her interest in language and translation is evident in poems like 'Gloss/Clós/ Glas', with its picture of a scholar 'raking the dictionaries' and finally confronted by 'the rags of language ... streaming like weathervanes' and brought up against a 'small locked door' with an unknown female presence 'panting on the other side' (*SP* 119). Locked doors, hidden spaces, the unknown at the heart of the known – these things go to the heart of Ní Chuilleanáin's poetry – but those 'rags' and 'dictionaries' remind us of the familiar foreignness of language itself in all its materiality.

Her work generates a powerful sense of speaking for a hidden, 'other' Ireland, like Thomas Kinsella's, and of following a pathway – among those 'narrow passages' – that is conspicuously unaligned with the mainstream of poetry in the British Isles and the United States. If this initially made her work less visible and recognisable to audiences outside Ireland, with recent publication by Faber in the United Kingdom and by Wake Forest in the United States, she is now a crucial presence on the larger map of contemporary poetry. In editing a volume called *Irish Women: Image and Achievement*, Ní Chuilleanáin aligned herself not only with the mythical Cailleach but women poets of her generation such as McGuckian and Ní Dhomhnaill, representing a newly enfranchised force in modern Irish writing. With her many poems about powerful religious women – 'St Margaret of Cortona', 'St Mary Magdalene Preaching at Marseilles', 'Sister Custos', 'The Girl Who Married the Reindeer' – she is more interested in women as agents, as empowered and empowering presences, than her contemporary Eavan Boland. For a time her colleague in Trinity College Dublin, Boland, in her poetry as well as essays such as *Object Lessons: The Life of the Woman Poet in Ireland*, always frames her experience and poetry explicitly within the frame of Irish history, feminism and critical debate. Less explicitly, Ní Chuilleanáin has played a major role in clearing a lyric space for other contemporary Irish women poets as well as offering a revisionary account of gender and religion.

III

Ní Chuilleanáin's poems are miniature mystery plays which map sites of cryptic revelation: dream-like theatres of memory which intimate larger cultural and psychological perspectives. 'Curtain', for example, opens 'I laid myself down and slept on the map of Europe, / it creaked and pulled all night', combining a sense of heavy materiality with oneiric strangeness as 'The dreams had bent my body and fused my bones'. Like a film, the poem cuts unnervingly to a 'square frame' of window which shows 'rolling domes' as 'dark oil-paint slid down the wall / Wiping out the way we had come'. We then shift scene and medium, as 'the measure changed'. The term suggests poetry, music and dance, and, staying in the same mode, as 'the warped foot staggered', the poem closes with a vision of a 'red-haired bard' rehearsing 'the bare words that make the verse hang right, / The skewed weights holding in their place like feathers' (S-F 58). Starting with the map of Europe, we end with a primal scene of Irish poetry figuring a 'red-haired bard'. Though the reference is unspecific, it evokes a poet such as the red-haired Eoghan Rua Ó Súilleabháin, one of the last great Munster bards, praised by Corkery for his 'mastery of form', 'grip on the lie of the human land' and the 'thirst for music' evident in his 'winged lyrics'.[21] Ní Chuilleanáin's lines about the verse hanging right take us back to the 'Curtain' of the title and the 'map' of the opening, while the reference to 'The skewed weights holding in their place like feathers' suggests the lightness and weight of the verse itself. If her idiom sounds strangely skewed, it also generates an uncanny sense of her own medium, with 'rehearsed' and 'verse' echoing each other in the penultimate line, and the final hexameter weighing 'weights' against 'words' and 'feathers'. We don't know the gender of the 'red-haired bard' – gender is refreshingly open in so many of her poems – and these uncanny, vertiginous effects of somehow being between places, languages and time zones are characteristic of Ní Chuilleanáin's poetry, where the space of the medium is suggested by the 'square frame' and titular 'curtains' which close it off from the world beyond.

In her essay on 'Where is Poetry?', Ní Chuilleanáin discusses poems in public places such as galleries or airport lounges, and in a Poetry Ireland exhibition of 'Rhyme and Resin' she notes that poetry offers 'the experience of entering meaning by a variety of passages' and that 'Seeing a poem slightly out of place' gives us a sense of 'the materiality of writing and the strangeness of words arranged in lines.'[22] 'Passages', with its simultaneously textual and architectural resonances, seems the right word for thinking about the author of 'The Architectural Metaphor'. That poem opens with a typically anecdotal description, as a guide introduces us to 'the buildings of the convent', which, we are told, is 'a good mile on the safe side of the border / Before the border was changed.' Borders change within the poem too, as we move from cloisters to laundry, and a hatch flies up to reveal 'the foundress, pale / In her funeral sheets, her face turned west / Searching for the rose-window.'

At this point, the camera angle changes abruptly several times, first showing the dead foundress as either sculpture or apparition gazing at that 'rose-window', which, we are told, 'shows her / What she never saw from any angle but this: / Weeds nesting in the churchyard, catching the late sun, / Herself at fourteen stumbling downhill / And landing, and crouching to watch / The sly limbering of the bantam hen / Foraging between gravestones' (*SP* 66–7). A poem without a first person, the initial viewpoint of a visitor shifts to that of the foundress, and both her unique post-mortem 'angle' on the churchyard and a memory of her 14-year-old self watching a hen. The title 'The Architectural Metaphor' suggests a controlling figurative logic to the poem, but in fact architecture triggers a multi-angled, multi-layered vision, in which space and time dissolve.

This borderland poem, with its conventual setting and architectural metaphors, reminds us that if she is a poet of vision Ní Chuilleanáin is also interested in the relationship between the visible and the invisible, as in 'The Brazen Serpent' where the wonderfully named Sister Custos calls the titular relic 'the real thing' before 'She veils it again and locks up', leaving her own history a 'blank sheet' (*SP* 68). This emphasis on the 'real thing', the 'materiality of writing' and 'a variety of passages' – the places we view things and where we view them from – is characteristic. Nevertheless, for Ní Chuilleanáin the material world remains cryptic, its elaborate visuality a theatre of concealment. Like her contemporaries Derek Mahon and Paul Durcan, she has written many poems about paintings, including recently 'A Musician's Gallery' and 'The Incidental Human Figures', as well as topography, as in the early ekphrastic sequence *Cork* revisiting her native city or poems like 'Crossing the Loire' reporting back on her travels, but all of them involve poetic topology, memory as architecture (or architecture as memory): time viewed in terms of space.

If her best poetry is luminous and often numinous – she is surely one of the most compelling religious poets of our time – it is also, I think anomalous, as her own terms of reference suggest. She is interested in non-homogenous space, in bringing different planes of experience together – the sacred and secular, the personal and mythical, the public and private – without any obvious resolution between them. In 'Finding Proteus', for example, which begins with 'Queen Méabh standing on the top of Tulsk', she imagines at the close that 'Up there,/ Dr Proteus hanging holds the perspective glass' and wants to 'tear it from her hand' (*BoB* 37). Her own protean work is reminiscent of the French philosopher Simone Weil's claim that 'A poet ... must simultaneously bear in mind matters on at least five or six different planes of composition.' These include 'the rules of versification', 'grammatical sequence', 'logical sequence', 'the purely musical sequence of sounds', 'the possibilities of suggestion' of every word and 'the psychological rhythm'. In this context, 'Inspiration is a tension on the part of the soul's faculties which renders possible the indispensable degree of concentration required for composition on a multiple plane.'[23] This is as good a description of Ní Chuilleanáin's poetry as any.

That reference to 'the soul's faculties' reminds us of the metaphysical dimension to so many of her most compelling poems, such as 'Stabat Mater', 'Teaching Daily in the Temple' or 'The Nave'. The last of these begins with the moment of composition (or prior to it), with the poet 'Learning at last to see, I must begin drawing.' She then casts 'abroad a line / That noses under stones' and 'threads off into the distance', leading the poem through a 'tangle of rickety laneways' into a church where 'the nave / Hums like a ship' and 'the uppermost gallery / Swings and revolves' (*S-F* 34). In the slow, unpredictable unwinding of the poem, we move vertiginously from the page through streets, past a 'carnival march', following 'wires' and 'curving banisters across 'the threshold' into the nave of an unspecified church which morphs into an actual and metaphoric ship (reflecting its Latin etymology): 'In the rigging clings / A saint whose cure is personal as a song / Performed aloud at a wake by a special call, / Or softly to a patient in her hospital ward.' We might compare the poem to Heaney's 'Lightenings' VII, in which 'the monks of Clonmacnoise' see a ship 'above them in the air' and a man 'climbed back / Out of the marvellous as he had known it.'[24] Nevertheless, Ní Chuilleanáin's poem, weaving as it does between figure and ground, topography and topology, literal and metaphoric, embodies architectural composition on many different planes at once, with no such clear demarcation between the ordinary and the marvellous.

When the poet says 'I cast abroad the line', we are reminded that this is a poem about poetry as well as drawing (lines are the basis of both). Though its material is communal and figurative, it is also 'as personal as a song', a notion that links poetry to mourning ('at a wake') and healing ('in her hospital ward') and aligning the poet with the typically ungendered figure of the saint in the rigging. Nobody else today has written religious poems like this, building on traditional iconography, but offering a new architecture of revelation. The same is true of 'Michael and the Angel', which begins arrestingly '*Stop*, said the angel. Stop what you are doing and listen', and goes on to conjure a vision set in both the past and present of how 'When the sloes are ripe in the hedge, you might still / Find the taste there, among the last of the grain' (*S-F* 22). If this refers to the 'grain of wheat' in St John's gospel, it is rooted among the 'sloes' and 'wood sorrell' of what the poem calls 'your way to school', confirming that Ní Chuilleanáin's poetry is as rooted in the world of everyday personal life as it is devoted to the realm of legend, myth, and the sacred. Like 'The Informant' and 'Sister Custos', the poet stands as mediator between different worlds.

NOTES

1. 'Acts and Monuments of an Unelected Nation: The Cailleach writes about the Renaissance', *Southern Review* 31.3 (Summer 1995): 570–80.
2. Julia Kristeva, *Strangers to Ourselves*, translated Leon S. Roudiez (New York: Columbia University Press, 1991), p. 1.
3. Nuala Ní Dhomhnaill in *Field Day Anthology of Irish Writing* V (Cork: University of Cork Press, 2002), p. 1292.
4. Quotations in this paragraph taken from Eiléan Ní Chuilleanáin, 'Acts and monuments of an unelected nation: the Cailleach writes about the Renaissance', *Southern Review* (31:3) [Summer 1995].
5. John Kerrigan, 'The Hidden Ireland: Eiléan Ní Chuilleanáin and Munster Poetry', *The Critical Quarterly* 40.4 (Winter 1998), 95.

6. James P. Myers, ed. *Writing Irish: Selected Interviews with Irish Writers from the Irish Literary Supplement* (New York: Syracuse University Press, 1999), p. 203.

7. *The Boys of the Bluehill* (Oldcastle: Gallery Press, 2015), p. 61. Subsequent quotations from Ní Chuilleanáin's poems are from *Selected Poems* (London: Faber, 2008), abbreviated *SP* in text, unless otherwise specified. Quotations from other collections will be referred to using the following abbreviations: *S-F* for *The Sun-Fish* (Oldcastle: Gallery, 2009), and *BoB* for *The Boys of Bluehill* (Oldcastle: Gallery, 2015).

8. For more on the Cailleach and the Hag of Beare, see Gearóid Ó Crualaoich, *The Book of the Cailleach: Stories of the Wise-Woman Healer* (Cork University Press, 2003) and Leanne O'Sullivan, *The Hag of Beare* (Newcastle: Carcanet, 2009).

9. Introducing *The Penguin Book of Contemporary Irish Poetry*, ed. Peter Fallon and Derek Mahon (London: Penguin, 1990), Derek Mahon notes that 'home is one of the words most frequently dwelt on', xxii.

10. 'The Redress of Poetry, Oxford Lectures by Seamus Heaney', *Poetry Ireland Review* 48 (Winter 1996), 77.

11. Julia Kristeva, *Strangers to Ourselves*, translated Leon S. Roudiez (New York: Columbia University Press, 1991), p. 191.

12. 'Nuns: A Subject for a Woman Writer' in Patricia Boyle Haberstroh, *My Self, My Muse* (Syracuse: Syracuse University Press, 2001), p. 22.

13. *Legend of the Walled-Up Wife* (Oldcastle: Gallery, 2011), p. 9.

14. On this, see Anne Mulhall, 'Forms of Exile: Reading *Cyphers*', *Irish University Review* 37.1 (Spring/Summer 2007), 2006–29.

15. Anne Fogarty, ed., *Irish University Review* Special Issue: Eiléan Ní Chuilleanáin 37.1 (Spring/Summer 2007); Patricia Haberstroh, *Women Creating Women: Contemporary Irish Women Poets* (Dublin: Attic Press, 1996).

16. John Kerrigan, 'Hidden Ireland: Eiléan Ní Chuilleanáin and Munster Poetry', *Critical Quarterly* 40.4 (Winter 1998), 76–100. See also Sean Dunne, ed., *Poets of Munster: An Anthology* (Brandon: Anvil Press, 1985).

17. Leslie Williams, 'The stone recalls its quarry: An Interview with Eiléan Ní Chuilleanáin', in Susan Shaw Sailer, *Representing Ireland: Gender, Class, Nationality* (Gainesville: University of Florida Press, 1997), p. 31.

18. 'The Borderlands of Irish Poetry', Elmer Andrews, ed., *Contemporary Irish Poetry: A Collection of Critical Essays* (London: Macmillan, 1992), p. 38.

19. 'Acts and Monuments of an Unelected Nation: The Cailleach writes about the Renaissance', *Southern Review* 31.3 (Summer 1995), 571.

20. Seamus Heaney, *Opened Ground: Poems 1966 – 1996* (London: Faber, 1998), p. 268.

21. Daniel Corkery, *The Hidden Ireland* (Cork: Mercier, 1924), p. 220.

22. Ní Chuilleanáin, 'Where is Poetry?'. *Poetry Ireland Review* 92 66 (2007).

23. Simone Weil, *The Need for Roots*, translated by A. F. Wills, with a Preface by T. S. Eliot (London: Routledge and Kegan Paul, 1952), p. 207.

24. Seamus Heaney, *Opened Ground: Poems 1966 – 96* (London: Faber, 1998), p. 364.

SELECTED FURTHER READING

Editions

Acts and Monuments (Dublin: Gallery, 1972).
Cork, with illustrations by Brian Lalor (Dublin: Gallery, 1977).
The Second Voyage (Dublin: Gallery, 1977).
The Rose-Geranium (Dublin: Gallery, 1981).
The Second Voyage (Dublin: Gallery, 1986).
The Magdalene Sermon(Oldcastle: Gallery, 1989).
The Brazen Serpent (Oldcastle: Gallery, 1994).
The Water Horse: Poems in Irish by Nuala Ní Dhomhnaiill with Translations into English by Medbh McGuckian and Eiléan Ní Chuilleanáin (Oldcastle: Gallery, 1999).
The Girl Who Married a Reindeer (Oldcastle: Gallery, 2001).
Ileana Mălăncioiu, *After the Raising of Lazarus: Poems Translated from the Romanian by Eiléan Ní Chuilleanáin* (Oldcastle: Gallery, 2005).
Selected Poems (Oldcastle: Gallery, 2008; London: Faber, 2008).
The Sun-Fish (Loughcrew: Gallery, 2009).
The Boys of Bluehill (Loughcrew: Gallery Press, 2015).

Interviews and essays

'Acts and Monuments of an Unelected Nation: The Cailleach writes about the Renaissance', *Southern Review* 31.3 (Summer 1995): 570–80.
'Borderlands of Irish Poetry' in Elmer Andrews, ed., *Contemporary Irish Poetry: A Collection of Critical Essays* (Basingstoke: Macmillan, 1992), pp. 25–40.
'Nuns: a Subject for a Woman Writer' in Patricia Boyle Haberstroh, *My Self, My Muse* (Syracuse: Syracuse University Press, 2001), pp. 18–31.
Haberstroh, Patricia, 'Interview with Eiléan Ní Chuilleanáin', *Irish University Review* Special Issue Eiléan Ní Chuilleanáin 37.1 (Spring/Summer 2007) 36–49.
Williams, Leslie, 'The stone recalls its quarry: An Interview with Eiléan Ní Chuilleanáin' in Susan Shaw Sailer, ed. *Representing Ireland: Gender, Class, Nationality* (Gainesville: University of Florida Press, 1997).

Critical

Batten, Guinn, 'Boland, McGuckian, Ní Chuilleanáin and the body of the nation', in Matthew Campbell, ed., *Cambridge Companion to Contemporary Irish Poetry* (Cambridge: Cambridge University Press, 2003), pp. 169–88.

Fogarty, Anne, ed. *Irish University Review* Special Issue Eiléan Ní Chuilleanáin 37.1 (Spring/Summer 2007).

Haberstroh, Patricia, *Women Creating Women: Contemporary Irish Women Poets* (Dublin: Attic Press, 1996).

Johnston, Dillon, 'Hundred-Pocketed Time': Eiléan Ní Chuilleanáin's Baroque Spaces

Kerrigan, John, 'The Hidden Ireland: Eiléan Ní Chuilleanáin and Munster Poetry', *The Critical Quarterly* 40.4 (Winter 1998).

McCarthy, Thomas, '"We could be in any city": Eiléan Ní Chuilleanáin and Cork' in *Irish University Review* 37.1.

25

JUSTIN QUINN

Eavan Boland

In her most recent book, *A Woman without a Country* (2014), Eavan Boland describes the dramatic changes that have overtaken her neighbourhood in Dundrum, in the suburbs of Dublin. In the preceding decade or so, Ireland underwent an economic upturn that powered the widespread construction of office buildings, residential houses and apartment buildings; and the effects were visible even in a quiet suburb such as Boland's. Neighbours' houses were sold in quick succession as people played the property market. The governments of those years also undertook larger construction works, such as the Luas light-rail system which supplemented Dublin public transport; a stylish cable-stayed bridge, named after the engineer William Dargan, was completed in 2004. Spanning a busy junction in Dundrum with the light-rail wagons passing over it, it became one of the many potent symbols of Ireland's success in the period. 'Luas' means speed.

Another dramatic building was the Dundrum Town Centre nearby. Its shops brought designer goods and services that were usually associated in the minds of Irish people with the larger metropolises of the world. It was all the more striking since Dundrum had been, in living memory, dairy pasture. It seemed to many people that the country had come very far very quickly. But for Boland, watching the people leaving the town centre in the twilight, it is a troubling development: 'Everyone leaving in the dusk with the single bag, / The way souls are said to enter the underworld / With one belonging. / And no one remembering.'[1] It seems, to her that more has been lost than gained – indeed, that she has lost her country.

For Boland wishes to make the suburban scene heft more ballast than it may at first seem capable of. The novelist John Updike stated his aim to 'give the mundane its beautiful due',[2] and in both cases this includes lyrical description of scenes and objects that may at first seem banal. From the 1970s on, the mainstay of Boland's work was to represent 'the life of a woman in a Dublin suburb with small children'; this may seem like a limited and modest theme, but Boland then remarks that she uses it to make 'a visionary claim'.[3] She has spoken of twilight as her favourite time of the day, and many of her poems find the speaker in the suburban dusk, considering her life, her street, her children, and the Dublin mountains in the background. But as an earlier poem demonstrates, suburbia is not all sweetness and light: it includes 'the lewd whispers of the goings-on, // the romperings, the rape on either side'.[4] This poem, 'Suburban Woman', is also alert to certain slants of light that undercut the stolid civic values of conformity – sexual, economic and religious:

> Morning: mistress of talcums, spun
> and second cottons, run tights
> she is, courtesan to the lethal
> rapine of routine. The room invites.
> She reaches to fluoresce the dawn.
> The kitchen lights like a brothel.[5]

On the face of it, a mother and wife living in the polite demesnes of Dundrum is geographically and socially distant from women who sell their bodies for money. Properly speaking, Ireland, as a republic, has no courtesans, but it has no shortage of prostitutes nor others, at higher levels, who trade sexual favours for social position and power. Through deft description, Boland illuminates how the life of a middle-class woman can have shades of such transactions; in the early 1970s, when this poem was written, it was incendiary to say such a thing. It is clinched with startling exactitude in the final line here, as the Dundrum kitchen is rhymed with the raw lighting of a brothel several miles down the road in Dublin's city centre, metonymically drawing together the bodies of housewives and prostitutes, who conduct their lives in the same light.

Again, like Updike, Boland used suburbia to approach a further subject, not content to use its scenery to set off individual dissatisfaction. In his Rabbit tetralogy, Updike uses his hero's miniscule slice of national life to take the temperature of the entire United States (his surname is Angstrom, a tiny unit of measurement). This grand ambition came under much fire at a time when ethnic minorities and women were protesting about their social and political status, precipitating similar critiques within culture also. How could a white, Harvard-educated, middle-class man hope to write a work that would have wide social import? Boland, also, wishes to take on the subject of the nation, in its many facets, as she stands on the porch of her Dundrum house in a summer twilight. How much could she see from that position?

Born in 1944 to a diplomat and a well-known painter, Boland spent much of her childhood abroad, first in London and then in New York, where her father had postings. In her poem 'After a Childhood away from Ireland' she describes the scene as the boat on which the family has travelled across the Atlantic docks on the south-west coast of Ireland: 'The engines / of the ship stopped. / There was an eerie / drawing near'.[6] The patron saint of Ireland, Patrick, is one of the shadows in this scene, as he too had grown up else-where, and came to Ireland at about the age of sixteen, eventually converting it to Christianity. There are also more recent ghosts in the scene, as many immigrants during the nineteenth century left Ireland from the same harbour to sail for America, often fleeing poverty and starvation. Here Boland marks another important transformation of the country. In 1922 part of the island gained independence from Britain, leaving six counties in Northern Ireland still part of the United Kingdom. Not all of Ireland's economic and social troubles can be blamed on British occupation of the island; in the later part of the nineteenth-century British rule in the country was increasingly benevo-lent – however, independence marked the new nation's improvement and by the mid-twentieth century the tide of immigration had been turned as Ireland briskly industrialised from the 1960s on. So, in Boland's poem we have a young Irish family in Cobh harbour returning from America, not setting out from it, as they believe their hopes for the future can be more properly realised at home than abroad. Literally, this is a new tide in Cobh harbour.

But the poem does not end there. The last two stanzas jump forward to when Boland herself has become a mother, as she goes up the stairs to check on her sleeping baby: 'I bend to kiss you. / Your cheeks / are brick pink.'[7] The final two words of the poem – the last two words quoted here – are startling in several ways. First, they are a half rhyme, each word a kind of anagram of the other, which creates a pleasing concluding cadence for the poem, a kind of clipped phonic punctuation. Second, they are visually accurate as the colour of brick often accrues in the cheeks of young children; this is all the more striking for the unlikeness of the two textures – hard and soft, abrasive and smooth. Third, most distantly but also most suggestively, bricks are something you build with – here a family is being built, but, as Boland will argue in her subsequent career, the story of the private individual and her family can have national ramifications of a clearly political kind.

Boland moved to the new suburb of Dundrum in 1971 with her husband Kevin Casey. She had attended Trinity College in Dublin, where she met fellow poets Michael Longley and Derek Mahon. At this time, Dublin literary life mostly orbited around several pubs in the city, among them the Palace Bar on Fleet Street and McDaid's on Harry Street. The presiding spirit of these locales was the older poet Patrick Kavanagh, who was renowned for his depictions of Irish rural life that had both lyrical and comic tones, as well as for his poems of Dublin city written towards the end of his life. If Irish poetry did not yet have an urban aspect, then Kavanagh's poetry was significant in bringing about this turn. In moving to Dundrum, Boland necessarily distanced herself from that life. Already she had gained significant attention for her poems written in an apprentice mode that she shared with Mahon and Longley, poems that employed traditional rhymes and metres, with a more formal mode of address, and which were rarely autobiographical or political in nature.

The semi-detached houses of Dundrum's new estates stretched for several kilometres to the foothills of the Dublin Mountains, and were a new element in the Irish landscape. Suburbia, in the sense that we understand now, had never really existed in Ireland. Boland was, to an extent, living an unmapped life. There she encountered experiences which, she believed, had not yet been dealt with in Irish poetry from a female standpoint. Irish poetry, in her view, had been structured around male experience and dealt with stories of heroism and sacrifice for the nation, excluding, say, a mother's tenderness for her child, the challenge of being a mother and wife in a new community, in a new place that had as yet no tradition. The people of these estates, like many people in Ireland at that time, were moving away from the oral folklore traditions of the country and had yet to forge the stories, to construct the images, that could guide them through this new territory. It was Boland's ambition to become the bard of this new era and new environment. The bricks of the house that they lived in were most likely only a few years older than the cheeks of the child described in the poem.

Like any vision of the future, Boland's stands on a critique of the past, and this has several elements. The first is the Irish language and its literary tradition. Poetry written in Gaelic, up to Renaissance times, was one of the finest traditions in Europe. It had absorbed Latin poetry over several centuries, and was fully aware of English and French models. It was maintained by aristocratic patronage and required long apprenticeship from its prospective poets. But as the power of the Irish-speaking political elite waned in the seventeenth century, so the social bases of Irish poetry was much diminished. During the famine of the 1840s several millions of Irish speakers were lost, either through emigration or starvation. The language never recovered its former status, and this wound was considered by many to be a constitutive element of Irish nationalism. In the following poem, 'My Country in Darkness', Boland is elegising one of the last bards of the old courtly order:

> The Gaelic world stretches out under a hawthorn tree
> and burns in the rain. This is its home,
> Its last frail shelter. All of it –
> Limerick, the Wild Geese and what went before –
> falters into cadence before he sleeps:
>
> He shut his eyes. Darkness falls on it.[8]

What is one to do as a poet when one is cut off from the taproot of what you believe to be your tradition? Although Boland can neither speak nor read Irish, she has argued that her identity as an Irish poet is constituted by this rupture. Throughout her poetry she makes frequent use of words such as 'wound' and 'scar', marks that are made on the language and the body politic of Ireland, and necessarily on its poetry also. The body of the moribund Gaelic poet described so plaintively here feeds the growth of the tradition in the island's new language of English.

Boland's second criticism of the Irish tradition concerns the way in which Gaelic poetry was appropriated for Irish nationalist cultural ideology. Beginning with the Young Irelanders of the mid-nineteenth century, some Irish poets married the modes of Victorian poetry with Irish themes, often drawing upon mythology and folklore that was gradually making its way into English translation (and which would later provide the basis of the Irish cultural revival at the end of the nineteenth century). This would become what Boland, in the poem, 'The Nineteenth-Century Poets', later called the 'toxic lyric', a type of poetry the legacy of which stretched well into the twentieth century.[9] In 'The Journey', Boland imagines this kind of poetry being written: 'Depend on it, somewhere a poet is wasting / his sweet uncluttered metres on the obvious // "emblem instead of the real thing".'[10] Deceived by the narcotic strains of nationalism, the male poet here is distracted from human experience ('the real thing') by what Yeats called 'character isolated by a deed'.[11]

Most important of all was feminism. At this time in Ireland, the feminist movement was gathering momentum, organising itself in social formations and challenging patriarchy in law, social practice and culture. Rather than the pubs and bars of inner-city Dublin, where Boland had begun her poetic apprenticeship, she now gravitated towards cafés such as Gaj's on Baggot Street, where she met with many of the women associated with the feminist movement, and herself became one of its leading figures.

Finding that her experience as a young suburban housewife and mother was somehow unamenable to the Irish poetic tradition that she had inherited, Boland sought to extend its thematic range to accommodate these salient elements of her autobiography. These were rooted in the everyday, not in elevated heroic deeds that might adorn a public building. She absorbed the ways in which American poets such as Adrienne Rich and Sylvia Plath explored new ways to represent gender relations. Rich, above all, provided her with models both for her poems and the critical prose that engaged with the Irish national tradition. The poetry of the past, she argued along with many American feminists, had depicted women as object, sexualised and aestheticised by the male gaze, and rarely if ever from the point of view of woman as subject. Iconic in this respect is Boland's poem 'Degas's Laundresses', about the French painter's visual representation of laundresses, which deconstructs the framework that the male artist has put on the image of the woman.[12] Many of Boland's poems are iconoclastic in this way, and among the fragments of older artistic modes of representation, she turns to her own experience as a suburban woman, unwilling to be configured as an object by the gaze of a male artist or the voice of a male powers, but as sovereign arranger of the story of her life, her city and her nation. She found the traditional lyric for that she had inherited along with her peers, Mahon and Longley, insufficient to the task that she had set herself. She thus began to loosen its ligatures, abandoning regular metre and rhyme in favour of more open forms. In one interview she remarked that 'I have been a poet who has been in some kind of dissident relationship since I was very young to the tradition and the structures of poetry', believing that this served as the description for both the thematic and formal ruptures offer poetry as she moved into the 1970s.[13]

Many critics have endorsed Boland's position and achievement. Anne Fogarty has remarked that '[m]ore forcefully and persuasively than any other contemporary Irish woman poet, Eavan Boland has explored and laid bare the psychic trauma caused by a wholly male-centred, national literary tradition'.[14] Yet, the terms of her position have been challenged by many other critics over the past few decades. In order to bring her position into sharper contrast, they argue, she has simplified many of the contours of Irish literary history, of gender issues and of politics. Reading her work, we often have the impression that the national tradition in Ireland is unified, bolstered by the heroic deeds of male warriors which are then memorialised as icons in the nation's cultural practice. However, Edna Longley, in reference to Boland's pamphlet, *A Kind of Scar: The Woman Poet in a National Tradition* (1989), remarks that she 'ignores the extent to which the North has destabilised the "nation". Troubled about "the woman poet", she takes the "national tradition" for granted – and perhaps thereby misses a source of her trouble.'[15] As I remarked earlier, in 1922 Ireland was separated into twenty-six counties, becoming what was called a free state in the Commonwealth of Nations, and six counties in the North remaining part of the Union of Great Britain and Northern Ireland. When Boland returned from New York with her family as a child in 1959, she became part of the elite of the nascent republic, whereas a decade later in Northern Ireland, sectarian violence would erupt, auguring the coming decades of what would be called the Troubles. The political and cultural debate of the two parts of Ireland then moved out of synchronisation, yet this is something that Boland's arguments have failed to take into consideration.

Guinn Batten and Dillon Johnson pointedly compare Boland with her contemporary Eiléan Ní Chuilleanáin. At the very time when Boland was arguing that female experience was excluded from the Irish poetic tradition, which was part and parcel of women's marginalisation in society, several miles down the road in another suburb, Ní Chuilleanáin 'moved in the quite different sphere of bohemian intellectual Dublin'.[16] This was 'a cosmopolitan group' with a 'shared commitment to the literature and culture of other European nations'.[17] In her refusal to consider the national tradition as monolithically patriarchal and impermeable to outside influence, the example of Ní Chuilleanáin's career indicates the inaccurate nature of Boland's critique.

Several critics, among them Gerardine Meaney, Brian Henry and Ríóna Ní Fhrighil, have argued that Boland, despite her ambition to disrupt the archetypal images of females in patriarchal poetry, has herself merely replaced one set of icons with another, failing to acknowledge the mechanisms by which such icons falsify experience. Of the images in one of Boland's poems, Meaney remarks that they are 'shocking in their stereotyping'.[18] In the poem 'The Achill Woman', Boland tells of her encounter with an old woman on the west coast of Ireland. This part of the country has always been the least Anglicised, and several pockets of native Irish speakers remain there to this day. Boland, however, has come from Dublin 'with one suitcase and a set text / of the Court poets of the Silver Age'.[19] She reproaches the young version of herself in the poem for failing 'to comprehend // the harmonies of servitude, / the grace music gives to flattery / and language borrows from ambition'.[20] The poem ends with 'the songs crying out their ironies'[21] over Boland's own ignorance. On the face of it, this poem would seem to show Boland in a critical light, yet the Achill woman herself is given little or no agency, and the ability to ironize and analyse is attributed solely to the speaker. Of the poem, Brian Henry remarks that it 'is an excellent example of Boland using the power of poetry to objectify other women while empowering herself'.[22]

One of the finest recent studies of Boland's work draws together many of these criticisms, from an angle that is integral to all conceptions of the Irish national tradition: that of the Irish language itself. Ríóna Ní Fhrighil's *Briathra, Béithe agus Banfhilí: Filíocht Eavan Boland agus Nuala Ní Dhomhnaill* [Words, Muses and Women Poets: The Poetry of Eavan Boland and Nuala Ní Dhomhnaill] (2008), is written in Irish, and thus comes at Boland's poetry from a viewpoint marginal to anglophone poetry; yet this also gives it a particular power and authority. Irish was the literary tradition that was supposed to have come to an end in the preceding centuries, in order to pass on its legacy to anglophone Irish poetry. Moreover,

Boland shares Ní Fhrighil's attention with a contemporary Irish-language poet of her own generation, Nuala Ní Dhomhnaill. These facts alone raise further questions about Boland's account in 'My Country in Darkness'.

Ní Fhrighil argues with several of Boland's positions. Following several previous critics, she shows how Boland was able to portray herself as a pioneer of Irish women's poetry only by erasing the significant achievements of her female forebears. What Ní Fhrighil identifies as the 'messianic' tone of some of poetry shores up the idea of Boland as sole saviour of the tradition.[23] She remarks that Boland 'sustains the reputation of her own pioneering status when she emphasises the absence of female poets in the preceding period'.[24] She also strongly challenges Boland's account of the history of Gaelic poetry. For instance, in her discussion of 'Caoineadh Airt Uí Laoghaire' by the eighteenth-century poet Eibhlín Dubh Ní Chonaill, Boland remarks that the poem's 'origins are obscured by the contemporary interpretations, most of them British or Anglo-Irish'.[25] Ní Fhrighil, who is familiar with these interpretations in both English and Irish, puts this obscuration down to Boland's 'own ignorance and the lack of knowledge of contemporary Irish-language criticism'.[26] Moreover, she says that Boland replicates the manoeuvres she elsewhere deplores: 'It is all too clear that there is a "mechanism of erasure" in the anglocentric commentary of Boland that does not take into consideration the implications of current debates on her own account of the female literary tradition.'[27]

Ní Fhrighil, like David Wheatley before her, draws attention to the persistence of Gaelic poetry into Boland's own time.[28] Even if one has no reading knowledge of the Irish language, there are enough translations available to make it clear that the Gaelic tradition did not die in the seventeenth century. Just as Longley pointed out the way that Boland's historical simplification of the nation overlooked Northern Irish political reality, Ní Fhrighil remarks: 'Despite her call to open culture and her assertion that cultural unity is undesirable, Boland gives little recognition to cultural differences in her discussion of Ireland's history and literary tradition.'[29]

Ní Fhrighil's book has had no impact on Boland criticism in subsequent years. One index of this is Jody Allen Randolph's study, *Eavan Boland* (2014), which only makes one passing mention of Ní Fhrighil, and in a context that suggests that her book is part of a rising chorus of appreciation, which it is not. To reproach Randolph for not having at least reading knowledge of Irish may seem unfair, since the subject of her study herself, Boland, has no Irish either. More generally, Irish literary criticism, whether written in Ireland or abroad, is not informed by knowledge of the Gaelic tradition nor its criticism. However, Boland, like many Anglophone Irish writers and their critics, makes large claims about the status of the Gaelic tradition, in order to define her own identity as an Irish writer. Ní Fhrighil's work gives us pause for thought, then, when it challenges the basis of those claims so thoroughly.

Do a particular writer's inaccurate accounts of literary history, national history and gender mean that we must take her their work less seriously? As Longley, again, has remarked, many of Boland's critics have allowed Boland to set the terms of her own reception.[30] Certainly, Boland's mature work was published at a time when the status of women in Ireland was changing dramatically, and it may seem that in criticising Boland's work, one is questioning the value of those social changes. The imperative mood, so favoured by Boland in her poems, gives the impression that she helped bring this new Ireland into being. Many embrace these changes without thinking that Boland is their best poet, or indeed a significant poet in this second half of the twentieth century. Stepping back further from the forceful story that Boland has told about her own poetic development within the Irish context, we may learn to see other ways of reading her work, such as suburbia, as I discussed at the outset – less compelling, perhaps, but still valuable as part of anglophone poetry in the period.

NOTES

I would like to acknowledge the assistance of Radvan Markus in the writing of this essay.

1. Eavan Boland, *A Woman without a Country* (Manchester: Carcanet, 2014), p. 66.
2. John Updike, *The Early Stories, 1953–1975* (New York: Alfred A. Knopf, 2003), p. xvii.
3. Jody Allen Randolph, 'An Interview with Eavan Boland', spec. issue on Eavan Boland, *Irish University Review* 23.1 (Spring/Summer 1993): 119.
4. Eavan Boland, *New Selected Poems* (Manchester: Carcanet, 2013), p. 14.
5. Boland, *New Selected*, p. 15.
6. Boland, *New Selected*, p. 40.
7. Boland, *New Selected*, p. 41.
8. Boland, *New Selected*, p. 151.
9. Boland, *Domestic Violence* (Manchester: Carcanet, 2007), p. 72.
10. Boland, *New Selected*, p. 73.
11. W. B. Yeats, *Collected Poems* (London: Macmillan, 1963), p. 392.
12. Boland, *New Selected*, pp. 45–46.
13. Belinda McKeon, 'Voices Amid the Verses', interview with Eavan Boland, *Irish Times* 15 March 2007, www.irishtimes.com/culture/violence-amid-the-verses-1.1199805.
14. Anne Fogarty, '"The Influence of Absences": Eavan Boland and the Silenced History of Irish Women's Poetry', *Colby Quarterly* 35.4 (Dec. 1999): 271.

15. Edna Longley, *The Living Stream: Literature and Revisionism in Ireland* (Newcastle upon Tyne: Bloodaxe Books, 1994), p. 187.

16. Guinn Batten and Dillon Johnston, 'Contemporary Irish Poetry in English: 1940–2000', *Cambridge History of Irish Literature*, eds Margaret Kelleher and Philip O'Leary, vol. 1 (Cambridge: Cambridge University Press, 2006), p. 401.

17. Batten and Johnston, 'Contemporary Irish Poetry', pp. 401–2.

18. Gerardine Meaney, 'Myth, History and the Politics of Subjectivity: Eavan Boland and Irish Women's Writing', *Women: A Cultural Review* 4.2 (1993): 146.

19. Boland, *New Selected*, p. 95.

20. Boland, *New Selected*, p. 96.

21. Boland, *New Selected*, p. 95.

22. Brian Henry, '"The Woman as Icon, The Woman as Poet", rev. of *An Origin Like Water: Collected Poems 1967–1997, Object Lessons* and *In a Time of Violence*, all by Eavan Boland', *Michigan Quarterly Review* 36.1 (Winter 1997): 200.

23. Ríona Ní Fhrighil, *Briathra, Béithe agus Banfhilí: Filíocht Eavan Boland agus Nuala Ní Dhomhnaill* (Dublin: An Clóchomhar Tta, 2008), p. 20.

24. 'ag cothú cháil a ceannródaíochta féin atá Boland nuair a leagann sí béim ar ghanntanas na mbanfhilí a chuaigh roimpi', Ní Fhrighil, *Briathra*, p. 20.

25. Eavan Boland, *A Journey with Two Maps: Becoming a Woman Poet* (New York: W. W. Norton, 2011), e-book.

26. 'lena haineolas féin agus leis an easpa cur amach atá aici ar chritic chomhaimseartha na Gaeilge', Ní Fhrighil, *Briathra*, p. 24.

27. 'Is ríléir gur "mechanism of erasure" atá i dtráchtaireacht Anglalárnach Boland nach dtugann aird ar na impleachtaí atá ag díospóireachtaí reatha dá cuntas féin ar thraidisiún liteartha na mban.' Ní Fhrighil, *Briathra*, p. 24.

28. For David Wheatley's analysis of Boland's relationship with Gaelic language and poetry see, 'Changing the Story: Eavan Boland and Literary History', *Irish Review* 31 (Spring/Summer 2004): 103–20.

29. 'In ainneoin a gairme chun oscailteachta i gcúrsaí cultúir agus a maímh nár chóir aontacht chultúir a shantú, is beag aitheantas a thugann Boland do dhifríochtaí cultúir sa phlé a dhéanann sí ar stair agus ar thraidisiún liteartha na hÉireann.' Ní Fhrighil, *Briathra*, p. 54.

30. Edna Longley, *Poetry and Posterity* (Highgreen: Bloodaxe Books, 2000), p. 246.

SELECTED FURTHER READING

Boland, Eavan. *New Selected Poems*. Manchester: Carcanet, 2013.

New Collected Poems. Manchester: Carcanet, 2005.

A Journey with Two Maps: Becoming a Woman Poet. Manchester: Carcanet, 2011.

Object Lessons: The Life of the Woman and the Poet in Our Time. Manchester: Carcanet, 1995.

Allen Randolph, Jody. *Eavan Boland*. Cork: Cork University Press, 2014.

Allen Randolph, Jody, and Anthony Roche, eds. Eavan Boland Special Issue. *Irish University Review* 23.1 (Spring/Summer 1993).

Batten, Guinn, and Dillon Johnston. 'Contemporary Irish Poetry in English: 1940–2000'. *Cambridge History of Irish Literature*, eds Margaret Kelleher and Philip O'Leary. vol. 1. Cambridge: Cambridge University Press, 2006), pp. 357–420.

Fogarty, Anne. '"The Influence of Absences": Eavan Boland and the Silenced History of Irish Women's Poetry', *Colby Quarterly* 35.4 (December 1999): 256–74.

Gelpi, Albert. '"Hazard and Death": The Poetry of Eavan Boland'. *Colby Quarterly* 35.4 (December 1999): 210–28.

Henry, Brian. '"The Woman as Icon, The Woman as Poet". Review of An Origin Like Water: Collected Poems 1967–1997, Object Lessons and In a Time of Violence, all by Eavan Boland'. *Michigan Quarterly Review* 36.1 (Winter 1997): 188–202.

Meaney, Gerardine. 'Myth, History and the Politics of Subjectivity: Eavan Boland and Irish Women's Writing'. *Women: A Cultural Review* 4.2 (1993): 136–53.

Ní Fhrighil, Ríona. *Briathra, Béithe agus Banfhilí: Filíocht Eavan Boland agus Nuala Ní Dhomhnaill*. Dublin: An Clóchomhar Tta, 2008.

Wheatley, David. 'Changing the Story: Eavan Boland and Literary History'. *Irish Review* 31 (Spring/Summer 2004): 103–20.

26

ALAN GILLIS

Paul Durcan

From his first publication in 1967 to his most recent (at the time of writing) in 2015, Paul Durcan has published more than twenty volumes of poetry, many of them voluminous. It's a spacious oeuvre that contains multitudes. To enter a Durcan poem is to enter a strange and unpredictable realm:

> Daddy and I were lovers
> From the beginning, and when I was six
> We got married in the church of Crinkle, near Birr.
> The *Irish Independent* photographed the wedding.
> My mother gave me away.
> My sister was best man.
> He was forty-two and a TV personality in Yorkshire,
> Close to his widowed mother in Mayo[1]

His opening lines reveal much about his verse: 'They do not like me at the local golf club' (41); 'Ted Rice was that abnormal creature – a normal man' (73); 'Don't suppose Derrylin will ever be prestigious as Auschwitz' (130); 'I decided to hunt down my wife' (147); 'Have you ever saved hay in Mayo in the rain?' (162); 'Edifying, edifying – you cry – edifying' (154); 'I loved Papa – even though he was an old bollox' (180); 'The answer to your question is that I am not your mother' (185); 'Did your bowels move today?' (231); 'My dear children of God, – I am an old cod' (247), 'Having photocopied Goya by moonlight, the IRA' (254); 'Tweet-tweet-tweet-tweet-tweet-tweet-tweet' (339); '*In the summer of '97 I lost my remote control*' (386); 'Paul Durcan would try the patience of the Queen of Tonga' (376).

As these openings suggest, his poems can be highly dramatic, or can plunge the reader into the telling of a yarn, with vivid immediacy. He is frequently entertaining, and often very funny. He is an overtly public poet, ceaselessly political: sometimes edgy, even confrontational. Few poets have condemned the conservative ideology and hypocrisies of State and Church, as well as the violence of the Troubles, more directly and more unremittingly within their verse. But Durcan is also one of Ireland's most confessional poets: an excavator of the confounding nature of the self, and a great love poet. His oeuvre incessantly explores the needs and afflictions of relationships and family, the great loneliness that pervades amid the welter of the world. Ultimately, the binding thread throughout his large body of work is the extent and manner in which the oeuvre is at once intensely personal and insistently public-minded.

Durcan's poems stress that individuality is shaped through communion with others, that the inner life is moulded by personal relationships and social formations. Conversely, the social sphere is always approached in terms of moral judgement, or ethical prescription, regarding the rights of personal autonomy, the sanctity of individual freedom. His poem 'Epistemology' reads, in full: 'If there is nobody to share the world with, / There is no world' (550). In this respect, like his beloved exemplar Patrick Kavanagh before him, Durcan would seem to have been influenced by W. H. Auden and Louis MacNeice. The latter wrote, in *Autumn Journal*: 'try and confine your / Self to yourself if you can'.[2] Perhaps all literature explores a continuum between self and society, but Durcan's verse is marked by extreme sensitivity to its fluid ebb and flow. It's as if a mere smile or frown from a passer-by, as if the slightest nuance of social good or ill picked up on the daily rounds of citizenship, could either leave the poet destroyed or else enraptured. Derek Mahon once quipped 'Durcan takes the madness of public life personally'. Nick Laird later added: 'he could also have said he takes his personal life publicly'.[3] This is spot-on regarding Durcan's tone, suggesting how he approaches the common ground of social being in heightened, even hyperbolic terms.

Fintan O'Toole has argued that Durcan 'writes out of a society that has become post-modern without ever really becoming modern'.[4] While James Joyce might have demurred, O'Toole primarily means to cast light on the sense of uneven development that has pervaded in Ireland, which is a dominant feature of Durcan's work. Global capital, rampant consumerism, information technology, urban sprawl – Durcan is ingenious in mapping how the emerging infrastructure of the contemporary sits incongruously with more residual aspects of Irish culture. Our age of multinational capital disrupts notions of being rooted to the land, rooted in tradition; it transmogrifies a culture formatively shaped by the Church, and by the sense of belonging to a tightly knit community. Durcan is the laureate of Irish culture's rapid transformations, of the ongoing metamorphosis of Irish sensibility. His verse gives voice to the fundamentally oxymoronic experience of contemporary life, where the very concept of cultural coherence becomes improvisatory. The majestic early poem 'The Hat Factory' expresses the paradoxes of Ireland's contribution to global trade with searing irony, while simultaneously turning the strange air of Ireland's unevenly developed new world into a thing of rhapsodic wonder.

It is tempting to label Durcan a surrealist. Surrealism originally sought to irrationally juxtapose images as a means of expressing the subconscious mind. But Durcan's work isn't quite interested in bringing forth the hidden depths of the subconscious. All the weirdness is on the surface. It is already out there, all around us. His work shows how the very essence of society is comprised of irrational juxtapositions. Since reality is already an oxymoron, many-angled and uneven, the surreal doesn't have to be summoned or willed. Durcan simply exaggerates to bring attention to what's in front of our eyes. Bizarre, eccentric, extravagant, whimsical, strange, odd, fantastic: this is the norm in his work. What best characterises his poetry is its oral immediacy, the vigour with which its speakers express the tumult of the ordinary. In 'Tullynoe: Tête à Tête in the Parish Priest's Parlour' (90), a conversation runs:

> 'He ... had the most expensive Toyota you can buy.'
> 'He had: well, it was only beautiful.'
> 'It was: he used to have an Audi.'
> 'He had: then he had an Avenger.'
> 'He had: and then he had a Volvo.'
> 'He had: in the beginning he had a lot of Volkses.'
> 'He had: he was a great man for the Volkses.'
> 'He was: did he once have an Escort?'
> 'He had not: he had a son a doctor.'
> 'He had: he had a Morris Minor too.'
> 'He had: and he had a sister a hairdresser in Kilmallock.'
> 'He had: he had another sister a hairdresser in Ballybunnion.'
> 'He had: he was put in a coffin which was put in his father's cart.'
> 'He was: his lady wife sat on top of the coffin driving the donkey.'

As this indicates, Durcan's verse is zestfully social. He is notable for his innovative manipulation of forms associated with everyday culture, not conventionally associated with the lyric poem. As Edna Longley claims, his 'methods not only draw on the ritual formulae of the Church, but imitate press-reports, television commentary, anecdote, advertising, ballads (not only Irish), blues, pop-songs, documentary programmes, revue-monologues, pub-talk'.[5] Much of the fun of this is conveyed in the poems' titles: 'Irish Hierarchy Bans Colour Photography' ('in accordance with tradition / No logical explanation would be provided' (71)); 'Minister Opens New Home For Battered Husbands'; 'Margaret Thatcher Joins IRA'; 'The Man With Five Penises'; 'Archbishop of Kerry to Have Abortion'; 'Cardinal Dies of Heart Attack in Dublin Brothel'; 'Priest Accused of Not Wearing a Condom';

'Diarrhoea Attack at Party Headquarters in Leningrad'; and so on. The opening lines of 'Wife Who Smashed Television Gets Jail' exemplify Durcan's skill in nailing a context and conveying a great deal of cultural information with dramatic economy: 'She came home, my Lord, and smashed in the television; / Me and the kids were peaceably watching *Kojak*' (29). The phrase 'my Lord' is implanted so deftly that one almost fails to notice it.

The familiarity of such modes provides a basis from which Durcan frequently freewheels with comedic riot. In the interview poem 'The Woman Who Keeps her Breasts in the Back Garden', the interviewee explains: 'I used to leave them out at night under the glorious stars / But then little men started coming in over the walls' (101). Moreover, Durcan is technically versatile. 'The Woman Who Keeps her Breasts' reads like an oral interview, as if heard in real time on the radio or television, while a poem published alongside it, 'Interview for a Job', offers the transcript of a job interview, but manipulates this form dramatically:

> – OK: so you want a job?
> – Yes, sir.
> – Well you can't have one.
> – I beg your pardon, sir?
> – You had one hell of a nerve applying for a job.
> You have no right to have a job here or anywhere.
> Get out of my office before I bellow for my Little Willie
> To kick you in the buck teeth and whack you on the bottom.
> – Thank you verra much, sir.
> – Don't mention it, girrul. (102)

It may be possible to identify 'straight' biographical poems in Durcan's early work, but the difference between what is personal and what is role-playing is in many ways immaterial. What comes through most strongly are voices. The interview, the report, the ballad, the yarn, the dialogue, the monologue: they all interfuse, when the work is read at large, weaving a multi-perspectival, unpredictable, many-peopled dramatic realm. This is taking the Yeatsian idea of the poetic mask to another level. Yeats's interest in masks was a means towards exploring the untold labyrinth of the inner self. In Durcan's early verse, the inner life isn't negated, but is levelled out, spun through the labyrinth of the social surface via dramatic encounters and narrative play. The difference between private and public becomes negligible as the lyric poem, and by extension inner subjectivity, become saturated in the warped discursive formations of an out-of-kilter culture.

One of the reasons why there is not too much of a leap between, say, a conventional ballad and a television skit, in Durcan's early work, is that his poems are in thrall to orality: the modes and registers of voices, the idiosyncratic music of their idioms. The news bulletin and the dramatic monologue, for example, are united in featuring the speaking voice in action. His verse fixates on the manner in which authority is assumed through aural means, and is mostly debased, by politician and priest. Since both these are the main, if easy, targets of his satire, the agents of much Irish ideological wrong, Durcan's exaggerated mimicry of their rhetorical means gives his political protests a specifically performative and dramatic aspect. Regarding the Church, Lucy Collins has argued: 'Durcan allows the linguistic aspects of litany and invocation to permeate the form and style of his work, most notably in his use of repetitive sentence structures. In this way he undermines the pieties of Irish society through a bizarre mimicry of their effects.'[6] Meanwhile, regarding politics, the empty rhetoric and spin of most ideologues are channelled through the media. And part of Durcan's edge stems from the way he intermingles Church, State, media and poetry in one antic performative realm.

Interestingly, John Goodby has drawn a link between oral literature and mass media, when contextualising Durcan, via the ideas of Walter J. Ong, 'who held that television broke down, for the first time, the barriers between print and oral tradition'. Goodby argues that Durcan's style 'represents an acceptance of the polyphonic, near-schizophrenic babel of images and voices through which contemporary society understands itself, his poetry attempting some form of literary equivalent'.[7] Reading Durcan thus parallels how channel-surfing brings a welter of disparate registers and modes into rapid juxtaposition. In turn, this suggests a tonal destabilisation that ultimately has an ethical effect. As we zap from, say, a news bulletin about an atrocity to a cartoon on another channel, or as the new bulletin itself sifts into a washing powder commercial, the serious – even the sacred – and the profane are problematically confused. This might be a context for the way in which many of Durcan's poems are kind of funny, plain daft, serious and edgy all at the same time. It can be well-nigh impossible to disentangle these 'levels', as the lines between satire and the sentimental, sincerity and parody, art and entertainment, visionary idealism and everyday mundaneness, fun and disruption, nonsense and truth become flummoxed.

It should be noted that this is an effect of Durcan's best work. His lesser poems are more sure of themselves. Likewise, his best poems tend to somehow combine the liturgical rhetoric noted by Collins with the polyphonic babel noted by Goodby. The ability to integrate colloquial immediacy with incantatory power is perhaps one of Durcan's finest poetic attributes. Thus, while his work is distinguished by his skill with dramatic and narrative poems, his best verse adds to this a highly potent lyricism. He is renowned for the brilliance of his public readings. Of course, this is bound up with his material – dramatic and entertaining – and with his facility for 'doing voices'. But it is also due to his manipulation of the emotional dynamics bound up in the temper and tempo of the linguistic stream. In his readings, a poem can get suddenly loud or go very quiet, can accelerate or slow down in a flash. His manipulation of silence is virtuosic. Aspects of this preclude a performative or actorly layering additional to the prosody of any given poem. However, it is also tied to an intrinsic push and pull within much of the work, as the banter, the invective, the aleatory swerves and all-round gallimaufry of his verse are orchestrated through cadence, repetition, refrain. This sets up a dynamic where a centrifugal or outward momentum is counterpointed by a centripetal or inward force.

Durcan announced his invocatory lyricism at the outset: one of his best poems is one of his earliest, 'Nessa'. This handles its ballad-form with great wit: 'Take off your pants, she said to me, / And I very nearly didn't'; while it is dominated by the hypnotism of its repeating refrain: 'She was a whirlpool, she was a whirlpool, / And I am very nearly drowned' (7). 'Nessa' demonstrated that Durcan was amply capable from the beginning of writing concentrated lyric poems in highly patterned forms. That he has mostly written instead in a loose free verse style is clearly a matter of choice. Yet aspects of conventional lyricism nonetheless permeate his best poems, especially through techniques of repetition. In 'Making love outside Áras an Uachtaráin' (68–9) – the official residence of the president of Ireland – the title becomes a repeated line: 'We both revered Irish patriots / And we dreamed our dreams of a green, green flag / Making love outside Áras an Uachtaráin'. The poem ends with De Valera taking action:

> I see him now in the heat-haze of the day
> Blindly stalking us down;
> And, levelling an ancient rifle, he says 'Stop
> Making love outside Áras an Uachtaráin'.

Such repeated lines and refrains feature throughout the oeuvre. Generally speaking, a refrain brings to a poem an element of communality – it's the bit where an audience might join in, modulating the inherent subjectivity of a lyric with broadened objectivity, shifting a poem's emphasis from its speaker towards the collective aether of its telling. The repetitive nature of the refrain also implants the effect of a perpetual return to the inevitability of some underlying emotion, force or reality that is either expressed in the poem or that lies behind it. Another of Durcan's poems is 'The Riding School' (285–6), an ekphrastic work that transposes a painting by Karel Dujardin to Belfast:

> *And I in my red blanket*
> *Under the Cave Hill Mountain*
> *Leading out the Grey of the Blues:*
> *The blindness of history in my eyes;*
> *The blindness of history in my hands.*

This is repeated four times, a counterpointed sub-song within the poem, which works to dilate the pressures of violent history into an expanse of space and time, enfolding the poem in what might be called dynamic stillness to profound effect.

One expects a refrain to add musicality and rhythmic propulsion to a poem. Tellingly, Durcan is frequently interested in playing with such expectation, warping the flow, creating an awkwardness that nonetheless clicks:

> Oh I've got the Drimoleague Blues, I've got the Drimoleague Blues,
> I've got the Drimoleague Blues so bad I can't move:
> Even if you were to plug in Drimoleague to every oil well in Arabia –
> I'd still have the Drimoleague Blues.   (86–87)

This repeats three times in a twenty-four-line poem. The mouthful of that penultimate line shouldn't work – almost doesn't work – yet somehow does, producing a musicality that is both out-of-step and in-time. The communality presupposed by the refrain, a matter of instinctually recognisable rhythm, is both subverted and upheld. The bond between inner subjectivity and broader cultural dispensation is renewed yet altered in a freshly lopsided balance.

This ramshackle inventiveness is something Durcan excels at, exploring strange ratios of imbalance and balance. Assuming the form of a poem says something about the form of its culture, the tenuousness of how things hold together or almost fall apart in his verse – his jazz-like mutations, tuned to the common ground – constitutes a major aspect of his poetic. 'The Bunamurry Scurry' (479–82) intensifies the lopsidedness of 'The Drimoleague Blues':

> *Once, before time began,*
> *When we were in our teens,*
> *It was the Dooagh Rock,*
> *The Inishbiggle Skiffle,*
> *The Dookinella March,*
> *The Crumpaun Jig,*
> *The Dooniver Hornpipe,*
> *The Saula Hucklebuck,*
> *The Valley Waltz,*
> *The Cabin Fever,*
> *But now in May ninety-nine,*
> *In the primes of our lives,*
> *It is the Bunnacurry Scurry.*

This repeats four times. What are we to make of it? Its excessiveness disrupts any sense that its function is to augment the time-flow of its poem. The lines assert confidence, yet in their over-seeded vim and vigour they betray implicit insecurity. In a poem partially about ageing, their sheer outlandishness leaves a faint whiff of subconscious desperation. The poem is proclaiming 'we are ok, we are doing grand', while its wilfulness makes this precarious. In such poems, the centripetal and the centrifugal are awkwardly dancing to a new tune, a weird and unstable sonic evolution of recognisable form.

Repeated lines fulfil many lyrical functions in Durcan's verse. A poem might conclude thus for resonance: 'It's not the soul that's the crux of the matter, it's the hole: // It's not the soul that's the crux of the matter, it's the hole' (83). Or a repeated line might constitute the beginning and end of a poem, creating an enveloped full-turn form to powerful effect, as in 'The Death by Heroin of Sid Vicious': 'There – but for the clutch of luck – go I' // 'There – but for the clutch of luck – go we all' (84–5). Or a repeated line might create a comic swerve which, through being repeated, transforms what might have been a surrealistic flash into the bedrock of the poem, as in 'And I do a small bit of sheepfarming on the side' in 'The Kilfenora Teaboy' (47–8). More broadly, repeated lines pervade Durcan's verse in a more casual manner. The early poem 'Phoenix Park Vespers' featured what would become a near-constant stylistic man-oeuvre when, in the midst of an otherwise straightforward and continuous free verse opening, it echoed itself: 'under the conifers of the Phoenix Park, / under the exceedingly lonely conifers of the Phoenix Park' (12). This repetition is not repeated, as it were, but stands alone. It has an intensifying affect, yet also seems arbitrary. Unpredictability is key to Durcan. As it happens, this repetition paves the way for a parallel of Phoenix Park with Babylon, à la Psalm 137 ('I squatted down and wept'). But more frequently, such repeated lines are more purely rhetorical, as if their speakers are buttressing themselves, so that one of Durcan's key incantatory effects is simultaneously a means of implanting colloquial contingency – the verisimilitude of speech.

The repetition of words can be a way of holding on to something, or of turning a reference to a thing or person into an invocation: 'If there be a heaven / heaven would be'; 'Let's drink to Teresa of Teresa's Bar' (32). Conversely, repetition effects can be used as a vehicle for the comedic, as in: 'He was by no means the only passenger smoking a cigarette / But he was the only naked passenger smoking a cigarette' (127); or: 'The main thing – the first and last thing – to say / About the poetry reading last night in the Royal Hibernian Hotel / Is that the Royal Hibernian Hotel does not exist' (152). The repetition here emphasises the solidity of the thing or person, while the comic alteration within the repetition transforms it. Durcan's effect is to simultaneously consolidate and explode normality.

Following the mention of *Kojak* in 'Wife Who Smashed Television Gets Jail', *Kojak* is mentioned again several times: 'we got there just before the finish of *Kojak*; / (My mother has a fondness for *Kojak*, my Lord)' (29). In 'Priest Accused of Not Wearing a Condom' the effect is amplified, repeating 'condom' incessantly: 'if he had known how to operate a condom, / He would most certainly have operated a condom'; '[he] should be given access to condom therapy'; 'he is lacking in condom consciousness'; and so on.[8] It is as if the mere mention of *Kojak* in a poem (not to mention a courtroom), or of condoms in a poem (not to mention a courtroom in connection with a Priest's sexual activity) is itself uproarious. The fact that this does indeed work – for this is as funny as contemporary poetry gets – tells us much about Durcan's livewire alertness to the nuance and idiomatic currency of diction. Moreover, that the effect depends upon the deadpan exactitude of the repetitions also demonstrates his skilful poetic technique. But what is interesting is how the formal vehicle of incantation is also the vehicle of absurdity.

In places, repetition triggers a virtual cancellation of meaning, where sound is in excess of sense. Sometimes this amplifies absurdity, zany yet empty: 'Ow: ow: ow: let's have a row: / Let's pink the pink floor pinker than pink: / I am a pink place in which a pink pig plashes' (88). Sometimes this creates a self-circling stasis, like a poetic dog chasing its semantic tail: 'Oh I know this mean town is not always mean / And I know that you do not always mean what you mean / And the meaning of meaning can both mean and not mean: / But I mean to say, I mean to say' (86). Sometimes such playful nullity is used to startling effect: '*Eat him, Bismark, eat him.* / *Eat him, Bismark, eat him.* // Nyum: nyum, nyum, nyum, nyum, nyum; *nyum*' (95). Sometimes it suddenly breaks into surprised meaning to even more startling effect: 'to kiss-with-my-tongue, kiss-with-my-tongue, kiss-with-my-tongue / Your big-eared, wide-eyed feet' (185). Or it can provide a rhetorical climax, a combustion where the imagination and the resourcefulness of words meet their outer limits: 'And what if you were a hatter / And you married a hatter / And all your sons and daughters worked as hatters / And you inhabited a hat-house all full of hats: / Hats, hats, hats, hats. / Hats' (44).

Finally, and perhaps most crucially, repetition also pervades through the broader rhetorical structures of Durcan's poetry. Rhetorical patterns provide a poem's means, or a speaker's means, of gaining a foothold; they provide a rhythm of assertion and reassertion, emphasising and directing presence and agency. In so doing, they simultaneously indicate a certain febrile precariousness – as if, without reiterative reassurance, they would be waylaid into a digressive limbo, fragmentary chaos. In the opening of 'The Haulier's Wife Meets Jesus on the Road Near Moone' (117–21), the basic act of saying where you're from takes six lines:

> I live in the town of Cahir,
> In the Glen of Aherlow,
> Not far from Peekaun
> In the townland of Toureen,
> At the foot of Galtee Mór
> In the County of Tipperary.

As each line gets its own place name, the specificity seems to have a counter-logical affect, ghosting the rhetorical act with a deracinating tenuousness, the sense of being adrift in a free-floating nowhere, a burlesque geography. Just as speakers might repeat lines as if to buttress their speech, bolster their performance, in a manner that often betrays subconscious insecurity, indicating how fragile the line is between emphatic sense and the inanity of chattering noise, so the recurring rhetorical cruxes and reiterative structures of Durcan's verse seem to evoke an implicit unease. The orality of his poetry, the aura of spoken language, is ultimately pitched against the backdrop of a void, an undercutting nullity, as if the white of the page and the silence it summons create an unspoken pressure, a wall of absurdity pressing in, against which the voices must push back. Hence the heartfelt and the parodic share the same poetic grounds, as it were, in a realm where sense and non-sense are constantly at battle.

To focus on the more flamboyant aspects of Durcan's early verse seems germane, as this work brought something new and different to Irish poetry. However, while remaining iconoclastic, his verse – from 1985's *The Berlin Wall Café* onwards – does become more settled. And while the inventively parodic still thrives in his mature verse, it frequently becomes more heartfelt and emotional. 'The Haulier's Wife Meets Jesus on the Road Near Moone' is the opening poem of *The Berlin Wall Café*, and signals a much richer level of affective intensity, more nuanced and textured, the speaker not a caricature but composed with full-blooded, yearning humanity. The poem might still be called surreal – it seems a high-point of magical realism in verse, if such a thing exists – yet the fantastical elements are fully in the service of a concern for the speaker's soul. Formally, a sense of unpredictability, of not knowing where things will go next, remains vital, while this centrifugal open-endedness is still crucially counterpointed by centripetal techniques (the poem ends with a return to the poem's emotional centre: 'Our night will come – he had smiled – our night will come'). But this inventiveness with the poem's ratio of balance and imbalance is likewise now at the service of a more compassionately engaged tone, the canvas extended to focus on the poignancy of the personal.

In Durcan's mature work, narrative poems begin to outnumber dramatic ones, and while the verse is still full of voices, a more straightforwardly biographical persona begins to overwhelmingly predominate. The best of these poems can only work when the poet-persona operates as a vehicle for the reader's own imaginative and emotional engagement – so that Durcan's experience becomes a kind of universal experience. Yet, over time, Durcan has been intent on making his oeuvre a biography of sorts. He was born in Dublin in 1944, to parents from County Mayo. His family feature heavily in his verse. He is related on his mother's side to John MacBride, husband of Maud Gonne, who was executed for his participation in the 1916 Easter Rising. When a student, Durcan was committed against his will, by his family, to a psychiatric hospital in Dublin, and later to a Harley Street clinic, where he was subjected to electric shock treatment and heavy dosages of barbiturates. His father was a barrister and circuit court judge: 'The President of the Circuit Court / Of the Republic of Ireland, / Appointed by the party of Fine Gael' (254). The book *Daddy, Daddy*, published in 1990, and many poems elsewhere explore Durcan's relationship with his father directly, who frequently comes to stand for negatively conservative, authoritarian, patriarchal aspects of Ireland at large. Meanwhile, many poems feature Durcan's wife, children and, more recently, grandchildren. He was divorced in 1984 and this break-up is the major subject of *The Berlin Wall Café*, and many poems elsewhere.

Durcan is often pitched as a loner (many poems deal directly with depression) and an outsider who gives voice to the marginalised and oppressed. Yet by the 1990s he had become something of a public celebrity, particularly associated with Mary Robinson's Presidency during that decade. As Edna Longley claims, his 'readiness to "speak for Ireland" in expansive and accessible terms' is 'a distinctive phenomenon'.[9] One aspect of his authenticity as national bard may well stem from the dual perspective that derives from his equal rootedness in the metropolis and the heartland. Durcan has lived in Dublin since the mid-1980s, but both Mayo and Dublin form two interestingly counterpointed homelands in his verse. However, he has lived in London and Cork as well, which also feature, while he has travelled widely, and tends to register many disparate places throughout the globe in his verse, so that his mature poetry has been defined by a simultaneous globalism and commitment to the local. In short, all of these facets have filtered into a tendency to implicitly address his biography as a figure for the state of the nation.

His many poems on his father form the eye of a vast storm of verse lambasting patriarchy, and masculinity more generally. Similarly, the poems of his marriage reflect a broader preoccupation with femininity. Durcan writes: 'all mystical entrances are through women's faces' (13). Women are incarnations of the ideal, manifestations of the sensuality, spirit and grace that patriarchy censors. His addresses to women are appeals to his own better nature, as much as anything. Perhaps this is an appropriation of femininity, more masculinist than feminist? He is certainly troubled by such matters. In the poems about his divorce he insistently lays all blame upon himself, finding within himself the latent fascism associated with his father. Yet the obsequiousness of some of these gestures appears unwittingly domineering. Nonetheless, at its heart, his verse perceives humanity as inescapably but fragilely pitched upon a kind of primal fault-line: an ontological gulf and bond between masculinity and femininity. This is perceived within individuals, between individuals and throughout the broader vistas of culture and history. Whichever way one construes the feminist politics of his work, he certainly insists this line between self and other is where all politics begins and ends.

Durcan's other main bugbear, the Catholic Church, is likewise central to his imagination. Viewed in the benevolence of its ideal form, shorn of the realpolitik of history, Catholicism offers a benign vision of connection and belonging. While narrative unpredictability remains a key element in much of his best work, a particular structure does unite several of his most ambitious and profound poems. 'The Beckett at the Gate' and 'Greetings to Our Friends in Brazil', for example, are poems in which everyday events or contexts gives rise to a considerable and extended epiphany. The relaxed, almost novelistic way in which such poems interweave incidental detail with recurring motifs to climax with expansive imaginative force are high-points of Durcan's achievement. The ending of 'Greetings to Our Friends in Brazil' (374) underlines how these poetic climaxes take place at a point where the difference between secular imagination and religious vision melts away.

If an epiphany is a glimpse of a deeper reality or truth behind the habitual surface of things, Durcan's epiphanies reflect a complex vision, intuiting a global phantasmagoria of longing and supplication behind the veneer of the everyday. These passages register the good and the ill in an even measure, through a kind of dilated entropy and redemptive limpidity which John Redmond has persuasively related to the conclusion of James Joyce's 'The Dead'.[10] Here is the basis for Durcan's thought: 'Although I am globally sad I am locally glad' (506). 'The Beckett at the Gate' shows the importance and daring of Durcan in keeping his vision grounded, centred upon the actuality of his environment, in a paean to Dublin:

> At Ringsend there was a full moon over
> The Sugar Loaf and the Wicklow Hills,
> And the crimson lights of the telecommunications aerial
> On the Three Rock Mountain were trembling
> And on the television transmitter in Donnybrook   (173)

At the apex of his imaginative abilities, Durcan remains true to the ordinariness of his environment. Perceiving the hurt and disparity of the world clearly, yet nonetheless embracing being-in-the-world, and yearning to reach out, his epiphanies incarnate the thought: 'There is nothing necessarily ignominious about anything' (179). Durcan is the Irish Neruda. He teaches that poetry is everywhere, that nothing is not extraordinary.

NOTES

1. Paul Durcan, 'Crinkle, Near Birr', *Life Is a Dream: 40 Years Reading Poems*, London: Harvill Secker, 2009, p. 235. Unless otherwise indicated, all poems cited hereafter are from this book, and all page references in brackets refer to it.
2. Louis MacNeice, *Collected Poems*, London: Faber and Faber, 2007, p. 136.
3. Derek Mahon cited in Nick Laird, 'Review: *The Art of Life* by Paul Durcan', *Guardian*, 26 March, 2005.
4. Fintan O'Toole, 'In the Light of Things as They Are: Paul Durcan's Ireland', pp. 26–41, *The Kilfenora Teaboy: A Study of Paul Durcan*, ed. Colm Tóibín, Dublin: New Island Books, 1996, p. 32.
5. Edna Longley, *The Living Stream: Literature and Revisionism in Ireland*, Newcastle upon Tyne: Bloodaxe Books, 1994, p. 218.
6. Lucy Collins, 'Irish Poets in the Public Sphere', pp. 209–28, *The Cambridge Companion to Contemporary Irish Poetry*, ed. Matthew Campbell, Cambridge: Cambridge University Press, 2003, p. 216.
7. John Goodby, *Irish Poetry Since 1950: From Stillness into History*, Manchester: Manchester University Press, 2000, p. 181.
8. Paul Durcan, 'Priest Accused of Not Wearing a Condom', *Going Home to Russia*, Belfast: Blackstaff Press, 1987, p. 19.
9. Longley, *The Living Stream*, p. 220.
10. John Redmond, 'Engagements with the Public Sphere in the Poetry of Paul Durcan and Brendan Kennelly', pp. 403–18, *The Oxford Handbook of Modern Irish Poetry*, eds. Fran Brearton and Alan Gillis, Oxford: Oxford University Press, 2012, p. 417.

SELECTED FURTHER READING

Editions

Endsville, with Brian Lynch, Dublin: New Writer's Press, 1967.
O Westport in the Light of Asia Minor, Dublin: Anna Livia Books/Dublin Magazine Press, 1975.
Teresa's Bar, Oldcastle: The Gallery Press, 1976.
Sam's Cross, Dublin: Profile Poetry, 1978.
Jesus, Break His Fall, Dublin: Raven Arts Press, 1980.
The Ark of the North: For Francis Stuart on His Eightieth Birthday, Dublin: Raven Arts Press, 1982.
The Selected Paul Durcan, ed. Edna Longley, Belfast: Blackstaff Press, 1982.

Jumping the Train Tracks with Angela, Manchester: Carcanet, 1984.
The Berlin Wall Café, Belfast: Blackstaff Press, 1985.
Going Home to Russia, Belfast: Blackstaff Press, 1987.
In the Land of Punt, with Gene Lambert, Dublin: Clashganna Mills Press, 1988.
Jesus and Angela: Poems, Belfast: Blackstaff Press, 1988.
Daddy, Daddy, Belfast: Blackstaff Press, 1990.
Crazy About Women, Dublin: The National Gallery of Ireland, 1991.
A Snail in My Prime: New and Selected Poems, London: Harvill Secker, 1993.
Give Me Your Hand, London: Macmillan, 1994.
Christmas Day, London: Harvill Secker, 1996.
Greetings to Our Friends in Brazil, London: Harvill Secker, 1999.
Cries of an Irish Caveman, London: Harvill Secker, 2001.
Paul Durcan's Diary, Dublin: New Island Books, 2003.
The Art of Life, London: Harvill Secker, 2004.
The Laughter of Mothers, London: Harvill Secker, 2007.
Life Is a Dream: 40 Years Reading Poems, London: Harvill Secker, 2009.
Praise in Which I Live and Move and Have My Being, London: Harvill Secker, 2012.
The Days of Surprise, London: Harvill Secker, 2015.

Secondary Material

Collins, Lucy 'Irish Poets in the Public Sphere', pp. 209–28, *The Cambridge Companion to Contemporary Irish Poetry*, ed. Matthew Campbell, Cambridge: Cambridge University Press, 2003.
Goodby, John, *Irish Poetry Since 1950: From Stillness into History*, Manchester: Manchester University Press, 2000.
Longley, Edna *The Living Stream: Literature and Revisionism in Ireland*, Newcastle upon Tyne: Bloodaxe Books, 1994.
McCracken, Kathleen, 'Masks and Voices: Dramatic Personas in the Poetry of Paul Durcan, pp. 107–20, *The Canadian Journal of Irish Studies*, vol. 13, No. 1 (June 1987).
Redmond, John, 'Engagements with the Public Sphere in the Poetry of Paul Durcan and Brendan Kennelly', pp. 403–18, *The Oxford Handbook of Modern Irish Poetry*, eds. Fran Brearton and Alan Gillis, Oxford: Oxford University Press, 2012.
Tóibín, Colm, ed., *The Kilfenora Teaboy: A Study of Paul Durcan*, Dublin: New Island Books, 1996.

27

NICHOLAS ALLEN

Ciaran Carson

In a literature captured by history, and a culture consumed by politics, Ciaran Carson is anomalous and elusive. His poetry, like his prose, which deserves separate mention for itself, is acutely conscious of its aesthetic relations to the work of other artists, as his serial versions of Ovid, Dante and Baudelaire suggest. But its material foundations are so much of Carson's own displaced time that these other poets are more spectres than anchors, the idea of ghostliness, or detachment, a common theme of his work. The objects that ballast Carson's imaginative world are the remnants of Belfast's imperial past, and its present, which persists in living memory as the violence of the Troubles. Empire marks every part of Carson's experience, from the dispossession of language to the naming of places.[1] His constant distrust of the symbolic landscape, and the melancholy paranoia that attends it, is a response to a sensory world overshadowed by the mechanisms of colonial war. This is not to get into the old arguments over the north of Ireland's status as a province, colony or state, however legitimate. Rather, Carson's experience of this fragmented culture leads his poetry into a labyrinth of association, the thread of which begins in his experience of alienation from a world ordered by violence and disruption.

In many respects, Carson shares these conditions with other writers of his time and place: Michael Longley's classicism and Paul Muldoon's allusive dexterity come to mind. Poetry, of course, is not an art of group comparison, and for every point of connection between Carson and his contemporaries there remains an aesthetic estrangement, which surfaced publicly in his negative review of Seamus Heaney's *North*.[2] Carson's is an anxious art of wavering frequency, a poetry that sees the world as it might have been could memory overcome experience. His poetry works a series of common themes and familiar territories over the course of his career, and the changes that emerge within it are formal and not subjective, a condition that reinforces the sense of enclosure that attends so much of Carson's work and the imprisonment that he resists by memory and vision.

The emblematic poem in this reading of Carson's work is 'The Ballad of *HMS Belfast*', which was published in *First Language* (1994). Its setting is significant for several reasons. Carson's *Last Night's Fun* is one of the best books ever published on traditional music and the ballad is a song associated throughout his poetry with the folk memory of rebellion, a context that becomes clear by the poem's final lines. *HMS Belfast* is a Royal Navy destroyer that served in World War II and which can be found today tied up on the Thames as a tourist attraction. Carson's connection of the sea to empire and war is suggestive, as is his construction of the boat as a kind of offshore society, such as he alludes to elsewhere in his versions of Baudelaire. Further, for a poet brought up in a house dedicated to the promotion of Esperanto, and of Irish, the idea of a first language is fraught, as is the date of the collection's publication, which coincides with the ceasefire that eventually brought a kind of peace to the north by century's end.[3] *First Language* is in this sense a work of art to compare with Joyce's *A Portrait of the Artist as a Young Man*, which was first published in 1916. Both books share the coincidence of a date of first publication with a transformative historical moment, the cultural background to which both inhabit just as that past is swept away. If *A Portrait* is a novel immersed in a late imperial Ireland made otherwise invisible by the Easter Rising, *First Language* is a collection submerged in the histories of a Belfast that its subjects have since been encouraged to forget.

'The Ballad of *HMS Belfast*' begins as nonsense verse, an April fool that sets a crew of 'Catestants and Protholics'[4] adrift on the perfume of alcohol and tobacco, the pub life of the city never far away from the poems. The co-ordinates of their fantastical journey are local and global, a cartography of associations generated from the collective memory of Belfast as an imperial city. The poet is the medium of this imagination and charts the journey in visionary dimensions, the under decks a dream of wealth, of 'state-rooms, crystal / chandeliers, / And salon bars'.[5] The ship's journey has two initial phases. The first is discovery and the second speculative, the voyage of the Beagle giving way to songs 'of Zanzibar and Montalban'.[6] The captain appears,

> like a grand Mikado,
> To bribe us with the Future: new Empires, Realms of Gold,
>   and precious ore
> Unheard-of since the days of Homer: we'd boldly go where
>   none had gone before.
> Ice to Archangel, tea to China, coals to Tyne: such would
>   be our cargo.[7]

The redundancy of this trade captures something of late-twentieth-century Belfast's condition, in which the old global vision of empire lingered even as the trades that connected it no longer held purchase. Belfast was one extremity of a global body in the last stages of decomposition, and Carson's poetry anatomises that which remains. The poem slumps towards a languid end as the sailors breathe in 'grass and opium and *kif*,[8] the manic energy of the previous stanzas gone, the poet awoken by a foghorn. He awakens by the docks, the Albert Clock above him:

> Then everything
>   began to click:
> I lay bound in iron chains, alone, my aisling gone, my sentence
>   passed.
> Grey Belfast dawn illuminated me, on board the prison ship
>   *Belfast*.[9]

The sharp return to imprisonment is a reminder of the other side of empire, which is dispossession, not trade (as does the click of the clock, which foreshadows the robotic chatter of surveillance machines in other poems more directly of the Troubles). Frequently in his poetry Carson uses the geography of public memorials as a commentary on the past oppression of the social imagination by political symbols. Prince Albert is one example, Queen Victoria another, as when he stubs a cigarette butt into the pedestal of her statue in a Belfast hospital. The most remarkable of these poems in 'The Brain of Edward Carson', also from *First Language*. This imagines an autopsy of the statue of the Unionist politician that stands grasping in front of Stormont. The poem cracks open the bronze skull to find the whirring mechanisms of an industrial empire, Edward Carson the hybrid symbol of man and machine, his bronze cast the logical end of a politics based on the industrious supremacy of God and Ulster. The poet deconstructs these ambitions in short order, Edward Carson pharaoh of a province 'opened up, hexagonal and intricate, / tectonic'.[10] This fantasy of mathematical possession fails in the final lines as the motif of embalmment falters:

> And then disintegration intervened, the brain eluded them:
>   Sphinxlike, catatonic.[11]

It is rare in Carson's poetry to find something that cannot be saved by memory. This laconic sketch of the passive brain of Ulster unionism is the poet's most pointed critique of the governing consciousness of the north of Ireland in the decades since partition. This is political poetry in the sense that it makes the sectarian inscrutable. The force of this suggestion only emerges in consideration of Carson's general, and extraordinary, attempt to generate memory as a bulwark against loss in a culture immiserated by violence and disenfranchisement. If restitution is not to be found in the established political system it is searched for in the detritus of the old city, which explains the impression a reader of Carson's poetry can have of watching scenes cut from *The Third Man*. The grey tones of the mid-century city are a function, perhaps, of a consciousness that remembers Belfast before the Troubles, but also a reflection of an art that finds its subjects in the fragments of the past, which take shape in the memory of things. Carson's poetry, like his prose, is remarkable for its material construction, which far outweighs its cast of people. Think, in comparison, of the many poems Carson's near contemporaries Seamus Heaney and Michael Longley dedicated to other people. Compare this, then, to one of Carson's canonical poems, 'Bloody Hand', from *Belfast Confetti* (1989):

> *Your man*, says the Man, *will walk into the bar like this –*
> here his fingers
> Mimic a pair of legs, one stiff at the knee – *so you'll know exactly*
> *What to do* . . .[12]

The Belfast demotic hides a whole series of dark associations. The dragging leg suggests a kneecapping, the gesture to 'your man' a perfect pitch of bar talk and murder. The poem connects this sectarian plot to the first colonisation of Ulster, when one brother beat another to its shore by cutting off his hand and throwing it aground. This idea pollutes the speaker's sense of his own body:

> My thumb is the hammer of a gun. The thumb goes up. The
> thumb goes down.[13]

In one sense, Carson is rewriting Heaney's poem 'Digging' in these lines; in another, he is playing with the idea of the marionette that surfaces so frequently in those moments in his poetry where the abstract meets the actual to the detriment of the human form. An extended version of this emerges in 'Dresden', from *The Irish for No* (1987). The city of Dresden was destroyed by Allied bombing in World War II, a bombardment that some regard as a war crime. Dresden was also famous as a centre for the production of china, and it is this that provides Carson with the imaginative connection to Ireland. The poem begins with the speaker's memory of a trip out of town to Carrick, which was once a Lough shore village in the rural hinterland of Belfast and is now swallowed by the late century city's outward expansion. There are images from the beginning of alarm and fall, the 'decrepit caravan'[14] of Horse Boyle surrounded by empty cans stacked to create an alarm if an intruder knocked them over. The scene shifts to an empty shop connected to a house from which an old woman appears, wreathed in the smell of a fry. The speaker plays the pose of innocent abroad in the sequences that follow, the first of which is Horse's reports of the outside world through the medium of his television, of violence in 'the Middle East, a mortar bomb attack in Mullaghbawn'.[15] This leads to a series of diversions, which are in part preparations for the poem's final stanzas, as when Horse compares the rocky ground of his parish to a reclaimed tip

Of broken delft and crockery ware[16]

This foreshadows the last sequence of the poem in which the reader discovers Horse's involvement in the bombing of Dresden during the war. This 'broke his heart',[17] the 'bone fragments'[18] of the splintered china a metaphor for the human destruction below. The return from memory to the present finds form in Horse's attachment to a porcelain figure that he remembers from child-hood and which stood on the family mantelpiece:

One day, reaching up to hold her yet again, his fingers stumbled,
    and she fell.
He lifted down a biscuit tin, and opened it.
It breathed an antique incense: things like pencils, snuff, tobacco.
His war medals. A broken rosary. And there, the milkmaid's
    creamy hand, the outstretched
Pitcher of milk, all that survived[19]

This is a pivotal passage in the reading of Carson's poetry. Its setting suggests an architecture for his art, which so disguises itself in the broken pieces of a damaged world. These pieces make their own shapes, as the fabric of poetry and the detritus of history, both of which Carson intertwines with such skill as to make the joins seem a natural part of his individual history. If this technique is evident in other poets of his place and time, and Michael Longley and Paul Muldoon share at least some characteristics with Carson, the effect is so intense and recurrent in his work that it becomes a foundational principle through which to see the world. The relationship between objects and poems differs in frequency throughout the poems but the correlation remains, and this is one of the ways in which the idea of Belfast becomes so critical to Carson's art. Place is so critical to Carson's art that it is easy to situate his poetry, without thinking, into an established mode that roots the writer into an organic, – and in Ireland, by implication, national – tradition. If this fails, an alternative is to corral the poetry in one set of contexts, Carson's poems of the Troubles his best known, the wide range of reading shrunk into the darkened bars of the paramilitaries. The cultural history of Belfast is more complex, and less fitting, to these narratives than Carson allows, and the material textures of his poetry are an admonition to the reduction of that place and the people who live there to ciphers for a literary tradition whose practices do not fit the social contours he draws.

'Dresden' is significant to this argument because it points the reader towards Belfast's muddled past as a quickly made imperial city whose modern core is built on stilts that stand in estuarial mud, its rivers culverted, the urban fringes touching the countryside from where so many of its dock and factory workers were drawn.[20] At the height of its productivity Belfast was a byword for imperial manufacture, the objects of which linger in the sensorium of 'Dresden', tobacco and medals two hints of a global past. The imperial history of Belfast has been so over-inscribed with conversations about identity that its material formation is often overlooked. The objects of its trade secured the idea of empire in Belfast; imperialism was an ideal whose boundaries were drawn by the exchange of the things that made it. Carson's sensitivity to the broken pieces of the world around him speaks to the persistence of these cultures of late empire in the city he inhabited. His poems are hyperlocal and global all at once, his memory of his personal past an orchestration also of the historical currents that shaped his poetic self. Read, for example, the early poem, 'Rubbish', which imagines the speaker as a young boy looking through a sick room window, dreaming of things to do:

> I could be sifting through
> The tip at the bottom of Ganges Street.
> Eggshells. Bricks. A broken hypodermic[21]

Belfast's terraced streets map the conquests of empire onto the Irish landscape and are a transnational resource that Carson turns to frequently. Their past pretension provides an ironic counterpoint to the contemporary mess the speaker more often finds himself in. The reminder of imperial fall is a recurrent motif in Carson's poetry and finds its local equivalent in industrial catastrophe. In another early poem, 'The Alhambra',

> The picture-house was next door
> To the laundry. I passed through clouds
> Of boiling steam to a foyer
> Marbled like the palaces of Pompeii.[22]

The child's capacity to extend the modesty of the working-class urban environment into the grand halls of ancient Rome suggests, however wryly, the continuing purchase of the epic imagination into modernity. That epic was founded most securely in the idea of Belfast's self-becoming as an industrial titan. Carson's memory poems are a subtle adjustment of this scale towards the individual, who remains stuck in the warp between official history and personal recollection:

> It is here I will kiss
> A girl who will never be my wife, watching
> The *Titanic* founder for the second time
> Through cascades of broken ice.[23]

The pressure point between private memory and public identity is one of Carson's key concerns and has two outcomes in his poetry, one of which is, like the second sinking of the Titanic, recurrence, and the other faultiness. The speaker is often trapped in a situation the outcome of which is always already known, and kept there by an inability to properly put together the available information in a useful answer. The archetypal poem of this phase is 'Belfast Confetti', from *The Irish for No* (1987), the title of which refers to the rain of bricks and pavers that flew in a Belfast riot. The poem draws the city as a syntactical map, its hyphens, periods and question marks so many notations in a score of violent instruments. The poem is a sonnet of two skewed stanzas. In the first, the speaker imagines the besieged city as under fire from a hail of 'exclamation marks'.[24] The proximity of language to the practice of violence causes a temporary blockage, the writer unable 'to complete a sentence in my head'.[25] The second stanza tries another way in, through a local streetscape of imperial misadventure:

> I know this labyrinth so well – Balaklava, Raglan, Inkerman,
>   Odessa Street –
> Why can't I escape? Every move is punctuated. Crimea Street.
>   Dead end again.[26]

The second stanza moves from the rioters to the military, the face masks, machines and radios of the security forces pitched against the interior life of the poet. Their chatter occupies the same frequency of the poem, crowding the space for the self to speak:

> What is
> My name? Where am I coming from? Where am I going?
> A fusillade of question marks.[27]

The melancholy of these last lines obscures the process that shaped their construction, the Troubles another function of late empire as material as the side streets, the cinema and the rubbish. Indeed, the proximity between all these processes is such that objects become animate, as in 'Night Patrol', in which Belfast is a hybrid of

> inner-city tubing: cables, sewers, a snarl
> of Portakabins ...
> a wire-grill and a voice-box uttering
> gobbledygook.[28]

Carson's poetry is punctuated with many moments of scrambled transmission. The sounds generated between mouth and machines are in contrast to the playfully anxious conversation carried on simultaneously between self and reader. Poems such as 'Army' and '33333' play a deadly game between language, action and consequence, the medium of which is a set of hand signals that connect the modern experience of Belfast to the historical myth of Ulster. In 'Army' soldiers make their way through city streets by snaking along walls and across corners. In '33333' the speaker visits the Holy Lands, an area near the university that takes its name from streets like Damascus, Jerusalem and Cairo. During the Troubles this was a relatively neutral space, populated by students, punks and hippies. It seemed subject to less obvious forms of surveillance than other flashpoint districts, which the speaker travels through in the 'synthetic leopard-skin bucket seat'[29] of an old Ford. By the time he makes it to the Gasworks,

> I start to ease back: I know this place like the back
> of my hand, except
> My hand is cut off at the wrist. We stop at an open door
> I never knew existed.[30]

The surreal distance between the strange and familiar registers a trauma that worries much of Carson's work. The bloodless cut has something of the quality of a fable, a tall tale that Carson works to extended form in *Fishing for Amber* and *Shamrock Tea*, and the depth of the association points back further than the Troubles as a source of the poet's anxiety. Carson grew up in a household of mixed language, his father famously an evangelist of Esperanto. He spoke Irish at a time when it was unwelcome, or at least unrecognised, and the historical loss of that language in the colonisation of Ulster stalks many of Carson's poems. 'The Irish for No' is one such meditation, a poem of four stanzas that dramatise miscommunication and loss. They do so through a filter of references that open the poem to the kind of cosmic comparisons that Carson would be the first to mock, were his tongue not firmly in his cheek to begin with. That kind of well-used metaphor is often the start of Carson's own linguistic deconstruction, dead language a mute object and a referent weighted to time past. 'The Irish for No' begins with the speaker walking through south Belfast, and overhearing part of two lovers' argument:

> *It's got nothing*, she was
> snarling, *nothing*
> *To do with politics*, and, before the bamboo curtain came down,
> *That goes for you too!*[31]

It is not far from street dispute to bar talk and the poem diverts shortly to a late night discussion in the Eglantine Inn over the possibility of translating an advertising slogan for a bank into Irish. '*The Ulster Bank – / the Bank / That Likes to Say Yes*'[32] is politics charged with comedy. The name of the bank ties commerce and Protestantism to the historical province, undermining as it does the more familiar fact that Ulster said no, to Home Rule and all that came after. Argument in the pub is a rebellion against the shameless capacity of advertising to absorb historical complexity without irony. This linguistic single dimension is anathema to Carson's aesthetic, both political and artistic. The broken flow of English he writes in is a window into the other languages he thinks of and in, and a resource for the imagination of alternative ways to proceed. It is impossible, of course, to translate the Ulster Bank's slogan into an Irish that all can agree on. The remarkable point of the poem is 'the dog's-leg short cut'[33] to a sideways critique of another poet in the fourth and final stanza. Up to this point the poem introduces two images of suffering from the Troubles: one a dead UDR corporal, the other a Belfast businessman. It is unclear which is fact and which fiction, and it soon becomes clear the apparent suffering is a cue to discuss something more to do with art than violence. The night the businessman 'drilled / Thirteen holes in his head',[34]

> the Milky Way
> trailed snowy brambles,
> The stars clustered thick as blackberries. They opened the door
> into the dark:
> *The murmurous haunt of flies on summer eves.* Empty jam-jars.[35]

The poems of John Keats and Seamus Heaney meet in this strange landscape, the direct quotation from 'Ode to a Nightingale' nestled between references to 'Clearances' and 'King of the Ditchbacks'.[36] The easy alliance between art, nature and the reconciliation of suffering to some integrative vision seems dishonest to Carson's speaker, and he extends the critique to include Derek Mahon in the allusion to Delft and 'blue clouds in porcelain'.[37] As we now know from Heather Clark's remarkable book on the northern poets, such infighting was not unusual among the clusters of writers who emerged from the north during the period of the Troubles (it is perhaps not unusual of poets at any time and place). The substantial point is what this poem tells the reader, if anything, of Carson's own perspective on writing and the North. The answer seems to reside in the half-light of the opened garage door, sight focused on the refuse of a life, senses attuned to the preservative smells of creosote, the debate ongoing as to whether '*yes* is *no*'.[38] The italics take the reader back to the first argument, the lovers squabbling from the balcony. This may itself be another fiction, an act of union in the making, the question of consent charged sexually and politically, as Heaney had already discovered. If this is so, the whole poem is not only a fiction but also a stage for argument, as the early allusion to *Romeo and Juliet* foresees.

'The Irish for No' is a playlet of indecision, the final scene of which points to the experience of objects as an alternative to a natural philosophy. This is a major break in a minor key, an alternate tradition hidden in the babble of pub talk and consumer debris. It is a formal departure, too – Carson building the objects of his art into the fabric of his poetry itself, as can be read in the longer prose poems such as 'Brick' and 'Intelligence', strange hybrids of imaginative memory that stray from the dominant lyric tradition of Irish poetry. 'Brick' is an anatomy of Belfast's foundations in the sleechy muck of the tidal zone, bricks the stays of which the city's underpinnings are made. The association evolves into vernacular uses of the word and a history, as such, of its linguistic origins. The vision is of rise and fall at rapid rate, the epic of the industrial age compressed into a moment of summary:

> As the tall chimneys and the catacomb-like kilns of the brickworks crumbled back into the earth, the very city recycled itself and disassembled buildings – churches, air-raid shelters, haberdashers, pawnshops – were poured into the sleech of the lough shore to make new land[39]

The impulse to match the imagination to a voyage of discovery runs through all of Carson's work, even if it comes to a dead stop with the *Titanic*, the sinking of which gives his writing an air of melancholy, the colour of which is the mizzle of a Belfast childhood. It is there in 'Drunk Boat', his version of Rimbaud's 'Le Bateau Ivre', and there in 'The Albatross', another version but this time after Baudelaire's 'L'Albatros'. 'The Albatross' is a metaphor for the poet, a creature of another element brought to the deck by taunting sailors, ungainly and uncertain, its gift for flight the undoing of its walking, as a stutter might be to speech. The bird's eye view informs 'Intelligence', which begins as a meditation on the variety of listening devices used by the British army, and the equally various tactics their subjects used to avoid them. The general thread of obscurity leads to a memory of Belfast from above, the young boy on the Black Mountain with his father, pointing to their house through the smoke from Gallaher's tobacco factory, a house

we strain our eyes to see through the smog, homing in through the terraces and
corner shops and spires and urinals to squat by the fire – coal-brick smoulder-
ing and hissing – while my father tells me a story[40]

This is the imaginative and emotional territory of *The Star Factory*, which is
among Carson's greatest achievements. The expansion of the poetic line into
a prose that is barely able to contain its associative charge is a strategy that
Carson retracts in his later collections, as in the sharper shards of *Breaking
News* (2003), in which

> Belfast
> is many
>
> places then
> as now
>
> all lie
> in ruins
>
> and
> it is
>
> as much
> as I can do
>
> to save
> even one
>
> from oblivion.[41]

The solitary impulse of this later poem brings to light that which is hidden in
the rich undergrowth of Carson's art, which is a loneliness whose presence
hides behind the thicket of associations his poetry tends to keep so carefully.
Loneliness, perhaps, is the wrong word, for a writer with such an advanced
social imagination. It is hard, though, not to think that the compulsive
attention to issues of surveillance, observation and the flamboyant release
of the self from convention into poetry, music and vision is not also a patrol
of the borders of a self unnaturally attuned to loss, whether it be of the
Troubles, of language or of a personal inclination beyond the critic's ken.
Carson's poetry is a remarkable body of art that speaks solely of that which
can only be imagined collectively. Individual and eccentric, it is brilliantly
democratic in its selective admission of the imperial past to the fractured
present. Map, memory and manifesto, it is an invitation to unwinding the
present into threads of the past knit together again from the edges, a poetry of
a time and place personally unknown and collectively familiar; a solidarity,
in the end, despite all experience to the contrary.

NOTES

1. For an introduction to Carson and contexts for his reading see Elmer Kennedy-Andrews, *Ciaran Carson: Critical Essays* (Dublin: Four Courts, 2009); Neal Alexander, *Ciaran Carson: Space, Place, Writing* (Liverpool: Liverpool University Press, 2010); and more broadly Peter McDonald, *Mistaken Identities: Poetry and Northern Ireland* (Oxford: Oxford University Press, 2000).
2. 'Escaped from the Massacre', *Honest Ulsterman*, 50 (Winter 1975), 184–6
3. A good introduction to this broader context is David McKittrick and David McVea, *Making Sense of the Troubles: The Story of the Conflict in Northern Ireland* (London: Penguin, 2012). See also Richard Kirkland, *Literature and Culture in Northern Ireland Since 1965: Moments of Danger* (London: Routledge, 1996).
4. Ciaran Carson, 'The Ballad of *HMS Belfast*', *Collected Poems*, ed. Peter Fallon (Loughcrew: Gallery Press, 2009), p. 274.
5. Ibid.
6. Ibid., p. 275.
7. Ibid.
8. Ibid., p. 276.
9. Ibid., p. 277.
10. Carson, 'The Brain of Edward Carson', *Collected Poems*, p. 234.
11. Ibid.
12. Carson, 'Bloody Hand', *Collected Poems*, p. 159.
13. Ibid.
14. Carson, 'Dresden', *Collected Poems*, p. 77.
15. Ibid., p. 78.
16. Ibid., p. 79.
17. Ibid., p. 80.
18. Ibid., p. 81.
19. Ibid.
20. For a general overview of the city's history, see S. J. Connolly, ed., *Belfast 400: People, Place and History* (Liverpool, Liverpool University Press, 2012). For the cultural contexts of the place's lesser-known history, see Nicholas Allen and Aaron Kelly, eds., *The Cities of Belfast* (Dublin: Four Courts, 2003).
21. Carson, 'Rubbish', *Collected Poems*, p. 34.
22. Carson, 'The Alhambra', *Collected Poems*, p. 48.
23. Ibid.
24. Carson, 'Belfast Confetti', *Collected Poems*, p. 93.
25. Ibid.
26. Ibid.
27. Ibid.
28. Carson, 'Night Patrol', *Collected Poems*, p. 96.
29. Carson, '33333', *Collected Poems*, p. 101.
30. Ibid.
31. Carson, 'The Irish for No', *Collected Poems*, p. 110.
32. Ibid.
33. Ibid.

34. Ibid., 111.
35. Ibid.
36. For further discussion, read Neal Alexander, *Ciaran Carson: Space, Place, Writing* (Liverpool: Liverpool University Press, 2010), 188.
37. Ibid.
38. Ibid.
39. Carson, 'Brick', *Collected Poems*, p. 180.
40. Carson, 'Intelligence', *Collected Poems*, p. 187.
41. Carson, 'Exile', *Collected Poems*, p. 466.

SELECTED FURTHER READING

Alexander, Neal, *Ciaran Carson: Space, Place, Writing* (Liverpool: Liverpool University Press, 2010).

Kennedy-Andrews, Elmer, *Ciaran Carson: Critical Essays* (Dublin: Four Courts, 2009).

Kirkland, Richard, *Literature and Culture in Northern Ireland Since 1965: Moments of Danger* (London: Routledge, 1996).

McDonald, Peter, *Mistaken Identities: Poetry and Northern Ireland* (Oxford: Oxford University Press, 2000).

McKittrick, David and David McVea, *Making Sense of the Troubles: The Story of the Conflict in Northern Ireland* (London: Penguin, 2012).

28

MARIA JOHNSTON

Medbh McGuckian

'They weren't sure whether it was poetry or just madness'.[1] In a 2007 interview, Medbh McGuckian recalls the perplexed reaction in the 1980s of Oxford University Press, her then-publisher, to the poems that would make up her fourth poetry collection, *Marconi's Cottage* (1991). As well as pointing attention to the atmosphere of bewilderment that surrounds McGuckian's work, such a telling observation should also prompt consideration of the significant relation between poetry and psychology across her oeuvre. Its brave territory takes in 'unexplored areas of the psyche', as fellow-Belfast-poet Michael Longley understands, and it is incontestable that such poetry, through its mind-bending twists and turns, has disturbed the landscape of contemporary poetry in Ireland and beyond in ways that have yet to be adequately understood.[2] Routinely labelled as 'baffling', 'obscure', McGuckian's poetry poses a particular intellectual challenge to her readers.

As the committed McGuckian scholar Shane Alcobia-Murphy describes: 'it is by now a critical commonplace to describe her poetry as "obscure", a term rarely used in approbation'.[3] Recognising McGuckian as 'a problematic figure', Peter Sirr highlights her awkward, outsider status: 'no contemporary Irish poet is as cautiously celebrated as McGuckian, as readers struggle to accommodate her lush and elusive rhetoric to their notions of where poems should properly go'.[4] Resisting the decorum of conventional structures of thought as she artfully breaks the poetic mould, McGuckian *properly* goes nowhere, for, as a fluctuating female self writing out of a disordered place and time – a 'very broken society', as she has termed it – trauma and technique in her work cannot be separated.[5] Self-consciously and subversively a woman poet (employing what she once termed a 'gynaecological metre'), the pressure that she puts on words in the act of composition – which is, in essence, an act of unmooring words from the work of others – is integral to an understanding of the mind of the poems as it moves and complicates.[6]

McGuckian's very method of composition suggests a profoundly troubled technique as her poems form themselves out of phrases searched for and cut out of published texts by other authors. That the source texts are never acknowledged makes for difficult work for the reader and, in this regard, the pioneering labours of Alcobia-Murphy as McGuckian's 'indefatigable sleuth' have been welcome and necessary.[7] For Alcobia-Murphy, her genius lies in her ability to 'respond imaginatively to a biography or critical essay – to the startling vividness and emotive acoustics of the words themselves – and subsequently dissect and re-combine the elements in a highly original fashion'.[8] That may be so, but the impulse behind this compositional process is difficult for many readers to come to terms with. It may not hamper the university-funded academic scholar who can dedicate time in the archive, sifting through the poet's library records and notebooks, but what are students to do with a poem that not only resists paraphrase but whose undisclosed sources remain frustratingly out of reach? Reading McGuckian is an 'insanely digressive business' for Leontia Flynn, who rounds off her analysis of McGuckian's 'Elegy for an Irish Speaker' with the disclaimer: 'Of course *all* of the above is probably recomposed of quotes in a way which, at any moment, might be revealed and undermine more creative critical constructions of it'.[9] 'Unaware of its true dialogism, the reader is likely to detect only disembodied voices', Alcobia-Murphy observes, contrasting McGuckian's stealthy procedures with Paul Muldoon's more 'intrusive literary allusions'.[10] It is far from a straightforward task to read, much less critically elucidate, McGuckian's work, but then the age we live in is not easy either, and universal difficulties are very much to the fore in McGuckian's Troubles-scarred imagination. Her poems are, to paraphrase that other connoisseur of chaos Wallace Stevens, poems of the mind in the act of finding what will suffice.

Reading across her oeuvre (sixteen collections to date), we become immediately aware of the many forms of personal and political trauma that are implicated throughout and of the very special pressures of religion, history, gender, and language that shape these poems into being. McGuckian's very methods suggest an anxious reading of the world for signs. Such a poetics of crisis sheds light on McGuckian as a poet of the city, a Belfast poet. As she told Rebecca Wilson:

> I was brought up in Belfast. I wouldn't have been a poet, I don't think, if I had lived anywhere else. I don't write about 'The Troubles' but in 1968 the conflict did filter into me – did give me a sense of dislocation, of being two people, or a divided personality.[11]

'Belfast is a dirty city but it is its own mind', McGuckian declared in a diary excerpt titled 'Women Are Trousers', which grants considerable insight into how McGuckian's reading and writing life cannot be separated from her day-to-day existence in a particular place and time.[12] As with Roy Fisher's

Birmingham, the fluid, fragmented city of Belfast is what McGuckian thinks with. As a writer she cannot think autobiographically without constantly referring to or quoting key moments from her own reading life. Thus, the entry for April 1970 is typical: 'I worried about America and continued with *Being and Nothingness*. Rotten afternoon with Sartre – all flesh and sex and conflict. Half-way through this ghastly absence. I had a cold bath with milk and cologne, my hair is reasonable after lime and lemon' (*WT*, 163–4). Emily Dickinson is quoted often – most tellingly, perhaps, her letter of 1862 that articulates the devastating reality of violent conflict: 'Sorrow seems more general than it did, and not just the estate of a few persons, since the war began' (*WT* 187). Citation of that letter reminds us of how McGuckian is a poet who, like Dickinson, must sing in her own style, 'off charnel steps'.

Entering Queen's University in 1968 to study English, it was here that Maeve T. P. McCaughan, an eighteen-year-old Catholic from north Belfast, would become the poet Medbh McGuckian. 'Met Paul Muldoon and liked him. Poetry reading with John Hewitt', the diary entry for 10 February 1972 records (*WT* 177). Fellow-student Muldoon, with his 'precocious wit and searing intelligence', quickly became a 'friend and inspiration' along with Ciaran Carson, who taught her 'a great deal about the craft'.[13] Seamus Heaney, first as educator, then mentor and friend, played a defining role:

> The big change for me in my evaluation and discernment of how to live through and survive what was happening around me, never mind understand it, was the year we had Seamus Heaney as a tutor in Honours English. ... I wrote a hopefully non-Wordsworthian sonnet, after the thirteen people were shot on the television[14]

McGuckian's effortful determination to become a poet is keenly felt from the diary entries of the time, and although she seeks to learn from Heaney's example ('I just transcribed the whole of *Death of a Naturalist* into my notebook because I wanted to do what he did'),[15] the ambition to write like no one else drives her relentlessly on: 'Bent and battered over a table, I want to use language, not study it or how others use it.'[16] Literature is not all that absorbs her: cinema, painting and music are all a major part of that vigorous life of the mind too.

'The shades of Emily Dickinson and Sylvia Plath might be looking over her shoulder', Muldoon discerned in his introduction to McGuckian's 1980 pamphlet *Single Ladies*, but 'neither is breathing down her neck'.[17] His attentiveness to her 'unique tone of voice' is evident as he quotes admiringly from two poems ('Faith' and 'Smoke'), and he would go on to include 'Smoke' in his 1986 *Faber Book of Contemporary Irish Poetry*. McGuckian is more often than not read with female precursors in mind, but reading her alongside

Muldoon opens the poetry up to its postmodern trickster quality; both are all too aware of how the meaning of the poem is always being deflected, both are poets who operate outside the frame, and both excel at throwing their voices. Their shared sensibility may be summed up by the lines from McGuckian's 'Spring' that Muldoon chooses to conclude with: 'There was my face at the window, / Frosted, so hard to see through', lines which could, it seems to me, be the closing shot of a Muldoon poem. Although his 'subtlety of rhyme and mastery of form' are, according to McGuckian, beyond her reach, she nonetheless regards him as 'the one I would emulate most, though, or be most anxious not to disappoint'.[18] In her poems too she converses with him, as in 'For A Young Matron' from *On Ballycastle Beach* (1988), a collection that in its 1995 Gallery Press reincarnation incorporates a number of dedications to her poet contemporaries. Thus, 'In the "Matron" poem I argue with Paul as to his decision to leave which I found unnerving at the time. ... I do say in that poem that family ties or a sense of rootedness and stubborn refusal to give up the struggle for freedom here made it worth my staying.'[19] The poem opens on a note of tension as Muldoon's 'new weather' becomes 'new dust', and, as we shall see, the intertextual resonances combine to voice a knotty lover's complaint to Muldoon as he starts a new life beyond Belfast:

> New dust in the heat-collecting
> Top floor. Her eyes
> Add a brown look
> With a bleached oak pencil.
>
> Approaching all colours
> From their peaks,
> We try to imagine each sentence
> In a crosstown light.[20]

As ever, there is far more going on here than it might at first seem. When we realise how the poem ingeniously composes itself out of phrases from Caroline Seebohm's biography of the pioneering American publishing magnate Condé Nast, Muldoon's departure from Belfast takes on the added gloss of a high-flying literary mover striking out for the penthouse life in the land of freedom and opportunity. 'With no air conditioning, no one else would contemplate inhabiting *the heat-collecting top floor*', Seebohm writes, that is except for Nast, who 'decided, daringly, to use the roof for a spectacular entertainment space – cooled, he trusted, by lingering *crosstown* breezes.'[21] Although, in her reading of the poem, Patricia Boyle Haberstroh asserts that 'the frustrated young matron speaking is a poet in the top floor of a house',[22] my own discovery of the Seebohm source leads me to suspect that the young matron of the title is in fact the upwardly mobile Muldoon, whose pretensions are being wickedly paralleled with the hapless subject of the following cautionary anecdote:

> Mrs. Van Rensselaer gleefully tells the story of the young matron, new in town, who wanted to impress New Yorkers by riding every day along the new bridle paths in Central Park. People indeed remarked on her expertise as a horsewoman, until one day it rained and the lady was mysteriously unable to dismount. It turned out that she had never ridden before she came to New York and had strapped herself into the saddle.[23]

The 'bleached oak writing tables' of the *Vogue* offices work their way into the first stanza also, as the business of writing and making one's way in the world animates the distressed heart of the poem.[24] Yet, despite the oblique admonitory jibes, admiration for Muldoon's daring, innovative flair is also evident, as, in the second stanza, McGuckian quotes Seebohm quoting from fashion designer Paul Poiret's autobiography: 'I approached all colors from their peaks, and gave life to exhausted hues.'[25] Although not quoted by McGuckian, what Poiret goes on to say seems to hold added import: 'But it was neither by returning life to colors nor by launching new forms ... that I rendered the greatest service to my epoch. It was by inspiring artists that I served the public of my time.' The subtext here is endlessly fascinating: the poet must be a revolutionary artist, innovator, an energising force, and Muldoon is set to be all of those things on the international stage. As if anticipating his later career as the *New Yorker*'s poetry editor, the third stanza has him critique lines by McGuckian: 'Why not forget this word, / He asks. It's edgeless / Echoless' (*OBB* 38). It must be said, however, that even with this source revealed to us, much still remains underground. What must not be lost in this account of the poem is the sheer originality of its construction, contrary as that word 'originality' might seem to the fact of the poem's composition. It was the startling image – 'approaching all colours / from their peaks' – that prompted my own Google search for origins as it called out to be deciphered. Far from being 'edgeless', much less 'echoless', this internally conflicted poem about art and isolation, art and responsibility, cuts to the quick in ways that would not have been apparent in the absence of the embedded source. It is the way the words are recast and made to move in new ways that creates the poem, compelling the reader to follow its leads to a centre that, designedly, never fully reveals itself.

Also in *On Ballycastle Beach*, 'The Time Before You', dedicated to Muldoon and conceived as 'a funeral rite' for him leaving Belfast, opens furtively: 'The secret of movement / Is not the secret itself / But the movement / Of there being a secret' (*OBB* 43).[26] Again, my own labours of reading into the poem led me to make more complicated sense of it in a way that would not have been possible had I accepted it at face value: the moments in this poem that seem most deeply intimate are in fact lifted from the correspondence of Robert Browning and Elizabeth Barrett. Thus, this excerpt from a letter of 1846 from Barrett to Browning:

> And to stand under a tree and feel the green shadow of the tree! I never knew before the difference of the *sensation* of a green shadow and a brown one. I seemed to feel that green shadow through and through me, till it went out at the soles of my feet and mixed with the other green below. Is it nonsense, or not?[27]

becomes in McGuckian's dizzying new arrangement:

> You ask the difference
> Between a green shadow
> And a brown one? Here
> Is a green answer.
>
> I can only say
> I feel that green shadow,
> That short, morning shadow,
> Through and through me.   (*OBB* 43–4)

In the letter, we find Barrett concerned that her deep-held feeling will be thought 'nonsense' by Browning, and the critical view that McGuckian herself has been writing nonsense has always accompanied reception of her work. Indeed, in his review of this same collection, Mark Ford charged McGuckian with being 'as helpless as Swinburne before the blandishments of fine-sounding nonsense'.[28] McGuckian's ability to pre-empt her critic's attacks turns the tables completely: the reviewer-as-cursory-reader will always be on the back foot. It is no coincidence that McGuckian would choose the famous correspondence between Browning and Barrett as the catalyst: poems, because of their built-in movement, their endlessly turning impetus, emerge as the supreme love-letters. 'By now you will have painted / The first of the sea fresh-staring / Yellow and changed its name' (*OBB* 44), the poem declares, thereby renovating an unremarkable description by Barrett of the newly painted Casa Lanfranchi in Pisa ('They have painted the front fresh staring yellow').[29] It is that adjectival phrase 'fresh staring' that doubtless caught McGuckian's painterly eye as she pays tribute to Muldoon's own extravagant transformative imagination. McGuckian's ability to rearrange sentences from literary letters into mobile poetic lines creates a new music of thought and feeling that does not shy away from imperative artistic questions but refashions them in ways that are vital and necessary; all the more so for being never resolved. 'I wish they could hear //

That we lived in one room / And littered a new poetry', the final lines proclaim, again quoting from a letter of Browning to Barrett that speaks to the needs of the poet for artistic community and interaction as well as lone experimentation.[30]

Much scholarly effort has been given over to McGuckian's interest in Russian models and sources, the use of feminist theory in her work and her debt to writers from the past, but her relationship with and relation to her contemporaries in her own immediate place of writing has received surprisingly little critical attention. Too often she is read as though she writes in a void, cut off from time, place or living literary relations. McGuckian is very much a poet of her literary milieu and Heaney, Carson, Muldoon and Longley were not just formative influences but, as Justin Quinn briefly proposes: 'Her early books . . . suggest that she is conducting a conversation with many of these figures, or at least a composite version of them'.[31] A reciprocity of influence marks her apprenticeship with Ciaran Carson. Just as she helped him as he worked on his first collection, he in turn was instrumental in directing McGuckian towards her chosen route: 'It was he who taught me to go to texts. . . . That you can draw on a resource. I owe him for that.'[32] As already mentioned, Heaney's importance was and remains substantial, and McGuckian's conversations with him span her career. For instance, in their introduction to McGuckian's *New Selected Poems* (2015), Faragó and Schrage-Früh consider McGuckian's early poem 'Eavesdropper' as a 'poetic response' to Heaney's 'Digging'.[33] McGuckian has herself pointed out how '"The Hollywood Bed" from *The Flower Master* [1982] owes much to Heaney's notion of the imperial male as the island of England, in "Act of Union"', while 'District Behind the Lines' from *Blaris Moor* (2015) was written as 'a reaction to' his 'District and Circle'.[34] Although counted with Muldoon and Heaney among her poetic 'father figures', Longley's relationship to McGuckian is perhaps less well-documented, yet that she has been in conversation with him since early in her career is clear.[35] 'Coleridge', also in *On Ballycastle Beach*, is dedicated to Longley. As Mary O'Connor interprets it, the poem centres on a 'father figure' as it 'foregrounds both the poet's gratitude for her inheritance from the Romantics, and the sense that she has left that relationship', but without knowledge of the source/s one doubts very much if such a clear-cut paraphrase can hold.[36]

Also in *On Ballycastle Beach*, the mysteriously wrought 'A Conversation Set to Flowers', which McGuckian has divulged was written for Longley, is, as my own research uncovered, built out of phrases from works by and about the writer Katherine Mansfield.[37] Thus, it opens:

That fine china (12) we conceived in spring
And lost in summer (98) has blown the final crumbs
Out of the book I was reading (242); though one
Is still bending over prams (27), an ice-blue peak (18)
Over the frills of houses.

The dress of ecru lace (48) you bought me
At the February sales is still all heart.
I cup my hands, thin as a window-pane
Unevenly blown, as if to hold
Some liquid in my palm (135), and the rings
Slide up and down (316).   (OBB 14)

As highlighted here, Antony Alpers' biography of Katherine Mansfield is the principal source. 'Conceived in the spring and lost in the summer' refers to a miscarriage that Mansfield suffered. The 'ice-blue peak' (of Tapuaenuku) could be seen from Mansfield's childhood summer home near Day's Bay where, as Alpers professes, she 'began to compose, *within herself*, her true place of origin'.[38] In a volume that has to do with processes of movement ('inward and outward, back and forward'), with the sea as a 'symbol of escape' and with Ballycastle Beach itself as a similarly enabling site of artistic growth, Mansfield may be regarded as a presiding spirit.[39] This poem, in its symphonically sensuous way, foregrounds what Longley himself has praised in McGuckian's work as 'stunning effects': 'the tumble of images – the tugging undertow of her rhythms'.[40] The repetition of 'apple/s' in the third stanza is hypnotic, while the final lines, with their self-reflexive quality ('A hill-wind blows at the book's edges / To open a page'), rotate the poem on its axis just as we think we've reached solid ground. It is a poem that turns on metamorphoses as one metaphor overtakes and overturns another, and the lines rush headlong into each other. Indeed, the source of the poem's title, from a 1917 letter written by Mansfield to Ottoline Morrell, underscores the poem's vivacious musical movement:

> Your glimpse of the garden – all flying green and gold made me wonder again *who* is going to write about that flower garden. ... There would be people walking in the garden – several *pairs* of people – their conversation their slow pacing – their glances as they pass one another ... A kind of, musically speaking, conversation *set* to flowers. Do you like the idea?[41]

As it turned out, it was Virginia Woolf whose story 'Kew Gardens' employs the same template. The almost-silent summoning of Woolf by McGuckian here seems significant as, despite the tumultuousness of their brief literary relationship, the intense conversations about art that took place between Woolf and Mansfield were essential to their developments as writers.

Perhaps McGuckian is nodding at the same sustaining interplay between herself and Longley; certainly their poetic worlds overlap at points. Yet while Longley's deft way with flowers and fauna is renowned, McGuckian has been dismissed for the same range of earthy interests: 'a wallpaper poet, a woman who writes about begonias'.[42]

On the one hand, one wants to savour the poem as it is before expanding the view but certain images cry out to be not only looked *at*, but looked *into*, such as this from the third stanza:

> And we both change into apples, my breasts
> And knees into apples, though you
> Are more apple than they could possibly be.   (*OBB* 14)

The more one contemplates this stanza's irresistible metamorphosis, the more one longs to know more about its origins in art. This led me to a powerful letter written by Mansfield to the still life painter Dorothy Brett in 1917:

> When I pass an apple stall I cannot help stopping and staring until I feel that I, myself, am changing into an apple, too, and that at any moment I can produce an apple, miraculously, out of my own being, like the conjuror produces the egg. When you paint apples do you feel that your breasts and your knees become apples, too? Or do you think this the greatest nonsense.[43]

Here again we have the writer presenting a crucial statement on her artistic technique yet concerned that her own unique perspective may be regarded as 'nonsense' by her reader. That McGuckian identifies with Mansfield as an artist seems obvious. Like Mansfield she reads the world for a truth that can only ever be partially glimpsed, is preoccupied with the idea of the self as fluid and is gifted with a painter's tactile feeling for line and colour. But the similarities go further. Mansfield, a Colonial from New Zealand who spent her adult life living between England and Europe, felt an outsider in the world of English letters and was deeply insecure about her talents and reputation. '[T]he people that I want to impress with my poetry, or have to keep up the standard with, are people like Heaney and Longley. There is a network of women who wouldn't dream of being heard by them at all', McGuckian remarked in 2007.[44] It is clearly this anxious solitary ambition coupled with decades-long poetic dialogues that sustain and enable her. Poetry may be a place for thought wherein such enlivening creative anxieties can find form if not resolution.

Included in a festschrift for Longley's seventieth birthday, 'A Hand-Stitched Balloon' continues the conversation between poets. An opulent tribute to Longley as 'the real botanist',[45] this organic poem seems to feel its way into the world, ripe with images from the earth to the stars:

Arils of peace-engorged late moon freezing
On the water, then the late dawn whispering
On our breath: the changing tree-presence
Time-deepens the orchardness of the tree-place,
And we love the veteran old trees for their ageing,
Their orchard practice – high, honest capturers
And players of weather and light – working trees
And companion trees, even, under the closed canopy,
The swastika they made out of larch trees.[46]

Here, it is tempting to see the 'veteran old trees' as poets, their 'orchard practice' their artistic vocations as 'capturers / and players of weather and light' while the 'closed canopy' is that space apart which they occupy singly and in company as 'working' and 'companion' poets. Any attempt to find echoes of Longley's poems in this meticulously woven, air-filled vessel leads nowhere. As my own searches illuminated, the poem-as-balloon is stitched together from quotations found from a range of sources, including *Tree Cultures: The Place of Trees and Trees in Their Place* by Owain Jones and Paul Cloke. The phrases that struck me as most imaginatively suggestive come from here, such as: 'Trees, because of their nature, are capturers or players of weather and light par excellence', 'each grave seems to have a companion tree', and terms such as 'orchardness' and 'tree-place', the latter being the title of a chapter that examines how 'trees are makers of places and places are makers of trees.'[47] If the protean, symbolically laden trees seem to occupy a role that is very close to that of the poet in the world – as makers of 'stunning acoustic and visual performances' who both shape and are shaped by the circumstances of a particular place and time – then McGuckian's reasons for mining this text to commemorate her relationship with Longley are readily apparent.[48]

As one reads McGuckian attuned to the possibility of underlying sources, one becomes more adept at lighting on the phrases that have come from elsewhere. However, simply typing lines into Google will not get the reader far. McGuckian is an artful editor. Her method of adding or deleting words, changing tenses, pronouns, and often making completely new sense of the original, makes any straightforward search impossible. Ultimately, although Google may provide a tip-off, the books then have to be read. Later on in the poem my sense that the lines 'He wanted to cut down all the trees / So he could collect stars from all over space' (which in fact fuses two sentences that are a number of pages apart) might lead somewhere brought me to Patricia Fara's groundbreaking study of women's contribution to science.[49] The 'he' is the astronomer William Herschel, whose sister Caroline not only assisted him but made some influential contributions of her own. McGuckian's image of the 'dark crater thirty miles wide / On Venus', comes from the same source and remembers, as Fara tells us, another of the 'forgotten women' of science: the Polish astronomer Elisabetha Hevelius.[50] When one remembers McGuckian's own account of her inaugural venture into the male-dominated world of poetry in Belfast, one can see how she might look to these women as lodestars: 'I remember going to a poetry reading in Belfast, I was about sixteen ... The poetry reading was like a secret society meeting – no other women in the room – and I remember this feeling of "I am here", like going to Mass.'[51] What draws McGuckian to extract and rework certain phrases and not others is something that eludes explanation. Associations build within her own mind as she reads and it is the multi-dimensional process of reading itself that is exposed. 'Like many of his apparently domestic settings, the dark environment extends the meaning',[52] McGuckian has written of Longley, and the same could be said of the work of this ostensibly stay-at-home poet as the underlying intertextual strata disrupt and proliferate the variety of surface meanings.

'Imagine contemporary poetry without it?' Peter Fallon said of McGuckian's poetry at the Dublin launch of *Blaris Moor* in 2015. Rather than 'traps / Through which you pick your way' (*OBB* 61), McGuckian's complex musical borrowings should be experienced as liquid, shimmering phrases in a work of infinite harmonic variations. Indeed, it is in such musical terms that McGuckian often accounts for her own methods: 'I did not take from his [Mandelstam's] poems but hoped to impose *my* rhythm on his prose to produce a different and, to my mind, original poetry.'[53] If one goes the distance, the effect is akin to hearing a soloist's bare melodic line being taken up by a shadow choir and transformed into a complex polyphony. 'Art always concerns me as a subject', she has stated, articulating her intentions for reader:

> If the poem is swallowed whole, it won't be digested. I want it to become part of the person, as I might recite a line from Dylan Thomas without understanding, but for the music.[54]

Flynn's probing study of McGuckian's first five collections concludes that 'a separation has occurred between the music of McGuckian's poetry and its borrowed "content"'.[55] Yet both Flynn's 'close reading' focus on the 'sound of sense' and Alcobia-Murphy's more detective-like strategies have their value and are, it seems to me, approaches that must go hand in hand. The poems that come out of McGuckian's studiously improvising mind demand to be turned over again and again in the reader's mind. 'I think that if someone had all the clues then it would be more of an enjoyable crossword puzzle, but for someone who didn't, they would just enjoy the sounds of the words on their own', McGuckian has opined.[56] The ideal reader will find her own way into the inexhaustible oeuvre of this singular poetic intellect – even if it means having her work cut out for her.

NOTES

1. Medbh McGuckian, in Shane Alcobia-Murphy and Richard Kirkland, 'Interview with Medbh McGuckian' in Alcobia-Murphy and Kirkland (eds.), *The Poetry of Medbh McGuckian: The Interior of Words* (Cork: Cork University Press, 2010), p. 195.
2. Michael Longley, 'Medbh McGuckian's poetry' (undated), Michael Longley Papers, Collection no. 744, Box 36, Folder 4, Robert W. Woodruff Library, Emory University.
3. Alcobia-Murphy, 'Introduction', *The Poetry of Medbh McGuckian*, p. 1.
4. Peter Sirr, '"How Things Begin to Happen": Notes on Eiléan Ní Chuilleanáin and Medbh McGuckian', *Southern Review*, 31.3 (Summer 1995), 450–68 (457).
5. McGuckian, poetry reading, Trinity College Dublin, 10 November 2004.
6. Ibid.
7. Quoted in Alcobia-Murphy, *Sympathetic Ink: Intertextual Relations in Northern Irish Poetry* (Liverpool: Liverpool University Press, 2006), p. 51.
8. Alcobia-Murphy, '"You Took Away My Biography": The Poetry of Medbh McGuckian', *Irish University Review*, 28.1 (Summer, 1998), 110–32 (124).
9. Leontia Flynn, *Reading Medbh McGuckian* (Dublin: Irish Academic Press, 2014), pp. 154–5.
10. Alcobia-Murphy, *Sympathetic Ink*, p. 244.
11. Rebecca Wilson, 'The Mutiny of Selves: An Interview with Medbh McGuckian', *Cencrastus*, 29 (1988), 17–21 (17).
12. McGuckian, 'Women are Trousers' in Kathryn Kirkpatrick (ed.), *Border Crossings: Irish Women Writers and National Identities* (Wolfhound Press, 2001), pp. 157–89. Hereafter cited in-text as *WT*.
13. McGuckian, 'Drawing Ballerinas' in Lizz Murphy (ed.), *Wee Girls: Women Writing from an Irish Perspective* (Melbourne: Spinifex Press, 1996), p. 195.
14. Ibid., p. 194.
15. Elin Holmsten, 'Double Doors: An Interview with Medbh McGuckian', *Nordic Irish Studies*, 3 (2004), 93–100 (100).
16. McGuckian, 'Rescuers and White Cloaks: Diary, 1968 – 1969' in Patricia Boyle (ed.), *My Self, My Muse: Irish Women Poets Reflect on Life and Art* (Syracuse University Press, 2001), p. 151.
17. Muldoon, 'Introduction', McGuckian, *Single Ladies* (Devon: Interim Press, 1980), n.p.
18. Kathleen McCracken, 'Medbh McGuckian', in James P. Myers (ed.), *Writing Irish: Selected Interviews with Irish Writers* (Syracuse University Press, 1991), p. 159.
19. Michaela Schrage-Früh, 'Uncharted Territory': An Interview with Medbh McGuckian: unpublished interview by Michaela Schrage-Früh, September 2004, n.p. Thanks to the author for making this interview available.

20. McGuckian, *On Ballycastle Beach* (Oldcastle: Gallery Press, 1996), p. 38; hereafter cited in-text as *OBB*.

21. Caroline Seebohm, *The Man Who Was Vogue: The Life and Time of Condé Nast* (New York: Viking Press, 1982), p. 2.

22. Patricia Boyle Haberstroh, *Women Creating Women: Contemporary Irish Women Poets* (New York: Syracuse University Press, 1996), p. 147.

23. Seebohm, *The Man Who Was Vogue*, p. 41.

24. Ibid, p. 60.

25. Ibid, p. 169.

26. McCracken, 'Medbh McGuckian', p. 160.

27. Elizabeth Barrett, in *The Letters of Robert Browning and Elizabeth Barrett Barrett*, vol. II (London: John Murray, 1934), p. 191.

28. Mark Ford, 'Sssnnnwhuffffll', *London Review of Books*, 11.2 (19 January 1989), 14–15.

29. Barrett, *Letters*, II, p. 464.

30. Browning, *Letters*, II, p. 352.

31. Justin Quinn, *The Cambridge Introduction to Modern Irish Poetry, 1800–2000* (Cambridge: Cambridge University Press, 2008), p. 167.

32. Alcobia-Murphy and Kirkland, 'Interview', p. 200.

33. McGuckian, in Borbála Faragó and Michaela Schrage-Früh (eds.), *The Unfixed Horizon: New Selected Poems* (Salem: Wake Forest University Press, 2015), p. xvi.

34. Alcobia-Murphy and Kirkland, 'Interview', p. 202.

35. McGuckian, in John Brown, *In the Chair: Interviews with Poets from the North of Ireland* (Clare: Salmon Publishing, 2002), p. 171.

36. Mary O'Connor, 'Medbh McGuckian' in Alexander G. Gonzalez (ed.), *Modern Irish Writers: A Bio-Critical Source Book* (Connecticut: Greenwood Press, 1997), pp. 183–4.

37. McGuckian, Reading at Rylands Library, 26 April 2014.

38. Antony Alpers, *The Life of Katherine Mansfield* (New York: Viking Press, 1980), pp. 98, 48, 18.

39. McGuckian, *In The Chair*, p. 179; McGuckian, 'Drawing Ballerinas', p. 198.

40. Longley, 'Medbh McGuckian's poetry', n.p.

41. Katherine Mansfield, quoted in Alpers, *The Life of Katherine Mansfield*, p. 250.

42. McGuckian, in 'Cómhra', *Southern Review*, 31.3 (1995), 581–614 (598).

43. Mansfield, in Alpers, *The Life of Katherine Mansfield*, p. 255.

44. Alcobia-Murphy and Kirkland, 'Interview', p. 1W9.

45. McGuckian, *In the Chair*, p. 171.

46. McGuckian, 'A Hand-Stitched Balloon' in Robin Robertson (ed.), *Love Poet, Carpenter: Michael Longley at Seventy* (London: Enitharmon, 2009), p. 84.

47. Owain Jones and Paul Cloke, *Tree Cultures: The Place of Trees and Trees in Their Place* (Oxford: Berg, 2002), pp. 91, xi, 138, 73.

48. Ibid., p. 91.

49. Patricia Fara, *Pandora's Breeches: Women, Science and Power in the Enlightenment* (London: Pimlico, 2004), pp. 157, 149.

50. Ibid., p. 130. McGuckian has added the adjective 'dark'.

51. McGuckian, 'Cómhra', p. 610.

52. McGuckian, 'Michael Longley as a Metaphysical', *Colby Quarterly*, 39.3 (2003), 215–20 (217).
53. Quoted in Alcobia-Murphy, 'You Took Away My Biography', p. 124.
54. In McCracken, 'Medbh McGuckian', p. 161.
55. Flynn, *Reading Medbh McGuckian*, p. 188.
56. McGuckian, quoted in Alcobia-Murphy, 'You Took Away My Biography', p. 121.

SELECTED FURTHER READING

Editions

Selected Poems: 1978–1994 (Oldcastle: Gallery Press, 1997).
The Unfixed Horizon; New Selected Poems, ed. Borbála Faragó and Michaela Schrage-Früh (Salem: Wake Forest University Press, 2015).

Critical

Alcobia-Murphy, Shane, *Medbh McGuckian: The Poetics of Exemplarity* (Aberdeen: AHRC Centre for Irish and Scottish Studies, 2012).
Alcobia-Murphy, Shane and Richard Kirkland (eds.), *The Poetry of Medbh McGuckian: The Interior of Words* (Cork: Cork University Press, 2010).
Faragó, Borbála, *Medbh McGuckian* (Cork: Cork University Press, 2014).
Flynn, Leontia, *Reading Medbh McGuckian* (Dublin: Irish Academic Press, 2014).

29

PETER MCDONALD

Paul Muldoon

I

In 1990, the thirty-eight-year-old Paul Muldoon seemed to have emerged as the most excitingly innovative narrative poet in contemporary literature. *Madoc: A Mystery*, published in that year, was his most ambitious work to date: its long title-poem is an extended conceit, in which Robert Southey and S. T. Coleridge are imagined as having actually carried out their Pantisocratic scheme to found a philosophical commune in America in the early nineteenth century. This imagined turn of events is pieced together through a huge series of short sections, each of which operates under the sign of a name from Western philosophical history. The unreal history described in the narrative turns out to be reconstructed in some future world, from deciphered images on the retina of a character called South.

This epic conception (albeit an epic of short poetic pieces that function as lyric pixels in making its big picture) developed from already impressive beginnings. Muldoon had composed three major narrative poems or sequences: '7, Middagh Street' in *Meeting the British* (1987), 'The More A Man Has The More A Man Wants' in *Quoof* (1983) and 'Immram' in *Why Brownlee Left* (1980), and all three works are among the most striking and important to have come from an Irish poet in the twentieth century. These great landmarks of the 1980s combine two distinctively Muldoonian areas, in bringing together capacious openness to the facts, to the raw data of history (literary, documentary and cultural), with a sense of style, of distinctive cadence in the poetic line, of rhetorical mastery and ease, and virtuoso feats of rhyme and formal arrangement, that gave Paul Muldoon an instantly identifiable voice.

The quality of Muldoon's volumes from the 1980s rests partly on his establishing there a completely persuasive, if persistently non-committal, habit of observation; and it is this which gives the 1980s narratives their stylistic *brio*. Another element of this style is its ability to intuit and half-suggest connections between apparently unrelated things – a 'metaphysical' poetic trait, perhaps, but not one likely to be mistaken for an imitation of John Donne, or even of William Empson. As early as *Mules* (1977), in his sonnet 'Ma', Muldoon could offer two pictures of his mother, one showing her 'bookish, sitting / Under a willow', the other on a motor-bike with a 'stranger' who is 'Not my father' but 'An American soldier, perhaps'. These are to be taken as the lives she lived, or might have lived. At the turn of the sonnet, the voice takes a turn towards a locality, not once seeming to return to 'Ma' herself:

> And the full moon
> Swaying over Keenaghan, the orchards and the cannery,
> Thins to a last yellow-hammer, and goes.
> The neighbours gather, all Keenaghan and Collegelands,
> There is story-telling. Old miners at Coalisland
> Going into the ground. Swinging, for fear of the gas,
> The soft flame of a canary.   (*P*, p. 49)

The rhymes are eye-catching as well as easy on the ear ('goes'/ 'gas', 'cannery'/ 'canary'), but their beguiling music covers a puzzle: where has 'Ma' gone? No answer is given, but a reader might wonder why exactly all the neighbours have gathered now, and what resonance that image of the Coalisland miners 'Going into the ground' might have. Something – more than just one thing, perhaps – is not being said; and the poem's aesthetic power resides in this very reticence.

The (always fallible) filling-in of gaps is of the essence in Muldoon's major narrative poems too, and is a basic principle of 'Madoc: A Mystery'. But there was something finally unsustainable in this procedure for Muldoon, and it may be that the long narrative of 1990 tested the principle to the point at which it failed. For this poem, the epic to cap his previous brief epics, is vulnerable to the accusation of being more style than substance: something is missing from the elaborate fantasy, and in the end damagingly so. That something is the charge of personal meaning which had energised Muldoon's shorter works, and had been suggested even at the very start of his career when, in *New Weather* (1973), he announced that 'Most of the world is centred / About ourselves' (*P*, p. 4). So, when South takes a tumble at the start of the narrative into 'the unruffled, waist-deep hedge / with its furbelow of thorns / and deckle-edged // razor-ribbon' (*P*, p. 203), Muldoon is recycling something from his previous book, diverting its power into merely narrative utility. In 'The Coney' from *Meeting the British*, it is Bugs Bunny who chooses to take the tumble, calling the shocked poet by his father's name:

> The moment he hit the water
> he lost his tattered
> bathing-togs

> to the swimming pool's pack of dogs.
> 'Come in': this flayed
> coney would parade
> and pirouette like honey on a spoon:
> 'Come on in, Paddy Muldoon.'   (*P*, p. 153)

There is more real mystery here than anything in 'Madoc: A Mystery', and more genuinely unfinished (perhaps unfinishable) business being done.

If 1990 saw the culmination of one kind of artistic development for Muldoon, his work as a poet afterwards had to twist back on itself, and in the process turn away from the more overtly narrative models on which some of its greatest successes had been built. Put like this, it is not just W. B. Yeats's habit of self-remaking in poetry which is being suggested: in a deeper-seated way, it is Yeats's conception of poetic experience as something privy to great contrary movements and tendencies, with the past and present rushing into and away from each other, and the poet's life pulled in different directions by its own facts and fictions, that Muldoon re-inhabits in his increasingly large-scale work after 1990. With this in mind, the present essay will turn Muldoon's development since then back on itself, in order to get a sense of the dynamics that have been in play.[1]

II

Of the many things there are to know in Muldoon's 2015 collection *One Thousand Things Worth Knowing*, facts connected to the keeping of domestic fowl are not the least. 'Charles Émile Jacque: *Poultry Among Trees*' includes a great deal of practical wisdom which could plausibly be drawn from its announced source in *Poultry Keeping for Dummies*,[2] as well as this:

> Their temperature being 106 centigrade
> might account for the quizzical
> view chickens take of history going in cycles,
> but I could divine from the jade
>
> of her exposed neck, the movement of her gizzard
> jewelled by broken oyster shells,
> one hen had ventured so far on the gravel shoals
> she'd become less hen than lizard.   (*OTTWK*, p. 15)

The different kinds of information here are differently unreliable. On the most straightforward level, these chickens are so hot that they're on the way to being cooked, for while the body temperature of a healthy chicken is indeed 106 degrees, that is in degrees Fahrenheit, and not centigrade. Maybe this high temperature is occasioned by the possibilities of rhyme, for 'centigrade' will be met by the word 'jade'. The chicken has been consuming the wrong things on 'the gravel shoals', but it is as much a stretch to see her gizzard 'jewelled' with 'jade' as it is to suggest that she is now 'less hen than lizard'. The tone, at once worldly wise and whimsical, also sounds in 'the quizzical / view chickens take of history going in cycles': 'quizzical' sits on both sides of the worldly/whimsical divide, for the poet's voice (like the reader's reaction) remains less than wholly convinced of the hens' critique of cyclical history.

But why should Muldoon's poultry be contemplating this in the first place? For the concept of 'history going in cycles' is certainly hard matter to digest, even if one is not oneself a chicken; and the poem leaves us in little doubt that there are dangers in swallowing hard things, however 'jewelled' they may appear. The other aspect of this glamorous richness, after all, is nothing more exclusive than 'gravel' and 'broken oyster shells' – these latter making for a moment of brief connection with the opening of T. S. Eliot's 'The Love Song of J. Alfred Prufrock'.[3] Equally tricky is the import of Muldoon's raising 'cycles of history' in this (utterly inappropriate) context; for just as fleetingly as the spirit of Eliot has been courted with 'oyster shells', so it is the ghost of Yeats who seems to appear for the moment (but only for the moment) these 'cycles' are adduced. Perhaps Muldoon's setting and tone here are glancing hints that such portentous cyclic visions are essentially for the birds. And it was Yeats, after all, who once grandly declared that 'As to the poultry yards, with them I have no concern.'[4] So, asking what a Muldoon poem is 'about' is importantly a matter of watching how that poem goes around and about the myriad things it is liable to include: the meaning is in the movement.

Already, it will be clear that Yeats's gyres are not quite absent from a lot of what Muldoon does – that is to say, the older poet's dominant intellectual image of contrary forces that swirl up all the data of art, of history and of life into interpenetrating whirls of energy, where time going forward meets time turning back, is altogether germane to the younger poet's imagination and ambition. This applies in several senses, but the most important of these is that of overall, volume-by-volume design in the Muldoon oeuvre. The dynamics of his collections are often those of diffusion and concentration, where both verbal and imagistic motifs are scattered with what at first reading can seem the abandon of sheer profusion, and they are then subject to gathering and re-combination, before being launched again in a final burst of re-configured energy and connection. Often, a Muldoon collection will close with major re-animation of its component parts in the shape of a long poem or sequence: for *One Thousand Things Worth Knowing*, this is the nineteen pages of sonnets that make up the piece entitled 'Dirty Data'. 'Dirty data' is 'data that contains erroneous information', and 'may also be used when referring to data that is in memory and not yet loaded into a database'. As if this wasn't bad enough, 'The complete removal of dirty data from a source is impractical or virtually impossible'.[5] In Muldoon's volumes, what goes around comes around, but it is not so much amplified or harmonised as (to use the language of computer files) corrupted there.

In terms of sheer quantity of information proffered, Muldoon outdoes Yeats, though he is more careful to be precise about his facts before distorting them into components of a personal fiction. Thus, 'Dirty Data' often addressees a 'Lew' who can be identified with Lewis Wallace (1827–1905), the author of *Ben-Hur: A Tale of the Christ* (1880). Wallace's connections with both Mexico and New Mexico feature in Muldoon's poem, but are caught up into cultural history of which he was ignorant: that of twentieth-century Ireland. While this can encompass the Troubles in Muldoon's own Northern Ireland, it also includes the point of seemingly random connection between Wallace and Ireland, in Seosamh MacGrianna's translation of *Ben-Hur* into Irish, *Ben Hur: Scéal fá Chríost* (1933). Muldoon's details are all correct enough; it is with his conjunctions of them that he ventures into the fictive, creating a seemingly endless string of coincidence which is less a string than a whirling vortex of recurrence, of a kind that Yeats would recognise. The coherence resides not in the subjects, but with the author who brings them together. In just five lines of 'Dirty Data', for example, Muldoon sweeps up a good deal of his own oeuvre along with the 'data' itself:

> It's easy to see how a UVF man posing as a B-Special
> became a privileged insider.
> Back in 1933, Mac Grianna had wondered if he should render "clockwise"
>   as *deisal*,
>
>   that being the direction in which a lobster (even one on a tether)
>   tended to move around a henge.   (*OTTWK*, p. 115)

The multiple allusions here are in significant part allusions to the works of Paul Muldoon, though they are at the same time recurring motifs in the 'Dirty Data' sequence itself.[6] A system of recurrence is certainly at the heart of things – and here, as with most of Muldoon's volumes, this is a recurrence of information, allusion and image which is mirrored by elaborate structures of formal recurrence in the verse's rhymes, repetitions and variations. A fully-informed reader must become a 'privileged insider' in more senses than one. 'Dirty Data' does not have room for one of *Ben-Hur*'s better-known lines; and this very fact may have a bearing on Muldoon's larger-scale works and their swirls of knowledge: 'Would you hurt a man keenest', Wallace writes, 'strike at his self-love'.[7]

Not that hurt is a concept at all lacking from Muldoon's poetry: consistently, the poems have been alert to – even keen on the track of – the kinds of physical and emotional suffering that go some way beyond a reader's readiness to feel sympathy, and near the point at which the eyes are more naturally turned away. *Maggot* (2010) is Muldoon's most distressing book, in this sense, though it is far from being his most distressed: it is more concerned to inflict than to register shock, and seems to belong to that part of the Yeatsian philosophy (and aesthetic) in which 'the blood-dimmed tide is loosed', and there is an 'Odour of blood on the ancestral stair', the violent moment at the cataclysmic turning of the gyres.[8] For Yeats, the violence is perhaps as extreme, but seldom quite as graphic as for Muldoon; and *Maggot* is not a book with interpretations to offer for the deaths and decompositions which it describes. Horrors may enter poems almost casually, as though feeling no need to account for their presence, as when a section of 'When the Pie Was Opened' ends with 'As if you might gather / yourself about a core / of high explosives packed into a vest' (*M*, p. 29), or a sonnet in the sequence 'Arion and the Dolphin' asks:

> What's not to love about this vestige
>
> of the tail of a water nymph
> who might learn within the week it's not the blue-green of a scaly femur
> but gangrene kicking into its second stage?   (*M*, p. 40)

'What's not to love?' (a returning motif in the sequence) is a carefully calibrated exercise in offhand tone, blatantly at odds with the image that is to follow it; an authorial voice in this poem is evidently inured to something that a reader can only with difficulty endure the sight of, and this act of poetic distancing is a key component of Muldoon's work. The same thing happens in 'Moryson's Fancy', where a grisly snippet of Elizabethan reportage from Ireland, in which three children are reduced to eating the corpse of their mother, gets recycled with attitude:

> Check out the cuffs. Check out the farthingales
> through which they so resolutely ate.
> Maybe they'll yet look into their mother's entrails
> and somehow haruspicate
>
> that the Muldoons will lose their hold on the ancient barony of Lurg
> and be reduced to ferrying pilgrims to Lough Derg.   (*M*, p. 22)

'The Muldoons' may seem to photo-bomb this scene of atrocity. Certainly, 'Check out' catastrophically misses the gravity of its occasion; and the fact that this is itself the aesthetic point of Muldoon's poem gives the reader's discomfort little in the way of alleviation.

'The Humors of Hakone' squats at the centre of *Maggot*, a sequence of nine twenty-line poems in quatrains that turn on the discovery of the body of a murdered woman in Japan. For Muldoon's speaker, the situation is that of a forensics drama, a kind of *CSI Tokyo*, in which elements that return become clues in a case, albeit clues that lead to no firm conclusion. The entire sequence is a gyrating arrangement of verbal motifs (notably, repetitions and variations on 'It was far too late to') and images, some of which are picked up from elsewhere in the volume. Mount Fuji, for instance, might seem to have a natural place in these proceedings, but it appears first as having 'yet to come to a head like a boil // about to crown its career' (*M*, p. 63): its appearance in this guise can only be attributed to the presence earlier in the book of the poem 'Myrrh', in which the speaker's mother deals with a boil on the back of his neck, leaving 'a little bloody pus / on this morning's poultice' (*M*, p. 17). The connection, then, is a real one in terms of the internal economy of Muldoon's poetry; what is more difficult to determine is the point of that connection – though the poet would seem to have already pre-empted questions about 'point' with another of the sequence's recurring images, that of 'A poem decomposing around what looked like an arrow' (*M*, p. 63). Some of the iterations of this image in 'the Humors of Hakone' make speculation about Muldoon's meta-poetic intentions almost unavoidable: 'Too late to insist that the body of a poem is no less sacred / than a temple with its banner gash // though both stink to high heaven', 'Too late to divine / that what was now merely the air pocket of a capsized boat // had been a poem decomposing around a quill' (*M*, p. 68). Finally, and with a calculated reflexivity, the speaker notes how 'the poem began to self-digest' (*M*, p. 70). The conclusion to which Muldoon seems anxious to push a reader is that his poems in *Maggot* not only eat themselves, but decompose before our very eyes.

Such gruesome prospects were not remote ones in Muldoon's previous full collection, *Horse Latitudes* (2006), though in this book the brooding on mortality does not quite speed up into a fascination with rotting away. The situations in this collection are often elegiac ones – ones, that is, in which although it may be too late to hope for escape from loss, it is not too late for memory, and the power which (however ambivalently) elegy can grant to the act of remembering. A long poem at the end of the book, 'Sillyhow Stride', splices two elegiac subjects, the singer-songwriter Warren Zevon, and Muldoon's own sister. This doubleness of focus may be felt to be problematic, a forced conjunction of familial and celebrity statuses, and the poem itself is one of Muldoon's most strained exercises, combining his customary formal procedures of repetition and kaleidoscopic rearrangement of elements with a thick literary cement in the shape of quotations from Donne. But this conflict of dual forces – of two distinct kinds of elegy, in fact – may still be to Muldoon's purpose, for the private and the public are categories which his poetry continually forces into collision.[9]

The finest elegies in *Horse Latitudes* are not the great theatres of private and public collision like 'Sillyhow Stride', but poems of narrower (and more concentrated) formal and intellectual control. 'Turkey Buzzards' is a virtuoso piece in terms of poetic shape – its twenty-five quatrains of alternating four-and two-beat lines, rhymed *abab* for the first eighteen stanzas, then rhymed in a more complex way across the remaining seven, all making up one long sentence – but it is also a feat of pained attention, in which the scavenger birds' activities are observed in an address to the poet's dying sister. A more uncomfortable subject for such an address could hardly be found, but the authorial voice is as unflinching in such niceties as it is in the face of the bloody dismemberments being contemplated ('making a / sweeping, too right, a sweeping cut / that's so blasé // it's hard to imagine, dear Sis, / why others shrink / from this sight' (*HL*, p. 80)). The buzzards' final turn (which is one with the poem's last turning in on itself, as it returns the final lines to the lines at the beginning) see them 'getting the hang at last / of being stripped // of their command of the vortex' (*HL*, p. 81): it is as if, even though Yeats's falcon cannot hear the falconer, these buzzards might yet hear an unflinching elegist, and forfeit their carrion.

And yet, within a dozen pages of *Horse Latitudes*, such hopes have expired. In the sestet of 'Hedge School', a sonnet that sees the poet thinking back to the remote family past of 'our great-great-grandmother' as well as his contemporary family life in the United States (where anxieties over Guantanamo Bay percolate into his daughter's learning of Latin verbs, 'forced to conjugate / *Guantánamo, amas amat*'), while quoting from Shakespeare (*The Comedy of Errors*) as he visits St Andrews in Scotland, 'all past and future mornings were impressed // on me':

> just now, dear Sis,
> as I sheltered in a doorway on Church Street in St. Andrews
> (where, in 673, another Maelduin was bishop),
>
> and tried to come up with a ruse
> for unsealing the *New Shorter Oxford English Dictionary* back in that corner shop
> and tracing the root of *metastasis*. (*HL*, p. 94)

But the Shakespearean promise earlier in the poem is being cruelly unfulfilled, for this will not prove a comedy, and there are few errors now: no mistakes from the poet about 'another Maelduin' having been Bishop,[10] nor about the location of the bookshop (J. & G. Innes Ltd), and no mistake about his sister's now metastasising cancer. In this, the rhyme for 'dear Sis', too, makes no mistake in its delayed (and final) arrival. Family, history and the supply of information are all brought together, with the poem as a process of discovery, paralleled by the contemplated (but unattempted) unwrapping of the shop's dictionary in search of 'the root of *metastasis*'. While that word's meaning in a medical sense is all too pressingly apparent, its earlier application in the field of formal rhetoric is not without relevance to this and others of Muldoon's poems: 'A rapid transition from one point or type of figure to another' (*OED* 'Metastasis', 1). Physical and poetic processes, in this respect, move horribly in step.

Fast movements like these between public and familial information, the historical and the intimate, are not to be separated from Muldoon's habitual rhetorical strategies. The poetry's formal rigour, too, is not above dealing with instances of *rigor mortis*; if it is to be understood as a container, of sorts, for all that comes his way, Muldoon's poetic form contains this in the sense that it keeps it in check. That is the case with the major poem in *Moy Sand and Gravel* (2002), 'At the Sign of the Black Horse, September 1999', in which an elaborate re-figuring of Yeats's 'Among School Children' stanza serves to accommodate information about the Muldoon home in New Jersey, home-cooking in the power-cuts after a hurricane, the family origins of the poet's wife in central Europe, and the resultant mixed Irish/Jewish heritage of the couple's newborn son. And of course, with forty-five eight-line stanzas, there is room for quite a lot here; furthermore, the length (and the Yeats stanza itself) repeats that of Muldoon's earlier 'Incantata' (in *The Annals of Chile* (1994)), to the extent of repeating that poem's rhymes and its circular structure, in which the final stanza rhymes with the first, the penultimate with the second and so on. The fact of the repetition may be as significant as the form itself, since part of Muldoon's meaning by now resides in the capacity of things to be repeated, as though large poetic structures were mirroring the cyclic patterns of experience that mark both private and public experiences through time. Inclusiveness is at one with pattern: while this could be thought of (approvingly) as ambitious in terms of literary effort, its ambition, because it admits of no clear boundaries between personal and public, is liable to cross the line between the conventionally acceptable and the unacceptable. How far, for instance, do the European Jewish origins on one side for the son of a tenured Ivy League professor at the end of the twentieth century entitle the poet to achieve a meaningful juxtaposition of the baby and those who died in Auschwitz-Birkenau? Does the rigour of Muldoon's formal procedures strengthen that measure of entitlement? Such questions are not easily answered, but the ethical queasiness behind them is not just factitious, any more than it is unreasonable to feel uncomfortable when faced with aspects of the private life of a family pressed into the same kind of service, as elements in the huge wheel of interconnection which Muldoon's poem becomes.

Besides the bits and pieces that at least started out as facts, Muldoon's vortex of information has plentiful room for the things that are not facts as such, but are imagined possibilities arising from the way things might have been. *Hay* (1998) is Muldoon's book of alternatives: of roads not taken in family and public history, but also of verbal mistakings, slips of the eye, of the pen, and of the printer. One whole poem is entitled 'Errata', with each of its forty lines devoted to the notional putting-right of an error ('For 'mother' read 'other''' ... 'For 'ludic' read 'lucid''' ... 'For 'ode' read 'code''' (*P*, p. 445)); another, which begins by considering 'A sentence of death, my love', ends by imagining a cruel reversal of the melodramatic announcement of a mistake in scenes of execution, when

> the rider whom we so eagerly
> awaited will leap from the saddle now, now to issue the decree
> that life is indeed no more than 'a misprint
> in the sentence of death.'   ('Now, Now', *P*, p. 407)

As this reversal (which turns out not to be a reversal, but a reversion to the poem's first words) implies, life, like written words, carries its cargo of unfulfilled but perfectly imaginable wrong turns. *Hay*'s concluding poem, a sequence of thirty sonnets entitled 'The Bangle (Slight Return)', splices the literary (Virgil's account of the sack of Troy), the journalistic (gourmet dinner in a Parisian restaurant) and the familial (the career of Muldoon's father as it might have been, had he emigrated to Australia), allowing these different might-have-beens to interweave and intercut, subject all the way to further levels of mistaking and verbal slippage. The effect is dizzying, but perhaps not more; and again, the sequence folds into itself many elements from elsewhere in the volume, so that local interpretations quickly slide into larger (and more baffling) aspects of Muldoon's pattern. There is a distinct feeling that only form stands between *Hay*'s articulations and a disabling inarticulacy. Even 'Errata' may be a mistake: '"For 'errata,'" Virgil smiled, "read 'corrigenda'"' (*P*, p. 475).

Are mistakes to be made, or to be corrected? The question arises naturally enough from Muldoon's previous collection, *The Annals of Chile* (1994). This is the poet's strongest single volume, both his most original and his most moving piece of sustained work. *Hay* deliberately swerves towards the poetics of error partly in reaction to its predecessor's disciplines of correction, which reach far into the familial history that the poet understands as being at the heart of his imaginative conditioning. Two poems in particular make *The Annals of Chile* the central work for Muldoon: 'Incantata', which is an elegy for the artist Mary Farl Powers, and 'Yarrow', the book's long concluding piece, partly an elegy for the poet's mother. There are formal links between the two works, but 'Yarrow' is on a bigger scale formally than 'Incantata', and addresses possibly the more intractable hurt. The two poems also establish alternative modes of articulation for art's relation to loss, 'Incantata' being attracted to the monumental, and 'Yarrow' more a series of wheels within wheels, where the multiple repetitions of sestina-like structures, all tangled within one another, start much more in the way of association than they could ever bring to a close. In 'Incantata', one stanza in particular concentrates the monumental (and directly Yeatsian) intent of Muldoon's grief:

> I thought of how art may be made, as it was by André Derain,
> of nothing more than a turn
> in the road where a swallow dips into the mire
> or plucks a strand of bloody wool from a strand of barbed wire
> in the aftermath of Chickamauga or Culloden
> and builds from pain, from misery, from a deep-seated hurt,
> a monument to the human heart
> that shines like a golden dome among roofs rain-glazed and leaden.
>
> (*P*, p. 335)

This is a moment of stillness, with the only turning its location at 'a turn / in the road'; the historical locations for 'deep-seated hurt' may be far-flung, but the swallow's building has a permanence which Muldoon's poetry only very rarely pauses to contemplate. Two images gesture beyond the immediate occasion: 'the mire' and 'a golden dome' lead us outwards – or backwards, or further in – to Yeats's 'Byzantium', with its 'mire of human veins' set against 'a starlit or a moonlit dome'.[11]

In 'Yarrow', nothing can stand still, so that grief, like all the other elements of this long poem, from Muldoon's boyhood adventure-story reading to the fictionalised sex-and-politics student world of a relationship with a woman appearing as 'S ——', must take its place in the whirling around of interpenetrating circular systems of recurrence and recall. At the poem's close, where all the various sestina-elements are woven together, the sound of grief and the noise of the machinery are one and the same:

> in a conventional envoy, her voice would be ever
> soft, gentle and low
> and the chrism of milfoil might over-
>
> flow
> as the great wheel
> came full circle; here a bittern's bibulous '*Orinochone O*'
>
> is counterpointed only by that corncrake, but the gulder-gowl

of a nightjar, I guess, above the open-cast mines,
by a quail's

indecipherable code; of a great cog-wheel, all that remains
is a rush of air – a wing-beat,
more like – past my head; even as I try to regain

my equilibrium, there's no more relief, no more respite
than when I scurried, click, down McParland's lane
with my arms crossed, click, under my armpits;   (P, pp. 391–2)

The truth in this poem is that there is no 'equilibrium' to be regained and, although its large formal structure might be regarded in one way as a closed system, 'Yarrow' in fact leaves everything open in the continual turning of its 'great wheel'. Like Yeats's gyres rather than his perfected Byzantium, 'Yarrow''s forces of connection and coherence are charged with the counter-forces that must bring about their ruin.

III

Prefacing his *Poems 1968–1998* (2001), Muldoon mentioned himself as 'the person through whom a poem was written' (P, p. xv). That formulation seems oddly self-distanced, but it is true to the deeper forces in this poet's aesthetic impulse, and to the dynamics that make his poems the things they are. Throughout, Muldoon has made himself a necessary part of the dramatic subject-matter which the circling, and continually self-ingesting, structures of his volumes require. An acknowledgement of this may be heard in Muldoon's remarks on Yeats's 'relationship, geographical and historical, to the material of the moment':[12]

> My sense is that it's part of our responsibility as reader to try, insofar as it's possible, to psych ourselves into that moment, as well as into the mind through which it made its way into this world, not only in terms of placing a text in its social context, but in terms of its relation to other texts.

The hope is that 'the mind' of the poet is up to the pressures of 'the moment'. Such a hope could be figured just as readily as an anxiety – as the anxiety behind *A Vision*, perhaps, as well as that behind Muldoon's books of poetry. But both the hope and the anxiety, for Muldoon as for Yeats, can also be understood as motive forces, unresting in their contrary movements and impulses as they generate the body of a poet's work.

*

Abbreviations

The following abbreviations have been used in the text for references to volumes of Paul Muldoon's poetry.

HL: *Horse Latitudes* (London: Faber and Faber, 2006)
M: *Maggot* (London: Faber and Faber, 2010)
MSG: *Moy Sand and Gravel* (London: Faber and Faber, 2002)
OTTWK: *One Thousand Things Worth Knowing* (London: Faber and Faber, 2015)
P: *Poems 1968–1998* (London: Faber and Faber, 2001)

NOTES

1. It will be objected that this is to short-change critically the significance and complexity of Muldoon's pre-1990 poetry. That is very likely to be so; however, the present critic has written before at length in praise of that work: see Peter McDonald, *Mistaken Identities: Poetry and Northern Ireland* (Oxford: Clarendon Press, 1997), ch.6.
2. Muldoon's admission, 'Though I might have taken the blueprint of a shack / from *Poultry Keeping for Dummies*' (*OTTWK*, p. 15), alludes to a text that is fictional, but it is only just so: Kimberley Willis and Robert T. Ludlow's book in the well-known *for Dummies* guidebook series is entitled *Raising Chickens for Dummies* (Hoboken: Wiley Publishing, 2009).
3. 'And sawdust restaurants with oyster-shells': 'The Love Song of J. Alfred Prufrock', l. 7. Christopher Ricks and Jim McCue (eds.), *The Poems of T. S. Eliot vol. 1: Collected and Uncollected Poems* (London: Faber and Faber, 2015), p. 5.
4. W. B. Yeats, letter to John O'Leary, 3 Feb. 1889, John Kelly and Eric Domville (eds.), *The Collected Letters of W. B. Yeats* vol.1 (Oxford: Clarendon Press, 1986), p. 138.
5. Definition of 'dirty data' from *Technopaedia*, www.techopedia.com/definition/1194/dirty-data, accessed 8 March 2016.
6. The B-Specials (an armed, part-time wing of the Ulster Special Constabulary, in existence from 1920 until 1970) feature in Muldoon's 'The Sightseers' from *Quoof* (1983) (*P68–98*, p. 111); 'deasil' is important to the poem 'Brazil' in *The Annals of Chile* (1994) (*P68–98*, p. 328); the lobster on a tether comes from the poem 'Something Else' in *Meeting the British* (1987), in which the French Symbolist Gerard de Nerval 'was given to promenade / a lobster on a gossamer thread' (*P68–98*, p. 173). This lobster is elsewhere in 'Dirty Data' too, where 'To add to the confusion, Ben's still trying to crack a lobster claw / with a lobster claw made of titanium' (*OTTWK*, p. 100).
7. Lewis Wallace, *Ben-Hur: A Tale of the Christ* (1880), vol. 2, p. 619.
8. W. B. Yeats, 'The Second Coming' and 'Blood and the Moon III', *The Variorum Edition of the Poems of W. B. Yeats*, eds. Peter Allt and Russell K. Alspatch (London: Macmillan, 1956), pp. 402, 482.

9. Another large-scale doubling in Muldoon's elegiac mode is the long opening poem of *One Thousand Things Worth Knowing*, 'Cuthbert and the Otters', in which an occasional meditation on St Cuthbert and the City of Durham is spliced with a personal lament for the death of Seamus Heaney. That these two subjects do not belong together (and indeed, to judge from the volume's Acknowledgements page, originated separately) is to be taken less as a weakness than as a deliberately staged disjunction.

10. Muldoon's date of 673 is wide of the mark for this, however, since the churchman in question died in 1055, and there were no Bishops of St Andrews in the seventh century.

11. W. B. Yeats, 'Byzantium', ll. 8 and 5, *Variorum Edition of the Poems*, p. 497.

12. Paul Muldoon, *The End of the Poem: Oxford Lectures on Poetry* (London: Faber and Faber, 2006), p. 27.

SELECTED FURTHER READING

Buxton, Rachel, *Robert Frost and Northern Irish Poetry* (Oxford: Oxford University Press, 2004), chapters 5–7.

Holdridge, Jefferson, *The Poetry of Paul Muldoon* (Dublin: Liffey Press, 2008).

Kendall, Tim, *Paul Muldoon* (Bridgend: Seren, 1996).

Kendall, Tim and McDonald, Peter (eds.) *Paul Muldoon: Critical Essays* (Liverpool: Liverpool University Press, 2004).

Kennedy-Andrews, Elmer (ed.), *Paul Muldoon: A Collection of Critical Essays* (Gerrards Cross: Colin Smythe, 2006).

Muldoon, Paul, 'Getting Round: Notes towards an *Ars Poetica*', *Essays in Criticism* vol. 48 no.2 (April 1998), pp. 107–28.

To Ireland, I (Oxford: Oxford University Press, 2000).

The End of the Poem: Oxford Lectures on Poetry (London: Faber and Faber, 2006).

Wills, Clair, *Reading Paul Muldoon* (Newcastle upon Tyne: Bloodaxe Books, 1998).

30

JOHN DILLON

Nuala Ní Dhomhnaill

When Nuala Ní Dhomhnaill was five years old, her parents sent her from Lancashire, England, to live with her Aunt and Uncle and her cousins in Ventry on the Dingle Peninsula on the West Coast of Ireland. At the time, she was able to understand Irish, but did not speak it. She recounts sitting at the table for dinner one night, not knowing how to speak Irish, and wanting the milk. When she tried the word 'bainne' the milk appeared, as if, she would later note, 'by magic.' 'Hey', she thought, 'this thing works!'[1] For Ní Dhomhnaill's readers, a similar sense of awe attends Ní Dhomhnaill's subsequent many collections of poetry. Her work arrests our attention with a kind of magic. In the tradition of the American poet Elizabeth Bishop or the Austrian philosopher Ludwig Wittgenstein, Ní Dhomhnaill's poetry simply urges the reader: 'Look'. Unlike any other Irish poet, Ní Dhomhnaill joins the past and the present in a way which startles us. Her work catches our attention in the deep bedrock of things which we too often taken for granted.

I

This early childhood experience is also indicative of Ní Dhomhnaill's sustained commitment to write in the Irish language. While an English-language tradition of Irish poetry, from Swift to Yeats to Heaney and Boland, has in the past dominated the syllabus and intellectual conversations, Ireland also has a robust tradition of poetry in Irish. And while Ní Dhomhnaill draws from both, she writes predominantly in Irish. In her essay 'Why I Choose to Write in Irish', Ní Dhomhnaill notes, 'If there is a level to our being that for want of any other word for it I might call "soul" (and I believe there is), then for some reason that I can never understand, the language that my soul speaks, and the place it comes from, is Irish.'[2] With the exception of a few early poems, all of Ní Dhomhnaill's poetry is written in Irish, and her decision to write in Irish has critically influenced the trajectory of her poetic career. At University College Cork, for instance, she was part of the *Innti* group which included members such as other Irish language poets Michael Davitt and Liam Ó Muirthile. This group of poets, which developed under the guidance of Seán Ó Tuama, emphasised a vibrant and changing approach to the Irish language as opposed to a pedantic one. Ní Dhomhnaill notes, in a now canonical interview with Medbh McGuckian and Laura O'Connor, 'One of the things that causes me to get up in the morning is the desire to take Irish back from that grey-faced Irish-revivalist male preserve.'[3] In key ways, Ní Dhomhnaill's poetry adds to the Irish language. Fortunately, for those who do not know Irish, Ní Dhomhnaill's poetry has been translated by many major poets into English as well as several other languages.

One of her best-known poems about Irish is 'Ceist na Teangan' (The Language Issue). This short poem, is a single question asked over sixteen lines:

Ceist na Teangan	The Language Issue
Cuirim mo dhóchas ar snámh	I place my hope on the water
i mbáidín teangan	in this little boat
faoi mar a leagfá naíonán	of the language, the way a body might put
i gcliabhán	an infant
a bheadh fite fuaite	in a basket of intertwined
de dhuilleoga feileastraim	iris leaves,
is bitiúman agus pic	its underside proofed
bheith cuimilte lena thóin	with bitumen and pitch,
ansan é a leagadh síos	then set the whole thing down amidst
i measc na ngiolcach	the sedge
is coigeal na mban sí	and bulrushes by the edge
le taobh na habhann,	of a river
féachaint n'fheadaraís	
cá dtabharfaidh an sruth é,	only to have it borne hither and thither,
féachaint, dála Mhaoise,	not knowing where it might end up;
an bhfóirfidh iníon Fhorainn?	in the lap, perhaps,
	of some Pharaoh's daughter.
	[trans. Paul Muldoon]

Like so many of Ní Dhomhnaill's poems, this poem presents a metaphor which we readily understand. On one level the narrative is eminently clear: Ní Dhomhnaill is putting her hope in the Irish language just as Moses' mother placed her son in a basket on the Nile. More broadly, 'Ceist na Teangan' is overtly responding to the precarious position of the Irish language in the twentieth and twenty-first centuries.

And Ní Dhomhnaill's poems often proceed in a straightforward manner, until we realise that there is something odd about her poetry. In this case, the metaphor doesn't quite match up because language is not something you can actually put in a boat. It is, of course, true that Ní Dhomhnaill, as a poet who writes in Irish, is literarily investing in Irish. And this somewhat strange play between language and life or the poem as a metaphor for the Pharaoh's basket also highlights Ní Dhomhnaill's more general love of language. Notice the lush vocabulary: the poem as vehicle is already winning us over with plant names such as 'coigeal na mban sí', which translates as 'distaff or spindle the banshees'. Sometimes, between the pages of her writing notebooks, she would even keep dried flowers and leaves that she had picked up. 'I know the name of every flower in Ireland in Irish', she has remarked. And there is a strange way in which Ní Dhomhnaill's use of plant names in this poem has an inherent and potent rhetorical effect.

Paul Muldoon translates 'Ceist na Teangan' as 'The Language Issue'. This translation, as other critics have noted, does justice to the complex meaning of 'ceist' as 'question', but also 'concern' and 'subject of discussion'. Muldoon has translated several of Ní Dhomhnaill's poems. In his translations, he preserves the nuance and precision of Ní Dhomhnaill's language. But best of all, he sustains a degree of play. To present a brief example: one collection of translations by Muldoon is called 'The Astrakhan Cloak', which is a play on the Irish word for translation (i.e. aistriúchán). The idea of an 'astrakhan cloak' is also, however, an analogy for understanding the process of translation. Is the process of translation like putting on a garment of clothing which imperfectly fits the original poem?

II

Ní Dhomhnaill's life is at times as fascinating as her poetry. When she was 19 years old, she met Dogan Leflef, a Turkish geologist, who was working on the Old Red Sandstone rocks of Munster in Cork. It was, she would later remark, 'love at first sight'. Ní Dhomhnaill's parents, however, did not approve of the engagement and to prevent her from marrying Leflef, she was made a ward of court. This tension between Ní Dhomhnaill and her parents, especially her mother, is described in poetic terms in her recent collection, *The Fifty Minute Mermaid*. In this collection, she uses the trope and lens of the mermaid in an effort to understand her relationship with her mother, and especially as her mother develops dementia. Not incidentally, it was also around this time that John Montague reputedly gave Ní Dhomhnaill a copy of the American poet John Berryman's *Dream Songs*. This was a key gift. In his poems, she recognises another poet who has suffered from periodic despair and depression. This collection is a critical counterbalance for Ní Dhomhnaill's tumultuous years in Ireland and her key transition from Ireland to Turkey in 1974. She would memorise Berryman's poems, recounting later on that she could recite several by heart.

Shortly after turning 21 years old, Ní Dhomhnaill and Leflef left for Utrecht, where they were married, and then headed to Istanbul before settling in Ankara, Turkey. In Ankara, Ní Dhomhnaill began to take account of her current situation: 'It was a completely different planet, but I learned how to survive'.

The move to Turkey was critical for Ní Dhomhaill for a number of reasons. It is a case where Joyce is exactly right in *Dubliners* that, 'But real adventures, I reflected, do not happen to people who remain at home: they must be sought abroad.'[4] And for this period of Ní Dhomhnaill's life there is a sense of adventure, including thrill and risk. First, while abroad, Ní Dhomhnaill acquired a self-reflective perspective. It allowed her to develop into herself beyond the at-times cliquish and coterie-esque scene of contemporary Dublin poetry. Second, Ní Dhomhnaill took on Turkish as a second language and Turkey as a second home. For instance, at the time, Ní Dhomhnaill was not welcomed by the social outings of the British Embassy in Turkey because 'she spoke Turkish to their children and not English'. And third, she acquired a geologic sense of time and place. This is attributable to her husband's profession as well as her context. From Ephesus to Miletus to Hagia Sophia in Istanbul, Ní Dhomhnaill developed a deep and layered understanding of history that is critical to her poetic project. She works with broad sweeps of history and tradition in a way that is unique. This particular understanding of history, tradition, and place is what separates Ní Dhomhnaill's work from that of many other Irish poets. In her home, there is a room that is full of books. Not with book shelves, but full in the way that you might fill a box full of books. The room is so full that books spill out of the door into the hallways. This is indicative of Ní Dhomhnaill's vast and layered knowledge of the past.

And it was in Turkey that Ní Dhomhnaill began to write poetry with a structured and routine approach. She recalls that she would go, 'Three hours a day in the Turkish American Association on Saturday. John Cheever, John Berryman. Half 10 to half 1 every Saturday morning. And then it became three hours 3 times a week.' Interestingly, Ní Dhomhnaill would often start her writing sessions by translating a John Berryman poem from English into Irish – 'I would use Berryman to get me going.'

Her first poems, however, are stylistically indebted to a tradition of what Máirtín Ó Cadhain called 'lirící beaga' or 'short lyrics.' In some ways, this is the poetry of Seán Ó Ríordáin and Máirtín Ó Direáin, who, along with Máire Mhac an tSaoi, were among the founding figures of contemporary poetry in Irish. Ó Cadhain's criticism of short lyrics was that a language could not survive in petrifying, jewel-like art. Ní Dhomhnaill's first collection, *An Dealg Droighin*, is divided up into three sections: 'Dánta Luatha' (Early Poems), 'Dánta ar Imirce' (Poems during Immigration) and 'Ar Fhilleadh ar Éirinn' (Returning to Ireland). And, in many ways, this first collection lays out the trajectory of her career. The early poetry has somewhat repetitive syntax and chiselled line breaks. These are in the tradition of 'liricí beaga' that Ó Cadhain is criticising. Nevertheless, Ní Dhomhnaill occasionally returns to this style, but with less rigid line breaks. Take, for instance, the short lyric 'Póg', which presses the short lyric into a much richer style of conversation:

Póg	Kiss
Do phóg fear eile mé	Straight on my mouth
i lár mo bheola,	another man's kiss.
do chuir sé a theanga	He put his tongue
isteach i mo bhéal.	between my lips.
Níor bhraitheas faic.	I was numb
Dúrt leis	and said to him
"Téir abhaile, a dheartháirín,	"Little man, go home
tánn tú ólta	you're drunk
is tá do bhean thall sa doras	your wife waits at the door."
ag fanacht."	
Ach nuair a chuimhním	But when I recall
ar do phógsa	*your* kiss
critheann mo chromáin	I shake, and all
is imíonn	that lies between my hips
a bhfuil eatarthu	liquifies
ina lacht.	to milk.
	[trans. Michael Hartnett]

Even in this short poem, we can see a conversational longer line influencing the line breaks and syntax. It is quite common for Ní Dhomhnaill to include dialogue in her poetry – a point to which we will return.

In Turkey, there was a breakthrough moment in Ní Dhomhnaill's development as a poet. We now know, based on archival research and interviews, that Ní Dhomhnaill is a voracious dreamer. In Turkey, she would keep a notebook and a pen beside her bed, and when awoke in the middle of the night she would write down her dreams. Sometimes in her dream records we literally see the red or black or green ink of her pen trailing down and off the page as she falls back asleep. She would often have big dreams, with long and complex narratives. These dream records span at least three decades of Ní Dhomhnaill's most creative period from 1970 to 2000 and are located in Boston College's Burns Library. At times, multiple dreams are recorded on an almost daily basis. These dreams, which have largely been overlooked by Ní Dhomhnaill's critics, form a key starting point in her creative process. In many cases, Ní Dhomhnaill first dreams the poem before writing it down. Then, she often typed up these handwritten dream records. There was also a period of time when she would code the dream records along certain recurring themes, such as 'horse' or 'foreign countries'. Ní Dhomhnaill's practice of recording dreams is indicative of her interest in the subconscious imagination as well as ideas of creativity and the lyric muse.

Stylistically, Ní Dhomhnaill's method of dream writing is reflected in a longer poetic line. While there are notable exceptions, her poetry becomes much more relaxed, the line breaks less punctuated and the syntax more conversational. This blending of writing and dreaming perhaps led her to develop this longer line. For instance, one day in April 1979 she records three dreams, the second of which begins, 'Sa tarna taibhreamh bhíos i bhfeighil ar an mbanphrionsa i dtír iasachta agus bhí béile mór le bheith ag a hathair an rí. Bhí dhá mhaighdeana coinnlithe, cúpla ab ea iad go raibh gruaig rua orthu, – in aonacht léi ach dúirt si leo dul ag snámh faoi bhun droichid.'[5] ('In the second dream, I was looking after some princess in a foreign country and her father, the king, was having a great feast. There were two ladies-in-waiting, twins who had red hair, along with her but she told them to go swimming under the bridge.') Already this dream shares some semblance to Ní Dhomhnaill's poetic preoccupations, such as her interest in myth and fairy tales. The poem which emerges from this dream is called 'Na Sceana Feola' (The Meat Knives), and it is strikingly similar:

Na Sceana Feola	The Meat Knives
Is tusa an bhanphrionsa	You are the princess
a éalaíonn amach as tigh a hathar	who creeps from her father's house
i lár an fhéasta.	at the feast's height.
Tugann tú leat	You take with you
na sceana feola éabharláimhe	the meat-knives,
mar uirlis chosanta, b'fhéidir,	knives with ivory handles
ar t'aistear.	for protection, perhaps,
	on your wanderings.
Cuireann tú iachall ar an mbeirt	
chailín coimhdeachta	You order your two
atá óg, rua agus ina gcúpla	ladies-in-waiting

tomadh san uisce	(who are two red-haired twins)
gan éadach, faoi bhun droichid	to dive in the water
agus fanacht,	naked, under a bridge,
faid is a théann tú ar aghaidh	and to wait,
go tigh do ghrá ghil.	while you go ahead
	to your darling's place.

[trans. Michael Hartnett]

To state the obvious, the poem is most definitely written from the dream. There are changes in perspective and language, but all in all, it is more akin to a revision than a different text. This change in perspective, however, is important. It is almost as if, in the dream, Ní Dhomhnaill is watching the narrative unfold and recounting the dream event. This method accounts for both the narrative quality that marks Ní Dhomhnaill's poetry as well as her long, conversational poetic line. It also explains the magic realism quality of her poetry – her poetry moves between the logical and the surreal in a way that is akin to a dream space. So many of Ní Dhomhnaill's poems feel as if she is recounting an actual event which she witnessed. This is a consequence of writing from dreaming.

III

No other contemporary Irish poet has so successfully blended a pre-modern oral tradition with contemporary affairs and concerns. Bo Almqvist, who has written on Ní Dhomhnaill's use of folklore, quotes Gabriel Rosenstock: 'No modern poet has mined folk material to such advantage.'[6] This is the most impressive aspect of Ní Dhomhnaill's work: she provides a method for jumping over the literary and aesthetic movements of Modernism and Postmodernism in a way that is convincing and believable. For W. B. Yeats, as well as many other Modernists writers such as F. G. Lorca, and Alexander Pushkin, the highest challenge was to find some way to translate a pre-modern art into a post-industrial, post-urban context. While European Modernists were only able to achieve this feat in the theatre, Ní Dhomhnaill accomplishes it in her poetry. Take, for instance, her encounter with the 'bean an leasa' or 'fairy fort woman' in 'An Crann' (As for the Quince). In folk belief, the fairy woman lived in a 'lios' or 'fairy mound', which would have been an actual mound on a farm or a patch of land that would not have been farmed or disturbed. For Ní Dhomhnaill, the 'bean an leasa' becomes a key trope or even mask:

Do tháinig bean an leasa	There came this bright young thing
le *Black & Decker*,	with a Black & Decker
do ghearr sí anuas mo chrann.	and cut down my quince-tree.
D'fhanas im óinseach ag féachaint uirthi	I stood with my mouth hanging open
faid a bhearraigh sí na brainsí	while one by one
ceann ar cheann.	she trimmed off the branches.

Note the way that Ní Dhomhnaill seamlessly blends the traditional folk figure of the 'bean an leasa' with a power tool made by Black & Decker. This is the type of verve and expansion that Ní Dhomhnaill brings to her use of the Irish language. Also note in the following stanza that Ní Dhomhnaill has hit her stride when it comes to rhythm and intonation of these more conversational poems. This is the type of adaptive approach to Irish when the language feels most alive:

Tháinig m'fhear céile abhaile tráthnóna.	When my husband got home that evening
Chonaic sé an crann.	and saw what had happened
Bhí an gomh dearg air,	he lost the rag,
ní nach ionadh. Dúirt sé	as you might imagine.
'Canathaobh nár stopais í?	'Why didn't you stop her?
Nó cad is dóigh léi?	What would she think
Cad a cheapfadh si	if I took the Black & Decker
dá bhfaighinnse *Black & Decker*	round to her place
is dul chun a tí	and cut down a quince-tree
agus crann ansúd a bhaineas léi,	belonging to her?
a ghearradh anuas sa ghairdín?'	What would she make of that?

Also note how, again, even though the narrative is clear, so much is left out for interpretation.

One of the reasons Ní Dhomhnaill returns to Ireland in 1980 is that she felt as if she was losing contact with the Irish language. Her children only spoke Turkish at the time, and she hoped that if they moved back to the Gaeltacht, the Irish-speaking area of West Kerry, they would learn Irish. Upon her return, she spent a great deal of time in The National Folklore Collection at University College Dublin, reading through local folktales told by storytellers she remembered from her childhood. At this time, Ní Dhomhnaill also made the key acquaintance of the great-storyteller Cáit Féiritéir. And in her writing notebooks we find hundreds of handwritten pages of phrases and words which she gathered out of the folklore archives. In short, when she returned to Ireland, she added to her use of the Irish language by delving into the National Folklore Collection, and this had very real payoffs for her first two collections.

Not only do Ní Dhomhnaill's first two collections, *An Dealg Droighin* and *Féar Suaithinseach*, begin with selections of folktales from Bab Féiritéir, but Ní

Dhomhnaill occasionally writes poems out of these folktales. And her poems have that type of quality where we believe in their truth even though they don't at times make any scientific sense. For instance, in 'Geasa' (The Bond), Ní Dhomhnaill outlines the dimension and gravity of the poetic space:

Má chuirim aon lámh ar an dtearmann beannaithe,	If I use my forbidden hand To raise a bridge across the river,
má thógaim droichead thar an abhainn,	All the work of the builders
gach a mbíonn tógtha isló ages na ceardaithe	Has been blown up by sunrise. [trans. Medbh McGuckian]
bíonn sé leagtha ar maidin romham.	

This poem, which draws from Bab Féiritéir's folktale 'An tSeanachailleach', has the same aesthetic quality of a folktale, where the rules of cause and effect do not need explanation or justification. This could be called cultural bedrock, or a rule unto itself. In the poem, there is no logical reason why the bridge continues to fall down. While Ní Dhomhnaill likes to point out that behind commonplace taboos there is often scientific justification, what strikes us here is the aesthetic quality of the poetry. In this sense, Ní Dhomhnaill has found a way to adopt this type of folkloric or aesthetic logic into the realm of the lyric. Ní Dhomhnaill's poetry overlaps with the oral tradition in its fascination with the seemingly illogical but aesthetically sound. Many of her poems are simply snippets of thought or life which strike us as remarkable, but we are not sure exactly why.

For Ní Dhomhnaill, these are some of the elements of her poetry: the Irish language, her life in Turkey, writing from dreaming, and a tradition of Irish folklore. These elements highlight a relationship with the past and tradition, which is unique to Ní Dhomhnaill in the Irish, English and American traditions. All of these aspects point to a valuable logic of poetry and aesthetic experience which is critical for narrative, history, and tradition. There are many other important themes to Ní Dhomhnaill's work, that have not been explored in this chapter, particularly the poet's relationship with her family and the way in which Ní Dhomhnaill has carved out space for female poets in a highly gendered tradition. Not only, though, is Ní Dhomhaill a master of blending the everyday with the miraculous, she is also a master of lyric craft. And to hear Ní Dhomhnaill read one of her poems in Irish is a great pleasure. It is almost as if we are invited into the dream space out of which Ní Dhomhnaill writes. To conclude with the opening of one of Ní Dhomhnaill's most lyric poems: 'Titim i nGrá' is translated by Paul Muldoon in *The Astrakhan Cloak*, and marks a high lyric threshold. Here we see the rift that leads to the lyric moment – which causes shivers down the spine. Seán Ó Ríordáin called it the 'geit' or 'startlement' of poetry.

Titim i nGrá	I Fall in Love
Titim i ngrá gach aon bhliain ins an bhfómhar leis na braonaíocha báistí ar ghloine tosaigh an chairr, leis an solas leicideach filiúil ag dul thar fóir na gcnoc ag íor na spéire os mo chomhair. Le duilleoga dreoite á gcuachadh i mo shlí go cruiceach, le muisiriúin, lúibíní díomais ar adhmad lofa, titim i ngrá fiú leis an gcré fhuar is an bogach Nuair a chuimhním gurb é atá á thuar dúinn fós, a stór.	I fall in love, in the fall of every year, with the smattering of rain on my windshield and the pale and wan light toppling over the sheer edge of my field of vision, with leaves strewn in my way, with the bracket-fungus screwed to a rotten log: I fall in love with bog and cold clay and what they hold in store for me and you, my dear. [trans. Paul Muldoon]

NOTES

1. This quotation and subsequent quotations of Nuala Ni Dhomhnaill are based on several conversations with the author, especially during April 2015 at the John J. Burns Library at Boston College.
2. Nuala Ní Dhomhnaill, *Selected Essays*, ed. Oona Frawley (Dublin: New Island, 2005).
3. Nuala Ní Dhomhnaill, Medbh McGuckian, and Laura O'Connor, 'Comhrá, with a Foreward and Afterward by Laura O'Connor', *The Southern Review*, 1995.
4. James Joyce, *Dubliners* (Dublin: The O'Brien Press, 2005).
5. Nuala Ni Dhomhnaill, Box 8, Folder 1–2, Nuala Ni Dhomhnaill Papers, 1974–2000 (MS1997–12), John J. Burns Library, Boston.
6. Bo Almqvist, 'Of Mermaids and Marriages. Seamus Heaney's "Maighdean Mara" and Nuala Ní Dhomhnaill's "an Mhaighdean Mhara" in the Light of Folk Tradition', *Béaloideas*, 1990; John Dillon, '*Writing by Night: Nuala Ní Dhomhnaill and the Dream Notebooks*', Winston-Salem: Wake Forrest University Press, 2016.

SELECTED FURTHER READING

Editions

The chronology and publication history of Ní Dhomhnaill's poetry is somewhat overlapping because her works were originally published solely in Irish and then as dual-language editions in English and Irish. Ní Dhomhnaill's work has also been translated in many other languages. What this also means is that a more recent collection with translations in English, such *The Fifty Minute Mermaid*, may include poems written many years ago. A good starting point for reading Ní Dhomhnaill's poetry in English is *The Astrakhan Cloak* (translated by Paul Muldoon) or *The Wake Forest Book of Irish Women's Poetry 1967–2000*. In Irish, Ní Dhomhnaill's first two collections, *An Dealg Droighin* and *Féar Suaithinseach* (published by Cló Mercier) are invaluable to the research scholar but difficult to track down.

Biographical

Ní Dhomhnaill, Nuala, *Selected Essays*, ed. Oona Frawley, Dublin: New Island, 2005.

Ní Dhomhnaill, Nuala, Medbh McGuckian, and Laura O'Connor, 'Comhrá, with a Foreward and Afterward by Laura O'Connor', *The Southern Review*, 31, no. 3, Summer 1995.

Critical

Almqvist, Bo, 'Of Mermaids and Marriages. Seamus Heaney's "Maighdean Mara" and Nuala Ní Dhomhnaill's "an Mhaighdean Mhara" in the Light of Folk Tradition', *Béaloideas*, IML 58, 1990, 1–74.

Nic Dhiarmada, Bríona, Téacs Baineann *Téacs Mná: Gnéithe de fhilíocht Nuala Ní Dhomhnaill*, Baile Átha Cliath (Dublin): An Clóchomhar Tta, 2005.

Sewell, Frank, *Modern Irish Poetry: A New Alhambra*, Oxford: Oxford University Press, 2001.

Shay, Cary A., *Of Mermaids and Others: An Introduction to the Poetry of Nuala Ní Dhomhnaill*, Dublin: Peter Lang, 2013.

FURTHER READING

Poets on Poetry

Goldsmith, Oliver, *Collected Letters of Oliver Goldsmith*, ed. Katherine C. Balderston, Cambridge, Cambridge University Press, 1928.

Moore, Thomas, *Letters of Thomas Moore*, ed. Wilfred S. Dowden, 2 vols., Oxford, Oxford University Press, 1964.

Mangan, James Clarence, *James Clarence Mangan: Selected Writings*, ed. Sean Ryder, Dublin: University College Dublin Press, 2004.

Yeats, William Butler, *Autobiographies*, London, Macmillan, 1955.

Mythologies, London, Macmillan, 1959.

Memoirs, ed. Denis Donoghue, London, Macmillan, 1972.

Kavanagh, Patrick, *Lapped Furrows. Correspondence 1933–1967 between Patrick and Peter Kavanagh: with Other Documents*, ed. Peter Kavanagh, New York, The Peter Kavanagh Hand Press, 1969.

A Poet's Country: Selected Prose, ed. Antoinette Quinn, Dublin, Lilliput Press, 2003.

MacNeice, Louis, *The Poetry of W.B. Yeats*, Oxford, Oxford University Press, 1941.

Selected Literary Criticism of Louis MacNeice, ed. Alan Heuser, Oxford, Clarendon, 1987.

The Strings Are False: An Unfinished Autobiography (1963), London, Faber & Faber, 2007.

Letters of Louis MacNeice, ed. Jonathan Allison, London, Faber & Faber, 2010.

Hewitt, John, *Ancestral Voices: The Selected Prose of John Hewitt*, ed. Tom Clyde, Belfast, Blackstaff Press, 1987.

A North Light: Twenty-five Years in a Municipal Art Gallery, eds. Frank Ferguson and Kathryn White, Dublin, Four Courts Press, 2013.

Kinsella, Thomas, *Prose Occasions 1951–2006*, ed. Andrew Fitzsimons, Manchester, Carcanet Press, 2009.

Murphy, Richard, *The Kick: A Life Among Writers*, London, Granta, 2002.

Clarke, Austin, *Reviews and Essays of Austin Clarke*, ed. Gregory Schirmer, Gerrards Cross, Colin Smythe, 1995.

Montague, John, *The Figure in the Cave, and Other Essays*, ed. Antoinette Quinn, Dublin, Lilliput Press, 1989.

Company: A Chosen Life, London, Duckworth, 2001.

The Pear is Ripe: A Memoir, Dublin, Liberties, 2007.

Heaney, Seamus, *Preoccupations: Selected Prose 1968 – 1978*, London, Faber & Faber, 1980.

Finders Keepers Selected Prose 1971–2001, London, Faber & Faber, 2002.

Stepping Stones: Interviews with Seamus Heaney, ed. by Dennis O'Driscoll, London, Faber & Faber, 2008.

Longley, Michael, *Tupenny Stung: Autobiographical Chapters*, Belfast, Lagan Press, 1994.

Mahon, Derek, *Selected Prose*, Loughcrew, Gallery Press, 2012.

Boland, Eavan, *Object Lessons: The Life of the Woman and the Poet in Our Time*, Manchester, Carcanet Press, 1995.

A Journey with Two Maps: Becoming a Woman Poet, Manchester, Carcanet Press, 2011.

Ni Chuilleanain, Eilean, *Irish Women: Image and Achievement*, Dublin, Arlen House, The Women's Press, 1985.

Muldoon, Paul, *Viewpoints: Poets in Conversation with John Haffenden*, London, Faber & Faber, 1981.

I am Ireland, Oxford, Oxford University Press, 2000.

The End of the Poem: Oxford Lectures on Poetry, London, Faber & Faber, 2006.

Sleeping with Monsters: Conversations with Scottish and Irish Women Poets, ed. Rebecca E. Wilson, Dublin, Wolfhound Press, 1990.

Poets Talking: Poet of the Month Interviews from BBC Radio 3, ed. Clive Wilmer, Manchester, Carcanet Press, 1994.

In the Chair: Interviews with Poets from the North of Ireland, ed. John Brown, Cliffs of Moher, Salmon Publishing, 2002.

Ni Dhomhnaill, Nuala, *Selected Essays*, ed. by Oona Frawley, Dublin, New Island, 2005.

Critics

Brearton, Fran and Gillis, Alan, eds., *The Oxford Handbook of Modern Irish Poetry*, Oxford, Oxford University Press, 2012.

Brown, Terence, *The Literature of Ireland: Culture and Criticism*, Cambridge, Cambridge University Press, 2010.

Campbell, Matthew, *The Cambridge Companion to Contemporary Irish Poetry*, Cambridge, Cambridge University Press, 2003.

Irish Poetry under the Union, 1801–1924, New York, Cambridge University Press, 2013.

Canny, Nicholas, *Making Ireland British, 1580–1650*, Oxford, Oxford University Press, 2001.

Clark, Heather, *The Ulster Renaissance, Poetry in Belfast 1962–1972*, Oxford, Oxford University Press, 2006.

Corkery, Daniel, *The Hidden Ireland*, Dublin, Gill & Macmillan, 1924.

Deane, Seamus, *Strange Country: Modernity and Nationhood in Irish Writing since 1790*, Oxford, Oxford University Press, 1997.

Gillis, Alan, *Irish Poetry of the 1930s*, Oxford: Oxford University Press, 2005.

Goodby, John, *Irish Poetry since 1950: From Stillness into History*, Manchester, Manchester University Press, 2000.

Kelleher, Margaret and O'Leary, Philip, eds., *The Cambridge History of Irish Literature*, 2 vols., Cambridge, Cambridge University Press, 2006.

Kiberd, Declan, *Irish Classics*, London, Granta, 2000.

Leersen, Joep, *Remembrance and Imagination: Patterns in the Historical and Literary Representation of Ireland in the Nineteenth Century*, Cork, Cork University Press, 1996.

Longley, Edna, *Poetry in the Wars*, Newcastle, Bloodaxe Books, 1986.

The Living Stream: Literature and Revisionism in Ireland, Newcastle, Bloodaxe Books, 1994.

Poetry and Posterity, Newcastle, Bloodaxe Books, 2000.

McCrea, Barry, *Languages of the Night, Minor Languages and the Literary Imagination in Twentieth-century Ireland and Europe*, New Haven, Yale University Press, 2015.

McDonald, Peter, *Mistaken Identities: Poetry and Northern Ireland*, Oxford, Oxford University Press, 2000.

Quinn, Justin, *The Cambridge Introduction to Modern Irish Poetry 1800–2000*, Cambridge, Cambridge University Press, 2008.

White, Harry, *Music and the Irish Literary Imagination*, Oxford, Oxford University Press, 2008.

Anthologies

Carpenter, Andrew, ed., *Verse in English from Eighteenth-Century Ireland*, Cork, Cork University Press, 1998.

Verse in English from Tudor and Stuart Ireland, Cork, Cork University Press, 2003.

Collins, Lucy, *Poetry by Women in Ireland: A Critical Anthology 1870–1970*, Liverpool, Liverpool University Press, 2012.

Crotty, Patrick, *The Penguin Book of Irish Poetry*, London, Penguin Books, 2010.

Davis, Wes, *An Anthology of Modern Irish Poetry*, Cambridge, MA, Belknap Press Harvard, 2010.

Dawe, Gerald, ed., *Earth Voices Whispering: An Anthology of Irish War Poetry, 1914–1945*, Belfast, The Blackstaff Press, 2008.

De Paor, Louis, *Leabhar na hAthghabhala / Poems of Repossession*, Northumberland, Bloodaxe Books, 2015.

Fallon, Peter and Mahon, Derek, eds., *Penguin Book of Contemporary Irish Poetry*, London, Penguin Books, 1991.

Guinness, Selina, ed., *New Irish Poets*, Northumberland, Bloodaxe Books, 2004.

Kinsella, Thomas, ed., *New Oxford Book of Irish Verse*, Oxford, Oxford University Press, 1986.

Mc Breen, Joan, ed., *The White Page/An Bhileog Bhan:Twentieth Century Irish Women Poets*, Cliffs of Moher, Salmon Poetry, 2007.

The Watchful Heart: A New Generation of Irish Poets, Cliffs of Moher, Salmon Poetry, 2009.

Morrissey, Sinead and Connolly, Stephen, eds. *The Future Always Makes Me Do Thirsty: New Poets from the North of Ireland*, Belfast, The Blackstaff Press, 2016.

Moylan, Terry, *The Indignant Muse: Poetry and Songs of the Irish Revolution*, Dublin, Lilliput Press, 2016.

Muldoon, Paul, *Faber Book of Contemporary Irish Poetry*, London, Faber & Faber, 1986.

O'Brien, Peggy, ed., *The Wake Forest Book of Contemporary Irish Women's Poetry 1967–2000*, Winston-Salem, Wake Forest Press, 1999.

Ó'Tuama, Seán, and Kinsella, Thomas, eds., *An Duanaire: Poems of the Dispossessed, 1600–1900*, Dublin, Dolmen Press, Bord Na Gaeilge, 1981.

INDEX

Compiled by Julitta Clancy, FSocInd
Note: page references in **bold** denote principal entries

Cambridge Companions to ...

AUTHORS

TOPICS